American History told by Contemporaries

BY THE SAME EDITOR

A Source-Book of American History

The *Source-Book* is independent of the four volumes of *Contemporaries*, and contains no articles which appear in the larger series.

THE MACMILLAN COMPANY
60 FIFTH AVENUE, NEW YORK

American History told by
Contemporaries

VOLUME V

TWENTIETH CENTURY UNITED STATES

1900–1929

THE MACMILLAN COMPANY
NEW YORK · BOSTON · CHICAGO · DALLAS
ATLANTA · SAN FRANCISCO

MACMILLAN & CO., Limited
LONDON · BOMBAY · CALCUTTA
MELBOURNE

THE MACMILLAN COMPANY
OF CANADA, Limited
TORONTO

American History told by Contemporaries

VOLUME V

TWENTIETH CENTURY UNITED STATES

1900–1929

EDITED BY

ALBERT BUSHNELL HART

PROFESSOR OF GOVERNMENT EMERITUS IN HARVARD UNIVERSITY

AUTHOR OF "FORMATION OF THE UNION," "SALMON P. CHASE,"
"MONROE DOCTRINE," "NATIONAL IDEALS HISTORICALLY TRACED,"
"AMERICAN HISTORY MAPS," ETC., ETC.
EDITOR OF "AMERICAN NATION," "AMERICAN YEAR BOOK,"
"COMMONWEALTH HISTORY OF MASSACHUSETTS," ETC., ETC.
HISTORIAN OF THE
U. S. GEORGE WASHINGTON BICENTENNIAL COMMISSION

WITH THE COLLABORATION OF

JOHN GOULD CURTIS

FORMERLY ASSISTANT IN GOVERNMENT IN HARVARD UNIVERSITY

NEW YORK

THE MACMILLAN COMPANY

1929

SET UP AND ELECTROTYPED BY T. MOREY & SON
PRINTED IN THE UNITED STATES OF AMERICA BY
THE BERWICK & SMITH CO.

Preface

In these modern days the significance of historical sources, as the only foundation of the study and teaching of history, government and international law, needs no defence or explanation. The fundamental idea that historical investigation and historical writing must be based on ascertained occurrences and expressions from personal experience, is now deeply rooted in the minds of historical writers, of teachers of history, and of publishers of historical books.

This method has been furthered by the World War, which presented tremendously important problems of historical evidence. For ten years a battle of books has raged, almost as full of animosity as the struggles of the armies in the field, upon the question of what actually took place in the cabinets of Europe immediately preceding the outbreak of hostilities. The dreadful question of the responsibility for that war has been subjected to the test of contemporary verbal statements, despatches, and telegrams; and also to subsequent explanations of responsible statesmen of the various countries involved. Never has there been such intensity of search and comparison of all publications, such delving in the intimate archives of the governments concerned, such concern over the exact wording of historical records.

That influence has also affected the attitude of the public mind in the United States of America toward the search for ascertained truth with regard to the connection of the United States with that gigantic struggle. Never in the history of the Republic has there been such an outpouring of intimate personal material and the contents of secret or revealed government archives, as during the last ten years.

It is not the purpose of this fifth volume of the *American History Told by Contemporaries* to devote disproportionate space to that controversy; but it has been found indispensable to print a body of carefully selected material relating to vital incidents and policies during the war. This volume recognizes the fact that every year of the last three decades has furnished absorbing problems; and recorded varying views and recollections of protagonists in American public life.

A glance at the Table of Contents will reveal the editor's conviction that the history of the United States is not concentrated in Washington nor in the national government. The real history of the United States involves millions of individuals and scores of concrete problems. Hence this volume follows the policy of the four preceding volumes in furnishing evidence that the complete history of our country involves the status of the people of the Nation; their origin; their spread over the land; their division into sections; their races; and the question of immigration. The industry of the American people is part of their history just as much as their politics.

On the other hand, we Americans are deeply interested in our governments—national, state, and local—as well as in the combination of public men in parties, and the antagonisms of party contests. Particular attention is therefore paid in the volume to the great figures who have come forward to represent the various ideas of their country-men. Numerous chapters are devoted to extracts from original discussions of the political questions of the time.

Other portions of the volume are devoted to vital questions of public welfare, including dependents and criminals, urban problems, labor problems, public utilities. Due space is allotted to the intellectual life of the American people, as shown in their education and their literature.

The greatest crisis of the United States Government in the field of this volume is the World War, a crisis paralleled as a period of national danger only by the American Revolution and the Civil War. Hence the efforts to reach a decision as to the responsible part which the United States took in the World War. This volume gives opportunity for some of the men who were deepest in those controversies to tell us what went on while the United States was a neutral; what brought the Nation to the issue of war; and what were the conditions of the struggle in field, camp, transport and hospital. No writer has as yet performed the task of furnishing a complete picture of the relation of the United States to European affairs; but the selections in this volume on the war and the subsequent readjustment will enable the student and reader to realize what those who were closest to the controversy believed, sought, proposed, and carried through.

In the last part of this volume the effort is made to give people who have been in the midst of the crisis the opportunity to make clear the confusion and difficulties of the status of the United States since the peace of 1919 toward the rest of the world—whether members of the League of Nations or outside of it. By the method of calling upon one writer after another to tell something of what he has seen, and what he believes to have been essential for the welfare of the Nation, controversial treatment of those questions is avoided.

A practical difficulty in making up this volume has been that substantially all the material, except extracts from public records, is copyrighted, and can be printed only with the consent of the original writer, his publisher, or other representatives. Some excellent pieces had to be omitted because the legal owner of the copyright could not be ascertained.

Throughout the process of the work Mr. John G. Curtis, of the Harvard Law School, has been an unfailing and sagacious aid. It is a fundamental condition of the work that it shall be as nearly as possible a letter-perfect transcript of the original sources; and in this and other necessary comparison with originals Miss Mabel F. Reed has been very efficient.

To these acknowledgments the editor must add his sense of personal indebtedness to the students and readers and libraries throughout the country whose support of the enterprise of the *American History told by Contemporaries*, during the thirty years since the publication of the first volume, has encouraged the author and his aids in the labor of unearthing and fitting together these two hundred and two extracts, from the original printed statements of a host of men and women in a variety of callings and experiences. The numerous constituency of readers is highly valued, because it is an evidence throughout the country that teachers and writers of history are depending upon actualities as a basis of historical knowledge, alongside the ripened judgments of the numerous investigators and writers, who also must usually base their results upon the records of the experience of other people.

ALBERT BUSHNELL HART

Widener Library
Cambridge, Mass.
October, 1929

Contents

PART I

PRACTICAL INTRODUCTION FOR TEACHERS, PUPILS, LIBRARIES, AND STUDENTS

CHAPTER I — SIGNIFICANCE AND DERIVATION OF SOURCES

PART II

THE LAND AND THE PEOPLE

CHAPTER II — POPULATION AND DISTRIBUTION

CHAPTER III — SECTIONS AND NEW STATES

Contents

PART III

GOVERNMENT AND DEPENDENCIES

CHAPTER V — PRESIDENT THEODORE ROOSEVELT

CHAPTER VI — NATIONAL ADMINISTRATION AND PROBLEMS

Government and Dependencies

PART IV

INTERNATIONAL ASPECTS

CHAPTER IX — EUROPEAN FOREIGN RELATIONS

PART V

DOMESTIC PROBLEMS AND ADVANCES

CHAPTER XII — CATASTROPHES

PART VI

ADMINISTRATION METHODS AND EXPEDIENTS

CHAPTER XVII — PARTY AND POLITICAL ORGANIZATION

CHAPTER XVIII — PUBLIC QUESTIONS IN STATES AND CITIES

PART VII

THE HUMAN RELATIONS

PART IX

THE ARTS AND SCIENCES

CHAPTER XXV — PHILANTHROPY AND CULTURAL ADVANCE

CHAPTER XXVI — EDUCATION

Contents

PAGE

PART XI

AFTERMATH OF THE WAR

PAGE

CHAPTER XXXVI — THE LEAGUE OF NATIONS AND THE WORLD COURT

CHAPTER XXXVII — THE PLACE OF THE UNITED STATES IN THE WORLD

American History told by Contemporaries

PART I

PRACTICAL INTRODUCTION
FOR TEACHERS, PUPILS, LIBRARIES, AND STUDENTS

CHAPTER I — SIGNIFICANCE AND DERIVATION OF SOURCES

1. Educative Value of Sources

DOWN to thirty years ago schools, colleges, and libraries had not yet accepted the idea that source materials could be used to advantage by beginners in systematic reading and study of history. Time and educational experience have gone far to establish those studies from the primary authorities which are the basis of most of our historical knowledge. The continued demand for the first four volumes of the *Contemporaries*, from the publication of the first volume in 1897, and the preparation of several other collections of source materials are evidences that students in secondary schools and colleges are more and more gaining practice in basing historical studies on first-hand accounts. They are learning to weigh the conflicting views of honest partisans, and to form their own opinions of the value of human evidence. Thus the inquiring mind acquires an experience of historic judgment.

Obviously great differences may develop in the testimony of two utterly honest witnesses to the same event, because no two people can see with the same eyes and hear with the same ears. Infinite are the forms and degrees of bias and prejudice which may result in great divergences of viewpoint and conflicts in the reports of results. Users of these sources will realize that the capacity and interest of each writer must be weighed with his words, to handicap or confirm their credibility. Unless the headnotes otherwise indicate, it may be assumed that the authors represented are competent and sincere. That they sometimes disagree with one another means simply that we are still spared the dullness of unanimity, that all questions have two sides, and that on both of them much may often justly be said.

Nowadays it is generally accepted that the reading of contemporary accounts imparts to the study of history a flavor of immediacy that makes for deeper interest and better recollection on the part of students. Naturally, brief extracts such as these will not be sufficient for all purposes, and in many instances it will prove desirable to read at greater length some of the authorities quoted here.

If Volume V lacks the zest of romantic records of pioneer adventure, or stirring tales of the struggle to maintain the Union, it does not necessarily deal with a less interesting time. True, governmental reforms are seldom exciting reading, and the aims even of the World War were perhaps less tangible than those of our earlier conflicts. But the first quarter of the Twentieth Century has been a time of swift social and industrial and political movement, and especially a time of the adaptation of science to the daily life of the people in such ways as to produce profound changes. They have been meaningful years.

————◆————

2. How to Find and Use Sources

GUIDES. The most thorough-going recent development of sources on current affairs is Milton Conover's *Working Manual of Original Sources in American Government* (rev. ed., 1928). A case system for the study of politics. An invaluable guide for those who wish to reach official and unofficial sources on recent questions of American history, government and politics.

The same method has been followed by Albert Bushnell Hart, editor of *The American Nation, a History*. The three last volumes, covering the same period as this fifth volume of the *American History Told by Contemporaries*, contain each a classified bibliography. These volumes are: J. H. Latané, *America as a World Power* [1897–1907]; F. A. Ogg, *National Progress* [1907–1917]; A. M. Schlesinger [1917–1929] in progress.

Channing, Hart and Turner, *Guide to the Reading and Study of American History* (rev. ed., 1912) contains many indications and discussions of sources. The sections 265–274 deal with the period from 1898 to 1910.

RECENT HISTORIES. The best histories of the United States contain classified and descriptive bibliographies, including sources. Sources are diligently used as a basis in all the recent elaborate histories of the United States, and especially in the following:

John S. Bassett, *Expansion and Reform, 1889–1926* (Epochs of American History, IV), has prefixed to each chapter an articulated bibliography of secondary works and of sources, brought down to date of publication; taking the captions in sequence, this is a comprehensive guide to the sources in the last three decades.

Edward Channing, *History of the United States* (6 vols. published). The volume VIII will include the period covered by Volume V of *American History told by Contemporaries*.

Charles A. Beard and William C. Bagley, the *American People* (2 vols., 1920).

Homer C. Hockett and Arthur M. Schlesinger, *Political and Social History of the United States* (second volume comes down to 1925).

James Ford Rhodes, *The McKinley and Roosevelt Administrations* (1897–1909).

Lester Burrell Shippee, *Recent American History* (1924)—Excellent lists of authorities.

Mark Sullivan, *Our Times, the United States*, 1900–1925 (2 vols., 1926, 1927).

David P. Muzzey, *The American Adventure* (2 vols., 1927).

Allen Johnson (editor), *Chronicles of America* (50 vols.). Original edition completed 1919; "Abraham Lincoln edition" published 1918–1921. The volumes bearing on the United States in the Twentieth Century are: Vol. 46, C. R. Fish, *Path of Empire;* Vol. 47, H. Howland, *Theodore Roosevelt and His Times*; Vol. 48, C. Seymour, *Woodrow Wilson and the World War*.

ANNUALS AND CYCLOPEDIAS. Valuable and continuing sources are found in most of the annual and cyclopedic works published in the United States. The most important of these are the following:

Encyclopedia of the Social Sciences, edited by E. R. A. Seligman. (In progress.)

New International Year Book (annual, 1908–1929).

World Almanac (annual).—Indispensable source of information for current happenings and statistics.

Official Congressional Directory for the use of the United States Congress (revised for each annual session).—Lists of legislative and some executive officials and judges. Maps of congressional districts.

Records of Political Events (annual).

Encyclopædia Britannica (several editions between 1902 and 1929).—Many American articles written by Americans. Also Supplementary Volumes (vols. I–III, 1926).—New Edition of the new *Encyclopedia Britannica* in progress in 1929.

Encyclopædia Britannica, These Eventful Years (2 vols., 1924).

The Americana Annual (connected with *Encyclopedia Americana* (1923–1926).

Statesman's Year Book (1864–1928).—An English standard publication with a large section on the United States.

New International Year Book (1898–1927).—General in character. Compiled articles on the United States.

Appleton's Annual Cyclopædia (New York, 1901–1903).—Series began in 1861. Many extracts from public documents.

American Year Book (annual volumes, 1910–1919; 1925–1928).—Prepared by a Board representing national learned societies. Brief articles by experts on progress of the year in many fields. Financed by the *New York Times*.

Dictionary of American Biography, edited by Allen Johnson; founded by Adolph S. Ochs (1928).—Will eventually include about 50 volumes.

PERIODICALS. Most of the serious periodicals contain valuable and quotable articles on history, politics, economics, social conditions and international relations. Especially serviceable for materials, such as are used in the *Contemporaries*, are the following:

New York Times Current History (monthly, 1914–1929).—Includes many monthly summaries of world conditions.

Annals of the American Academy of Political and Social Science (quarterly).

Political Science Quarterly, with supplements.—Discussions of pending questions of government.

American Historical Review (quarterly).—Articles in its field, reviews, and current information.

American Political Science Review (quarterly).—On governmental affairs, in the same lines as the preceding titles.

Foreign Affairs (quarterly).—Many informational articles.

American Journal of International Law (quarterly).—Many narrative articles.

Foreign Policy Association issues many publications of current material.

Economic Geography (quarterly).

American Review of Reviews (monthly).

Forum (monthly).—Many political articles.

Nation (weekly).—Founded in 1866: ultra liberal

World's Work (monthly).

New Republic (weekly).—Critical and somewhat destructive.

Atlantic Monthly (founded in 1853).

Outlook and Independent (weekly).—Many articles on current events.

North American Review (monthly).—Successor to a famous and solid publication founded in 1815.

The Historical Outlook (monthly).—Pays special attention to the use of sources in teaching.

DIPLOMACY. In the field of government and diplomacy access to the sources is aided by A. C. McLaughlin and Albert Bushnell Hart (editors), *Cyclopedia of American Government* (3 vols., 1914–1916)—Includes many biographical entries down to 1916.

Detailed bibliography on diplomacy in Channing, Hart and Turner, *Guide*, §§ 266–268.

Bibliographical aids in *Journal of International Law*, many entries.

Parker T. Moon, *Syllabus on International Relations* (1925).—Very full and helpful.

Charles C. Hyde, *International Law Chiefly as Interpreted and Applied by the United States* (2 vols., 1922).—A work of immense research, abounding in bibliography, including many unusual sources.

Arthur N. Holcombe, *The Political Parties of Today* (1924).—Standard textbook with references.

P. O. Ray, *Political Parties and Practical Politics* (1924).—Bibliographies include sources.

NEWSPAPERS. A vast amount of original material finds its way into the columns of the daily press, especially in reports of speeches and documents, and personal narratives and arguments by public men. Among the newspapers are:

United States Daily, published in Washington; prints significant sources from day to day.

New York Times. The most powerful daily in the United States. "All the news that's fit to print" on politics and public questions from day to day.

The principal newspapers in the large cities, including the *Springfield Republican*.

ROOSEVELT PERIOD. A considerable number of sources are grouped about Theodore Roosevelt and his time.

Hermann Hagedorn, *Americanism of Theodore Roosevelt* (1923).—Classified extracts.

Theodore Roosevelt, *Autobiography* (1913).

Theodore Roosevelt, *Works* (limited edition, 24 vols.).

Theodore Roosevelt, *Works* (popular edition, 22 vols.).

Joseph B. Bishop, *Theodore Roosevelt and His Times as Shown in His Own Letters* (1920).

William D. Lewis, *Life of Theodore Roosevelt* (1919).

Howard C. Hill, *Roosevelt and the Caribbean* (1927).

Albert Bushnell Hart (editor), *Roosevelt Encyclopedia*.—An alphabetical register of Theodore Roosevelt's views upon public and other questions, in progress in 1929.

Robert M. LaFollette, *Autobiography* (1913).

H. H. Kohlsaat, *From McKinley to Harding* (1922).

WOODROW WILSON. Similarly numerous sources have been published bearing on Woodrow Wilson and the United States in the World War.

Edgar E. Robinson and Victor J. West, *The Foreign Policy of Woodrow Wilson* (1913–1917). (Extracts.)

Ray Stannard Baker and William E. Dodd (editors), *The Public Papers of Woodrow Wilson* (1925–1926).

Albert Shaw (editor), *Woodrow Wilson. Messages and Papers* (1917–1918).

A. B. Hart (editor), *Selected Addresses and Public Papers of Woodrow Wilson* (1918).

Ray Stanwood Baker, *Woodrow Wilson and World Settlement* (3 vols., 1923).—Includes a volume of documents.

International Ideals (1919).—Collection from Woodrow Wilson material.

WORLD WAR.

A. E. McKinley (editor), *Collected Materials for the Study of the War* (1918).

James W. Gerard, *My Four Years in Germany* (1917).

John B. McMaster, *The United States and the World War* (1918).

Lester B. Shippee, *Recent American History (1865–1922)*.—Very useful bibliographies of source material and narrative histories at the end of each chapter.

Burton J. Hendrick, *Life and Letters of Walter H. Page* (3 vols., 1921).

Many contemporary collections, official and private.

PEACE OF VERSAILLES.

Bernard M. Baruch, *Making of the Reparation and Economic Sections of the Treaty* (1920).

Ray Stanwood Baker, *Woodrow Wilson and World Settlement* (3 vols., 1922).—Includes a volume of documents.

Robert Lansing, *The Peace Negotiations, a Personal Narrative* (1921).

Joseph B. Tumulty, *Woodrow Wilson as I Knew Him* (1921).

Charles Shipley, *Intimate Papers of Colonel House* (4 vols., 1926–1928).

Henry Cabot Lodge, *The Senate and the League of Nations* (1924).

William E. Dodd, *Woodrow Wilson and his Work*.

---

3. Classification of Official Materials in This Volume

RECORDS of various kinds furnish extremely valuable material: first, the *Congressional Record* from which have been taken speeches by Wadsworth (No. 126), Lodge (No. 171), and Borah (No. 193). Extracts from presidential addresses are represented by Roosevelt (No. 111) and Wilson (Nos. 40, 87).

Diplomatic correspondence will be found in the following: Root (No. 51), Page (No. 166), Wilson (Nos. 168, 201).

Extracts have been made from official publications of the executive departments and separate bureaus of the government: the Department of Agriculture (Nos. 72, 81), the War Department (No. 59), the Bureau of the Budget (No. 70), the Children's Bureau (No. 114), the Smithsonian Institution (Nos. 73, 152), and the opinions of the

Supreme Court (Nos. 83, 85, 112). Among official utterances of public officials are extracts from the Governor of Samoa (No. 37) and the Director of the Budget (No. 70).

PUBLIC PAPERS. Somewhat less use has been made of speeches in Congress and the Senate than in earlier volumes. Addresses in the Senate comprise those of Wadsworth (No. 126), Lodge (No. 171), and Borah (No. 193). A single Senate document is quoted (No. 60). Presidential messages and diplomatic communications are represented by Roosevelt (Nos. 47, 111) and Wilson (Nos. 40, 87, 168, 201). Other officials of the national government speaking in the line of office are Root (No. 51), Taft (No. 34), Hughes (No. 45), Weeks (No. 58), Dawes (No. 70), and McAdoo (No. 69). Military and naval officers making formal reports include Evans (No. 37), Goethals (No. 39), Greely (No. 59), and Pershing (No. 184). Completing the official material are three reports of decisions by the United States Supreme Court (Nos. 83, 85, 112).

STATESMEN. Probably of equal value to the student are the unofficial utterances of public men, such as Bryan (No. 84), Roosevelt (Nos. 10 and 31), Hay (No. 24), Cortelyou (No. 28), Root (No. 123), LaFollette (No. 86), Underwood (No. 27), Wilson (No. 204), Daniels (No. 129), and Houston (No. 132).

PERSONS IN GOVERNMENT SERVICE. Large use has been made of addresses by public officials, as Cortelyou (No. 28), Taft (No. 34), Hughes (No. 45), Weeks (No. 58), McAdoo (No. 69), Wilson (No. 204). Books and magazine articles by public men in or out of office have been drawn upon, as Underwood (No. 27), Goethals (No. 39), Myers (No. 52), Houston (No. 132), besides part of a speech in the Massachusetts Constitutional Convention of 1917 (No. 95). See also National Civil Service Reform League (No. 49).

MILITARY AND NAVAL. Official reports by military and naval officers include Captain Waldo Evans (No. 37), Major General Greely (No. 59), General Pershing (No. 184). Unofficial writings of military and naval officers are by Lieutenant Colonel Goethals (No. 39), Rear Admiral Mahan (No. 54), Lieutenant Commander Mannix (No. 55), Lieutenant Commander Green (No. 57), Colonel Bingham (No. 183), Captain Frothingham (Nos. 187, 190).

4. Observers and Critics of American Conditions

PUBLIC AFFAIRS. A variety of leaders in civil affairs are represented in the selections: in business by Markham (No. 17) and Ford (No. 154); in science by Lindbergh (No. 68) and Chanute (No. 152); in agriculture by Lowden (No. 80), Davenport (No. 76), and Butterfield (No. 77); in education by Pritchett (No. 117), Wirt (No. 139), and Eliot (No. 141); and in reforms by Older (No. 94), Johnson (No. 95), Adams (No. 100), Lindsey (No. 104), Eliot (No. 106), Darrow (No. 107), and Sanville (No. 118). Biographers, recording episodes in the lives of eminent men, are Low (No. 130), Bok (No. 135), Russell (No. 134), Hammond (No. 153), Macfarland (No. 121), Parkman (No. 116), Blossom (No. 62), and Davis (No. 110).

OBSERVERS. Numerous extracts are printed from observers and critics of conditions and affairs—in large part either journalists or academic men—during the years before the World War: Lowell (No. 53), Beard (No. 90), Young (No. 91), Riis (No. 19), Ogg (Nos. 21 and 88), Kohlsaat (No. 24), Myers (No. 52), Rhodes (No. 25), Holcombe (Nos. 29 and 96), Foulke (No. 30), Hart (Nos. 13 and 98), Howe (No. 12), Frankfurter (No. 122), Gardner (No. 97), Pearson (No. 146), and Eastman (No. 119).

PUBLIC SERVICE. H. H. Kohlsaat (No. 23), A. N. Holcombe (Nos. 29, 96), W. D. Foulke (No. 30), Theodore Roosevelt (No. 31), D. L. Merritt (No. 32), W. J. Bryan (No. 84), F. A. Ogg (No. 88), Albert Halstead (No. 89), C. A. Beard (No. 90), J. T. Young (No. 91), W. B. Munro (No. 93), Max Eastman (No. 119), E. G. Robinson (No. 131), V. J. West (No. 131), J. C. Welliver (No. 157), J. S. Bassett (No. 197). State and local political activities are presented by Fremont Older (No. 94), A. B. Hart (No. 98), Raymond Moley (No. 109), G. W. Johnson (No. 198).

INTERNATIONAL RELATIONS have been treated by Leopold Grahame (No. 41), C. C. Thach (No. 42), W. R. Shepherd (No. 44), A. L. Lowell (No. 53), Henry Macfarland (No. 121), C. C. Hyde (No. 165), Bishop William Lawrence (No. 202), M. O. Hudson (No. 203), William Phillips (No. 205), C. W. Eliot (No. 206), Mark Sullivan (No. 207),

A. A. Young (No. 108). The problems of immigration have been analyzed by Theodore Roosevelt (No. 10), J. A. Riis (No. 19), F. C. Ogg (No. 21), J. B. Connolly (No. 18), R. de C. Ward (No. 22). Foreign statesmen and critics have contributed some interesting pieces: Wu Ting-Fang (No. 9), Lord Charnwood (No. 26), Sir A. Maurice Low (No. 130).

LEGISLATIVE AND JUDICIARY. Problems of legislation are treated by A. B. Hart (No. 98), Glenn Frank (No. 105), C. W. Eliot (No. 106), C. S. Darrow (No. 107), William Seagle (No. 108).

CRITICS OF THE COURTS are E. F. Baldwin (No. 101), J. T. Young (No. 102), Fabian Franklin (No. 103), B. B. Lindsay (No. 104), Felix Frankfurter (No. 122), Raymond Moley (No. 109).

PERSONAL AND AUTOBIOGRAPHIC. Selections from autobiographies and biographies and other writings concern the following eminent persons: Booker T. Washington (No. 20), John Hay (Nos. 24, 47, 121), Theodore Roosevelt (No. 26), T. J. Hill (No. 62), Fremont Older (No. 94), Tom Johnson (No. 95), J. J. Davis (No. 110), Jane Addams (No. 116), Judge Holmes (No. 122), J. C. Choate (No. 123), Admiral Sims (No. 124), Elihu Root (No. 125), H. C. Lodge (Nos. 126, 202), Eugene Debs (No. 127), W. E. Borah (No. 128), Woodrow Wilson (Nos. 129, 130, 131), D. F. Houston (No. 132), Theodore Thomas (No. 134), Edward Bok (No. 135), C. W. Eliot (No. 141), John Burroughs (No. 144), Mark Twain (No. 145), C. P. Steinmetz (No. 153), Henry Ford (No. 154), W. H. Page (Nos. 166, 167), President Warren G. Harding (No. 195), President Calvin Coolidge (No. 196).

SOCIAL AND ECONOMIC WRITINGS on industries and general economics: Crowther (No. 11), Howe (No. 12), Harger (Nos. 14, 15), Markham (No. 17), Rhodes (No. 25), Emory (No. 46), Weyl (No. 48), Blossom (No. 62), Thrasher (No. 63), Allen (No. 65), Olsen (No. 72), Howland (No. 74), Davenport (No. 76), Butterfield (No. 77), Greeley (No. 78), Smith (No. 79), Lowden (No. 89), Hochbaum (No. 81), Schoffelmayer (No. 82), Harlan (No. 83), Bryan (No. 84), Lurton (No. 85).

SCIENTIFIC MEN. Scientists, engineers, inventors, etc., are Octave Chanute (No. 152), John Hays Hammond (No. 153), Henry Ford (No. 154), E. A. Mills (No. 162).

THE AMERICAN TRAVELLERS are Belmore Browne (No. 35), C. K. London (No. 36), Knowlton Mixer (No. 43). Foreign travellers are J. T. Muirhead (No. 7), Wu Ting-Fang (No. 9). Another foreign critic is Sir A. M. Low (No. 130).

CRITICS. The professions are represented by many authoritative writers. The opinions of academic critics of the affairs of this period are represented by Van Norman (No. 8), A. B. Hart (Nos. 13, 98), Ogg (No. 21, 88), Shepherd (No. 44), Miner (No. 33), Lowell (No. 53), Holcombe (Nos. 29, 96), Davenport (No. 76), Butterfield (No. 77), Beard (No. 90), Young (Nos. 91, 102), Munro (No. 93), Eliot (Nos. 106, 141, 206), Pritchett (No. 117), Wirt (No. 139), Hazard (No. 163), Hyde (No. 165), Bassett (Nos. 192, 197), Chafee (No. 194), Abbott (No. 199), Hudson (No. 203).

---

5. Classification of Economic and Social Selections

ECONOMIC. The effects of modern inventions on social and economic life are presented by Albert (No. 65), Stout (No. 67), Lindbergh (No. 68), Smith (No. 79), McNamee (No. 158), Pound (No. 159). Writers on financial matters are Carrick (No. 73), Hendrick (No. 113), Frank (No. 136).

SOCIAL CONDITIONS. Competent writers are H. E. Van Norman (No. 8), C. W. Eliot (No. 104), Glenn Frank (No. 105), C. S. Darrow (No. 107), Mary H. Parkman (No. 116), Vachel Lindsay (No. 149), M. A. Abbott (No. 199). Racial problems are handled by Hart (No. 13), Riis (No. 19), Scott (No. 20), Stowe (No. 20), Ogg (No. 21). Critics of philanthropic methods are Frank (No. 136), McGee (No. 138). Athletics and amusements are presented by Putnam (No. 16), McNamee (No. 158), Casey (No. 161).

LITERARY ACTIVITIES. The intellectual life of the American people in the period is set forth in a variety of aspects in the following selections on the arts: Russell (No. 134), Bok (No. 135), Mumford (No. 137), Gross (No. 164). Critics of educational efforts are Pritchett (No. 117), C. W. Eliot (No. 141), Slosson (No. 142), Gavit (No. 143), M. A. Abbott (No. 199). Critics of literature are Pearson (No. 146), Boynton (No. 147), Van Doren (No. 148), De Rochemont (No. 150).

Pieces in verse are numerous, written by Wallace Irwin (Nos. 38, 50), Vachel Lindsay (No. 149), "Neri" (No. 151), "Wamp" (No. 151), Caroline Hazard (No. 163), Michael Gross (No. 164), "P. W." (No. 164), Alan Seegar (Nos. 169, 180), Joyce Kilmer (No. 178), E. B. Comstock (No. 189).

The following women authors are represented: Luella Miner (No. 33), Charmian K. London (No. 36), Mary C. Blossom (No. 62), Mary R. Parkman (No. 116), Florence L. Sanville (No. 118), Jane Addams (No. 120), Caroline Hazard (No. 163), Katherine Mayo (No. 186).

Newspaper editorials and staff articles have been taken from *Literary Digest* (Nos. 56, 172), *Outlook* (No. 64), *New Republic* (Nos. 71, 92), *Nation* (No. 127), *New York Times* (No. 200), *New York Times Current History* (Nos. 155, 156, 191).

Foreign writers who comment on Americans are Wu Ting-Fang (No. 9), Charnwood (No. 26), Masefield (No. 179), and Low (No. 130).

CORRESPONDENTS AND CRITICS are Luella Miner (No. 33), anonymous correspondent of the *Literary Digest* (No. 56), C. C. Hyde (No. 165), R. W. Bruère (No. 170), F. C. Howe (No. 173), F. H. Rindge, Jr. (No. 174), R. B. Fosdick (No. 175), Theodore Roosevelt (No. 176), R. H. Davis (No. 177), John Masefield (No. 179), H. S. Canby (No. 181), E. L. James (No. 185), Katherine Mayo (No. 186), Albert Kinross (No. 188), J. S. Bassett (No. 192), Zechariah Chafee, Jr. (No. 194). Critics in particular of art and literature comprise Bok (No. 135), Mumford (No. 137), Page (No. 133), Boynton (No. 147), and Van Doren (No. 148).

OBSERVERS ON ECONOMICS AND FINANCE are Dawes (No. 70), McAdoo (No. 69), Olsen (No. 72), Carrick (No. 73), Young (No. 208), Howland (No. 74), Newell (No. 75), Greeley (No. 76), and Smith (No. 79).

6. Classification of Selections on the World War

PARTICIPANTS. Reports and reminiscences of participants have been taken out of F. C. Howe (No. 173), F. H. Rindge, Jr., (No. 174), R. H. Davis (No. 177), Colonel Hiram Bingham (No. 183). Eyewitnesses have given invaluable accounts of important events, particularly W. H. Page (No. 166), Katherine Mayo (No. 186), Albert Kinross (No. 188).

Post-Bellum Writings on similar subjects, as they came up after the War, include Eliot (No. 206), Ward (No. 22), Lowry (No. 124), Shepherd (No. 44), Munro (No. 93), Bassett (No. 197), Abbott (No. 199), Lawrence (No. 202), Hudson (No. 203), and Phillips (No. 205).

Observers in the Field. From observers, correspondents, and critics of the World War have been selected: Roosevelt (No. 176), Hyde (No. 165), Bruère (No. 170), Page (No. 166), Grattan (No. 167), Canby (No. 181), Bingham (No. 183), James (No. 185), Fosdick (No. 175), Rindge (No. 174), Chafee (No. 194), Howe (No. 173), Ogg (No. 88), and Keough (No. 140).

PART II

THE LAND AND THE PEOPLE

CHAPTER II — POPULATION AND DISTRIBUTION

7. A Traveler at the Opening of the Century (1900)

BY JAMES FULLARTON MUIRHEAD

Muirhead, an Englishman, lived some two years in the United States about the time this was written. Engaged in gathering material for the Baedeker *Guide* to the United States, he traveled widely and had an opportunity to view the entire country with the unprejudiced eyes of a stranger.—For similar general accounts of the state of the country, see Mark Sullivan, *Our Times, the United States* [1900–1925]; Frederic Austin Ogg, *National Progress, 1907–1917* [*American Nation*, vol. XXVII]; Charles Austin Beard, *Contemporary American History, 1887–1913;* E. B. Andrews, *The United States in Recent Times;* Albert Perry Brigham, *United States of America;* and such periodicals as *World's Work, Century, Review of Reviews,* and *Outlook* for appropriate years; *American Year Book,* for years 1910–1920, 1925.

NEXT to the interest and beauty of the places to be visited, perhaps the two things in which a visitor to a new country has most concern are the means of moving from point to point and the accommodation provided for him at his nightly stopping-places—in brief, its conveyances and its inns. During the year or more I spent in almost continuous traveling in the United States I had abundant opportunity of testing both of these. In all I must have slept in over two hundred different beds, ranging from one in a hotel-chamber so gorgeous that it seemed almost as indelicate to go to bed in it as to undress in the drawing-room, down through the berths of Pullman cars and river steamboats, to an open air couch of balsam boughs in the Adirondack forests. My means of locomotion included a safety bicycle, an Adirondack canoe, the back of a horse, the omni-

14

present buggy, a bob-sleigh, a "cutter," a "booby," four-horse "stages," river, lake and sea-going steamers, horse-cars, cable-cars, electric cars, mountain elevators, narrow-gauge railways, and the Vestibuled Limited Express from New York to Chicago.

Perhaps it is significant of the amount of truth in many of the assertions made about traveling in the United States that I traversed about 35,000 miles in the various ways indicated above without a scratch and almost without serious detention or delay. Once we were nearly swamped in a sudden squall in a mountain lake, and once we had a minute or two's unpleasant experience of the iron-shod heels of our horse *inside* the buggy, the unfortunate animal having hitched his hind-legs over the dash-board and nearly kicking out our brains in his frantic efforts to get free. These, however, were accidents that might have happened anywhere, and if my experiences by road and rail in America prove anything, they prove that traveling in the United States is just as safe as in Europe. Some varieties of it are rougher than anything of the kind I know in the Old World; but on the other hand much of it is far pleasanter. The European system of small railway compartments, in spite of its advantage of privacy and quiet, would be simply unendurable in the long journeys that have to be made in the western hemisphere. The journey of twenty-four to thirty hours from New York to Chicago, if made by the Vestibuled Limited, is probably less fatiguing than the day-journey of half the time from London to Edinburgh. The comforts of this superb train include those of the drawing-room, the dining-room, the smoking-room, and the library. These apartments are perfectly ventilated by compressed air and lighted by movable electric lights, while in winter they are warmed to an agreeable temperature by steam-pipes. Card-tables and a selection of the daily papers minister to the traveler's amusement, while bulletin boards give the latest Stock Exchange quotations and the reports of the Government Weather Bureau. Those who desire it may enjoy a bath *en route*, or avail themselves of the services of a lady's maid, a barber, a stenographer, and a type-writer. There is even a small and carefully selected medicine chest within reach; and the way in which the minor delicacies of life are consulted may be illustrated by the fact that powdered soap is provided in the lavatories, so that no one may have to use the same cake of soap as his neighbor.

No one who has not tried both can appreciate the immense difference in comfort given by the opportunity to move about in the train. No matter how pleasant one's companions are in an English first-class compartment, their *enforced* proximity makes one heartily sick of them before many hours have elapsed; while a conversation with Daisy Miller in the American parlour car is rendered doubly delightful by the consciousness that you may at any moment transfer yourself and your *bons mots* to Lydia Blood at the other end of the car, or retire with Gilead P. Beck to the snug little smoking-room. The great size and weight of the American cars make them very steady on well-laid tracks like those of the Pennsylvania Railway, and thus letter-writing need not be a lost art on a railway journey. Even when the permanent way is inferior, the same cause often makes the vibration less than on the admirable road-beds of England. . . .

Travelers who prefer the privacy of the European system may combine it with the liberty of the American system by hiring, at a small extra rate, the so-called "drawing-room" or "state-room," a small compartment containing four seats or berths, divided by partitions from the rest of the parlour car. The ordinary carriage or "day coach" corresponds to the English second-class carriage, or, rather, to the excellent third-class carriages on such railways as the Midland. It does not, I think, excel them in comfort except in the greater size, the greater liberty of motion, and the element of variety afforded by the greater number of fellow-passengers. The seats are disposed on each side of a narrow central aisle, and are so arranged that the occupants can ride forward or backward as they prefer. Each seat holds two persons, but with some difficulty if either has any amplitude of bulk. The space for the legs is also very limited. . . . The windows are another weak point. They move vertically as ours do, but up instead of down; and they are frequently made so that they cannot be opened more than a few inches. The handles by which they are lifted are very small, and afford very little purchase; and the windows are frequently so stiff that it requires a strong man to move them. I have often seen half a dozen passengers struggle in vain with a refractory glass, and finally have to call in the help of the brawny brakeman. . . . The windows are all furnished with small slatted blinds, which can be arranged in hot weather so as to exclude the sun and let in the air. . . . At intervals the brakeman carries round a pitcher of

iced water, which he serves gratis to all who want it; and it is a pleasant sight on sultry summer days to see how the children welcome his
coming. In some cases there is a permanent filter of ice-water with a
tap in a corner of the car. At each end of the car is a lavatory, one
for men and one for women. In spite, then, of the discomforts noted
above, it may be asserted that the poor man is more comfortable on a
long journey than in Europe; and that on a short journey the American
system affords more entertainment than the European. . . .

A feature connected with the American railway system that should
not be overlooked is the mass of literature prepared by the railway
companies and distributed gratis to their passengers. The illustrated
pamphlets issued by the larger companies are marvels of paper and
typography, with really charming illustrations and a text that is often
clever and witty enough to suggest that authors of repute are sometimes tempted to lend their anonymous pens for this kind of work.
But even the tiniest little "one-horse" railway distributes neat little
"folders," showing conclusively that its tracks lead through the
Elysian Fields and end at the Garden of Eden. A conspicuous feature
in all hotel offices is a large rack containing packages of these gaily
coloured folders, contributed by perhaps fifty different railways for
the use of the hotel guests. . . .

The United States is proverbially the paradise of what it is, perhaps,
now behind the times to term the gentler sex. The path of woman,
old or new, in America is made smooth in all directions, and as a rule
she has the best of the accommodation and the lion's share of the attention wherever she goes. But this is emphatically not the case on
the parlour car. No attempt is made there to divide the sexes or to
respect the privacy of a lady. If there are twelve men and four women
on the car, the latter are not grouped by themselves, but are scattered
among the men, either in lower or upper berths, as the number of
their tickets or the courtesy of the men dictates. The lavatory and
dressing-room for men at one end of the car has two or more "set
bowls" (fixed in basins), and can be used by several dressers at once.
The parallel accommodation for ladies barely holds one, and its door
is provided with a lock, which enables a selfish bang-frizzler and
rouge-layer to occupy it for an hour while a queue of her unhappy
sisters remains outside. It is difficult to see why a small portion
at one end of the car should not be reserved for ladies, and separ-

ated at night from the rest of the car by a curtain across the central aisle. . . .

The speed of American trains is as a rule slower than that of English ones, though there are some brilliant exceptions to this rule. I never remember dawdling along in so slow and apparently purposeless a manner as in crossing the arid deserts of Arizona—unless, indeed, it was in traveling by the Manchester and Milford line in Wales. The train on the branch between Raymond (a starting point for the Yosemite) and the main line went so cannily that the engine-driver (an excellent marksman) shot rabbits from the engine, while the fireman jumped down, picked them up, and clambered on again at the end of the train. The only time the train had to be stopped for him was when the engineer had a successful right and left, the victims of which expired at some distance from each other. It should be said that there was absolutely no reason to hurry on this trip, as we had "lashins" of time to spare for our connection at the junction, and the passengers were all much interested in the sport. . . .

Coaching in America is, as a rule, anything but a pleasure. It is true that the chance of being held up by "road agents" is to-day practically non-existent, and that the spectacle of a crowd of yelling Apaches making a stage-coach the pin-cushion for their arrows is now to be seen nowhere but in Buffalo Bill's Wild West Show. But the roads! . . . Even in the State of New York I have been in a stage that was temporarily checked by a hole two feet deep in the centre of the road, and that had to be emptied *and held up* while passing another part of the same road. In Virginia I drove over a road, leading to one of the most frequented resorts of the State, which it is simple truth to state offered worse going than any ordinary ploughed field. The wheels were often almost entirely submerged in liquid mud, and it is still a mystery to me how the tackle held together. To be jolted off one's seat so violently as to strike the top of the carriage was not a unique experience. Nor was the spending of ten hours in making thirty miles with four horses. In the Yellowstone one of the coaches of our party settled down in the midst of a slough of despond on the highway, from which it was finally extricated *backwards* by the combined efforts of twelve horses borrowed from the other coaches. Misery makes strange bedfellows, and the ingredients of a Christmas pudding are not more thoroughly shaken together or more inextricably mingled than stage-coach passengers in America are apt to be. The difficulties of the roads have developed the skill, courage, and readiness of the stage-coach men to an extraordinary degree, and I have never seen bolder or more dexterous driving than when California Bill or Colorado Jack rushed his team of four young horses down the breakneck slopes of these terrible highways. After one particularly hair-raising descent the driver condescended to explain that he was afraid to come down more slowly, lest the hind wheels should skid on the smooth rocky outcrop in the road and swing the vehicle sideways into the abyss. In coming out of the Yosemite, owing to some disturbance of the ordinary traffic arrangements our coach met the incoming stage at a part of the road so narrow that it seemed absolutely impossible for the two to pass each other. On the one side was a yawning precipice, on the other the mountain rose steeply from the roadside. The off-wheels of the incoming coach were tilted up on the hillside as far as they could be without an upset. In vain; our hubs still locked. We were then allowed to dismount. Our coach was backed down for fifty yards or so. Small heaps of stone were piled opposite the hubs of the stationary coach. Our driver whipped his horses to a gallop, ran his near-wheels over these stones so that their hubs were raised *above* those of the near-wheels of the other coach, and successfully made the dare-devil passage, in which he had not more than a couple of inches' margin to save him from precipitation into eternity. I hardly knew which to admire most—the ingenuity which thus made good in altitude what it lacked in latitude, or the phlegm with which the occupants of the other coach retained their seats throughout the entire episode. . . .

The transition from traveling facilities to the telegraphic and postal services is natural. The telegraphs of the United States are not in the hands of the government, but are controlled by private companies, of which the Western Union, with its headquarters in New York, is *facile princeps*. This company possesses the largest telegraph system in the world, having 21,000 offices and 750,000 miles of wire. It also leases or uses seven Atlantic cables. In this, however, as in many other cases, size does not necessarily connote quality. . . .

The postal service also struck me as on the whole less prompt and accurate than that of Great Britain. The comparative infrequency of fully equipped post-offices is certainly an inconvenience. . . .

No remarks on the possible inferiority of the American telegraph and postal systems would be fair if unaccompanied by a tribute to the wonderful development of the use of the telephone. New York has (or had very recently) more than twice as many subscribers to the telephonic exchanges as London, and some American towns possess one telephone for every twenty inhabitants, while the ratio in the British metropolis is 1:3,000. . . .

The generalisations made in travelers' books about the hotels of America seem to me as fallacious as most of the generalisations about this chameleon among nations. Some of the American hotels I stayed at were about the best of their kind in the world, others about the worst, others again about half-way between these extremes. On the whole, I liked the so-called "American system" of an inclusive price by the day, covering everything except such purely voluntary extras as wine; and it seems to me that an ideal hotel on this system would leave very little to wish for. The large American way of looking at things makes a man prefer to give twenty shillings per day for all he needs and consumes rather than be bothered with a bill for sixteen to seventeen shillings, including such items (not disdained even by the swellest European hotels) as one penny for stationery or a shilling for lights. . . .

In houses on the American system the price generally varies according to the style of room selected; but most of the inconvenience of a bedchamber near the top of the house is obviated by the universal service of easy-running "elevators" or lifts. (By the way, the persistent manner in which the elevators are used on all occasions is often amusing. An American lady who has some twenty shallow steps to descend to the ground floor will rather wait patiently five minutes for the elevator than walk downstairs.)

Traveler's tales as to the system of "tipping" in American hotels differ widely. The truth is probably as far from the indignant Briton's assertion, based probably on one flagrant instance in New York, that "it is ten times worse than in England and tantamount to robbery with violence," as from the patriotic American's assurance that "The thing, sir, is absolutely unknown in our free and enlightened country; no American citizen would demean himself to accept a gratuity." To judge from my own experience, I should say that the practice was quite as common in such cities as Boston, New York, and Philadelphia as in Europe, and more onerous because the amounts expected are larger. A dollar goes no farther than a shilling. Moreover, the gratuity is usually given in the form of "refreshers" from day to day, so that the vengeance of the disappointed is less easily evaded. . . .

Wine or beer is much less frequently drunk at meals than in Europe, though the amount of alcoholic liquor seen on the tables of a hotel would be a very misleading measure of the amount consumed. The men have a curious habit of flocking to the bar-room immediately after dinner to imbibe the stimulant that preference, or custom, or the fear of their wives has deprived them of during the meal. Wine is generally poor and dear. The mixed drinks at the bar are fascinating and probably very indigestible. . . .

The real national beverage is, however, ice-water. Of this I have little more to say than to warn the British visitor to suspend his judgment until he has been some time in the country. I certainly was not prejudiced in favour of this chilly draught when I started for the United States, but I soon came to find it natural and even necessary, and as much so from the dry hot air of the stove-heated room in winter as from the natural ambition of the mercury in summer. The habit so easily formed was as uneasily unlearned when I returned to civilisation. On the whole, it may be philosophic to conclude that a universal habit in any country has some solid if cryptic reason for its existence, and to surmise that the drinking of ice-water is not so deadly in the States as it might be elsewhere. It certainly is universal enough. When you ring a bell or look at a waiter, ice-water is immediately brought to you. Each meal is started with a full tumbler of that fluid, and the observant darkey rarely allows the tide to ebb until the meal is concluded. Ice-water is provided gratuitously and copiously on trains, in waiting-rooms, even sometimes in the public fountains. If, finally, I were asked to name the characteristic sound of the United States, which would tell you of your whereabouts if transported to America in an instant of time, it would be the musical tinkle of the ice in the small white pitchers that the bell-boys in hotels seem perennially carrying along all the corridors, day and night, year in and year out.

James Fullarton Muirhead, *America: The Land of Contrasts: A Briton's View of his American Kin* (London and New York, John Lane, 3rd ed., 1902), 221–272 *passim*. Reprinted by permission of the author.

8. Rural Conveniences (1912)

BY PROFESSOR HERBERT EVERETT VAN NORMAN

Van Norman was, at the time of writing, Professor of Dairy Husbandry at Pennsylvania State College. He has held many official positions in agricultural institutions; published *First Lesson in Dairying* (1908) and many articles, bulletins, etc., on dairying and agricultural subjects.—For material on farm life, see such periodicals as *Country Gentleman*, *Rural New-Yorker*, and *Successful Farming*. For more detailed accounts of particular rural conveniences, see No. 63 below on Rural Free Delivery; No. 65 on Automobiles; and No. 159 on Telephones.

FOR many years a serious problem, receiving the consideration of the student of rural problems was the drift from country to city and the causes which underlay it. Gradually conditions are changing and there is a decided movement toward the country. Careful analysis of the situation suggests that a large factor in the changed condition and increased interest in country life is the development of rural conveniences which make country living more enjoyable, not to emphasize their importance as commercial factors. The perfection and wide introduction of the telephone, rural delivery and interurban electric railway are revolutionizing the sentiment in many communities and are making marked changes in every community where they have been introduced. . . .

Business appointments, social appointments, discussions of social and church plans, to say nothing of the mere friendly exchange of greeting over the telephone have probably compensated every owner of a rural telephone many times over for the expense of it if all business advantages were ignored.

In spite of the fact that on some rural lines there are from three to twenty 'phones, many of which are called into play in response to a summons which only demands one answer, the subscriber would not be without its convenience because of its lack of privacy. At some seasons of the year the general summons to the 'phone gives notice that central is ready to report the weather bureau's prognostication for the following day. When haying and harvest or late seeding are in progress the notice of a probable change in the weather may mean the saving of part or all of a crop that would otherwise have been lost.

The rural delivery of mail has stimulated correspondence between friends and family. The certainty that the letter if written will reach the postoffice at the latest within twenty-four hours and that the answer will be delivered to the door even though every member of the family is too busy to go to the postoffice, makes for a sense of nearness which can hardly be realized unless one has experienced the sense of isolation when six or seven miles from the postoffice and "too busy to go for the mail." The business advantage resulting from a quick communication with the merchant and factory is again a factor the value of which statistics do not report. To know that the letter mailed to-day will reach its destination on the morrow in time for necessary repairs to be shipped on the express is an economic advantage which is having a desirable influence. The increase in the circulation of city dailies, agricultural weeklies and innumerable monthly magazines, social, religious and literary, has been very great. In no place is the truth of the saying "that the more one has the more one wants" greater than in the increasing use of reading matter because of rural delivery.

The regularity of market reports with its resulting closer understanding of market conditions and better judgment as to when to sell are only incidents of the conveniences that rural mail service affords. This usefulness will be added to immeasurably when the nation inaugurates a parcel post that will make possible the quick exchange of moderate sized packages between country and city at a moderate cost and with the promptness now possible in the exchange of written communications.

The interurban car line connecting the country and the town has both a commercial and a social influence in a community. To know that one has only to dress and "be ready for the 7.05 car" in order to attend a social function, a church gathering, an instructive lecture or an evening entertainment or other recreation and finish in time to catch the last car for home is conducive to rural contentment. To be free from the necessity of hitching up the horse by the light of a lantern before one dresses for the evening function; to know that one enters a social circle with the atmosphere of the house rather than of the stable; to know that after the evening pleasure is over horse and rig will not have to be cared for, and to know that a spirited horse is not standing out exposed to weather, even with a blanket on, while his owner listens to the lecture increases very materially the attractiveness of the evening diversion. This is especially true if in weighing the attractions and disadvantages early rising on the morrow is one of the drawbacks to the evening's social or educational event. . . .

Increasingly, the interurban car is becoming a systematic means of marketing products. Hundreds of thousands of gallons of milk, cream and packages of butter are regularly shipped from the farm gate to the city distributor or consumer. Market garden products, live and dressed poultry, eggs, dressed pork and mutton are all handled on many interurban lines. In some fruit sections four and five cars may be seen standing on the siding being loaded with fruit at a station where there is not a farm building in sight. Seven o'clock the following morning will find these products in the great markets of the city, fifty, sixty or even a hundred miles away. When car load shipments justify it the private siding for loading of hay, grain and other bulky crops may be secured at the individual farm.

The delivery of morning and evening papers in a territory not supplied by rural mail is often accomplished by means of the interurban car.

The automobile, by some considered a luxury, is in many sections rapidly becoming an economic factor of no small importance. The actual time saved in the delivery of milk and cream to the creamery or shipping station or the delivery of other perishable farm products; the quick securing of repairs; the rapid movement of farm labor from one job to another; the reduced time necessary to be absent from the farm work in order to transact business in town and get back are matters of vital importance, independent of any sentiment. The pleasure and contentment of the family which the automobile makes possible because of the evening automobile ride for diversion or the exchange of social courtesies and the attendance upon meetings of various kinds is not to be overlooked. The great distance that may be covered, at the same time the fact that the evening pleasure with the automobile does not lessen the efficiency of the farm motive power on the following day, as is the case when the farm team must be hitched into the pleasure vehicle, is a factor which the student of farm conditions should not overlook. From a half to an hour's distance from railroad, church and social activities is the maximum desirable limit for a farm home. With the ordinary team and conveyances this restricts the distance to not over six or seven miles. With the automobile this may be increased to from nine to twelve miles and yet the farmer will feel nearer to town and his neighbors because of his automobile than he did with his horse-drawn vehicle.

The perfection and reliability of the automobile is rapidly introducing into the rural life problem a new factor in the personnel of the city business man who finds that the thirty to fifty minutes trip from home to office daily will, when taken in his automobile, permit him to live in the country where his children may have country air and freedom, and where he can forget city business problems in an effort to develop plant and animal life, whether it takes the form of generous lawns and gardens or a systematic farm business.

The influence of this transplanted city dweller on the social life, the labor problem and the farm practice of his new environment are subjects for study which the automobile and the interurban electric car have largely made possible. Probably no one factor has been a greater stimulus to the development of country roads with their economic importance in the movement of farm products aside from pleasure than has the rural and city-owned automobile.

Aside from questions of relative remuneration, social intercourse and educational opportunities, it is the conveniences made possible by the telephone, rural mail deliveries, interurban car line and automobile that are the greatest factors in the rapidly changing rural and urban sentiment toward farm life, and are hastening the day when the successful farmer will be recognized as of the true aristocracy of the nation.

H. E. Van Norman, in *Annals of the American Academy of Political and Social Science* (Philadelphia, March, 1912), XL, 163-167 *passim*.

------◆------

9. A Chinese View of American Manners (1914)

BY MINISTER WU TING-FANG

Wu Ting-Fang was Chinese Minister to the United States 1897–1902, and 1907–1909. Notably distinguished for his wit and social grace, he viewed American peculiarities with tolerance and interest.

MUCH has been written and more said about American manners, or, rather, the American lack of manners. Americans have frequently been criticized for their bad breeding, and many sarcastic references to American deportment have been made in my presence.

I have even been told (I do not know how true it is) that European diplomats dislike being stationed in America, because of their aversion to the American way of doing things.

Much, too, has been written and said about Chinese manners, not only by foreigners, but also by Chinese. One of the classics which our youth have to know by heart is devoted almost entirely to manners. There has also been much adverse criticism of our manners or our excess of manners, though I have never heard that any diplomats have, on this account, objected to being sent to China. We Chinese are, therefore, in the same boat as the Americans. In regard to manners, neither of us finds much favor with foreigners, though for diametrically opposite reasons; the Americans are accused of observing too few formalities, and we of observing too many.

The Americans are direct and straightforward. They will tell you to your face that they like you, and occasionally they also have very little hesitation in telling you that they do not like you. They say frankly just what they think. It is immaterial to them that their remarks are personal, perhaps uncomplimentary.

The directness of Americans is seen not only in what they say, but in the way they say it. They come directly to the point, without much preface or introduction; much less is there any circumlocution or "beating about the bush." When they come to see you they say their say and then take their departure; moreover, they say it in the most terse, concise, and unambiguous manner. In this respect what a contrast they are to us! We always approach one another with preliminary greetings. Then we talk of the weather, of politics or friends —of anything, in fact, which is as far as possible from the object of the visit. Only after this introduction do we broach the subject uppermost in our minds, and throughout the conversation polite courtesies are exchanged whenever the opportunity arises. These elaborate preludes and interludes may, to the strenuous, ever-in-a-hurry American, seem useless and superfluous, but they serve a good purpose. Like the common courtesies and civilities of life, they pave the way for the speakers, especially if they are strangers; they improve their tempers and place them generally on terms of mutual understanding. It is said that some years ago a foreign consul in China, having a serious complaint to make on behalf of his nation, called on the Taotai, the highest local authority in the port. He found the

Chinese official so genial and polite that after half an hour's conversation he advised the complainant to settle the trouble amicably without bothering the Chinese officials about the matter. A good deal may be said on behalf of both systems. The American practice has at least the merit of saving time, an all-important object with the American people. When we recall that this remarkable nation will spend millions of dollars to build a tunnel under a river or to shorten a curve in a railroad, merely that they may save two or three minutes, we are not surprised at the abruptness of their speech.

Americans act up to their Declaration of Independence, especially the principle it enunciates concerning the equality of man. They lay so much importance of this that they do not confine its application to social intercourse. In fact, I think this doctrine is the basis of the so-called American manners. All men are deemed socially equal, whether as friend and friend, as President and citizen, as employer and employee, as master and servant, or as parent and child. Their relationship may be such that one is entitled to demand, and the other to render, certain acts of obedience and a certain amount of respect, but outside that they are on the same level. . . .

The youth of America have not unnaturally caught the spirit of their elders, so that even children consider themselves almost on a par with their parents, while the parents, on the other hand, also treat them as if they were equals, and allow them the utmost freedom. While a Chinese child renders unquestioning obedience to his parents' orders, such obedience as a soldier yields to his superior officer, the American child must have the whys and the wherefores duly explained to him, and the reason for his obedience made clear. It is not his parent that he obeys, but expediency and the dictates of reason. Here we see the clear-headed, sound, common-sense business man in the making. The early training of the boy has laid the foundation for the future man. . . .

Even the domestic servant does not lose this precious American heritage of equality. I have nothing to say against that worthy individual, the American servant (if one can be found). On the contrary, none is more faithful or more efficient. But in some respects he is unique among the servants of the world. He does not see that there is any inequality between him and his master. His master—or should I say his employer?—pays him certain wages to do certain work, and he does it, but outside the bounds of this contract they are still man and man, citizen and citizen.

We of the Old World are accustomed to regard domestic service as a profession in which the members work for advancement, without much thought of ever changing their position. A few clever persons may ultimately adopt another profession and, according to our antiquated, conservative ways of thinking, rise higher in the social scale, but for the large majority the dignity of a butler or a house-keeper is the height of their ambition, the crowning-point in their career. Not so the American servant. Strictly speaking, there are no servants in America. The man or the woman, as the case may be, who happens for the moment to be your servant is only servant for the time being. He has no intention of making domestic service his profession, of being a servant for the whole of his life. To be subject to the will of others, even in the small degree to which American servants are subordinate, is offensive to an American's pride of citizenship; it is contrary to his conception of American equality. He is a servant only for the time and until he finds something better to do. He accepts a menial position only as a stepping-stone to some more independent employment. Is it to be wondered at that American servants have manners different from their brethren in other coun-tries? When foreigners find that American servants are not like servants in their own country, they should not resent their behavior. It does not denote disrespect, it is merely the outcrop of their natural independence and aspirations. . . .

Few people are more warm-hearted, genial, and sociable than the Americans. I do not dwell on this, because it is quite unnecessary. The fact is perfectly familiar to all who have the slightest knowledge of them. Their kindness and warmth to strangers are particularly pleasant, and are appreciated by their visitors. In some other coun-tries the people, though not unsociable, surround themselves with so much reserve that strangers are at first chilled and repulsed, although there are no pleasanter or more hospitable persons anywhere to be found when once you have broken the ice and learned to know them; but it is the stranger who must make the first advances, for they themselves will make no effort to become acquainted, and their manner is such as to discourage any efforts on the part of the visitor. You may travel with them for hours in the same car, sit opposite to them, and all the while they will shelter themselves behind a news-paper, the broad sheets of which effectively prohibit any attempts at closer acquaintance. . . .

How different are the manners of an American! You can hardly take a walk or go for any distance in a train without being addressed by a stranger, and not infrequently making a friend. In some coun-tries the fact that you are a foreigner only thickens the ice; in America it thaws it. This delightful trait in the American character is also traceable to the same cause as that which has helped us to explain the other peculiarities which have been mentioned. To good Ameri-cans not only are the citizens of America born equal, but the citizens of the world are also born equal.

Wu Ting-Fang, *American Dinners and American Manners*, in *Harper's Magazine*, March, 1914 (New York), 526–533 *passim*.

———◆———

10. Hyphenated Americanism (1916)

BY EX-PRESIDENT THEODORE ROOSEVELT

This is a kind of essay on patriotism and national spirit, in Roosevelt's charac-teristic style.—For Roosevelt see Nos. 23–26 below.

WE must recognize that it is a cardinal sin against democracy to support a man for public office because he belongs to a given creed or to oppose him because he belongs to a given creed. It is just as evil as to draw the line between class and class, between occupation and occupation in political life. No man who tries to draw either line is a good American. True Americanism demands that we judge each man on his conduct, that we so judge him in public life. The line of cleavage drawn on principle and conduct in public affairs is never in any healthy community identical with the line of cleavage between creed and creed or between class and class. On the contrary, where the community life is healthy, these lines of cleavage almost always run nearly at right angles to one another. It is eminently necessary to all of us that we should have able and honest public officials in the nation, in the city, in the state. If we make a serious and resolute effort to get such officials of the right kind, men who shall not only be honest but shall be able and shall take the right view of public questions, we will find as a matter of fact that the men we thus choose will be drawn from the professors of every creed and from among men who do not adhere to any creed.

For thirty-five years I have been more or less actively engaged in public life, in the performance of my political duties, now in a public position, now in a private position. I have fought with all the fervor I possessed for the various causes in which with all my heart I believed; and in every fight I thus made I have had with me and against me Catholics, Protestants and Jews. There have been times when I have had to make the fight for or against some man of each creed on grounds of plain public morality, unconnected with questions of public policy. There were other times when I have made such a fight for or against a given man, not on grounds of public morality, for he may have been morally a good man, but on account of his attitude on questions of public policy, of governmental principle. In both cases, I have always found myself fighting beside, and fighting against, men of every creed. The one sure way to have secured the defeat of every good principle worth fighting for would have been to have permitted the fight to be changed into one along sectarian lines and inspired by the spirit of sectarian bitterness, either for the purpose of putting into public life or of keeping out of public life the believers in any given creed. Such conduct represents an assault upon Americanism. The man guilty of it is not a good American.

I hold that in this country there must be complete severance of Church and State; that public moneys shall not be used for the purpose of advancing any particular creed; and therefore that the public schools shall be non-sectarian and no public moneys appropriated for sectarian schools. As a necessary corollary to this, not only the pupils but the members of the teaching force and the school officials of all kinds must be treated exactly on a par, no matter what their creed; and there must be no more discrimination against Jew or Catholic or Protestant than discrimination in favor of Jew, Catholic or Protestant. Whoever makes such discrimination is an enemy of the public schools.

What is true of creed is no less true of nationality. There is no room in this country for hyphenated Americans. When I refer to hyphenated Americanism, I do not refer to naturalized Americans. Some of the very best Americans I have ever known were naturalized Americans, Americans born abroad. But a hyphenated American is not an American at all. This is just as true of the man who puts "native" before the hyphen as of the man who puts German or Irish or English or French before the hyphen. Americanism is a matter of the spirit and of the soul. Our allegiance must be purely to the United States. We must unsparingly condemn any man who holds any other allegiance. But if he is heartily and singly loyal to this Republic, then no matter where he was born, he is just as good an American as any one else. . . .

When in 1909 our battle fleet returned from its voyage around the world, Admirals Wainwright and Schroeder represented the best traditions and the most efficient action in our navy; one was of old American blood and of English descent; the other was the son of German immigrants. But one was not a native-American and the other a German-American. Each was an American pure and simple. Each bore allegiance only to the flag of the United States. Each would have been incapable of considering the interests of Germany or of England or of any other country except the United States. . . .

For an American citizen to vote as a German-American, an Irish-American or an English-American is to be a traitor to American institutions; and those hyphenated Americans who terrorize American politicians by threats of the foreign vote are engaged in treason to the American Republic.

Now this is a declaration of principles. How are we in practical fashion to secure the making of these principles part of the very fiber of our national life? First and foremost let us all resolve that in this country hereafter we shall place far less emphasis upon the question of right and much greater emphasis upon the matter of duty. A republic can't succeed and won't succeed in the tremendous international stress of the modern world unless its citizens possess that form of high-minded patriotism which consists of individual rights. . . .

We should meet this situation by on the one hand seeing that these immigrants get all their rights as American citizens, and on the other hand insisting that they live up to their duties as American citizens. Any discrimination against aliens is a wrong, for it tends to put the immigrant at a disadvantage and to cause him to feel bitterness and resentment during the very years when he should be preparing himself for American citizenship. If an immigrant is not fit to become a citizen, he should not be allowed to come here. If he is fit, he should be given all the rights to earn his own livelihood, and to better himself, that any man can have. Take such a matter as the illiteracy test; I entirely agree with those who feel that many very excellent possible citizens would be barred improperly by an illiteracy test. But why do you not admit aliens under a bond to learn to read and write English within a certain time? It would then be a duty to see that they were given ample opportunity to learn to read and write and that they were deported if they failed to take advantage of the opportunity. No man can be a good citizen if he is not at least in process of learning to speak the language of his fellow-citizens. And an alien who remains here without learning to speak English for more than a certain number of years should at the end of that time be treated as having refused to take the preliminary steps necessary to complete Americanization and should be deported. But there should be no denial or limitation of the alien's opportunity to work, to own property and to take advantage of civic opportunities. Special legislation should deal with the aliens who do not come here to be made citizens. But the alien who comes here intending to become a citizen should be helped in every way to advance himself, should be removed from every possible disadvantage and in return should be required under penalty of being sent back to the country from which he came, to prove that he is in good faith fitting himself to be an American citizen. We should set a high standard and insist on men reaching it; but if they do reach it we should treat them as on a full equality with ourselves.

From *Fear God and Take Your Own Part*, by Theodore Roosevelt (copyright 1916, George H. Doran Company), 359–370 *passim*.

11.   The Flapper: A National Institution (1926)

BY SAMUEL CROWTHER

Crowther is a journalist who has written on a wide variety of subjects, most of them with an economic slant.—Bibliography: Harold U. Faulkner, American Economic History; Garet Garrett, The American Omen; and frequent popular articles in Collier's Weekly and The Saturday Evening Post.

IT was not so long ago that going to a bootblack was an extravagance—fool-and-his-money affair, or diversion of improvident traveling salesmen. Then shines were five cents. To-day they are ten, and we take them as a matter of course.

During the past several months I have traveled from coast to coast and from Fargo, N. D., to El Paso, Tex.—through all the states and in all the cities and many of the towns. I did not find a town of over two thousand—and I doubt if there is one—where Jeanette or Lucille or Marie is not running a "beauty parlor" or a "beauty shoppe" and doing fairly well. In Sioux Falls, S. D., I counted three in two blocks—and Sioux Falls is supposed to be broke.

Polishing shoes and polishing hands and faces have become great industries, earning many millions a year. In a small Middle West city I saw, in the wholesale district, a store devoted entirely to selling beauty-parlor aprons. Every fair-sized city has its "beauty school" and also you can learn by mail.

But why bother about such trivialities as shining shoes and steaming faces—does not this just go to show that the males are growing laxer and the females more vain? It means a lot more.

It means more than the figures any statistician might assemble—it means that we to-day are rich enough to go in for luxuries not just in the big cities but everywhere in our land. It means that we are all rich in a way, for there are not enough of the really rich to keep so many places going.

Consider the flapper and how she grows. I was not on a flapper hunt; my primary purpose was to see what was going on in this country. I had heard many doleful tales—we were riding to a fall; our people were not working but demanding extravagant wages for going through the motions of work; money was being spent and not saved; numerous homely virtues of our forefathers had been scrapped; we were all in hock for automobiles, radios, diamond rings, and the thousand and one knickknacks that you can buy for a dollar down and a dollar when they catch you; and the country had to get back to normalcy or perish. I have not yet been able to discover exactly what normalcy is, but as far as I can make out it is intimately connected with 1913 and Canton flannel nighties.

I was told that people were skimping on necessities in order to indulge in luxuries; that retail dealers were nervous and bought only from hand to mouth, because they could not know from one day to the next what their business would be; that the consumption of the country was far below productive capacity, and that we simply had to have a drastic readjustment.

I talked with bankers, business men and farmers, and also I kept my eyes and my ears open, and I reached the conclusion that our only trouble is that we have not yet awakened to what this country really is—what has happened, what is happening or what can happen.

We have been measuring it with old measures. We have been thinking, "For the poor always ye have with you." We cannot comprehend that to America has come a new order of things—that dire poverty is as rare as small pox and as obsolete; that we are in the midst of a great experiment the like of which the world has never even dreamed of, and that it lies with us to carry on or to funk.

Our national machine is wondrously strong. It hit many a wicked bump in the three years from 1920 to 1923, and those bumps, which would have smashed any other machine, merely tuned ours up—as one tunes up a new motor car. . . .

But we have built up our machine by good management which pays high wages. We have an enormous stock of good managers. We have only a few bad ones and they are principally in the textiles and in coal. But over and above all and more powerful than anything is this—our people have the will to be prosperous. That is the great fact which shows out all over the country—and it is nowhere more evident than in the flapper. . . .

The real flapper is what used to be known as the "poor working girl"—who, if the accounts are true, dragged herself off day by day to work until someone came along and married her. Sometimes she was a Cinderella, but more often she graduated a household drudge.

The flapper of to-day is a very different person. In dress she is as standardized as a chain hotel—and incidentally hotel bedrooms are becoming so alike that you can remember what city you are in only by tacking a local newspaper on the wall. Barring size, flappers at a hundred feet are as standardized as Ford cars. As far as dress goes, they are a simplified national product. . . . There is no distinction between the town flapper and the farm flapper—the automobile has wiped them out. There is no distinction in the cut of clothing between the rich flapper and the poor flapper—national advertising has attended to that. The rich flapper has better clothing than the poor one, but a block away they are all flappers.

The outstanding characteristic of the flapper is not her uniform but her independence and her will to be prosperous.

She is no clinging vine. I was in the office of the president of a good-sized bank on the Pacific Coast when his daughter and several of her high-school friends burst in—flappers all. We got to talking and I found that these girls, not one of whom had any need to work, all intended to find jobs during the summer, and they thought that most of the girls in school would do the same. They all wanted to know how to make a living—and to have a good time doing it. That seems to be common everywhere.

Girls will no longer marry men who can merely support them— they can support themselves better than can many of the men of their own age. They have awakened to the fact that the "superior sex" stuff is all bunk. They will not meekly bow their heads to the valiant man who roars, "Where is that dress I bought you three years ago?" . . .

The flapper wants to look well, and she is willing to provide for herself—employers everywhere told me that the women were doing better work than the men, and they do seem to be mentally more alert. All of which means that the man who marries the modern flapper has got to provide for her—she will not be merely an unpaid servant. And this in turn means that the men have got to work— than which nothing better could happen for the country. The flapper is to-day our most important national institution. . . .

The will to be prosperous has brought prosperity. We have practically no poverty, and I judge that at least two-thirds of what little we have is voluntary.

The rest is due to accident or disease and must clearly be distinguished from destitution, for its amount is negligible and can easily be cared for by the communities in which it exists. There is work at fair wages for anyone who will go after it—some will not go after it.

For instance, in southern Ohio, near Ironton, I found many squatter shacks—filthy huts thrown together from any old thing and standing in seas of mud. Lounging about were always a big, brutish, dull-eyed man and a slatternly, barefoot, tired-looking woman, with any-where from half a dozen pale, ill-nourished, half-dressed children—not a few of whom had the look of imbeciles. These men were soft-coal miners. They have had almost no work since 1919, yet they persist in being miners.

An engineer told me that on a big excavating job near by he had offered these men six dollars a day, but not one of them would take a job. He actually had to import his labor. The miners shuffled over every day to see how things were coming, but not one of them would work even for a single day. That is what I mean by voluntary poverty.

We have the same sort of thing through the mountains in the South, and we have the white trash and the shiftless Negro, but the tremen-dous industrial expansion of the South—for there are cotton mills going up nearly everywhere—is drawing down the mountaineers and taking the white trash and making human beings of them, while the Negro is leaving the South and scattering far and wide through the industries of the Middle West.

Nearly all our backward people have felt the touch of money. They have increased their wants. They all want automobiles, and the women, and especially the girls, want clothes. They are learning that they can get the things they want only by work. . . .

Within a generation the regular payment of wages will completely have transformed the South. The daughters and the sons nowhere are content just to live!

The purchasing power of the South Atlantic States, although it is still small as compared with that of the North Atlantic States, is probably fifty times what it was before the World War. And that is the sort of thing which is going on everywhere. This country is not static. It is in flux; it is ridiculous to talk of the country in terms of European economics—for instance, to talk of saturation points. We do not even know what there is to saturate—we are changing so mightily.

Samuel Crowther, "Aren't We All Rich Now?" in *Collier's* (New York, November 7, 1926), 9–10 *passim.*

CHAPTER III — SECTIONS AND NEW STATES

12. The Great Empire by the Lakes (1900)

BY FREDERIC C. HOWE

Howe was Commissioner of Immigration at the port of New York, 1914–1919; has written many books on political and social subjects.—For material on the general subject of this chapter see such periodicals as *World's Work, Century,* and *Review of Reviews;* also consult *Readers' Guide* under names of states, and of sections, such as New England.

PROBABLY the greatest industrial phenomenon of the past ten years, unless it be the trust development, is the consummation of the dreams of far-sighted business men, by which the iron mines of Lake Superior have been linked with the coal and coke fields of Pennsylvania. This has led to the tremendous development of the iron and steel industry in the Pittsburg and Cleveland districts. Human labor has been reduced to an insignificant item in all the processes, from the extraction of the crude ore from the earth, to the production of the finished product at the furnace nearly a thousand miles away. Railroads have been built from Pittsburg to Lake Erie, as have immense docks and cavernous iron steamships, as large as ocean liners, designed almost exclusively for the transportation of ore, coal, and grain. All the essentials of production, including the mines, steamships, railroads, docks, and furnaces, have been combined under one hand. At the present time Carnegie, the American Steel & Wire Company, and the National Steel Company own their own boats and do at least a part of their own carrying business. These companies also own their own mines.

Coincident with this consolidation there has occurred a revolution in industrial methods before which earlier achievements sink into insignificance. A few decades ago the blast furnace was an enlarged blacksmith shop, and the finished product, whether a steel rail or horseshoe nail, was largely the result of manual labor. By present processes, from the moment the steam scoop, handling tons of native ore, touches the soil in Minnesota or Michigan until the raw material issues as a hundred-pound steel rail on the banks of the Monongahela River, the element of human labor is scarce appreciable. Trains in the Superior district are loaded by steam scoops. At the docks the cars are unloaded into bins or pockets. From these pockets, ships of five to seven thousand gross tons' capacity are loaded in a few hours' time, through chute attachments running into the holds of the vessels.

In the Mesabi range a half dozen men will mine five thousand tons of ore in a few hours. An ore vessel is loaded almost without the use of pickax or shovel. Gravitation does the work formerly done by man. On the lower lakes the vessels are unloaded in a few hours' time by hoisting-devices or clam-like scoops which will do the work of sixty men and transport ten tons of ore in a single clasp of the scoop. Steel cars with a capacity of sixty tons are unloaded at the furnaces by immense cranes which pick the cars clear from the tracks, transport them to an ore pile, and dump them as simply and easily, and with as much precision, as if they were but buckets of sand. The earth is tapped, and genii-like enginery, with man's hand on the throttle, turns out the finished product.

And as if by the prevision of nature, the vast coal regions of western Pennsylvania, Ohio, and West Virginia furnish return cargoes to the upper lakes. These return cargoes greatly reduce freight rates. The coal tonnage of the lakes for the year 1899 amounted to 9,000,000 tons, which was taken from the bituminous coal fields of these states and transported to its destination, by the aid of the same sort of machinery as is used in the handling of ore.

Inferior only in importance to the iron ore and coal industry is that of the copper mines of the upper Peninsula of Michigan. The long, projecting promontory on the southern shore of Lake Superior, known as Keweenaw Point, is dotted with copper mines, of which the Calumet and Hecla is the chief. From these mines are extracted millions of dollars' worth of native copper every year. This region supplies a large part of the world's copper, and the mines yield fabulous returns to those who anticipated the future of this industry. The stock of the Calumet and Hecla mine, of the par value of twenty-five dollars per share, is now quoted at seven hundred and sixty dollars per share. Upon this stock but twelve dollars and fifty cents has ever been paid in. And some of the iron mines in the Lake Superior ranges show a commercial standing only less remarkable.

From the watershed of the Great Lakes, moreover, is taken a large part of the lumber supply for the eastern and central states, while to the south of Lake Erie, in western Pennsylvania, Ohio, West Virginia, and Indiana, are the great oil fields, which supply not only America, but the world, with petroleum. Salt in immense quantities is secured from the region about Cleveland, while the building-stones of the upper lakes are among the most beautiful that we have.

Nature has been lavish of her riches in this Great Lakes region. She has created here an empire richer than that of the Incas. For while the precious metals are not found, those which furnish the sinews of modern commerce abound in quantities to supply the world.

The dividends of one copper mine in the Lake Superior district, whose capital stock is but $2,500,000, amounted in the year 1899 to $10,000,000. In 1898 the same mine declared dividends of $5,000,000. Some of the iron mines of the same district distribute the total capital value of their mines in dividends each year. And during the past ten years hundreds of persons have been enriched from the iron, coal, copper, oil, and gas fields of this region. Could these bounties have been preserved to the state, the problems of finance would have been easy of solution.

The great power tunnel by which the forces of Niagara are utilized for the generation of power, as well as a similar power canal in construction at Sault Ste. Marie, Michigan, evidence again the way nature is forced to do man's work while he stands by. And the secret of the phenomenal development of this region lies in this fact. It has been brought about by the harnessing of force and the utilization of man's ingenuity and the engineer's skill. From mine to mill a thousand miles away, with two breakages in carriage, is as simple, if not a simpler process than a like breakage in freight at the Hudson River. The element of labor cost in a ton of ore from mine to furnace has been reduced to insignificance. It amounts to but a few cents. The forces of steam, hydraulics, pneumatics, and electricity have achieved this result.

One of the great, if not *the* great, problem of the last generation has been the reduction of transportation charges. By this cheapening of carriage cost space has been annihilated. To us this problem was basic. Our distances are so great. How well we have succeeded is seen in the low railroad and steamboat freight rates. On the Great Lakes the charges for carrying a ton of freight one mile are less than one-tenth of one cent. Railroad freights in competition are about four times as much. To-day the eyes of European engineers are turned on the transportation systems of America.

But transportation on the lakes includes something more than delivery from port to port. It involves the transfer from railroad to boat and from boat to railroad. And these processes have become as much a part of lake transportation as the carriage. In this respect inventive ingenuity has kept pace with our demands, and transfers at the docks are now accomplished by immense machinery, which seems to operate with almost human intelligence.

It is through the waterways of the Great Lakes that a large portion of the grain of the world is carried. By reason of the low water freight charges, the prairies of the West are able to lay their products down in the European market at a price otherwise impossible. The significance of these great waterways, not only to the states of the West, but to the civilization of the world, cannot be overstated.

And far-seeing men of this region are now casting their eyes toward the markets of the world. Plans have been matured to place the coal fields of Ohio, West Virginia, and Pennsylvania in immediate touch with European ports. Within a short time a fleet of boats will carry coal between Newport News and Europe. The former point will be connected with the interior by a railroad. This will mean a fuel economy to European cities of from one dollar to two dollars a ton. One may safely say that the next generation will see the coal fields and iron mines of America supplying the European consumer, much as the wheat fields of the West now supply the English artisan. Within the next year and a half it is freely expected that American ore will be landed in the Clyde. To-day America is "carrying coals to Newcastle."

Frederic C. Howe, in *World's Work*, November, 1900 (New York), I, 409–412 *passim*.

13. Remedies for the Southern Problem (1905)

BY PROFESSOR ALBERT BUSHNELL HART

The author, Professor of Government in Harvard University, has written on a great variety of subjects concerned with American History.—For further information by him on the present subject, see A. B. Hart, *The Southern South.*

. . . THE first and most obvious remedy is to remove the supposed cause. This idea of deportation of the negroes was suggested more than a century ago by Thomas Jefferson and was later urged by Lincoln. An instant objection is that it is resisted by nearly every one of the nine million negroes, South and North alike. They no more wish to cross the ocean eastward than their ancestors did to come westward. The negroes in general are attached to their homes and would probably fight rather than add to the repeated failures of attempts to build up civilized communities of American negroes in Africa, which is the only region available for such an emigration. An equally strong objection is that the white people absolutely will not permit the negro to leave the country. When in 1889 attempts were made to draw negroes to Kansas the boats that were carrying them were stopped by armed men and the negroes were driven back with the shotgun. On the other hand, in a number of communities, especially in the mountains, the poor whites will not permit the negroes to come in; and, for that matter, there is a town of several thousand people in southern Ohio where no negro has ever been allowed to stop over night. Nevertheless, where the negro is there he stays; and for the very simple reason that without him or her there would be no breakfast in the big house, no wood cut for the fires, no cotton raised, no babies dressed—for the real confidence of the whites in the negro race is shown by their almost universal practice of committing their little children to negro nurses. To deport the negro would mean the social disruption as well as the economic ruin of the greater part of the South, and the fierce and brutal advocacy of that method which one hears occasionally from Southern men is simply a piece of acting.

For there is no substitute in sight, since the South has never been able to attract foreign immigrants. The census of 1900 shows that the eleven States that seceded in 1861 have 11,400,000 native whites, 7,200,000 negroes and only 350,000 people of foreign birth, of whom two-thirds are in Louisiana and Texas, while the rest of the Union shows 45,300,000 native whites, 1,600,000 negroes and 10,000,000 foreigners. The figures explain themselves: most immigrants work with their hands and avoid regions where there is a poor opportunity for their children, and where handwork classes them with a servile race. The only foreign element now seeking the South is the Italian, some thousands of whom are to be found in the Mississippi bottoms; but their influx is likely to be checked when they discover that they, like the negroes, are to be excluded from the suffrage wherever they come to be in the majority or to exercise the balance of power.

A remedy not publicly advocated, yet practiced in some remote parts of the South, is peonage. It is not necessary to go to the length of some State laws which assume to legalize contracts by which the laborer agrees to work or else to accept a whipping and a bull pen; servitude is realized if they are deliberately kept in such a condition of debt and dependence that they cannot acquire land or move about freely. The testimony of people who have visited rural plantations is that in many places great advantage is taken of the ignorance of the negro; that he is cheated in his efforts to buy land, that in some places he is a serf, tied to the land. Inasmuch as probably a majority of the intelligent people of the South insist that the negro was better off in slavery than in freedom, there is in some regions insufficient healthy public sentiment to protect the rural laborer.

Another method widely applied in the South has been put by Senator Tillman in the sententious form: "We shall have to send a few more negroes to hell." This brute method is a deliberate attempt to keep the race down by occasionally shooting negroes because they are bad, or loose-tongued, or influential, or acquiring property; and by insisting that the murder of a white man, or sometimes even a saucy speech by a negro to a white man, is to be followed by swift, relentless and often tormenting death. In every case of passionate conflict between two races the higher one loses most, because it has most to lose; and lynch law as a remedy for the lawlessness of the negroes has the disadvantage of demoralizing the white race, and eventually of exposing white men to the uncontrollable passions of other white men. The usual, tho not the real, justification for lynching is that nothing else can protect or avenge white women. Rapes and lynchings aggravate but do not cause race hostility. Any Southern State might forthwith reduce both the negro crime and that of his white executioners by following a useful precedent of slavery times—by providing a special tribunal of reputable men, not necessarily lawyers, with summary process, testimony behind closed doors if desirable, and quick but civilized punishment for aggravated crimes of violence, committed by whites or blacks.

Another remedy is education. It would be very unjust to leave the impression that the white people of the South as a community approve of solving the negro question by aggravating it. Indeed, the South has made great sacrifices since the Civil War to educate the negro, tho it somewhat exaggerates its benefactions by dwelling on the fact that the negroes pay two per cent. of the taxes and furnish nearly one-half of the school children. One of the most influential newspapers in the South recently threatened to cut off the funds for negro education if Northern benefactors did not cease giving money to negro schools. In New York and Chicago there is no protest because the people who furnish nineteen-twentieths of the school children pay only one-twentieth of the taxes. The South, however, begins to realize that reducing the present illiteracy in the South among both negroes and whites is not all the battle. Your negro chamber-maid may have been through eight years' study in the city schools and yet remain incredibly ignorant and brutish. Still the North also has learned that ability to read, write and cipher will not make model citizens out of the morally degraded. In many ways the most hopeful thing for the negro is the work of institutions like Fisk, Atlanta and Talladega, which aim to train future professional men and women and especially teachers.

Hence the great interest now felt by good people in the South in industrial education for negroes, and sometimes even for whites. This is partly due to the success of Hampton, Tuskegee, Calhoun and other like institutions, which have proven the expansion of mind resulting from the more intelligent forms of handiwork combined with a judicious use of books. In these schools a great part of the good is done by the character of the teachers, and nobody can see the fine body of young, alert minds trained by the best universities of the country which make up the faculty, say of Tuskegee, without hopefulness that they will train as well as instruct. Yet from the Southern point of view their success will raise the same ultimate difficulty as other forms of education for the negroes. Notwithstanding the influence of a few notable men, at the head of whom is Booker T. Washington, the whites in general do not wish to see leaders and organizers arise among the negroes; they distrust the negro preachers and have a contempt for negro professors, lawyers and physicians. If industrial education produces good blacksmiths, carpenters and domestic servants the South will be pleased, tho perhaps the trades unions will have something to say; but the South does not wish to see political and social leaders springing up among the negroes, lest they attempt such organization of the negroes as would give them power over the white race. . . .

Any remedy for the ills that beset the South must recognize that the condition of the negroes is discouraging; that in forty years of freedom they have made less progress than white people expected; that as a race they have little sense of truth and perhaps of sexual morality; that they furnish great numbers of idlers and many criminals. This dark picture must, however, include also about half the poor whites, who, tho far superior to the negroes in intellect, match them in ignorance and overmatch them in blood-thirstiness. These are the conditions from which the community must extricate itself or admit that it cannot civilize its own people.

It is perfectly true, and we of the North must candidly acknowledge and appreciate it, that many Southerners are making genuine and self-sacrificing effort to upraise their colored neighbors, by personal interest in their education, by protection of their rights, by example of moderation and respect for law, by appreciation (so far as the color line admits) of their best men. These are the white people who ought to solve the problem if anybody, yet they are precisely the people who see the only solution in a very slow elevation of the colored race, during which many things may come in to accentuate the race problem.

On one side the remedy is the slow uplifting of the negro race, the practice of those homely virtues of industry, steadiness, thrift and habits of saving which have made the Northern communities what they are. The Southern people are right in demanding that the negroes themselves shall discourage and discountenance the criminals of their race, and make it their business to help to bring to legal, orderly punishment the desperate criminals who arouse the most fearful resentment of the whites. The negroes must be taught to respect and honor the best members of their own race and to bring up their children to follow such models. That is the way, and the only way, in which a race can rise.

But how can the negroes be expected to respect and admire what the whites despise? Can the poor white call the thriftlessness of the negro hopeless? Is the negro to set the example of lawabiding to the white man? Are the Southern whites to abjure the duty of the highest in the community to make the standard of coolness, patience and observance of law? Why does not the white man, who boasts of his interest in and aid to the negro during slavery, do more to educate him now? The other day a South Carolina storekeeper who stepped into a negro school and made a speech of encouragement found himself in danger of mobbing and made an abject recantation. Why not everywhere put cultivated white teachers into the negro schools, such as are employed in Charleston? Why should not negroes of high character be honored by degrees from institutions of learning? Why do not the white people with good will open the door of opportunity to a few places in the public service to negroes whom they recognize as qualified?

The reason is simple; the Southern whites have an unfounded and unformulated fear that somehow white supremacy is endangered; and they see no halting place between acknowledging that some negroes are men of character and "permitting your daughter to marry a nigger." The true remedy for the Southerner is to do with the negro exactly what his brethren are doing up North with the Pole, the Slovak and the Hungarian. Why does he not make the best of a bad job and not the worst? Why not set before the negro every possible inducement to rise, by facilitating the purchase of land, by opening new industries, by granting to the best negroes such scanty rewards as the white man's color line permits? The Southern white community may well ponder the meaning of one of Booker Washington's noblest utterances: "I will never allow any man to drag me down by making me hate him!"

Albert Bushnell Hart, in *Independent* (New York, 1905), LVIII, 993–996 *passim*.

14. Arizona and New Mexico (1911)

BY CHARLES MOREAU HARGER

Harger is a journalist and a frequent contributor to periodicals. Has been director and lecturer in the Department of Journalism, University of Kansas. Editor of the Abilene (Kansas) *Daily Reflector*.—Bibliography as in No. 12 above.

FOR centuries 235,000 square miles of gray desert, blue hills, mesas, and valleys dozed under almost cloudless skies. The awakening has come in two distinct periods. Said an old ranchman of New Mexico: "Eighteen years ago I moved here from Illinois. Practically all the Americans in New Mexcio were from Arkansas, Tennessee, Texas, Missouri. They drifted in after the war, just as Northerners went to Kansas and Nebraska. They were stockmen; so are their descendants to-day. Ten years ago, when irrigation became a feature of agriculture, families from Illinois, Indiana, and Ohio arrived on homeseekers' excursions. Later, Nebraska, Iowa, and Kansas furnished settlers, until now we have folks from all over the East."

In Arizona the mines brought the first American residents. They came seeking copper, gold, silver. Later came the farmer and the home-builder. To-day on the streets of Phoenix or Bisbee is a cosmopolitan assembly representing every section of the Nation.

So on its 122,000 square miles New Mexico has 327,000 population; Arizona on its 113,000 square miles has 200,000. While historically and physically having much in common, the Territories are temperamentally far apart. "It comes from their varied settlement," explained ex-Governor J. H. Kibbey, of Arizona. "New Mexico's valleys run north and south, and the early Mexican sheep-herders pastured their flocks far northward. When given grants for more or less valuable services to ruler or conqueror, they chose lands with which they were familiar. The American settlers, westward bound, found a start made toward civilization, and stopped there in large numbers. In Arizona the valleys extend east and west, and the herders were less likely to cross deserts to reach them. The discovery of mines brought the Americans, and not until a later era came the farmer."

So one State is pastoral, the other devoted more largely to mines, and each harbors a grievance against the East. "We have not received a square deal," said Governor R. E. Sloan, of Arizona. "The East has looked upon the Southwest as yet existing in the wild and woolly frontier period, with cowboys 'shooting up ' the towns, with terrorism frequently rampant. On the contrary, no Eastern State community is better behaved or has a higher average of citizenship than these new States." . . .

In one direction do both States look for industrial progress—irrigation. Their mines produce great wealth, likely to increase as the hills are more thoroughly tested; their lumber camps are important. But mines and lumber camps do not bring homes; they attract migratory laborers whose interest is ephemeral. The farm makes for development of a social life. Only by irrigation can either State hope to build up such a feature. Month after month of cloudless skies and pulsating sunlight will not, even on good soil, raise crops. "Dry farming " is a delusion when the season is too dry. "Thousands of settlers have tried it and failed," said a Territorial officer. "No amount of cultivation can bring moisture from dry skies, and in most years it is a doubtful venture." Unless combined with ranching, the settler is unwise to seek a competency by that route. Better twenty acres under ditch than two hundred on the unwatered prairie. The expense of intensive culture necessary to raise crops with a minimum of rainfall is not repaid by the production. This hundreds of disappointed families have discovered.

Each State has its special pride in irrigation enterprise. New Mexico has approximately 500,000 acres under ditch, with 3,000,000 more amenable to artificial watering. It will take decades to utilize it all, but some day the waters of the Rio Grande and its tributaries, with the flow of smaller streams and surface moisture, will be conserved. The Pecos Valley is already practically all under the plow; the Mesilla Valley is rapidly being improved as settlers realize its possibilities. The Government Reclamation Service is expending millions in projects that will fertilize vast areas. Of these, that of the Rio Grande is largest. On that river, seventy-five miles north of Las Cruces, is located one of the greatest natural reservoir sites in the world. Below this site is the Mesilla Valley; then for twenty miles north of El Paso, and for a like distance below that city, in Texas, is another large area of extremely fertile land. Immediately across the river, in the Republic of Mexico, and in the vicinity of the city of Juarez, are found, approximately, 25,000 acres of equally valuable soil. Here the Elephant Butte project, to cost $9,000,000, one of the most important in the Reclamation Service undertakings, is to be constructed. For Mexico's share Congress appropriated $1,000,000. The total area watered will be 180,000 acres—110,000 in New Mexico, 45,000 in Texas, and 25,000 in Mexico. In three or four years some storage will be provided.

Nearer completion is Arizona's portion in the Service's notable work—the Roosevelt Dam on the Salt River, to be dedicated by Mr. Roosevelt next March. Here the Salt River Valley lies like an outstretched hand reaching westward, with a rock-bound gateway at the wrist. The great bulwark of masonry, built at a cost of $6,000,000, rears its 240 feet, a massive retainer of a lake covering 17,000 acres. Behind it flood waters will be held to be spread out over 200,000 acres, with an additional 40,000 acres to be irrigated by pumping. Here will be demonstrated, as in other similar projects, the possibilities of an acre. Where a man can take $705.65 in asparagus from 1¾ acres and $980 from one acre of blackberries, or where 7½ acres of mixed berries and melons yield net $3,200, or ten acres of oranges produce 1,800 boxes which return an average of $4 per box, it is clear that only a few will care to own more than they can well cultivate.

"Agriculture," said Governor W. J. Mills, of New Mexico, "is the hope of the Southwest, winning to us men who are worthy as citizens and successful as managers." . . .

The Southwest has peculiar problems, such as face no other part of our Nation. Chief among them is that of the Mexican population— the politician does not say "Mexican," he refers to "our Spanish-American friends." There are plenty of them. In New Mexico 135,000, 41 per cent of the population, according to the Census supervisor, are Spanish-Americans. Many more have some Spanish blood. There are towns and counties wholly dominated by them in politics and business. Once the Territory was theirs, but American immigration has changed that, and to-day the "native" occupies a secondary place. But he must be reckoned in every accounting.

When the Constitutional Convention met, October 3, of the one hundred delegates, thirty were Mexican. All were Republicans, and added their votes to that of forty-one Americans, making seventy-one Republicans to twenty-nine Democrats. In some of the precincts the ballots for the election of delegates were printed in Spanish. This was the excuse expressed by a Territorial officer: "The precincts where this was done have an almost wholly Mexican population. The voters are men who cannot read or write English, though they can speak and understand it. It was simpler to print the ballots so they could read them than to take each voter into the booth and explain the wording of the ballot. With the next generation there will be no such problem. Every school in the Territory teaches English to every pupil. Spanish is taught only as an additional language in the high schools. All must know English; but the earlier generation will never learn it."

This Mexican population is of two classes: a large portion the laborers, the sheepmen; a smaller part men of means, shrewd business managers. Curiously, in view of the usual conception of the Mexican, he is given a good reputation by those who know him best. "I have had twenty years' experience with him," said the manager of a one-hundred-thousand-acre ranch. "I have never found better laborers or men who would keep a contract more faithfully. They do not strike, and, treated well, they remain with you. I have bought tens of thousands of sheep of Mexican shepherds without a written contract, and never had one fail to do as he agreed—which is more than I can say for some American stock-owners. We must have laborers, and this class furnishes them. Without them it would be difficult to develop a definite place in the Southwest." . . .

In Arizona there is the Mormon question. Two members of the Church of the Latter-Day Saints were elected members of the Arizona Convention. Said Governor Sloan: "It has been repeatedly charged that the Mormon vote in Arizona is thirty per cent of the total; it is not more than ten per cent. The people of this sect are farmers and good citizens. They are prohibitionists and not polygamists. There is no indication that they will ever be a large factor in the State's politics. The Mexican population is not more than fifteen per cent, mostly itinerants, and likewise no important factor in politics, for the American population is increasing, while the Spanish-American stands still. We have had clean Legislatures, no scandals, and have an ambition to make this a good State for the farmer and business man alike. With our 400,000 acres now in cultivation we can support twice the present population. Eventually there will be 1,250,000 acres tilled, and every acre extraordinarily productive. We want settlers and capital, and propose to give both square treatment."

This last sentence is the key to the sentiment of the dweller in the Southwest. Men and money are needed. Irrigation enterprises cannot pay unless settlers come to till the lands. Here and there a plunger has equipped a great ranch house, making a mansion in the desert. He has lived like a king, impressing every titled visitor— and then departed. Such investors are not wanted. The future will depend on the worker, the man who comes to stay. Owing to the vast distances and the waste desert lands, there can never be a network of railways such as has covered Oklahoma and other parts of the Middle West. Two trunk lines with some branches constitute practically all the railway facilities likely to be had for many years. The new States will be disposed to consider this in their statutes, as they will the work of capital that has developed the mines and stored the waters; but there is a strong undercurrent of disposition to regulate corporations and secure for the citizen his full rights.

In New Mexico, where the Republican majority is overwhelming, primaries, initiative and referendum, and similar progressive ideas have not been indorsed. The Constitution is to be, as Governor Mills expressed it, "safe and sane," with the idea of submitting additional propositions to the votors separately. The Mexican voters, being largely sheepmen, are generally high-tariff advocates, and this accounts for much of their allegiance to Republicanism. In Arizona the Democrats are in large majority, the Constitutional Convention having forty-four Democrats to eight Republicans, no Spanish-American delegate being elected. The Constitution will contain many "Progressive" sections. In neither State is equal suffrage or prohibition likely to carry. The initiative and referendum will probably be a part of Arizona's organic law. These differences indicate the variation in settlement and business interests in the two new States. . .

A clear-headed, energetic people is developing the new States, eager to make them, in Western parlance, "a good place to live in." That success will come is inevitable. The era of the "bad man" has passed—it is punishable by heavy fine to carry concealed weapons in either State. The era of the home-builder is at hand.

Set amid twenty miles of brown-gray prairie was a tiny adobe dwelling, an adobe-walled corral, and a bit of plowed ground. Thoughtfully, from the observation platform of the California Limited, a passenger watched it. "My father," he commented, "once started West by ox-team. In mid-Iowa he became discouraged, squatted on a claim, farmed for three years, then sold out for two hundred dollars and went back East. To-day, part of the business section of Des Moines is built on that farm. It may be—"

The suggestion lent keener interests to that dull-brown group fast blending into the hazy distance.

Into every beginning in the new States enters some vision of the future. In a half-century more, it may be—Who knows?

Charles Moreau Harger, *Our Two New States*, in *Outlook*, January 28, 1911 (New York), XCVII, 165–176 *passim*.

---

15. The Oil Fields of Oklahoma (1919)

BY CHARLES MOREAU HARGER

For Harger, see No. 14 above.—Bibliography as in No. 12 above; see also Walter S. Tower, *The Story of Oil*.

FOR the past decade oil booms have centered in the mid-continent field—Texas, Oklahoma, and Kansas—which has succeeded the eastern territory as the great source of petroleum supply, producing nearly half the output of the United States. From the first well in southeast Kansas in the middle nineties, it has spread until in scarcely a county west of the Mississippi has there not been search for the wealth millions of years old, settled in pools formed by the changing structure of earth. These pools may be large or small; they may be under such compression that when tapped the black flood will rise to the surface or may require pumping—but always fortune beckons if once the underground store of oil can be found.

Location and development are systematized to the limit of ingenuity, the outgrowth of years of experience. At the beginning is the spying out of the land. Three men in a Ford car, carrying spades, pickaxes, tripods, and levels, come quietly into town, putting up at the second best hotel. For days and weeks they travel over the country measuring, digging, taking notes of slopes, valleys, hills, and the outcropping ledges of rocks. Then as quietly they depart.

A little later come three other men—alert, well-dressed—who put up at the best hotel. They hire motor-cars and drive over a portion of the country, stopping at every farm in a selected portion.

"We want to lease your farm for oil," is their introduction. "If we can get, say 10,000 to 25,000 acres leased, we will put down a well inside of a year, and you will know whether or not there is oil there."

"What are you paying for leases?" comes back the question.

It is explained that one dollar will be paid for a lease on the farm for one year, the farmer to get one-eighth of all the oil produced on his land, delivered free to the pipe-line. If no well is drilled in a year in that territory, the leases may be renewed by paying a dollar an acre from year to year. No leases, no well. The farmer signs; so do his neighbors, and suddenly the county wakes to the first ebullition of an oil boom.

This is "wildcatting," or exploring new territory. The first men were geologists or locators, and they reported that the surface conditions were good. They do not pretend to say where oil certainly is, but claim to be able to determine with fair exactness where conditions are favorable.

"Of course," explained an oilman with long experience, "no one can tell with certainty what is hundreds of feet underground, but study and experiments of the past few years have given a great volume of facts on which to base opinions. Oil is found only where geologic strata have been bent by upheavals in the past. There may be structures where there is no oil, but there is no oil where the structure is not favorable. Chance of success is increased by surface indications, but, after all, it is a gamble. Geology plays a more important part in the location of every oil country removed from proved fields than a few years ago, because conditions are better understood. Hence, the developers fall into two classes: companies that pay high prices for leases in proved territory, and the wildcatters. The first play a comparatively safe game, with high expense and smaller profits. The wildcatters pay little or nothing for leases in unknown country. Their geologists choose the likely places for drilling. If a few good wells are brought in, their profits are large. Theirs is really the gamble end of the oil business, for the chances are in favor of the operator in country already producing oil."

From their study the locators, or geologists, report indications of oil at 2,000 to 3,000 feet, the usual depth at which wells are drilled in the interior. Leases secured, the financial operations begin. The interest in the leases may be sold outright to one of the great producing and distributing companies or their subsidiaries. These constantly explore new territory, setting aside a few hundred thousand dollars each year to maintain production—for every pool has its limit of content. One company last year drilled forty wells, only three of which were good producers.

A large leased acreage in a field that has been passed on by experts is a tangible asset. The promoters may decide to finance it themselves. A derrick is erected; drill, engine, workmen appear, and down goes a test hole Chinaward. Up to this time the only activity has been that of the geologists and the lease writers; now is reared the pyramid of speculation which has attracted millions from capitalists large and small.

With leases on 25,000 acres and a well being drilled, the promoter makes a trip east. To brokers he presents his plans, tells of the favorable reports, and day by day receives telegrams telling how many hundred feet the drill has penetrated. "It is a good wildcat prospect," he declares, and sells two-thirds of his leases for, say, $3 an acre, taking home $50,000. He can finish the well, costing these days $30,000 to $40,000, and if it is a dry hole his profit is still sure. The eastern broker sells the leases, either outright or in undivided interest, on a basis of $5 or more an acre, and the buyers are "in the oil game." Each proudly announces that he has "oil interests" and confidently awaits the outcome.

Or the promoters may organize the Bounding Billow Oil & Gas Company, retaining 51 per cent of the stock and the management, and take pages in such newspapers as will accept their advertising announcing the sale of 10,000,000 shares at five cents a share, "well now drilling and prices to advance next week." On an even less basis than this two Oklahoma sharps, recently arrested, took in over $500,000 from trusting investors. . . .

But out in Fragrant Hill township the drill is pounding away, sinking deeper each day into the earth. At 1,800 feet it strikes "oil-sand," a layer of sand sprinkled with particles of oil. Excitement rises locally. Every farmer has retained the statutory one-eighth royalty in the oil to be produced on his place, and those nearest the well commence to figure in millions. No company can lease the entire product of the farm. Those living nearest the well plan on moving to the city and buying a flock of limousines. Here enters the next step in the high finance of the oil game.

To the farm adjoining the well rolls a big blue racing car carrying another kind of promoter.

"What will you take for one-fourth of your royalty?" he asks.

The farm owner is torn by conflicting interests. If oil were sure, he should keep his entire property, if no oil is under his property, now is the time to possess some real money. In the end he sells one-fourth of his one-eighth for, say, $10,000, and the promoter is to receive one thirty-second of the production, if any.

This fraction is capitalized for $100,000, divided into 1,000 "units" of $100 each; or into 5,000 units of $20 each; or, if the promoter has soaring imagination, into 5,000,000 units of two cents each. This procedure has for a long time evaded the blue sky law, as it was held technically to be selling an actual interest in the outcome, and not stock in a company. . . .

Who buys? Every class, from the banker to the laborer; from the widow to the sales-girl and school-teacher. One grade teacher borrowed on her salary contract to invest $400 in units last year—that she sold out eventually for $1,000 did not alter the fact that she took long chances. Of 4,059 wells completed in the established fields of Oklahoma the first six months of 1919, 1,124 were dry holes. In unproved territory it is a gambling chance, and production may in the successful instances be so small as to return no profit. It is stated that the average production of all wells in the United States now producing oil is four and one-half barrels a day.

Supposing the men with the tripods and levels did guess right. The well when it is down 2,600 feet suddenly becomes a fountain of oil, sending forth 3,000 barrels a day worth $2.25 to $2.70 a barrel! Then is the thrill of a lifetime The value of the leases held by a single company, or by smaller investors down east, soars; units of royalties near by, marketed at $20 each, go up to $100 and more; royalties on all the surrounding farms jump to tens of thousands cash; other wells are started as rapidly as machinery can be secured. . . .

If the well be a "duster," a dry hole, the entire pyramid collapses, except for the promoters, who move on to other financial hunting-grounds, having so planned that they win, no matter who loses.

Charles Moreau Harger, *Romance of the Oil Fields*, in *Scribner's Magazine*, November, 1919 (New York), 616–623 *passim*.

◆

16. Sport in the West (1922)

BY GEORGE PALMER PUTNAM

Putnam is the present active head of the publishing firm of G. P. Putnam's Sons. Author of *The Southland of North America* (1913); *In the Oregon Country; The Smiting of the Rock* (1918).—Bibliography as in No. 12 above; see also such heads as Rodeos and Wild West, in the *Readers' Guide*.

. . . EACH year there are a number of these rodeos, or round-ups, throughout the West, perhaps the most notable of them being held at Pendleton, Oregon. . . .

The Round-up is a great deal more than a merely "Wild West show." It is wild and Western enough and reminiscent of the picturesque past. But it is much more than an exhibition. It is a competition. It is a pennant race in which America's best horsemen and most competent cowboys compete.

Pendleton itself is a prosperous town in the heart of the wheat and cattle country of eastern Oregon. Normally, I suppose, its population is some fifteen thousand. But during the three days of the Round-Up, when it is the focus of interest for most of the Pacific Northwest and an increasing number of Eastern seeing-America-first-ers, it expands miraculously to thrice that size. Well over thirty thousand enthusiasts paid admission on the last day of this year's show. Which at that compares pretty well with a Polo Grounds attendance, especially considering that Pendleton is some three thousand miles from Eastern population centers and that the whole State of Oregon hasn't as many people as Brooklyn.

Consider, then, a frontier town—albeit a modern one with paved streets, porcelain tubs, elevators, and all the metropolitan trimmings—entirely turned over for three hectic days to the show, which the town itself owns and conducts, not for profit but for the downright glamour of it and the glory of the West that was and is. Cowboy clothes are the order of the day—woolly "chaps," swashbuckling spurs clinking from leather boots, broad-rimmed Stetsons, gay-colored silk shirts and scarfs, and, above all, gaudy vests hued like unto the aurora borealis.

"Assuredly," as Charles Hanson Towne punned it, "here is where the vest begins."

There is a saying, epitomizing generosity, that one "would give you his shirt." Just that happened in Pendleton, for our hosts at once insisted that we exchange our becollared drab affairs for their own giddy silk creations. In celebration of which hospitable transfer Wallace Irwin perpetrated a song that forthwith became the popular Round-Up hit and doubtless by now echoes merrily throughout cowland, to the tune of "Tourelay":

> When I was in Oregon scratching the dirt,
> I met a young cowboy who gave me his shirt.
> The shirt it was silk, and the shirt it was red,
> So I held out my hand and these fine words I said:
> "Cowboy, O Cowboy, I hope you do well,
> You're a good-natured, bulldogging son of a swell."
> So I put on the shirt, and I tucked in the tail,
> And beat it back East on the Oregon Trail.

The show itself is staged on a quarter-mile track and in an arena at its center, the whole surrounded by bleachers and grand stands. There is, of course, racing of all kinds—bareback, pony express (where the riders shift the saddle from one horse to another at each change), Indian squaw, and most picturesque of all, the wild-horse race, which last is an unexampled epic of concentrated excitement. A score of absolutely unbroken horses—animals who have felt neither bridle nor saddle—snorting, raging, are turned into the track. At a signal a group of mounted cowboys go after them, each ultimately roping one. Then, in a welter of wild-eyed, fighting, biting, rolling, bucking creatures, the rider and his assistant somehow contrive to get a bandage over the horse's eyes, which, after frantic struggles, quiets him enough to make saddling possible. Then off with the eye bandages and on with the race—and often enough, off with the rider! Remember, no horse ever has been ridden. Their one interest is to get rid of saddle and rider. They have no intention whatever of going around the track. Instead they buck and "sunfish," actually roll over on the ground, and generally mill around like four-footed demons gone mad.

A wonderfully unforgettable sight is that concentrated inferno of insane horse-flesh and roistering fearless man-flesh. This year, just to see a lean buckaroo named Punch Guyette ride the bereft cayuse which luck wished on him—ride him right side up and upside down, horse and rider somehow somersaulting quite completely, with Punch remaining in the saddle, all with a whoop and a laugh, was in itself quite worth the trip from New York.

And that wild-horse race is, of course, only a detail, a sort of curtain-raiser, a tasty appetizer for the big events. The contests for bucking, bull-dogging, and roping are the top-line attractions. And working up to the championship decisions of the last day are a welter of hair-raising elimination trials, so that the fifty or so riders are put through their paces, under all sorts of circumstances, and the crowd is fairly saturated with a veritable saturnalia of exciting sights.

Those Round-Up names mean little to us back here. Suffice to say that Yakima Canutt (who this year rode third in the bucking) is a Babe Ruth of cowland. Howard Tegland, world champion, and Ray Bell—who wears a neat white collar even when astride twelve hundred pounds of horse-hided insanity—are every bit as well known out there as Dempsey and, say, Harold Bell Wright; while the Western reputations of marvelous woman riders like Mable Strickland and Bonnie McCarroll rank right up with Mary Pickford and Elsie Ferguson.

The bucking horses which supply the motive power, so to speak, for the riding contests are the pick of the untamable "bad" animals of all the West. Their names become historic. There are "Lena" (no lady she!), "U-tell-Em," "Bill McAdoo," "Wiggles," "Angel," and others. This year two especially bad-mannered beasts were christened "Doc Traprock" and "George Putnam." Neither, we regret to state, succeeded in unseating his rider!

The matter of getting the saddle on a "bad horse" is a problem in itself, solved by the "wranglers." Ultimately the rider gets aboard, but not necessarily for long, for horses know every trick imaginable likely to encourage an immediate divorce between themselves and the unwelcome stranger perched upon their hurricane deck. Be the horse a trained bucker or an outlaw, he can be counted upon for all sorts of gymnastics, ranging from the "side wind" and "sunfish" and "weave" to the straight buck and the high dive, not to mention the pleasant trick of rearing and falling back on the rider.

They ride with only a halter, no reins or bridle being used. And they must ride with style—ride "slick"—that is, straight up, with a close seat, and "no daylight showing." And really to impress the judges the rider must "rake" the shoulders and rump of his horse with his blunted spurs, and "fan" the animal at every jump, swinging his hat with a full arm sweep. And, above all, he must not "pull leather" or touch the saddle with either hand.

And then the roping. That means to ride after a wild Texas long-horn steer, get a lasso around his horns, throw him, and "hogtie" him by fastening his four feet together while the cow-pony at the other end of the rope holds the steer helpless on the ground. And it must all be done under two minutes.

But, from the standpoint of individual muscular prowess and sheer human grit, "bulldogging" is the showiest event of all. The steer is driven out of a chute, and he emerges much as a limited mail train comes out of a tunnel. They give him about thirty feet start, and then the man starts after him on a horse running like a scared jack-rabbit. The horse draws alongside and the man leans over, hooks an arm around the steer's horn, and slides from the saddle. The horse goes on, so does the steer for a few jumps, the man dragging through the dust and acting as a brake. Finally the two come to rest. Then the man reaches for the steer's nose and, clasping his hands around it with the horn between his arms, leans backward and tries to throw the animal. Sometimes the steer shakes him loose, sometimes it whirls and tosses him, but we have seen a man bring down an animal in seventeen seconds from the time he started after him. They call it bulldogging, but it's the greatest wrestling in the world.

And let this be clear: there is no cruelty to animals. The broken bones—and necks too—are the lot of two-legged contestants. Not an animal this year was injured. It is the men and the women who take the big risks and get the real hurts.

"Let 'er buck!"

"Ride 'em, cowboy!"

Those cries of the Round-Up echo still in our ears, and the memory of all that goes with them is a magnet that inevitably will draw us again westward to this courageous competition—an epic of sportsmanship so essentially American.

George Palmer Putnam, *The Pendleton Round-Up*, in *Outlook*, October 25, 1922 (New York), CXXXII, 330–331 *passim.*

———————◆———————

17. The Strategy of Locating a Railroad (1925)

BY CHARLES H. MARKHAM

Markham, who died in 1927, began his railway career as a section laborer; at his death he was President of the Illinois Central Railroad.—For bibliography on Railroads, see No. 84 below.

. . . GEOGRAPHICALLY, the Illinois Central System is located almost in the heart of the North American continent. The fourteen states of the Mississippi Valley in which it operates embrace one-third of the total population of the United States. It connects many of the great industrial and commercial centers of the Mississippi Valley, including Chicago, the second largest city on the continent, and in many respects the leading commercial city of the world; St. Louis, the great manufacturing and distributing center; New Orleans, the second largest port in the country; Birmingham, the "Pittsburgh of the South"; Memphis, the world's leading hardwood lumber market; Omaha, the manufacturing and commercial metropolis of Nebraska, and such other important cities as Sioux City, Sioux Falls, Fort Dodge, Waterloo, Dubuque, Rockford, Madison, Peoria, Bloomington, Springfield, Indianapolis, Decatur, Evansville, East St. Louis, Louisville, Paducah, Jackson, Tenn., Jackson, Miss., Vicksburg, Natchez, Baton Rouge, Hattiesburg and Gulfport.

Unlike many railroads which have to depend on single crops or industries for most of their tonnage and therefore suffer seriously when those crops or industries meet with reverses, the Illinois Central System traverses a region the agricultural, mineral, lumbering and manufacturing production of which is highly diversified. It is consequently little affected by the failure of any one harvest or the slowing down of any one industry. The fourteen states in which the Illinois Central System operates embrace only 26 per cent of the total land area of the United States, but they produce 34 per cent of the nation's bituminous coal, 34 per cent of its lumber, 38 per cent of its cotton, 49 per cent of its tobacco, 69 per cent of its corn, 33 per cent of its wheat, 64 per cent of its oats, 66 per cent of its rice and 46 per cent of its livestock. They contain 37 per cent of the country's railway mileage, or one-eighth of the total railway mileage of the world.

The wide range of climate traversed by the Illinois Central System has an important bearing on the traffic which flows over its lines. The northernmost extremity of the system is at Albert Lea, Minn., north of the 43d parallel, with a mean temperature in January of about 14° and in July of about 82°, and an annual precipitation of about 27 inches. So wide is the climatic variation that while the northern part of the railroad is blanketed in snow and ice and experiencing sub-zero weather, fields of strawberries and vegetables are ripening under the warm Louisiana sun at the southern end of the line, and peach trees are in bloom along the balmy Gulf Coast of Southern Mississippi. Many of the agricultural and forest products of the South are native to that region and cannot be grown successfully in the North, and many of the hardier agricultural products of the North do not thrive in the sub-tropical climate of the Southern states. Hence the interchange of Southern products, such as Southern pine lumber, cotton and cotton-seed products, winter vegetables, fruits, tobacco, berries, sugar, rice and pecans, for the grains, packing house products and hardier fruits and vegetables of the North furnishes the railroad with a large and important part of its tonnage.

The advantages of being a pioneer railroad probably more than offset the disadvantages. The Illinois Central System reached most of what now are the populous centers of its territory when they were scarcely more than settlements. It was the forerunner of hundreds of towns and cities along its lines. Naturally, therefore, it acquired the advantage of exceedingly favorable locations in many of these centers which it would be difficult if not impossible to acquire today.

At Chicago, for example, the Illinois Central terminal occupies a location along the Lake front immediately adjacent to the "Loop" business district, a property that could not be obtained by a railroad today at any price. When this right-of-way was acquired, Chicago had a population of 30,000. . . .

Another pronounced geographical advantage which the Illinois Central has is that of traversing the comparatively level country of the Mississippi Valley. Not only did the level topography and light timber growth through this territory render construction easier and less expensive than would have been the case through a more rugged country, but it enabled the construction of a straighter and smoother roadway. Ninety per cent of the original road in Illinois was straight, and the few curves were of such wide radius as to render them an almost negligible factor in the operation of trains. The long and steep grades that have to be overcome on nearly all the Eastern and Western railroads are not so great a factor on the Illinois Central System. The advantages of its comparatively straight and level track enable the operation of long, heavy trains at a much lower tractive effort than is required on the majority of railroads.

Seventy-one per cent of all land in the fourteen states in which the Illinois Central System operates is in farms compared with 43 per cent in the thirty-four other states of the Union. In 1923 these fourteen states furnished more than 40 per cent of the total agricultural production of the United States. It is therefore manifest that the Illinois Central System, traversing this rich agricultural region, carries a vast traffic of agricultural products. Although the Illinois Central System embraces only about one-thirty-eighth of the railway mileage of the country, one in every twenty-four carloads of agricultural products handled by the Class 1 railroads of the United States in 1924 originated on the Illinois Central System.

When the Illinois Central Railroad was projected, except for the lead and zinc mines of northwestern Illinois and southwestern Wisconsin, the mineral resources of the Mississippi Valley were entirely undeveloped. Coal had not come into extensive use as fuel. In 1855 the mining of 20,000 tons of coal in the vicinity of LaSalle and DuQuoin, Ill., for domestic consumption in those and neighboring towns led the president of the Illinois Central in his annual report to make the prophetic statement that he was "fully persuaded that coal traffic would eventually become one of the most important elements of profit to the road." By means of railway transportation the coal mines of Illinois, Indiana and Kentucky found markets at Chicago, St. Louis, Indianapolis, Louisville, Memphis and other populous industrial centers. As the territory developed and the railroads helped to create markets, such commodities as sand, gravel, stone, clay and fluorspar came to contribute substantially to the system's freight tonnage. In 1919 there were 3,868 producing mines and quarries, employing 254,234 workmen in the fourteen states of the Mississippi Valley in which the Illinois Central System operates, and their total production that year was valued at $660,000,000, or 21 per cent of the total value of all mine and quarry products in the United States. In 1924 the Illinois Central System transported 25,703,690 tons of mineral products, approximately two-thirds of which was coal.

The strategic position of the Illinois Central System in relation to the lumber industry is at once apparent. The United States uses about two-fifths of the total world consumption of wood and wood products. Not many years ago the states of Michigan, Minnesota and Wisconsin produced a surplus of forest products, and because of the short haul they were the principal sources of supply for the consuming states of Illinois, Indiana, Iowa, Ohio and Missouri. Today, however, with the exception of Maine and New Hampshire, every state north of the Ohio and Potomac rivers and east of the Rocky Mountains, as well as Kentucky, consumes more lumber than it produces, while Louisiana, Mississippi, eastern Texas, Arkansas and Alabama form the principal lumber-producing region and the main source of surplus lumber supply east of the Rocky Mountains.

During 1922 the fourteen states in which the Illinois Central System operates produced 10,853,000,000 feet of lumber, or 34.5 per cent of the total lumber production of the United States. The four states of Louisiana, Mississippi, Arkansas and Alabama milled 8,494,000,000 feet, or 26.9 per cent of the total production in the country. Therefore, the Illinois Central System, with its network of lines traversing the principal lumber-producing regions of Mississippi, affording direct connections with lumber-producing points in Louisiana, Alabama and Arkansas and serving directly the great markets of the Central West, is most advantageously located as a lumber carrier. . . .

The vast agricultural, mineral and lumber resources of the states of the Mississippi Valley, their excellent transportation facilities, their central location with respect to population and accessibility of fuel and raw materials, have given the territory traversed by the lines of the Illinois Central System every advantage in manufacturing, and the phenomenal industrial growth of the Mississippi Valley region has contributed greatly to the economic strength of the railroad. . . .

At New Orleans, the second largest port in the United States in total tonnage of exports and imports and total net tonnage of shipping engaged in foreign trade, the Illinois Central System owns extensive docks, elevators and warehouses, equipped with modern loading and unloading machinery.

The recent acquisition of the Gulf & Ship Island Railroad has added a second Gulf port to the Illinois Central System. At Gulfport, the only deep-water harbor on the Mississippi Coast, the system now owns a pier more than a mile in length and a wharf several hundred feet in length, where cargoes are loaded and unloaded directly between cars and ships. Gulfport is one of the leading lumber and naval stores ports on the Gulf Coast.

The Ocean Steamship Company, a subsidiary of the Central of Georgia Railway Company (which is, as noted, a part of the greater Illinois Central System), owns commodious marine terminals at Savannah, Ga., the largest naval stores port of the country and the third largest cotton port in the world.

A fourth deep-water port on the Illinois Central System is at Baton Rouge, on the lower Mississippi River. Baton Rouge is now a port of entry under United States customs regulations. . . .

In common with other latitudinal railroads engaged in the transportation of transcontinental tonnage, the Illinois Central System's line between Chicago and Omaha suffers from canal competition, but new traffic has developed to and from the Panama Canal over the longitudinal lines of the system. The Panama Canal may therefore well be considered an asset to the Illinois Central System, because of its geographical location, although a liability to the latitudinal transcontinental lines. As the trade of the United States continues to grow with the increasing industrialization of its people, the growth of its population, and the development of its interest in foreign markets, the Panama Canal will become of increasing importance as a factor in the business of the Illinois Central; an importance that even today is significant, and of consideration in the policies of the system. . . .

Charles H. Markham, *The Illinois Central System*, in *Economic Geography* (Worcester, Clark University, 1926), II, 4–15 *passim*.

CHAPTER IV — IMMIGRATION AND RACE ELEMENTS

18. Landing in New York (1901)

BY JAMES B. CONNOLLY

Connolly served in the infantry in the Spanish War, later in U. S. Navy. Correspondent of *Collier's* in Mexico in 1914 and in European waters in 1918. He is the author of some exceptionally good books and articles about the sea.

AT ten o'clock in the evening the big French liner from Havre came to anchor in the harbor of New York, and six hundred immigrants, Armenian, Greek, Turk, Italian, French, what not, craned over her rail to look on the fascinating lights of the immense city of their new land. They were told that the ship would move no further that night, and that it would be well to go below and get some sleep; but they paid no attention, and dawn found them still there, wakefully gazing.

Not until the last night-light died out did these watchers go below, and then it was to hurry bags and bundles on deck. At five o'clock every one of them was up on his toes ready to step ashore at the word, but it was seven o'clock before they were allowed to move, and then it was to make ready for the doctors, who had just climbed aboard.

Down one long gangway and up the other we were marched—citizens and foreigners alike; nationality made no difference where all were mere "steerage." At the rate of forty to the minute we went by the doctor and his staff, who stood in the waist and reviewed us. As some of us in approaching failed to uncover, the ship's man addressed us; "Your chapeaux, messieurs, your chapeaux." We did not understand, "For the hair diseases," he said.

So we doffed our chapeaux, although it looked ridiculously like a salute to the doctors. And they must have had miraculous eyes

if they detected any but the most rampant disease by the brief looks
they gave to the immigrants' heads.

After this inspection the steerage dragged up its very last bags
and bundles and chests. Six hundred of them there were, and with
all their belongings they camped on deck. They made a pretty
tight fit for one deck, and on one deck they had to stay. Later, it
was like prying the first block out of a square of paving to get them
started.

It was a blistering morning in July, and for two hours we sizzled
in the blaze, until at last some blessed body up ahead said we might
move. We moved, at first with glacial slowness, but in a little while
more rapidly. By the time one little bunch reached the head of the
gangplank, we were moving beyond all question. The people half a
dozen numbers ahead of us were bumping down the runway like cakes
of ice down a chute, and yet a man said, "Hurry! hurry!"

Cakes of ice may be skidded with speed when the runs are well
greased, but they do not always stop gracefully. A band of Armenians,
with bundles behind and before them, went clattering before us down
the cleated runway like men thrown down-stairs.

Two men at the foot "kept tab." One had to use a baseball umpire's indicator for his count, but the other, a greater brain, thought
that he needed no mechanical aid to keep his reckoning. He counted
us by a system of fours; but presently the struggling throng confused
him and he grew wrathy. His system broke down when his companion
counted one of us as number three hundred and sixty-eight, and he had
only reached number three hundred and sixty-four.

On the dock it was a noisy assemblage. Here was where Volapük
or any other universal language would have been worth everybody's
knowing. These friendless people stood helplessly about, waiting for
somebody to come and tell them what to do. Officials who might have
made things a bit easier for them seemed to prefer to add to their
bewilderment. Some that sought aid were waved away with arrogant
indifference. "We'll get around to you," was a reply that bore not
the slightest relation to the timorous question. All the Jacks in office
scorned these poor people, and they were made to feel it. To the command of any loud-voiced truckman they jumped aside like rabbits, and
beneath the mere look of anything in uniform they shrank like mice.

A lifeless-looking man behind a small stand-up desk was registering the lucky ones with "papers"—the naturalized Americans who had been home for a visit. He might have been registering ordinary cattle of no pedigree. His ambition, seemingly, was to be regarded as a man who could be flustered by nothing on top of this earth. He only moved his fingers to fill in blank lines on one big sheet and a lot of little slips. His jaws seemed made to chew tobacco—he did not move them to speak.

Some citizens, native born, American by every word and action, approached this impassive creature, saying: "We are American citizens who have come third class. Can we be passed out?"

"Passport?"

"No; but if——"

"Any sworn statements that you are American citizens?"

"No. We did not anticipate anything like this. If you will look at these——"

"Don't want to look. If you have no regular papers stand aside."

An Italian who could just say "Yes," "No," and "Feeladelfy" then presented his stamped credentials, and was passed out. Another, who had no credentials, stood ready to make affidavit that he was born in America sixty years ago. He had to get an interpreter to tell his story. His dismissal was as abrupt as ours.

The great body had no papers, had no hope of any shorter cut to liberty than by way of Ellis Island, and so waited patiently with their packs beside them. They never wandered far away from their packs. By and by they were told the inspector wished them to get in line and be ready for him. They hurried to arrange themselves in a row with their bundles opened up. In about an hour the inspector walked along the line, chalking his initials about as fast as he could step from one to the other. There was little suspicion of valuable stuffs concealed there.

After a time we learned that to get out we had only to swear that we were born in America and were citizens. Then we "went for" the man behind the desk, who could have attended to us before, and he took our abuse as, doubtless, he would have taken our praise—without changing a muscle. Given our slips, we hurried out of that darkened dock, out into the free sunshine of West Street. There we took a good long look at the United States. Travelling in immigrant fashion was all right after one had done with it.

When we left, the first batch of our fellow voyagers were being marched on the Ellis Island barge. We saw a bunch of them later— after they were clear of the Immigration Bureau. It was in the shadow of Castle Garden. They were being driven away by a boisterous man of their own kind, who was talking to them like a jolly father. Perhaps he was making clear to them that now they were recognized fixtures in this land of promise, and that all their troubles were past.

James B. Connolly, in *Youth's Companion*, March 14, 1901 (Boston), iii after 136.

———◆———

19. Our Italian Laborers (1901)

BY JACOB A. RIIS

Riis, a native of Denmark, came to the United States as a young man, worked as a police-court reporter in New York City, and interested himself in the problems of the tenement district. He was responsible for many reforms, as he has already told in his books, *A Ten Years' War; An Account of the Battle with the Slum in New York* (Boston, 1900), and his autobiography, *The Making of an American* (New York, 1902).—Bibliography: *Jacob A. Riis; A Sketch of His Life and Work;* Theodore Roosevelt, "Reformed through Social Work" in *Fortnightly Review* (1901), 739–747.

EVER in the hollow by the railroad-track, a little way from my home, stand two huts, if the term can be applied to structures having almost no sides, but consisting mainly of roofs oddly made of old boards, shingles and broken branches thrown down by a great storm that swept the country in the early fall. From the roof of one hut a crazy stovepipe sticks out; the fireplace of the other is just outside, where a door should have been, and there the occupants were busy cooking something in a pan.

At first sight I thought the huts harbored tramps who had halted on their annual migration southward, but before I caught sight of the men I knew by their chatter that they were Italian laborers employed in repairing the road-bed near by. The thicket was their kitchen, parlor and living-room. They might have found quarters much worse on a sunny day.

Soon after the men camped there thieves made a raid on our village. First our hen-coops suffered, then our silver drawers. There was

great excitement for a season, and public indignation, in its search
for a victim, hovered for a while about the settlement in the hollow.
That was a mistake, as the event proved, and I am glad to say I had
no share in it. I knew the Italian too well for that.

He is not a thief. His boy may, does often enough, become corrupted by the city slum and its idleness, but with his immigrant
father the police have rarely any concern. Even the bandit from
across the sea works peacefully enough with pick and shovel here.
It is only when the slum swallows him up from the moment of his
coming and claims him for its own, or when his angry passions are
excited by his Sunday game of cards that he falls back into his old
evil ways.

The Mulberry Bend in New York is the great market where the
padrone finds his countrymen just come over the sea, waiting to be
hired and shipped in squads to the jobs that are waiting. The padrone
is the middleman who knows what every big contractor is doing,
even what he is thinking of doing, and is ever ready to enlist from a
dozen to a thousand men with shovels, and ship them by the next
train to wherever they may be needed. The "banker" in the Bend
is the padrone's backer, who furnishes the capital to run the
"business," which begins as soon as the men are shipped.

The contractor houses them sometimes, in barracks of rough boards
put up for the occasion; sometimes, if the job is on the railroad and
is not to last long, in a couple of old freight-cars side-tracked as near
the job as may be. A few cars can hold a great many Italian navvies,
for they pack well.

It may happen that they are quartered in old barns or farmhouses,
the owners of which are willing to let them for ready money. Into
them swarm the swarthy Italians by scores, stowing themselves in
every nook and cranny from cellar to attic, and away up in the
cockloft.

As near to the men as may be, the padrone opens his store, and
stocks it with macaroni and such other simple viands as his customers
require. Once or twice a week he lays in a supply of stale bread,
their chief food. It is cheap and it is healthy, if not exactly palatable.
Thus he makes a double profit on his men, for each of them pays
him a regular percentage on his pay for getting him the job. These
items together, small for the individual but large in the aggregate,

are enough to make the padrone and his banker rich in a few busy years.

Their client, the navvy, is not envious. He is willing that they shall make a good thing of him for themselves, so long as he has his share. His thrift insures his own prosperity. It is a common observation on works where Italians are employed in numbers that with their dollar and quarter a day they draw more cash at the end of the month than the highly paid engineers. The reason is simple; they save rigidly.

Stale bread and flour are cheap; they make their macaroni as often as they buy it readymade; the woods for a mile around furnish their fuel; field, meadow and swamp contribute to their larder in a way truly amazing to one used only to civilized city life.

The camp-fire is lighted against the bluff when the evening shades begin to fall. A hole dug in the bank horizontally serves as the fireplace; another scooped out over it, straight up, makes the chimney. When the kitchen is ready, the pot is boiling in no time.

To it the men foraging after their day's work bring what they find; some carry fagots for the fire from the thicket, others bring by the armful greens that no one of that neighborhood thought of as good to eat. Young dandelions, young milkweed, sour sorrel and the weed called "lamb's quarters" are delicacies. A slice of bacon or anything else that comes handy gives a flavor to the mess—a dead bird, a land-turtle, or even a mud-turtle. It all goes into the pot. Italian navvies are "death on turtles." The result of it all is a broth not unpalatable to one who has the courage to taste it, and which they swallow with great gusto.

The meal over and their few chores done, the men squat by the fires for a game of cards and a smoke. Generally some one among them has a guitar, perhaps a harp, at least an accordion, and the echoes of the summer night are awakened by the sweetly seductive strains of "Santa Lucia" or some Sicilian love-song.

The fierce-looking men in their red flannel shirts, wide open at the sunburned throat, with the firelight playing upon their dark faces, make a striking figure suggestive enough of savage mountaineers fresh from a raid on weakling lowlanders and their wealth; but whatever was their trade abroad, here it is honest. Even the farmer's hen-coops are safe, if the turtles in his swamp-lot are not.

Midnight finds them bundled in their barracks, on straw or on the solid planks, usually packed close together. Rude bunks are nailed up two tiers high if there is room, and twenty or thirty sleep where Americans would see space for two. In the space left by the bunks, lines are strung and their clothes hung up to dry.

Once a week the camp takes a wash. On Saturday evening all go to the near-by stream, where the men soak their shirts while they sit smoking on the bank. The most venturesome jump in with clothes on, and wash them in that way, but bathing is not popular among them as a sport. As a sanitary measure it is not even dreamed of.

The soaked clothes, wrung out on the bank, are spread on the roof of their barracks over night, or hung out to dry on the next tree, and are fit for Sunday wear in the morning, there being no church to demand an extra polishing-up.

If it were not for his manner of spending Sunday or Sunday afternoon, the Italian would be an ideal navvy. He does not go off carousing, is hardy and not afraid of work. Sunday morning he manages to put in mending his clothes or cobbling in camp, if he has not a wife in the Bend whom he goes to see. But as the afternoon wears on in idleness, the gaming that is his besetting vice tempts him, and then, with the darkness, the padrone's profits are likely to be curtailed by a general fight in which knives are trumps.

The history of the building of the aqueduct dams, the ship-canal and other great works of like character near New York City records many such bloody fights, often over a few wretched pennies. The police are usually in time to carry out the dead, rarely to prevent murder. In spite of this, the Italian navvy is, as a rule, a man of peace as he is one of hard work, and a most important person in the accomplishment of the great enterprises that mark the progress of our country.

Although he works for less than the imperious Irishman, he manages to make his wage go vastly farther. At the end of his job, when camp is broken in the late fall, he goes away with his pockets lined with gold, perhaps to the city to watch for another job, perhaps over the ocean to buy a farm or a hillside vineyard at home. His shovel, his loaf of stale bread and the umbrella that were his inseparable companions here are left behind.

He sets sail in a brand-new corduroy suit, with a heavy silver chain to his watch, to return, if he does not settle among his own, with his wife and little ones to make his home with us for good; showing thus in the best of all ways that he appreciates the advantages of his new-found freedom, and is going to try the best of it according to his light.

Jacob A. Riis, in *Youth's Companion*, January 17, 1901 (Boston), 111.

———◆———

20. A Self-Made Negro (1910)

BY EMMETT J. SCOTT AND LYMAN BEECHER STOWE (1916)

Scott was at one time Booker T. Washington's private secretary; he was secretary of Tuskegee Institute and later of Howard University, both schools for negroes. Stowe, grandson of Harriet Beecher Stowe, is the author (with his father) of *Harriet Beecher Stowe—The Story of Her Life* (1911); (with W. R. George) of *Made and Remade* (1912); (with Dr. J. Goricar) of *The Inside Story of Austro-German Intrigue* (1919). Booker Washington wrote on negro problems. Some of his more important works are: *Sowing and Reaping* (Boston, 1900); *The Story of my Life and Work* (1900); *Up from Slavery* (1901); *The Future of the American Negro* (1902); *Character Building* (1903); *Working with the Hands* (1904); *Tuskegee and Its People* (1905); *Putting the Most into Life* (1906); *Life of Frederick Douglass* (1907); *The Negro in Business* (1907); *The Story of the Negro* (1909).—Bibliography: See B. F. Riley, *The Life and Times of Booker T. Washington* (New York, 1916).

BOOKER WASHINGTON was always emphasizing the necessity of better conditions right here and now instead of in a distant future or in heaven. He was constantly combating the tendency in his people—a tendency common to all people but naturally particularly strong in those having a heritage of slavery—to substitute the anticipated bliss of a future life for effective efforts to improve the conditions of this present life. He was always telling them to put their energies into societies for the preservation of health and improvement of living conditions, instead of into the too numerous and popular sick benefit and death benefit organizations.

At the next stop of the party Mr. Washington was introduced to the assembled townspeople by a graduate of Tuskegee Institute, who was one of their leading citizens and most successful farmers. In this talk he urged the people to get more land and keep it and to grow something besides cotton. He said they should not lean upon others and should not go to town on Saturdays to "draw upon" the merchants, but should stay at home and "draw every day from their own soil corn, peas, beans, and hogs." He urged the men to give their wives more time to work around the house and to raise vegetables. (This, of course, instead of requiring them to work in the fields with the men as is so common.) He urged especially that they take their wives into their confidence and make them their partners as well as their companions. He assured them that if they took their wives into partnership they would accumulate more and get along better in every way.

There was no advice given by him more constantly or insistently in speaking to the plain people of his race, whether in country or city, than this injunction to the men to take their wives into their confidence and make them their partners. He recognized that the home was the basis of all progress and civilization for his race, as well as all other races, and that the wife and mother is primarily the conservator of the home.

One of the stops of the trip was at a little hamlet called Damascus. Here, in characteristic fashion, he told the people how much richer they were in soil and all natural advantages than were the inhabitants of the original Damascus in the Holy Land. He then argued that having these great natural advantages, much was to be expected of them, etc. Like all great preachers, teachers, and leaders of men he seized upon the names, incidents, and conditions immediately about him and from them drew lessons of fundamental import and universal application.

The efforts of the Negro farmers on these trips to get a word of approval from their great leader were often pathetic. One old man had a good breed of pigs of which he was particularly proud. He contrived to be found feeding them beside the road just as the great man and his party were passing. The simple ruse succeeded. Mr. Washington and his companions stopped and every one admired the proud and excited old man's pigs. And then after the pigs had been duly admired, he led them to a rough plank table upon which he had displayed in tremulous anticipation of this dramatic moment a huge pumpkin, some perfectly developed ears of corn, and a lusty cabbage. After these objects had also been admired the old man decoyed the party into the little whitewashed cottage where his wife had her hour of triumph in displaying her jars of preserves, pickles, cans of vegetables, dried fruits, and syrup together with quilts and other needle-work all carefully arranged for this hoped-for inspection.

The basic teaching of all these tours was: "Make your own little heaven right here and now. Do it by putting business methods into your farming, by growing things in your garden the year around, by building and keeping attractive and comfortable homes for your children so they will stay at home and not go to the cities, by keeping your bodies and your surroundings clean, by staying in one place, by getting a good teacher and a good preacher, by building a good school and church, by letting your wife be your partner in all you do, by keeping out of debt, by cultivating friendly relations with your neighbors both white and black."

Mr. Washington was constantly bringing up in the Tuskegee faculty meetings cases of distress among the colored people of the county, which he had personally discovered while off hunting or riding, and planning ways and means to relieve them. Apparently it never occurred to him that technically, at least, the fate of these poor persons was not his affair nor that of his school. At one such meeting he told of having come upon while hunting a tumbledown cabin in the woods, within it a half-paralyzed old Negro obviously unable to care for his simple wants. Mr. Washington had stopped, built a fire in his stove, and otherwise made him comfortable temporarily, but some provision for the old man's care must be made at once. One of the teachers knew about the old man and stated that he had such an ugly temper that he had driven off his wife, son, and daughter who had until recently lived with him and taken care of him. The young teacher seemed to feel that the old man had brought his troubles upon his own head and so deserved little sympathy. Mr. Washington would not for a moment agree to this. He replied that if the old fellow was so unfortunate as to have a bad temper as well as his physical infirmities that was no reason why he should be allowed to suffer privation. He delegated one of the teachers to look up the old man's family at once and see if they could be prevailed upon to support him and to report at the next meeting what had been arranged. In the meantime he would send some one out to the cabin daily to take him food and attend to his wants.

At another faculty meeting he brought up the plight of an old woman who was about to be evicted from her little shack on the out-

skirts of the town because of her inability to pay the nominal rent
which she was charged. He arranged to have her rent paid out of a
sum of money which he always had included in the school budget
for the relief of such cases. In such ways he was constantly impressing upon his associates the idea that was ever a mainspring of his
own life—namely, that it was always and everywhere the duty of the
more fortunate to help the less fortunate.

Emmett J. Scott and Lyman Beecher Stowe, *Booker T. Washington, Builder of a
Civilization* (New York, Doubleday Page, 1916), 139–143.

------◆------

21. The Japanese Problem (1913)

BY PROFESSOR FREDERIC AUSTIN OGG (1918)

Ogg is Professor of Political Science at the University of Wisconsin.—Bibliography: George H. Blakeslee, *Japan and Japanese-American Relations;* K. K.
Kawakami, *The Real Japanese Question;* H. A. Millis, *The Japanese Problem in
the United States;* P. J. Treat, *Japan and the United States.*

. . . THE people of the far West had long believed that their
section of the country was in danger of being flooded with
Asiatics, and that unless repressive steps were taken they would be
saddled with a permanent race problem like the negro question in the
South. Exclusion acts wrung from Congress in 1880–1884 were a
sufficient safeguard against the Chinese. By 1895, however, high
wages began to attract Japanese and Korean laborers, many of whom
reached the mainland after a sojourn in Hawaii. In 1900 there were
in the coast states only 18,269 Japanese; but after 1903 the influx rose,
and native laborers and shopkeepers seemed likely to be displaced on
a large scale by orientals. Japanese capitalists, too, were seeking a
footing in important industries. In this new form, the "yellow peril"
stirred the coast communities profoundly. Organized labor set up a
cry for exclusion; and the political leaders, the press, and a large part
of the public gave hearty support. Race prejudice played its part,
but the mainspring of the protest was the fear of economic competition.

On October 11, 1906, the board of education of San Francisco cast
a brand into the tinder by passing a resolution that thereafter all Chi-

nese, Japanese, and Korean pupils should be given instruction in an "oriental" school, and not, as previously, in the ordinary schools. Coming at a time when Japanese pride was more than usually exalted, this action was keenly resented. The Tokio authorities made inquiries, and then demanded that Japanese residents in California be protected in the full enjoyment of the rights guaranteed them by the treaty of 1894. In 1907 a tentative settlement was reached in a "gentleman's agreement" to the effect that San Francisco should admit to the ordinary schools oriental children not over sixteen years of age, while the Japanese authorities should withhold passports from laborers bound for the United States, except returning residents and members of their families. An order of President Roosevelt, March 14, 1907, issued under authority of a new immigration act, further restrained the immigration of oriental laborers; and within two years the number of Japanese annually entering the country was reduced to a tenth of its former proportions. February 24, 1911, the United States Senate ratified a new treaty of commerce and navigation with Japan, which was accompanied by a Japanese note to the effect that the Mikado's government was "fully prepared to maintain with equal effectiveness the limitation and control which they have for the past three years exercised in regulation of emigration of laborers to the United States."

The real issue in 1906–1907 was not school attendance, but the right of the Japanese to migrate to the Pacific coast states and to enjoy there the same privileges as other aliens. Agitation therefore continued, and in 1913 it bore fruit in a bill introduced in the California legislature prohibiting the holding of land, through either purchase or lease, by aliens ineligible to citizenship under United States law. Several states, including New York and Texas, had laws unconditionally prohibiting ownership of real property by aliens. The Tokio authorities objected to the California proposal, however, on the ground that it was aimed solely at the Japanese (who under the naturalization laws were ineligible to citizenship), and that it was a discrimination in violation of the treaty of 1911. After asking in vain that the measure be modified, President Wilson sent Secretary Bryan to Sacramento to explain to the governor and legislature the views of the officials at Washington. Nevertheless, the legislature passed a substitute measure, known as the Webb alien landholding bill, which received the governor's signature May 19, 1913.

On its face, the bill passed was less offensive than its original, for it did not contain the phrase "ineligible to citizenship," which had been the basis of the Japanese protest. The real object was attained, however, by the provision that, whereas aliens eligible to citizenship should be allowed to acquire and hold land on the same terms as citizens, all other aliens should have only such landholding rights as should be guaranteed to them by treaty. No treaty with Japan conferred the right of land ownership; so that Japanese residents of the state, while continuing to be capable of owning real property used for residence or commercial purposes, and while permitted to lease land for a term not exceeding three years, were henceforth disqualified to become land-owners. Existing holdings were not affected.

The law was drawn to minimize legal objections. Its effect, however, was to deny to Japanese residents rights which they, in common with other aliens, had hitherto possessed; and on this ground the Tokio government renewed its protest. The State Department urged that no rights were denied, and that, in any event, the courts were open for the adjudication of the question. But the Japanese authorities preferred to consider the situation on the plane of international and inter-racial honor and fair play; for the real source of their dissatisfaction was the stigma which was felt to have been placed upon the Japanese as a people by the refusal of the United States to admit Japanese settlers to citizenship.

The suggestion of a new treaty was eventually dropped; and after a fruitless exchange of notes, the controversy (overshadowed, from 1914, by the European war) languished. That in the course of time it would be revived, nobody doubted. Indeed, in the early months of 1917 the legislatures of Oregon, Idaho, and one or two other Pacific states debated land-holding measures resembling that which brought the difficulty to a head in California.

Certain facts lent the situation an ominous aspect. Japan and the United States must always confront each other across the Pacific. Economic competition between them was certain to increase. An outlet for surplus population was for Japan a growing necessity. The Japanese are a proud people, quick to resent any hint that they are an inferior race. They are extraordinarily polite, and they expect unfailing courtesy from those who undertake to deal with them as equals. The events of 1906–1907 and 1913 revealed in both countries a jingo press, as well as a tendency to indiscreet and violent acts. Not a few sober-minded Americans were convinced that Japan, having triumphed first over China, then over Russia, had chosen the United States as her third great antagonist; and that through conquests in Latin America, or in some way, she would bring on a conflict whenever the time seemed ripe. Nervous persons recalled that never since the modernization of her armies had the empire suffered defeat.

Fortunately, there were offsets to these causes of alarm. The official attitude of each government toward the other was always correct; diplomatic language was careful and courteous. For a decade the "gentleman's agreement" was faithfully carried out, and it yielded every immediate result that could have been attained by statutes or by treaty. The situation was saved by the fact that the Japanese plans for national development admitted of no heavy emigration to the United States; the end in view was rather colonization in Korea and elsewhere, under the Japanese flag. Furthermore, the United States was not alone in seeking to prevent the entrance of orientals; Australia and other British dominions had gone even further. If the country could discover some means of attaining its purpose without branding the Japanese as an inferior people, there was no reason—so far, at all events, as the immigration question was concerned—why earlier friendliness should not be restored. The old relation of mentor and pupil, however, could never be revived; for Japan had outgrown the need of tutelage.

Frederic Austin Ogg, *National Progress* [American Nation, XXVII] (New York, Harper's, 1918), 307–312.

22.   Our New Immigration Policy (1924)

BY PROFESSOR ROBERT DE COURCY WARD

Ward, an eminent American meteorologist and professor of that science at Harvard University, has long taken a deep interest in immigration problems.— Bibliography: J. W. Jenks and W. J. Lauck, *The Immigration Problem* (N. Y., 1922); Gino Speranza, *Race or Nation: the Conflict of Divided Loyalties* (Indianapolis, 1925); H. P. Fairchild, *The Melting Pot Mistake* (Boston, 1926); R. L. Garis, *Immigration Restriction* (N. Y., 1927); Madison Grant and C. S. Davison, editors, *The Founders of the Republic on Immigration, Naturalization and Aliens* (N. Y., 1928); E. R. Lewis, *America: Nation or Confusion* (N. Y., 1928).

FOR a round hundred years it was a national ideal that the United States should be the asylum for the poor and the oppressed of every land. This very early came to be known as the "traditional" American attitude towards immigration. Curiously enough, there has always been a fundamental error in the popular conception of this tradition. This noble ideal of a refuge, open to all, had its roots in economic conditions far more than in any altruistic spirit or world philanthropy. For many decades the country was very sparsely settled. There was abundant free land. Labor was scarce. The number of immigrants was still very small, and nearly all of them were sturdy pioneers, essentially homogeneous and readily assimilated. There was, therefore, little need to worry about any immigration "problems," and it was comforting to the consciences of our ancestors to keep the doors wide open. . . .

During the last decade of the nineteenth century a distinct change in public opinion began to manifest itself. Of slow growth at first, the new views soon spread more and more rapidly until they have finally been embodied in the new immigration law. . . . The reason for the gradual reversal of the earlier American policy of free immigration to one of steadily increasing restriction was the very marked change in the general character of immigration which began in the decade 1880–1890. It is significant that in the period 1871–1880 the "old" immigration from northern and western Europe amounted to slightly over 2,000,000 persons while the "new" immigration, from southern and eastern Europe and near Asia, numbered only 180,000. In the years 1897–1914, the period immediately preceding the war, the "old" contributed about 3,000,000 while the "new" contributed over 10,000,000. The number of arriving aliens was increasing with enormous rapidity. Their racial origins and their characteristics were changing. It was at this point that a real and very serious immigration "problem" arose. The newer immigrants generally had different and lower standards of living. They often retained their loyalty to their native countries. They read their own foreign language newspapers. Barriers of every kind separated them from the native population and from earlier immigrants from northern and western Europe. . . .

Americans began to realize that the ideal of furnishing an asylum for all the world's oppressed was coming into conflict with changed economic and social conditions. The cold facts were that the supply of public land was practically exhausted; that acute labor problems, aggravated by the influx of ignorant and unskilled aliens, had arisen; that the large cities were becoming congested with foreigners; that there were too many immigrants for proper assimilation; that large numbers of mentally and physically unfit, and of the economically undesirable, had come to the United States. Those who still honestly clung to the idea of maintaining in the United States a haven of refuge for the oppressed, one by one realized that America can only be such a haven if conditions here are better than they are in the lands from which our immigrants come, and that the only way to maintain our economic, political, educational, and social standards is by means of restriction.

The fallacies of the Melting Pot theory had also become obvious. Years before the war it had become increasingly apparent that the Melting Pot was no longer successfully performing its function; that the American population was losing its homogeneous character; that various nationalities of recent immigrants were forming more and more compact racial "blocs," each bloc tenaciously maintaining its own racial character, customs, and traditions. The United States was fast becoming, as Theodore Roosevelt expressed it, a "polyglot boarding house." . . .

What goes into the Melting Pot determines what shall come out of it. If the material fed in is a varied assortment of nationalities, to a considerable extent physically and mentally below par, there can be no hope of producing a superior or even of maintaining a homogeneous race. It is often said, and with truth, that each of

the different alien peoples coming to America has something to contribute to American civilization. But what America needs is desirable
additions to, and not inferior substitutes for, what it already possesses.
There is nothing in biological discovery or principles which would
lead to the hope that only the virtues of the various races which were
going to make up the future American would survive and the vices
be eliminated. The public consciousness awakened to the realization
that, to quote Dr. Henry Fairfield Osborn, "education and environment do not fundamentally alter racial values. . . . The true spirit
of American democracy, that all men are born with equal rights and
duties, has been confused with the political sophistry that all men
are born with equal character and ability to govern themselves and
others, and with the educational sophistry that education and environment will offset the handicap of ancestry."

In another important respect public opinion underwent a striking
change in the decade or two before the war, namely in regard to the
relation of immigration to the need for labor. So accustomed had
Americans become to seeing vast numbers of foreign laborers flocking
into the factories, and mills, and coal mines that it had come to be
an axiom that the need for labor could only be supplied by a constant
and unlimited inflow of immigration. From the time of the first
agitation for restriction down to the present, large employers of
"cheap labor" have always insisted that the development of industry
and the prosperity of the country absolutely depend upon a free
inflow of alien labor. Of late years, however, it has been seen that
cheap foreign labor may often be so cheap that it is dear at any
price; that it is usually, in the long run, both socially and politically
very expensive; that a tremendously rapid development of the country
is by no means altogether desirable. . . .

Thus American public opinion had for twenty-five or thirty years
before the war been gradually crystallizing in favor of more restriction. . . . The report of the United States Immigration Commission,
completed in 1917, which recommended restriction "as demanded by
economic, moral, and social considerations," was a very convincing
official pronouncement on the question, and did much to convert the
nation as a whole to the necessity of prompt action. This commission,
it should be noted, suggested a percentage limitation of immigration.

Then came the Great War. Patriotic Americans who had been in doubt on the question of restriction became aggressive restrictionists. Those who had been advocating further effective legislation saw the tide turning their way with irresistible force. . . . The lessons of the war, and the prospect of a vast immigration following it, suddenly fanned into a brighter flame the smouldering fire of sentiment in favor of restriction. The result was that in the Emergency Act of 1921 the United States for the first time placed a definite numerical limit on immigration.

With the three per cent law expiring on June 30, 1924, Congress was faced with the necessity of providing adequate legislation to take the place of the Emergency Act. . . .

The main provisions of the Act of 1924 may, for the sake of simplicity and clearness, be grouped under three heads, (1) those dealing with limitation of numbers; (2) those providing for selection; (3) those based on humanitarian motives.

(1) *Limitation.* For three years, or until June 30, 1927, the annual quota is fixed at two per cent of the number of foreign-born of each nationality in this country in 1890. This will admit, within the quota, somewhat over 160,000. . . .

Sec. 11 (b) of the Immigration Act of 1924 reads as follows: "The annual quota of any nationality for the fiscal year beginning July 1, 1927, and for each fiscal year thereafter, shall be a number which bears the same ratio to 150,000 as the number of inhabitants in continental United States in 1920 having that national origin bears to the number of inhabitants in continental United States in 1920, but the minimum quota of any nationality shall be 100." This is Senator Reed's racial origins provision. It cuts straight through the controversy as to whether the quotas should be based on the census of 1890 or that of 1910. It bases the quotas not upon the numbers of those composing the various alien colonies or foreign "blocs" now in the country, ignoring the native-born, but divides them among the nationalities in accordance with the national origins of the whole population. The fairness of such an apportionment cannot be disputed. It declares, in effect, that what we now are racially we propose to remain. Against such a stand there can be no ground for opposition. Each year's immigration, as Commissioner Curran put it, is to be "an exact miniature of what we are as to stock." This is bedrock immigration policy. It is one of the fairest and most constructive provisions which has ever been embodied in any immigration law. . . .

(2) *Selection.* Another important feature of the new law is the attempt, for the first time, to exercise some control over immigration at the source. Intending immigrants must apply to United States consular officers abroad for "immigration visas." These papers are to contain answers to questions essentially the same as those asked the immigrant on his arrival at our ports, together with full information as to the alien's family status, his occupation, personal appearance, ability to speak, read and write, addresses of relations, destination, personal and family institutional history, etc. In addition, the alien must furnish, if available, copies of his "dossier" and prison and military record, and copies of all other available public records concerning him kept by the government to which he owes allegiance. "The application is to be signed by the alien in the presence of the consular officer, and verified by oath administered by that officer. No immigration visa is to be issued if it appears to the consular officer, from statements in the application or in the papers submitted therewith, that the immigrant is inadmissible to the United States under the immigration laws," nor "if the consular officer knows or has reason to believe that the immigrant is inadmissible to the United States under the immigration laws." . . .

The new plan is the first real attempt on the part of the United States to exercise some control over the kind of immigrants who shall come here. Hitherto this matter has been left practically altogether in the hands of foreign countries, some of which have certainly had no hesitation about making it easy for their own least desirable citizens to come to America.

(3) *Humanitarian Provisions.* The new law contains many provisions based on broad humanitarian motives. The immigration visa plan should reduce hardships to a minimum, prevent the division of families, and put an end to deportations on account of arrivals in excess of the quotas. Congestion at Ellis Island, with its attendant hardships, will be done away with, and it will therefore be possible to make the medical and general examinations more thorough and more effective. Further, "an immigrant who is the unmarried child under eighteen years of age, or the wife, of a citizen of the United States who resided therein at the time of filing a petition" is admis-

sible as a "non-quota" immigrant provided there is no medical or other ground for exclusion; and in the issuance of immigration visas preference, up to fifty per cent of the annual quota of any nationality, is to be given to an alien "who is the unmarried child under twenty-one years of age, the father, the mother, the husband, or the wife, of a citizen of the United States who is twenty-one years of age or over." These two provisions should surely be sufficiently liberal in preventing the separation of families. Indeed, experience may show that these exceptions in favor of near blood relatives are too liberal, and are open to abuse, in which case they can be modified by law. Among the humanitarian sections mention may further be made of the permission to reënter the United States after temporary absence, and the admission, as non-quota immigrants, of ministers, professors (including their wives and unmarried children under eighteen), and *bona fide* students.

Further, more effective provision is made for preventing the embarkation of aliens who fall into the excluded classes by increasing the fines on the transportation companies in cases where such aliens are brought to the United States. If intending immigrants of this sort are kept from sailing, hardship and suffering are very greatly reduced. Heavy fines on the transportation companies prevent these companies from taking the passage money from aliens who may later be deported. In each case the Secretary of Labor is to satisfy himself, before imposing the fine, that the existence of the disease, or disability might have been detected by competent examination, medical or otherwise, or by "reasonable precaution" at the time of foreign embarkation. In addition, the steamship company is to refund to the alien the price of his ticket from initial point of departure to the port of arrival. All these provisions are distinctly humane, and in the interests of the alien as well as of the United States.

In all, it can truthfully be said in regard to the Act of 1924 that no immigration measure has had such careful drafting and such diligent, humane and disinterested consideration. It is an emphatic national decision that, to quote President Coolidge, "America must be kept American." It is based on bedrock principles. It marks a turning point in American civilization.

Robert De C. Ward, in *Foreign Affairs* (New York, 1924), III, 100–110 *passim*. Reprinted by permission.

PART III

GOVERNMENT AND DEPENDENCIES

CHAPTER V — PRESIDENT THEODORE ROOSEVELT

23. Roosevelt and Hanna (1901)

BY HERMANN H. KOHLSAAT (1923)

Kohlsaat (1853–1929) was connected with the bakery lunch industry, which grew into the great lunch and wholesale bakery business of H. H. Kohlsaat and Co. In 1891 he became part owner of the Chicago *Inter-Ocean*, and in 1894 editor of the Chicago *Times-Herald;* he was editor of the Chicago *Evening Post* from 1894 to 1901, of the Chicago *Record-Herald* from 1910 to 1912, and of the Chicago *Inter-Ocean* in 1913.—For Roosevelt, see the volumes from which Nos. 23–26 are taken, also Joseph Bucklin Bishop, *Theodore Roosevelt and his Time;* Howard C. Hill, *Roosevelt and the Caribbean; Roosevelt's Autobiography,* and his works. See also Nos. 31 and 47 below; also *Roosevelt Encyclopedia* (in progress).

ROOSEVELT occupied a drawing-room. He asked me to sit with him. His mind was working like a trip-hammer. He talked of many things he was going to do.

Part of the time I was in the second Pullman. An hour or two after leaving Buffalo Mark Hanna came to my seat. He was in an intensely bitter state of mind. He damned Roosevelt and said: "I told William McKinley it was a mistake to nominate that wild man at Philadelphia. I asked him if he realized what would happen if he should die. Now look, that damned cowboy is President of the United States!"

I tried to reason with him; told him Roosevelt did not want to be "shot into the Presidency," but could not mollify him.

A little later I asked Roosevelt how he and Mark Hanna got along. He said: "Hanna treats me like a boy. He calls me 'Teddy.'" I asked him if he realized what it meant if he and Hanna quarrelled, and told him Hanna held the Republican organization in the hollow of his hand; that he was the leader in the senate and could defeat any measure that he, Roosevelt, proposed, and make his administration a failure. I cited the Garfield-Conkling row.

Roosevelt said "What can I do about it? Give him complete control of the patronage!" I said: "Hanna would resent any such suggestion." I told him Hanna was heart-broken. He saw his best friend gone. All his hopes crushed.

Finally I made the suggestion he invite Hanna to take supper with him alone in his drawing-room. That he must not say anything in the presence of the waiter that could be repeated, as the newspaper men would pounce upon the poor colored boy when they arrived in Washington. That after the plates and cloth were removed, to let the table remain, calling his attention to the awful gap between the front and back seat of a Pullman sleeper. When they were alone, to say: "Old man, I want you to be my friend. I know you cannot give me the love and affection you gave McKinley, but I want you to give me just as much as you can. I need you. Will you be my friend?" Then put your hands, palms up, on the table. If he puts his hands in his pockets, you are a goner, but if he puts his hands in yours, you can bet on him for life." Roosevelt said: "All right, I'll try it!"

Later, as I sat in the forward coach, I saw the waiter whisper in Senator Hanna's ear. He hesitated a moment, and then nodded his head. He came to my seat at the other end of the car and said: "That damned cowboy wants me to take supper with him, alone. Damn him!" I said: "Mark, you are acting like a child. Go and meet him half-way."

Shortly after, he disappeared into Roosevelt's car. I was very nervous, but as an hour passed and thirty minutes more, Hanna came in, and I knew by his face, as he limped toward my seat, that it was "all right." With a smile which the late Volney Foster said "would grease a wagon," Hanna said: "He's a pretty good little cuss, after all!" When I asked him what took place, he told of Roosevelt's putting his hands on the table, and as near as one man can quote another, he told what Roosevelt said, repeating what I had told Roosevelt to say. "What did you do, Mark?" He answered: "Putting my hands in his I said: 'I will be your friend on two conditions: first that you carry out McKinley's policies, as you promised.' Roosevelt answered: 'All right, I will.' 'Second, that you quit calling me "old man." If you don't I'll call you "Teddy."' 'All right. You call me "Teddy" and I'll call you "old man."'" From that moment Roosevelt and Hanna were staunch, loyal friends. The only rift was for a few weeks late in 1903, when some anti-Roosevelt people tried to get Mark Hanna into the race for the Presidency.

All of Roosevelt's own writings and his numerous biographers tell of his friendly relations with Hanna, but are silent as to how it came about.

Hermann H. Kohlsaat, *From McKinley to Harding* (New York, Scribner's, 1923), 100–103.

---

24. A Statesman's View of a President (1904)

BY SECRETARY JOHN HAY (1904)

For Hay, see No. 121 below.—Bibliography as in No. 23 above.

1904. *Jan.* 17.—THE President came in for an hour and talked very amusingly on many matters. Among others he spoke of a letter he had received from an old lady in Canada denouncing him for having drunk a toast to Helen [Hay] at her wedding two years ago. The good soul had waited two years, hoping that the pulpit or the press would take up this enormity. "Think," she said, "of the effect on your friends, on your children, on your own immortal soul, of such a thoughtless act."

March 14.—We lunched with the President; Cardinal Gibbons, the Hengelmüllers, Thayers, and others were there. . . . The Cardinal told the President he hoped earnestly for his election. He is deeply disgusted with the campaign of Gorman against the negroes. He told the President that he had seen a memorial drawn up by an eminent lawyer in favor of paying a large sum to Colombia for her rights in

Panama. He would not tell the name of the eminent lawyer, but a light of recognition came into his cold blue eye when the President told him that X. favored paying the money to Reyes, as that would strengthen the Liberals as against the Clericals!

March 18.—At the Cabinet meeting to-day the President said some one had written asking if he wanted to annex any more Islands. He answered, "about as much as a gorged anaconda wants to swallow a porcupine wrong end to." . . . He was *orienting* some one, when it was observed that the man was doubtless conscientious. "Well," he burst out, "if a man has a conscience which leads him to do things like that, he should take it out and look at it—for it is unhealthy."

March 20.—The President talked of the situation, which seems to him very rosy; he thinks that Congress will adjourn by the first of May and that everything will go smoothly during the summer; that Parker will probably be nominated by the Democrats, but that he will not be formidable. The things that annoy him most are trifles; such as the cost of the White House improvements, the upholstering of the *Mayflower*, etc. He has heard that some people in New York have said he was a grotesque figure in the White House, and wonders what they mean.

March 27.—The President is much preoccupied about the Chairmanship of the National Committee. His mind is now turned to Root. I should be glad if he would take it: it would still further extend his reputation and his national standing, to carry on a campaign which is sure to be interesting and wholesome, and crowned by a great success. It would be an advantage also to the party to keep its best men like Root and Taft, etc., as much to the front as possible for the sake of the contrast, etc.

April 5.—At the Cabinet meeting this morning it was suggested that——would be a good candidate to carry Maryland—(which Gary says we will carry anyhow). Taft said: "Mr. President, are you particular about your company?" T. answered: "I am a liberal man," and said no more.

Shaw told a good story about poor Senator——. He and some more grafters had agreed to press a certain bill through the—— Legislature, and had been paid for it. As the session drew near its close the lobbyist grew alarmed and went to see——, who demanded a supplement. The man said: "What can I say to my principals, who thought this matter settled? " "Tell them," said———thoughtfully, "that I'm acting damn strange."

April 10.—The President came in and talked mostly about the situation in New York, which annoys him greatly and somewhat alarms him. He sees a good many lions in the path—but I told him of the far greater beasts that appeared to some people as in Lincoln's way, which turned out to be only bobcats after all.

April 26.—At the Cabinet this morning the President talked of his Japanese wrestler, who is giving him lessons in Jiu Jitsu. He says the muscles of his throat are so powerfully developed by training that it is impossible for any ordinary man to strangle him. If the President succeeds, once in a while, in getting the better of him, he says, "Good! lovely! "

May 8.—The President was reading Emerson's "Days" and came to the wonderful closing line; " I, too late, Under her solemn fillet saw the scorn." I said, "I fancy you do not know what that means." "O, do I not? Perhaps the greatest men do not, but I in my soul know I am but the average man, and that only marvelous good fortune has brought me where I am."

May 12.—Bade the President good-bye. He said, with jeering good nature, he hoped I would enjoy my well-earned rest. [Mr. Hay was going to make an address at the World's Fair in St. Louis.]

June 5.—[The President] spoke of his own speeches, saying he knew there was not much in them except a certain sincerity and kind of commonplace morality which put him *en rapport* with the people he talked with. He told me with singular humor and recklessness of the way X and the late lamented Holls tried to put him on his guard against me.

June 21.—The President returned from Valley Forge yesterday and we all congratulated him at the Cabinet meeting to-day on his sermon on Sunday. It seems it was entirely impromptu, Knox having asked him to speak only just before Church time. K. says the question what is to become of Roosevelt after 1908 is easily answered. He should be made a Bishop.

August 11.—I dined with the President last night. . . . After dinner we adjourned to the library and the President read his letter of acceptance. I was struck with the readiness with which he accepted every suggestion which was made.

August 13.—I went to the White House this morning and found the President screaming with delight over a proposition in the [New York] *Evening Post* that Wayne MacVeagh should be Secretary of State in Parker's Cabinet. So the dear Wayne has wearied of waiting for my envied shoes at the hands of Roosevelt.

October 17.—I lunched at the White House—nobody else but Yves Guyot and Theodore Stanton. The President talked with great energy and perfect ease the most curious French I ever listened to. It was absolutely lawless as to grammar and occasionally bankrupt in substantives; but he had not the least difficulty in making himself understood, and one subject did not worry him more than another.

October 23.—The President came in this morning badly bunged about the head and face. It did not occur to me till after he had gone that I had come so near a fatal elevation to a short term of the Presidency.[1] *Dei avertite omen!*

He was in high spirits, though he always speaks of the election as uncertain. I showed him Lincoln's Pledge of August, 1864, written when he thought McClellan might be elected. He was much impressed, and went on as he often does to compare Lincoln's great trials with what he calls his little ones. He asked me to read Stannard Baker's article about him in *McClure's* which he likes.

October 30.—The President came in for an hour. We talked awhile about the campaign and at last he said: "It seems a cheap sort of thing to say, and I would not say [it] to other people, but laying aside my own great personal interests and hopes,—for of course I desire intensely to succeed,—I have the greatest pride that in this fight we are not only making it on clearly avowed principles, but we have the principles and the record to avow. How can I help being a little proud when I contrast the men and the considerations by which I am attacked, and those by which I am defended? "

November 3.—The President's fall from his horse ten days ago, might have been very serious. He landed fairly on his head, and his neck and shoulders were severely wrenched. For a few days there seemed a possibility of meningitis. But he is strong and well-knit, and the spine escaped injury. I am thankful to have escaped a four months' troubled term of the Presidency. Strange that twice I have

[1] There being no Vice-President, Mr. Hay, as Secretary of State, stood next in line of succession to the Presidency.

come so hideously near it—once at Lenox and now with a hole-in-a-bridge. The President will of course outlive me, but he will not live to be old. . . .

November 8.—I went over to the White House at a quarter after nine, thinking the returns must have begun to come in by that time. I found the Red Parlor full of people, the President in the midst of them with his hands full of telegrams. I asked him if he had anything decisive as yet. He said: "Yes, Judge Parker has sent his congratulations." . . . Everywhere the majorities are overwhelming. . . . "I am glad," said Roosevelt, "to be President in my own right."

November 12.—The papers this morning announce on the authority of the President that I am to remain Secretary of State for the next four years. He did it in a moment of emotion,—I cannot exactly see why,—for he has never discussed the matter with me and I have never said I would stay. I have always deprecated the idea, saying there was not four years' work in me; now I shall have to go along awhile longer, as it would be a scandal to contradict him. . . .

J. B. Bishop told me to-day of the tumultuous dinner last night at the White House and the speechless amazement of John Morley at the *faconde* of the President. He said afterwards to Bishop: "The two things in America which seem to me most extraordinary are Niagara Falls and President Roosevelt."

November 20.—I read the President's message in the afternoon. . . . Made several suggestions as to changes and omissions. The President came in just as I had finished, and we went over the matters together. He accepted my ideas with that singular amiability and open-mindedness which form so striking a contrast with the general idea of his brusque and arbitrary character.

William Roscoe Thayer, *The Life and Letters of John Hay* (Boston, Houghton Mifflin, 1915), II, 351–360 *passim.* Reprinted by special permission of the publishers.

25. Roosevelt the Trust Buster (1904)

BY JAMES FORD RHODES (1922)

Rhodes (1848–1927), for years a business man, trained himself as an historian. He received honorary degrees from several American universities and from Oxford, and was awarded the Loubat Prize (Berlin Academy of Science, 1901), the gold medal of the National Institute of Arts and Letters (1919), and the Pulitzer Prize (Columbia University, 1918). He was a member of many learned societies. He wrote *History of the United States from the Compromise of 1850* (7 vols., 1893–1906), *From Hayes to McKinley, 1877–1896* (1919), and *The McKinley and Roosevelt Administrations, 1897–1909* (1922); also *Historical Essays* (1909); *History of the Civil War* (1917).

THE Northern Pacific and Great Northern railroads ran from Lake Superior to Puget Sound on the Pacific coast, and on through traffic were competing lines; but for a number of years their relations had been altogether friendly. Both desired a terminal in Chicago which should connect with their St. Paul-Minneapolis lines, and after much discussion and negotiation acquired the Chicago, Burlington and Quincy. James J. Hill, as honest a man as ever lived, whose career from early poverty to superfluous wealth was noted for the confidence other men reposed in him, may be said to be the hero of the merger of the three railroads. He formed a company called the Northern Securities which was to own the C., B. and Q. property as well as that of the other two. This was a holding company whose officers should manage the three railroads and divide the dividends among the stockholders of the Northern Pacific and Great Northern; the Chicago, Burlington and Quincy stockholders were paid by joint bonds of the two purchasing railroads.

Hill's idea in making the merger was for the sake of no vulgar profit but to render the stock of the Northern Securities Company an investment to men and their heirs who would have a great protection in the event of the death of those now in control. Hill and his attorneys studied the precedents, laws and regulations and especially the decision of the United States Supreme Court in the Knight case, arriving at the conclusion that the Anti-Trust Act of 1890 did not apply to such a merger; they went forward therefore with their plans. And if James J. Hill could have left men who would carry on business as he had carried it on, the merger could not be said to interfere with the public good.

But he had to reckon with Theodore Roosevelt, who was antagonistic to the operations of large financiers and believed that it was incumbent on him as President to protect the public against their operations. While Roosevelt liked Hill, he did not consider J. Pierpont Morgan, who was an active coadjutor with Hill in this enterprise, a good financial adviser. When Morgan heard of the President's opposition to the merger he went to Washington and said to him, "If we have done anything wrong send your man (meaning Attorney-General Knox) to my man (naming one of his lawyers) and they can fix it up." "That can't be done," said the President. "We don't want to fix it up," added Knox who assisted at this interview, "we want to stop it." Morgan inquired, "Are you going to attack my other interests, the Steel Trust and the others?" "Certainly not," replied the President, "unless we find out that in any case they have done something that we regard as wrong."

When Morgan went away Roosevelt expressed his opinion, saying to Knox: "That is a most illuminating illustration of the Wall Street point of view. Mr. Morgan could not help regarding me as a big rival operator, who either intended to ruin all his interests or else could be induced to come to an agreement to ruin none." Roosevelt considered Hill a good financial adviser but said that he had to be on the watch that Hill, in giving him counsel, had not an eye to his own interest. Still Roosevelt appreciated a man who from nothing had amassed a fortune of sixty millions, although he did not rate as the highest ability the acquiring of wealth in this country of enormous resources. His heroes were drawn from another class.

It is interesting to note the conflict between these two honest men. Roosevelt requested an opinion from Attorney-General Knox, who on February 19, 1902, authorized the publication of the following statement: "Sometime ago the President requested an opinion as to the legality of this merger, and I have recently given him one to the effect that, in my judgment, it violates the provisions of the Sherman Act of 1890 (the Anti-Trust Act), whereupon he directed that suitable action should be taken to have the question judicially determined." This was a bomb shell in Wall Street and the beginning of the active hostility of the large financial interests to Theodore Roosevelt, who directed the course of his Attorney-General.

Knox knew the ground well, as before McKinley had drawn him

from the active practice of his profession, he was a corporation lawyer. He began suit in the United States Circuit Court in St. Paul on March 10, 1902; and on April 9, 1903, a decision was rendered by four Circuit judges sitting in St. Louis. This tribunal "decreed that, as the combination known as the Northern Securities Company violated the Anti-Trust Act of 1890, that Company is enjoined from attempting to acquire further stock of the Northern Pacific or Great Northern Railways; it is further enjoined from voting the stock already acquired or attempting to exercise any control whatsoever. The Northern Pacific and Great Northern are enjoined from permitting any such action on the part of the Securities Company and from paying to that Company any dividends on stock which it now claims to own."

The case went to the United States Supreme Court, the majority opinion of which was written by Justice Harlan (March 14, 1904), which took the ground that the merger was opposed to the Anti-Trust Act of 1890 and therefore illegal; the decree of the lower Court was affirmed. It was given out that the Court had decided in favor of the Government by 5 to 4; but Justice Brewer, in stating his agreement in the main with the four others, differed in some degree, so that it was jocularly said that the Government had won by $4\frac{5}{8}$ to $4\frac{3}{8}$. Many were vitally interested in the decision and the gossip of the day put Justice Holmes, who was appointed by Roosevelt, on the side of the Government. It was a great surprise therefore that when the decision was known, he should be found on the other side, giving the grounds of his judgment. Gossip of the day was also concerned with two other judges who were counted against the Government, but as matter of fact concurred with Harlan in his opinion. This gossip redounded to the majesty of the Court.

Hill's opinion soon after Knox's announcement was given in a private letter. "It really seems hard," he wrote, "when we look back on what we have done and know that we have led all Western companies in opening the country and carrying at the lowest rates, that we should be compelled to fight for our lives against the political adventurers who have never done anything but pose and draw a salary." But when the Supreme Court decision, which he thought would be favorable to his enterprise, was rendered, he said, "We must all bow to the law of the land," and steps were taken to undo the work of combination. Through the decisions of the Courts, no property was sacrificed, but shares, which had been transferred to the Securities Company, were returned to their original owners; but any such holding company as the Northern Securities was forbidden.

No one who has read carefully the life of Hill can do otherwise than feel sympathy with the man when one of his darling projects was defeated, but as we look at it now, President Roosevelt was right and the decision of the Court was sound. While this combination as directed by Hill may not have been against the public good, the mischief lay in the precedent, for, were this merger approved, a few men by successive steps might have controlled the railroad system of the country. . . .

Roosevelt's idea of the Knight case, which had been decided by the United States Supreme Court in January, 1895, with but one dissenting voice, was that such a merger as that involved in the Northern Securities case could be reached only by the action of the States themselves; but by the decision of the same court in the actual (*i. e.* the Northern Securities) case the nation might act and for this Roosevelt contended. He thus wrote: "By a vote of five to four the Supreme Court reversed its decision in the Knight case, and in the Northern Securities case sustained the Government. The power to deal with industrial monopoly and suppress it and to control and regulate combinations, of which the Knight case had deprived the Federal Government, was thus restored to it by the Northern Securities case."

From the day of Knox's statement, the line was drawn between Roosevelt and the large financial interests of the country. A goodly part of the history of his administration is due to that conflict, and as Roosevelt was effective as a fighter, he was ready to throw down the gauntlet.

"The Northern Securities Suit," he wrote during August, 1904, "is one of the great achievements of my administration. I look back upon it with great pride for through it we emphasized the fact that the most powerful men in this country were held to accountability before the law."

James Ford Rhodes, *The McKinley and Roosevelt Administrations* (New York, Macmillan, 1922), 221–227 *passim*.

26.   An Outsider's View of Roosevelt as Peacemaker (1905)

BY LORD CHARNWOOD (1924)

Lord Charnwood, an English political observer and biographer, has written also an excellent biography of Lincoln.

AND now it must be briefly said how, in 1905, the President of the United States, having done much to enhance his country's strength and having made his personality quietly felt in more than one land across the seas, became one of the greatest figures then before the world, as a devoted and most successful peacemaker. Many of us can remember vividly how the struggle between the compact and trained strength of Japan, and the decayed, giant might of Russia, exerted at a vast distance, came to a deadlock, in which national pride and national suspiciousness withheld each country from seeking peace, although neither could gain anything by further fighting except at a ruinous cost.

Early in this year Roosevelt, with his vividly sympathetic comprehension of the characters and situations of other countries, began anxiously to brood on the question whether neighbors could do no neighborly service. An Englishman, who, about this time, had a strange intermittent talk with him, while he simultaneously attended a Cabinet meeting in the next room, is reported to have brought home a quaint account of his emphatic self-contradictory declarations, that there was nothing that could possibly be done and also that the war must stop. It was the odd, superficial token of an intense, self-restrained watchfulness. The detailed story now before us of his intervention cannot usefully be abridged. Its effect upon every careful reader must be the same. I have used the word devoted, since no weaker word can well be applied to a man who, with overabundant work on his hands, put, as he did, his immense industry and resourcefulness to the severest strain which they ever underwent, unsolicited, in a high cause, in which rebuff and failure were most probable, and in which success, if it was to come, would very likely demand his trading all the credit and lustre to others.

His task was, at first, one of incessantly feeling his way, not only with Japan and Russia, but with France, England, and Germany.

It should be said clearly that the only noticeable help which he found in these three neutral countries came from the German Emperor, whose help was zealous and valuable, and of whom his critical and humorous estimate became tinged with real gratitude. At a later stage when the combatant Powers showed coy signs of a wish for peace; later still when each was willing to negotiate, if, and if, and if; last of all when their plenipotentiaries had met in America, and, like their armies, come to a deadlock from which only a strong arm could free them the difficulty of the task never abated. His letters to Sir George Trevelyan, Mr. St. Loe Strachey, and others throw exceedingly pleasant lights upon the whole of this performance in diplomacy. At the close of August it ended with actual peace, just when matters had begun to seem quite hopeless. It had exacted of him throughout not only ability and courage, but unfailing patience and the sympathetic tact of a gentleman whose quality, if not always exhibited, was often almost as conspicuous as Lincoln's.

He was, too, helped here by his many appreciations of a race so distant from us as the Japanese. The large subject of American relations with the Far East cannot here be opened up, but it may be said that the same right feeling that he showed in his attitude toward the dark races which are palpably inferior, governed him also in his various dealings with other races which, though we can never regard them from a superior standpoint, present quite as difficult a problem of human relationships. If his intervention in the Japanese struggle with Russia —in which by the way *Realpolitik* would have bidden an American statesman to let the Japanese exhaust themselves—may be dismissed so briefly, it is because in this instance nothing but frank eulogy would be in place.

Lord Charnwood, *Theodore Roosevelt* (Boston, Atlantic Monthly Press, 1924), 146–148.

CHAPTER VI — NATIONAL ADMINISTRATION AND PROBLEMS

27. The Corrupting Power of Public Patronage (1901)

BY CONGRESSMAN OSCAR W. UNDERWOOD

Underwood (1862–1929) was a Representative in Congress from Alabama from 1895 to 1915, and was Chairman of the Ways and Means Committee; he was Senator from 1915 to 1927, and Democratic floor leader. He was a prominent candidate for the presidential nomination in 1924.—Bibliography: William Dudley Foulke, *Fighting the Spoilsmen.*

FROM the commencement of our government, the question of the appointment and removal of civil employees has harassed and annoyed those charged by the people with the administration of public affairs, and at times has greatly embarrassed and seriously menaced the successful determination and execution of great governmental policies and public undertakings. The makers of the Constitution realized the danger that must threaten a republican government, should the subordinate offices become the spoils of partisan victory; and after many days' debate as to whether the power of appointment should be vested in the two Houses of Congress, or solely with the Executive, or with the Executive and the Senate jointly, they finally determined on the latter course. They provided certain other limitations on the power of appointments to office, such as:

No senator or representative shall, during the time for which he was elected, be appointed to any civil office under the authority of the United States, which shall have been created, or the emoluments whereof shall have been increased, during such time; and no person holding any office under the United States shall be a member of either House during his continuance in office.

These limitations were wise, but not far-reaching enough to guard against the dangerous abuse of the power of patronage. . . .

Although the abuses that once existed have been checked by the present Civil Service Commission, there are still many flagrant violations of the law taking place every day. So long as it is left optional with the several heads of departments to select from the names certified to them from the Civil Service Commission, or to reject the entire list without giving a trial to the men thus certified, there is bound to be more or less partisan politics shown in the selections. The result is that a new Administration succeeding one of the opposite party will surely find the great majority of the civil service positions in the hands of its political opponents; and a cry will be raised by its own partisans for an equal distribution of the places, which of necessity will destroy any civil service system ever created.

I did not, however, commence this article with the intention of discussing the evils or shortcomings of our present system, but rather to call attention to the dangerous influence exerted by the spoils system on the legislation of the country. You sometimes hear some blatant reviler of the characters of other men, who has never had an opportunity of gaining correct information, denounce senators and representatives in Congress as guilty of corruption and other high crimes and misdemeanors. I do not contend that corrupt men do not sometimes enter in the professions, or among business men; but I do say, after six years' service in the House of Representatives, that I have never heard of any member of Congress being corrupted by the use of money. Taking the 357 representatives as a whole, I am sure that their moral character will not suffer in a comparison with that of the same number of citizens chosen as you come to them from any religious denomination in the land. This of necessity is so. The American people are an honest, God-fearing constituency; and, as a rule, the men they send to represent them reflect their moral character as well as their views on great political questions.

Wherein, then, is the complaint? It is that the pressure brought by the people at home on their representatives to secure offices for them gives the executive branch of the government a dangerous power in influencing legislation.

A new Administration is returned to power. Mr. Blank belongs to the same party as the President-elect. He probably comes to Washington with campaign pledges to honor; or, if he has been wise and made no ante-election promises, he has many true and tried friends and political followers who are justly entitled to his support, and for whom he desires to obtain some of the appointive offices. The new Administration has a policy it desires to carry out, which requires legislation, and bills are, therefore, introduced by the party leader. Mr. Blank finds that some of these measures are not to the interest of his constituency; or, as a man of independent thought, he conscientiously believes they will not be beneficial to the country. He calls on the Cabinet officers to secure his friend's appointment. He is met with pleasant words, and is told that his friend seems to be well endorsed, but that the matter cannot be determined at present.

Mr. Blank is then asked what he thinks in regard to the Administration measures. The member of the Cabinet is greatly astonished that he cannot support the Administration, and asks him to read somebody's report, and consider it from the standpoint of a party man, etc. After he has made his fourth or fifth call, with the same result, he will begin to hear from his friend, who tells him that congressmen from adjacent districts have received appointments, and that the people at home cannot understand why he cannot do something for his district. The question that he has now to decide is whether he shall submit to become a tool in the hands of the Administration, secure the offices, and drift with the party tides, or whether he shall be a representative of the people, determining for himself what best conserves their interest and meets the demands of justice and right. To do this he must return to face angry friends, and must meet the opposition of an unfriendly Administration. Within the last four years I have seen at least two men of great ability retire from public life rather than surrender their own individuality; being unwilling to remain and contend against a hostile Administration. When the Porto Rican bill was first reported to the House, over thirty members of the Administration party declared themselves against it; but as the debate progressed it was understood by all that the Administration whip was being brought into use to bring the recalcitrants into line. One of the original opponents had the courage to announce openly that he had changed his views because the President had requested him to do so. And, on the final vote, only eight had the courage to support their original conviction.

I do not wish to be understood, from what I have said above, as contending that the present Administration alone is responsible for this state of affairs. It has existed with all parties and all administrations almost since the beginning of the government. All that I contend is that from decade to decade it has grown worse instead of better.

If the Democratic party has stood for one thing more than another, it has been for a policy of opposition to a permanent increase of the standing army; yet I have seen the solid phalanx of the opposition in the House of Representatives broken, in the passage of an army bill, by the distribution of patronage. When the cry for place is heard from the editor's son, the banker's son, the lawyer's son, the farmer's son—in truth, everybody's son—the guardian of the liberties of the people, the keeper of the public treasury, must, indeed, be a bold man. The bill providing for the holding of an International Exposition at St. Louis and that creating a Spanish War Claims Commission were passed, after being at first defeated, by making the Commission non-partisan, so that the advocates of the bills secured a number of candidates for the places from almost every State, to work on their delegations. The fact that a member of Congress is regarded as the means through which patronage is distributed has so affected legislation as to cause the unnecessary expenditure of millions of dollars and the passage of bills that otherwise would never have become law.

The framers of the Constitution contemplated that the legislative branch of the government should be separate and distinct from the executive, in order that one might be a check upon the other. This was a wise provision; and, if our government is to last, it must be guarded with the utmost care. It can only be done by prohibiting by law the representative of the people from having any voice in the appointment of the government offices, either directly or indirectly, and making him ineligible for an appointive office under the government for at least two years after the term for which he has been elected has expired. Make his sole business that of legislation, let all fear of punishment or hope of reward come only from his constituency, and the majesty of the people as the rulers of this country will be maintained.

Oscar W. Underwood, in *Forum*, July, 1901 (New York), XXXI, 557–560.

28.   The Department of Commerce and Labor (1903)

BY SECRETARY GEORGE B. CORTELYOU

Cortelyou was personal secretary to Presidents McKinley and Roosevelt; by the latter he was appointed the first Secretary of the Department of Commerce and Labor; and he served also as Postmaster-General and Secretary of the Treasury. Has been in business since 1909.—Bibliography: *Annual Reports* of the Secretary of Commerce.   See No. 89, below.

CONGRESS has declared it to be the province and duty of the Department of Commerce and Labor to "foster, promote, and develop the foreign and domestic commerce, the mining, manufacturing, shipping, and fishery industries, the labor interests, and the transportation facilities of the United States."

One of the most important methods of aiding commerce is to give to those engaged in it such definite information regarding existing conditions as will enable them intelligently to determine the classes of articles which can be most profitably produced, the sections to which they should be distributed, and the agencies through which they can best be placed before the prospective customers.   In all of this work the new Department is actively engaged.

The Census Bureau, which in the year 1900 gathered the statistics of population, manufactures, and agriculture, is now engaged in collecting and compiling information on other subjects having important relation to our industries, and is also preparing to take, a year hence, another census of our manufactures, thus giving a quinquennial instead of decennial statement, which in the past has been our sole information on the subject of manufactures.   In addition, its statistics on cotton production are now presented at frequent intervals, and in conjunction with special investigations ordered by Congress, it is giving to the country a fuller knowledge of the great factors of our commerce than ever before.

The Bureau of Statistics of the Department publishes, for the benefit of our commercial interests, such information as it is able to collect with the coöperation of the various governmental offices and commercial organizations.   It also gathers and publishes from month to month statements of the concentration of the principal articles at certain internal points and their transportation therefrom to various parts of the country and to the seaboard for exportation. This work, a comparatively new one, is carried on by the Bureau largely through the coöperation of commercial bodies, the press, and the large organizations engaged in transportation. In like manner information is collected and distributed regarding exports and imports. Material for use in manufacture is forming a steadily growing share in our imports, while the home market for articles in a form ready for consumption is more fully supplied year by year by our own producers and manufacturers. Manufacturers' materials in 1860 formed 26 per cent of our total imports; in 1880, 37 per cent; in 1900, 46 per cent, and in 1903, 48 per cent, while the imports of articles manufactured in a state ready for consumption have decreased in about the same proportion.

Monthly statements of the total exports of the various articles of production and of the countries to which exported are presented by the Bureau of Statistics and distributed to individuals and to commercial and industrial organizations. In addition, statements are issued at the close of each fiscal year showing the distribution by countries of every article exported and the quantity and value sent to each country during each year of the previous decade. Semiweekly statements of commercial conditions are prepared and distributed to the press and to commercial organizations, thus giving the widest possible publicity to the latest available information regarding commercial conditions.

Still another important undertaking of the Department is the publication and distribution of commercial information collected by the consular service of the United States—a service composed of more than 300 men scattered throughout the world, who report regularly upon the opportunities for American commerce in their respective districts. These reports are forwarded by the consuls through the State Department to the Department of Commerce and Labor for publication and distribution. In addition to the information thus obtained, the Department of Commerce and Labor from time to time calls upon the consuls for special information for which inquiry has been received from merchants and manufacturers. The consular reports are issued daily in printed form, and distributed to the press, to commercial bodies, and to a limited number of individuals. It is through this service that the American commercial public is kept in close and constant touch with trade conditions and opportunities throughout the world.

Another valuable agency is the Bureau of Labor of the Department. Its investigations are not confined to conditions in the United States, but are extended to other countries and to the relations which labor conditions there bear to production and commerce and labor in the United States. The information thus obtained is published periodically and widely distributed.

Other branches of the Department's work in the interest of commerce and industry include the Light-House Establishment with its thousands of employees engaged in maintaining aids and safeguards to commerce on the coast and inland waterways; the Coast and Geodetic Survey with its corps of skilled men engaged in surveys of our coast; the Steamboat-Inspection Service, which contributes largely to the safety of persons and capital engaged in commerce by water, both along the coast and upon the interior waterways of the country; the Bureau of Navigation, which has to do with matters relating to the shipping interests of the United States; the Bureau of Fisheries, which in promoting the development of our fresh and salt water fisheries contributes largely to the food supplies entering into the commerce of the country; the Bureau of Immigration, which protects the country against violations of the laws governing immigration; and the Bureau of Standards, which is intrusted with the care and use of the national standards of measure, with the development of methods of measurement, and with the dissemination of knowledge concerning these subjects as applied in the arts, sciences, and industries.

Of the new Bureaus created by the act establishing the Department of Commerce and Labor, the Bureau of Corporations is engaged in the necessary foundation work for its duties under the law, and will eventually become a valuable agency for the extension of our domestic and foreign commerce. The Bureau of Manufactures is not yet organized, owing to lack of appropriations. Funds available in present legislation will make possible an early beginning of the work of this Bureau.

Provision was made in the estimates for this year for an appropriation to be expended under the immediate direction of the Secretary for special investigations of trade conditions at home and abroad, with the object of promoting the domestic and foreign commerce of the United States, and for other purposes. Important instruments in the promotion of trade are the agents dispatched from time to time by foreign governments to study commercial opportunities in other countries. Military and naval experts are sent abroad by our Government to report on conditions that are of interest to their respective Departments. In the daily competition of international trade there is even greater need of intelligent outposts abroad. Special agents are also required in the Department itself to inspect the branches of its services in different localities and to secure uniform, businesslike, and economical methods. The need of such agents in other Departments has been met by appropriations, and there is of course a similar need in this new Department.

No appropriation has yet been made for this service, but I am convinced that when its importance is made more apparent to Congress favorable action will be taken.

In addition to the measures that have been taken for the reorganization and improvement of existing branches of the statistical service, it is proposed to establish an office for the collection and distribution of foreign-tariff information, this being one of the directions in which the Department's work can apparently be extended with great advantage. A small initial appropriation has been received for this purpose.

Nations are inclined to regulate their commercial intercourse by means of a double system of tariffs, permitting preferences through commercial treaties. The current agitation in Great Britain for a departure from traditional policy in order to increase commerce between the members of the British Empire may have marked effects upon American trade and incidentally upon American labor.

The industrial and economic facts which accompany such movements must be closely, intelligently, and unremittingly watched. A few competent employees, acting directly under the head of the Department, will suffice for this purpose. From the small expenditure proposed excellent results may be obtained. There is at present no Government office in the United States engaged systematically in the work of collecting information regarding foreign tariffs and making that information available to our exporters. The Department has received frequent inquiries for such information, and has been impressed with the importance of providing a medium to supply it.

You have been kept advised from time to time of what the new Department is doing on these lines. Too much must not be expected in the initial months of its existence. It will coöperate with you and you must coöperate with it. There must be mutual understanding and mutual support. It will not attempt the impossible. Its sphere lies in what will be well-defined limits. It is a branch of the Federal Government, and as such must adhere strictly to the lines marked out for its jurisdiction and not inject itself into fields of private endeavor where it does not belong. It can do a great work for the commerce and industry of this country, but the results it will achieve will be measured by the foresight and the intelligence and the conservatism with which it carries on its work as one of the great agencies in the extension of our domestic and foreign trade.

The promise held out for the new Department presupposes proper equipment. As it demonstrates its usefulness, I am confident Congress will increase its appropriations to a point adequate to its needs. Like all new institutions it is bound to have its early struggles for recognition. Congress and the Chief Executive have given it work to do. Whether well or ill equipped, it will do this work in the best manner possible. It seeks nothing it should not have. It will ask for support only on its merits, but as it demonstrates its usefulness in the scheme of our Government, it will have whatever recognition and commendation it may be entitled to receive.

The new Department has to deal in a large way with great business enterprises. It has approached these problems with conservatism and impartiality. It has some jurisdiction over the interests represented by the toilers of the country, and it will do its share in securing a recognition of labor's rights and the encouragement of better feeling and fairer dealing. It is made the statistical Department of the Government, and it will make its statistics non-partisan, impartial, and as accurate as they can be made. It has to do with marine interests. It will advance those interests in every proper manner, and I am sure it is not heresy to state in this presence that it will lend the weight of its influence to the building up of the American merchant marine. It has supervision over the difficult problems of immigration and Chinese exclusion. There are inconsistencies in the laws relating to them. There are grave hardships constantly coming up in the execution of these laws. Not infrequently they present obstacles to the development of our commerce. But they are founded on the good old doctrine of self-preservation, and must be fairly enforced until more satisfactory legislation can be devised. These and other problems to the solution of which the Department must give its best energies are among the most important confronting our people to-day. If the Department can do its legitimate share in their solution, if its personnel can be raised to a high standard, if its expenditures can be kept at the lowest figure consistent with good administration, if, in a word, it can be conducted as a business establishment for the encouragement of good feeling and better understanding between all interests having to do with our trade and industrial relations—the employer and the employee, the accumulator of wealth, and the toiler in the counting room or the shop or the factory who contributes to it—if it can be a potent force for enlightenment and progress in these busy years of the nation's development, all who have an interest in its success will feel that their confidence has not been misplaced and that they have contributed to the establishment and advancement of a factor in our national life.

Address of Secretary Cortelyou before the American Academy of Political and Social Science, April 8, 1904 (Washington, Government Printing Office, 1904), 12–25.

---

29. Distinctions among Parties (1900–1908)

BY PROFESSOR ARTHUR N. HOLCOMBE (1924)

Holcombe is Professor of Government at Harvard. He held several important executive posts in Washington during the World War. He is the author of *Public Ownership of Telephones* (1911); *State Government in the United States* (1916); *Foundations of the Commonwealth* (1923). Bibliography: Kirk Harold Porter, *National Party Platforms;* Edward Stanwood, *History of the Presidency*, II; James Albert Woodburn, *Political Parties and Party Problems in the United States.*

THEODORE ROOSEVELT was a vigorous writer of history, as well as the foremost apostle of the strenuous life in modern politics, and took sides in the partisan controversies of earlier times no less energetically than in those of his own day. He was an ardent admirer of the leading Federalist statesmen, and wrote a life of one of Hamilton's closest associates, Gouverneur Morris. In his writings and also in his speeches he did much to revive the vogue of the great Federalist leader and popularize the Republican tradition. Roosevelt detested Jefferson with a fervor that carried conviction to many of his followers, and expressed his feeling with a freedom that undoubtedly helped the Democrats to revive their old tradition. Many lesser leaders shared the Rooseveltian point of view. Thus the realignment of parties, brought about by the "sound money" campaign, was followed by a corresponding readjustment of the partisan traditions. The "business" interests and capitalistic elements in the Republican party were doubtless grateful for the change, but those who cherished the original Republican ideals observed the new spirit of their party with concern and even alarm. The Eastern wing of the Republican party, in which the former elements were strongest, rejoiced most at the new spirit; the Republicans in the West, where the spirit of the earlier Radical Republicanism found the most friendly soil, felt the greatest misgiving. The conflict of ideals within the Republican party was not so sharp as that between the two wings of the Democratic party, the urban Democracy of New York and the rest of the Northeast, on the one hand, and on the other the agrarian Democracy of the South and West. But the conflict was sharp enough to have a place in any account of the causes of the division of the party during the campaign of 1912.

The effect of the new Republican tradition upon the unity of the party would have been more serious if Theodore Roosevelt had not become its official leader. Roosevelt was as great an idealist in his way as Bryan, and was not the man to permit the leader of a rival party to monopolize the appeal to human disinterestedness. "Aggressive fighting for the right," he declared, "is the noblest sport the world affords." And he seemed to practice what he preached. . . .

A more substantial cause of dissension within the Republican party was the mutual jealousy on the part of the two principal interests which constituted the bulk of its strength, the manufacturers and "business men" of the Northeast, and the grain growers of the old and new Northwest. . . . The feeling grew that the Eastern manufacturers had received more than their share of consideration from the party leaders, and that the interest of the farmers was being neglected.

This feeling was strengthened by the struggles which took place at Washington over the regulation of the railroads, the "trusts," and "big business" generally. The inadequacy of the Interstate Commerce Act of 1887 for the prevention of objectionable practices by the railroads had long since become manifest. The failure of the Sherman Anti-trust Act of 1890 to check the growth of huge combinations of capital and to protect the public against the menace of monopoly was plain. The need of some control over the great meat packers and other food manufacturers had been dramatically revealed to the general public. And the danger in permitting the unregulated exploitation of the natural resources of the country, especially that of the forests by the lumber interests, was becoming widely recognized. But the dominant elements in the Republican party seemed to be unalterably opposed to all effective measures for the conservation of natural resources, for the supervision of the packers and food manufacturers, for the restraint of the "great corporations," and for the regulation of the railroads. The Senators and Representatives from the sections where urban and industrial interests were strong would take no action, and seemed unmindful of the interests of the farmers and of the masses of consumers. The country was prosperous, and the business interests, which had suffered such a fright at the climax of the campaign for the free coinage of silver, wished for relief from further agitation. The new Republican policy of colonial expansion had provided fresh markets for American manufactures and fresh fields for American industry and enterprise. In 1900 the gold standard had at last been firmly established by law. There was little more that the business interests wanted from the federal government in the line of legislation. In opposition to further agitation they presented a united front.

The point of view of this wing of the party was stated most effectively by the foremost leader of the Conservative Republicans, Senator Hanna of Ohio. Mark Hanna had not rested content with his successful management of the campaign which resulted in the election of his friend, McKinley, to the Presidency. He entered the Senate, where he gradually acquired the most influential place among the ambitious and realistic politicians who represented the urban and industrial interests in the Republican party. After McKinley's death he became their favorite candidate for the succession to the Presidency, when the "temperamental" Roosevelt's accidental term should expire. In this rôle Hanna's political utterances attracted universal attention. Speaking at Steubenville, Ohio, in the campaign of 1903, he began as follows: "Two years ago I suggested to the people, in view of the prosperous time, that they knew their business. They replied that they did. One year ago I suggested that they leave well enough alone. They replied that they would. This year I suggested that they stand pat, and they will reply, 'You bet.' "

This was language which the American business man could understand. It voiced his own state of mind. He liked it. The farmer also could understand it. But he did not like it so well. To be sure, he, like the business man, was prosperous. . . . But the increased influence of the business interests made the farmer uneasy. The power of money in politics seemed to have grown greatly and to have become dangerous. People became more sensitive about corruption, both in politics and in American life generally. The era of muck-raking began.

There was little difficulty in holding the two wings of the Republican party together at the campaign of 1904. Mark Hanna had died and there was no other candidate about whom the "stand-patters" could rally. Roosevelt's personal popularity easily gained him his renomination. The Gold Democrats secured control of the Democratic organization and Republican grain growers had no reason to prefer their leadership to that of the Conservative Republicans. Indeed, so many of the Democratic grain growers in the West and even former populists preferred the Republican candidate to that of their own party that the entire West was carried by the Republicans for the first time since 1888. The Republican leaders were more concerned over their chances in New York than on the Western prairies and plains. But Roosevelt had not yet fully exposed his hand, and the Stand-patters did not call for a show-down.

There was also little difficulty in holding the party together in 1908. Roosevelt had done much which the Stand-patters greatly regretted. He had forced through the Congress, against the bitter opposition of Conservative Republicans, many measures which business interests deemed unnecessary and improper. Conspicuous among these were the Hepburn Act, providing effective regulation of the railroads, the Meat Inspection and Pure Food and Drugs Acts, providing effective supervision of the food industries, and the Employers' Liability Act, providing more adequate relief for railroad employees, injured in the course of duty. He had also given a tremendous impetus to the causes of conservation and trust regulation and had made it generally far more difficult for predatory interests to secure undeserved advantages at the expense of the public. But after all, plenty of opportunity remained for legitimate businesses to make satisfactory profits. Moreover, Roosevelt enforced the law without fear or favor. He had not hesitated to help big business and even Wall Street itself, when the occasion seemed to require, as during the panic of 1907. He had set a new standard of efficiency and integrity in the public service, and he was about to hand over his leadership to a successor in whose ability to maintain that standard of efficiency and integrity business interests generally had confidence. Finally, the Stand-patters did not have such an attractive alternative in 1908 as in 1904, for the Gold Democrats had been compelled to surrender the leadership of their party again to the agrarian Democracy of the South and West.

The Western Republicans were also content in 1908 to hold their place in the combination of interests which constituted the Republican party. If Roosevelt had not done much to gratify the special sectional interests of the Western grain growers, he had shown himself extraordinarily sensitive to what may be termed the common human interests. The regulation of railroad rates had not resulted in any special reductions for the particular benefit of farmers and stockmen, but it had removed the fear of uncontrollable power. The prosecution of the "trusts" had not brought noticeable reductions of prices, but it had diminished the menace of unfair competition and oppressive practices. The Reclamation Act and the new policy of conservation had not yet revolutionized the process of settlement in the Far West, but it at least held out the promise of equal opportunity to the small homesteader. If the influence of money continued to seem excessive in public affairs, there was the possibility of correcting that through suitable changes in the laws of the states. The small farmers and wage-earners were not chiefly dependent on the federal government for corrupt practices acts and laws regulating the use of money in elections. They were not at all dependent on federal government for direct primaries, the initiative, referendum, and recall, and other measures designed to make their representatives more responsive to their wishes. Roosevelt at least had mightily contributed to the creation of an atmosphere in politics which made it easier for other leaders to finish the work, and his successor in the leadership of the party might be expected to push the good work along. The matter of the tariff remained indeed a cause of discontent in the corn belt and among the grain growers everywhere, but the Republican platform of 1908 promised a revision of the tariff, and it was supposed that this would mean a downward revision, at least on articles which the farmer had to buy. . . .

The Taft administration made a record of substantial achievement, if it be judged merely by the number and importance of the measures which were enacted into law and by its methods of law enforcement. It began with the revision of the tariff in 1909. The Payne-Aldrich Act provided not only a whole new set of tariff schedules, but also a Tariff Commission to investigate the operation of the new rates and supply the Congress with information concerning the need for further changes. In the following year a permanent Commission on Economy and Efficiency was created to assist the President in the supervision of administration, and several other measures were enacted which were designed to provide for the more economical and efficient enforcement of the laws. The most notable of these measures was the act amending the Railroad Rate Regulation Act of 1906, which broadened the powers of the Interstate Commerce Commission and created a Commerce Court to review the Commission's orders and decrees. A Court of Customs Appeals was also created in order to improve the administration of the tariff law, and in 1911 the organization and procedure of the federal courts was greatly improved by the reform of the Circuit Courts of Appeal and the enactment of a Judicial Code. The execution of certain policies which the administration inherited from its predecessor became the subject of adverse criticism, especially the policy of conservation of natural resources, and the President was compelled to make changes in his Cabinet in order to placate the critics; but in general the Taft administration more than sustained the expectations of the Conservative Republicans with respect to his management of the business of government. It set new standards of performance in the economical and efficient conduct of public affairs.

But the agrarian wing of the Republican party did not judge the Taft administration by these achievements. The corn and wheat growers were more concerned with matters of legislative policy. The revision of the tariff seemed to them much more serviceable to the manufacturers and other urban interests within the party and to the wool growers of the Mountain section than to the farmers of the Mid-Western prairies and plains. Hot controversy broke out as to whether the tariff had been revised upward or downward, and neither wing of the party was satisfied with the result. The urban interests desired lower rates on food and raw materials, while maintaining the existing level of protection on manufactures. The agrarian interests demanded lower rates on clothing, farm equipment, and supplies, but opposed any letting down of the bars which kept the produce of foreign, especially Canadian, farms out of the domestic market. The wool growers and cattlemen wanted ample protection for their products, but the woollen manufacturers and boot-and-shoe manufacturers were beginning to look abroad for additional markets and fought vigorously for the lowest possible manufacturing costs. New England and Pennsylvania and the urban interests of the industrial Northeast generally clung fast to protection for manufactured goods. The Pacific Coast was interested likewise in protection for manufactures. California was also specially interested in protection for its subtropical fruits and nuts, while the Pacific Northwest was specially interested in the protection of lumber and fish. The Mountain section had nothing to gain by the protection of any of these commodities, but it was greatly interested in wool and hides and hence interested indirectly also in the prosperity of the textile and leather industries. The Central sections, where the grain growers predominated, were increasingly disposed to doubt the value of all kinds of protection. The reconciliation of these diverse interests was too great a task for the Taft administration. The expectations of the dominant interests in each of the various sections were excessive, and in the end those which were most powerful at Washington prevailed over the others.

Arthur N. Holcombe, *The Political Parties of To-Day* (New York, Harper's, 1924), 252–264 *passim*.

30. The Campaign of 1912

BY WILLIAM DUDLEY FOULKE (1922)

Foulke, journalist and author, has been for many years interested in civil service reform; he was President of the National Municipal League. In 1885 he joined the National Civil Service Reform League, and formed the Indiana C. S. R. League. Served on Civil Service Commission 1899–1903, under appointment of President Roosevelt. In 1899 he was chairman of the committee of the National Civil Service Reform League to represent it at Washington. Author of *Slav or Saxon* (1887); *Maya, a Story of the Yucatan* (1900); *Protean Papers* (1903); *Lyrics of War and Peace* (1916): *Fighting the Spoilsmen* (1919).—Bibliography: Edward Stanwood, *History of the Presidency*, II, Ch. iv; *American Year Book*, 1912; William J. Bryan, *Tale of Two Conventions*.

. . . THE differences between Mr. Taft and the Progressives were not confined to the tariff. Controversies arose in regard to the conservation policy inaugurated by Roosevelt and endorsed by the Republican Convention. President Taft made an unfortunate mistake in appointing Richard A. Ballinger Secretary of the Interior as the successor to James R. Garfield and in removing Gifford Pinchot from the Forestry Bureau. These controversies still further separated the President from the Progressive members of his party, to which group Garfield and Pinchot belonged.

In the meantime (in June, 1910) Mr. Roosevelt had returned from his African and European journey. He was disappointed at the President's course and believed it would hurt the Republican Party, but during a visit which Lucius B. Swift and I paid to him at Oyster Bay he told us that he hoped his friends would not do anything which would make their ultimate support of Mr. Taft impossible, since it was extremely likely that he would be renominated, although it was not probable that he would be re-elected. At that time and for some time afterwards, Mr. Roosevelt had no intention of running for the presidency himself.

It seemed clear that Mr. Taft's policy was not to the liking of the people. In the election of 1910 the Democrats gained heavily in the House of Representatives, though the Progressive candidates suffered less than others. The breach between them and the President kept growing wider until finally a measure to reduce the tariff was passed by a coalition of Democrats and Progressives and vetoed by the President.

In opposition to Mr. Taft's views, Col. Roosevelt declared himself a Progressive. Since he had declined to be a candidate and had asked his friends to see to it that no movement was made to bring him forward, a conference of Progressive Republicans endorsed Senator La Follette. But a speaking tour throughout the country had ended disastrously for him, and it was found that his candidacy was impossible. There was now no one else to lead the Progressives with any chance of success, and Roosevelt at last, in the latter part of February, 1912, declared that "his hat was in the ring," and that he had determined to make the race.

He was at once accused of ingratitude to Taft. The matter was considered as if it were a question of personal obligation and not of public duty. Yet it was Taft who had pledged himself to carry out the Roosevelt policies; and it was Roosevelt who had returned from Africa to find the President allied with his former opponents. Was Roosevelt now to discredit his own record, or was he to hold up the standard he had always maintained? If personal obligations could be considered, it was Taft and not Roosevelt who had first disregarded them. But the demands of public duty ought in any event to be paramount.

Mr. Taft seemed to be quite unconscious of the real character of his political companionships. He declared in a conversation with an Indiana man, "I am just as much opposed to bosses as is your own wild fanatic, the untamed Col. Wm. Dudley Foulke."

And yet men like Penrose, Cannon, Aldrich, Lorimer, Guggenheim, Hemenway, Gallinger, even George B. Cox, the boss of Cincinnati, and other politicians of similar character, were working with all their might to get him nominated. They wanted an "opponent" with whom they could get on comfortably.

It was about this time that Roosevelt addressed the Constitutional Convention of Ohio, then sitting at Columbus, and spoke in favour of direct primaries and of the initiative, referendum and recall, including the recall of decisions and even of judges. This last proposition exposed him to widespread criticism.

There was a vigorous contest in the primaries and in the district nominating conventions between the Taft men and the Roosevelt men. Wherever the question was submitted to the Republican voters, as in Pennsylvania, Illinois, and even in Mr. Taft's own State of

Ohio, Roosevelt carried all before him. But the State and district conventions, manipulated as they were by political leaders, were generally for Taft. Thus in Indianapolis the local chairman declared that the Roosevelt men would not be allowed to carry a single ward! He excluded the Roosevelt watchers from the polls, the primaries were packed, and Roosevelt did not get a single Indianapolis delegate to the State Convention. In that convention men who were fraudulently elected were allowed to sit in judgment upon each other's credentials, and thus delegates at large were chosen to the national convention. In other States, Washington, California, Texas, Alabama, and elsewhere, similar frauds were committed.

The campaign soon became bitter and personal. Charges were made by Roosevelt and Taft against each other. Taft declared Roosevelt had garbled his speeches, had not given him "a square deal," and had disregarded the promise not to accept another nomination. Roosevelt charged the President with violating confidential correspondence, with intentional misrepresentation, and with a responsibility for the alliance between crooked politics and crooked business; and he reminded the President: "It is a bad trait to bite the hand that feeds you."

It remained to be decided by the Republican National Convention at Chicago whether the voters of the party or its machine leaders and manipulators should nominate the President. There were 254 contested seats. The members of the National Committee, selected four years before and composed largely of reactionary politicians, some of whom had been discredited in their own States, now seated 235 Taft delegates. This gave Taft a majority on the preliminary roll call. The delegates thus seated voted in favour of each other's credentials, and Taft was nominated.

What would the Progressives do? Should they permit a convention controlled by fraud thus to deliver the party into the hands of its reactionary elements by the nomination of a candidate who was not the choice of the vast majority of its members? Ought they thus to perpetuate misrule? They determined to organise a party of their own. Mr. Roosevelt was under no illusions as to the probable outcome of this course. He wrote me on July 1st that he felt the Democrats would probably win if a progressive man should be nominated, adding, "But of course there is no use of my getting into a fight in a half-hearted fashion, and I could not expect Republicans to follow me out if they were merely to endorse the Democratic Convention. So I hoisted the flag and will win or fall under it."

Progressive conventions were held in the various States and districts, and delegates were sent to a national convention, which met on August 5th in Chicago. I was one of the delegates from my own district and was placed on the committee on resolutions to prepare the platform. Roosevelt, as the guest of the convention, delivered what he called "A Confession of Faith." The convention was filled with a kind of religious enthusiasm which reached its climax when he concluded.

The committee on resolutions had plenty to do on account of the great length of the platform and the vast number of questions considered. The original draft when read to us took more than an hour in delivery. I protested vigorously, and in our efforts to shorten and modify it we spent two whole nights, besides much of the intervening day. We got it down to less than half of its original dimensions, but it was still far too long.

In spite of hard work we had a good time on that committee. Professor William Draper Lewis, of the University of Pennsylvania, was chairman and controlled our discussions with great skill. William Allen White, Chester Rowell, Gifford Pinchot and other enthusiastic souls made things as lively as possible and the final product was one of the most notable platforms ever adopted by a political convention.

It is astonishing, now that the Progressive Party is gone, to see how many of the things it advocated have been actually written into the laws either of the Federal Government or of various States.

Again I took an active part in the campaign. The strongest attack made against Mr. Roosevelt was upon the ground that he was a candidate for a "third term." Mr. Taft had warned the people against the man who intended to hold office for life, and the Democratic platform had favoured a single term and a constitutional amendment making a President ineligible for re-election. I considered this objection in my speeches and reminded my hearers that the question had been carefully weighed by the convention in Philadelphia when the Federal Constitution was adopted. That convention finally held that there ought to be no limit as to the number of terms for which a candidate should be eligible. The reason Washington had declined a second re-election was not because it would have been injurious to the public, but because he was personally weary of continuous service and believed he was entitled to seek the repose of Mt. Vernon.

It was further objected that since Roosevelt had said, when he was last elected in 1904, that he would not accept another term, he should therefore not accept it now, although he had been out of office four years. The thing he then had in mind was the question of successive terms, with the danger in the control of patronage which this might involve. But even if it had applied for all time, he had no right to bind himself to abstain from future service by such a declaration. When Washington laid down his command of the army at the end of the Revolution he stated in his circular letter to the Governors, his "determination of not taking any share in public business thereafter," but duty called him to the executive chair and he obeyed. Every criticism of Roosevelt for becoming a candidate on this ground would apply also to Washington.

But neither the excellence of the Progressive platform nor of the candidate could offset the fact that the Democrats were united while their opponents were hopelessly divided. Woodrow Wilson was elected President by an enormous plurality, though not by a majority of all the votes.

William Dudley Foulke, *A Hoosier Autobiography* (New York, Oxford University Press, 1922), 157–163.

———◆———

31. The Bolter's Justification (1912)

BY EX-PRESIDENT THEODORE ROOSEVELT

For a detailed account of the circumstances which led to the holding of a bolting convention in 1912, see No. 30, above.

. . . THE big bosses and the intensely conservative representatives of the moneyed interests have sometimes been divided from one another in the past. But they were a unit at Chicago, just as they have tended to become more and more a unit during recent years throughout the Union. Mr. Taft in the statement he made when informed that he had received the fraudulent nomination practically announced that the end justified the means, and that it was so important to beat me and the forces I represented in order "to save the Constitution" or to "save the State"—the same kind of excuse that the men of the Red Terror advanced for their actions— that it would not do to look closely into the methods by which the feat had been accomplished.   This, of course, is the attitude frankly taken by political bosses of the stamp of Mr. Penrose and Mr. Barnes. Neither Mr. Barnes nor Mr. Penrose cares a rap for the Republican party as it was organized in the days of Lincoln—they probably have not the slightest idea what the Republican party of those days was, and would regard with measureless scorn the men who founded the party if they were still alive.   They object to me because they know that the triumph of the forces which for the moment I head means their elimination from politics.   They are fighting for their lives. . . .

The representatives of big business, and the thousands of smaller men who in panicky fashion follow their lead, are actuated by slightly different motives.   These representatives of big business work hand in glove with the big political bosses, although in social life they are rather ashamed of the association.   The trouble with these men is fundamental.   They do not believe in the rule of the people.   They do believe in special privilege.   They live in a democracy, and there- fore they are obliged to pay lip loyalty to democratic forms.   But they thoroughly distrust democracy.   Some of them are honestly convinced that the rule of the people jeopardizes property; that it is right and proper that privileges should exist; and that privileges and special interest, masquerading as property rights, should stand above human rights.   Others have no honest convictions of any kind, and merely feel that they wish to exploit their fellows without interference.   But the two classes, however different their standards of morality, act in combination.   They may not like the bosses, and some of them may even disapprove of the particular kinds of political immorality obtain- ing among the bosses.   But they regard the retention of privilege as a vital matter.   They feel, that is, that this question is too important to permit their indulging their personal likings, or even their moral prejudices, if to do so would jeopardize privilege.   They feel that under actually existing conditions privilege is only safe so long as the bosses are kept in power.   They trust in the courts and the great

corporation lawyers; and they become uneasy lest the people themselves insist on exercising control over the action of the courts when
the courts buttress privilege. The important thing to them is to
prevent the Government being made in fact what it is in theory.
In their eyes it is vitally necessary that the people shall not be allowed
to rule. They like to keep the people contented, if possible, to cajole
them, to swindle them, to dole out to them gifts of one kind or another.
But they are bound that the people shall not rule themselves and
control their own destinies; for they think that in such event privilege
would be in real danger. Therefore they approve any action necessary
to prevent the triumph of the principles for which I stand. They
rather prefer that the action shall be legal; they rather prefer that it
shall be moral; but they will not hesitate because of any prejudice
in favor of legality or morality if their object can be achieved only
through illegal and immoral methods.

These men regard themselves as the foremost upholders of order
and property. They are very severe in denunciation of that species
of class consciousness which has made certain labor men condone the
actions of the McNamaras, and which has just been openly avowed as
an excuse for violence and lawlessness by certain representatives of
the Industrial Workers of the World. I join with these wealthy men
in their condemnation of those labor people—I believe very few in
number—who excuse violence and murder on the ground that they
are necessary in order to get justice and redress wrong; but I also
point out to these same wealthy men that they are themselves showing
in peculiarly gross form this same class consciousness when, in the
fancied interest of property, and in the real interest of privilege,
they encourage and condone theft and fraud such as that by
which their representatives and agents secured control of the
Chicago Convention. These very wealthy men, these big political
bosses who stole that Convention, are by their actions encouraging exactly the kind of lawless feeling of which, when shown
by other classes, they stand in such dread, and for which they feel
such horror. If the representatives of privilege encourage and condone
the theft of the Presidency in the fancied interest of their own class,
they cannot expect to have their protests heeded when they declaim
against outrage and violence by labor men in the fancied interest
of *their* own class. The worst blow that can be struck against the

cause of law and order is that struck by the big men of great wealth who by corruption try to overthrow the will of the people. They are acting in a spirit of as naked class selfishness as that which was shown by the fanatical extremists among the labor men who condoned the McNamara dynamiting. They are condoning a far worse outrage, infinitely more far-reaching in the damage done to the country as a whole. They fear the people; they care more about retaining the benefits of privilege than they care for honesty or patriotism; and therefore they encourage and condone the theft from the people of their right to rule the country.

These big financial men and big political bosses are able to act as they have acted largely because a considerable number of respectable men, men of means and of good social and business standing, especially in New York and New England, support them in their actions. This support is partly obtained by choking the sources of information by the use of the daily press. Most of the papers of large circulation, and most of the papers that affect a severe respectability, in New York, Boston, and other Northeastern cities are directly or indirectly controlled by the money of the big special interests; and, as many worthy citizens obtain most of their information on public affairs from these papers, and are wholly unaware that the sources of their information are poisoned, they are naturally misled as regards the rights and wrongs of any issue as to which the big interests deem it expedient that they should be misinformed. These papers rarely have any very strong party bias; at least, if they do have a party preference, it is weak compared to the intensity with which they fear and hate any man who believes in fundamental reforms affecting the social and industrial conditions of the people as a whole—although they are willing enough to support small rose-water reforms, or reforms of large sound and small substance which do not affect privilege. Most of these papers cordially supported Judge Parker against me for President in the election of 1904, in the contest for the nomination this year they ardently supported Mr. Taft; they now, for the most part, support Dr. Wilson, although some still cling to Mr. Taft. What they really wish is to beat me, because they dread the success of the principles of which in this particular crisis I am the exponent. They may individually prefer Judge Parker or Mr. Taft, or Dr. Wilson; but the differences among the three they regard as negligible when compared with the deep gulf which they feel separates all three of them from me.

In addition to the respectable support which comes from individuals who are misinformed, there is also a considerable body of support from respectable men who do know something of the issue at stake. They are men who find life easy, who live softly, and who, instead of feeling that their own good fortune makes it incumbent on them actively to work for betterment in the life conditions of others, are overcome by the fear that any such effort to improve the general welfare would jar the present system sufficiently to cause them inconvenience. These men abound in the New York and Boston social and business or professional clubs, in the Boards of Trade and Chambers of Commerce, in the Bar Associations, in the residential districts where people of means and leisure dwell. They are free from physical toil and hardship; they live under conditions that tell for ease, that indeed tend rather to too much self-indulgent softness, and therefore, alas! to that dreadful selfishness which is born of fear when they become alarmed lest the system which has brought about these pleasant conditions may be changed. These men are not hard-hearted; they are charitably inclined; but their vision is narrow, their sympathies are restricted by their inability to realize the feelings and needs of less fortunate men of harder lives, and they become panic stricken when required to face the question as to whether our social system really does justice to these other less fortunate men. When not thus moved by selfish fear, they stand for morality in public and private life. But when they become persuaded that the social system which makes their lives relatively effortless and easy is endangered by a given man or by a proposed reform, they develop a panic-born immorality which makes them not merely excuse, but eagerly commend, the theft of a nominating convention, or any other rascality which in their estimation helps to "save society," or to "preserve the Constitution," or to "repel assaults on the courts"; for these men under such conditions follow the lead of the great corporation owners and great corporation lawyers in treating the Constitution and the courts—quite without warrant—as instruments designed to protect privilege and vested wrong and to prevent the people from really ruling themselves. They have apparently been educated to the point of feeling all this in accentuated form about me, and about the changes I champion. They do not know that most of the things I advocate have been successfully tried out in a few of our own States— Wisconsin, for instance, and even Massachusetts—and in foreign countries such as Germany, Denmark, England, New Zealand, Switzerland. I am merely trying to get this country to be wise in time—which is nine-tenths of wisdom. I wish to see our less fortunate citizens avoid the dreadful excesses of syndicalism and the like to which their fellows abroad have been prone. This can only be accomplished if our people as a whole will formulate and reduce certain great moral principles which most of us are now dimly beginning to see shape themselves from the confused welter of our business and our politics. If we do not at least keep step with "the march of the world conscience," it will be an evil thing for us and for all mankind. Moreover, I most earnestly desire that this movement for justice to the plain people, the common people, this effort to make moral and economic conditions easier for the average man and average woman, shall owe its strength neither to fear nor to greed, but to the honest desire of our people as a whole to treat all men and women fairly and kindly. I most earnestly hope that in this movement for social and industrial justice and betterment the lead may be taken by those among us to whom fate has been kind, who have themselves nothing material to gain from the movement, and not by those who are sullen with a sense of personal wrong. This country will not permanently be a good place for any of us to live in unless we make it a reasonably good place for all of us to live in.

Theodore Roosevelt, *Two Phases of the Chicago Convention*, in *Outlook* (New York, 1912), CI, 628–630 *passim*.

32. The Task of the Presidency (1925)

BY DIXON MERRITT

Merritt is a journalist and editor, with a long and varied experience. During the war he was employed on emergency work in the office of the Assistant Secretary of Agriculture. Washington representative of the *Outlook* after 1923. Author of *Audubon in Kentucky* (1908); *History of Tennessee* (1913); *The Department of Agriculture in the War* (1919); *The Seventeen-Year Locust* (1919). Merritt's description of President Coolidge's household and of a typical day's routine will give an idea of the President's life. For Coolidge see also No. 197 below; William Allen White, *Calvin Coolidge;* E. E. Whiting, *President Coolidge.*

MR. COOLIDGE is out of bed before seven o'clock. He always was, no matter what job he had. With Richard H. Jervis, of the Secret Service, at his elbow, he goes walking, and he steps along at a pretty lively clip, usually through the parked places not far from the White House.

At eight o'clock, just when practically all other Government workers are doing the same thing, the President sits down to breakfast. He does not have to hurry so much as most others do because his office is not so far from his house. He is at his desk when the rest are, at nine o'clock.

After that, for a clear four hours, the President sits at his desk and talks to people who want to tell him something or from whom he wants to extract information. He does no other work than this during the morning except on Tuesdays and Fridays, when Cabinet meetings are held.

At one o'clock the President goes home to lunch, a privilege that not one Government worker in a thousand has. Frequently he takes some friends with him, and sometimes very important matters are discussed at the luncheon table.

In the afternoon the President sees no one except those who assist him with his work. He is not in to callers. He reads documents that require his attention, studies out the problems that he must solve, performs generally the real work of the Presidential office. Frequently he takes a nap, sometimes on a couch in his office, sometimes in his bedroom at the White House proper. The only afternoon interruption he has is on Friday, when he sees the newspaper correspondents.

About five o'clock—half an hour after the general run of Government workers have left their desks—Mr. Coolidge shuts up shop and goes for a walk with two members of the Secret Service as his inescapable companions. The parked places are not sought for the afternoon ramble. Frequently he goes through the main business district, stopping now and then in front of shop windows. When held up by traffic at street intersections, he usually catches the "go" sign before the Secret Service man does and is out at least three steps ahead.

By seven o'clock the President is home and ready for dinner. Sometimes he sees friends in the evening, but usually they are gone and he is in bed by a little after ten o'clock—when nearly everybody else in Washington is swearing at static.

And that is "all there is to" the routine of being President of the United States in the year 1925.

If it seems to you that this does not at all comprehend the multiplicity of duties that must be performed at the White House, the answer is that the White House is a business institution where employees, grown old in the service, do their own particular tasks without bothering anybody else about them. Except for the private secretary to the President—who is misnamed and should be called the political secretary to the President—the White House force does not change much from one Administration to another, or from one decade to another. A majority of those in important positions have been there twenty years, some thirty years, a few forty. And they are organized as a series of sifters, of finer and finer mesh the nearer they approach the President. No man gets through the last sifter unless he has real business with the President. . . .

Time was—twice—when letters actually composed by the President were not so uncommon as they are now. Presidents Roosevelt and Wilson dictated a large percentage of the letters that bore their names. No other President of recent times has done so, and Mr. Coolidge does less of it than most of the others did. But even Mr. Wilson dictated an average of not more than twenty-five letters a day, and President Roosevelt only slightly more.

The total number of letters answered at the White House in an average day when Congress is not in session is about 150. When Congress is in session, the average is about doubled. Under exceptional circumstances, the number may shoot up to 1,000 a day, and even more. But the regular run of mail to be answered at the White House is not heavy. Many an obscure office in an executive department handles several times as many letters.

When a Message is to be written, or a speech, the President does not write it in the sense that the ordinary man understands as writing a speech. When the Message to Congress is to be prepared, the White House asks the various Cabinet officers and heads of departments for material which they think should be included in the Message. Each Cabinet officer sends word down the line to his bureau chiefs and his specialists on various subjects. Finally, a great mass of memoranda comes to each Cabinet member. His assistant, a specialist on information in that department, digests them, and this digest forms the basis of a memorandum which the Cabinet member sends to the White House for inclusion in the Message. The White House staff goes over this material, sifts out the least important, arranges the more important, and informs the President of what is on hand. He decides which of the many subjects shall be treated in his Message, and the material bearing on those subjects is whipped into shape for his use. A corps of able assistants are at the call of the President for the final preparation of the Message.

When this point was reached, Wilson used to sit down at a typewriter and peck out the Message with his own fingers, but other Presidents have performed the task in a less laborious way. Wilson produced better literature than most of the others have done, but the others have dealt just as adequately with current problems. A Message of the President is no less a Message of the President because it is not actually written or even not actually dictated by him. . . .

The persons so far noticed are only a few of those who aid the President in his work. The social side of the President's job constitutes no small part of the total. The aids on that side are no less efficient than those on the official side.

Inside the main door of the White House proper is the office of the head usher. I. H. Hoover has presided over it for twenty-two years and has been connected with it for almost forty years. All who enter the front door are routed by him.

There is a social secretary to the President's wife. Miss Laura Harlan, one of the newest of the regular White House staff, occupies this position. But assisting her in her work is W. E. Rockwell, who has worked on the social side of life at the White House for a great many years. Under the direction of Miss Harlan and Mr. Rockwell the bulk of the preliminary social work is done.

When social functions are actually on, the burden falls on Colonel Cheney, military aid to the President, and on Captain Andrews, naval aid and commander of the Mayflower.

The President has many assistants in various of his duties who are not on the roll of White House employees at all. An employee anywhere in the Government may be detailed to the White House. A law passed a few years ago put a stop to the making of details from one department to another, but the White House was specifically excepted.

The Secret Service men, about a dozen of whom are constantly on duty at the White House, are employees of the Treasury Department and under the supervision of Secretary Mellon. All of the household servants, all of the doormen, all of the gardeners and laborers about the grounds, are on the payroll and under the supervision of the Superintendent of Buildings and Grounds of the District of Columbia.

W. M. Parnell, a bonded custodian, is responsible for the safety of every teaspoon in the White House. Likewise Arthur Brooks, another bonded custodian, is responsible for all the property in the Executive Offices, down to the rubber bands and paper clips.

Take it all in all, the White House staff is one of the most comprehensive and one of the most efficient business organizations in the Government not merely, but anywhere in the United States. Every President when he begins his duties has ready to his hand something that most men strive for through a lifetime and few ever attain— a staff of tried subordinates, each a competent specialist in his own line. . . .

The heart of the present misconception of the terrible weight of the President's work is in the belief that two Presidents recently have been worked to death. The fact is that Wilson, though he was one of the hardest workers that the White House has known, was in better health there than he ever was anywhere else. He came to the White House a frail man suffering from a chronic disease. He had worked himself to death in his years as a teacher. It was his custom all his life to work ceaselessly for days on end, until he was exhausted, and then to sleep the clock around twice. He picked up weight and vitality after he came to the White House. The improvement in his appearance was a marvel to those who knew him earlier. The war, the trips to Paris, the final trip to take his appeal to the country—these did break him down, but he would probably have died sooner than he did if he had never left Princeton.

Harding was almost the opposite of Wilson in nearly every particular. Hard work was out of his line. The duties of the Presidency irked him terribly, but it is not true that the weight of responsibility wrecked him. Those who knew him at work say that he was practically impervious to worry. Harding simply got sick and died. If there is anything more than that to the story, it is locked behind that secret door to which the pry of the reporter does not constitute a key.

We have now in the White House another man who came there none too robust. Mr. Coolidge has gained eight pounds since he became President, and the change in his appearance, while not as striking as the improvement that Wilson underwent, is marked. Very clearly, he is not a man worked to death. His former private secretary, Mr. Slemp, recently said in a magazine article, "Calvin Coolidge will thrive on the tasks of the Presidency." . . .

The hopeful sign is that during all these recent years the tendency has been toward relieving the President of burdens and leaving him more nearly free to devote himself to uninterrupted study of the great problems of the country. . . .

When we have relieved the President of his burdens which are mainly political, he will be able with our help to struggle along under his burdens which are purely official.

Dixon L. Merritt, *Calvin Coolidge and His Job*, in *Outlook* (New York, 1925), CXL, 103–107 *passim*.

CHAPTER VII — PACIFIC DEPENDENCIES AND POLICIES

33. Prisoners in Peking (1900)

BY PROFESSOR LUELLA MINER

Professor Miner held a chair in the American College at Tungchau, China, at the time of the Boxer Rebellion of 1900. The purpose of that movement was in part to drive foreigners out of China.—Bibliography: Kenneth S. Latourette, *Development of China;* W. W. Rockhill, "Affairs in China," in *United States Foreign Relations* (1901); A. B. Hart, *The Obvious Orient* (1911).

June 15.— ABOUT ten o'clock the most horrible noise began in the southern city, just on the opposite side of the city wall. It was a horde of Boxers going through their rites, burning incense, crying, "Kill the foreign devils! Kill the secondary foreign devils! (Christians.) Kill! Kill! Kill!" They called other things, but I could only distinguish the "kill!" There may have been from twenty to fifty thousand voices, not all Boxers, swelling that mad tumult. After two or three hours the noise suddenly ceased. The Boxers in their indiscriminate pillaging had looted a Mohammedan bank. The Mohammedans gathered a band of three hundred, pursued them, and got back their money, after which the mob dispersed.

Our lines of defense have been extended to include all the streets bordering on this mission property—three or four streets and alleys being under martial law—and all passers-by are challenged. The same conditions prevail on Legation Street—stray Boxers are captured and passers-by are challenged. The missionaries and Chinese who have weapons all help in guard duty. There are barbed-wire barricades at the end of each street. . . . This morning four of the missionaries took their guns and, accompanied by the Chinese to do the buying, started out to the shops, and came back with everything they tried to get. Of course they paid the shopkeepers, though they did have to take out their pistols before business opened up very briskly.

Now, in the compound and adjoining streets we have barricade within barricade of barbed wire or brick, all the walls and some of the small buildings having been torn up to get brick. This is said to be the best fortified place in the city now, thanks to the free labor of our numerous refugees, and if we had a Gatling or machine gun we would feel quite safe. . . .

Evening.—This forenoon ten Americans and twenty Russians went to the south cathedral, where the Boxers were looting, burning, and killing, killed seventy Boxers, captured ten, and took Catholic refugees to a place near the British Legation. In the afternoon twenty-five Germans and an equal number of French went to the same place, with much the same result, though not quite so many Boxers were killed, I think.

Mr. Tewksbury, Dr. Ingram, Mr. Ewing, and Dr. Inglis just went to the city gate near us, closed it, and brought the key here with them. The official in charge of the gate will be obliged to come here in the morning to get the key before the gate can be opened. . . .

June 18.—We have now spent ten full days in this place, and may be obliged to spend many more, for we can get no word from our foreign troops who left Tientsin a week ago yesterday. Since the trouble broke out in the city we have sent three messengers, offering a high reward if they should get through to Captain McCalla and inform him of our peril, but they have all returned reporting that it was impossible to get through the hordes of Boxers between us and our army. . . .

We are more effectively cut off from the world than ever, for no couriers can now be found to carry mail to Tientsin for the Imperial post-office. We have been surprised that they have succeeded in keeping up the service so long. We hope that in two or three days communication will be open again. We hear that vast numbers of Boxers attacked the railroad station in Tientsin and were repulsed with great slaughter. It is rumored that the relief army is now only ten or fifteen miles from us, but we cannot be sure.

Placards are being distributed everywhere in the city commanding that this place and Legation Street be destroyed to-day. Word to the same effect has also been brought in by some of our Christian Chinese who are staying outside. It is said that the Chinese general Tung-Fu-Hsiang has told the Boxers that if they do not wipe out these remaining foreign places soon, he will take his soldiers off and will not help them any more. Another fire has been started near us in the southern city, and five fires can be seen in the western part of this city, far away from us. . . .

Over seventy of us American missionaries live, eat, and sleep in the little church at the British Legation, though a few of the ladies sleep in Lady Macdonald's ballroom, two or three in the billiard-room, and some of the men outdoors. In the church we all sleep on the floor or on the church seats. There are thirty-five in our Congregational crowd, about twenty Methodists, and sixteen Presbyterians. We eat by denominations, but there is only one tiny stove to cook over, so we cannot cook much. If we are besieged long, we shall have to go on short rations. In fact, we are now leaving most of the canned meats for the men, who are doing hard work outside, watching and fortifying. . . .

Yesterday afternoon, after several hours of firing, all under the cover of buildings or barricades, a white flag was run up by the Chinese soldiers north of us, close by the wall of the Imperial City. Then the message was sent that there was an Imperial edict commanding the soldiers to stop shooting and setting fires and to protect the Foreign Ministers. The edict would be sent to us later. Few of us were taken in by this subterfuge, though some thought there really might be a genuine edict forthcoming, occasioned by the possible nearness of the relief army. The Government would be quite capable of laying down arms in such an event, and pretending that it was only the mob which had been fighting the foreigners. No copy of an edict was sent us later, and when the Chinese soldiers made attacks at midnight on this place—the American Legation and the refuge—they were the only surprised ones, for extra precautions were taken last night to guard against attack. . . .

Some horses which were turned into the street between our barricades have been shot, and consequently we have a new delicacy added to our bill of fare. We call it "French roast beef." This morning it was prepared in the form of curry to eat with our rice. After eating our cornmeal mush there was a break in the meal, and when someone asked Miss Haven, who was helping to wait on the table, what was the reason for the delay, she patly replied, "The horse has not been curried yet." . . .

July 18.—About two o'clock this afternoon—four weeks to an hour from the time when we took refuge in this Legation—we received our first authentic message from the outside world. On June 30 a Methodist young man was sent by the Japanese Minister as a messenger to Tientsin, and he has just returned, bringing a letter from the Japanese Consul in Tientsin, stating that foreign troops numbering 33,300 will leave Tientsin about the 20th, day after tomorrow, for the relief of Peking. In a way, this is discouraging, for now we cannot hope day by day for their arrival; but with this great force they will come up with practically no resistance, and the strain and stress of this terrible siege is over. . . .

August 14.—At last our ears have heard the sweet music for which we have been listening for two months—the cannonading of the relief army—so plainly that we know that intense desire and imagination are not deceiving us, as so many times before. Our deliverance is at hand. Last night was a fearful one. There were at least six distinct attacks, the first beginning about eight in the evening, and there was almost incessant firing between these attacks. Our implacable foes seemed determined to use to the utmost this last chance to wipe us out. Our garrison returned fire more than at any other time, for now they are not afraid of exhausting their ammunition. . . .

It was a little after two in the afternoon, as I was sitting writing under the trees in the tennis-court, where I have spent so many hours during these past weeks, when an American marine from the city wall ran into the yard shouting, "The troops are inside the city—almost here!" There was a wild rush for the south end of the compound, and there, sheltered by the barricades, we stood and saw the first of the relief army straggling up the streets. And who do you think they were? Black-faced, high-turbaned troops, Rajpunts from India—great, fierce-looking fellows, but their faces were beaming with joy, and they hurrahed louder than we did. There were British officers with them, and one of them stooped in passing and kissed a pale-faced girlie who looked as if she needed to be rescued by a relief army. All that afternoon the troops came streaming in, Sihks,

Bengal Lancers, English soldiers, and, most welcome of all, our American boys.

Luella Miner, *A Prisoner in Peking*, in *Outlook*, November 10, 17, 24, 1900 (New York), 641–671 *passim*.

---◆---

34. Progress in the Philippines (1907)

BY SECRETARY WILLIAM HOWARD TAFT

Chief Justice Taft was Secretary of War in Roosevelt's Cabinet. In February 1900, he was placed at the head of a commission to exercise legislative jurisdiction in the Philippines; and, from July 4, 1901, to February 1, 1904, he was Governor-General. He was sent to represent the government of the United States at the first opening of the Philippine Assembly—one of the steps toward self-government by the Islands.—Bibliography: Charles B. Elliott, *The Philippines to the End of Commission Government;* J. A. Le Roy, *Americans in the Philippines;* D. C. Worcester, *Philippines, Past and Present;* J. G. Schurman, *Philippine Affairs;* W. Cameron Forbes, *The Philippine Islands*.

GENTLEMEN OF THE ASSEMBLY: President Roosevelt has sent me to convey to you and the Filipino people his congratulations upon another step in the enlargement of popular self-government in these Islands. I have the greatest personal pleasure in being the bearer of this message. It is intended for each and every member of the Assembly, no matter what his views upon the issues which were presented in the late electoral campaign. It assumes that he is loyal to the government in which he now proposes, under oath of allegiance, to take part. It does not assume that he may not have a wish to bring about, either soon or in the far future, by peaceable means, a transfer of sovereignty; but it does assume that while the present government endures, he will loyally do all he lawfully can to uphold its authority and to make it useful to the Filipino people.

I am aware that, in view of the issues discussed at the election of this Assembly, I am expected to say something regarding the policy of the United States toward these Islands. Before attempting any such task, it is well to make clear the fact that I can not speak with the authority of one who may control that policy. . . .

Our Philippine policy has been subjected to the severest condemnation by critics who occupy points of view as widely apart as the two poles. There are those who say that we have gone too fast, that we have counted on the capacity of the Filipino for political development with a foolish confidence leading to what they regard as the disastrous result of this election. There are others who assert that we have denied the Filipino that which is every man's birthright—to govern himself—and have been guilty of tyranny and a violation of American principles in not turning the government over to the people of the Islands at once.

With your permission, I propose to consider our policy in the light of the events of the six years during which it has been pursued, to array the difficulties of the situation which we have had to meet and to mention in some detail what has been accomplished. . . .

Let us consider in some detail what progress has been made:

First. To repeat what I have said, the Islands are in a state of tranquillity. On this very day of the opening of the National Assembly, there has never been a time in the history of the Islands when peace and good order have prevailed more generally. The difficulties presented by the controversies arising with and concerning the Roman Catholic Church have either been completely settled or are in process of satisfactory adjustment on a basis of justice and equity.

Second. Most noteworthy progress has been made in the spread of general education. One of the obstacles to the development of this people speaking half a dozen or more different native dialects was a lack of common language, which would furnish a medium of sympathetic touch with modern thought and civilization. The dense ignorance of a very large proportion of the people emphasized the necessity for a general educational system. English was the language of the sovereign power, English was the business language of the Orient, English was the language in which was thought and written the history of free institutions and popular government, and English was the language to which the common people turned with eagerness to learn. A system of education was built up, and to-day upward of half a million children are being taught to read, write, and recite English. It is not an exaggeration to assert that now more native Filipinos speak English than Spanish, although Spanish was the language of the ruling race in these Islands for more than two hundred and fifty years. English is not so beautiful as the Spanish language, but it is more likely to prove of use to the Filipinos for the reasons I have given. The strongest basis for our confidence in the future of the Filipino people is the eagerness with which the opportunities extended for education in English have been seized by the poor and ignorant parents of these Islands for their children. It is alike pathetic and encouraging.

I am not one of those who believe that much of the public money should be expended here for university or advanced education. Perhaps one institution merely to form a type of higher education may be established at Manila or at some other suitable place in the Islands, and special schools to develop needed scientific professions may be useful, but the great part of the public funds expended for education should be used in the spread of primary education and of industrial education—that education which shall fit young men to be good farmers, good mechanics, good skilled laborers, and shall teach them the dignity of labor and that it is no disgrace for the son of a good family to learn his trade and earn his livelihood by it. The higher education is well for those who can use it to advantage, but it too often fits a man to do things for which there is no demand, and unfits him for work which there are too few to do. The enlargement of opportunity for higher education may well await private beneficence or be postponed to a period when the calls upon the Island Treasury for other more important improvements have ceased. We have laid the foundation of a primary and industrial educational system here which, if the same spirit continues in the Government, will prove to be the most lasting benefit which has been conferred on these Islands by Americans.

Third. We have introduced here a health department which is gradually teaching the people the necessity for sanitation. In the years to come, when the great discoveries of the world are recited, that which will appear to have played as large a part as any in the world's progress in the current hundred years will be the discovery of proper sanitary methods for avoiding disease in the Tropics. The introduction of such methods, the gradual teaching of the people the simple facts affecting hygiene, unpopular and difficult as the process of education has been, will prove to be another one of the great benefits given by Americans to this people. . . .

Fourth. A judicial system has been established in the Islands which has taught the Filipinos the possibility of the independence of a judiciary. This must be of enduring good to the people of the Islands. The personnel of the judges is divided between Americans and Filipinos, both for the purpose of aiding the Americans to learn and administer civil law and of enabling the Filipinos to learn and administer justice according to a system prevailing in a country where the judiciary is absolutely independent of the executive or legislative branches of the Government. Charges have been made that individual judges and particular courts have not been free from executive control and have not been without prejudices arising from the race of the particular judge who sat in the court, but on the whole an impartial review of the six years' history of the administration of justice will show that the system has been productive of the greatest good and that right has been sustained without fear or favor. It is entirely natural that a system which departs from the principles of that in which one has been educated should at times attract his severe animadversion, and as the system here administered partakes of two systems, it is subject to the criticism of those trained in each. . . .

Fifth. We come to the matter of public improvements. The port of Manila has been made into a harbor which is now as secure as any in the Orient, and which, with the docking facilities that are now being rapidly constructed, will be as convenient and as free from charge and burden as any along the Asiatic coast. The improvements in Iloilo and Cebu harbors, the other two important ports of the Islands, are also rapidly progressing. Road building has proceeded in the Islands, both at the instance of the Central Government and through the agency of the provinces. The difficulties of road building and road maintaining in the Philippines are little understood by those not familiar with the difficulty of securing proper material to resist the enormous wear and tear caused by the torrential downpours of the rainy season. Progress in this direction must necessarily be gradual, for the Islands are a poor country, comparatively speaking, and roads are expensive. . . .

When the Americans came to the Islands there was one railroad 120 miles long, and that was all. In spite of circumstances, which I have already detailed, making capital reluctant to come here, contracts have now been entered into, that are in the course of fulfillment, which in five years will give to the Islands a railroad mileage of 1,000 miles. The construction of these roads will involve the investment of twenty to thirty millions of dollars, and that in itself means an added prosperity to the country, additional demands for labor, and the quickening of all the nerves of trade. When the work is finished, it means a great additional profit to agriculture, a very great enlargement of the export capacity of the Islands, and a substantial elevation of the material condition of the people. . . .

The government now maintains and operates a more complete system of posts, telephones, and telegraphs than ever before in the history of the Islands. Seventy-five per cent of the 652 municipalities now established in these Islands have post-offices, in 235 of which there are now opened for business postal savings banks. The telegraph or telephone now connects all of the provincial capitals with Manila and more than 90 offices are now open for business. Appropriation has been made to provide for a system of rural free delivery. . . .

Sixth. We have inaugurated a civil service law for the selection of civil servants upon the merit system. On the whole it has worked well. It has grown with our experience and has improved with the disclosure of its defects.

One of the burning questions which constantly presents itself in respect to the civil service of a Government like this is, how far it shall be American and how far Filipino. In the outset it was essential that most of the civil servants of the government should be Americans. The government was English speaking, and the practical difficulty of having subordinates who did not speak that language prevented large employment of Filipinos. Then their lack of knowledge of the American governmental and business methods had the same tendency. The avowed policy of the government has been to employ Filipinos wherever, as between them and Americans, the Filipinos can do equally good work. This has given rise to frequent and bitter criticism, because it has been improperly assumed that every time that there has been a vacancy, it could be filled by a Filipino. There are two great advantages in the employment of Filipinos—one is that this is the government of the Filipinos and they ought to be employed where they can be, and the other is that their employment is a matter of economy for the government, because they are able to live more cheaply and economically in the Islands than Americans and so can afford to receive less salary. There has therefore been a constant reduction of American employees and an increase of Filipinos. This has not been without its disadvantage because it makes competent American employees feel an uncertainty of tenure, and materially affects their hope of promotion and their interest in the government of which they are a part. This disadvantage I believe can be largely obviated. . . .

Seventh. In the progress which has been made, I should mention the land system, the provision for homestead settlement, for free patents, and for perfecting of imperfect titles by land registration. The homestead settlements under the law were very few for several years, but I am delighted to learn that during 1907 they reached 4,000 and the free patents applied for were 10,600. It is probable that the machinery for land registration, though necessary, is too expensive, and it will be for you to decide whether, in view of the great public benefit that good land titles will bring to the country, it may not be wise to reduce the cost of registration to the landowner and charge the expense to the government. Capital will not be advanced to the farmer unless his title is good, and the great benefit of an agricultural bank can never be realized until the registration of titles is greatly increased. . . .

The condition of agriculture in the Islands while generally much improved in the last three years is still unsatisfactory in many parts of the Islands, due not only to the continued scarcity of cattle but also to the destructive effect of the typhoon of 1905 upon the hemp culture. This has properly led to the suspension of the land tax for another year and the meeting of half the deficit in provincial and municipal treasuries thus produced, out of the central treasury.

The production of rice has, however, materially increased. It is also a source of satisfaction to note that the exports from the Islands, which are wholly agricultural, are larger in value by half a million gold dollars than ever in the history of the Islands. One of the chief duties of this Assembly is to devote its attention and practical knowledge to measures for the relief of agriculture.

Eighth. The financial condition of the Philippine government is quite satisfactory, and so, too, is the state of the money and currency of the Islands. There is a bonded indebtedness for the purchase of the friar lands amounting to $7,000,000, for the waterworks and sewage of Manila of $3,000,000, and for public works amounting to $3,500,000. Sinking funds have been established for all of these. The price paid for the friar lands was a round one and may result, after the lands are disposed of, in some net pecuniary loss to the Government, but the political benefit of the purchase was a full justification. The lands will be disposed of to the tenants as rapidly as the public interest will permit. . . .

Before discussing the Assembly, I wish to give attention to one report that has been spread to the four corners of the globe, and which, if credited, might have a pernicious effect in these Islands. I refer to the statement that the American Government is about to sell the Islands to some Asiatic or European power. Those who credit such a report little understand the motives which actuated the American people in accepting the burden of this Government. The majority of the American people are still in favor of carrying out our Philippine policy as a great altruistic work. . . . I do not hesitate to pronounce the report that the Government contemplates the transfer of these Islands to any foreign power as utterly without foundation. It has never entered the mind of a single person in the Government responsible for the Administration.

Address of the Secretary of War at Inauguration of Philippine Assembly, October 16, 1907 (Manila, Bureau of Printing, 1907), 81–94 *passim*.

———◆———

35. Alaska (1914)

BY BELMORE BROWNE

This is an artist's account of our northernmost Territory, which was once called "Seward's Folly" and was regarded as a tremendous extravagance when Secretary Seward negotiated its purchase in 1867 for $7,200,000. It was organized as a Territory in 1912. Mr. Browne, the artist-author, has written several books about the Northwest.—General bibliography: W. F. Willoughby, *Territories and Dependencies;* W. D. Boyce, *United States Colonies and Dependencies.* Special bibliography on Alaska: Scott C. Bone, *Alaska, its Past, Present and Future* (1924); J. Nichols, *Alaska* (1924); A. W. Greely, *Handbook of Alaska* (1925); John J. Underwood, *Alaska, and Empire in the Making* (1925); Mrs. Ella (Rhoads) Higginson, *Alaska, the Great Country* (1926); G. W. Spicer, *Constitutional Status and Government of Alaska* (1927).

ONE reason why Alaska is not better understood is that it went down on the map under one name; for in reality the "big land up yonder" possesses about as many different kinds of climate and geographic features as Newfoundland, Labrador, New Brunswick,

Iceland, the North Pole, and—yes, Pennsylvania. The reasons for these differences in climate are first the Japan Current, and secondly the great mountain barriers that follow the coast from the southernmost boundary to the island of Attu. This huge stretch of coast is as long as the distance that separates New York and San Francisco, and lying in a great semicircle athwart the course of the Japan Current it absorbs the warmth of the current-born winds of the South Pacific.

Even then, if the coast were low and flat, the winds would pass inland, and their influence would be distributed over a much larger area; but the towering mountains form a wall along the entire coast, and hold the humid clouds back until they have cast down their last drop of moisture. The result is that at some parts of this coast the winters are warmer than those of New York. This in a general way holds true of Southeastern Alaska. At the northern part of the circle, formed by Cook Inlet, the Kenai Peninsula, Prince William Sound, and the Fairweather Range, heavy falls of snow take the place of rain. The unusual snowfall, which reaches as much as sixty feet in a season, accounts for the large number of glaciers along the coast; but close to the beaches the effect of the snow is neutralized by the salt water. Thus we have already divided this long strip of coast into two parts,— the southern or rainy part, and the northern or snowy part.

Back from the coast lies the mountainous strip, and inside of this protecting wall we come to what Alaskans call the "Interior." The Interior is by far the largest part of Alaska, and is formed, roughly, by the valleys of the Yukon, the Tanana, the Kuskokwim, the great wilderness of mountains and tundra that lies between the Yukon and the Arctic Ocean. Here again we find a difference in the climate; for the same mountains that make the coast wet in turn keep the Interior dry, by shutting out the moist winds of the Pacific. The result is that the Interior is dry and cold, and the snowfall is in consequence very light.

Beginning our travels in Southeastern Alaska necessitates going by water; for a strip of British Columbia 450 miles in length separates Alaska from the state of Washington. As you leave Puget Sound behind the scenery grows more beautiful, until at the southern boundary line the steamer enters a wilderness of rugged islands that stretch away like a solid wall along the fiord-gashed coast.

Shortly after crossing the line you come to Ketchikan, the southernmost town of importance in Alaska. The entire population turns out at sound of the whistle, for the arrival of a steamer is an important event and in a few minutes you find yourself in the thick of an Alaska crowd. The resultant feeling is one of satisfaction; for the composite picture resolves itself into a blend of broad shoulders, clear brown skins, good-natured smiles, and unlimited self-confidence.

As you steam onward you begin to realize the extent of the natural obstacles that the Alaskan is called upon to overcome. To the westward stretch islands, nothing but islands; to the eastward rises the Coast Range, with deep-green fiords running away through their snow-streaked walls,—a maze of waterways that makes your head swim, and increases your respect for the men who unraveled it. Now and then the Pacific breaks through the protecting islands, and the steamer rolls slowly to the pulse of the sea; while schools of whales *blow* against the distant headlands. A few years ago the whales cruised these waters in safety; but now small, power-driven whalers, armed with bomb guns, are ceaselessly searching among the islands, and every year finds the fleet working farther north.

During the days that follow you are always hemmed in by fiords, mountains, and islands. Among the natural harbors are copper mines and salmon canneries. When the steamer stops by the rough wharves you will see Alaska Indians loading the cases of fish, pulling the nets, or paddling their high-prowed canoes. They are a strong, smooth-skinned, black-haired lot, and look for all the world like the Japanese that work beside them.

A short walk ashore will take you to a salmon river, where the fish are jammed in solid silver masses in the pools. Beyond lies a mosquito-haunted jungle of devils-club, down timber, berry bushes, and twisted alders. Here a day's travel is computed in yards instead of miles, and if you are hardy enough to force your way through it you will return to the steamer with increased respect for the pioneer, and many rents in your clothing and anatomy.

For 350 miles the steamer glides northward through the Alaska Archipelago. As it advances the mountains carry a heavier mantle of snow, and an occasional glacier sweeps downward out of blue mountain fastnesses and joins the sea; but you are still lost in a maze of rugged islands when you enter Gastineau Channel and see Juneau lying at the feet of towering mountains.

Juneau is the capital of Alaska, and in addition is the most picturesquely situated settlement on the Alaska coast. Huge mountains tower above the huddled houses, and a white government building lends dignity to the town. Across the channel clouds of steam rising above a great scar in the mountainside mark the site of Treadwell, the largest gold stampmill in the world, and on a quiet day you can hear the subdued roar of the hammers, ceaselessly crushing the precious quartz.

North of Juneau, on another waterway, lies Skagway, the saltwater terminus of the White Pass & Yukon Railroad. Skagway was the Mecca of gold seekers in the days of the Klondike rush; for it was over these mountains that the line of human ants crawled on their way to the Yukon. The successful ones sometimes spent months in reaching their goal. Now the railroad takes you across in a few hours. Farther still to the westward lies Sitka, the little settlement wherein were enacted many of the lurid pages of Alaska's early history. Under Russian rule it was the most important settlement in Alaska. . . .

At Sitka Southeastern Alaska comes to an end, and it is at this point that the tourist steamers turn back. In reality, however, we have reached only the gateway; for to see the real Alaska, the land of immense distances, of stupendous glaciers and towering mountains, you must travel northward for many days beyond the floe-dotted waters of Icy Strait. Once you have left the islands behind there is no turning aside until, having skirted 300 miles of icebound coast, you enter the calm waters of Price William Sound. Every foot of this bleak beach is backed by the huge, ice-capped peaks of the Fairweather and St. Elias Ranges. Nowhere in the world is there more impressive scenery.

On the second day you come to a great headland of naked rock which rises above a smother of foam, and beyond the uneasy surging of the sea tells of hidden reefs that girdle it. This is Cape St. Elias. A more grim and impressive headland could not be imagined. Behind its bulwarks of cliffs and reefs lies Yakutat Bay, the only harbor for large boats on this coast. It is a quiet little harbor, far removed from the outside world. The steamer comes to rest before a salmon cannery, where a short railroad brings the silver fish from a near-by river. Yakutat Indians paddle over the water in their queerly fashioned canoes, and on clear days Mount St. Elias hangs like a cloud in the northern sky.

The great peak stands on the 141st meridian, and it forms the monument that marks the point where the Alaska boundary turns from the coast and stretches away 600 miles to the Arctic. Around it lies the sea of ice called the Malaspina Glacier. Topographers tell us that this glacier, including the snowfields that feed it, covers 5,000 square miles. . . .

Among these wild surroundings the Alaska prospector is hard at work, and many mines, ranging from small veins to the large copper deposits on Latouche Island, speak of the richness of the region.

Fox raising is being practised with success on some of the more isolated islands, and as you go farther westward to the mountains and valleys of the Kenai Peninsula you come to a splendid hunting ground, where the white sheep and the world's largest moose abound.

Between the Kenai Peninsula and Attu, the westernmost of the Aleutian Islands, lies more than 15,000 miles of coast before you enter the great sweep of Bering Sea and the Arctic. In the entire stretch of more than 7,000 miles Nome is the only town well known in the outside world.

Besides being one of the world's greatest mining camps, Nome each winter is the scene of the Alaska dog team races. The race is called the All-Alaska Sweepstake, and is participated in by the pick of northern dog teams, over a 400-mile course. From the viewpoint of endurance, physical condition, and courage it is the world's greatest sporting event.

Contrary to general opinion, wintertime is the season of travel; and when the snow is packed hard the jingle of dog bells is heard throughout the land. Almost every pound of freight that is moved in Alaska in the winter is pulled by dogs, and from the time that the ice closes navigation they become the most important factor in transportation. Inheriting the courage and endurance of their wolf ancestors, they perform the hardest labor on the smallest food supply. Money, thought, and labor are spent lavishly in perfecting the teams, and from the decorated harness, with its red pompons and silver bells, down to the skilfully constructed "Nome" sleds, every detail speaks of strength and service.

Although I have traveled for many years in Alaska, it was my last journey through the Interior that opened my eyes to the possibilities of our great northern possession.   What I saw was a huge land of rolling uplands trampled by wild game, of great rivers teeming with edible fish, of rich valleys where adventurous farmers were already breaking the soil, of mines of copper and coal and gold; in fact, a land of golden opportunities, or, in the language of our last frontier, "a white man's country."

Belmore Browne, *Alaska*, in *The Mentor*, December 1, 1914 (New York), No. 72, 2–11.

———————◆———————

36. Patriarchal Hawaii (1916)

BY CHARMIAN K. LONDON (1922)

Mrs. London is the widow of the widely known American novelist, Jack London. Besides *Our Hawaii*, she has published *The Log of the Snark* (1917) and *The Book of Jack London* (2 vols., 1921).

HAWAII is a Paradise—and I can never cease proclaiming it; but I must append one word of qualification: *Hawaii is a paradise for the well-to-do*.   It is not a paradise for the unskilled laborer from the mainland, nor for the person without capital from the mainland.   The one great industry of the islands is sugar.   The unskilled labor for the plantations is already here.   Also, the white unskilled laborer, with a higher standard of living, cannot compete with coolie labor, and, further, the white laborer cannot and will not work in the canefields.

For the person without capital, dreaming to start on a shoestring and become a capitalist, Hawaii is the last place in the world.   It must be remembered that Hawaii is very old—comparatively. When California was a huge cattle ranch for hides and tallow (the meat being left where it was skinned), Hawaii was publishing newspapers and boasting schools of higher learning.   During the early years of the gold rush, before the soil of California was scratched with a plow, Hawaii kept a fleet of ships busy carrying her wheat, and flour, and potatoes to California, while California was sending her children down to Hawaii to be educated. The shoestring days are past. The land and industries of Hawaii are owned by old families and large corporations, and Hawaii is only so large.

But the homesteader may object, saying that he has read the reports of the millions of acres of government land in Hawaii which are his for the homesteading. But he must remember that the vastly larger portion of this government land is naked lava rock and not worth ten cents a square mile to a homesteader, and that much of the remaining land, while rich in soil values, is worthless because it is without water. The small portion of good government land is leased by the plantations. Of course, when these leases expire, they may be homesteaded. It has been done in the past. But such homesteaders, after making good their titles, almost invariably sell out their holdings in fee simple to the plantations. There is reason for it. There are various reasons for it.

Even the skilled laborer is needed only in small, definite numbers. Perhaps I cannot do better than quote the warning circulated by the Hawaiian Promotion Committee: "No American is advised to come here in search of employment unless he has some definite work in prospect, or means enough to maintain himself for some months and to launch into some enterprise. Clerical positions are well filled; common labor is largely performed by Japanese or native Hawaiians, and the ranks of skilled labor are also well supplied."

For be it understood that Hawaii is patriarchial rather than democratic. Economically it is owned and operated in a fashion that is a combination of twentieth century, machine-civilization methods and of medieval feudal methods. Its rich lands, devoted to sugar, are farmed not merely as scientifically as any land is farmed anywhere in the world, but, if anything, more scientifically. The last word in machinery is vocal here, the last word in fertilizing and agronomy, and the last word in scientific expertness. In the employ of the Planters' Association is a corps of scientific investigators who wage unceasing war on the insect and vegetable pests and who are on the travel in the remotest parts of the world recruiting and shipping to Hawaii insect and micro-organic allies for the war.

The Sugar Planters' Association and the several sugar factors or financial agencies control sugar, and, since sugar is king, control the destiny and welfare of the Islands. And they are able to do this, under the peculiar conditions that obtain, far more efficiently than it could be done by the population of Hawaii were it a democratic commonwealth, which it essentially is not. Much of the stock in these corporations is owned in small lots by members of the small business and professional classes. The larger blocks are held by families who, earlier in the game, ran their small plantations for themselves, but who learned that they could not do it so well and so profitably as the corporations which, with centralized management, could hire far better brains for the entire operation of the industry, from planting to marketing, than was possessed by the heads of the families. As a result, absentee ownership or landlordship has come about. Finding the work done better for them than they could do it themselves, they prefer to live in their Honolulu and seaside and mountain homes, to travel much, and to develop a cosmopolitanism and culture that never misses shocking the traveler or newcomer with surprise. All of which makes this class in Hawaii as cosmopolitan as any class to be found the world over. Of course, there are notable exceptions to this practice of absentee landlordism, and such men run their own plantations and corporations and are active as sugar factors and in the management of the Planters' Association.

Yet will I dare to assert that no owning class on the mainland is so conscious of its social responsibility as is this owning class of Hawaii, and especially that portion of it which has descended out of the old missionary stock. Its charities, missions, social settlements, kindergartens, schools, hospitals, homes, and other philanthropic enterprises are many; its activities are unceasing; and some of its members contribute from twenty-five to fifty per cent of their incomes to the work for the general good.

But all the foregoing, it must be remembered, is not democratic nor communal but is distinctly feudal. The coolie and peasant labor possesses no vote, while Hawaii is after all only a territory, its governor appointed by the President of the United States, its one delegate sitting in Congress at Washington but denied the right to vote in that body. Under such conditions, it is patent that the small class of large land-owners finds it not too difficult to control the small vote in local politics. Some of the large land-owners are Hawaiian or part Hawaiian, as are practically all the smaller land-owners. And these and the land-holding whites are knit together by a common interest, by social equality, and, in many cases, by the closer bonds of affection and blood relationship.

Interesting, even menacing, problems loom large for Hawaii in the not distant future. Let but one of these be considered, namely, the Japanese and citizenship. Granting that no Japanese immigrant can ever become naturalized, nevertheless remains the irrefragable law and fact that every male Japanese, Hawaii-born, by his birth is automatically a citizen of the United States. Since practically every other person in all Hawaii is Japanese, it is merely a matter of time when the Hawaii-born Japanese vote will not only be larger than any other Hawaiian vote, but will be practically equal to all other votes combined. When such time comes, it looks as if the Japanese will have the dominant say in local politics. If Hawaii should get statehood, a Japanese governor of the State of Hawaii would be not merely possible but very probable.

Charmian K. London, *Our Hawaii—Islands and Islanders* (New York, Macmillan, 1922), 26–30.

———————◆———————

37. Samoa (1921)

BY CAPTAIN WALDO EVANS

Captain Evans writes as Naval Governor of American Samoa.—Bibliography as in No. 35 above.

ON February 19, 1900, an Executive order was signed by the President, reading as follows:

The island of Tutuila, of the Samoan group, and all other islands of the group east of longitude 171° west of Greenwich, are hereby placed under the control of the Department of the Navy for a naval station.

The Secretary of the Navy shall take such steps as are necessary to establish the authority of the United States and to give to the islands the necessary protection. . . .

Beginning with 1905, the commandant, upon nomination by the Secretary of the Navy, has been given by the President of the United States a commission as governor, and his authority in civil matters is derived therefrom.

The islands have been known officially as "Naval Station, Tutuila," but the Navy Department has now adopted the name "American Samoa," by which name they are now called. . . .

In 1903 full information as to the conditions in American Samoa was furnished to Congress, but that body failed to legislate for the islands and has never defined their political status. . . .

All of the Samoan Islands are of volcanic formation, having been probably thrown up from the ocean bed by some mighty convulsion of nature. All are mountainous.

The Island of Tutuila, of irregular shape, is about 18 miles long and from 5 to 6 miles wide in the widest part. It is estimated that it contains 40.2 square miles of land. A mountain ridge extends nearly the whole length of the island, with spurs on each side, and with indentations of deep valleys. The aspect is extremely rugged, but more so in the eastern than in the western part. There is very little level land except at the foot of the mountains along the coast, and with the exception of a broad fertile plain in the southwestern part of the island. On this plain are several villages of importance and extensive cultivations of coconut trees.

The north side is bold and precipitous, with a few level spaces here and there, barely large enough to support a village. The mountains are wooded to the top, the whole island being a mass of tropical vegetation, extremely beautiful to the eye of the traveler.

Pago Pago Bay, the safest and best harbor in the South Seas, has its entrance to the southward and nearly cuts the island in twain. It is formed in the crater of an immense volcano, the south side broken away and open to the sea. About a mile from the harbor mouth it turns sharply to the westward, giving the harbor the appearance of the foot of a stocking, with the United States naval station situated on the instep, facing north and entirely sheltered from seaward. The sea can not be seen from ships at anchor inside the harbor, the ships lying quietly in smooth water during the heaviest gales. High mountains encompass the harbor, villages nestling comfortably on the narrow strip of level land along the shore. Pago Pago, the most important village of the island, is at the extreme toe of the stocking, to follow the simile. Fagatogo lies behind the naval station. Aua, Lepua, and other small villages are on the north shore. The harbor is well buoyed and lighted and may be safely entered by the largest vessels by night or day. . . .

The climate is tropical. The southeast winds blow strongly from May until November; during the other months of the year the winds are variable, frequently from the west and northwest. Severe gales and occasional hurricanes have been experienced. . . .

The seat of government is at the naval station in Pago Pago Bay. The governor is at the head of the government. He is also the commandant of the naval station and commands the station ship. The secretary of native affairs, an executive official, has cognizance of all native affairs and native officials, acting under the direction of the governor. The position of chief customs officer is held by a naval officer, so appointed by the governor. The public works officer of the naval station acts in the same capacity in the island government, and as such is superintendent of roads. The captain of the yard, or executive officer of the naval station, is sheriff and responsible for the public safety. The island treasurer is a naval supply officer, who also acts as the general store keeper of the naval station. The public health officer is the senior medical officer, who, in addition to his naval duties, has direct charge of the Samoan Hospital and outlying dispensaries and is responsible for quarantine regulations and the sanitary conditions of the islands. The navy chaplain is superintendent of education for the island government.

American Samoa is divided into three general administrative divisions—Eastern District of Tutuila, Western District of Tutuila, and Manua District—these corresponding to the Samoan political divisions which have existed from early days. Each district is administered by a native district governor appointed by the governor. The districts are divided into counties, each administered by a county chief. These are also very ancient political divisions, each ruled by one high chief. The county chiefs are appointed by the governor, but the selection is limited, as the office is usually given to the chief whose name entitles him to it by Samoan custom—an hereditary position which is held during good behavior. District governors are chosen from the rank of county chiefs. . . .

The soil is a rich mold upon the slopes and even upon the precipitous mountain sides, while the valleys and level tracts are a deep alluvial deposit of the same, the whole a decomposition of vegetable matter, with only a slight proportion of decomposed lava. . . .

Lava beds descend to the sea in many places, with black and forbidding faces. The "iron-bound coast" extends for several miles east of Leone Bay, the edge of a great lava bed, against which the sea roars unceasingly. The sea has cut tunnels in the lava, breaking through the crust many yards inland; the air compressed within the tunnels or chambers by the surges of the sea forces the imprisoned water high into the air through these inland "blowholes" with a geyserlike effect. On a stormy day the sight is a magnificent one.

The hills and valleys are rocky, but the volcanic rock is still disintegrating. Many landslides occur during the wet season from this cause. . . .

The most important product of the soil of Samoa is the coconut ("niu"). This tree gives meat, drink, and shelter to the Samoans. It grows anywhere it is planted—in the sand on the coast where the roots are laved by the sea, on plateaus, on the slopes, and even on the mountain ridges, where it stands out like a sentinel against the sky. . . .

From the husk of the coconut (coir) the men plait sennit, with which they bind together the parts of canoes and all parts of the framework of the houses without the use of nails. The shell is used for drinking cups and for fuel. The leaves are used to make rough baskets, rough mats, and to place on the thatches of the houses to hold them down in windy weather, and when dry the leaves are used as torches. From the midrib of the leaves crude brooms are made. The wood of the trunk is too perishable to be of any great value, but it is used rough hewn for rafters in the native houses, and whole sections of the trunk are sometimes used for rustic bridges over streams. The water of the green nuts is used for drink, and in some villages where there are no springs it is their only beverage. It is slightly sweet, delicate, and wholesome. . . .

The chief usefulness of the coconut is the copra produced from it.

Copra is the dried kernel of the ripe coconut. It is the principal—in fact the only—export from American Samoa. It is shipped to foreign countries, where oil is expressed from it. This oil is in great demand in the manufacture of coconut butters of various kinds, soaps, salad oil, and for other purposes. . . .

The Samoans are the true Polynesians, probably the finest physical specimens of the race. In appearance they are of a light reddish-brown or copper color, well formed, erect in bearing and handsome in features. The face has many of the distinctive marks of the European.

The nose is straight, the chin firm and strong, the cheek bones rather prominent, and the forehead high. The hair is black and soft—sometimes wavy. There is nothing about them to suggest the Negro. The men are tall, proud in bearing, muscular in limbs and torso, seldom corpulent—withal, a very handsome race of men. The women, while fit mothers for a race of strong men, are not often noticeably beautiful in features. In girlhood and early womanhood they have beautiful figures, but, like other natives of the Tropics, they do not retain a good figure long. They are graceful, light-hearted, and merry; their eyes are soft and dark, with an expression of gentleness and meekness.

The Samoan does not like to work. For this trait he has been severely criticized, but the critics do not take into consideration his life and environment. His wants are few; the climate demands that little clothing be worn; nature is prodigal of her favors; and the heat of the day is not conducive to exertion. It is customary for the Samoans to rise at daylight, and do the hardest work of the day before the sun is high. Their food is easily produced; breadfruit requires no cultivation; bananas, taro, and yams require little beyond the planting; pigs and chickens are raised to a considerable extent, but are generally reserved for food at feasts, not for ordinary daily use. The men and women fish on the reefs. There are certain fish which women catch, and these are to be found under stones on the reef; the women also collect clams and other shell fish. Men spear the fish from canoes, or while standing on the reef, and they also use the hook and line in deep water, by day and by night. This kind of labor the Samoan likes. He will row or paddle in his boat for hours at a time with no fatigue, but it is not easy to induce him to do a day's work in the towns. There are, however, notable exceptions to this rule, and when there is a proper incentive the Samoan is capable of the hardest kind of work. There is no desire to amass wealth. By the simple communistic system under which the Samoans live, each person contributes the profits of his industry to the family fund, and there is no incentive for one person to work harder than his fellow laborer; the drone fares as well in the good things of life as the worker. Energy and ambition must be manifested in the head of the family in order to produce any increase in prosperity. . . .

The people are generous and hospitable to a remarkable degree. Any stranger is given a cordial welcome in any house, given food and sleeping accommodations. There are so few foreigners in these islands that this admirable trait has not been stamped out by imposition or abuse of confidence. The child born out of wedlock labors under no disadvantages, and an erring girl is soon forgiven by her family and by the community. There is no polygamy.

The art of falsehood is extensively practiced, but open, barefaced perjury in the courts is rare. In criminal trials the alibi is practically unknown. Petty theft is common, but grand larceny, burglary, and robbery seldom occur. . . .

The dress of the people consists of a "lavalava" or loin cloth, and in the case of women of a waist or upper garment of some kind, sometimes of a long, loose gown. The men consider it undignified to appear without a shirt or coat or both on occasions of ceremony, such as attending church, visiting foreigners, or receiving distinguished guests, but on ordinary occasions they wear no clothing, but the "lavalava." The women wear only the "lavalava" in their own homes or where only Samoans may see them, but it is usually considered immodest for them to expose the bust in the presence of foreigners, except when unmarried girls take part in some Samoan ceremony such as dancing the siva, the national dance. On ceremonial occasions the men and women frequently wear their fine mats or tapas as clothing.

Tattooing, though prohibited in the Manua group, is universally practiced in Tutuila. A young man is not supposed to meet other men on equal terms until he has been tattooed. . . . The missionaries at first attempted to abolish the practice, and laws were made against it, but to no avail. The custom will doubtless disappear in the course of time, as there is little to recommend it. The operation is painful, and the young man is usually laid up for several weeks following the tattooing, which, in itself, takes three or four days with intervals of rest between. The women usually are not tattooed at all, but some of them have numerous small designs tattooed on the legs and the back of the hands.

American Samoa; A General Report by the Governor (Washington, Government Printing Office, 1922), 10–25 *passim.*

CHAPTER VIII — LATIN-AMERICAN POLICIES

38. Monroe Doctrinings (1906)

BY WALLACE IRWIN

Wallace Irwin, journalist, editor, and author of many volumes in many veins, has reduced to verse, largely humorous, a great deal of contemporary history and politics. Another example is No. 50 below.

WE have got our little foot in the Canal,
　　We have got the languid Cuban 'neath our eyes,
We have placed our index finger on the lazy San Dominger,
　　And we're teaching Porto Rico to be wise.
We are asking Mister Castro won't he please
　　Discontinue his piratical campaigns;
Yet the dark-skinned Latin Jingo only mutters, "Dirty *Gringo!*"
　　Which is all the thanks we're getting for our pains.

Here's a bumper to the doctrine of Monroe, roe, roe,
　　And the neighbors whom we cannot let alone;
Through the thirst for diagnosis we're inserting our proboscis
　　Into everybody's business but our own.

We are worrying from Texas to the Horn,
　　We are training guns on Germany's advance,
While we shake the mail-clad mitten at the hunger of the Briton,
　　And suggest, "Monsieur, keep off the map!" to France.
Does the gentle South American rejoice
　　At our fatherly protection from the Powers?
No, alas! the dusky Jingo merely hisses, "Yankee *Gringo!*"
　　To reward this large philanthropy of ours.

Here's a bumper to the doctrine of Monroe, roe, roe,
　　Which we follow when we've nothing else to do,
While we spend our golden billions to protect the rag-tag millions,
　　And I think they're making fun of us, don't you?

Wallace Irwin, *Random Rhymes and Odd Numbers* (New York, Macmillan, 1906), 199–200.

39. The Panama Canal (1909)

BY LIEUTENANT COLONEL GEORGE W. GOETHALS

Goethals was an Army officer who acted as Chairman and Chief Engineer of the Isthmian Canal Commission, and first Civil Governor of the Canal Zone. Received thanks of Congress (1915) for "distinguished service in constructing the Panama Canal," and (1918) was awarded the D. S. M. for especially meritorious and conspicuous service in reorganizing the Quartermaster's Department during the World War.—Bibliography: Howard C. Hill, *Roosevelt and the Caribbean;* M. W. Williams, *Anglo-American Isthmian Diplomacy;* P. Buneau-Varilla, *Panama, the Creation, Destruction, and Resurrection;* and *Reports of Congressional Investigations in Canal History* (House Docs., 62d Congress, 2 Sess., No. 680, and Senate Docs., 63d Congress, 2 Sess., No. 474).

THE United States, not unmindful of the advantages of an isthmian canal, had from time to time made investigations and surveys of the various routes. With a view to government ownership and control Congress directed an investigation of the Nicaraguan Canal for which a concession had been granted to a private company. The resulting report brought about such a discussion of the advantages of the Panama route to the Nicaraguan route, that by an act of Congress, approved March 3, 1889, a commission was appointed to

make full and complete investigation of the Isthmus of Panama, with a view to the construction of a canal . . . to connect the Atlantic and Pacific oceans . . . and particularly to investigate the two routes known respectively as the Nicaragua route and the Panama route, with a view to determining the most practicable and feasible route for such canal, together with the approximate and probable cost of constructing a canal at each of the two or more of said routes.

The commission reported on November 16, 1901, in favor of Panama, and recommended the lock type of canal. The plan consisted of a sea-level section from Colon to Bohio, where a dam across the Chagres Valley created a summit level 82 to 90 feet above the sea, reached by two locks. The lake or summit level extended from Bohio to Pedro Miguel, where two locks connected it with a pool 28 feet above mean tide, extending to Miraflores, the location of the final lock. The ruling bottom width of the canal prism was fixed at 150 feet, increased at the curves and in the submerged channels. In Panama Bay the width was fixed at 200 feet, and in the artificial channel in Limon Bay 500 feet was adopted, with turning places 800 feet wide. The minimum depth was 35 feet, and the locks were to have usable lengths of 740 feet and widths of 84 feet. The commission assessed the value of the rights, franchises, concessions, lands, unfinished work, plans, and other property, including the railroad of the New Panama Canal Company, at $40,000,000.

By an act of Congress, approved June 28, 1902, the President of the United States was authorized to acquire, at a cost not exceeding $40,000,000, the property rights of the New Panama Canal Company on the Isthmus of Panama, and also to secure from the Republic of Colombia perpetual control of a strip of land not less than 6 miles wide, extending from the Caribbean Sea to the Pacific Ocean, and

the right . . . to excavate, construct, and to perpetually maintain, operate, and protect thereon a canal of such depth, and capacity as will afford convenient passage of ships of the greatest tonnage and draft now in use.

In event the provisions for the purchase, and for securing the necessary concession from Colombia could not be carried out, the President was authorized to secure the rights necessary for the construction of the Nicaraguan Canal.

To enable the President to carry out these provisions certain sums were appropriated and a bond issue, not to exceed one hundred and thirty millions of dollars, was authorized. By this act Congress, in accepting the estimates accompanying the report of the commission of 1901, adopted the type proposed by the board, or a lock canal.

Pursuant to the legislation, negotiations were entered into with Colombia and with the New Panama Canal Company, with the end that a treaty was made with the Republic of Panama granting to the United States control of a 10-mile strip, constituting the Canal Zone, with the right to construct, maintain, and operate a canal. This treaty was ratified by the Republic of Panama on December 2, 1903, and by the United States on February 23, 1904.

The formal transfer of the property of the New Panama Canal Company on the Isthmus was made on May 4, 1904, after which the United States began the organization of a force for the construction of the lock type of canal, in the meantime continuing the excavation by utilizing the French material and equipment and such labor as was procurable on the Isthmus. . . .

On June 29, 1906, Congress provided that a lock type of canal be constructed across the Isthmus of Panama, of the general type proposed by the minority of the Board of Consulting Engineers, and work has continued along these lines. As originally proposed, the plan consisted of a practically straight channel 500 feet wide, 41 feet deep from deep water in the Caribbean to Gatun, where an ascent to the 85-foot level was made by three locks in flight. The level is maintained by a dam approximately 7,700 feet long, one-half mile wide at the base, 100 feet wide at the top, constructed to 135 feet above mean tide. The lake formed by this dam, 171 square miles in extent, carried navigation to Pedro Miguel, where a lock of 30-feet lift carried the vessel down to a lake 55 feet above mean tide, extending to Sosa Hill, where two locks overcame the difference of level between the lake surface and the Pacific. Nineteen and eight-hundredths miles of the distance from Gatun to Sosa Hill had a channel 1,000 feet at the bottom, a minimum channel for 4½ miles through Culebra of 200 feet at the bottom. The balance of the distance varied in width to 800 feet, the larger portion of the entire canal being not less than 500 feet. The depth of water was fixed at 45 feet. The lake assured a perfect control of the Chagres River. . . . .

We are justly proud of the organization for the prosecution of the work. The force originally organized by Mr. John F. Stevens for the attack upon the continental divide has been modified and enlarged as the necessities of the situation required, until at the present time it approaches the perfection of a huge machine, and all are working together to a common end. The manner in which the work is being done and the spirit of enthusiasm that is manifested by all forcibly strikes everyone who visits the works.

The main object of our being there is the construction of the canal; everything else is subordinate to it, and the work of every department is directed to the accomplishment of that object.

In addition to the department of construction and engineering, there are the departments of sanitation and civil administration, the quartermaster's and subsistence departments, the purchasing department organized in the United States, the legal department, and the departments of examination of accounts and disbursements. Subordinated to, but acting in conjunction with, the commission is the Panama Railroad.

Too much credit cannot be given to the department of sanitation, which, in conjunction with the division of municipal engineering, has wrought such a change in the conditions as they existed in 1904 as to make the construction of the canal possible. This department is subdivided into the health department, which has charge of the hospitals, supervision of health matters in Panama and Colon, and of the quarantine, and into the sanitary inspection department, which looks after the destruction of the mosquito by various methods, by grass and brush cutting, the draining of various swampy areas, and the oiling of unavoidable pools and stagnant streams.

According to the statistics of the health department, based on the death rate, the Canal Zone is one of the heathiest communities in the world, but in this connection it must be remembered that our population consists of men and women in the prime of life, with few if any of the aged, and that a number of the sick are returned to the United States before death overtakes them.

George W. Goethals, *The Isthmian Canal* (Washington, Government Printing Office, 1909), 3–21 *passim*.

———◆———

40. Relations of the United States with Mexico (1913)

BY PRESIDENT WOODROW WILSON

This is one of the first official documents to give evidence of President Wilson's methods in diplomacy and international relations. In this negotiation he employed a personal representative rather than the diplomatic service. Later, during the World War, he relied for information and negotiation on his friend, Colonel House. —For Wilson, see Nos. 129–132 below. For other matter by Wilson, see Nos. 168, 201, 204.—Bibliography: C. W. Barron, *The Mexican Problem;* S. G. Inman, *Intervention in Mexico;* Chester L. Jones, *Mexico and Its Reconstruction;* P. F. Martin, *Mexico in the Twentieth Century.*

GENTLEMEN of the Congress, it is clearly my duty to lay before you, very fully and without reservation, the facts concerning our present relations with the Republic of Mexico. The deplorable posture of affairs in Mexico I need not describe, but I deem it my duty to speak very frankly of what this Government has done and should seek to do in fulfillment of its obligation to Mexico herself, as a friend and neighbor, and to American citizens whose lives and vital interests are daily affected by the distressing conditions which now obtain beyond our southern border.

Those conditions touch us very nearly. Not merely because they lie at our very doors. That of course makes us more vividly and more constantly conscious of them, and every instinct of neighborly interest and sympathy is aroused and quickened by them; but that is only one element in the determination of our duty. We are glad to call ourselves the friends of Mexico, and we shall, I hope, have many an occasion, in happier times as well as in these days of trouble and confusion, to show that our friendship is genuine and disinterested, capable of sacrifice and every generous manifestation. The peace, prosperity, and contentment of Mexico mean more, much more, to us than merely an enlarged field for our commerce and enterprise. They mean an enlargement of the field of self-government and the realization of the hopes and rights of a nation with whose best aspirations, so long suppressed and disappointed, we deeply sympathize. We shall yet prove to the Mexican people that we know how to serve them without first thinking how we shall serve ourselves. . . .

. . . The future has much in store for Mexico, as for all the States of Central America; but the best gifts can come to her only if she be ready and free to receive them and to enjoy them honorably. America in particular—America north and south and upon both continents— waits upon the development of Mexico; and that development can be sound and lasting only if it be the product of a genuine freedom, a just and ordered government founded upon law. Only so can it be peaceful or fruitful of the benefits of peace. Mexico has a great and enviable future before her, if only she choose and attain the paths of honest constitutional government.

The present circumstances of the Republic, I deeply regret to say, do not seem to promise even the foundations of such a peace. We have waited many months, months full of peril and anxiety, for the conditions there to improve, and they have not improved. They have grown worse, rather. The territory in some sort controlled by the provisional authorities at Mexico City has grown smaller, not larger. The prospect of the pacification of the country, even by arms, has seemed to grow more and more remote; and its pacification by the authorities at the capital is evidently impossible by any other means than by force. Difficulties more and more entangle those who claim to constitute the legitimate government of the Republic. They have not made good their claim in fact. Their successes in the field have proved only temporary. War and disorder, devastation and confusion, seem to threaten to become the settled fortune of the distracted country. As friends we could wait no longer for a solution which every week seemed further away. It was our duty at least to volunteer our good offices—to offer to assist, if we might, in effecting some arrangements which would bring relief and peace and set up a universally acknowledged political authority there.

Accordingly, I took the liberty of sending the Hon. John Lind, formerly governor of Minnesota, as my personal spokesman and representative, to the City of Mexico, with the following instructions:

Press very earnestly upon the attention of those who are now exercising authority or wielding influence in Mexico the following considerations and advice:

The Government of the United States does not feel at liberty any longer to stand inactively by while it becomes daily more and more evident that no real progress is being made toward the establishment of a government at the City of Mexico which the country will obey and respect.

The Government of the United States does not stand in the same case with the other great Governments of the world in respect of what is happening or what is likely to happen in Mexico. We offer our good offices, not only because of our genuine desire to play the part of a friend, but also because we are expected by the powers of the world to act as Mexico's nearest friend.

We wish to act in these circumstances in the spirit of the most earnest and disinterested friendship. It is our purpose in whatever we do or propose in this perplexing and distressing situation not only to pay the most scrupulous regard to the sovereignty and independence of Mexico—that we take as a matter of course to which we are bound by every obligation of right and honor—but also to give every possible evidence that we act in the interest of Mexico alone, and not in the interest of any person or body of persons who may have personal or property claims in Mexico which they may feel that they have the right to press. We are seeking to counsel Mexico for her own good and in the interest of her own peace, and not for any other purpose whatever. The Government of the United States would deem itself discredited if it had any selfish or ulterior purpose in transactions where the peace, happiness, and prosperity of a whole people are involved. It is acting as its friendship for Mexico, not as any selfish interest, dictates.

The present situation in Mexico is incompatible with the fulfillment of international obligations on the part of Mexico, with the civilized development of Mexico herself, and with the maintenance of tolerable political and economic conditions in Central America. It is upon no common occasion, therefore, that the United States offers her counsel and assistance. All America cries out for a settlement.

A satisfactory settlement seems to us to be conditioned on—

(a) An immediate cessation of fighting throughout Mexico, a definite armistice solemnly entered into and scrupulously observed.

(b) Security given for an early and free election in which all will agree to take part.

(c) The consent of Gen. Huerta to bind himself not to be a candidate for election as President of the Republic at this election.

(d) The agreement of all parties to abide by the results of the election and co-operate in the most loyal way in organizing and supporting the new administration.

The Government of the United States will be glad to play any part in this settlement or in its carrying out which it can play honorably and consistently with international right. It pledges itself to recognize and in every way possible and proper to assist the administration chosen and set up in Mexico in the way and on the conditions suggested.

Taking all the existing conditions into consideration, the Government of the United States can conceive of no reasons sufficient to justify those who are now attempting to shape the policy or exercise the authority of Mexico in declining the offices of friendship thus offered. Can Mexico give the civilized world a satisfactory reason for rejecting our good offices? If Mexico can suggest any better way in which to show our friendship, serve the people of Mexico, and meet our international obligations, we are more than willing to consider the suggestion.

Mr. Lind executed his delicate and difficult mission with singular tact, firmness, and good judgment, and made clear to the authorities at the City of Mexico not only the purpose of his visit but also the spirit in which it had been undertaken. But the proposals he submitted were rejected, in a note the full text of which I take the liberty of laying before you.

I am led to believe that they were rejected partly because the authorities at Mexico City had been grossly misinformed and misled upon two points. They did not realize the spirit of the American people in this matter, their earnest friendliness and yet sober determination that some just solution be found for the Mexican difficulties; and they did not believe that the present administration spoke, through Mr. Lind, for the people of the United States. The effect of this unfortunate misunderstanding on their part is to leave them singularly isolated and without friends who can effectively aid them. So long as the misunderstanding continues we can only await the time of their awakening to a realization of the actual facts. We can not thrust our good office upon them. The situation must be given a little more time to work itself out in the new circumstances; and I believe that only a little while will be necessary. For the circumstances are new. The rejection of our friendship makes them new and will inevitably bring its own alterations in the whole aspect of affairs. The actual situation of the authorities at Mexico City will presently be revealed.

Meanwhile, what is it our duty to do? Clearly, everything that we do must be rooted in patience and done with calm and disinterested deliberation. Impatience on our part would be childish, and would be fraught with every risk of wrong and folly. We can afford to exercise the self-restraint of a really great nation which realizes its own strength and scorns to misuse it. . . .

While we wait the contest of the rival forces will undoubtedly for a little while be sharper than ever, just because it will be plain that an end must be made of the existing situation, and that very promptly; and with the increased activity of the contending factions will come, it is to be feared, increased danger to the non-combatants in Mexico as well as to those actually in the field of battle. The position of outsiders is always particularly trying and full of hazard where there is civil strife and a whole country is upset. We should earnestly urge all Americans to leave Mexico at once, and should assist them to get away in every way possible—not because we would mean to slacken in the least our efforts to safeguard their lives and their interests, but because it is imperative that they should take no unnecessary risks when it is physically possible for them to leave the country. We should let every one who assumes to exercise authority in any part of Mexico know in the most unequivocal way that we shall vigilantly watch the fortunes of those Americans who can not get away, and shall hold those responsible for their sufferings and losses to a definite reckoning. That can be and will be made plain beyond the possibility of a misunderstanding.

For the rest, I deem it my duty to exercise the authority conferred upon me by the law of March 14, 1912, to see to it that neither side to the struggle now going on in Mexico receive any assistance from this side the border. I shall follow the best practice of nations in the matter of neutrality by forbidding the exportation of arms or munitions of war of any kind from the United States to any part of the Republic of Mexico—a policy suggested by several interesting precedents and certainly dictated by many manifest considerations of practical expediency. We can not in the circumstances be the partisans of either party to the contest that now distracts Mexico or constitute ourselves the virtual umpire between them. . . .

. . . The steady pressure of moral force will before many days break the barriers of pride and prejudice down, and we shall triumph as Mexico's friends sooner than we could triumph as her enemies—and how much more handsomely, with how much higher and finer satisfactions of conscience and of honor!

Address to Congress, August 27, 1913, in *Congressional Record*, L, 3803.

———◆———

41. The Latin View of the Monroe Doctrine (1914)

BY LEOPOLD GRAHAME

Grahame is the author of *Argentine Railways* (1916).—Bibliography: Alejandro Alvarez, *The Monroe Doctrine;* Albert Bushnell Hart, *The Monroe Doctrine.* See H. Sherill, *Modernizing the Monroe Doctrine.*

ALTHOUGH there are many conflicting opinions as to the ramifications of the Monroe Doctrine, it seems to me that the Latin view is that which must ultimately prevail in defining its status. The issue is clean-cut. It is whether the Monroe Doctrine is to be unilateral, or continental, in its operation; and upon this issue the retention of the doctrine as an integral part of the national policy of the United States must alone be determined. . . .

It has been urged by many eminent public men, including ex-President Roosevelt, that the very conditions which led to the adoption of the Monroe Doctrine conferred upon the United States not only by implication, but by necessity, the right to extend its protection of the Latin republics to the point of active intervention when the existence of disturbing conditions in any one of them might be thought to jeopardize its national independence. It should be remembered, however, that the United States has never assumed responsibility for the acts of those countries, but has, on the contrary, always maintained that, whilst it would not sanction the acquisition or occupation of the territory of an American republic by a foreign power, it would assist such power to protect its subjects from moral or material injury in cases of national wrong-doing; and to that extent the doctrine, though not incorporated into international law, has been accepted without reserve by practically all of the European governments. Nor, indeed, are there to be found, so far as I am aware, any historical records to sustain the contention that the Monroe Doctrine is anything more than a logical culmination of an order of political ideas initiated by the declaration of American independence to separate the interests of the two hemispheres and to prevent European intervention in the internal affairs of the countries on this side of the Atlantic.

Let me ask in what cases the relations of a Latin republic with a European government might call for the reassertion of the Monroe Doctrine by the United States? The answer, I think, would be civil wars and insurrections; outrages inflicted upon foreigners; failure to fulfil contracts with them; their unlawful expulsion; and default in payment of public or private debts. These, in the abstract, would constitute the most likely reasons for a possible future application of the Monroe Doctrine; and within the last ten years we have had practical demonstration of the willingness of the great powers of Europe to accept the American view and to submit the differences arising out of such matters to the judicial methods of international courts of arbitration. Thus, the Monroe Doctrine, in its original and real sense, is universally established and admitted; and I cannot conceive either the moral or legal grounds upon which the United States can lay claim, in regard to the Latin republics, to a right so admittedly and so strongly denied to the nations of Europe.

We know from the fully recorded proceedings of the negotiations between President Monroe and the British government, preceding the formal declaration of the doctrine, that Mr. Canning, whilst adhering to its principles, steadfastly refused to allow the British government to become an official party to its formal establishment. The American minister, Mr. Rush, repeatedly informed his government of his belief that Great Britain had suspicions that the United States entertained designs of securing commercial advantages and of creating a hegemony on the American continent. Is it, then, surprising that, with latter-day occurrences in mind, the Latin-American republics should also entertain suspicions as to the motives underlying the various and frequently strained interpretations placed upon the Monroe Doctrine by many leaders of American thought?

It must be borne in mind that although successive Presidents of the United States, in recent years, have often stated, with undoubted sincerity, that this country has no idea of obtaining an inch of Latin-

American territory by conquest, circumstances have arisen to justify the belief in many of the smaller republics of this continent that their complete independence is not quite so secure as they would wish. Common sense points to the conclusion that if, rightly or wrongly, the British government harbored doubts in the matter of American policy, in the early twenties of the nineteenth century, even in the face of the solemn declarations of such men as Monroe, Clay, Adams, Madison, Jefferson, Rush, Gallatin, and other equally conscientious and patriotic citizens, it can hardly be a matter of surprise that the Latin-American sense of security has been weakened by what has transpired in the recent past in the policy of the United States towards the sister republics. I do not for one moment assume or believe, that enlightened public opinion in this country, official or unofficial, regards either as desirable, or justifiable, encroachments upon the sovereign rights of the Latin-American nations. On the contrary, I assume and believe that the main purpose of the policy of the United States in relation to the other republics is to maintain and perpetuate their absolute independence. Therefore, I would further ask, what advantages are to be secured by the extension of the scope of the Monroe Doctrine beyond that so specifically expressed by its original founders?

The people of Latin America are of common origin. Their emancipation was secured by arduous struggles with their former oppressors; and an attack upon the dearly-bought independence of any one of the republics is reflected throughout them all. Their view of the Monroe Doctrine is that, although it has its origin in the United States, it is part of the international law of the American continent, where each nation is a distinct unit, with equal freedom and sovereignty and with no prerogative extended to any single one of them to control a continental policy. They regard the Monroe Doctrine as an instrument designed to proclaim the existence, in the western hemisphere, of independent nations, with the right to implant laws and institutions for the government of free people, without interference or dictation at the hands of the monarchies of Europe; but those republics would consider their last condition as worse than their first, if a distorted interpretation of the doctrine were to lead to any of them becoming, what, for all practical purposes, would be vassals of the United States. . . .

. . . The doubts and suspicions of the Latin republics as to the ultimate aims of the United States are accentuated by the widening of the Monroe Doctrine to ends never contemplated by its authors. It is such incidents as those which have occurred in Mexico, in Nicaragua and in Colombia, that have led to a growing belief in the supposed desire on the part of the United States to establish a suzerainty over some of the republics of Central and South America; and, even though there be no payment of a money tribute, or no open claim to the right of intervention in the internal affairs of the other states, the repetition of such acts as are here indicated, would, to all intents and purposes, confer the power of suzerainty upon the United States. . . .

Ex-President Roosevelt truly describes the situation when he says that the Monroe Doctrine is looked upon with favor and is even welcomed as an American policy by the leading statesmen of South America; but what they approve and welcome is the Monroe Doctrine as they view it; and not as it is viewed by a great number of the public men of the United States. The Argentine Republic has special reasons for gratitude for the past existence of the Monroe Doctrine, not least amongst which are, that it was the first of the Latin-American republics to be recognized by the United States; and that it was enabled, largely through the re-assertion of that doctrine, to remain over a long period in undisturbed possession of the extensive and then undeveloped Patagonian territory, which is now becoming such a valuable national asset. Yet, knowing as I do, the honorable and liberty-loving character of the Argentine people, I venture to assert that there is not a public man of that country who would sanction, for one moment, the further endorsement of the Monroe Doctrine, if he believed it implied a claim to intervention in the domestic concerns of even the least important of the American republics. . . .

Looking at all these circumstances and at the change of conditions in all the American republics from those existing in their early stages of nationhood, there would appear to be little reason and less justification for the assumption, by the United States, of anything in the nature of protectorate over them. This country has the right to adopt measures to secure the fullest protection of its citizens and their interests on the borders of a turbulent neighbor, such as every nation enjoys in other parts of the world; but it derives no prescriptive right from the Monroe Doctrine to encroach upon the independence of any other sovereign state.

Briefly summarized, the situation, as already stated, must be viewed alike from the standpoints of justice and expediency. Justice unquestionably demands the complete independence of all the republics of the New World. To deny this is to stultify the utterances of every President of the United States since the declaration of its independence. On the other hand, expediency dictates that "honesty is the best policy;" and that moral as well as material loss must necessarily follow the pursuance of a course of action which would alienate the sympathies and friendship of the twenty independent nations described as the Latin Republics of America. In other words, it would involve the sacrifice of commercial and industrial expansion to political considerations that would bring no corresponding advantages. The really sane view of the Monroe Doctrine is that its provisions should be enforced only against those who seek to violate them and not against those in whose interest they were framed.

Leopold Grahame, in *Annals of the American Academy of Political and Social Science* (Philadelphia, July, 1914), LIV, 57–62 *passim*.

———————◆———————

42. The Modern Monroe Doctrine (1920)

BY CHARLES C. THACH

Thach is Associate in History and Political Science at John Hopkins University. He is the author of *The Creation of the Presidency, 1775–1789* (Johns Hopkins Studies in History and Political Science, Series XI, no. 4).—Bibliography as in No. 41 above.

. . . SUCH *was* the Monroe Doctrine, a statement of the right of the Latin-American peoples to work out their own salvation free from outside interference, and of the interest that the United States had in the preservation of this right from European interference. For some seventy-five years it stood the wear and tear of actual operation remarkably well. Polk, to be sure, added a new provision, and one which was scarcely a logical deduction from the original principle, namely, that a Latin-American State could not even voluntarily alienate territory to a European Power. The annexation of Texas, despite claims to the contrary, was no violation either of the letter or the spirit of the doctrine, which, indeed, had contemplated just such a voluntary accession to the Union, not only of Texas, but also of Cuba. Even the forcible annexation of California and New Mexico was not so black as it has been painted, for Mexico did her fair share in making the war inevitable and the territory in question was practically masterless long before it began.

The growth of American interest in a trans-isthmian canal, however, led to the enunciation of a doctrine which was certainly not in accord with the original principle that Latin-America could do with its own as seemed best to itself. This doctrine, the so-called doctrine of "paramount interest," was to the effect that the United States claimed the exclusive right to protect and guarantee any canal built across Central America. This, obviously, was a clear denial of the right of the States possessing canal routes to enter into what agreements they chose concerning their territory. But, in any event, the new doctrine scarcely came to any practical importance during the period prior to 1898.

On the other hand, the two chief applications of it in those years were in complete accord with the spirit of the original message. When Seward finally brought about the downfall of the Maximilian government in Mexico during the sixties by forcing Napoleon III to withdraw his troops he was undoubtedly protecting the Mexicans from a rule which had been forced on them by a European Power and was maintained only by its troops. Similarly, when Grover Cleveland forced Great Britain to arbitrate her dispute with Venezuela, he was, he thought, preventing a European Power from acquiring, by virtue of her superior might, the territory of a defenceless neighbor.

But Cleveland was the last of the old order. McKinley, Roosevelt, Taft, Knox, Wilson, Hughes, differing *toto cœlo* from each other in other respects, have been as one in transforming the Monroe Doctrine from one of national independence and non-intervention into one of American suzerainty and intervention. It has been a singularly hypocritical and unedifying performance. All have given lip service to the doctrine, have proclaimed it the ark of the covenant of our foreign policy. All have heaped Latin-America with fine phrases about independence, equality and sovereignty. And all have busied themselves in denying, so far as their acts went, all three, until finally the nation today stands committed to a policy which seeks to determine the very form and personnel of the Latin-American governments, and which denies that right of revolution which, as it happens, is the basic principle of the very doctrine which we have always professed to revere and apply.

It began with the Spanish War. Our purpose, we declared at the outset, was not to "exercise sovereignty, jurisdiction or control" over Cuba, but "to leave the government and control of the island to its people." But, with the war over, we established a protectorate, despite Cuba's opposition. We annexed Porto Rico, whose right to determine her own affairs amounted to nothing in the face of the desire of the United States to keep her. The basic assumption of the original doctrine, that the Latin-Americans had both the right and the capacity to work out their own future, went overboard once and forever.

If Mr. Roosevelt did not intervene in the Panama "revolution" then intervention has lost all meaning. A rebellion of a portion of Colombia, if not actively fomented by American agents, was certainly assured of success by American troops, American recognition, and a guarantee treaty. Santo Domingo came next, and with it a "modification," and "extension" of the Monroe Doctrine that completely reversed its original significance. This modification took the form of the "doctrine of preventive intervention," by virtue of which the United States has claimed and exercised the right to intervene in the affairs of any Latin-American State whenever, *in its opinion*, a state of affairs threatens to arise which may produce European intervention, which, in turn, may produce occupation of territory, which *may* ultimately produce annexation. If this is a doctrine of non-intervention, of national independence, then, of course, black is white.

Followed Mr. Taft and Mr. Knox. The region of Central America was their especial preserve. "The United States," said Mr. Taft, "has been glad to encourage and support American bankers who were willing to lend a helping hand to the financial rehabilitation of such countries, because the financial rehabilitation and the protection of their customs-houses from being the prey of would-be dictators would remove at one stroke the menace of foreign creditors and the menace of revolutionary disorder." American bankers, those notorious extenders of the helping hand, were no longer, it would seem, "foreign" to Central America. And the "sacred right of revolution" had become mere "revolutionary disorder."

Nor did the great crusade for the rights of small nations produce a change so far as the small nations of America were concerned. The Great Crusader himself informed the Pan-American Scientific Congress that the Monroe Doctrine had set up a partial protectorate over Latin-America and that it contained no pledge concerning the method in which we would exercise the powers that flowed from it. Nicaragua was bribed into a treaty that made her, to considerable degree, our ward, thus partially consummating an abortive plan fathered by Mr. Taft, which looked toward the creation of a complete protectorate. Santo Domingo and Haiti found that their world was much safer for deserving Democrats than for democracy, which, for purposes relating to this hemisphere, was interpreted to be synonymous with government by the marines. Mexico, too, discovered that her government had, for the future, to conform to the ideals of governmental morality entertained by the administration then in power in the United States. Huerta, not so conforming, got no recognition, and hence no credit and no arms. Without these, his existence was, of course, impossible and power passed from him to successors who had our approval.

And what of the Hon. Charles Evans Hughes? As might have been expected from so distinguished a former ornament of the Supreme Bench, he jettisoned morality and took legality aboard. No Latin-American government, the edict went forth, would be recognized if it was of revolutionary origin, or if its ideas concerning private property and the right of the State in relation thereto did not conform with those of the United States. More than that, revolutionists could get no arms here, but established governments might. Legitimacy, as a hundred years ago, became the order of the day.

Charles C. Thach, *The Monroe Doctrine*, in *American Mercury*, February, 1925 (New York), IV, 140–142.

43.   American Coöperation in Porto Rico (1925)

BY KNOWLTON MIXER

Mixer is a lawyer practising in New York.—Bibliography as in No. 35 above; also L. S. Rowe, *The United States and Porto Rico.*

WHEN the invading forces of the United States landed in Porto Rico our officers found a people suffering from the results of the oppression of centuries. Ninety per cent. of the population were unable to read or write in any language and were more densely ignorant than those of any South American country. The people had had no experience whatever in self-government. Initiative had been proscribed; they had learned simply to do as they were ordered by their superiors and to accept whatever was given them in return. They suffered from social conditions which were the result of ignorance and the neglect of their government. The originally fertile lands of the Island were impoverished by a century of cultivation without refreshment and commerce languished, epidemics were common with this people, underfed and overcrowded, chronically the victims of hookworm, malaria and tuberculosis.

In the twenty-five years of American rule the population has increased fifty per cent. The birth rate has advanced and the death rate has been reduced so that the net increase of population per year is now approximately 22,000. Epidemics have been abolished and measurable progress has been made in the fight against hookworm, malaria and tuberculosis.

Under the old régime practically no public school system existed. Nine-tenths of the people were rural and there were no rural schools. There are now more than 2,000 rural schools while above 200,000 pupils are enrolled in graded, high schools and technical schools throughout the Island. For education the Insular Government is expending annually $4,000,000, more than a third of its budget.

Illiteracy has been reduced in the average to fifty-five per cent. of the population but in the cities it has been reduced to thirty-seven per cent. The rural school is becoming a real factor for progress in the country. The growing system of farm and technical schools for boys and the teaching of domestic science for girls are training the present generation to take care of itself and are both raising the standard of living and pointing the way to attain it.

A complete University with six departments and an enrollment of more than 2,000 students has been established and maintained.

During the American period ten million dollars have been spent on roads, an investment which has increased the value of the lands opened to commerce many times the sum expended. To make these lands of the interior available to commerce this construction of roads has been a prime necessity for the Island's development. . . .

A large expenditure, also constructive in character, has been made for irrigation, which has increased the productivity of the lands affected at least fifty per cent. . . .

The manifold expenditures for the public good have been accomplished without undue taxation, in fact the resulting taxes are very much less than those of the United States. . . .

Even in the coffee trade which has advanced the least of the basic industries, because of its lack of protection under the U. S. tariff, the production is again as large as during the Spanish régime and the price is approaching the pre-Spanish war figure. It is at least bringing as high a price in the American market as the best South American coffees. . . .

The production of sugar has not only made extraordinary advances in volume but has achieved a high standard in method, which places Porto Rico in the front rank of producing countries. The harmonious coöperation between government officials and the Centrale managers in the work of improvement may be credited with the present satisfactory situation.

The tobacco trade has witnessed an enormous improvement in organization and quality of product and this has brought a corresponding increase in price. The large increase in export is in leaf tobacco which last year reached more than 23,000,000 lbs. This is not an entirely satisfactory phase of growth for the Island, since if this large volume of leaf had been manufactured into cigars in the Island, employment would have been furnished a larger number of tobacco workers. It is possible that this outcome is the result of strikes which have been frequent and prolonged.

Fruit is entirely an American industry in inception and development. Its importance as an economic factor grows yearly and the industry seems, at present, to be on a thoroughly satisfactory basis, particularly as to the production of grape fruit and pineapples.

It would be surprising if this universal improvement of business conditions should not bring with it some measure of betterment for the worker whose labor makes such results possible. His advance in wages and rise in living standards would doubtless follow in direct ratio if it were not for the fact that his labor is constantly in surplus, his supply always greater than the demand.

That his condition is improving, however, is shown by the Governor's report for 1924 in which he says that a marked improvement in the conditions of labor has been shown during the year. Wages have increased, living conditions have improved, unemployment has decreased. The activities of government in welfare work, education of the children, prevention and treatment of disease and sanitary measures of all kinds have been greatly extended and the chief beneficiaries of all these are the workmen.

The attitude of the present administration is that the condition of the working man is the responsibility of the Government and that every effort possible, within the field of government operations, must be made to raise the standard of his living to an approximation of that on the mainland. This point of view, if adhered to, will inevitably result in a marked improvement within a few years. . . .

The labor legislation enacted during the American régime manifests a sincere desire to overcome so far as government can, the handicaps of labor due to ignorance and past neglect. These laws aided by the spread of education are beginning to make themselves felt in a higher standard of living and morals.

In summing up the results of American control for a quarter of a century in his inaugural address, the present Governor touched on the underlying explanation of this unexampled progress. He said: "I doubt if anywhere, any isolated section, a part of any other nation, can show a like record. It proves, does it not, that our relations are mutually beneficial?

"We have, on the part of the general government, granted the greatest possible measure of liberty. You have privileges in some regards of greater worth than those enjoyed by any other part of the Union. You have a constantly increasing measure of local self-government and you have given to the world a splendid example of what may be done in less than a single generation by a liberty-loving, capable and intelligent people under republican institutions."

The reasons for this progress, though largely native to our fundamental reactions as a nation, are worth analyzing, since wherever they may be applied with the same sincerity of purpose, similar results may confidently be expected.

The results were made possible then by the active participation in Island affairs of the United States government, first exemplified under the military government by the establishment of the fundamentals of liberty, the freedom of speech and the press and education, the protection of property, the abolishment of extreme punishment for crimes and the reformation of the judiciary.

The early grant of civil government provided a school for citizenship of the most effective sort. This was supplemented by frequent hearings before the Insular Affairs Committees of the House and Senate to whose members, Porto Ricans, representing all parties, have had an opportunity to express their criticism and their desires. To the insistent demand for citizenship from Porto Rico, Congress finally yielded and granted not only that badge of equality but a measure of almost complete autonomy in the Jones law. . . .

With a very few exceptions the United States has sent men of the best type to represent the nation in its coöperation with the Island representatives. The Island leaders have at times complained that they were made subject to men who knew nothing of their language nor history and were not in sympathy with their traditions. There has, however, been but one short period in recent years when that criticism could be justly applied. With this exception the largest measure of sympathy with the Island needs and coöperation in its advancement have been manifested by those who have been sent from the United States. . . .

Protection and stability have been given the Island through the Public Health Service and military control and as a consequence of this high financial credit has been established which enables the Island treasury to borrow at low rates of interest. This high credit enables the Government to complete public work of great productive value to the country at a low cost and at the same time makes it possible to employ thousands of laborers at remunerative wages.

In general the Government has been sustained by the loyalty and coöperation of the Porto Ricans. This friendly and coöperative spirit was particularly marked in the early years of civil government when the best of local talent was devoted to the joint effort of building up the country. . . .

The keen desire manifested by the people for education and their grateful acceptance and coöperation with the various plans for their betterment, when they have understood them, have been important factors in the Island's progress. . . .

In spite of the extraordinary progress made in the past twenty-five years, the underlying problem of the Island is not yet solved, since the regeneration of the farm laborer has but just begun. That a start has been made is a great step in advance. Particularly is it a hopeful sign that all political parties have accepted this problem as their responsibility and that one party, whose power is expanding rapidly, that is, the Socialist, has made the welfare of the working man its sole objective. In short, the outlook of the rural farm laborer has never in his history been as bright as it is today. He has a long way to go before he can reach the standard of his brothers on the continent but he is on the way. He is at least a citizen of the United States and this, in the opinion of Mr. Travieso, the first native secretary of the Island and the mayor of San Juan, is the greatest achievement of the Porto Rican during the past twenty-five years. His immediate response to the grant of citizenship in 1917 was his registration for the national army to the number of 121,000 men. His loyalty at that moment of the nation's need was beyond question and many times the actual number enlisted would gladly have volunteered for service overseas if places could have been found for them.

Knowlton Mixer, *Porto Rico* (New York, Macmillan, 1926), 273–285 *passim.*

44. Uncle Sam, Imperialist (1927)

BY PROFESSOR WILLIAM R. SHEPHERD

Shepherd is Seth Low Professor of History at Columbia University. He was United States delegate to the first Pan-American Scientific Congress at Santiago, Chile, in 1908–1909, and secretary of the United States delegation at the fourth International Conference of American States at Buenos Aires in 1910. He has also been otherwise specially concerned with international affairs within the Americas, and has published a number of books concerning the Hispanic nations of the New World and the relations of the United States therewith.—Bibliography as in No. 41 above.

IN about thirty years we have created two new republics—Cuba and Panama; converted both of them and three other Latin-American countries—the Dominican Republic, Nicaragua and Haiti—into virtual protectorates; intervened by force at least thirty times in the internal affairs of nine supposedly sovereign and independent nations; made the period of intervention last anywhere from a few days to a dozen years; enlarged our investments from a paltry two or three hundred millions of dollars to the tidy sum of upwards of three billions, and installed in four states our own collectors of customs to insure payment. Incidentally, we have annexed Porto Rico and the Virgin Islands, built a canal, secured an option to construct another and gathered in several naval stations.

The causes for our entry into so close a relationship with the five little republics may easily be recalled. In 1898 the United States declared war on Spain for the liberation of Cuba from what we regarded as Spanish misrule. The immediate motive, beyond doubt, was one of good will toward a people suffering from oppression in an island that lay very near our own shores.

Meanwhile Americans had long been cherishing the idea of constructing a canal somewhere in the nether portion of the North American Continent. Whether it should be run through the Colombian province of Panama or through the Republic of Nicaragua was the question until 1903, when a timely revolution in the province solved the difficulty in favor of the Panama route. Thereafter it became a foregone conclusion that the second new nation which we had godfathered within five years would grant to the United States all the rights and privileges which the building and control of a canal might warrant.

Hardly had the construction of the new waterway begun, when the financial distress of another small state, the Dominican Republic, awoke fears on the part of the American government lest the situation prompt European creditors to take measures for a collection of their debts, likely to impinge upon some one of our numerous interpretations of the Monroe Doctrine. Hence, in order to forestall that possibility, in 1905 the United States assumed financial guardianship itself.

From the Dominican Republic the next step was directed, in 1912, to Nicaragua. Here two motives came into operation. One was the determination of the United States not to allow an option to be acquired by some foreign power for the construction of a canal that would not only compete with the Panama waterway, but would also be a potential menace to our control of the latter. The other motive was, to quiet political disturbances that threatened injury to Americans and foreigners and their respective property. The fact that the gentleman who in 1927 claims to be president of Nicaragua happens to be the same aspirant whom we installed in office fifteen years ago lends enchantment to the present tangle there.

In 1915 the Colossus of the North again stepped back on to the island for the eastern end of which he had already assumed the financial management. At the western end lay a Negro republic called Haiti, squirming under a series of despotic presidencies tempered by frequent assassination. Here an unusually horrible slaughter of political prisoners and the violation of a foreign legation compelled the United States to intervene, for fear the European nation concerned might do something detrimental, again, to the Monroe Doctrine. Although the protection of foreign and American lives and property was involved, the basic motive for the landing of Marines in Haiti, as in the case of Cuba, was humanitarian.

Whatever the direct motives for these several courses of action, through them all has run the advancement of our own economic, as well as political, welfare. This country of ours has become powerful in proportion as its southern neighbors have remained weak. We have known how to utilize our resources; they have not. Because they have not and we want what lies in their soil and under it, our captains of industry, aided by the government of the United States, have put themselves increasingly into the position of showing them how the things nature has provided should be turned to account.

In our virtual protectorates we have followed two quite distinct procedures: one toward Cuba, Panama and Nicaragua; the other toward the Dominican Republic and Haiti. Both of them have the same aims: to encourage American economic enterprise and to promote the material benefit of the peoples concerned. Neither course of action has been motivated so much by a determination to exact reparation for injury committed, as by a desire to prevent such injury. Lest Americans and their property, as well as foreigners and theirs, should suffer damage and the Monroe Doctrine be exposed to infringement, the plan has been to avert the possibility of either. Commonly, the intervention has been asked by interested parties, native, American or European, with or without sufficient reason. Whether the inhabitants of the countries affected relish it or not, is something not taken into account.

So far as Cuba, Panama and Nicaragua are concerned, the United States has aided the local authorities to maintain order and adopt other salutary measures for the general objects in view. Since 1909 Cuba has remained under its own rulers. The same has always been true of Panama and Nicaragua, even if the personnel of the functionaries has sometimes been determined by the United States.

Toward the Dominican Republic and Haiti, on the other hand, the action taken has been quite ruthless. Because of political commotions and a disposition to incur indebtedness beyond what the American guardian thought proper, in 1916 the Dominican government was practically abolished. In its place an American military régime was set up, which stayed on until 1924. Haiti, a year earlier, had undergone a similar fate, except that the native administration still continues under the military supervision of an American officer, now styled a "High Commissioner."

From the standpoint of the rights presumed to attach to states which are reputed to be "sovereign and independent," certainly the plight of the Dominican Republic and Haiti is much less enviable than that of their three fellows. To be sure, the American military rulers have built roads and railways, improved ports, bettered sanitary conditions and enlarged educational facilities, but their action has been accompanied at times by harshness and cruelty to individual natives, especially in the Negro republic. Both of the little states, also, have been compelled to assent to treaties providing for huge loans.

These advances from American financiers will contribute, no doubt, to the material welfare of the countries concerned; so they will to our own. Doubtless, too, the opposition to American influence there and in all of the republics under our tutelage where similar loans have been the order of the day, is political, rather than the result of actual wrongs inflicted. But is political opposition on the part of reluctant wards toward their self-appointed mentor nothing of any moment?

A much more intriguing question now presents itself. Is there a possible ratio between the extent of American governmental control and the manner of its exercise, on the one side, and the increase in American investments, on the other? Has there been any apparent connection between the growth of American financial interests and a tendency of our Department of State to practice, through diplomatic pressure, with Marines posted in the background, political interference in the internal affairs of the republics? Let us cite the case of Cuba.

In the joint resolution of April, 1898, which brought on the war with Spain, Congress declared that the United States disclaimed any intention to exercise control over Cuba except for its pacification, and would leave the government and control of the island to its own people. Events, however, soon indicated that the government was indeed to be left, but not the control. Three years later, the so-called "Platt Amendment," which the Cubans were obliged to incorporate into their constitution, provided among other things that the United States was to possess the right to intervene in the republic for the preservation of its independence and the maintenance of a government capable of protecting life, property and individual liberty, and that Cuba should contract no excessive indebtedness. The former of these stipulations the United States has enforced on several occasions. The application of the latter appears to stand in quite a different category, although in essence the ultimate means employed have been the same.

In 1904 the first loan contract made with Cuba by an American banking house provided for no financial administration by Americans, and contained no allusions to the government of the United States as a party to the agreement. From that time onward, moreover, such contracts regularly have stipulated that the amount loaned constitutes a lien upon the customs revenue, or even on all sources of public income, of the country concerned, as security for the interest on, and amortization of, the bonds as issued. These in turn, as to both principal and interest, are exempt from domestic taxation.

Beginning in 1905, sometimes by "executive agreement" between the President of the United States and the appropriate authorities in a given republic when the Senate would not assent, sometimes by formal treaty, no fewer than five methods have been devised for insuring payment. As the table shows [not reprinted], in Cuba the customs revenues are administered by Cuban officials; in the Dominican Republic, by an American General Receiver, named by the President of the United States; in Nicaragua, by an American Collector, acting under the orders of a High Commission, one of whose three members is chosen by our Department of State and one by American bondholders. In Haiti, the entire revenue system of the country is in the hands of an American General Receiver and an American Financial Advisor, appointed by the president of the republic on the nomination of the President of the United States, who also appoints the High Commissioner over all. The case of El Salvador, not one of the virtual protectorates, and yet illustrative of the fifth method, is even more significant. For the service of a loan, contracted in 1922, the collection of 70 per cent, and, if necessary, all, of its customs revenues is attended to by an American official chosen by an American corporation with the approval of our Department of State. Nor are extensive loans likely to be made anywhere in Latin America without seeking in advance the approval of that branch of our national administration.

Considering the financial relationship of Cuba to the United States, . . . between 1899 and 1916 the estimated amount of American investments in the island increased from $50,000,000 to $400,000,000; whereas between 1916 and 1925 it rose to $1,360,000,000. But it was precisely during these nine years that the influence of our government over Cuban political and financial affairs became altogether marked. After 1918, and acting in compliance with a series of memoranda from an army officer of high rank, sent as personal representative of the President of the United States and later appointed American ambassador to the republic, the Cuban congress passed a large number of enactments aimed at improving political and economic conditions. They included: new electoral laws; suspension of certain provisions of the civil service law, so as to permit the president of Cuba to shift the personnel of administrative departments; facilitation of the removal of judges; revision of the tariff; changes in the budget; reorganization of the system of accounting; the clearing up of indebtedness, and the floating of an American loan of $50,000,000, placed as a lien upon the entire national revenue and under the virtual guarantee of the government of the United States. All of this might argue that the jurisdiction of the United States over the financial concerns of Cuba has made some progress since 1901, when the republic was obligated only to contract no excessive indebtedness!

In handling the affairs of our neighbors in and around the Caribbean, with or without their coöperation, four general policies have been brought into play. They may be designated by as many words: *regulation, annexation, neutralization,* and *abstention.* Certain islands have been annexed; a Central American country (Honduras) has been neutralized and, where the political and economic interests of the United States have seemed to permit it, abstention from interference in internal situations or international relations among the several republics has been practiced. But the general policy most in vogue has been that of regulation, whereby whatever those neighbors do is subject in greater or less degree to American control. For its exercise, four methods of action have been followed: (1) recognition of a particular government; (2) the severance of diplomatic relations—which means the same thing as the newly coined and misleading expression, "withdrawal of recognition"; (3) the levying or the lifting of an embargo on the shipment of arms and munitions, and (4) military intervention.

Phases of this policy of regulation are visible just now in our dealings with little Nicaragua and Panama and with bigger Mexico. The legitimate successor to an erstwhile president in Nicaragua, not recognized by the United States, is forcibly prevented from taking his official seat, because our government regards another person as better suited to our interests, political and economic. The allegation that the installation of the personage who is not our candidate might imperil the canal which we have not begun to construct is—amusing. The supposition that, in collaboration with Mexico, he and his band of partisans might conjure up the "spectre of a Mexican-fostered Bolshevist hegemony intervening between the United States and the

Panama Canal" is—terrifying, indeed, to the richest and most powerful nation on earth! If the United States recognizes one "president"
in Nicaragua, Mexico mustn't recognize another; if, for the benefit
of its protégé, the United States lifts an embargo on the shipment of
arms and munitions, Mexico has no business to allow Mexican armaments and soldiers of fortune to be used for the advantage of its own
alleged disciple. As to Panama, that small state has been induced to
enter into a treaty of alliance with this country, whereby it stands
pledged to coöperate in the military defense of the Canal, despite its
solemn obligations as a member of the League of Nations.

The nigger in the Nicaraguan wood-pile is evidently the issue—on
quite different grounds—between the United States and its neighbor
immediately to the south of the Rio Grande. In order to enforce our
will, we appear to menace Mexico with the threat of severing diplomatic relations and lifting the embargo on arms and munitions, which
would result, probably, in putting the country anew into the throes of
civil war. Yet the problem need not be solved in this fashion. With
all due respect for "national honor and vital interests," the matters
in dispute might be adjusted by a resort to the Permanent Court of
International Arbitration at The Hague, of which the United States
is a sponsor.

Our country may not "covet an inch of our neighbors' territory";
yet somehow it seems to have been exemplifying on this side of the
Atlantic what John Galsworthy described as a characteristic of the
motherland on the other—"the possessive instinct of the nation on
the move." Of the measures we have taken in the Caribbean, the
eventual outcome is painfully clear. If we go on as we have begun,
the American empire must ultimately bestride the entire area. Politically, the republics within it may remain "sovereign and independent"—in the language of diplomacy. Economically, they would
become a happy hunting ground for American capitalists, upheld
and protected by their government. The Monroe Doctrine then will
deserve the definition given in the Covenant of the League of Nations:
a "regional understanding" about a sphere of influence for a great
power.

Of this broadening out of the United States over its huge preserve,
bounded by the wall of the Monroe Doctrine, the nations of Europe
doubtless would disapprove. Even though we are only emulating

their own example elsewhere in the world, they are likely to object
to such behavior on our part, just as the Latin-American republics
still outside the sphere will cherish resentment. Both will vent their
feelings in hard words, if nothing worse. But what does that matter?
Business is business. And southward the course of empire takes its
way.

William R. Shepherd, in *New Republic*, January 26, 1927 (New York), XLIX,
266–269.

---

45. Pan-American Problems (1928)

BY EX-SECRETARY CHARLES EVANS HUGHES

Hughes, eminent lawyer and statesman, has twice been Governor of New York,
served on the United States Supreme Court from 1910 to 1916, was defeated for
the Presidency in 1916, acted as Secretary of State under Harding and Coolidge,
1921–1925, and was appointed a member of the Permanent Court of International
Justice at The Hague in 1928. The speech quoted here was made in his capacity
as Chairman of the United States delegation to the sixth Pan-American Conference, held in Havana, 1928.

WE cherish the thought that Cuba in her liberty and independence is the vindication of the idealism of the people of
the United States. It is that idealism which, at the beginning, during
the struggles of over 100 years ago nurtured our policy in this hemisphere. It is that idealism which has ever been the guardian of our
liberty at home.

You will find us keen in trade, zealous for the advantages of commercial intercourse, but no one knows us well who fails to recognize,
despite all our shortcomings, the dominance among us of the ideals
of independence and democracy. These brought us to the aid of
Cuba in 1898 and again summoned us with imperative command to
take our part in the titanic contest of the World War.

You cannot adequately explain the United States in statistics of
population, of commerce or of wealth. There is a power above all
these which gives final direction to our public opinion and establishes
the standards of our statesmanship, according to which we take
measure of executives and legislators.

If you would find what we worship in our inmost thought, do not rest content with going to our marts, but visit our shrines. We like to be thought shrewd, but we erect no monuments to mere shrewdness. We reserve our highest veneration for the greatest exemplars of liberty and independence—Washington, Jefferson and Lincoln. They are still, and I trust ever will be, the true spokesmen of the American spirit.

But this idealism is that of a practical and industrious people. We rejoice with you in the material gains of progress. With vast and increasing populations there must be opportunities well used to give talent its proper place and workers their full reward, or we should have the discontent that leads to anarchy rather than the coöperative efforts which give better standards of living and a wider-diffused prosperity.

The advancement of civilization is in the care of the factory, the plantation, the markets of commerce as well as the halls of learning. Progress must have its economic basis, and the commercial movement between North America and Latin America is one which in the main is equally satisfactory to the statesman and the economist. The steady development of our commercial exchanges reflects the contrasts of products and of industrial needs.

We could not be satisfied with the expansion of commercial relations if these contacts failed to develop a better understanding and a more comprehensive and sympathetic view of the lives and the problems of our peoples.

There is no guarantee of friendship in disregard of differences. The differences in individuals, groups and nations save life from monotony and give to our contacts a never-failing fascination. But, however noteworthy the varieties of our particular environments, our resemblances are more fundamental than our differences. Even our problems, to the keen observer, have many elements in common.

Underneath the superficial contrasts there is the bond of fellowship between democratic peoples in their age-long quest of solidarity, efficiency and equal justice. It may be a long journey to our goal, but we are on the way. At the sixth Pan-American Conference we are taking counsel together to help us onward.

Pan-Americanism rests upon four pillars. The first is independence. It is the firm policy of the United States to respect the territorial integrity of the American republics. We have no policy of aggression. We wish for all of them, not simply those great in area and population and wealth, but for every one, to the very smallest, strength and not weakness. What a fatuous idea it would be to think that the United States desired that any of these States should be weak or the prey of disorder. There is no promise for the United States in that. We do not wish their territory. We have troubles enough at home without seeking responsibilities abroad. The rights we assert for ourselves we accord to others.

Nothing could be happier for the United States than that all the countries in the region of the Caribbean should be strong, self-sufficient, fulfilling their destiny, settling their problems, with peace at home and the fulfillment of their obligations abroad. It is in the strength of these Powers, as equal and responsible States, and not in the weakness of any, that lies our confidence for future tranquillity and the mutual benefits of intercourse.

The second pillar of Pan-Americanism is stability. Independence is not enough. Independence gives opportunity, but stability is essential to take advantage of it. It is our desire to encourage stability in the interest of independence. Let me recall to you an illustration: Several years ago, in circumstances which it is not necessary for me to review, the United States entered Santo Domingo. But what did we do? Did we endeavor to stay? On the contrary, we labored to get out. It would have been very easy to remain, but the Government of the United States was most solicitous to arrange for the termination of its occupation and the withdrawal of its forces, and endeavored earnestly and successfully to aid the Dominican people in establishing a sound basis for an independent Government. The leaders of all parties were brought together for conversation. A plan of evacuation was agreed upon; arrangements were made for the provisional Government and for the establishment of a permanent Government. These arrangements were carried out and the United States withdrew. It was my happy privilege to be associated with these endeavors which had this successful fruition. If we had cherished an imperialistic purpose we should have remained in Santo Domingo; but we withdrew. We would leave Haiti at any time that we had reasonable expectations of stability and could be assured that the withdrawal would not be the occasion for a recurrence of bloodshed.

Meanwhile, we are endeavoring in every important direction to assist in the establishment of conditions for stability and prosperity, not that we may stay in Haiti, but that we may get out at the earliest opportunity. We are at this moment in Nicaragua, but what we are doing there and the commitments we have made are at the request of both parties and in the interest of peace and order and a fair election. We have no desire to stay. We wish Nicaragua to be strong, prosperous and independent. We entered to meet an imperative but temporary exigency; and we shall retire as soon as it is possible.

The third pillar of Pan-Americanism is mutual good-will. Strong and stable Governments that do not trust each other afford no assurance of peace and beneficent collaboration. Good-will does not mean identity of views. It is not jeopardized by candid, but at all times friendly, expressions, albeit there are differences of opinion. The enemies of good-will are on every hand. There are those who seek to find in every act a wrongful motive; who poison the air with suspicion; who will never be content. Good-will rests on mutual respect, upon a common appreciation that each harbors no mistrust of the other. We desire the wide dissemination of information, but, unfortunately, good works, the calm and quiet efforts of those who have the good-will of nations at heart, rarely contain elements of sensation. The enemies of our peace and happiness often get the centre of the stage and their declamations fill the air. But this need not discourage us. In the case of an honorable individual, we know that it is his reputation with his intimates—with those who know his purposes and activities—that gradually extends in ever-widening circles until it becomes proof against any possible assault. So it is with nations.

The fourth pillar of Pan-Americanism is coöperation. Peace and good-will are not ends, but means. They give us the promise, but not fruit. It is in our working together that we reap the benefits which friendly relations should bestow. Coöperation among the Pan-American States does not mean the organization of a superstate. It does not mean that any of the twenty-one American republics or any group of these republics will attempt to dominate others. It is the coöperation of equals for common advantage in those directions where there is prospect of success. Coöperation does not mean that we should ignore difference in conditions and in the varied circumstances surrounding our lives. It means mutual helpfulness, where we can be of assistance by doing together what we cannot so well do alone. It is not for us to be wearied with futile anxieties about the future. It is for us, in our day and generation to play our part. And if we do that with sincerity of purpose and an earnest desire to advance the cause of civilization so far as it is in our keeping, future generations will rejoice in the inheritance of our labors.

Address before American Chamber of Commerce, Havana, Cuba, January 20, 1928. In *New York Times Current History*, March, 1928 (New York), 861–862.

PART IV

INTERNATIONAL ASPECTS

CHAPTER IX — EUROPEAN FOREIGN RELATIONS

46. The Consular Service Aids Trade (1901)

BY FREDERICK L. EMORY

Emory (1867–1921) was Professor of Mechanics and Applied Mathematics at West Virginia University. He was a contributor to technical publications.—On foreign trade, see bibliography with No. 48 below.—On the diplomatic service in general, see No. 205 below.

OUR progress in foreign markets is the more extraordinary because of the general lack, until very recently, of organized or intelligent effort by our manufacturers or by our exporters to cater to any but our own consumers. With most defective and inefficient methods, we have surprised ourselves and the world at large by suddenly emerging from our absorption in domestic trade as a potent factor of international commerce.

The same result has been reached in a branch of our Government machinery which a few years ago seemed but little likely to challenge the emulation of other countries, and is still the object of much well-meaning but ignorant criticism, not by foreigners, but by would-be reformers at home. For it is only lately that the consular service of the United States has come to be regarded by the best authorities abroad as the most efficient organization of its kind in the world for spreading the sale of goods, for stimulating home industry and enterprise, and for informing exporters as to trade conditions in every important market of the globe.

186

In view of the demand from various quarters for reforms in our consular system, this, doubtless, will be regarded as a surprising statement, but it is one that is abundantly borne out by the facts. It is the fashion to argue that, because the consular service is largely made up of men appointed for merely political or personal reasons, therefore its fruits must necessarily be bad. But it sometimes happens that a system confessedly faulty produces some good results; and paradoxical as it may seem, there are foreign experts who consider the frequent changes in our consular corps, which most of our reformers denounce as wholly pernicious, to be one of the reasons which explain the admittedly greater usefulness of American consuls in promoting trade.

Six years ago the commercial world of Great Britain was beginning to take note of the practical character of the reports on commerce and industry by American consuls, and the promptness with which they were printed and distributed by the Department of State. The British Chambers of Commerce were called upon by the Executive Council to consider "the action taken by the Government of the United States and by other governments by means of special consular reports, in order to supply their traders with information up to date with regard to openings for business in foreign countries," and the opinion was expressed that the practical value of the reports of British consuls "would be much increased if they afforded more direct and early suggestions and details with respect to trade questions of present interest." The local chambers of commerce were, therefore, invited to make suggestions as to trade inquiries by consuls for submission to the Foreign Office. . . .

The British agitation of the subject continued, and about a year ago a commercial intelligence branch of the Board of Trade (a government bureau) was established, and the organ of the board, the Board of Trade Journal, was converted from a monthly into a weekly periodical, in order that consular and other commercial reports of current interest might be given more promptly to the public. . . .

Germany, with her splendidly equipped commercial schools and admirable machinery for extending foreign trade, seems also to consider her facilities deficient by comparison with the American in the matter of procuring and promptly distributing commercial information, and has recently begun the publication, declaredly "after the mode of the United States Department of State," of special consular reports upon trade matters, products, economic questions, etc., prepared by German consuls in reply to interrogatories or specific instructions from the government.

Dr. Vosberg-Rekow, the head of the Central Bureau for preparing commercial treaties, in a recent book upon commercial treaties, in which he expresses the opinion that the United States is likely to be Germany's strongest rival in industrial competition, speaks of our consular officers in Europe as "inspectors of our exports and vigilant sentinels who spy out every trade opening or advantage and promptly report it." In another place he says:—

"The Americans have acted judiciously in establishing a system which is of the greatest advantage to themselves, but costly and inconvenient to their competitors. In all countries with which it has trade relations, the United States has stationed consuls and consular agents. Every shipment of goods to a United States port must pass through the hands of these officials, and the amount, value, place of origin, market price ruling in the country of production, method of production, etc., are noted. The consuls thus dive deeply into the economic condition of their districts and obtain information the result of which is discernible in the steadily increasing exportations of their home country."

Among the practical business men who appeared before the Committee on Foreign Relations at the hearing in May last, there was one who put his finger on a weak spot which seems fully to justify the demand for legislative reform. "I have come to believe," he said, "that the lack in our consular service is owing more to the short tenure of office than to the quality of the material that is originally appointed, and any bill that will give opportunity for our consuls to perfect themselves in the requirements which all must gain when they take the field, will add to the efficiency of the service."

Perhaps there would not be so much opposition to consular reform if it concentrated itself upon the effort to obtain greater stability of tenure and an equitable system of rewards for meritorious service and to secure a much needed elasticity in permitting the transfer, at the option of the Department of State, of any consular officer from one post to another, as occasion required. It is but natural that the present incumbents and their friends should antagonize a movement which proposes to make their continuance in office depend upon a drastic scheme of examinations. No doubt, they would be much more placable, if assured that they were not to be rudely jostled or perhaps thrown out by the reform, so long as they continued to do satisfactory work.

The truth is that the politician who is appointed to a consular post is usually something besides a mere party worker. As a rule, he is a newspaper man, a merchant, a manufacturer (even if it be only in a small way), who is more or less in touch with business affairs, and there are but few who rely upon politics exclusively as a means of support. And it must be admitted that even with the handicap of the "spoils" instinct, he sometimes does better work for our business men than would a carefully trained neophyte who has never rubbed about in practical life.

Undoubtedly, the movement which is rapidly gaining headway in our colleges for special courses to train young men for the diplomatic and consular services is a wholesome feature of the general tendency toward the adoption of more intelligent, more scientific, methods in our government service, and also in the development of our export trade. Training of this kind is an excellent specific for the evils complained of, but the experience of other countries proves that it is easy to take an overdose. By all means give us educated consuls; but may it not be found wiser to insist that they shall first have served an apprenticeship (such as most of the present consuls have served) in a newspaper office, a countinghouse, a workshop, or a bank?

The same considerations do not apply to the diplomatic service, which is essentially a polite profession in which the greater the degree of intellectual and social training, the better the results. In this field, the special courses of colleges and the test of academic attainments can work no serious harm, but, on the contrary, should prove most helpful. The burden of all the demands of reform in the consular service is greater efficiency in trade, and how is this to be secured if not by making it a primary qualification of consular officers that they shall have a practical knowledge of and adaptability for the most important of the duties they are to discharge?

Frederick L. Emory, *Our Consuls and Our Trade*, in *World's Work*, May, 1901 (New York), II, 751–757 *passim*.

47. Warning to the German Emperor (1902)

BY EX-PRESIDENT THEODORE ROOSEVELT AND SECRETARY
JOHN HAY

The last two paragraphs are by John Hay; the rest is quoted from Roosevelt, for whom see Nos. 23–26 above.—Bibliography as in No. 23 above.

THERE is now no reason why I should not speak of the facts connected with the disagreement between the United States and Germany over the Venezuela matter in the early part of my administration as President, and of the final amicable settlement of the disagreement.

At that time the Venezuelan Dictator-President Castro had committed various offences against different European nations, including Germany and England. The English Government was then endeavoring to keep on good terms with Germany, and on this occasion acted jointly with her. Germany sent a squadron of war vessels to the Venezuelan coast, and they were accompanied by some English war vessels. There was no objection whatever to Castro's being punished, as long as the punishment did not take the form of seizure of territory and its more or less permanent occupation by some Old-World Power. At this particular point such seizure of territory would have been a direct menace to the United States, because it would have threatened or partially controlled the approach to the projected Isthmian Canal.

I speedily became convinced that Germany was the leader, and the really formidable party in the transaction; and that England was merely following Germany's lead in rather half-hearted fashion. I became convinced that England would not back Germany in the event of a clash over the matter between Germany and the United States, but would remain neutral; I did not desire that she should do more than remain neutral. I also became convinced that Germany intended to seize some Venezuelan harbor and turn it into a strongly fortified place of arms, on the model of Kiauchau, with a view to exercising some degree of control over the future Isthmian Canal, and over South American affairs generally.

For some time the usual methods of diplomatic intercourse were tried. Germany declined to agree to arbitrate the question at issue between her and Venezuela, and declined to say that she would not take possession of Venezuelan territory, merely saying that such possession would be "temporary"—which might mean anything. I finally decided that no useful purpose would be served by further delay, and I took action accordingly. I assembled our battle fleet, under Admiral Dewey, near Porto Rico, for "manœuvres," with instructions that the fleet should be kept in hand and in fighting trim, and should be ready to sail at an hour's notice. The fact that the fleet was in West Indian waters was of course generally known; but I believe that the Secretary of the Navy, and Admiral Dewey, and perhaps his Chief of Staff, and the Secretary of State, John Hay, were the only persons who knew about the order for the fleet to be ready to sail at an hour's notice. I told John Hay that I would now see the German Ambassador, Herr von Holleben, myself, and that I intended to bring matters to an early conclusion. Our navy was in very efficient condition, being superior to the German navy.

I saw the Ambassador, and explained that in view of the presence of the German squadron on the Venezuelan coast I could not permit longer delay in answering my request for an arbitration, and that I could not acquiesce in any seizure of Venezuelan territory. The Ambassador responded that his Government could not agree to arbitrate, and that there was no intention to take "permanent" possession of Venezuelan territory. I answered that Kiauchau was not a "permanent" possession of Germany's—that I understood that it was merely held by a ninety-nine years' lease; and that I did not intend to have another Kiauchau, held by similar tenure, on the approach to the Isthmian Canal. The Ambassador repeated that his Government would not agree to arbitrate. I then asked him to inform his Government that if no notification for arbitration came within a certain specified number of days I should be obliged to order Dewey to take his fleet to the Venezuelan coast and see that the German forces did not take possession of any territory. He expressed very grave concern, and asked me if I realized the serious consequences that would follow such action; consequences so serious to both countries that he dreaded to give them a name. I answered that I had thoroughly counted the cost before I decided on the step, and asked him to look at the map, as a glance would show him that there was no spot in the world where Germany in the event of a conflict with the United States would be at a greater disadvantage than in the Caribbean Sea.

A few days later the Ambassador came to see me, talked pleasantly on several subjects, and rose to go. I asked him if he had any answer to make from his Government to my request, and when he said no, I informed him that in such event it was useless to wait as long as I had intended, and that Dewey would be ordered to sail twenty-four hours in advance of the time I had set. He expressed deep apprehension, and said that his Government would not arbitrate. However, less than twenty-four hours before the time I had appointed for cabling the order to Dewey, the Embassy notified me that His Imperial Majesty the German Emperor had directed him to request me to undertake the arbitration myself. I felt, and publicly expressed, great gratification at this outcome, and great appreciation of the course the German Government had finally agreed to take. Later I received the consent of the German Government to have the arbitration undertaken by the Hague Tribunal, and not by me. . . .

The German and British Governments firmly counted on our well-established jellyfish squashiness and felt sure they had a free hand. The Kaiser and Junker party especially had everything cut and dried, and counted the affair as accomplished. The first time, Holleben informed his Government that probably Roosevelt's attitude was a bluff; but on second thought went to his friend Buenz for advice, as B. knew the American people better than any German living, and was a close friend of Roosevelt's (I introduced him) and hence a good judge of the situation. Buenz at once assured him that Roosevelt was not bluffing, and that he could count on his doing as threatened; and that in a conversation Roosevelt had shown that he had an intimate knowledge of the strength and condition of the German fleet which was . . . [then] no match for ours.

Holleben was obliged to eat his own words and telegraph in hot haste to Berlin, where his message fell like a bombshell. You know the rest. This resulted in Holleben's being recalled and dismissed from the diplomatic service.

William Roscoe Thayer, *Life and Letters of John Hay* (Boston, Houghton Mifflin, 1915), II, 411–416 *passim*. Reprinted by special permission of the publishers.

48.   America and European Competitors (1916)

BY WALTER E. WEYL

Weyl (1873–1919) was statistical expert on international commerce for the United States Bureau of Statistics. He conducted investigations for the U. S. Department of Labor in 1898, in Mexico in 1901, and in Porto Rico. Author of *The Passenger Traffic of Railways* (1901), *The New Democracy* (1911), *American World Policies* (1917); also various bulletins for the Department of Labor.—Bibliography: Harold U. Faulkner, *American Economic History;* Garet Garrett, *The American Omen;* Clarence F. Jones, *Commerce of South America;* and various pamphlet publications of the Department of Commerce.

IT is true that the world market constantly expands, but the producing capacity of the manufacturing nations also increases and competition becomes ever more severe. The more rapidly America invades the markets which Europe has hitherto held, the more she squeezes them, the more bitter the feeling against her will become.

That bitterness of feeling (in the conditions preceding the present war) was more likely to arise in Germany than in England and more likely in England than in France. We have spoken of these as rival nations, but there are intensities of rivalry varying in proportion to the similarity of products and of methods of production. Germany, like the United States, is a newcomer in international industry, pushing and aggressive. More scientific and better organised than we, she possesses far more meagre resources. We both have trusts or cartels, and both manufacture huge quantities of cheap, standardised products. Our competition therefore is of the keenest, and is likely to grow more intense, if, as seems likely, Germany recovers from the effects of this war. Less keen is our competition with Great Britain. Like an old firm, grown rich and conservative, Great Britain is not pushing, not scientific, not well organised. We are gaining on her in those branches of manufacture which permit standardisation and production in huge quantities, and have no hope, and but little wish, of competing in articles of high finish and therefore high labour cost. With France we compete still less, since much of her export trade is in articles of taste and luxury, in which we are hopelessly inferior.

In this battle for the world market, the United States has the disadvantage of coming late and of being intellectually unprepared. On the other hand, not only have we superior natural resources, but also the advantage that to us success is not vital. Whatever trade we gain is a mere improvement of a situation already good. We are playing "on velvet." Finally, like Germany, we have the advantage of large scale production by strong corporations working with what is practically a bounty upon exports. Because of their control of a protected home market, our great corporations can make their sales at home cover all initial and constant costs, and as these costs need not be applied to exports, we are able to sell goods cheaper in Rio Janeiro or Lima than in Chicago or New York. They are able to "dump" their surplus goods. . . .

If our foreign commerce was gaining before the war, it has made even greater progress since the outbreak of hostilities. While Germany's foreign commerce has been temporarily destroyed and that of Great Britain has been hampered by the war, our total commerce has immensely increased. In the year 1915 we exported over a billion dollars in excess of our exports of 1913, our exports in the latter year exceeding those of the United Kingdom or of any other country in any year of its history. This development, it is true, was abnormal and consisted partly in increases in prices and temporary deflections in trade. Nevertheless, while many American industries, especially those engaged in the manufacture of war munitions, will suffer severely at the end of the war, and while our export of such commodities will dwindle, the war cannot but result in a relative advantage to American manufacturers of export commodities.

Moreover, the war by destroying established connections between neutral countries and their natural purveyors of manufactured goods in Europe has opened the way to future extension of American exports. Like a protective tariff, it gives an initial advantage to Americans, and helps them to overcome the early handicaps. It induces American manufacturers to think in terms of foreign markets instead of concentrating their attention upon a protected home market. In the beginning, it is true, the buying capacity of certain countries, such as those of South America, was diminished by the shattering of financial arrangements with Europe. But such a condition is purely temporary. . . .

American manufacturers are to-day determined to secure an increased share of this expanding market. They are slowly learning that you cannot push your goods, in South America let us say, unless you learn to pack your goods, have studied local requirements, are willing to print catalogues in Spanish and Portuguese, and have your salesmen know these languages. In the past Americans have been hampered by their unwillingness or inability to extend long credits, but this drawback is being removed by the improvement of banking facilities. The government, moreover, now seeks actively to promote American trade with foreign countries, and especially with Latin America. A new merchant marine is epected to give additional facilities to American exporters and enable them to meet their British and German competitors on more nearly equal terms. Moreover, the United States is learning that in the export trade coöperation is desirable, and the Federal Trade Commission seems about to grant permission to manufacturers to combine for the conduct of business in foreign countries.

All this does not mean that American manufacturers are completely to displace their European competitors in South America and other markets. Competition after the war will be severe, and whatever the course of wages and employment in Europe, a measure of success for industrial countries like Great Britain, Germany and Belgium is absolutely essential to the maintenance of their populations. Desperate efforts will be made by these nations to reëstablish their foreign business. A great part of South America is as near to London and Rotterdam as to New York, and much of the trade and of its future increase will revert to Europe. In the years to come, however, more than in the present or past, the United States will be a formidable competitor for the world-markets, and will incur enmity and jealousy in the attempt to maintain and improve its position. A similar development is taking place in the field of investment. In former years, British, French, Dutch, Belgian and German financiers were requested, indeed begged, to invest their surplus capital in American enterprises. To these financiers we went cap in hand, and they did not lend their money cheaply. The complementary relation between lending Europe and borrowing America was productive of the friendship of mutual benefit. To-day we are still a debtor. We ourselves have a large capital, and in the main go to Europe merely for the sale of safer and less remunerative bonds, while the common stock of new enterprises is likely to remain in America. Or we graciously "let Europe in on a good thing," conferring, not asking, a favour. In the meantime, we are paying off our indebtedness as is indicated by the balance of trade, which since 1876 has almost invariably been strongly in our favour. . . .

Even to-day (Nov. 1, 1916) there is still a probable excess of our debts over our credits with foreign nations of at least two billions of dollars. In comparison with our total wealth, however (estimated by the census of 1910 at 207 billions and since then largely increased), this indebtedness seems comparatively small. The national income is rapidly expanding and as the chance to secure exceptionally large profits in railroad and industrial enterprises diminishes there is an increased temptation for surplus capital to flow abroad. Whether or not we shall again have recourse to the fund of European capital in developing our immense resources, it is hardly to be doubted that we shall increasingly invest in foreign countries, and especially in Mexico, and elsewhere in the Americas.

Such a development is entirely legitimate and within bounds desirable both for the United States and to the countries to which our capital (and trade) will go. The possible field of investment in Latin America and the Orient, to say nothing of other regions, is still immensely great, and as capital develops these areas their international trade will also grow. There is no reason why the United States should not take its part both in the investment of capital and the development of trade with these non-industrial countries.

As we so invest and trade, however, we must recognise the direction in which our policy is leading us and the dangers, both from within and without, that we are liable to incur. The more we invest the more we shall come into competition with the investing nations of Europe. We are already urged to put capital into South America on the just plea that trade follows investment, and the same forces that are pushing our trade outward will seek opportunities for investment in the mines and railroads of the politically backward countries. Like European nations, we too shall seek for valuable concessions, and may be tempted (and herein lies the danger) to use political pressure to secure investment opportunities. What happened in Morocco, Persia, Egypt, where the financial interests of rival nations brought them to the verge of war, may occur in Mexico, Venezuela or

Colombia, and the United States may be one of the parties involved.

We seem thus to be entering upon an economic competition not entirely unlike that which existed between Germany and England. We too have gone over to a policy of extending our foreign markets and of protecting our foreign investments. More and more we shall be interested in politically and industrially backward countries, to which we shall sell and in which we shall invest. Inevitably we shall face outwards. We shall not be permitted by our own financiers, manufacturers and merchants, to say nothing of those of Europe, to hold completely aloof. We have seen, even in the present Mexican crisis, how American investment tended to precipitate a conflict. We have learned the same lesson from England, France and Germany. As we expand both industrially and financially beyond our political borders we are placed in new, difficult and complicated international relations, and are forced to determine for ourselves the rôle that America must play in this great development. We can no longer stand aside and do nothing, for that is the worst and most dangerous of policies. We must either plunge into national competitive imperialism, with all its profits and dangers, following our financiers wherever they lead, or must seek out some method by which the economic needs and desires of rival industrial nations may be compromised and appeased, so that foreign trade may go on and capital develop backward lands without the interested nations flying at each other's throat. Isolation, aloofness, a hermit life among the nations is no longer safe or possible. Whatever our decision the United States must face the new problem that presents itself, the problem of the economic expansion of the industrial nations throughout the world.

Walter E. Weyl, *American World Policies* (New York, Macmillan, 1917), 61–71 *passim*.

49. Appointment of Ministers (1919)

FROM THE REPORT OF THE NATIONAL CIVIL SERVICE REFORM LEAGUE

With the Civil Service Reform League was actively associated William Dudley Foulke, for whom see No. 30 above. The aim of this organization was to make merit, and not political connections and services, the basis of retention and promotion in the government service. See also No. 205 below.—Bibliography: F. Van Dyne, *Our Foreign Service*.

AT the meeting of the Council of the National Civil Service Reform League, July 26, 1918, President Richard H. Dana, reading a summary of the report of the special War Committee, said:

It seems imperative that the League should take a fearless, uncompromising stand on the application of the merit principle to foreign service all along the line, especially in view of the shameless barter of these positions.

The governing body of the League, its Council, accepting the report of the War Committee, voted unanimously:

That the League advocates the extension of the merit principle to all grades of the consular and diplomatic services.

An examination shows that all other great nations do apply such a rule to their foreign service, including the highest grade of Ambassador. A contrary impression seems to prevail in the minds of many Senators, who allege that the custom of Great Britain is to appoint distinguished citizens outside the service. In point of fact there are very few such instances. . . .

Members of the British service have expressed the opinion that their Government could not expect to get first-class men to enter the service if secretaries could not look forward to promotion to the highest posts. The failure to observe the merit principle causes the service to work in a vicious circle and brings its own specious excuse. Thanks to the salary situation and the quota rule a smaller number of really able men will enter the service and the supporters of political appointment then point to the quality of the men in the service as a justification for passing them over. Yet, even with this justification, a careful examination of the political appoin.ments actually made in our service compared with the men serving in the highest service grades of the diplomatic and consular service will be found not unfavorable to the latter. . . .

In theory, the appointment of the most distinguished citizens of the Republic to the post of Minister or Ambassador is excellent, and there is no doubt that the practice has certain real advantages. The prime consideration is, alas, that it provides places for "deserving Democrats" or Republicans, as the case may be. The real significance of Mr. Bryan's euphemistic designation of "deserving" is clear when we examine the relationship between diplomatic appointments and campaign contributions.

Hon. William Dudley Foulke has ably discussed this matter in "Fighting the Spoilsmen." He gives the names of appointees who made "deserving" contributions to the campaign fund. The editorial in the New York *Sun* of February 24, 1919, is likewise to the point. Representative Rogers also discussed this subject in his speech in Congress. It is not fair to arraign the present administration as the sole offender on this score. This remnant of the Jacksonian spoils system has been retained and applied in varying degrees by all preceding administrations. William Roscoe Thayer, in his "Life of John Hay," publishes some interesting correspondence relative to the appointment of the Ambassador to London.

It is no adequate answer to point to exceptional instances—the Choates and Bryces—in justification of a system which has meant the appointment of men like Cameron of Pennsylvania, or Sullivan, the notorious minister to Santo Domingo. Even in our consular service the old political appointment system has to its credit such distinguished names as Nathaniel Hawthorne, William D. Howells and Bret Harte, but the general average under the spoils system was low and the whole service sadly inefficient. The rank and file of the consular appointments were then much below the present, and our service suffered. The other branch of the service now needs men thoroughly qualified by training—men who speak French and the language of the country to which they are sent.

The second alleged advantage in making appointments from without the service is one more openly defended. It is said to give the President representatives who view the great questions of policy from the same angle as he does. This is said to make for political harmony. But when we come to study the question we find that the value of this argument is more apparent than real. The prevalent idea is that an Ambassador is a political office like that of a Cabinet Member, and that he should represent the personal views of the administration. In actual practice the President is more likely to secure the close coöperation of which he stands in need from diplomats of career than he will from the heterogeneous group forced upon his consideration for preferment by politicians. Furthermore, we must remember that several months elapse before the President has cleaned his diplomatic slate and secured his new representatives. Take, for example, the ambassadorial appointments when President Wilson succeeded a Republican administration. An examination will show that the administration had to work for no inconsiderable period through the agency of the appointees of the other party. . . . If the argument of the defenders of political appointments were sound, it would be inadvisable to allow these hangovers to remain at their posts one moment after the change of administration.

As against the merits, alleged or real, of the system of political appointments we must balance the inconvenience of a quaternial rotation of posts. A man who comes new to his work requires some time to familiarize himself with the technique and the mere routine of his new office. Until he has acquired this he is at a disadvantage with his colleagues of the diplomatic corps, who can always block his suggestions by some technical objection. Furthermore, a man new to the service cannot expect to hold the influence nor so easily gather political information as his experienced professional colleagues. All the other countries have tried the political appointment system and long ago discarded it as less satisfactory. With occasional exceptions justified by extraordinary circumstances they depend upon professional diplomats.

The experience of other services has shown that the political heads of the State have no difficulty in securing the effective coöperation of the diplomatic representatives abroad. And, be it noted, that political considerations are of much greater relative importance in the relations of European countries than has hitherto been the case with the United States.

In truth, the President is often forced to send abroad men who are not in harmony with his own ideals. Lincoln sent Cameron to Russia, and instances abound where diplomats have been appointed to get rid of a troublesome rival rather than to secure the coöperation of a sympathetic supporter.

After all, it is only in a few posts where personal policies or party politics are of importance in relation to the direction of foreign affairs, and even in these posts we repeat the statement that the President often has little real opportunity to select those who are in close political communion with him. This is shown by the frequency with which President Wilson has had recourse to special emissaries—Dr. Bayard Hale, Commissioner Lind, and especially Colonel E. M. House. Possibly the condition which we have been discussing may have something to do with the resignations of many of the men whom President Wilson had appointed—Ambassador Mayre from Petrograd, Ambassador Sharp from Paris, Minister Page from Rome, Minister Van Dyke from The Hague, and others.

The abuses which result from the application of the political appointment system to Ambassadors are less than in the case of Ministers because of the brighter light of publicity which beats down upon appointments to the more important posts, but when we come to far-off States of second rank, the abuses of the political appointment system become glaring. . . .

At the present time one of the causes for the opposition to the application of the merit principle to the diplomatic service is the impression which results from the extreme rapidity with which these promotions sometimes occur. A single administration may make several promotions of the same individual, so that he seems to stand to a certain extent in the light of its political protégé. The cause of these rapid promotions is the rapid rate at which good men leave our service and the wholesale transfer of places with the change of administration. When an adequate increase of salary has been made and the merit principle applied to the promotions of secretaries to Ministers, we may expect that the majority of men in the service will receive promotion under the Presidents belonging to both of the political parties.

Report on The Foreign Service by National Civil Service Reform League (New York, 1919), 45–55 *passim.*

CHAPTER X — PLANS FOR WORLD PEACE

50. Clasp Hands, Ye Nations! (1905)

BY WALLACE IRWIN (1906)

This brief poem relates to the ending of the Russo-Japanese War, which had reached an impasse, with the victorious Japanese virtually exhausted, when Roosevelt offered his good offices as peacemaker. Representatives of the belligerents met, at his invitation, at Portsmouth, N. H., August 5, 1905. Roosevelt's suggestions were of the utmost help in enabling them to agree.—For Irwin, see No. 38 above.—Bibliography: Tyler Dennett, *Roosevelt and the Russo-Japanese War*.

(The Peace of Portsmouth)

CLASP hands, ye Nations, and thank God
    The bitter tragedy is done!
Corn shall be planted in the sod
    That vengeance long has trod upon.
Clasp hands, ye Foes, across the path
    By life-blood dampened as by dew;
The curtains of Almighty wrath
    Roll back and let the sunlight through!

In those long camps where armies lie
    Between the battle and despair
I think I hear a mighty sigh
    Rise up to heaven like a prayer:
"Giver of Peace, our lives are dear
    And we have felt the pains of men;
Thank God the blessed end is here
    And we may see our homes again!"

Peace! and the grass may grow once more
    Among the gullies and the stones
Where War might still have festered o'er
    A continent of skulls and bones.

> Peace! and the fleets of commerce choose
>   Safe paths on the untroubled deep
> Where, buried in the crawling ooze,
>   The Navies of Misfortune sleep.
>
> Clasp hands, ye Nations, in the prayer
>   That hell's fierce work for good be done;
> That such a trial by fire may bear
>   New splendor to the Rising Sun;
> And that the Peasants of the North
>   Through suffering have found a way
> To summon Light and Freedom forth
>   To strike the prison-chains away!

Wallace Irwin, *Random Rhymes and Odd Numbers* (New York, Macmillan, 1906), 268–269.

---

51. America's Peace Policy (1907)

BY SECRETARY ELIHU ROOT

Root, eminent lawyer, jurist, was Secretary of War in the Cabinets of McKinley and Roosevelt; in that position he was responsible for the creation of the Army General Staff in 1903. Later he served, with great distinction, as Secretary of State. Senator from New York 1909–1915. He has been a strong supporter of the World Court of International Justice. His speeches and state papers have been published by the Harvard University Press.—Bibliography: W. M. Mallory (compiler), *Treaties and Conventions, 1776–1909* (Senate Docs., 61 Congress, 2 Sess., No. 357); numerous publications of the World Peace Foundation; publications of the League of Nations; Joseph H. Choate, *The Two Hague Conferences.* See also No. 123 below.

GENTLEMEN,—You have been appointed delegates plenipotentiary to represent the United States at a Second Peace Conference which is to meet at The Hague on the 15th of June, 1907. . . .

It is not expedient that you should be limited by too rigid instructions upon the various questions which are to be discussed, for such a course, if pursued generally with all the delegates, would make the discussion useless and the Conference a mere formality. You will, however, keep in mind the following observations regarding the general policy of the United States upon these questions:

1. In the discussions upon every question it is important to remember that the object of the Conference is agreement, and not compulsion. If such conferences are to be made occasions for trying to force nations into positions which they consider against their interests, the Powers cannot be expected to send representatives to them. It is important also that the agreements reached shall be genuine and not reluctant. Otherwise, they will inevitably fail to receive approval when submitted for the ratification of the Powers represented. Comparison of views and frank and considerate explanation and discussion may frequently resolve doubts, obviate difficulties, and lead to real agreement upon matters which at the outset have appeared unsurmountable. . . .

The immediate results of such a conference must always be limited to a small part of the field which the more sanguine have hoped to see covered; but each successive conference will make the positions reached in the preceding conference its point of departure, and will bring to the consideration of further advances toward international agreement opinions affected by the acceptance and application of the . previous agreements. Each conference will inevitably make further progress, and, by successive steps, results may be accomplished which have formerly appeared impossible. . . .

2. The policy of the United States to avoid entangling alliances and to refrain from any interference or participation in the political affairs of Europe must be kept in mind, and may impose upon you some degree of reserve in respect of some of the questions which are discussed by the Conference. . . .

3. The First Conference adopted the following resolutions:

The Conference is of opinion that the restriction of military charges, which are at present a heavy burden on the world, is extremely desirable for the increase of the material and moral welfare of mankind.

The Conference expresses the wish that the Governments, taking into consideration the proposals made at the Conference, may examine the possibility of an agreement as to the limitation of armed forces by land and sea and of war budgets.

Under these circumstances this Government has been and still is of the opinion that this subject should be regarded as unfinished business, and that the Second Conference should ascertain and give full consideration to the results of such examination as the Governments may have given to the possibility of an agreement pursuant to the wish expressed by the First Conference. We think that there should be a sincere effort to learn whether, by conference and discussion, some practicable formula may not be worked out which would have the effect of limiting or retarding the increase of armaments.

There is, however, reason to believe not only that there has been the examination by the respective Governments for which the First Conference expressed a wish, but that discussion of its results has been forestalled by a process of direct communication between a majority of the Governments having the greatest immediate interest in the subject. These communications have been going on actively among the different Governments for nearly a year, and as a result at least four of the European Powers have announced their unwillingness to continue the discussion in the Conference. . . .

If any European power proposes consideration of the subject, you will vote in favor of consideration and do everything you properly can to promote it. If, on the other hand, no European Power proposes consideration of the subject, and no new and affirmative evidence is presented to satisfy you that a useful purpose would be subserved by your making such a proposal, you may assume that the limitations above stated by way of guidance to your action preclude you from asking the Conference to consider the subject.

4. The other subject which the United States specifically reserved the right to propose for consideration is the attainment of an agreement to observe some limitation upon the use of force for the collection of ordinary public debts arising out of contract.

It has long been the established policy of the United States not to use its Army and Navy for the collection of ordinary contract debts due to its citizens by other Governments. This Government has not considered the use of force for such a purpose consistent with that respect for the independent sovereignty of other members of the family of nations which is the most important principle of international law and the chief protection of weak nations against the oppression of the strong. It seems to us that the practice is injurious in its general effect upon the relation of nations and upon the welfare of weak and disordered States, whose development ought to be encouraged in the interests of civilization; that it offers frequent temptation to bullying and oppression and to unnecessary and unjustifiable warfare. It is doubtless true that the non-payment of such debts may be accomplished by such circumstances of fraud and wrong-doing or violation of treaties as to justify the use of force; but we should be glad to see an international consideration of this subject which would discriminate between such cases and the simple non-performance of a contract with a private person, and a resolution in favor of reliance upon peaceful means in cases of the latter class. . . .

5. In the general field of arbitration two lines of advance are clearly indicated. The first is to provide for obligatory arbitration as broad in scope as now appears to be practicable, and the second is to increase the effectiveness of the system, so that nations may more readily have recourse to it voluntarily.

You are familiar with the numerous expressions in favor of the settlement of international disputes by arbitration on the part both of the Congress and of the Executive of the United States.

So many separate treaties of arbitration have been made between individual countries that there is little cause to doubt that the time is now ripe for a decided advance in this direction. . . .

In December, 1904, and January, 1905, my predecessor, Mr. Hay, concluded separate arbitration treaties between the United States and Great Britain, France, Germany, Spain, Portugal, Italy, Switzerland, Austria-Hungary, Sweden and Norway, and Mexico. . . . The first article of each of these treaties was as follows:

Differences which may arise of a legal nature, or relating to the interpretation of treaties existing between the two Contracting Parties, and which it may not have been possible to settle by diplomacy, shall be referred to the Permanent Court of Arbitration established at The Hague by the Convention of the 29th July, 1899, provided, nevertheless, that they do not affect the vital interests, the independence, or the honor of the two Contracting States, and do not concern the interests of third Parties.

To this extent you may go in agreeing to a general treaty of arbitration, and to secure such a treaty you should use your best and most earnest efforts. . . .

. . . There can be no doubt that the principal objection to arbitration rests not upon the unwillingness of nations to submit their controversies to impartial arbitration, but upon an apprehension that the arbitration to which they submit may not be impartial. It has been a very general practice for arbitrators to act, not as judges deciding questions of fact and law upon the record before them under a sense of judicial responsibility, but as negotiators effecting settlements of the questions brought before them in accordance with the tradition and usages and subject to all the considerations and influences which affect diplomatic agents. The two methods are radically different, proceed upon different standards of honorable obligation, and frequently lead to widely differing results. It very frequently happens that a nation which would be very willing to submit its differences to an impartial judicial determination is unwilling to subject them to this kind of diplomatic process. If there could be a tribunal which would pass upon questions between nations with the same impartial and impersonal judgment that the Supreme Court of the United States gives to questions arising between citizens of the different States, or between foreign citizens and the citizens of the United States, there can be no doubt that nations would be much more ready to submit their controversies to its decision than they are now to take the chances of arbitration. It should be your effort to bring about in the Second Conference a development of The Hague Tribunal into a permanent tribunal composed of judges who are judicial officers and nothing else, who are paid adequate salaries, who have no other occupation, and who will devote their entire time to the trial and decision of international causes by judicial methods and under a sense of judicial responsibility. These judges should be so selected from the different countries that the different systems of law and procedure and the principal languages shall be fairly represented. The court should be made of such dignity, consideration and rank that the best and ablest jurist will accept appointment to it, and that the whole world will have absolute confidence in its judgments. . . .

6. You will maintain the traditional policy of the United States regarding the immunity of private property of belligerents at sea. . . .

7. Since the code of rules for the government of military operations on land was adopted by the First Peace Conference there have been occasions for its application under very severe conditions, notably in the South African war and the war between Japan and Russia. Doubtless the Powers involved in those conflicts have had occasion to observe many particulars in which useful additions or improvements might be made. You will consider their suggestions with a view to

reducing, so far as is practicable, the evils of war and protecting the rights of neutrals. . . .

8. The clause of the program relating to the rights and duties of neutrals is of very great importance and in itself would furnish matter for useful discussion sufficient to occupy the time and justify the labors of the Conference.

The various subjects which the Conference may be called upon to consider are likely to bring out proposals which should be considered in their relation to each other, as standing in the following order of substantial importance:

(1) Provisions tending to prevent disagreements between nations.

(2) Provisions tending to dispose of disagreements without war.

(3) Provisions tending to preserve the rights and interests of neutrals.

(4) Provisions tending to mitigate the evils of war to belligerents.

The relative importance of these classes of provisions should always be kept in mind. No rules should be adopted for the purpose of mitigating the evils of war to belligerents which will tend strongly to destroy the rights of neutrals, and no rules should be adopted regarding the rights of neutrals which will tend strongly to bring about war. It is of the highest importance that not only the rights, but the duties of neutrals shall be most clearly and distinctly defined and understood, not only because the evils which belligerent nations bring upon themselves ought not to be allowed to spread to their peaceful neighbors and inflict unnecessary injury upon the rest of mankind, but because misunderstandings regarding the rights and duties of neutrals constantly tend to involve them in controversy with one or the other belligerent.

For both of these reasons, special consideration should be given to an agreement upon what shall be deemed to constitute contraband of war. . . . You should do all in your power to bring about an agreement upon what is to constitute contraband; and it is very desirable that the list should be limited as narrowly as possible. . . .

Following the precedent established by the commission to the First Conference, all your reports and communications to this Government will be made to the Department of State for proper consideration and eventual preservation in the archives. The records of your commission will be kept by your secretary, Mr. Chandler Hale.

Should you be in doubt at any time regarding the meaning or effect of these instructions, or should you consider at any time that there is occasion for special instructions, you will communicate freely, with the Department of State by telegraph. It is the President's earnest wish that you may contribute materially to the effective work of the Conference and that its deliberations may result in making national justice more certain and international peace more secure.

I am, gentlemen, your obedient servant,

ELIHU ROOT.

Instructions to the American Delegates to The Hague Conferences [*World Peace Foundation Pamphlet Series*, Vol. III, No. 4], 13–27 *passim*.

———◆———

52. Results of the Hague Convention (1914)

BY DENYS P. MYERS

Myers was Secretary of the World Peace Foundation, and possesses an exceptionally broad fund of information on matters related to the promotion of international peace.—Bibliography as in No. 51 above.

THE greater bulk of the international statute law written at The Hague has dealt with the prospect of war or its conduct. This is not surprising, since that abnormal condition of the modern state must, by reason of its abnormality, be more clearly limited and defined than the condition of peace, in which problems are far more diverse and usually not of equally critical character. The Third Conference—if it takes place under conditions similar to its predecessors and is not superseded by a closer international federative body—will inevitably make additions to the statute law of war, and for the first time will probably take long steps toward codifying the regulation of peaceful relations between nations.

It is the Hague Convention for the Pacific Settlement of International Disputes which has been most in the public eye and by which the work at The Hague has been publicly judged. This Convention consists of four constructive parts relating to the maintenance of general peace, good offices and mediation, international commissions of inquiry, and international arbitration. The extent to which these methods have been used is the test of the Convention. The first part is declaratory that "the contracting powers agree to use their best efforts to insure the pacific settlement of international differences." The part referring to good offices and mediation relates to the proffering of assistance by a third party respecting differences between two states. It is provided that "the exercise of this right can never be regarded by either of the parties in dispute as an unfriendly act." The provisions of this part have found their application since 1899 in many instances of international strained feeling. The mediation of the United States in Central and South America has several times resulted in smoothing over serious difficulties; and at a more recent period the European powers were acting as mediators under this convention throughout almost the whole course of the Turko-Italian War and throughout all of the Turko-Balkan and Inter-Balkan conflicts. It is generally accepted in diplomatic circles that this mediation facilitated peace negotiations and hastened their conclusion. The success of mediation by Brazil, Argentina, and Chile in the Mexican difficulty in the spring of 1914, saving the United States from a threatened war, is perhaps in itself a complete justification of this part of the Convention. The European war came about only after the failure of several mediation proposals and had hardly begun before President Wilson had tendered his good offices.

The part referring to international commissions of inquiry was intended to set up machinery "to facilitate a solution of disputes by elucidating the facts by means of an impartial and conscientious investigation." It is not intended to pass on the quality of facts and actions, but simply to determine what actually occurred. Twice this machinery has been availed of, both times successfully. The cases are tabulated in an accompanying table [not reprinted here], the historical details being as follows:

1. The Russian fleet, Admiral Rozhdestvensky, on the way to the Far East, suspected the presence of Japanese war vessels in the North Sea and on October 22, 1904, fired by mistake on the English fleet of Hull trawler fishermen. Two men were killed, six wounded, the *Crane* sunk and five trawlers damaged. On November 25, 1904, it was agreed to refer the incident to a commission for report. The commission met at Paris and in February, 1905, the report was made. As

a result of the facts established by it, Russia voluntarily paid to Great Britain about $300,000 as damages.

2. On January 25, 1912, during the Turko-Italian War, the French steamer *Tavignano* was seized by the Italian torpedo boat *Fulmine* in the roads of Raz Zira. On the same day and in the same roads the Italian torpedo boat *Canopo* fired on the Tunisian mahones *Kamouna* and *Gaulois*. Accounts of the circumstances surrounding these incidents were so at variance that France and Italy could reach no decision upon them and by agreement of April 15, 1912, the incidents were referred to a commission for investigation and report. The commission reported on July 23, 1912, and the report was accepted. . . .

The part of the Convention referring to international arbitration is the one most generally known. It provides for arbitration at The Hague, establishes technical rules therefor, provides a bureau corresponding to the familiar office of clerk of court, and lays down general rules for the selection of judges. Choice of arbitrators is now rather clumsy, and the American project for a Judicial Arbitral Court brought up at the Second Conference was designed to remedy this by providing a court holding regular sessions. At present "each contracting power selects four persons at the most, of known competency in questions of international law, of the highest moral reputation, and disposed to accept the duties of arbitrator." These persons form the so-called Permanent Court, in reality a panel of judges. When states have a question to arbitrate the arbitrators are chosen from the list of this panel, three or five members being named by a method previously agreed upon. One is designated president, and the court so constituted hears the case and renders the decision. The court was declared formed by a note of the Dutch Minister of Foreign Affairs of April 9, 1901, a little more than thirteen years ago. From that date to May 22, 1902, it awaited business. From then until the present time business has always been pending before the court in some stage, except the period from August 8, 1905, to March 14, 1908.

An accompanying table [not reprinted here], shows the details of the cases heard by the court, but as that table is official it does not indicate the results. It is therefore of interest to state the character of the awards:

1. United States *vs.* Mexico regarding Pius funds of the Californias; decision rendered, October 14, 1902; award of $1,420,682.67 (Mexican) to United States.

2. Germany, Great Britain and Italy *vs.* Venezuela (Belgium, Spain, United States, France, Mexico, Netherlands, and Sweden and Norway associated with defendant) regarding right of preference claimed by blockading powers; decision rendered, February 22, 1904; award favored plaintiffs' right of preference for payment of claims as being blockading powers.

3. Germany, France and Great Britain *vs.* Japan regarding perpetual leases in Japan; decision rendered, May 22, 1905; favorable to plaintiffs, who secured exemption from taxation of structures on perpetually leased land.

4. France *vs.* Great Britain regarding dhows of Mascat; decision rendered, August 8, 1905; held that only Mascat natives enjoying French protection by treaty were entitled to fly the French flag.

5. Germany *vs.* France regarding deserters of Casablanca; decision rendered, May 22, 1909; held, in detail, that German consular officers erroneously aided deserters from the French Foreign Legion and that French military authorities erroneously failed to respect the protection granted to the deserters.

6. Norway *vs.* Sweden regarding maritime frontier; decision rendered, October 23, 1909; boundary line traced by the Court.

7. United States *vs.* Great Britain regarding North Atlantic Coast fisheries; decision rendered, September 7, 1910, decision detailed, equitably apportioning rights of parties under treaty of 1818.

8. United States *vs.* Venezuela regarding claims of the Orinoco Company; decision rendered, October 25, 1910; held that the awards against Venezuela by an umpire were void, that the claims were founded, and, in addition to the sums allowed by the earlier award, allowed the United States sums of $19,200, $1,053, $28,845.20 and $769.22 on the four points reviewed, with interest at 3 per cent.

9. France *vs.* Great Britain regarding the arrest and restitution of Savarkar; decision rendered, February 24, 1911; held that the British Government was not required to restore Savarkar to the French Government, to whose jurisdiction he had escaped from imprisonment on a British ship in a French harbor.

10. Italy *vs.* Peru regarding the claim of Canevaro Brothers;

decision rendered, May 3, 1912; held that Peru should pay the Canevaros £39,811 8s. 1d. in Peruvian bonds on the claim and £9,388 17s. 1d. in gold as interest from January 1, 1889, to July 31, 1912.

11. Russia vs. Turkey regarding arrears of interest claimed for Russian indemnitaries for damages sustained during the war of 1877; decision rendered, November 11, 1912; held that Turkey was not required to pay Russia damages for failing to pay interest on the Russian claims.

12. France vs. Italy regarding seizure of the *Manouba;* decision rendered, May 6, 1913; award sustained Italian right of temporary seizure of ship and arrest of Turkish (belligerent) passengers and awarded France 4,000 francs for losses and damages proved.

13. France vs. Italy regarding seizure of the *Carthage;* decision rendered, May 6, 1913; award denied belligerent's (Italy's) right to seize a mail steamer temporarily and awarded France 160,000 francs for losses and damages proved.

14. France vs. Italy regarding seizure of the *Tavignano* and cannon shots fired at the Tunisian mahones *Kamouna* and *Gaulois;* litigants agreed after court convened to settle affairs directly.

15. Netherlands vs. Portugal regarding the Dutch-Portuguese frontiers in the island of Timor; decision rendered, August, 1914; award favored the contention of the Netherlands.

16. Spain, France, and Great Britain vs. Portugal regarding seizure of religious property in Portugal; decision pending.

17. Italy vs. Austria-Hungary regarding responsibility for loss of two fishing vessels by Austro-Hungarian submarine automatic contact mines defective in mechanism; submission agreed upon.

Denys P. Myers, *The Record of The Hague* [*World Peace Foundation Pamphlet Series*], Vol. IV, No. 6, Part III], 6–10.

53.   A League to Enforce Peace (1915)

BY PRESIDENT A. LAWRENCE LOWELL

Lowell, after service as Professor of Government at Harvard, was elected President of the University in 1909. He is an authority of international standing in his field. See also Nos. 201–204.—Bibliography as in No. 51 above.

IN spite of its ominous sound, the suggestion of a league of nations to enforce peace has no connection with any effort to stop the present war. It is aimed solely at preventing future conflicts after the terrific struggle now raging has come to an end; and yet this is not a bad time for people in private life to bring forward proposals of such a nature. Owing to the vast number of soldiers under arms, to the proportion of men and women in the warring countries who suffer acutely, to the extent of the devastation and misery, it is probable that, whatever the result may be, the people of all nations will be more anxious to prevent the outbreak of another war than ever before in the history of the world. The time is not yet ripe for governments to take action, but it is ripe for public discussion of practicable means to reduce the danger of future breaches of international peace.

The nations of the world to-day are in much the position of frontier settlements in America half a century ago, before orderly government was set up. The men there were in the main well disposed, but in the absence of an authority that could enforce order each man, feeling no other security from attack, carried arms which he was prepared to use if danger threatened. The first step, when affrays became unbearable, was the formation of a vigilance committee, supported by the enrollment of all good citizens, to prevent men from shooting one another and to punish offenders. People did not wait for a gradual improvement by the preaching of higher ethics and a better civilization. They felt that violence must be met by force, and, when the show of force was strong enough, violence ceased. In time the vigilance committee was replaced by the policeman and by the sheriff with the *posse comitatus*. The policeman and the sheriff maintain order because they have the bulk of the community behind them, and no country has yet reached, or is likely for an indefinite period to reach, such a state of civilization that it can wholly dispense with the police.

Treaties for the arbitration of international disputes are good. They have proved an effective method of settling questions that would otherwise have bred ill-feeling without directly causing war; but when passion runs high, and deep-rooted interests or sentiments are at stake, there is need of the sheriff with his *posse* to enforce the obligation. There are, no doubt, differences in the conception of justice and right, divergencies of civilization, so profound that people will fight over them, and face even the prospect of disaster in war rather than submit. Yet even in such cases it is worth while to postpone the conflict, to have a public discussion of the question at issue before an impartial tribunal, and thus give to the people of the countries involved a chance to consider, before hostilities begin, whether the risk and suffering of war is really worth while. No sensible man expects to abolish wars altogether, but we ought to seek to reduce the probability of war as much as possible. It is on these grounds that the suggestion has been put forth of a league of nations to enforce peace.

Without attempting to cover details of operation, which are, indeed, of vital importance and will require careful study by experts in international law and diplomacy, the proposal contains four points stated as general objects. The first is that before resorting to arms the members of the league shall submit disputes with one another, if justiciable, to an international tribunal; second, that in like manner they shall submit non-justiciable questions (that is such as cannot be decided on the basis of strict international law) to an international council of conciliation, which shall recommend a fair and amicable solution; third, that if any member of the league wages war against another before submitting the question in dispute to the tribunal or council, all the other members shall jointly use forthwith both their economic and military forces against the state that so breaks the peace; and, fourth, that the signatory powers shall endeavor to codify and improve the rules of international law.

The kernel of the proposal, the feature in which it differs from other plans, lies in the third point, obliging all the members of the league to declare war on any member violating the pact of peace. This is the provision that provokes both adherence and opposition; and at first it certainly gives one a shock that a people should be asked to pledge itself to go to war over a quarrel which is not of its making, in which it has no interest, and in which it may believe that substantial justice lies on the other side. If, indeed, the nations of the earth could maintain complete isolation, could pursue each its own destiny without regard to the rest, if they were not affected by a war between two others or liable to be drawn into it; if, in short, there were no overwhelming common interest in securing universal peace, the provision would be intolerable. It would be as bad as the liability of an individual to take part in the *posse comitatus* of a community with which he had nothing in common. But in every civilized country the public force is employed to prevent any man, however just his claim, from vindicating his own right with his own hand instead of going to law; and every citizen is bound, when needed, to assist in preventing him, because that is the only way to restrain private war, and the maintenance of order is of paramount importance for every one. Surely the family of nations has a like interest in restraining war between states. . . .

What is true of this country is true of others. To agree to abide by the result of an arbitration, on every non-justiciable question of every nature whatsoever, on pain of compulsion in any form by the whole world, would involve a greater cession of sovereignty than nations would now be willing to concede. This appears, indeed, perfectly clearly from the discussions at the Hague Conference of 1907. But to exclude differences that do not turn on questions of international law from the cases where a state must present the matter to a tribunal or council of conciliation before beginning hostilities, would leave very little check upon the outbreak of war. Almost every conflict between European nations for more than half a century has been based upon some dissension which could not be decided by strict rules of law, and in which a violation of international law or of treaty rights has usually not even been used as an excuse. . . .

No one will claim that a league to enforce peace, such as is proposed, would wholly prevent war, but it would greatly reduce the probability of hostilities. It would take away the advantage of surprise, of catching the enemy unprepared for a sudden attack. It would give a chance for public opinion on the nature of the controversy to be formed throughout the world and in the militant country. The latter is of great importance, for the moment war is declared argument about its merits is at once stifled. Passion runs too high for calm debate, and patriotism forces people to support their government. But a trial before an international tribunal would give time for discussion while emotion is not yet highly inflamed. Men opposed to war would be able to urge its injustice, to ask whether, after all, the object is worth sacrifice, and they would get a hearing from their fellow citizens which they cannot get after war begins. The mere delay, the interval for consideration, would be an immense gain for the prospect of a peaceful settlement. . . .

A suggestion more commonly made is that the members of the league of nations, instead of pledging themselves to use their military forces forthwith against any of their number that commits a breach of the peace, should agree to hold at once a conference, and take such measures—diplomatic, economic, or military—as may be necessary to prevent war. The objection to this is that it weakens very seriously the sanction. Conferences are apt to shrink from decisive action. . . .

A conference is an excellent thing. The proposal of a league to enforce peace by no means excludes it; but the important matter, the effective principle, is that every member of the league should know that whether a conference meets or not, or whatever action it may take or fail to take, all the members of the league have pledged themselves to declare war forthwith on any member that commits a breach of the peace before submitting its case to the international tribunal or council of conciliation. Such a pledge, and such a pledge alone, can have the strong deterrent influence, and thus furnish the sanction, that is needed. Of course the pledge may not be kept. Like other treaties it may be broken by the parties to it. Nations are composed of human beings with human weaknesses, and one of these is a disinclination to perform an agreement when it involves a sacrifice. Nevertheless, nations, like men, often do have enough sense of honor, of duty, or of ultimate self-interest to carry out their contracts at no little immediate sacrifice. They are certainly more likely to do a thing if they have pledged themselves to it than if they have not; and any nation would be running a terrible risk that went to war in the hope that the other members of the league would break their pledges. . . .

There are many agreements in private business which are not easy to embody in formal contracts; agreements where, as in this case, the execution of the terms calls for immediate action, and where redress after an elaborate trial of the facts affords no real reparation. But, if the object sought is good, men do not condemn it on account of the difficulty in devising provisions that will accomplish the result desired; certainly not until they have tried to devise them. It may, indeed, prove impossible to draft a code of specific acts that will cover the ground; it may be impracticable to draft it so as to avoid issues of fact that can be determined only after a long sifting of evidence which would come too late; but surely that is no reason for failure to make the attempt. We are not making a treaty among nations. We are merely putting forward a suggestion for reducing war which seems to merit consideration.

A second difficulty that will sometimes arise is the rule of conduct to be followed pending the presentation of the question to the international tribunal. The continuance or cessation of the acts complained of may appear to be, and may even be in fact, more important than the final decision. This has been brought to our attention forcibly by the sinking of the *Lusitania*. We should have no objection to submitting to arbitration the question of the right of submarines to torpedo merchant ships without warning, provided Germany abandoned the practice pending the arbitration; and Germany would probably have no objection to submitting the question to a tribunal on the understanding that the practice was to continue until the decision was rendered, because by that time the war would be over. This difficulty is inherent in every plan for the arbitration of international disputes, although more serious in a league whose members bind themselves to prevent by force the outbreak of war. It would be necessary to give the tribunal summary authority to decree a *modus vivendi*, to empower it, like a court of equity, to issue a temporary injunction.

In short, the proposal for a league to enforce peace cannot meet all possible contingencies. It cannot prevent all future wars, nor does any sensible person believe that any plan can do so in the present state of civilization. But it can prevent some wars that would otherwise take place, and, if it does that, it will have done much good.

A. Lawrence Lowell, in *Atlantic Monthly*, September, 1915 (Boston, 1915), 5–18 *passim*.

CHAPTER XI — THE NATIONAL DEFENCE

54. Fortify the Panama Canal (1911)

BY REAR-ADMIRAL A. T. MAHAN

Admiral Mahan (1840–1914) was a naval officer and achieved great distinction as a writer of naval history. His suggestions in his famous books on the influence of sea power upon history, and upon the French Revolution and Empire (1890 and 1892), caused a change in the naval policies of the United States, Great Britain, and Germany.—For the Panama Canal, see No. 39 above.

IN approaching the question of fortifying the Panama Canal, it is well to remember at once that the Canal Zone, with the qualified exceptions of the cities of Colon and Panama, is United States territory. In the treaty of cession there is a clause providing for the extradition of offenders between the Zone and the Republic of Panama. Being, therefore, territory rather than property, to ask guarantees of neutrality from foreign states is to constitute over ourselves a kind of protectorate. It would also contravene our traditional policies, by inviting the participation of non-American states in the assuring of American conditions; a lapse the more marked when it is remembered that the Zone has become ours by acquisition from another American commonwealth. How grievously the nation resented co-partnership in the affairs of the Isthmus is testified by the whole history of the Clayton-Bulwer Treaty; a resentment which verged so closely on bitterness during the final twenty years of the discussion as to be a warning against any reconstitution of similar conditions. We should have perpetual discussions with foreign nations about American affairs; such as have enlivened and not sweetened much of Great Britain's occupancy of Egypt.

It is also to be remembered that, besides being American soil, the Panama Canal Zone cannot be looked upon as an isolated position such as the Philippines. The loss of the Philippines by war, as a material result, would be to us like the loss of a little finger, perhaps of a single joint of it. The Philippines to us are less a property than a charge. The Canal Zone, on the contrary, must be regarded in its geographical and military relations—the two adjectives are in this connection almost identical—to the United States as a whole and to other specific American stations. . . .

Upon the general question of seacoast fortification, as distinct from the special question of fortifying the Panama Canal, the reasons why fortification is an essential complement of a navy are twofold. Seacoast fortification supplies a navy with fortified bases, strictly analogous to the fortresses, or temporarily fortified positions, which are the home or the advanced bases of an army in campaign. To argue the advantage—nay, the need—of these would be to discuss military art from its foundation. It is sufficient to say that all military history testifies to it. One of the most distinguished of the opponents of the first Napoleon said: "An army which has to insure the protection of unfortified bases is crippled in all its movements." In a naval campaign the navy is the mobile army—in the field. It, too, requires bases concerning the security of which it need feel no apprehension.

The second office of seacoast fortification is that of simple protection. It is gravely argued that, because a recent international stipulation provides that unfortified seaports shall not be bombarded, therefore protection is unnecessary and even inexpedient. . . . An undefended neutrality of the Canal Zone would forbid an enemy's bombarding; but it would not deter his occupation, if at war with the United States, because the position is too valuable not to be secured, if possible.

To apply these general considerations to the specific case of the Panama Canal. What will be the value of the Canal to the United States, and, incidentally, to the United States Navy? Primarily, and above all, it will be the most important link in the line of communications between our Atlantic and Pacific coasts. There is throughout the whole length and extension of our seacoast, from Maine to Puget Sound, no single position or reach of water comparable to Panama in this respect. Communications, the free access of an army to its source of supplies,—or rather the free passage of supplies to it,—and the ability of one part of the army to reach the other for material support, or of the whole to move to any particular point of a theatre of war—communications, in this sense, are the most important factor in war. Communications dominate war in all its aspects. On a battle-field the connection of the several divisions of an army must be such that an enemy cannot break through. Advancing in campaign, the relations of army corps to each other must be such that they can unite before the enemy attacks either in force. Concentration, of which we hear so much and so justly, means simply communications so preserved as to enable the whole to live and the parts to unite betimes. . . .

The question of fortifying the Canal, therefore, is the question of preserving an essential line of naval communications. But, it will be replied, you beg the question; the navy will protect its own communications, the Canal not least. Will, then, the navy be tied to the Canal, or will it protect it by a big detachment, by dividing its numbers while the bulk of the fleet goes to some other assigned duty? Yes, it is replied, the money spent for fortifications, which are immobile, will be given to ships, which, though mobile, will remain for defence of the Canal and yet, if required, can go to reinforce the fleet. Just so; if required, they will go away. One advantage of fortifications is that, being established in moments of calm consideration, they cannot be moved in moments of real or panicky pressure. . . .

It is often argued that, because an enemy intending the invasion of a country situated as the United States is must primarily possess a competent navy, therefore, the best defence against invasion on either large or small scale is a mobile navy. This is perfectly true, and applies with equal or greater force to the maintenance of oversea dependencies, such as Hawaii, Guantánamo and the Canal Zone. A navy at least equal to the enemy's is essential to their preservation, but it does not follow that the navy must be immediately present at either or all. A navy does not protect by local presence, but by action upon the lines of communication; that is, upon the sea. Hence fallacy enters with the further assertion that all money spent on fortifications had better be spent on ships. The question is one of proportion. Coast fortification may be pushed, at times has been pushed, to an extravagant extent. But for the defence of points, the tenure of which is essential to military operations,—the operations of a fleet,—fixed works are better than floating because they secure the same aggregate gun defence at much less cost; or, if you prefer it so stated, much greater defensive strength for the same cost. In addition to the fact that they cannot be moved under popular apprehension,—such as kept the Flying Squadron in Hampton Roads during the war with Spain, a measure which would have cost the country dear with a more active enemy,—guns in forts cost far less, under normal conditions, than those in ships. Forts need no floating power, no motive machinery, no long storage of fuel. Moreover, they are less vulnerable; for the solidity of the ground permits the accumulation of armor or other protective covering, and they have not to dread the submarine or the floating-mine.

Guns on ships are also necessarily massed within the length of the ship, presenting a concentrated target, whereas on shore they may be dispersed indefinitely, and largely concealed, which is the modern practice. For such reasons, while vessels have usually been able to run by forts through an *unobstructed* channel, the same amount of artillery in ships has rarely been able to stand up against forts. Even with superior fire, ships have been able to dominate land-works only under peculiar conditions, which the all-big-gun ship does not possess; the conditions of very rapid fire from very numerous pieces at very close range. No one is going to take a ten-million-dollar battleship over an unexplored mine-field to get near the same number of guns ashore; nor will it be attempted to engage at a distance, because the ship is so much more open to fatal injury by a chance shot. . . .

Granting, then, that the United States intends to make sure of the use of the Canal in war, fortification will insure that peculiar end more cheaply, with less danger of losing the position, than the same amount of money expended in war-ships, unless there are abnormal peculiarities of the ground of which I not have heard. It is to be taken for granted that the Board of Fortification, checked as it should be by a naval representation, will not pile Ossa on Pelion in needless multiplication of defences, but will have a due regard to the fundamental fact that the defences exist for the Canal, and not the Canal for the sake of being defended. That is, it will be remembered that from the broad military point of view, which includes the entire military establishment of the country as a composite whole—army, navy, coast defence—the value of the Canal is not its impregnability as a position, but its usefulness to the navy as the offensive defender of the whole national coast-line—Atlantic, Gulf and Pacific.

A. T. Mahan, in *North American Review* (New York, 1911), CXCIII, 331–336.

55. The Light Cavalry of the Seas (1914)

BY LIEUTENANT-COMMANDER D. PRATT MANNIX

Lieutenant-Commander Mannix (still serving, 1928, with a destroyer squadron) is distinguished as the first American to duplicate Leander's historic feat of swimming the Hellespont.—See also, on the convoy work of destroyers in the World War, No. 189 below.

THE torpedo flotilla of the Atlantic fleet as now organized consists of twenty-five destroyers divided into five divisions of five boats each. Their duties are almost precisely the same as those performed by the cavalry of a land army. Just as the mounted men are the "eyes of the army" so are the destroyers the "eyes of the fleet."

The general characteristics of these vessels are as follows: length, 300 feet; beam, 26 feet; displacement, 850 tons. They draw about ten feet of water, and each boat carries four officers and a hundred men. Their armament consists of three double torpedo tubes and five semi-automatic three-inch guns. Armor protection they have none, depending on their high speed (about thirty knots or thirty-four statute miles an hour) and the fact that most of their work is done at night.

As the name implies, torpedo-boat destroyers were originally built to combat the smaller torpedo-boat, which had become such a serious menace to the battle-ships and large cruisers that search-lights and rapid-fire guns could not be depended upon for protection. Gradually, however, the duties of the destroyer were extended until they included all that was formerly done by the torpedo-boat and much besides. The mere fact that a modern destroyer is three or four times as large as one of the earlier boats renders it so much more seaworthy and capable of carrying so much more fuel that the radius of action of torpedo-craft has been enormously increased, and they have become more and more dangerous to an enemy's fleet.

The duties of the modern flotilla may be tabulated in this way:

(1) Scouting. This comprises locating and reporting the position of the enemy and keeping in touch with him as long as may be necessary.

(2) Protection of one's own fleet from night attacks of the enemy's

destroyers. This includes not only locating and reporting the position of the hostile torpedo-craft, but, if necessary, attacking them with your guns and sinking or driving them away before they can force home an attack against your battle-ships.

(3) Attacking the battle-ships of the enemy with your torpedoes. This is, of course, the paramount duty of every vessel in the flotilla.

(4) In addition to the above "regular" duties, destroyers are frequently used in what might be called "gunboat work"; patrolling the enemy's coast; running up his rivers where the big ships cannot go; overtaking and capturing his merchant-vessels and firing on troops and field-batteries ashore. In the recent Turco-Italian War, although the Turkish navy remained at anchor most of the time, the Italian destroyers were constantly engaged, blockading, landing troops, and even attacking fortified towns.

In scouting, many different systems may be used. Most of these are confidential and cannot be divulged, but a general idea of the problem that confronts the flotilla may readily be given. Suppose a hostile fleet is making preparations to leave Europe, with the evident intention of attacking some point on our coast-line, or, as would be more probable, of seizing some island in the West Indies, establishing a base there, and directing operations against either the Panama Canal or the mainland. As long as that fleet is in or near Europe we can follow its movements from day to day. That is what our diplomatic agents and secret-service men are for, and they would cable, in cipher of course, detailed reports, not only of the fleet's location but of the number and types of vessels comprising it, the amount of ammunition and provisions on board, the state of discipline of the crews, and everything that could possibly be of assistance to us in preparing to defend ourselves.

Now, suppose the hostile fleet weigh their anchors, and, steaming past the rock of Gibraltar, head out to sea. In a few hours they are out of sight; they can steer any course they wish and travel at any rate of speed up to their maximum. It will not be many days before the people of our country will be asking themselves: "Where are they? When will they appear off our coasts, and what will be their first point of attack?"

We have certain facts to help us. No modern ship can keep the seas for months at a time as did the fleets of a hundred years ago.

They must coal. We know the coal capacity and also, roughly, the coal-consumption at various speeds of all foreign war-ships just as they know ours. Hence we are certain that after a comparatively short time at sea the enemy must put in somewhere to fill his bunkers. If, however, they take their colliers with them, as a large fleet would undoubtedly do, even this becomes uncertain, as it is not impossible, in smooth weather, to coal at sea. Should such a force evade our battle-ships and effect a landing either in the West Indies or on the mainland they might do untold damage before they were overcome and their ships destroyed. Most of the school histories carefully slur over the fact that a few thousand British soldiers and sailors, under General Ross and Admiral Cockburn, marched to Washington, burned the national capitol, and escaped to their ships with trifling losses.

It is the destroyers' duty to locate the enemy as soon as possible and notify our fleet of dreadnaughts so that they can attack before he succeeds in landing his forces. His position, within certain wide limits of latitude and longitude, can generally be established by reports from merchant-ships who have seen him and ports where he has stopped for coal or repairs. This gives us a "scouting area," which the flotilla must carefully patrol by day and night.

The simplest type of such a patrol is to form the boats in a line with wide intervals between them, just as a skirmish-line is formed ashore. These intervals should be as large as possible, but not so great that an enemy's vessel could slip through without being seen by at least one of the destroyers. On a clear day they might be twenty miles apart; a division of five could then cover a hundred miles of the ocean.

The boats being in position, at a certain hour previously designated they start steaming toward the enemy, all making exactly the same speed in order to keep their proper station or "dress" in the scouting-line. Lookouts on the bridges carefully watch for any sign of smoke on the horizon, which is usually the first indication of the presence of a stranger. Anything seen must immediately be investigated, and, if necessary, reported by wireless to the battle-ships either directly or, if they be far distant, through a chain of vessels which relay the message along until it reaches the admiral. Should the stranger be harmless he is allowed to proceed, but if he prove to be one of the enemy's scouts, his location is at once sent broadcast by the wireless of the destroyer discovering him, and every effort is made to find the hostile battle-ships, which are probably not far from their scout. When contact is made with the big ships a general wireless call is sent out for all destroyers to assemble in that vicinity. Here they wait, taking advantage of their superior speed to keep just outside the range of the big guns, until night falls, when they may either attack or continue "tracking" the enemy, being careful not to lose touch for a moment and sending repeated reports to their admiral of what he is doing.

Of course, the hostile fleet will make every effort to keep these reports from getting through by "interfering" with their own wireless, and the best method of avoiding this interference is being constantly studied by all navies.

D. Pratt Mannix, *The Light Cavalry of the Seas* in *Scribner's*, May, 1914 (New York), 573–583.

———————◆———————

56. Mobilization "Blunders" (1916)

FROM THE LITERARY DIGEST

This article attempts to reflect newspaper opinion of the National Guard mobilization for Mexican border service. Parenthetical abbreviations following newspaper names indicate editorial adherence to one or another of the leading political faiths. —Bibliography as in No. 40 above; see also Roger Batchelder, *Watching and Waiting on the Border*.

IT is within "neither the possibilities nor the space of one newspaper," remarks the Buffalo *News* (Rep.), to record the deficiencies that followed the President's call of the National Guard for service on the Mexican border. "Regiments with uniforms for only a third of their membership, armories without reserve supplies of any kind, batteries without guns, troops without horses, rifles but no cartridges, food but no cooking outfits, tents but no blankets"; "if there had been any worse way to handle the mobilization of the National Guard," concludes the Newark *Star-Eagle* (Ind.); " or any better way to expose the national unfitness for war, the people in authority would have hastened, one suspects, to adopt it." . . .

"On every side," according to the Boston *Transcript* (Rep.), "appear evidences of our unpreparedness that prove every charge of incompetency brought against the executive and legislative branches of the Government, which have ignored the lessons of the European War." The mobilization was "far too slow and awkward," in the opinion of the New York *Tribune* (Rep.). The spirit and the collective reliability of the men are acknowledged by the Boston *News Bureau* (Ind.), as by many another critic, "but the machine, when tested, worked badly."

"The physical discomforts visited on the men in delays, the lack of supplies, including food, and in inadequate accommodations are the fruits. State mobilizing-points were proved not equal to the unloading strain. The sudden call upon railroad facilities, in the midst of a busy traffic season, could not by any skill be perfectly met.

"But there are some still bigger symptoms. Two in particular point their own moral. One is the demonstration that neither an army nor the means of equipping and moving it can be improvised. The other is that a nation, for proper defense, needs a unified national control of its forces." . . .

But when we turn from the general criticism of the National Guard mobilization to the concrete instances of inefficiency, we find the critics promptly answered and their allegations circumstantially denied. Take the matter of hardships *en-route* to Mexico. "Our boys may never get into a battle," remarked the Philadelphia *Press* (Rep.), "but they will have a story of hardship, discomfort, and even suffering to relate on their return because of the negligent and unscientific method of their transportation." In the first place, as the Buffalo *News* (Rep.) puts it, we "sent 2,000 of our best young men away in the past month in cars that the European immigrants would decline with scorn." And then the "failure of the authorities to provide ample food for the militiamen on their long trip to the Mexican border" was characterized as "disgraceful" by the Brooklyn *Standard Union* (Rep.). This refers to the stories of hungry Guardsmen raiding lunch-rooms and provision shops in Erie, Cleveland, and Kansas City. The Philadelphia *Record* (Dem.) suspects there is political animus in these stories and the charges founded on them. It calls attention to a letter sent to the Associated Press by the men of the 69th New York, one of the "starving regiments," stating that "our meals are being served to us regularly and in a sufficient quantity to satisfy our appetites." A General Staff officer in Washington was quoted by the New York *Tribune* as saying:

"The Guardsmen have got to learn to take care of themselves. . . . Any units that have run short of food on the five-day trip to the border have themselves to blame, as their supply was sufficient for ten days.

"As for the complaint that men had to travel in day coaches, we had to take what we could get at the outset. Troops were needed to stop the gaps in our border patrol,—and we couldn't get enough tourist sleepers."

The Boston *Transcript* (Rep.) and the Minneapolis *Tribune* point to the great advance made in camp sanitation since the days of the Chickamauga camp. The New Orleans *Times-Picayune* (Dem.) is so well satisfied as to declare that "never in this country's history was an army of citizen soldiers better looked after and cared for." Senator Wadsworth, though a Republican, declared on the floor of the Senate his belief that "the mobilization was performed as satisfactorily as could have been expected." "The task was performed with remarkable skill," in the Washington *Post's* (Ind.) opinion; "rather creditably on the whole," says the Dallas *News* (Dem.), nearer the border. In its Washington correspondence, the Chicago *Daily News* (Ind.) quotes Major Douglas MacArthur as saying enthusiastically, "When one considers the number of men moved and the distances they were moved, the recent mobilization of the militia on the Mexican border was the best job of its kind done by any country." This demonstration of the usefulness of the State militia as the nation's second line of defense gives the hitherto skeptical St. Louis *Post Dispatch* (Ind.) "more assurance than discouragement." It has, the New York *Times* thinks, "already decreased the prejudice against the Federalization plan."

Staff article in *Literary Digest*, August 5, 1916 (New York), 287–289.

57. "Stand by to Ram!" (1922)

BY LIEUTENANT-COMMANDER FITZHUGH GREEN (1926)

Green, no longer in active naval service, has devoted himself to Arctic exploration and to writing, mostly on subjects related to explorers and their work. He was co-author with C. A. Lindbergh of *We* (1928). This account of heroism typifies the infinite variety of situations that may call for action by our defensive forces, even in peace time.

U. S. NAVY GENERAL ORDER NO. 123

The Navy Department takes pleasure in announcing the award of a Medal of Honor to Lieutenant Commander W. A. Edwards, U. S. Navy, for heroism in rescuing 482 men, women and children from the French military transport Vinh-Long, destroyed by fire in the Sea of Marmora, Turkey, on December 16, 1922.

FOR reasons best known to itself the French Government suppressed the true story of the Vinh-Long's calamity. Lately we have been given to understand that "now it can be told."

It is well worth telling. The feat of rescuing a whole shipload of humanity with a frail and tiny torpedo-boat destroyer was an extraordinary one, and the method of rescue was, so far as can be learned, unique in the annals of the sea. Moreover, courage and audacity of the first order were required to carry it out. Surely American boldness at its best is a thrilling thing to see.

The first streaks of dawn on that December morning revealed two vessels in the Sea of Marmora on parallel courses headed for Constantinople. One was the big French transport Vinh-Long, loaded with troops and their families. The other was the little American destroyer Bainbridge. Three miles of black choppy seas separated the pair.

One of the Vinh-Long's French quartermasters came off his mid watch at 4 A. M. Before turning in he lit a cigarette. From his hammock a few moments later he tossed the smoking butt, he *thought*, to the steel deck beneath him. Instead he tossed it in a spit-kid containing rubbish. How Death must have grinned!

Presently a flicker of flame lighted the small compartment. Men snored on. The flame rose. A puff of breeze carried it toward the bulkhead, where a leaking gasoline drum stood.

Abruptly a second flame flared up: the gasoline. A man aroused and shouted the alarm. But before the jangling firebells could start there came an explosion that shocked all hands and the passengers wide-awake. A tank of hydrogen, meant for a French army dirigible, had gone off right above the burning gasoline.

Terrible fear seized the hearts of those aboard the transport. She carried a cargo of ammunition. Fire could mean only one thing: complete destruction of the ship and of 500 helpless human beings in her. Nothing short of a miracle could save them.

Commander Edwards tells it:

"My officer of the watch had in the meantime sighted a vessel to starboard. While he strove to make her out in the dim early morning light he suddenly saw a flash of fire near her stern. Sensibly he put his helm hard over and sent word to me. This was simple routine of the sea. There was no indication that my big crisis was getting close.

"I was sleeping in the emergency cabin opening on the bridge. Glancing out, I saw I had time to throw an old uniform over my pajamas before we came within hail.

"'Away Fire and Rescue Party,' I told the watch officer. He stepped to the general alarm. Gongs echoed between our decks. Our boatswain's mate took up the word. As we swung to for me to hail the Frenchmen, I saw my men lined up ready to man our small dories with pumps, axes, pulmotors and other rescue apparatus.

"'Very smart outfit,' I thought. 'Now we'll see what we can do with it.' It never occurred to me that when the end came my boats would scarcely count.

"I jammed my megaphone to my lips and let go with a good loud yell:

"'Ship ahoy! Can we be of assistance?

"I saw the French captain at the end of his bridge ready to answer me. Smoke billowed out of his after hatch. Hose played on the flames. Orders were being shouted. A confused mass of sailors and soldiers, women and children, were visible roaming anxiously about the decks. Boats were being got ready for lowering.

"He raised his megaphone. I strained my ears. But his words never came.

"His ship answered for him. Out of her waist rose a wide tongue of yellow flame. With it went a cloud of wreckage. The big after mast sprang skyward as if released by a spring. A terrific roar deafened us. The transport had blown up amidships. This was my first hint of the dreadful experience just ahead.

"At my signal our boats went down. They did not wait for orders to pick up the torn wretches who had been blown into the sea. Also there were those who, maddened by fear, began throwing themselves over the transport's side.

"I did some fast thinking. Remember, it was dark. I hadn't any idea how many people there were aboard the French ship. My complement was less than 100. I knew a destroyer could crowd 300 on her decks. Little did I reckon on the total of nearly 500 human beings I was to be deluged with a few minutes later.

"Just then one of my boats returned with a semihysterical fellow from the burning ship, 'She's loaded with powder!' he literally screamed at me. 'She will blow up in a moment! You will be blown up too!' Another explosion interrupted his frenzy. My worst fears were realized.

"I told my watch officer to have men stand by to flood our magazines, which carried their full allowance of high explosives. One lucky shot from the crazy Vinh-Long and we would start popping the way she was. Moreover, the water was now covered with flaming fuel oil."

Sooner or later every commanding officer finds himself in a position involving the safety of others. In such a jam he must decide what is the best course to take. His decision may mean great peril, even death, to those under him. But his power, like his responsibility, is at sea supreme.

"Of course," says the young commander, "my whole impulse was to do what I could for the poor wretches on the blazing ship before me. But I could not forget that I had nearly a hundred fine young Americans on my own vessel. They were ready to obey my every order. The sight of men dying did not make them flinch. But I confess I flinched inwardly when I thought of asking them to do what now seemed the only right and decent thing for a ship of the United States Navy to do."

It was all a matter of seconds. But Edwards made his decision after real thought. "The greatest good to the greatest number," was the keynote of his next move. He would put his little boat along-side the Vinh-Long, with all her explosives!

"Stand by your lines!" he ordered.

Deck hands spread quickly to the coils of rope that were faked down near chocks on the destroyer's main deck.

Crash—bang! Again on the transport. More screams, and smoke clouds slit by flame. But the Yankee sailors did not falter.

"She's a warm baby, all right!" one lad remarked with a grin. Five minutes later he was under the surgeon's care, his flesh seared by a fragment of hot steel.

A scene more violent than before now ensued. The Vinh-Long's passengers knew that their ship might at any moment be blown to bits beneath their feet. They stampeded to the rail. For a moment it looked as if the Bainbridge would be swamped by the human cata-ract that poured upon her.

But, as before, the drama was harshly interrupted—this time by an explosion so terrific that it nearly threw all hands off their feet. All were temporarily blinded.

How anyone survived that burst, or why both ships were not in-stantly sunk, one cannot say. Indeed, Edwards cannot even remem-ber what occurred in the succeeding moments. All he knows is that when he regained his senses the destroyer was some distance away from the transport and lying at right angles to her. Every mooring line had been severed.

Says the commander: "I glanced at the black mass of humanity huddled near the Vinh-Long's bow. The flames aft were reaching toward them. Minor explosions continued."

"No serious damage aboard—yet, sir," reported the watch officer, saluting. There was an ominous note in his "yet."

Now came the superb feat of the day. The American captain had to act quickly and with success or all was lost. With a daring and resourcefulness worthy of the best traditions of the United States Navy, Edwards threw all hope into a final stroke of seafaring genius.

"Stand by to ram!" he cried. "Check water-tight doors! Flood the forward magazines without orders if necessary! '

He rang up the engine telegraphs: "Full speed ahead." He knew if he could cut deep into the Vinh-Long's hull he would flood her between-decks. This might check the fire. And it would give those still aboard her a chance to escape. Of course, he realized such a move might also be the end of the Bainbridge.

Coolly Edwards had the helmsman put her on a point near the transport's bridge. Perfect seamanship was required or the destroyer would only sink herself. But the knifelike stem crunched into the steel plates and the bold maneuver was successful.

Knowing that every second counted, no effort was made to control the rush to escape from the floating charnel house. Nor did the mob need any urging. Death was at their heels.

All the while the flames came closer. The minor explosions grew more frequent. Suddenly those on the destroyer's bridge became conscious of a lunatic on the forecastle. One could see he was a French officer, despite the shredded condition of his uniform, which clung in rags about him. He sprang into the air and waved his arms at the bridge. He was yelling hoarsely in his own tongue.

Then Edwards got him. He was telling what the smoke and uproar hid: that everyone alive was off the Vinh-Long.

"I nearly yanked our engine telegraphs out by their roots throwing them into reverse," says the commander. "We backed clear of the blazing wreck. Our skins, most of them, were whole, and we were still afloat.

"But our work was not yet done. Aboard us some were dead; others were dying. Anguished screams of those burned were heart-rending.

"Leaving the slowly sinking transport behind us, we put on all speed for Constantinople. A few hours later we sighted the French flagship in the harbor. I had already radioed for medical help."

The first one aboard was the French rear admiral commanding naval forces in the Levant. In Latin fashion he hugged Edwards and kissed him on both cheeks. Charitably he directed that at once all survivors be transferred to his flagship. As there was not an inch of standing room aboard the American destroyer, this was a relief.

In the next breath he began inquiring excitedly for Madame somebody. Edwards couldn't make out the name.

Just then the plump female figure of a middle-aged Frenchwoman emerged from the forward hatch. She wore the jumper and pants of an American bluejacket. All began to chuckle, and Edwards was on the point of calling the French admiral's attention to the grotesque figure.

But at that moment the admiral sprang forward. In two jumps he reached the betrousered lady. With straining arms he embraced her. Tears streamed down his cheeks as he showered her with kisses.

"*It is Madame Grand-Clement, wife of Vice Admiral Grand-Clement, my boss!*" he finally shouted over his shoulder.

Fitzhugh Green, in *Collier's* (New York, 1926), LXXVIII, No. 19, 19 ss.

------◆------

58. Peace-Time Work of the Army (1923)

BY SECRETARY JOHN W. WEEKS

Weeks (1860–1926), a Massachusetts banker, was appointed Secretary of War by President Harding in 1921; he held the same position in the Coolidge Cabinet until his resignation in 1925. The emphasis here put upon the non-military work of the Army was doubtless in part intended to counteract the influence of post-war pacifism, which in some quarters favored the reduction of our military forces to almost negligible proportions.

THE construction of the Panama Canal was merely one of a continuous series of projects conducted by the Army engineers for the development of our waterways. Beginning with the construction of the old Chesapeake and Ohio Canal and the Erie Canal, they have continued their activities upon practically every navigable waterway in our country, and their work has been of such uniform excellence that there is a general acceptance of the belief that our governmental engineering projects are unexcelled by any other country on earth. . . .

There are however many other fields in which the Army has contributed. A former engineer officer is at present at the head of the Chemical Warfare Service of the Army. . . .

Few Americans realize that the deadly mustard gas, as well as some of the chlorine compounds developed by the Army, are being experimented with successfully in the prevention of influenza and other diseases of the respiratory tracts. This discovery grew through the knowledge that during the great influenza epidemics, the employees of some of the war gas factories were practically immune to the disease. Extensive arrangements are made in the laboratories of the Chemical Warfare Service to conduct research into the possibilities for constructive use of other gases and liquids developed for defense. Tear gases have become generally recognized as valuable in the action of police against outlaws and in protection of banks and other buildings against burglars and safe robbers. Investigations of various war gases have led to valuable contributions to the American dye industry, as well as to chemical production generally. . . .

In the pest destruction experiments, the Army Air Service has been called in to investigate means of spraying liquids over the growing crops. The Department of Agriculture are calling for more planes for this purpose than we can possibly provide. Our Air Service is fully occupied with the development of commercial aviation, the protection of forests, and preparation for defense, in addition to activity against pests. In 1922 we were unable to provide planes for forest protection in the State of California, and the California Forester expressed the opinion that this was the direct cause of an increase of 23% in incendiary fires in that year. Air patrols are frequently able to discover new fires which escape the observation of ground observers, and have been the first to report a considerable percentage of destructive fires. The Air Service have also been called upon to experiment in the spraying of fruit trees from the air. There are now even efforts to develop a process of actual seeding from the air. I need not impress upon you the general importance of our Air Service as a defensive proposition. I do wish to impress upon Americans the fact that in preparing for defense, the Air Service are also preparing the way for commercial air development. . . .

I am often challenged in the statement that the Army developed the steel industry. It can be proven. The dominating influences in steel development have been the provision of markets, the adaptation of the use of steel, and the standardization of steel specifications. The Army was the original market for steel products, opened up an ever increasing field for its employment, and led the entire industry in specifications for design. High grade steel dates from the Civil War when the Army demanded superior gun metal. . . .

I have mentioned our work in colonization at the Panama Canal. Colonization is one of the severest tests of the ideals of a nation. As our country grew older this burden was thrust upon it, through acquisition of Alaska, Hawaii, Cuba, Porto Rico, the Philippines, and Guam, as well as the Panama Canal Zone. Our burdens have been successfully carried, and the major part of the task was that of the Army. When gold was discovered in Alaska, it was the Army that opened the harbors, and built the roads and trails leading to the mines. Americans settled this new country, and were protected from lawlessness and mob rule by the Army. . . .

Just as in Alaska, the Army has a record of accomplishment in other possessions. Building up public utilities, eradicating terrible diseases, educating the children, attending even to spiritual needs, creating the institutions of self-government and protecting these from aggression—in all of these has the Army left its seal, which is the seal of Americanism upon our possessions. In the Philippines, where tribes once fought continuously, we have built roads, railroads, schools, and churches, and have done more in twenty years than was done before in centuries, to make the Filipinos a unified people. To the Cuban we brought freedom and civilization. One of the greatest influences for good in Cuba today is the American Ambassador, an American Army officer who gained his experience in the Philippines.

In speaking of our tropical ventures, I cannot overlook the work of Army medical men. The countries to the south of us, as well as tropical countries throughout the world, were once ravaged by yellow fever and malignant malaria. The French enterprise at Panama was completely blocked because 75% of the employees lost their lives from disease within a few months of their arrival. In 1901, a group of medical officers, headed by Dr. Walter Reed of the Army, determined definitely that yellow fever is transmitted by the mosquito. Within a few months of the discovery, Havana was cleared of the disease that had ravaged it for 150 years. One can now live in Panama with as much assurance of health as though one were living in Continental United States. When we took over the administration of Porto Rico, the entire population was enervated by the results of what was then called "tropical anemia." Army officers demonstrated that this disease is a hookworm infection and these people have been redeemed from a plague that would have forever hindered their development. They have also played a considerable part in the elimination of pellagra, and one of them made the first discovery of Malta Fever in this country.

All of this work of the Medical Department had a bearing upon the health of America. It moreover was preparing our officers to administer our war armies without the great disease losses of former wars. During the Civil War, smallpox claimed over 7,000 victims, during the World War only 14. In the Civil War malaria claimed 15,000—in the World War, 25. In the Spanish-American War, 20,000 men suffered from typhoid—in the World War we had 2,000 cases—a contrast between twenty per cent and one-twentieth of one per cent, of the totals engaged in these wars. This marked progress leads us to wonder if there was anything else that our medical men could give to Americans who entered the armies. We find indeed that there was. We are shocked to discover that approximately half of our young men who were examined for service, had physical disabilities of some sort. We should be pleased to realize that after a comparatively short time in service, under the supervision of our physical trainers and our medical men, the recruits were generally developed into fine specimens of American manhood. This is no exaggeration. Because of prevention measures taken against such diseases as typhoid, there is moreover no doubt that the prevalence of these diseases has been greatly decreased throughout our general population. . . .

A most vital element in national defense, more important perhaps than during peace time industry, is the question of transportation. I have called your attention to the work of the Army in building railroads, canals, harbors, and improving waterways generally. The Public Roads Bureau has been given at cost, over a quarter billion dollars worth of material for public road construction. Trucks and tractors and many other manufactured elements are standardized throughout Army organizations, and this process of standardization has been recognized of great value to the industries. One concern reports a 20% gain in sales through adoption of certain features recommended by army equipment experts. The Ordnance Department has periodic conferences with manufacturers relative to such matters. Finally, there is one phase of transportational problems that is even more directly an interest of the Army. The World War proved to be a great drain upon our stock of horses and mules and the standards have become rather depleted. The Army Remount Service have been given leadership in the effort to elevate the standard. With the close coöperation of the Department of Agriculture and civilian horse associations they have established a record of successful breeding that compares favorably with the best European records, and that assures us a timely solution for this vital problem.

We could not afford to maintain a great pioneer organization to perform such functions as I have described alone. Such benefits can come only from some organized and trained public body which produces them as by-products and still performs its primary tasks. The Army is being trained primarily for emergency use. It is not limited to the emergency of war. When the Mississippi overflows its banks, it is the Army that is called upon for protection, supply, and relief. After the San Francisco Fire in 1906, it was the Army that took charge of disorder and administered the emergency relief forces until civilian organization could be formed. In the Galveston flood, the Mount Pelée disaster, during the floods on the Ohio in 1912, and in nearly every grave civil emergency in our history, the Army made similar records of accomplishment for which there are huge files of grateful letters of appreciation. . . .

Many Americans are surprised that the Army is able to accomplish what it does in the way of civic accomplishment. They forget that the War Department is one of the greatest administrative schools in the country. I have looked up the record of former regular officers and I was really amazed at its excellence. There is scarcely a high office under the Government to say nothing of high achievement in private life, that has not been attained to by army officers. Statesmen, lawyers, financiers, authors, even artists of world renown—all had their training in the service of the Regular Army. I might point to a few examples at the present day. The Governor General of the Philippines, our most important foreign possession, the head of the Bureau of the Budget, a new undertaking that is absorbing the minds of our statesmen—the President of the Radio Corporation of America —the Ambassador to Cuba—the Governor of the Panama Canal Zone—the head of the Veterans' Bureau—all of these are posts of predominant importance, and all are held by public servants who have been until recently officers of the Regular Army. . . .

Next to the belief that army officers are incapable of handling big business and finance, which I trust I have counteracted by the few brief proofs to the contrary which I have just offered, there is among our citizens the belief that we pay too much for our army. This belief is fostered by certain pacifist organizations which are continually circulating incorrect and misleading statistics relative to the cost of national defense. Typical of this false propaganda was a recent statement purporting to be an official analysis of the Budget, wherein it was claimed that 85% of our Budget will go for past and future wars. The real report of the Budget proves that but 13.5% of the Federal Budget is for present national defense and only 32.7% for purposes relating to past wars as well as present defense, including pensions, insurance and similar items. One cannot condemn too severely the tactics of those who thus seek to mislead the American public concerning such a vital matter as national defense. . . .

An analysis of city and state governmental budgets in thirteen of our largest cities indicates that out of every dollar of taxes approximately 2½ cents is spent for the upkeep of our army, and about 6 cents for army and navy together. If the radical pacifists succeeded in their desire to do away with our entire military organization the result would merely reduce the dollar of taxation to about 97½ cents. Such a policy of false economy would be laughed at by a business man, preparing for the insurance of his property. . . .

Americans need not be afraid of militarism as long as their own hearts are set against war. They need have no fear of the growth of a militaristic class, as long as they take the interest in national defense that the responsibilities of citizenship demand of them. They should, however, be on guard against the dangers of going too far in the desire for peace. We should obey the words of our past leaders who urged us to be industrious and constructive, but to resist alike the coercion and the aggression of those who would interfere with our destiny. . . .

John W. Weeks, *Other Things the Army Does besides Fight*, address before Los Angeles Chamber of Commerce, May 21, 1923 (Washington, Government Printing Office, 1923), 4-18 *passim*.

PART V

DOMESTIC PROBLEMS AND ADVANCES

CHAPTER XII — CATASTROPHES

59. The San Francisco Disaster (1906)

BY MAJOR–GENERAL ADOLPHUS W. GREELY

Greely, soldier and Arctic explorer, was the ranking Army officer on duty in San Francisco at the time of the earthquake and fire of 1906. This account quotes at length the report of Funston, who was actually on the ground at the moment of the catastrophe. Californians always refer to it as "the fire." The water mains were shattered by the earthquake. Greely is the author of a long list of works on scientific subjects—mainly climatology and meteorology—connected with his profession. He was the first volunteer private soldier of the Civil War to reach the grade of brigadier-general, U. S. A.—Bibliography: contemporary periodicals.

HEADQUARTERS PACIFIC DIVISION, SAN FRANCISCO, CAL.,
JULY 30, 1906

SIR: In accordance with the instructions of the Hon. William H. Taft, Secretary of War, under date of June 29, 1906, I have the honor to submit herewith a comprehensive report of the services of the United States Army in connection with the recent earthquake and conflagration in the city of San Francisco, Cal., and the relief measures rendered necessary by these disasters. . . .

The report of operations of Brigadier-General Funston, who was temporarily in command during my absence, from April 18 to 22, follows in full:

I have the honor to make the following report of the work of the troops in connection with the recent earthquake and conflagration in the city of San Francisco, from the morning of the 18th of April, 1906, until the return of the division commander on the 22d of the same month:

I was living at 1310 Washington street, near Jones, and was awakened by the earthquake shock at 5.16 a. m. of April 18. Realizing from the intensity and duration of the shock that serious damage to the city, with attendant loss of life, must have occurred, I dressed, and, finding that the street cars were not running, hastened on foot to the business part of the city. My route was down Jones street to California and along that street to Sansome. That portion of California street between Jones and Powell being one of the most elevated in the city, I had noticed that columns of smoke were arising in various localities, particularly in the region south of Market street. Reaching Sansome I saw that several fires were already burning fiercely in the banking district and that the firemen who were on the scene were quite helpless owing to lack of water. This, in connection with the number of fires I had seen from the higher part of California street, convinced me that a most serious conflagration was at hand, and that, owing to the great extent of the area in which fires had already appeared, the police force of the city would be totally inadequate to maintain order and prevent looting and establish and hold the proper fire lines in order that the fire department might not be hampered in its work. By this time the streets were full of people, somewhat alarmed but by no means panic stricken. Encountering a patrolman, I inquired of him how I could most quickly communicate with the Mayor or Chief of Police, and was informed that the entire telephone system was paralyzed, but that he felt sure that both of those officials would immediately repair to the Hall of Justice on Portsmouth Square, which surmise proved correct. I requested this man to hasten to the Hall of Justice and leave word for the Chief of Police that I would at once order out all available troops and place them at his disposal. There being no means of transportation available and quick action being imperative, I then ran from the corner of Sansome and California streets to the quartermaster's stable, on Pine street, between Leavenworth and Hyde, a distance of slightly more than a mile, directed my carriage driver to saddle a horse, and, while he was doing so, hastily wrote on a leaf from a notebook a brief note addressed to the commanding officer, Presidio, directing him to turn out the entire garrison and report for duty to the Chief of Police at the Hall of Justice. The man was directed to stop at Fort Mason on his way to the Presidio and give a verbal message to the same effect to the commanding officer of that post. From here I proceeded on foot to the headquarters of the Department of California, Phelan Building, at the corner of Market street and Grant avenue, a distance of about a mile. Here I found several officers of the staffs of the Pacific Division and the Department of California, as well as a number of clerks and messengers who had already, under the direction of the chief clerk, Mr. A. R. Holzheid, engaged in getting the more important records in shape for removal from the building, if necessary. At about 7.45 a. m. arrived the first troops from Fort Mason, Companies C and D, of the Engineers, Capt. M. L. Walker commanding. These troops had already been reported to the Mayor and the Chief of Police, and had been directed by the former to guard the banking district and send patrols along Market street to prevent looting. The arrival of these troops was greeted with demonstrations of approval by the many people on the streets. At about 8 a. m. the garrison from the Presidio, consisting of the 10th, 29th, 38th, 66th, 67th, 70th, and 105th Companies of Coast Artillery, Troops I and K, 14th Cavalry, and the 1st, 9th, and 24th Field Batteries, Col. Charles Morris, Artillery Corps, commanding, began to arrive. Detachments were sent to guard the mint and post-office, while the remainder assisted the police in keeping the dense crowds of onlookers away from close proximity to the fire and in patrolling the streets to prevent the people from breaking into stores and saloons. Most fortunately the latter had already been ordered closed by the Mayor, so that one source of danger had been removed. . . .

Early in the morning, shortly after it was seen that a serious conflagration was at hand, the acting chief of the fire department had sent a message to the Presidio, requesting that all available explosives, with a detail to handle them, be sent to check the fire; as the earthquake had broken the water mains and the fire department was practically helpless. The commanding officer of the Presidio ordered Capt. Le Vert Coleman, post ordnance officer, to provide the necessary explosives. . . . While many of the older and more fragile buildings could be destroyed by high explosives, it was found that the modern steel-and-concrete buildings were practically impervious to anything except enormous charges. . . .

About 10 a. m. the commissary depot was destroyed, and I wired an estimate of the extent of the disaster. I considered it necessary to make an estimate of the number who would be rendered homeless by the fire in case the conflagration could be checked within reasonable bounds. I asked, therefore, for tents and rations for 30,000 people. As the fire progressed, however, it became evident that not 30,000, but probably more than 100,000, people would be homeless before midnight. Telegraphic request was therefore made that all available tents and rations be forwarded as soon as possible. This step was considered necessary, as it seemed then that all supply warehouses, not only for food but for bedding and shelter, would inevitably be destroyed without the hope of saving even a small percentage of their contents. A fact which made the saving of property most difficult was that no wagons of any kind appeared to be in the vicinity of the fire to carry away any goods that it might have been possible to save. . . .

Anxious inquiries were made as to the extent of the injuries to the water system. No water appearing in any of the pipes in the vicinity of Fort Mason or, in fact, any part of the city covered by the troops, it appeared for the time that a water famine was inevitable. Steps were at once taken to have an examination made of all the available sources of water supply outside the regular Spring Valley supply, and it was found that there was an independent water supply in Golden Gate Park, where were also lakes of fresh water of considerable size. . . .

By the night of the 19th about 250,000 people or more must have been encamped or sleeping out in the open in the various military reservations, parks, and open spaces of the city.

The Pacific Squadron having arrived on the 19th, Admiral C. F. Goodrich, commanding, sent ashore an officer and offered to land a force to assist in the work being done by the troops. The offer was most gladly accepted. . . .

The division commander, Maj.-Gen. A. W. Greely, having returned to the city on the evening of the 22d, I relinquished command of the Pacific Division, which command I had exercised simultaneously with that of the department of California, and from that time exercised command of the department alone. . . .

Without exception the officers of the division and department staffs performed their duties so conscientiously and energetically that it is a difficult, if not impossible, matter to make distinctions in bestowing praise upon them. . . .

As I have already officially stated, the terrible days of earthquake and fire in San Francisco were almost absolutely free from disorder, drunkenness, and crime. The orderly and law-abiding spirit of the people as a whole rendered the maintenance of public peace a comparatively easy task. Having in view the extent of ruin, the devastation of property, and the desperate condition of the vast numbers of hungry and homeless, there might reasonably have been expected many casualties from violence and disorder. . . .

In these days of earthquake and fire it was my misfortune to take no active part. There remained on my return, April 22, duties less striking, but nevertheless of import to the city. . . .

The existent conditions in San Francisco were of the most appalling character. While incapable of satisfactory description or adequate expression, yet roughly summarized they were as follows: On April 18 this was a city of 500,000 inhabitants, the commercial emporium of the Pacific coast, a great industrial and manufacturing center, adorned with magnificent buildings, equipped with extensive local transportation, provided with the most modern sanitary appliances, and having an abundant water supply. On April 21 these triumphs of human effort, this center of civilization, had become a scene of indescribable desolation, more than 200,000 residents having fled from the burnt district alone, leaving several hundred dead under its smoldering ashes. The entire community of 450,000, deprived of all modern conveniences and necessities, had, in forty-eight hours, not only been relegated to conditions of primitive life, but were also hampered by ruins and débris. Its entire business districts and adjacent territory had been ravaged by fire. The burnt area covered 3,400 acres, as against 2,100 in Chicago and 50 in Boston. Of the 261 miles of electric and cable railways not a mile remained in operation. While probably 1,500 teams were uninjured, yet, as a whole, they had been withdrawn with the refugees to the outlying districts. Practically all travel had to be on foot, the few automobiles having been impressed by the authorities. The intricate masses of iron, brick, and débris were supplemented in the unburned area by fallen buildings and chimneys, which made all travel circuitous and extremely difficult. The city telephone system was interrupted; every telegraph office and station had been destroyed. All the banks, deposit vaults, and trust buildings were in ruins. Not a hotel of note or importance was left standing. The great apartment houses had vanished. Of the thousands of wholesale and large retail establishments scarce half a dozen were saved, and these in remote districts. Even buildings spared by the fire were damaged as to chimneys, so that all food of the entire city was cooked over camp fires in the open streets.

Two hundred and twenty-five thousand people were not only homeless, losing all real and personal property, but also were deprived of their means of present sustenance and future livelihood. Food, water, shelter, clothing, medicines, and sewerage were all lacking. Failing even for drinking purposes, water had to be brought long distances. Every large bakery was destroyed or interrupted. While milk and country produce were plentiful in the suburbs, local transportation was entirely interrupted so that even people of great wealth could obtain food only by charity or public relief. In short, all those things which are deemed essential to the support, comfort, and decency of a well-ordered life were destroyed or wanting.

The quarter of a million people driven into the streets by the flames escaped as a rule only with the clothing they wore. Thousands upon thousands had fled to the open country, but tens of thousands upon tens of thousands remained in the parks, generally in stupor or exhaustion after days of terror and struggle. . . .

This report would be incomplete if it did not recognize the sterling qualities of the people of San Francisco. Almost without exception these people suffered financially, varying from small losses to total ruin. It is safe to say that nearly 200,000 persons were brought to a state of complete destitution, beyond the clothing they wore or carried in their arms. The majority of the community was reduced from conditions of comfort to dependence upon public charity, yet in all my experiences I have never seen a woman in tears, nor heard a man whining over his losses. Besides this spirit of cheerful courage, they exhibited qualities of resourcefulness and self-respect which must command the admiration of the world. Within two months the bread line, which at first exceeded 300,000, was reduced to a comparative handful—less than 5 per cent of the original number.

Maj.-Gen. Adolphus W. Greely, *Special Report on Army Relief Operations at San Francisco* (Washington, Government Printing Office, 1906), 5–47 *passim*.

———————◆———————

60. The Sinking of the *Titanic* (1912)

FROM THE REPORT OF THE SENATE COMMITTEE ON COMMERCE

After the *Titanic* disaster of April 14–15, 1912, the survivors were brought to the United States, and this circumstance, together with the fact that many of those lost were American citizens, led the Senate of the United States to direct an examination of as many of the witnesses as were available, and an investigation into the circumstances of the disaster.

ON the third day out ice warnings were received by the wireless operators on the *Titanic*, and the testimony is conclusive that at least three of these warnings came direct to the commander of the Titanic on the day of the accident, the first about noon, from the *Baltic*, of the White Star Line. It will be noted that this message places icebergs within 5 miles of the track which the *Titanic* was following, and near the place where the accident occurred. The message from the commander of the *Baltic* is as follows:

STEAMSHIP "BALTIC," *April 14, 1912.*

Capt. SMITH, *Titanic:*
   Have had moderate variable winds and clear fine weather since leaving. Greek steamer *Athinai* reports passing icebergs and large quantity of field ice to-day in latitude 41.51 north, longitude 49.52 west. Last night we spoke German oil tank *Deutschland*, Stettin to Philadelphia, not under control; short of coal; latitude 40.52 north, longitude 55.11. Wishes to be reported to New York and other steamers. Wish you and *Titanic* all success.

COMMANDER.

The second message was received by the *Titanic* from the *Californian*, of the Leyland Line, at 5.35 p. m. New York time, Sunday afternoon, reporting ice about 19 miles to the northward of the track which the *Titanic* was following. This message was as follows:

Latitude 42.3 north, longitude 49.9 west. Three large bergs 5 miles to the southward of us. Regards. (Sig.) Lord.

The third message was transmitted from the *Amerika* via the *Titanic* and Cape Race to the Hydrographic Office in Washington, D. C., reporting ice about 19 miles to the southward of the course being followed by the *Titanic*, and reads as follows:

STEAMSHIP "AMERIKA," *VIA* "TITANIC" AND CAPE RACE, N. F.,
April 14, 1912.
HYDROGRAPHIC OFFICE, *Washington, D. C.:*
  Amerika passed two large icebergs in 41.27 N., 50.8 W., on the 14th of April.
  K. N. U. T.

This message was actually received at the Hydrographic Office in Washington at 10.51 p. m., April 14.

The fourth message was sent to the *Titanic* at 9.05 p. m. New York time, on Sunday, the 14th of April, approximately an hour before the accident occurred. The message reads as follows:

We are stopped and surrounded by ice.

To this the operator of the *Titanic* replied:

Shut up. I am busy. I am working Cape Race.

While this was the last message sent by the *Californian* to the *Titanic*, the evidence shows that the operator of the *Californian* kept the telephones on his head, and heard the *Titanic* talking to Cape Race up to within a few minutes of the time of the accident, when he "put the phones down, took off his clothes, and turned in."

The *Baltic's* operator on that Sunday overheard ice reports going to the *Titanic* from the *Prinz Friedrich Wilhelm*, and from the *Amerika*, while the *Carpathia* on the same day overheard the *Parisian* talking about ice with other ships.

This enables the committee to say that the ice positions so definitely reported to the *Titanic* just preceding the accident located ice on both sides of the track or lane which the *Titanic* was following, and in her immediate vicinity. No general discussion took place among the officers; no conference was called to consider these warnings; no heed was given to them. The speed was not relaxed, the lookout was not increased, and the only vigilance displayed by the officer of the watch was by instructions to the lookouts to keep "a sharp lookout for ice." It should be said, however, that the testimony shows that Capt. Smith remarked to Officer Lightoller, who was the officer doing duty on the bridge until 10 o'clock ship's time, or 8.27 o'clock New York time, "If it was in a slight degree hazy there would be no doubt we should have to go very slowly" and "If in the slightest degree doubtful, let me know." The evidence is that it was exceptionally clear. There was no haze, and the ship's speed was not reduced.

The speed of the *Titanic* was gradually increased after leaving Queenstown. The first day's run was 464 miles, the second day's run was 519 miles, the third day's run was 546 miles. Just prior to the collision the ship was making her maximum speed of the voyage—not less than 21 knots, or 24¼ miles per hour.

At 11.46 p. m. ship's time, or 10.13 p. m. New York time, Sunday evening, April 14, the lookout signalled the bridge and telephoned the officer of the watch, "Iceberg right ahead." The officer of the watch, Mr. Murdock, immediately ordered the quatermaster at the wheel to put the helm "hard astarboard," and reversed the engines; but while the sixth officer standing behind the quartermaster at the wheel reported to officer Murdock "The helm is hard astarboard," the *Titanic* struck the ice. The impact, while not violent enough to disturb the passengers or crew, or to arrest the ship's progress, rolled the vessel slightly and tore the steel plating above the turn of the bilge.

The testimony shows that coincident with the collision air was heard whistling or hissing from the overflow pipe to the forepeak tank, indicating the escape of air from that tank because of the inrush of water. Practically at once, the forepeak tank, No. 1 hold, No. 2 hold, No. 3 hold, and the forward boiler room, filled with water, the presence of which was immediately reported from the mail room and the racquet court and trunk room in No. 3 hold, and also from the firemen's quarters in No. 1 hold. Leading Fireman Barret saw the water rushing into the forward fireroom from a tear about two feet above the stokehold floor plates and about twenty feet below the water line, which tear extended into the coal bunker at the forward end of the second fireroom.

The reports received by the captain after various inspections of the ship must have acquainted him promptly with its serious condition, and when interrogated by President Ismay, he so expressed himself. It is believed, also, that this serious condition was promptly realized by the chief engineer and by the builders' representative, Mr. Andrews, none of whom survived.

No general alarm was sounded, no whistle blown, and no systematic warning was given the passengers. Within 15 or 20 minutes the captain visited the wireless room and instructed the operator to get assistance, sending out the distress call, C. Q. D.

This distress call was heard by the wireless station at Cape Race that evening at 10.25 p. m. New York time, together with the report that she had struck an iceberg, and at the same time was accidentally overheard by the *Mount Temple*, which ship immediately turned around toward the *Titanic*. Within two or three minutes a reply was received from the *Frankfurt*. Within 10 minutes the wireless operator of the *Carpathia* fortunately and largely by chance heard the *Titanic's* C. Q. D. call, which he reported at once to the bridge and to the captain. The *Carpathia* was immediately turned around and reported her latitude and longitude to the *Titanic*, together with the fact that she was steaming full speed toward the stricken ship. The *Frankfurt*, however, did not give her latitude or longitude, and after waiting 20 minutes asked the operator of the *Titanic*, "What is matter?" To this the *Titanic* operator replied that he was a fool.

In view of the fact that no position had been given by the *Frankfurt*, and that her exact distance from the *Titanic* was unknown at that time, the answer of the operator of the *Titanic* was scarcely such as prudence would have dictated. Notwithstanding this, however, the *Frankfurt* was overheard by the *Mount Temple* to report, "Our captain will go for you." Communication was promptly established with the *Olympic* and the *Baltic*, and the *Caronia*, some 800 miles to the eastward, overheard the *Titanic's* C. Q. D. call. The wireless messages of the *Titanic* were recorded in part by the Cape Race station and by the *Mount Temple*, and in part by the *Baltic*. The *Mount Temple* last heard the *Titanic* after the accident at 11.47 p. m. New York time. The *Baltic* and the *Carpathia* lost touch about the same time, the last message they received being "Engine room getting flooded." The *Virginian* last heard the *Titanic's* signals at 12.27 New York time, and reported them blurred, and ending abruptly.

Sixteen witnesses from the *Titanic*, including officers and experienced seamen, and passengers of sound judgment, testified to seeing the light of a ship in the distance, and some of the lifeboats were directed to pull for that light, to leave the passengers and to return to the side of the *Titanic*. The *Titanic* fired distress rockets and attempted to signal by the electric lamp and Morse code to this vessel. At about the same time the officers of the *Californian* admit seeing rockets in the general direction of the *Titanic* and say that they immediately displayed a powerful Morse lamp, which could be easily seen a distance of 10 miles, while several of the crew of the *Californian* testify that the side lights of a large vessel going at full speed were plainly visible from the lower deck of the *Californian* at 11.30 p. m. ship's time, just before the accident. There is no evidence that any rockets were fired by any vessel between the *Titanic* and the *Californian*, although every eye on the *Titanic* was searching the horizon for possible assistance.

The committee is forced to the inevitable conclusion that the *Californian*, controlled by the same company, was nearer the *Titanic* than the 19 miles reported by her captain, and that her officers and crew saw the distress signals of the *Titanic* and failed to respond to them in accordance with the dictates of humanity, international usage, and the requirements of law. The only reply to the distress signals was a counter signal from a large white light which was flashed for nearly two hours from the mast of the *Californian*. In our opinion such conduct, whether arising from indifference or gross carelessness, is most reprehensible, and places upon the commander of the *Californian* a grave responsibility. The wireless operator of the *Californian* was not aroused until 3.30 a. m. New York time, on the morning of the 15th, after considerable conversation between officers and members of the crew had taken place aboard that ship regarding these distress signals or rockets, and was directed by the chief officer to see if there was anything the matter, as a ship had been firing rockets during the night. The inquiry this set on foot immediately disclosed the fact that the *Titanic* had sunk. Had assistance been promptly proffered, or had the wireless operator of the *Californian* remained a few minutes longer at his post on Sunday evening, that ship might have had the proud distinction of rescuing the lives of the passengers and crew of the *Titanic*.

When Captain Smith received the reports as to the water entering the ship, he promptly gave the order to clear away the lifeboats and later orders were given to put women and children into the boats. During this time distress rockets were fired at frequent intervals.

The lack of preparation was at this time most noticeable. There was no system adopted for loading the boats; there was great indecision as to the deck from which the boats were to be loaded; there was wide diversity of opinion as to the number of the crew necessary to man each boat; there was no direction whatever as to the number of passengers to be carried by each boat, and no uniformity in loading them. On one side only women and children were put in the boats, while on the other side there was almost an equal proportion of men and women put into the boats, the women and children being given the preference in all cases. The failure to utilize all lifeboats to their recognized capacity for safety unquestionably resulted in the needless sacrifice of several hundred lives which might otherwise have been saved.

The testimony is definite that, except in isolated instances, there was no panic. In loading boats no distinction was made between first-, second-, and third-class passengers, although the proportion of lost is larger among third-class passengers than in either of the other classes. Women and children, without discrimination, were given preference.

The committee deems the course followed by Captain Rostron of the *Carpathia* as deserving of the highest praise and worthy of especial recognition. Captain Rostron fully realized all the risk involved. He doubled his lookouts, doubled his fireroom force, and notwithstanding such risk pushed his ship at her very highest limit of speed through the many dangers of the night to the relief of the stricken vessel. His detailed instructions issued in anticipation of the rescue of the *Titanic* are a marvel of systematic preparation and completeness, evincing such solicitude as calls for the highest commendation. The precautions he adopted enabled him to steer his course between and around icebergs until he stopped his engines at 4 o'clock in the morning in the vicinity of the accident, where he proceeded to pick up the *Titanic's* lifeboats with the survivors.

The first boat was picked up at 4.10 a. m. Monday, and the last of the survivors was on board by 8.30 a. m., after which Captain Rostron made arrangements to "hold service, a short prayer of thankfulness for those rescued, and a short burial service for those who were lost."

"Titanic" Disaster, Report of the Committee on Commerce, United States Senate (Washington, Government Printing Office, 1912), 6–15 *passim*.

———◆———

61. Saving New Orleans (1927)

BY L. C. SPEERS

Recurrent floods of the Mississippi and its tributary rivers have led to the development of elaborate protective systems. That for the city of New Orleans is only an example. For related material, see contemporary periodical accounts, notably of the Ohio floods of 1912, and of relief work under Secretary of Commerce Hoover in the greatest of all Mississippi floods, that of 1927.

LAST to receive the impact of the crest of the heaviest flood that ever swept down the Mississippi will be the levees that half encircle New Orleans. Will they hold? The eyes of a nation are focused on these man-made embankments that hold the fate of the gay and lovely metropolis of the South, our chief foreign trade port after New York. Bienville laid out the city not flush with but below the level of the great river. The safeguarding levees, according to tests by Federal, State and City engineers, will surely hold.

Three weeks ago New Orleans awoke to the realization that the supreme test of the Mississippi levee system was at hand, for the Mississippi's highest flood was being reinforced by the maximum discharges of her capacious tributaries, the Missouri, the Ohio, the Arkansas, the St. Francis, the Yazoo and the Red. These waters were roaring southward with a crest such as was never before recorded. With the crest still weeks away the Mississippi was rising to record heights. In the emergency New Orleans mobilized for the battle of defense. John Klorer, who has had seventeen years' experience in levee engineering since graduation from Tulane, was voted, as Commissioner of Public Property in the Government of New Orleans, "plenary power to do all things necessary and requisite" to preserve the safety of the city.

Klorer, grown gray-haired in the fight to hold the Mississippi constantly in check, decided that the emergency demanded the dynamiting of the main levee system south of New Orleans. This, he promised, would guarantee safety to the city. Without dissent, and with her historic smile, New Orleans told Klorer to go ahead and she would pay the bill.

It is seldom that one man is invested with such complete control of the safety of a city of 425,000 inhabitants as John Klorer exercises during the present peril. The correspondent of THE NEW YORK TIMES asked him to describe the problem of saving the city, urging that all America loves New Orleans and is interested in her history— in preserving old St. Louis cathedral, the house built by the French of New Orleans as a refuge for Napoleon Bonaparte, the field of Chalmette where Jackson defeated the British, the picturesque French Quarter and that part of New Orleans that is as modern as New York.

"To understand the problem of defense against the record-breaking flood it is necessary to consider the topography of New Orleans," he answered.

"Its site was chosen more for military and strategic reasons than for the advantages it possessed as a commercial depot.

"As is the case near all alluvial streams, the highest land is immediately alongside the river; from the banks it slopes gradually toward the interior. The levees are only artificial elevations of the banks, and these levees are the highest land in New Orleans. On the commercial front the levees are not apparent, because the ground has been filled in artificially. On the riverfront levees are sixteen to twenty feet, and some portions of the city are as much as twenty feet below the level of the high waterline.

"These sections are also one to two feet below Gulf level. Behind the city is Lake Pontchartrain, subject to a tidal rise of about one foot and a storm rise of five to six feet. Thus it is necessary to protect New Orleans not only from water invasion in the front but from a similar invasion in the rear, and on both sides. New Orleans is, therefore, entirely surrounded by levees.

"Of this line of defense, about twenty-five miles are on the riverfront, divided equally between the left and right bank. About forty miles comprise the outer walls. Counting the levees with which the waterways penetrating the city from the lake must be prevented from overflowing their banks into the city, New Orleans is protected by about 106 miles of these embankments.

"A part of the interior levee system is known as the Upper Protection Levee. It runs from the river to the lake and is about six miles long. This was built after the Sauve crevasse of 1849, fifteen or twenty miles above the city, which spilled a good deal of backwater into New Orleans. Its purpose is to keep the city dry in the event of a break in the levees within forty miles upstream.

"The river levees are the strongest on the entire Mississippi. There was never any apprehension that they would break, despite the fact that a flood stage of twenty-four feet and possibly more was forecast in April, because of the river heights further upstream.

"Water has not pressed against the upper protection levee sufficiently to be an annual remainder to build that structure as strong as possible; and as the years passed without a crevasse above the city there was such a slackening in vigilance that about twenty-five years ago the municipal authorities permitted a large drainage canal to be excavated along the foot of this levee. This weakening to the foundation makes it rather problematical whether this upper protection levee could hold out the eight or ten feet of water that would be poured against the city by a crevasse a few miles above the city limits.

"When the water levels up-river began to rise high late this Spring and when in April the Government meteorologist at New Orleans forecast a flood stage of 24 feet, with the possibility that the water would rise a foot higher if the winds were unfavorable, a very real alarm was felt here. There was even fear that the levees at New Orleans would break because they had never been called upon to stand such a rush of water.

"This fear was not seriously entertained by engineers who understood conditions. Engineers, however, did entertain grave apprehensions regarding the levees in the country adjoining the city. This fear was concerned, not only with the Upper Protection Levees, but also with the lake front levee, for if the Mississippi poured a sizable crevasse into Lake Pontchartrain its level would be raised three feet, if not more.

"The Levee Board threw all of its resources behind strengthening the hundred-odd miles of embankment that protect New Orleans on its front, rear and sides. A committee of citizens appointed by Mayor O'Keefe, acting upon technical advice, concluded that the situation required further safeguards. They advised cutting the levee below the city, near the old Poydras crevasse, that in 1922 had taken two and a half feet off the river.

"The cross-section of the riverfront levees at New Orleans is much more than the standard established by the Mississippi River Commission. But in some places the height was not up to grade, a fact due to wharfs that had been built, and to other reasons. The problem in this sector therefore involved only topping the levee to take care of the ultimate inches of flood water that might develop.

"This problem was complicated by the distance from which material had to be moved. For there are no bluffs or hills in the city limits. It was necessary to haul material from a distance of 40 to 50 miles, and so a transportation as well as a construction problem had to be solved. The material was assembled by railroad excavating machines, packed into sacks and shipped into New Orleans, where the sand bags were built into stout ramparts along the levee tops to a height of 3 feet in places. About 7 miles of levee were raised in this manner.

"The interior levee system was raised by portable excavating machines. The material, in the main, was obtained on the water side of the levee and placed against a line of boarding erected on the crown of the levee. About 10 miles were raised 2 to 3 feet in this manner. Nearly 1,200 men were employed on this work. The cost to the city may be estimated at $200,000.

"Because of the possibility that some person or persons of unsound mentality in the section below the city, where the levee was cut to relieve the pressure, might break the levees at New Orleans in reprisal it was necessary to police the ramparts closely. Electric lights were erected on the crown of the levee, tools were assembled, frequent telephone stations were established.

"Agreement was reached with the authorities of all Bernard and Plaquemines parishes below the city to cut the levee at the station named Caernarvon, two miles below the natural crevasse of five years before. The New Orleans Levee Board agreed to reimburse the residents for all property losses by a special tax which it had the authority to levy in time of emergency.

"The cutting of this levee began on April 29 and continued for two weeks gradually, lest the run-off of water, developing too suddenly, should cause the sloughing of the banks upstream. About 35 tons of dynamite were used to break this levee, a fact which testifies to the strength of these embankments, and the dynamite was aided by powerful eroding influences of the current, once the opening was started. The break was allowed to reach a width of about 3,000 feet.

"The cost of breaking this levee was about $25,000. The total of the indemnity to the property holders cannot be accurately estimated at present. If it is $2,000,000, the protective devices with which New Orleans has supplemented the levees to meet this year's flood have cost nearly $2,500,000.

"The results have been everything that we expected and hoped. The river today is at least two and a half feet lower than it would have been had it not been for the Point-a-la-Hache and Caernarvon breaks."

New York Times, May 15, 1927.

CHAPTER XIII — TRANSPORTATION AND COMMUNICATION

62. James J. Hill, Builder of a Frontier (1901)

BY MARY C. BLOSSOM

Hill, though a good part of his work was accomplished before the period covered by this volume, was one of the great guiding powers behind our present-day system of transportation. His energy and his capacity for inspiring loyalty were tremendous, and perhaps his most striking memorial is the fact that the region which he opened is often referred to as "the Jim Hill country." See also No. 83 below.— Bibliography: J. G. Pyle, *Life of J. J. Hill*.

FORTY–FIVE years ago there went into the great new country of Minnesota a young Scotch-Irish farmer from Canada. He was the sixteenth of his name in direct line of descent, hardy and alert. At the age of eighteen in the straggling village of St. Paul he became check-clerk and caretaker of freight at the steamboat landing. . . .

In 1862 the first ten miles of railroad in the state were finished with great effort. It ran from the levee in St. Paul to the riverside in St. Anthony, and was known as the St. Paul and Pacific Railroad, of which Mr. Hill later became the agent. . . .

There is no record of an enterprise of Mr. Hill's in which he has not succeeded. In his enterprises, of course, he uses the same agents that others use, but with a sense of proportion and with a concentration of utility that makes his power reach twice as far and accomplish twice as much as most other men. . . .

For several years the St. Paul and Pacific system of railroads, consisting of 437 miles of completed track, was in bad condition. It was mortgaged, the roadbed was not good, the time was one of great depression in the financial world, the stockholders, mostly Holland capitalists, were weary with delay and misfortune. Because of his faith in the future of the region that he knew so well, Mr. Hill formed a syndicate of five persons which soon gained possession of the road,

and in June, 1870, the system was consolidated into a single ownership as the St. Paul, Minnesota & Manitoba Railroad Company.
The task was not an easy one; the untiring industry and foresight of
the moving spirit were taxed to the utmost. At a time when he was
striving to complete a certain piece of road in order not to lose a land
grant, he worked night and day, personally supervising the construction, laying ties under most adverse conditions, and getting water
out of the way as best he could. The service of a friend who labored
with him unceasingly in this hour of need has never been forgotten.
To crown their efforts the road was completed two days before the
appointed time.

Later it was extended to the Pacific coast, traversing vast tracts
of land without human habitation. The track was well laid but the
stations were often only freight cars, remote from one another, and
remote from other human settlements. Dismal predictions were
made, but not for a moment did the unflinching courage and purpose
of the leader waver. The Cascade Mountains were rich in lumber of
a growth so large as to be useful for purposes not previously possible
for single trees. Some of the trees had gained four or five hundred
rings, proving them to have been large when Columbus discovered
America. Coal fields were discovered, and a branch road carried their
produce for the use of the main line. Settlements were formed for
preparing the lumber for shipment; and Mr. Hill was all along the
line, giving words of practical advice to newcomers, telling them the
kind of stock they ought to keep, and how to get it, and what to feed
it, and giving them many other bits of practical assistance. While
the work was going on through this region, Mr. Hill rode over the
rough mountains on horseback, deciding problems of tunnels and the
like. He knows the cost of a bridge as well as his engineers, and more
than once he has torn up specifications and saved money by using
his own plans. One reason why the road has held its own while others
failed, is that before putting it into operation he spent $5,000,000 in
grading. It was Mr. Hill who taught the workers in the lumber
country to alternate the thick and thin ends of the shingle so as to
make flat, square packages, and thus economize space in the cars.
He is sometimes called exacting with the employees of the road. It
is because the work must be done the best way; and, when a division
superintendent is not packing his freight to the best advantage, he

is not retained because he is a nice old man, but his place is taken by a man who can load cars well. In some cases it may not seem sufficient consideration of the individual, but great forces often do not consider individuals.

There is nothing Mr. Hill feels more keenly than his responsibility to his stockholders. Before the panic of 1893, $30,000,000 had been provided by Mr. Hill for the road; and when the financial crash came, as this money was not in use, Mr. Hill lent it to relieve the strain, saved many men from ruin, and helped to preserve confidence. There are two old ladies in New Hampshire who had put $10,000 into the Manitoba road; and to this day Mr. Hill says to the stockholders at the meetings: "We still keep faith with the old ladies." The confidence felt in him by European investors is profound. He and Lord Roberts are close friends, and all of Lord Roberts' possessions beside his campbed and his uniform and his recent grants by Parliament are invested in the Great Northern railroad.

The first year the road was in operation, 1890, trade was paralyzed, the competition was great, and the country along the route was yet unsettled; but the mind which had planned the great enterprise had provided for its success. The officers of the road offered to have their salaries cut down, Mr. Hill receiving none; and reductions were made, ranging from large sums down to ten cents a day from some of the employees. When 10,000 men receive ten cents less a day the saving amounts to a considerable sum.

To ship valuable lumber eastward was an excellent plan; but to send empty cars after it was out of the question; so Mr. Hill conceived the idea of shipping grain for the Japanese steamers to carry to the Orient. An agent was sent to China and Japan to find out what the cost of wheat must be to compete with rice; and the result was the Japanese Navigation Company, the third largest steamship company in the world, began to carry large shipments of grain to China and Japan. This was a foresighted piece of work surely. These boats were soon found to be inadequate for the shipment of the grain, lumber, cotton, steel rails, tobacco and silver which soon became a part of our exports to the Orient. Two large new steamers are therefore now in process of construction at New London for the Oriental trade. . . .

The question of docks for these large steamers was the next that came up. Seattle, the western terminus of the road, is built on the side of a hill, which continues to slope very gradually under the water. Moreover, there is in the water a very destructive mollusk called the teredo or shipworm, which burrows into wood and soon destroys every kind of timber. The fertile brain of Mr. Hill met this difficulty also. He caused thousands of tons of brush which the teredo cannot penetrate, to be carried and dumped into the water in two sections, leaving a channel between. Then the channel was found not to be deep enough; so out of this a huge hydraulic pump removed the mud and gravel and forced them into the brush, making quite a compact mass. Then creosoted piles, prepared by a very expensive process, were found to be impervious to the dreaded teredo, and were driven outside the brush and gravel. In this way a depth of forty-six feet of water has been provided for the great steamers when they shall begin their work.

The original 437 miles of completed road of which Mr. Hill took charge as manager, now number as the Great Northern System, 6,000 miles. In 1883 he became president of the company. While other transcontinental roads have collapsed and gone into the hands of receivers, the Great Northern has never once defaulted the interest on its bonds or passed a dividend. The road extends from Puget Sound to St. Paul, or during the season of navigation to Duluth and Superior, where it connects for Buffalo with its own two most luxurious steamers. A fleet of six freight vessels are added to these. The grain ships moving through the "Soo" give that canal rank over the Suez in point of tonnage.

In developing this great scheme of his life, the plan has increased enormously in the process. Besides laying the foundation of a great fortune, it has in its fulfilment opened a very rich and vast new country, reached out to new markets for many American products, and brought benefit to great numbers of people. All along the line of his road he has encouraged the most diversified and productive farming, and he has introduced new methods and labor-saving devices. . . .

Mr. Hill is often spoken of as a puzzle. Like other elemental forces he is not easily understood. He is a figure of world-wide reputation and a man of remarkable intellectual endowment, of a great constructive genius, of a marvelous capacity for detail, inventive and of untiring industry; and behind all his qualities is the force of an indomitable will. For years he has been the embodiment of one great idea.

He may discharge an employee who has served him fifteen years, with no word of explanation and apparently with no effort to adjust the fault, whatever it may be—because that man causes friction in his vast machine. Yet he will care for and speak in the tenderest way of an unhappy little dog that has fled to him for protection. He will give a large sum of money to save a friend in danger of financial disaster; he puts his mighty hand on the political machine and without an instant's delay retains for a fellow-citizen of integrity the office he has filled well: he expresses civic pride in many ways. As the head and energy of the great industry that he has built up and with his touch on every part of it, he looks upon every man in its employ as an instrument that does or does not do its work. He is capable of being touched and influenced by a spiritual personality like that of the beautiful old priest whose portrait stands in his library; and he can feel contempt for the less powerful than those who are on his own plane. A warm sympathy for old friends comes to the surface in his nature; he takes up the roll of his old militia comrades and recounts each name without faltering. . . .

On the other hand, Mr. Hill has displayed the greatest consideration towards certain of the old employees who were personal friends of his at an early day. A superintendent, one of the pioneer railroaders of Minnesota, was retained on full pay long after his physical condition incapacitated him for effective service. An assistant was provided to relieve him of actual responsibility, and when he died, leaving his family with little property, Mr. Hill gave the widow $10,000 to maintain herself and children. So secretly was this good deed performed that it did not become known till long afterwards. The unvarying desire to remember and aid the friends of his less prosperous days is characteristic of Mr. Hill.

Mary C. Blossom, *James J. Hill*, in *World's Work*, May, 1901 (New York), 721–728 *passim*.

63. Rural Free Delivery (1903)

BY MAX BENNET THRASHER

At the time of its introduction, the Rural Free Delivery service was, like all in-novations, viewed with suspicion and disapproval in some quarters. The event, of course, has proved it indispensable.

RURAL free delivery is as yet so much of a novelty in this coun-try that when, a few months ago, a rural mail carrier in Michi-gan invited me to spend a day driving with him over his thirty-mile route, I was glad to avail myself of the opportunity which his invita-tion afforded me to see something of the actual working of a system which in about five years has grown from an experiment, at an expense of $25,000 a year, to 14,000 actual working routes this year, operated at a cost of $8,000,000, and asking for half as much more next year to provide for the extension of the system.

I was the more interested in rural free delivery from the fact that the establishment of a route in my home town in New Hampshire had been proposed not long since, and so strongly opposed by some of the citizens that the project had been abandoned. The reasons given for the opposition were generally that small local offices at a distance from the railroads would be discontinued, and the patrons did not believe they would be so satisfactorily served by the new arrangement. I think this feeling arose in the main from the rather common dis-trust of any innovation, especially when it has to do with an institu-tion so old and respected as the post office. Moreover, the local office is usually located in a country store. The merchant, fearing that the doing away with the office will injure this trade, argues that it ought to be retained, and arrays on his side all those who are at-tached to him by friendship or by accounts of more or less long stand-ing on the store's ledger.

I was told that all these objections had been made to the establish-ment of the routes running out from Cassopolis, Mich., the town in which I was staying at the time, and that a day's drive among the people would enable me to judge how they felt about rural free de-livery after a little less than a year's trial, the first route from that office having been put in operation October 1st, 1901.

There are four routes in operation from the Cassopolis post office now. I was to go over Route No. 1, the first to be established. The carrier on this route, Mr. G. B. Warner, was formerly a farmer living several miles out of town and in the district which he now serves. He therefore had the advantage of being well acquainted beforehand with many of the patrons of the route and much of the country over which he now drives daily. This route covers twenty-nine miles. This, I was told, was a little longer than the average, twenty-five miles being reckoned a practical working distance.

We left the post office at Cassopolis at 8.30 A. M. and were back there at 5 P. M. There were 109 boxes on the route over which we drove, and we stopped at over one hundred of them. Into those boxes we distributed 264 papers, 37 letters, 8 postals, 12 circulars and 2 packages. The day was Friday, and on account of the fact that so many weekly papers are printed in the middle of the week, the number of papers delivered that day was considerably above the average. When the route was established there were only five daily papers taken in the district which it was to serve. When I rode over it there were sixty-five. . . .

About twenty-five monthly magazines are taken on this route.

The average number of pieces of mail delivered monthly by the carrier with whom I rode at that time was 5,200. Since the route was established the carrier had issued 262 money orders and registered 64 letters. The extension of the money order system is one of the benefits of rural delivery. Few of the small discontinued country offices were authorized to issue money orders. We issued two money orders during the trip I made. One of these happened to be asked for by a man whom I had been told was one of the most violent opponents to the establishment of the route. I asked this man—a farmer—how he liked the system.

"Wal," he said, "I'll be honest with you. I fit it jest the best I knew how. I thought we didn't want it. But if I was to sell my farm to-morrow, and go to look for another to buy, I'd give five dollars to an acre more for a place where they had rural delivery than I would for one where they hadn't." One other farmer with whom I talked was even more emphatic. He declared that he would never again own a farm at any price outside the limits of rural free delivery.

We made the trip in a small, light, covered wagon, built expressly for this purpose, so as to secure the comfort and convenience of the carrier with the least possible weight. . . . In the bottom of the front end of the wagon and in easy reach of the driver's seat is a set of pigeon holes in which he arranges his mail as he drives, so as to have it convenient for delivery. This man must have had between fifty and seventy-five pounds of mail when he started out that morning. Delivery begins about two miles out from the post office.

The exterior of the cart is painted a light blue, and from its size and color the vehicle is conspicuous a long way off on the country roads. The carrier wears the gray uniform of the regular postal service. Each carrier is required to furnish his own wagon and the horses to draw it, and to provide for the keep of the horses. Two horses are necessary, so that they may have alternate days in which to rest. It takes a pretty good horse to draw such a wagon over twenty-five to thirty miles of country roads in all kinds of weather, at all seasons of the year, making a hundred or more stops, and yet the horse must be docile enough so that he will halt at a word from the driver, when the wagon is alongside a box, and stand there until he gets the word to go on, since both the driver's hands must be occupied in opening the box and depositing the mail in it. For all this and his own services the carrier receives $600 a year.

The Department requires each man living on a route, who wishes the service, to furnish an iron box and set it up on a post of suitable height at some point on the route convenient to the carrier. Those who do not do this must go to town for their mail. Where a man lives off the route as laid out by the Department's agent his box is set up at the nearest convenient point and he comes to it for his mail. With few exceptions the boxes are so near the houses that a signal affixed to the end of each can be seen from the house. When the owner of a box leaves mail in it for the carrier to collect he raises the signal, to attract the carrier's attention; when the carrier has put mail in the box, he leaves the signal raised. . . .

The fact that the Department insisted on certain requirements as to boxes was one of the things which made trouble in the establishing of the route. These requirements in the main are that the boxes must be of iron, and one of some dozen or so kinds approved of by the Department as suitable. These boxes are not made by the Department, but by private firms. The farmer is obliged to buy the box and set it up, at a cost of about $2 to $3. Many farmers insisted that they should be allowed to set up a homemade wooden box. Some claimed that they could not afford to pay for the required iron box. I suspect that the real reason in most cases was because they objected to being—as they thought—"dictated to." A few men held out for a time after the route was established and did not provide boxes, but eventually they all got into line. . . .

The rural carrier is a daily connecting link between the farmer and the world. By his help the farmers are sure of their mail every day. Without it people who live three miles or more from a post office rarely get their mail oftener than once a week, unless some one goes to town on an errand and brings back the mail for a whole neighborhood. In this case the mail is apt to be left at some central point for chance distribution, which may cause delay or loss. . . .

Along the whole route I improved every opportunity to talk with men and women about rural delivery. I did not find any who did not approve of it, and most were enthusiastic. One man said: "It's one of the things that seems to bring back to us farmers some of the money we've been paying out for years for taxes"—indirect taxes in the way of duties, I infer he meant. "Congress votes money, lots of it," he went on, "for armies, and war ships, and river and harbor improvements, and public buildings in cities and towns, and a good many of us live and die and never see none of 'em. But here is something that comes right to our very doors, and we can't help seeing and feeling the good of our money."

Max Bennet Thrasher, *Thirty Miles with a Rural Carrier*, in *Independent*, February 5, 1903 (New York), LV, 311–317 *passim*.

64. Parcel Post (1913)

FROM THE OUTLOOK

The United States was slow to adopt the Parcel Post system, a device which had already shown its worth in several foreign countries. Complications described by this author were subsequently smoothed out by modifications in the classifying of mail matter.—Bibliography: *American Year Book*, 1913.

THE parcel post is already in active competition with the express companies. How seriously the competition is felt does not yet appear, but that the effect is material and will increase seems unquestionable. This of course is true only on small parcels, for the parcel post limit is eleven pounds, and above that weight the express monopoly is undisturbed. . . .

So long as the express companies keep their rates for the lighter parcels at the present figures, there seems to be every reason why the use of the parcel post should continue to increase. There is one element, however, which gives the express companies an advantage even on the parcels within the eleven-pound limit. The express rates automatically carry with them insurance against loss. In the parcel post, however, a parcel must be definitely insured through the payment of an additional fee of ten cents in practically the same way that a letter is registered. The addition of this fee to the various rates in the table above [not reprinted] will naturally decrease the difference in favor of the parcel post. But even if the insurance fee is paid, in almost every case the resulting post-office rates are the lower.

This comparison of rates suggests that, as far as it goes, the parcel post ought to be popular. But is it popular?

Thus far there are available figures for only one month. In the first two weeks of its operation there were despatched from the fifty largest post-offices in the country six million parcels. In the second two weeks there were despatched eight and a half-million parcels— a gain for the second half-month of two and one-half million parcels, or over forty per cent. The whole number of parcels despatched during the month was fourteen and a half million. The Post-Office Department has found from experience that the business done by the fifty largest post-offices is about one-half the postal business of the

entire country.   There were evidently, therefore, not far from thirty
million parcels handled by the parcel post during the first month. . . .

The parcel post is here.   Incidentally, we need not be too proud of
that fact.   Forty countries of the world had the parcel post before we
did.   But at last we have it; and we have begun to use it with a will.
Thirty million parcels a month is a good record, especially when it
means probably fourteen million more parcels than would have been
carried if we had continued to stick to our old fourth-class-cent-an-
ounce-four-pound-limit plan.   It is a new tool, but we are learning
rapidly to use it.   Already it is adopted for local deliveries by shoe
dealers, men's furnishing stores, department stores.   One big concern
in St. Louis is reported to be dispensing with three-quarters of its
delivery wagons.   Department stores are also using the parcel post
for deliveries to all parts of the country. . . .

Among the articles carried in the post, and many of them new to
it, are pitchforks, crutches, raw oysters and clams, strawberries,
squirrels (dressed), beefsteak, umbrellas, pieces of machinery, sides
of bacon, buckets of molasses, fishing rods, bricks, and eggs.   A dealer
in Maryland proposes to deliver ice-cream by parcel post, and a dairyman to deliver cream in the same way.   Brick manufacturers of the
country have sent a brick house by parcel post to the Clay Products
Exposition at Chicago.   The house, it should perhaps be said, was
sent one brick at a time, each of the manufacturers contributing his
quota.

We are learning to use the parcel post, but we have a great deal
yet to learn.   Old habits are hard to change, and as a people we have
a deeply ingrained habit of looking upon the post-office as an institution with the strictest limitations in regard to the sending of parcels.
We must get used to the widened limits and form the habit of taking
advantage of them.   There are fascinating possibilities, many of them
in the direction of helps in solving that most vexed of problems, the
high cost of living.

May not the parcel post help to bring the farmer and the ultimate
consumer of farm products nearer together?   May it not tend, if not
to the elimination of that much-objurated personage, the middleman, at least to his sobering and possible reformation, through the
building up of a wholesome competition?   Why should not the farmer
living within fifty miles of a city build up a trade in eggs, butter,

fruits, and garden "sass" to the comfort of his and his customers' pockets as well as their palates and digestions? . . .

We have the parcel post now and we shall never be without it. As a people we are many times slow about taking a step forward, but once it is taken, we very seldom look back and practically never step back. But we shall probably find plenty of room for improvement. Already questions are beginning to raise their heads. For instance, why should a package of blank books weighing four pounds be carried for from 5 to 30 cents within a distance of a thousand miles, while a four-pound package of printed books costs 32 cents for carriage regardless of the distance? Why should the post-office be able to carry eleven pounds of blank books and only four pounds of printed books? . . .

Let us suppose that a farmer living on a rural free delivery route wants to send ten pounds of dried peas by mail to a friend living in the town from which the route starts. If the peas are intended for planting in his friend's garden, he will pay eighty cents postage on the parcel. If the peas, on the other hand, are intended for the concoction of pea soup, the postage will be fourteen cents. If the peas are sent to a friend nearly a thousand miles away, the postage will still be eighty cents for the peas to be planted but seventy-two cents for the peas to be eaten. If the peas are sent from coast to coast, the postage on the to-be-planted peas will still be eighty cents; the postage on the to-be-made-into-soup peas will be $1.20.

If the sender does not know what his friend intends to use the peas for, a very pretty problem will present itself to the postman and the farmer. . . .

The great need in relation to the parcel post, as in relation to the whole postal service, is simplification. We now have seven or eight classifications of postal matter bearing different rates. There is need for but three:

First Class. Letters and sealed matter.

Second Class. Newspapers and periodicals mailed in bulk by publishers.

Third Class. Parcels.

Such a classification would make for convenience, efficiency, and economy. . . .

Until we have the postal service so organized that costs, profits and losses, wastes and extravagances, can be determined quickly and accurately, we shall have no basis for intelligent and effective improvement. If the parcel post shall provide an incentive to such an examination of the postal service as will make clear its defects and its needs and shall lead to improvements in the direction of business efficiency and extended public service, the country will have added reason for welcoming its establishment.

Staff article, *A Million a Day*, in *Outlook*, March 15, 1913 (New York), CIII, 580–585 *passim*.

---

65. The Wizardry of the Automobile (1922)

BY ALLEN D. ALBERT

Albert, the eminent editor and sociologist who wrote this account of the effect of the widespread adoption of the automobile as a means of transportation, has specialized since 1906 in causes of city growth and programmes of city development. He has seen the automobile, from being a mere curiosity at the beginning of the century, achieve a popularity such that over twenty million cars are now in use.— For the influence of the automobile on country life, see No. 8 above. For a description of the modern traffic problem, see No. 99 below. For an account of automobile manufacturing, see No. 154 below.

WE have in 1921 about nine million motor-cars in the United States, hardly a third as many as our horses. Yet I think there can be no serious question that the motor-car has come to be more important to us socially than the horse.

The most comprehensive change it has wrought for us has been the general widening of the circle of our life. City folk feel this in the evening and at the week-end. Farmer folk feel it from early morning till bedtime every day.

Our mail comes to our R. F. D. box usually not later than eleven in the morning, and ours is the last delivery but one on our route. Some who work, in every town, now have year-round houses in the country. There is, in fact, a tangible and powerful movement directly opposite to that of the retired farmer. He came to town to rest; city folk are going to the country to rest, and in the era of the automobile they do not lose the diversions that appealed so strongly to the retired farmer. . . .

We may expect these new country homes to affect the quality of American farm life positively and fundamentally. It is the younger generation of business men who are building country houses outside our smaller cities, and wherever they build they are enlivening the countryside with visiting, and landscape gardening, and the giving of parties. . . .

There are absorbing stories in the rusty little cars parked these days before the high school in the county-seat. This one brings two brothers eleven miles from a farm where neither parent had more than four months of schooling in any year or passed beyond the sixth grade. This one bears the daughter of a dairyman, who tells you with a steady look into your eyes that she has never learned to milk and never intends to learn. This one picks up the high-school students of three families from Wintergreen Bottoms, a community hopelessly sullen and lawless unless its children save it.

Farm men race to town to meetings of the farm bureau; farm women to meetings of the domestic-science clubs; all of them to the circus or the movies; or the winter concert season. In our youth such expeditions would have required half a day in travel. In our motoring middle life they require less than half an hour each way.

We have the doctor within easy call. We can patronize the steam laundry. Our butter and poultry customers do their own delivering. In some of the older farming sections now, as in most of the new, some of us whose children have absorbed high-school standards find ourselves joining the country club and playing golf in hours when our fathers would have been chopping feed or mending fence. . . .

I wish I could believe that our new ease of transportation had strengthened the church by widening the radius of its service. Some of our farmer families do in fact drive eight or ten miles to worship, but not many of them. And as an offset to these few, any town clergyman can cite the loss of leading families of city members who automobile away most of the Sunday mornings excepting Easter. . . . Without the automobile or some similar new agent of transport, probably we never could have had any advance in co-operation so worth while as the farm bureau, the woman's club, the parent-teacher association. The motor-carriage isolates us as it transports us but it gives us more of fellowship at the end of the journey.

The point is that the cost of a such a gain should be paid knowingly and kept as low as possible. Our car-owners who take no part in community movements are making the community poorer by paying the cost without any compensating gain. And I, for one, do not expect it ever to be established that the welfare of any such community movement necessarily involves the weakening of the church. . . .

The same machine that hurries the surgeon to the bedside of the child with a broken foot will hurry the yeggman in his getaway from a hold-up. The boy who acts the pig in his home will not suddenly become considerate of others when given absolute control of a vehicle swifter and heavier than the others on the street. Traffic squads are already making his control far from absolute in the more travelled thoroughfares. Within such limits it is to be expected that he and his highwayman associates will shortly be checked by some device that will stop all vehicular movement within a fixed limit on the sounding of an alarm. The car that persists in shooting ahead will thus be brought into clear view, while if the joyrider or the thief stopped with the others ordinarily, he would only await capture.

In the country the control must come by other methods. State constabulary is the means most often urged. What the "Mounted" do in Canada and the State police in New York and Pennsylvania, it is argued, can be done on a larger scale for the making safe of our country roads.

Present systems, headed by sheriffs and manned by constables, are for practical uses of patrol, non-existent. The plain truth is that on this continent there are only small areas in which the rural highways are not totally undefended against wrongdoers. . . .

Electric interurbans are holding their own against the new competition somewhat better than the steam roads; but not invariably, and not on many routes with success to warrant hope of any imminent extensions.

General touring by motor-car has, of course, only begun. It must be expected to double and quadruple within a few seasons. Its increase will include a series of social changes of the greatest interest to those who love the picturesque.

Most of our municipalities will have auto camps by to-morrow.

The wayside inn is even now being restored to its prominence of stage-coach days. Those who have seen the blackboards in front of farm-houses may share my expectation of an important if not a radical short-circuiting of present methods in marketing farm produce.

Best of all and most important of all, we shall steady down as a people more and more out of our rushing from place to place and come inevitably nearer, I think, to an appreciation of the beauty of the countryside.

Allen D. Albert, *The Social Influence of the Automobile*, in *Scribner's Magazine*, May, 1922 (New York), LXII, 685–688.

———◆———

66. Road Improvement (1924)

BY T. WARREN ALLEN AND OTHERS

The development of a federal system of highways has been part of the work of the Bureau of Public Roads of the Department of Agriculture. Elaborate experiments have been necessary to settle upon the precise kind of engineering procedure to assure serviceable roads for every purpose without extravagance.—Bibliography: periodicals of automobile clubs, such as *The American Motorist*, report almost monthly the progress of improved highways.

. . . BEFORE entering into a discussion of the various types of improvement and their purposes, there are certain widely entertained erroneous ideas the falsity of which should be apparent.

The first is the idea that an improved road is a luxury to be enjoyed if it can be afforded, but not essential to the economic health of the community. It is an idea that had its origin in the early days of the automobile when the motor vehicle was thought to be merely a toy for the wealthy few, and road improvement was thought to be in the interest of only this special class. Although there are now almost enough motor vehicles in use to provide one for every family, this erroneous idea still persists, and one often hears, in objection to a particular proposal for road improvement, the statement that the cost is too great, or that to undertake it would increase taxes to the breaking point. Such statements are based upon the assumption that improved roads are in the nature of luxuries, desirable if they can be afforded but not to be considered unless there is available for their construction a surplus of income not required for more necessary things.

A brief examination of the purpose of roads and the effect of their improvement is sufficient to dispel this false idea. A road is merely a route over which persons and things are moved from place to place, as in all civilized communities they must be moved. A man may walk along it carrying his load upon his back; he may pile a larger load upon a wagon and cause a team of horses or oxen to draw it for him with less expenditure of labor and time; or he may now load a motor truck with a still larger burden and move it still more rapidly. He may content himself with the wearying, time-consuming delays and obstructions of a rutted trail that runs up hill and down over bowlders and through creeks, twisting and turning around every natural obstacle, and thereby increasing the distance he must travel in going from point to point; or he may cut the hills and fill the valleys, and bridge the streams and straighten the course and thereby enable himself to move a larger load in less time with the same expenditure of effort; in other words, at the same cost. If he chooses the latter course, a certain amount of effort is required to improve the road, and that effort entails a certain cost, but he recognizes that the cost of improving the road is less than the cost of toiling over it in its unimproved condition. For the movement of every vehicle over a road there is a certain cost, a cost which is less if the road be improved than if it be left in a state of nature. Multiply the reduction in the cost of operating one vehicle by the number of vehicles which use the road in a year and the result is the greatest annual sum it is proper to pay to improve the road and maintain it in its improved state. It thus appears that the only limit that may properly be placed upon the expenditure for highway improvement is the aggregate amount of the saving in vehicular operating costs resulting from the improvement, an amount which depends upon the number of vehicles using the road. Because of the great multiplication of motor vehicles it has now come about that the numbers of vehicles using our main roads are so great that the accumulated savings resulting from road improvement will more than pay the cost of the most expensive types of road. It must be clear, therefore, that improved roads are not a luxury to be enjoyed if we have the means and put aside if we have not. The fact is that we lose more by not improving them than it costs to improve them; so that we may say that we pay for improved roads whether we have them or not, and we pay less if we have them than if we have not.

The second erroneous idea is that all roads should be "hard surface"; that no road improvement is worth while unless it results in a "hard surface." The so-called hard-surfaced roads are the concrete, brick, bituminous concrete, sheet asphalt, and various stone and wood-block pavements. All of them are expensive. To insist that all roads should be surfaced with one of these types of material would be luxurious road making indeed. The answer to those who propose such a plan has already been given. It has been shown that the maximum amount which it is proper to spend for the improvement of a given road is the sum of the individual savings accruing from the improvement to the owners of each of the vehicles driven over it. For, after all, those who use the roads are the citizens who pay for them by their taxes; and we can not properly require these citizens or road users to pay more for the building and maintenance of a road than they recover in the way of reduced costs of vehicular operation. Clearly what we spend for the improvement of any given road should always be less than the sum total of savings from the improvement. Otherwise the expenditure for the road is not a paying investment. Fortunately it is not impossible to make a material improvement in the condition of a road without hard-surfacing it, and these lesser improvements are quite effective in reducing the cost of travel.

To grade and drain an unimproved road costs much less than to hard-surface it, and substantially reduces the cost of moving vehicles over the road. If the vehicles that use the road are comparatively few in number, an unsurfaced but graded and drained road can be maintained in satisfactory condition by dragging at very low cost. The cost is so small that the savings accruing from the operation of very few vehicles will more than pay it. If the number of vehicles using the road is great enough to make it impracticable to maintain an unsurfaced road in continuous good condition, the road may be surfaced with sand-clay or gravel which, while it will entail an additional expenditure for improvement, will be more than compensated for by the greater multiplication of individual operating savings resulting from the greater traffic. In a similar manner, if the traffic is heavier than a gravel road will carry, a surface of bituminous macadam may be economically applied; and it is not until the traffic reaches a very considerable density that one of the hard-surfaced types is required or can be economically justified. When that point is reached a hard-surfaced road should be built.

To build and maintain a mile of any one of these types requires a certain annual expenditure of public funds, an expenditure which is greater for the higher than for the lower types; but for any type the required annual expenditure is well within the yearly savings in the cost of operating the number of vehicles which it will carry without destruction. From this course of reasoning it follows that all roads should be improved to the maximum degree the traffic will justify, but no road should be improved to an extent in excess of its earning capacity. The return to the public in the form of economic transportation is the sole measure of the worth of the improvement. Hard surfaces are required on our main, heavily traveled thoroughfares, but to say that all roads should be hard surfaced is merely another way of urging expenditure in excess of income.

The third erroneous idea can be disposed of in less space than has been required for the first two. It is that there is such a thing as a permanent road. It is this delusion that has been responsible for the unhealthy disregard of the maintenance of our roads in the past. Following the will-o'-the-wisp of the "permanent road" we have in the past allowed some of our new roads to go to pieces for lack of necessary repair. Fortunately there is none of the State highway departments which now suffers from this delusion. It is thoroughly understood by these public agencies which are in charge of the more important road work of the country that all roads, regardless of type, gradually depreciate and wear out under the wheels of vehicles and the action of the elements. They know that to keep a road in continuously good condition they must start maintaining it the day its construction is completed; they know, moreover, that no matter how well they repair it the time will come eventually when it will need an entirely new surface, and they set aside the required sum from their available revenues to pay for the maintenance and reconstruction of the roads as such maintenance and reconstruction are required. They consider this recurring expense as a part of the cost of the road to be thrown into the balance with the construction cost and weighed against the multiplied operating savings in determining the type of road to build for any given traffic condition.

T. Warren Allen and Others, *Highways and Highway Transportation*, in *Agriculture Yearbook, 1924* (Washington, Government Printing Office, 1925), 109–112.

◆

67. Flivvers of the Air (1926)

BY WILLIAM B. STOUT

Stout, after an extensive experience as engineer and designer of automobiles, turned his attention to aircraft, and became general manager of the Stout Metal Airplane Company, the airplane division of the Ford Motor Company. This article suggests the probable line of development of air travel in the United States, in part influenced, of course, by what has already been done in Europe.—Bibliography: current periodicals.

TWO broad general fields for the airplane are already open. The first use and the one for which we are now fitted is the service of the airplane as a common carrier. The second is as a personal machine which will be as cheap, as reliable and as convenient as an automobile.

We are already much farther along in the first field than most people realize, while the personal plane is not far off.

No man can safely say what the eventual plane is going to look like or what it will be able to do, and I shall not attempt to be a prophet. There is no point in trying to be one, for the present utility of the airplane is a big enough subject in itself.

Within a year the effects of the air travel will begin to be felt throughout the country. We already have more planes in commercial use than any other country—although not more per capita. We have now about fifteen privately owned air lines in operation or ready to operate as soon as planes can be had. All these lines will carry express matter, and most of them have mail contracts.

It is becoming general for towns and cities to set up landing fields and hangars for the free use of these companies and, what is more important, the companies are being backed by practical business men and bankers of sufficient means to finish what they start.

It is not at all unlikely that we shall soon see an air boom—like the radio boom and the real-estate boom. It is the next thing in order.

American pilots are now flying upward of twenty thousand miles a day over regular routes. The mail routes of the country approach nine thousand miles. Business and banking are using the air mail as a matter of course, and the postage, though high, is not expensive considering the time saved. Also the private lines are being used for jewelry and other valuable articles where the interest charge in transit is important.

One direct result of these services will be to release a large amount of money that is now tied up in goods in transit. Every addition to speed in transportation tends to the lowering of prices to the consumer without the producer getting less. It also brings the producer and the consumer closer together. In addition the speed makes available additional markets to relieve any shortage.

The passenger lines are bound to grow. Our large three-engine machine which is already being flown does away with the possibility of having to come down for engine trouble, since the machine will fly on any two of the engines. Byrd's machine on his North Pole trip had three engines and propellers. He had some difficulties with one engine and might have had to turn back had that been his only engine, but with the assurance of the other two engines he was able to carry on.

With the planes which we now have or can build, it is possible to maintain a daily passenger service from New York to Chicago on a six-hour schedule and from New York to San Francisco on a thirty-hour schedule. The Chicago trip can be made without changing. The fare need not be more than double the present railroad fare.

Starting a service to Europe is only a question of someone putting up the money. We can build a six-engine plane, running on never more than four engines, which will make the crossing in twenty-four hours with great regularity, for the plane can go above or around storms. And also it can take an absolutely direct route, winter and summer.

A plane for this service can be built to operate at two hundred dollars an hour, which includes depreciation and all expenses. It would hold twenty passengers. At a fare of five hundred dollars, the gross revenue would be ten thousand dollars a trip and the expense forty-eight hundred dollars. This gives an ample margin and the fare is only about double the best minimum passage on the fast liners. The enterprise is both mechanically and financially feasible. . . .

Almost everyone now says flying is dangerous. The public is suspicious of the airplane—probably because it has no visible means of support. People were suspicious of the automobile when it first came in, and the man who would drive one of the newfangled things had a leg on the dare-devil cup. . . .

But when the Germans some time back had to send fifty millions in gold to London, how did they send it? By air. Why? Because they figured that the airplane was the safest and quickest way to get the money across the Channel.

This is not to say that flying is perfectly safe. It is not perfectly safe. No form of transportation is or can be absolutely safe and many airplanes are distinctly unsafe. But the fact which few people realize is that nowadays accidents do not happen to well-constructed planes while they are in the air. The single point of danger is in a forced landing on unsuitable ground. The safest position for an airplane is high in the air, going at a speed of one hundred miles an hour or more. A mother writing to her son in the aviation corps counseled him to fly "low and slow." She did not know she was advising him to kill himself.

The old planes were dangerous in the air. They did not have the power to make the speed necessary for control and also they did not have the power to rise above storms and fog.

The old aviators dreaded the nose dive and the tail spin because their wings were not strong enough to stand the strain of checking the dive or the spin. Today both the dive and the spin are recognized parts of military flying and a plane which will not do either at the will of the pilot would be of little use in combat.

Involuntary spins and dives can be prevented by the design—as put into commercial planes; but no aviator now bothers about spinning or diving, for it is as easy to get out of either as to take a motor car out of a skid.

Storms and fog—especially fog—are still dreaded by airmen, but no more so than by ships at sea.

In the Ford Air Service between Dearborn and Cleveland and between Dearborn and Chicago, we are experimenting with a radio arrangement for guiding the pilot through the fog. If he is on the true course he hears "Dearborn"; if he goes to the left he hears only "Dear," and to the right only "born." He can keep his distance above the earth by the instruments before him, and the radio beacon will hold him exactly in his course.

The other large safety item—the provision of landing fields—is equally neglected. All the present types of planes require a fairly level open space of considerable size in which to land. As the planes are developed, the amount of space required will be cut down, but taking the situation as it now stands, the provision of a large number of air ports would cut the element of danger in flying to a negligible figure.

In Europe the air lines last year covered a distance equal to two hundred and forty times around the earth, with casualties too few to mention.

The government air mail, with by no means the most modern planes, has been maintaining a service from New York to San Francisco daily both ways, and for nearly two years has been flying night and day. In two years the day service, going under all sorts of weather conditions, has not had a fatality. The night service has not been so fortunate, but all its accidents have been due to the experimental nature of night flying, which used to be thought impossible.

Two general styles of planes are now being built—the biplane and the monoplane. Each has its advantages, for every plane is a compromise. . . .

I strongly favor the metal monoplane for many reasons. For instance, the flow of air around the wings is not influenced by an adjacent wing or anything close at hand. Again, in a biplane the upper wing lifts often two-thirds of the total load and the lower wing is there largely for structural purposes. The entire advantage of the biplane is structural, but at a great aërodynamic disadvantage.

I believe the monoplane in one form or another will entirely displace the biplane for load-carrying work and eventually in practically every field.

I was led into the thought of making a metal plane because such a plane would not be bothered by heat or cold or any weather and might be left out in the open for days without harm.

Going into metal meant only the monoplane with a thick wing.

The next step was to find the metal, and finally I found duralumin, which is a mixture of copper and aluminum and as strong as structural steel. It is noncorrosive and so light that a plane with a sixty-foot wing spread and capable of carrying a ton of freight weighs no more than a first-class sedan car.

The plane being metal, it can be made with interchangeable parts and almost entirely by machinery; thus the human element of skill in construction is eliminated. This is a step toward the practice followed in the manufacture of automobiles. . . .

The personal plane has not yet come into being, but it is hardly more than five years away.

The small personal plane will carry the pilot and a passenger. It will be small enough to be housed in any fair-sized garage, but really will not need housing, for it will have nothing about it to be hurt by the weather. . . .

The air flivver may seem fantastic, but that is only because aviation has been made so mysterious. This plane, as well as the larger development of the commercial plane, will depend upon the bettering of engine design. . . .

The airplane engine of the future will be more reliable and able to run wide open for at least a week, day and night, without stopping, before it can be considered reliable enough for air work; it must be lighter than present-day engines, and air-cooled—it is as foolish to water-cool an airplane as it is to air-cool a motor boat. . . .

And the landing is going to be of steadily less moment, excepting with the large machines. It will soon be possible to land a small plane at forty miles an hour, and stop it within the same distance that an automobile going at that pace can stop.

William B. Stout, in *The Country Gentleman*, December, 1926 (Philadelphia), 14 ss. Copyright by The Curtis Publishing Co.

68. An Epochal Flight (1927)

BY CAPTAIN CHARLES A. LINDBERGH

Although some sixty others had preceded him in trans-Atlantic flights by air-plane and dirigible, Lindbergh attracted unequalled attention. He was the first to make the flight entirely alone; and his entire success in landing exactly where he planned, as well as his youth and winning personality, made an immense impression on the popular mind. He was promptly promoted to a colonelcy in the National Guard.—Bibliography: Charles A. Lindbergh, *We* (1928); Gerald R. Gage, *"Plucky" Lindbergh* (1927); all newspapers and periodicals of the time, in which an unprecedented amount of space was devoted to Lindbergh and his flight.

WELL, here I am in the hands of American Ambassador Her-rick. From what I have seen of it, I am sure I am going to like Paris.

It isn't part of my plans to fly back to the United States, although that doesn't mean I have finished my flying career. If I thought that was going to be the result of my flight across the Atlantic, you may be sure I would never have undertaken it. Indeed, I hope that I will be able to do some flying over here in Europe—that is, if the souvenir hunters left enough of my plane last night.

Incidentally, that reception I got was the most dangerous part of the whole flight. If wind and storm had handled me as vigorously as that Reception Committee of Fifty Thousand I would never have reached Paris and I wouldn't be eating a 3-o'clock-in-the-afternoon breakfast here in Uncle Sam's Embassy.

There's one thing I wish to get straight about this flight. They call me "Lucky," but luck isn't enough. As a matter of fact, I had what I regarded and still regard as the best existing plane to make the flight from New York to Paris. I had what I regard as the best engine, and I was equipped with what were in the circumstances the best possible instruments for making such efforts. I hope I made good use of what I had.

That I landed with considerable gasoline left means that I had recalled the fact that so many flights had failed because of lack of fuel, and that was one mistake I tried to avoid.

All in all, I couldn't complain of the weather. It wasn't what was predicted. It was worse in some places and better in others. In fact, it was so bad once that for a moment there came over me the temptation to turn back. But then I figured it was probably just as bad behind me as in front of me, so I kept on toward Paris.

As you know, we (that's my ship and I) took off rather suddenly. We had a report somewhere around 4 o'clock in the afternoon before that the weather would be fine, so we thought we would try it.

We had been told we might expect good weather mostly during the whole of the way. But we struck fog and rain over the coast not far from the start. Actually, it was comparatively easy to get to New-foundland, but real bad weather began just after dark, after leaving Newfoundland, and continued until about four hours before daybreak. We hadn't expected that at all, and it sort of took us by surprise, morally and physically. That was when I began to think about turning back.

Then sleet began, and, as all aviators know, in a sleet storm one may be forced down in a very few minutes. It got worse and worse. There, above and below me, and on both sides, was that driving storm. I made several detours trying to get out of it, but in vain. I flew as low as ten feet above the water and then mounted up to ten thousand feet. Along toward morning the storm eased off, and I came down to a comparatively low level.

I had seen one ship just before losing sight of Newfoundland, and I saw the glow of several others afterward through the mist and storm. During the day I saw no ships until near Ireland.

I had, as I said, no trouble before I hit the storm I referred to. We had taken off at 7:55 in the morning. The field was slightly damp and soft, so the take-off was longer than it would have been other-wise. I had no trouble getting over the houses and trees. I kept out of the way of every obstacle and was careful not to take any unnecessary chances. As soon as I cleared everything, the motor was throttled down to three-fourths and kept there during the whole flight, except when I tried to climb over the storm.

Soon after starting I was out of sight of land for 300 miles, from Cape Cod over the sea to Nova Scotia. The motor was acting per-fectly and was carrying well the huge load of 451 gallons of gasoline and 20 gallons of oil, which gave my ship the greatest cruising radius of any plane of its type.

I passed over St. John's, N. F., purposely going out of my way a few miles to check up. I went right through the narrow pass, going down so low that it could be definitely established where I was at that hour. That was the last place I saw before taking to the open sea.

I had made preparations before I started for a forced landing if it became necessary, but after I started I never thought much about the possibility of such a landing. I was ready for it, but I saw no use thinking about it, inasmuch as one place would have been about as good or as bad as another.

Despite the talk about my periscope, I had no trouble in regard to visibility. The view I had on both sides was quite good enough for navigating the ocean, and the purpose of the periscope was only to enable me to see any obstacle directly in front of me. The periscope was useful in starting from New York and landing in Paris. Other than that I used it very little. I kept a map in front of me and an instrument showing practically where I was all of the time.

Shortly after leaving Newfoundland I began to see icebergs. There was a low fog and even through it I could make out bergs clearly. It began to get very cold, but I was well prepared for cold. I had on ordinary flying clothing, but I was down in the cockpit, which protected me, and I never suffered from the weather.

Within an hour after leaving the coast it became dark. Then I struck clouds and decided to try to get over them. For a while I succeeded, at a height of 10,000 feet. I flew at this height until early morning. The engine was working beautifully and I was not sleepy at all. I felt just as if I was driving a motor car over a smooth road, only it was easier.

Then it began to get light and the clouds got higher. I went under some and over others. There was sleet in all of those clouds and the sleet began to cling to the plane. That worried me a great deal and I debated whether I should keep on or go back. I decided I must not think any more about going back. I realized that it was henceforth only a question of getting there. It was too far to turn back.

The engine was working perfectly and that cheered me. I was going along a hundred miles an hour and I knew that if the motor kept on turning I would get there. After that I thought only about navigating, and then I thought that I wasn't so badly off after all.

It was true that the flight was thirty-four hours long, and that at almost any moment in it a forced landing might be what you might call "rather interesting," but I remembered that the flying boys I knew back home spent some hours almost every week in bad flying when a forced landing would have been just as bad for them as a forced landing would have been for me. Those boys don't get credit for it, that's all, and without doubt in a few years many people will be taking just as many chances as I took.

The only real danger I had was at night. In the daytime I knew where I was going, but in the evening and at night it was largely a matter of guesswork. However, my instruments were so good that I never could get more than 200 miles off my course, and that was easy to correct, and I had enough extra gasoline to take care of a number of such deviations. All in all, the trip over the Atlantic, especially the latter half, was much better than I expected.

Laymen have made a great deal of the fact that I sailed without a navigator and without the ordinary stock of navigation instruments, but my real director was my earth inductor compass. I also had a magnetic compass, but it was the inductor compass which guided me so faithfully that I hit the Irish coast only three miles from the theoretic point that I might have hit it if I had had a navigator. I replaced a navigator's weight by the inductor compass. The compass behaved so admirably that I am ashamed to hear any one talk about my luck. Maybe I am lucky, but all the same I knew at every moment where I was going.

The inductor compass is based on the principle of the relation between the earth's magnetic field and the magnetic field generated at the compass. When the course had been set so that the needle registered zero on this compass, any deviation, from any cause, would cause the needle to swing away from zero in the direction of the error. By flying the plane with the needle at an equal distance on the other side of zero and for about the same time the error had been committed, the plane would be back on her course again. This inductor compass was so accurate that I really needed no other guide.

Fairly early in the afternoon I saw a fleet of fishing boats. On some of them I could see no one, but on one of them I saw some men and flew down, almost touching the craft and yelled at them, asking if I was on the right road to Ireland.

They just stared. Maybe they didn't hear me. Maybe I didn't hear them. Or maybe they thought I was just a crazy fool.

An hour later I saw land. I have forgotten just what time it was.

It must have been shortly before 4 o'clock. It was rocky land and all my study told me it was Ireland. And it was Ireland!

I slowed down and flew low enough to study the land and be sure of where I was; and, believe me, it was a beautiful sight. It was the most wonderful looking piece of natural scenery I have ever beheld.

After I had made up my mind that it was Ireland, the right place for me to strike rather than Spain or some other country, the rest was child's play. I had my course all marked out carefully from approximately the place where I hit the coast, and you know it is quite easy to fly over strange territory if you have good maps and your course prepared.

I flew quite low over Ireland to be seen, but apparently no great attention was paid to me. I also flew low over England, mounted a little over the Channel and then came down close to land when I passed a little west of Cherbourg. From Cherbourg I headed for the Seine and followed it up-stream.

I noticed it gets dark much later over here than in New York and I was thankful for that. What especially pleased me was the ease with which I followed my course after hitting the coast of Ireland.

When I was about half an hour away from Paris I began to see rockets and Very lights sent up from the airfield, and I knew I was all right.

I saw an immense vertical electric sign, which I made out to be the Eiffel Tower. I circled Paris once and immediately saw Le Bourget [the aviation field], although I didn't know at first what it was. I saw a lot of lights, but in the dark I couldn't make out any hangars. I sent Morse signals as I flew over the field, but no one appears to have heard them. The only mistake in all my calculations was that I thought Le Bourget was northeast rather than east of Paris.

Fearing for a moment that the field I had seen—remember that I couldn't see the crowd—was some other airfield than Le Bourget, I flew back over Paris to the northwest, looking for Le Bourget. I was slightly confused by the fact that whereas in America when a ship is to land, beacons are put out when floodlights are turned on, at Le Bourget both beacons and floodlights were going at the same time.

I was anxious to land where I was being awaited. So when I didn't find another airfield, I flew back toward the first lights I had seen, and flying low I saw the lights of numberless automobiles. I decided that was the right place, and I landed.

I appreciated the reception which had been prepared for me, and had intended taxiing up to the front of the hangars, but no sooner had my plane touched the ground than a human sea swept toward it. I saw there was danger of killing people with my propeller, and I quickly came to a stop.

That reception was the most dangerous part of the trip. Never in my life have I seen anything like that human sea. It isn't clear to me yet just what happened. Before I knew it I had been hoisted out of the cockpit, and one moment was on the shoulders of some men and the next moment on the ground.

It seemed to be even more dangerous for my plane than for me. I saw one man tear away the switch and another took something out of the cockpit. Then, when they started cutting pieces of cloth from the wings, I struggled to get back to the plane, but it was impossible.

A brave man with good intentions tried to clear a way for me with a club. Swinging the club back, he caught me on the back of the head.

It isn't true that I was exhausted. I was tired, but I wasn't exhausted.

Several French officers asked me to come away with them and I went, casting anxious glances at my ship. I haven't seen it since, but I am afraid it suffered. I would regret that very much because I want to use it again.

But I must remember that crowd did welcome me. Good Lord! There must have been a million of them. Other men will fly the Atlantic as I did, but I think it safe to guess that none of them will get any warmer reception than I got.

Finally I got to Ambassador Herrick's house and I have certainly been all right since then. . . .

I didn't bring any extra clothes with me. I am wearing a borrowed suit now. It was a case of clothes or gasoline, and I took the gasoline. I have a check on a Paris bank and am going to cash it tomorrow morning, buy shirts, socks and other things. I expect to have a good time in Paris.

But I do want to do a little flying over here.

Charles A. Lindbergh, in *The New York Times*, May 23, 1927; copyright by The New York Times Company, and reprinted by permission.

CHAPTER XIV — NATIONAL FINANCE

69. The Liberty Loan (1917)

BY SECRETARY WILLIAM GIBBS McADOO

McAdoo, a lawyer and railroad man by profession, was Secretary of the Treasury (1913–1918) and Director-General of Railways (1917–1919) under the Wilson administration. This is part of one of the addresses made by him as Secretary of the Treasury, in the effort to crystallize public sentiment in support of the First Liberty Loan. Before the war was over, a tremendous organization of bankers and financiers had been assembled to solve the financial problems involved.—Bibliography: Harvey E. Fisk, *Our Public Debt, an Historical Sketch with a Description of the United States Securities* (1919); Alexander D. Noyes, *Financial Chapters of the War* (1916); Noyes, *The War Period of American Finance, 1918–1925* (1926); Dewey, *Financial History of the United States;* American Academy of Political and Social Science, *Financing the War* (1918); Jacob H. Hollander, *War Borrowing* (1919); Ernest L. Bogart, *War Costs and their Financing* (1921).

· · · WARS can not be fought without money. The very first step in this war, the most effective step that we could take, was to provide the money for its conduct. The Congress quickly passed an act authorizing a credit of $5,000,000,000, and empowered the Secretary of the Treasury, with the approval of the President, to extend to the allied Governments making war with us against the enemies of our country, credits not exceeding $3,000,000,-000. Since that law was passed—it was only passed on the 24th of April, less than a month ago—the financial machinery of your Government has been speeded up to top notch to give relief to the allies in Europe, in order that they might be able to make their units in the trenches, their machinery which is there on the ground, tell to the utmost, and tell, if possible, so effectively that it might not be necessary to send American soldiers to the battle fields. As a result, we have already extended in credits to these Governments—Great Britain, France, Italy, Russia, and Belgium—something like $745,-000,000, and we shall have to extend before this year is out, if the war lasts that long, not $3,000,000,000 of credits, but probably five billions or six billions. But it makes no difference how much credit we extend, we are extending it for a service which is essential, as I said before, for your own protection, if no other grave issues were involved in this struggle.

This initial financing was not an easy thing to do. The Congress authorized the Secretary of the Treasury to issue, in addition to bonds, $3,000,000,000 of one-year debt certificates. Their purpose is to bridge over any chasms, so to speak, so that if the Treasury is short at any time, because of extraordinary demands, we can sell these temporary certificates, supply the need, and then sell bonds to take up these certificates. We have been selling temporary debt certificates in anticipation of the sale of these Liberty bonds. The first issue of bonds,—$2,000,000,000,—has not been determined by any arbitrary decision or judgment; it has been determined by the actual necessities of the situation. It is the least possible sum that we can afford to provide for the immediate conduct of the war. We are trying to spread the payment for the bonds over as large a period as possible, so that there shall be no interference with business. This money is not going to be taken out of the country. All of this financing is largely a matter of shifting credits; it is not going to involve any loss of gold; it is not going to involve any loss of values. These moneys are going to be put back into circulation, put back promptly into the channels of business and circulated and recirculated to take care of the abnormal prosperity of the country, a prosperity that will be greater in the present year than ever before in our history. As we sell these bonds we take back from the foreign governments, under the terms of the act, their obligations, having practically the same maturity as ours, bearing the same rate of interest as ours, so that as their obligations mature the proceeds will be employed to pay off the obligations issued by this Government to provide them with credit. So you can see, fellow citizens, that in extending credit to our allies we are not giving anything to them. So far as that is concerned, for the purposes of this war, I would be willing to give them anything to gain success, but they don't ask that. They are glad and grateful that the American Government is willing to give them the benefit of its matchless credit, a credit greater and stronger than any nation on the face of the globe. We give them credit at the same price our Government has to pay you, its people, for the use of the money, because we do not want to make any profit on our allies. We do not

want to profit by the blood that they must shed upon the battle field
in the same cause in which we are engaged.

What can you do to make this loan a success? You have got to
work, gentlemen, to make this loan a success. America never before
was offered a $2,000,000,000 issue of bonds. This Government never
has had to borrow so much money at one time. The money is in the
country and can be had if you men will simply say that the Government can have it. The annual increase of our wealth is estimated
to be fifty billions of dollars. You are asked not to give anything
to your Government, but merely to invest 4 per cent of the annual
increase of wealth in this country, to take back from your Government the strongest security on the face of God's earth, and to receive
in return for it 3½ per cent per annum, exempted from all taxation,
with the further provision that if the Government issues any other
bonds during the period of this war at a higher rate of interest than
3½ per cent every man who has bought a 3½ per cent bond may turn
it in and get a new bond at the higher rate of interest. Could anything be fairer than that? Could anything be more secure than an
obligation of your Government, an obligation backed not alone by
the honor of the American people—which of itself is sufficient—but
backed also by the resources of the richest nation in the world, a
nation whose aggregate wealth to-day is two hundred and fifty billions
of dollars; so that you take no risk, my friends, in buying these
bonds.

This bond offering is not going to be successful of its own momentum.
Every man and woman in this country must realize that the first
duty they can perform for their country is to take some of these bonds.
Those who are not able to take some of these bonds ought to begin saving monthly to take some of them; and if they can not save monthly,
or at all, they ought to make some man or woman who is able to
take some of these bonds subscribe. If you do that, my friends,
this first issue of $2,000,000,000 will be largely oversubscribed. It
depends, however, upon you. Your Government can not do what
you can do for your Government. A government is not worth a continental unless it has the support of the people of the country. And
one thing that makes me glad—I ought not to be glad that there is
a war—but I can not help feeling a certain amount of reverent ela-
tion that God has called us to this great duty, not alone to vindicate

the ideals that inspire us but also because it has, for the time being, eliminated detestable partisanism from our national life and made us one solid people. As one people, my friends, with such an ideal, the Republic is invincible and irresistible, and there can be no doubt whatever of the outcome. I want you to give a thunderous reply on the 15th of June—Liberty bond subscription day—to the enemies of your country.

William Gibbs McAdoo, Address at a meeting of business men and bankers of Iowa, in Des Moines, May 21, 1917. *Senate Document No. 40, 65th Congress, 1st Session* (Washington, Government Printing Office, 1917), 6–8.

———————◆———————

70. Benefits of the Budget (1922)

BY DIRECTOR CHARLES G. DAWES

Dawes, a Chicago banker, was the first Director of the Bureau of the Budget, the aim of which was to put government expenditures on a truly business basis. His name was given to the "Dawes Plan" for German reparations payments (1924) in the formulation of which he had a part and on account of which he was awarded a half of the Nobel Peace Prize for 1926. In 1924 he was elected Vice-President of the United States and promptly announced plans for the revision of the rules of debate governing the Senate. In 1929 he was appointed Ambassador to Great Britain.—Bibliography: Rufus C. Dawes, *The Dawes Plan in the Making* (1925); George P. Auld, *The Dawes Plan and the New Economics* (1927); Carl Bergmann, *The History of Reparations* (1927).

. . . THE budget law is the product of nonpartisanship in Congress. In the first year's work of the budget, members of both parties, in Congress and out, have earnestly contributed time and effort to the furthering of its efficiency. It has no administrative functions. It is a small organization, consisting of the Director of the Budget, the assistant director, four advisers of the director's selection, to be compensated at the rate of $6,000 per year, the balance of the organization being secured under civil service rules at salaries not exceeding $5,000 per year. The major part of its force is engaged in gathering and compiling information from the departments, upon which advice to the Executive may be based not only as to the money which will be required in the operations of Government, but as to how it can be more economically and efficiently expended to carry out the policies imposed by higher legislative and executive authority. . . .

The results accomplished, while primarily due to this Executive pressure, could not have been achieved without the coöperation of the rank and file of Government employees who have commendably responded to the directions of the President as transmitted to them by the heads of the departments and establishments. Numerous examples of the interest and ingenuity which have been exhibited by the individual employee in office and field have come to the attention of this office, and this spirit, no less than that of the head of the department or establishment, has been a factor contributing to the savings accomplished.

In treating governmental business questions the clarifying method is always reached through the adoption of the point of view which would be taken in a private enterprise confronting analogous questions in its business. The idea that governmental business can be successfully administered under a different set of principles or different methods than private business is a fallacy which has already cost this Government too dearly to be further encouraged as a basis for partisan discussion.

An appropriation by Congress is simply an authorization of expenditure. If Congress overestimates the necessity for expenditure and makes an overappropriation it does not necessarily follow that the unspent portion of an appropriation is a real saving. On the other hand, if Congress underestimates the necessity for expenditure in its appropriations it does not follow that an excess expenditure by a department is necessarily an evidence of extravagance. Where a portion of a given appropriation is unspent it may indicate a saving, provided the money was unspent because of more economical and efficient functioning of a governmental activity. In like manner, where, in expenditure, a fixed congressional appropriation has been exceeded, it may represent extravagance if the excess expenditure was occasioned by the inefficient functioning of a governmental activity.

Indirect savings, resulting from such improvements in the functioning of governmental business activities as make unnecessary the expenditure of money which otherwise would have to be appropriated by Congress, must be determined by consideration of the facts, without any reference whatever to the subject of congressional appropriations. The question of the relation of appropriations to the subject of real savings is only incidental as being one of the factors discussed in consideration of the actual facts relating to the savings under discussion. If the only factor to be considered in estimating real savings was the relation of actual expenditures to the appropriation program outlined by Congress all it would be necessary to do to apparently save money would be, at the beginning of any fiscal year, to make appropriations so large that under no possibility could all of them be spent and thereby, at the end of the year, "save" the unspent portion of the appropriation, incidentally avoiding any deficiency appropriation. Deficiency appropriations, therefore, are not necessarily the evidence of extravagance, nor is the unspent portion of appropriations necessarily an evidence of economy.

In a private business fixed appropriations are always considered as the maximum of the amount of money to be spent in administration, never the minimum, as has been the case in Government. While in private business appropriation limitations are imposed to check extravagance, they are not allowed to operate either to prevent economy or to destroy efficiency. Appropriation limits in congressional efforts to secure real economy in administration in the past have failed, because the departments, unsubjected to Executive pressure, have organized themselves to spend the maximum amount appropriated and then, up to this year, have practically relaxed efforts to save under it. An authorized standard of expenditures in Government, based upon appropriations, without intervening Executive supervision, is fatal to economy. From the beginning of our Government, for proper business administration, there should have been interposed, as there is at the present time, Executive control and Executive responsibility over the business organization, and between the business organization and the congressional appropriating power.

This report is an effort to determine what the real savings of Government have been during the current fiscal year. Economies and savings will be estimated as similar ones would be in private business organization—by consideration of the facts which are involved. . . .

The estimates of this report relate to the largest business in the world, conducted over a great territory. The machinery of investigation is limited, and even were it not limited the short time available for preparation involves the liability of some error in estimates. The governmental business machine has, for the present fiscal year, functioned with a sense of responsibility to a central control, with resulting marked improvement, the full extent of which can only be developed by time.

The Bureau of the Budget is an impersonal, impartial, and nonpartisan business agent. In this particular report where its estimates may become a basis of contention in an approaching political contest, its figures should be conservative and meet the test of examination, not only in the present but in the future when existing partisan differences are forgotten and the record for impartiality and nonpartisanship of the Budget Bureau is considered in retrospect by the unprejudiced mind of the governmental economist and student. It will be noted from the table covering gross expenditures and estimates that the Director of the Budget, out of total estimated expenditures of $3,922,372,030 for 1922, classifies only $1,765,875,672 as being generally subject to Executive control in the operation of the routine business of Government. These figures compare with actual expenditures under the same categories in 1921 of $2,673,435,079.77, segregated out of a total expenditure for 1921 of $5,538,040,689.30. The reduction in the ordinary expenditures for the operation of the routine business of Government generally subject to Executive control over governmental expenditures in 1922 is estimated by the Director of the Budget in this report at the lesser sum of $250,134,385.03. He feels reasonably assured that this estimate of economies and savings attributable to the new system is an underestimate, but that if an error has been made in this regard the savings and economies are still so large as to vindicate it, and will at the same time emphasize the indispensable policy of the Budget Bureau to have its estimates conformable to the principles of business conservatism. In these figures the Director of the Budget has found it impossible to make any reliable estimate of some indefinite general savings, such as those incident to the corrected system of purchasing which has been established in the Government, by which competition between departments and the overlapping and acquiring of unnecessary surplus has been avoided. On the basis of the original estimates made by the different departments and establishments there have been eliminated, after

due consideration of the facts involved, in the neighborhood of $150,-
000,000 claimed economies.

Charles G. Dawes, *Report of the Director of the Bureau of the Budget*, May 8, 1922
(Washington, Government Printing Office, 1922), 3–5 *passim*.

---

71. Our War Debtors (1922)

FROM THE NEW REPUBLIC

This editorial is based on the views of Herbert Hoover, later President of the United
States, whose sound knowledge of economics and personal familiarity with Euro-
pean conditions qualified him to analyze the situation. For Hoover, see No. 200
below.—Bibliography: Harvey E. Fisk, *The Inter-Ally Debts: an Analysis of War
and Post-War Public Finance, 1914–1923* (1924); Harold G. Moulton and Leo
Pasvolsky, *World-War Debt Settlements* (1926); John F. Bass and H. G. Moulton,
America and the Balance Sheet of Europe (1922); National Industrial Conference
Board, *The Inter-Ally Debts and the United States* (1925).

ON the economics of the Allied debts Mr. Hoover has spoken with
characteristic vigor. The debts are not the crushing burden
that advocates of cancellation are in the habit of considering them.
Three hundred and fifty millions a year from our Continental debtors
would represent only a minute fraction of their total national incomes,
and only from two to twelve per cent of their actual budgets. There
is not one of them that does not waste a larger percentage in military
parading or other pernicious extravagance. Neither is there any
financial impracticability in finding $350,000,000 in bills of exchange
to be transmitted to America. In the long run there will be plenty
of paper to be found, drawn against American tourist expenditures,
American investments abroad and American tropical imports. Finally, the notion that we should be injured by the influx of goods in
payment of the debts is a pure delusion. We can take a modest sum
like that in goods that do not compete with our own productions.
Mr. Hoover could have made his case even stronger if he had not been
the spokesman of a high tariff administration. Even if the $350,000,-
000 were sent here in the form of goods competing with our own
products, the volume is too insignificant to affect prices or employment appreciably. We consume at least thirty-five billions of such

goods, one hundred times the assumed import. Besides, since the $350,000,000 would be gratis, it would not reduce by one dollar the purchasing power to be applied to domestic products. And it is this purchasing power which sustains prices.

Mr. Hoover has performed a valuable service for American intelligence in clearing away some of the cobwebs that have accumulated around the debt problem. But a demonstration of the abstract feasibility of debt payment does not bring us appreciably nearer to practical results. European opinion as reflected by the press is as firmly convinced as ever of the impossibility of payment. European economists do not believe that the debts will ever be paid. Nor do we see how Mr. Hoover can believe it.

For the European nations, though they may be individually sane in their policies, are collectively mad, and that collective madness stands in the way of the economic recovery which must precede debt payment. It is collective madness which has saddled upon a depleted and impoverished Europe military establishments actually larger and more costly than those under which the continent groaned in its pre-war strength. It is collective madness which makes every state adopt a menacing attitude toward its neighbor, to the disturbance of all orderly economic and social development. It is collective madness which has multiplied customs barriers and embargo lines when the obvious need of the times is the freest practicable movement of trade.

It is easy to speculate about collective interests, but not very profitable. For there is no collective Europe, but a group of intensely competitive states, each forced to look chiefly to itself for security and even existence. France spends an excessive part of her income on soldiering. How could she do otherwise? She fears Germany, and with good reason, for however broken down and friendless the Germans may be now, history is a long story, and may some day give Germany a chance to avenge on France the injuries that France, England and America inflicted on her. In the present state of world organization France is far from safe. Armed as she is at present, she is not so safe as America would be if she had not one soldier, not one ship. And does anyone here propose to save $350,000,000 a year by utterly abolishing our army and navy?

Poland menaces Russia and Russia menaces Poland. Collectively that is idiotic. But has Russia any guarantee against Polish aggression except her power to inspire a wholesome fear in the Poles? Has Poland any different guarantee of her continued independence? Czecho-Slovakia is pursuing a policy of extreme protection designed incidentally to ruin the industries of Austria, potentially a valuable customer and supporter. Why should she not, in a world where industrial power and national security go hand in hand? American industry could better do entirely without customs duties than any of the succession states in Central Europe could forego customs rates that are destructive of the collective interest. How many American industrialists, or statesmen, even, are out for absolute free trade?

Now, so long as the collective madness of Europe persists, no nation will scamp its expenditures for defence, for military railroads and highways, for industrial subsidies, in order to pay its debts to America. No nation will add to the burden under which its taxpayers are staggering for any such purpose. It is not that the nations of Europe are insensitive to the point of honor—assuming that they regard the American claims as debts of honor, which is unlikely. No political party can govern if it taxes too heavily or strips the country of national defences. Has anyone heard of a party in France or Italy, Poland or Jugoslavia or Czecho-Slovakia which is aiming at power on a platform of debt payment?

Whatever helps to restore sanity to Europe brings debt payment nearer, or what is far more important, brings Europe nearer to the point where she can take her proper place in world trade. Did Mr. Hoover's speech make any such contribution to European sanity? That has not been its immediate effect. On the contrary, the effect on the debtor states has been to strengthen the absurd belief that America has, and has had, no other interest in European welfare than self-interest. Apparently it has strengthened the French determination to proceed drastically to collect what she can from Germany. It has by no means lightened the fear in France and Italy that francs and lire may presently plunge to the abyss after the marks and kronen and rubles.

But Mr. Hoover was not primarily concerned, we surmise, with the immediate effect upon European public sentiment. As a member of the commission charged with the refunding of the Allied debts, he may be in a position to exert a considerable influence upon European policy. If the European negotiators believed that the debts had already been virtually cancelled by American popular opinion, they would be disposed both to resist any movement toward fixing definite conditions for payment and to reject forthwith any proposal for the consideration of policies conducive to peace and international prosperity. The attitude of the bankers' convention may have given our debtors a mistaken view of American leniency. It was essential to our future diplomatic action that Mr. Hoover should correct any such misapprehension.

Whether America can exert any influence upon European policy at this late date is somewhat doubtful. If she can, her best leverage consists of the debts. And it cannot be made too plain to Europe that we regard those debts as valid and binding.

Editorial, *Hoover on the Debts*, in *New Republic* (New York, 1922), XXXII, 234–235.

———◆———

72. Federal Farm Loans (1924)

BY NILS A. OLSEN AND OTHERS

The system of Federal Farm Loans was a device to ameliorate the financial difficulties of agriculture. As this description shows, its machinery is somewhat complicated, and the formalities necessary to borrow in this way have doubtless operated to limit its use. Olsen is associated with the Bureau of Agricultural Economics of the Department of Agriculture.—Bibliography: Herbert Myrick, *Rural Credits System for the United States*.

. . . A FARM mortgage credit system which would more adequately serve the needs of farmers was created by the Federal farm loan act in 1916. This measure provides for two classes of credit institutions—the Federal land banks, which operate under Government direction and supervision, and the joint-stock land banks, which are privately owned and managed institutions but operate under the supervision of the Federal Government. The general direction of the Federal farm loan system is in the hands of the Federal Farm Loan Board. This board is composed of seven members, six of whom are appointed by the President with the advice and consent of the Senate. The Secretary of the Treasury is chairman ex officio of the board. This board exercises careful supervision over the activities of both Federal and joint-stock land banks. It gives special attention to the adequacy of security taken for the funds advanced, as well as to the marketing of the bonds through which funds for making loans are obtained.

For the purpose of administering the Federal land banks the country has been divided into 12 districts, each of which is served by one bank. Each bank had originally a paid-up capital stock of $750,000. The total original capital stock of the 12 banks was therefore, $9,000,-000, of which $8,892,130 was subscribed by the United States Treasury. The law provided that the capital stock subscribed by the Government should be gradually retired through repurchase by the local national farm loan associations. By December 31, 1924, seven of the banks had completely repaid their capital stock, and the five remaining banks had outstanding the sum of $1,670,965 of the original stock subscribed by the Treasury.

The Federal land banks were in the beginning managed by five directors appointed by the Federal Farm Loan Board. At the time the original act was passed it was the intention that the control of each bank should pass to the borrowers as soon as the subscription to the stock amounted to $100,000. Control should then be vested in nine directors, six of whom were to be chosen to represent the public interest. From an early date, however, it was felt by the board that the control of the Federal land banks by borrowers would be unwise. The coöperative features of the system did not develop as expected. Once their loans were obtained, borrowers often ceased to participate actively in the work of the local farm loan associations. It was also believed that farmer control of the banks would interfere with the sale of bonds in adequate volume. An amendment was accordingly passed in 1923 which gives the Federal Loan Board at least as much control over the Federal land bank directors as that of the local associations. This amendment provides for seven directors. The Federal Farm Loan Board appoints three district directors and the national farm loan associations elect three local directors. The seventh member, who is a director at large, is appointed by the board from the three persons obtaining the greatest number of votes for director at large from the associations. It is thus apparent that the original plan to make the Federal land banks strictly coöperative institutions has not been realized.

The Federal land banks operate locally through national farm loan associations, which were intended to be the active part of the system. These associations may be organized by 10 or more farmers desiring loans amounting to at least $20,000 and are chartered by the Federal Farm Loan Board. At the present time over 4,600 national farm loan associations have been organized in all parts of the country. Practically every county in the United States is now served by one or more of these associations. . . .

The Federal land banks make loans only to actual farmers or to those who intend to become farmers. With few exceptions these loans are made through local national farm loan associations. Every borrower is required to subscribe to the extent of 5 per cent of his loan in the stock of the local national farm loan association. The association in turn must subscribe to an equal amount in the stock of the Federal land bank. Every borrower is liable to twice the amount of his stock for losses that may be incurred by the association.

Originally the maximum loan that could be made by the Federal land banks was $10,000. By an amendment passed in March, 1923, the maximum was raised to $25,000. The average size of loans made since the organization of the system to date is $3,065. The largest loans have been made in Iowa, where they average $7,509, and the smallest in Arkansas, where they average $1,706. These loans can be made up to 50 per cent of the appraised value of the land plus 20 per cent of the appraised value of the insured permanent improvements. In no case can the loan exceed $100 per acre. The final appraisals on which these loans are based are made by special land-bank appraisers, appointed by the Federal Farm Loan Board. Under the act the land must be appraised on the basis of its value for agricultural purposes and its earning power. These appraisals in the past have been conservatively made, and this fact no doubt has contributed to the growing popularity of the Federal farm loan bonds. The interest rate on Federal farm loans may not exceed 6 per cent and may be even lower, depending upon the rate paid on the bonds. Loans may be made for terms ranging from 5 to 40 years at the option of the borrower. Most of them, however, are made for terms ranging from 33 to 35 years. At the end of five years all or a part of the loan may be repaid. Payments are made on the amortization plan, whereby annual or semiannual installments are paid covering the interest and a part of the principal until the loan is liquidated. . . .

The Federal land banks began their operations in the fall of 1917. Their growth was fairly rapid until the summer of 1919, when court action was brought to test the constitutionality of the Federal farm loan act. In the spring of 1921 the act was declared constitutional, and from then on the system grew rapidly.

During the two years 1918–1919 an average of $128,636,000 in loans were closed annually; in the two following years the annual average dropped to $81,942,000. With the full resumption of their activities in 1921 a large demand for loans developed, and during the three years 1922–1924 an annual average of $193,999,000 loans were closed. This record is splendid evidence of the manner in which the Federal land banks responded to the needs of the farmer during the years of depression. Since 1924 there has been a decline in the volume of loans made by the banks, which reflects a decreasing demand for farm mortgage credit. The Federal land banks in a very short time have become leading sources of farm mortgage credit. In January, 1920, it is estimated that their loans amounted to 3.7 per cent of the total farm mortgage debt, as compared with over 9 per cent in January, 1924.

The loans of the Federal land banks are distributed quite uniformly over the entire country. In fact, the Federal land banks have been especially helpful in accommodating farmers in regions where other agencies have supplied such credit in inadequate amounts and often at high costs. The Federal land banks thus have been one of the most important channels through which capital could flow freely into regions most in need of such credit. . . .

While the Federal land banks perhaps have not materially aided the landless farmer, they have helped to reduce and equalize interest rates and have assisted farmers in refunding their debts on more favorable terms. It should no longer be necessary for the farmer to have his mortgage credit in the form of short-term loans, subject to frequent renewals. With the advent of long-time amortized loans such as are made by the Federal land banks, the danger of foreclosure in time of depression no doubt will be greatly reduced.

The Federal farm loan act also provided for land banks organized and owned by lenders. These banks are known as joint-stock land banks. While they are privately organized and managed institutions, they also operate under the supervision of the Federal Farm Loan Board. A joint-stock land bank may be organized by 10 or more persons with a minimum capital stock of $250,000. The plan under which they are operated is very similar to that of the Federal land banks. . . .

At the time the Federal farm loan act was passed it was thought the joint-stock land banks would play only a minor rôle in financing the mortgage credit needs of the farmer. As a matter of fact, the growth of such banks in the early years of the system was slow. By November 30, 1918, only nine joint-stock land banks had been organized, and further development was practically stopped when the constitutionality of the act was challenged. Since the constitutionality of the act was set at rest the development of joint-stock land banks has been very rapid. . . .

At the beginning of this year there were 64 joint-stock land banks operating in most sections of the country. The major portion of their loans, however, are being made in the better farming regions. This is somewhat in contrast to the policy of the Federal land banks, the loans of which are more uniformly distributed over the entire country. It is also significant that the loans made by the joint-stock land banks are materially larger than those of the Federal land banks. Since their organization the loans of the joint-stock land banks have averaged $7,714, compared with an average of $3,065 for the Federal land banks. The joint-stock land banks, as previously stated, are permitted to make loans up to $50,000, and this no doubt has been an advantage in their competition with the Federal land banks.

Nils A. Olsen and Others, *Farm Credit*, in *Agriculture Yearbook, 1924* (Washington, Government Printing Office, 1925), 198–208 *passim*.

73. The Federal Reserve System (1926)

BY KRICKEL K. CARRICK

The booklet from which this extract is taken was prepared by Carrick, a member of the staff of the Federal Reserve Bank of Boston, and is an example of the way in which large organizations are attempting to explain their technical functions to the public in simple language.—Bibliography: E. W. Kemmerer, *A B C of the Federal Reserve System;* H. P. Willis, *The Federal Reserve System.*

. . . THE function of the Federal Reserve Board may be best summed up by the statement that the Board is the supervisory and governing body of the system. It is composed of eight members; two members, the Secretary of the Treasury and the Comptroller of the Currency, are members ex-officio and the other six members are appointed by the President for terms of ten years each. The President, in selecting the six appointive members, is required to have due regard to the financial, agricultural, industrial and commercial interests and the geographical divisions of the country, and no two appointive members may be from the same Federal reserve district. . . .

The country is divided geographically into twelve Federal reserve districts and in each district there is a Federal reserve bank, named for the city where located. . . .

Each Federal reserve bank is chartered for twenty years from the date of its organization and is a corporation separate and distinct from the other eleven reserve banks. . . .

The board of directors is composed of nine members equally divided into three classes, which are designated by the letters A, B and C. The member or stockholding banks are divided by the Federal Reserve Board into three groups, each group being composed as far as possible of banks of similar size and each group choosing one class A director and one class B director. In other words, the member banks elect six of the nine directors. Class A directors must be representative of the stockholding banks and may be and usually are active executive officers of member banks and obviously, since they represent banks, they represent the principal lending element in the community. Class B directors may not be officers, directors or employees of any bank and must be "actively engaged in their district in commerce, agriculture or some other industrial pursuit," so that they may naturally be expected to represent the borrowing element in the community. The three class C directors are appointed by the Federal Reserve Board and since they may not be either officers, directors, employees or stockholders of any bank, are representative of the public and its general economic interest. One of the class C directors has a dual capacity, being designated chairman of the board of directors and "Federal reserve agent," in which latter capacity he is required to maintain an office of the Federal Reserve Board on the premises of the bank. Another of the class C directors is designated deputy chairman and exercises the powers of the chairman when necessary. The terms of office of all directors are three years, so arranged that the term of one director of each class expires each year. . . .

All national banks in existence when the Act was passed were given a certain period within which to determine whether they would become member banks by subscribing for stock in their district reserve banks, or discontinue operation under national charters. . . .

Any State bank or trust company which is of specified size may apply to the Federal Reserve Board for admission to the system and, subject to such conditions as the Board may prescribe, may be admitted to membership. . . . These national and State bank members are the only stockholders in the Federal reserve banks and their capital stock subscriptions, just as in an ordinary bank, constitute the first source of funds with which the reserve banks operate.

The second source of funds used by a Federal reserve bank is in the reserve deposits of member banks. The country having found by experience that scattered reserves could not be of maximum usefulness, the Federal Reserve Act has brought about a pooling of such funds by requiring every member bank, national or State, to carry all of its legal reserve on deposit with its Federal reserve bank. It may carry such money in its own vault as its officers think best, but the only money which now counts as legal reserve is that which is left with the reserve bank. However, since a pooled reserve need not be as large as one individually held, the original reserve requirements of the Act were reduced below the reserves required of a national bank before the system was started and later the Act was amended so as to reduce still further the reserve required, partly because it was concluded that a lower reserve would suffice and partly to compensate member banks for inability to count cash in vault as reserve. To most member banks these two reductions meant that a large amount of funds was freed for them to loan or invest. The reserve which a member bank must now keep with its reserve bank is a sum equal to three per cent of the member bank's time deposits plus seven, ten or thirteen per cent of deposits payable on demand, depending on the location of the member bank. . . .

Having assembled the reserves of the member banks of the country into the twelve "reservoirs,"—the Federal reserve banks,—upon the theory that when so assembled some of the reserve funds might be drawn out to help member banks having a temporary or seasonal demand in excess of their own ability to supply, Congress provided a very simple arrangement for affording such help. Any member bank, large or small, city or country, may ask its Federal reserve bank to discount for it, that is, to buy from the member bank upon the latter's indorsement, certain "paper," that is, notes and drafts, etc., which the member bank owns. The kinds of notes, etc., upon which a member bank may thus replenish its funds, generally referred to as "eligible paper," are specified in the Federal Reserve Act and the Federal Reserve Board is given the power to determine whether particular classes of paper come within the specifications. Generally speaking, paper to be eligible must be a note or draft, etc., issued or drawn for the purpose of producing, purchasing, carrying or marketing goods, agricultural products or live stock and it must have a definite maturity at the time of rediscount of not more than 90 days, except that if for an agricultural purpose or based upon live stock, its maturity may be not more than nine months. . . .

Besides borrowing by means of the rediscount of eligible paper, a bank may secure an advance from its Federal reserve bank by giving its own note direct. In such a case the note must mature within fifteen days and it must be secured either by Government securities or by paper which is eligible for discount as previously described, or by certain drafts and bankers' acceptances of kinds which a Federal reserve bank may purchase in the open market. . . .

Probably the most important services furnished by the Federal reserve banks are their primary functions, namely the rediscount of commercial paper or loans to member banks and the ability to furnish currency, with which should be grouped, as of co-ordinate importance, their open market operations. . . .

Scarcely less important than the primary services is the collection of checks. Under regulations made by the Federal Reserve Board, the twelve Federal reserve banks are acting virtually as nation-wide clearing houses for their member banks and for such non-member banks as maintain certain balances with the reserve banks, and by far the greater portion of out-of-town checks are today collected through the reserve banks almost as directly as checks on banks in the same place are collected through the familiar general clearing house exchange or direct exchange between banks. Out-of-town checks deposited with a Federal reserve bank are sent direct to the places where payable and as a rule direct to the banks on which drawn, except that if drawn on banks in another Federal reserve district they are sent to the reserve bank of that district, which presents them direct. This direct forwarding and settlement cut in half the average time which was required to collect out-of-town checks under the old indirect routing, in many instances effecting an even greater saving of time. Obviously, if the proceeds of out-of-town checks can be obtained more quickly, they can be sooner used, and the importance of this saving of time to business and banking is apparent, from the estimate generally accepted that over 95% of the commercial transactions of the country are settled by checks. Furthermore, the Federal reserve banks are able to collect checks drawn on 90% or more of the banks of the country without payment of the old "exchange" charge, another great saving to commerce. Checks deposited by a member bank are credited to its reserve account if the proceeds can be obtained immediately by the reserve bank; otherwise, credit to the reserve account is deferred for the length of time which it takes the reserve bank to obtain the proceeds, as shown by a time schedule governing the matter and applying to checks drawn on banks in different parts of the country.

The Federal reserve banks also collect miscellaneous items such as notes, drafts, bonds, coupons, etc., collection being made through direct routing and presentation in much the same manner as in the case of checks. . . .

Member banks wishing to create balances or pay funds in another part of the country may do so by means of wire transfers through their reserve banks without loss of time and, if transfers are for multiples of $100, at no cost to member banks except where made for the benefit of a designated customer, when a charge is made for the cost of the telegram. The convenience of this service as compared with an express shipment may be illustrated by the case of a member bank wishing to transfer $10,000 from Boston to San Francisco. By express it would take five days to get the money there, the expressage would be $32.50 and the loss of interest $8.22; while if made by wire through the Federal reserve bank for the account of a member bank, there would be no charge to the member bank and the time taken would normally be a few minutes only. Such transfers are accomplished by means of wire advices from the sending to the receiving Federal reserve bank and through the medium of the "Gold Settlement Fund," which is a fund of gold carried in Washington, D. C., by the twelve Federal reserve banks. Each Federal reserve bank advises the Federal Reserve Board daily by wire of its credits to each of the other eleven reserve banks, whether those credits arise out of the wire transfers mentioned here or out of other transactions, appropriate entries then being made in the books of the Gold Settlement Fund. This daily settlement between the reserve banks through this fund is one of the chief reasons why the reserve banks are able to save so much time on the collection of checks payable in other Federal reserve districts,— payment for such checks when collected comes back through a wire credit in the Gold Settlement Fund. . . .

Lest too much may be expected of the Federal Reserve System, it is well to bear in mind that its purposes, functions, scope and influence, though broad, have limitations. That it can be a cure-all for all financial ills or for general economic derangements is beyond the range of possibility. It cannot be a preventive of business depressions, which may always be expected when development and production get too far ahead of economic needs. Nothing in the Federal Reserve Act nor in the history of that measure imposes any duty or responsibility upon it to attempt to influence prices, either in the interest of the producer or for the advantage of the consumer. That it may prevent financial panics, however, is a different matter, and competent students for the most part believe that the danger of another financial panic in this country, such as that of 1907, is so small as to be negligible.

Nor does the reserve bank constitute a sort of guarantor of deposits in member banks. The solvency of any bank, member or non-member, is still the care and responsibility of the officers and directors of such bank and in proportion as the official management is capable, careful and conscientious in the same proportion will that bank be solvent and reliable. At the same time, membership in the system, though not a guaranty, is a bulwark of strength for any well managed bank, because in the event of a seasonal demand for funds in excess of the member bank's own ability to meet, for the movement of crops or goods, or in the event of panicky apprehension on the part of customers, the member bank has in its Federal reserve bank an institution of unusual strength to which it may turn for extra funds, and if it is a well managed bank it will have in its possession the kinds of assets upon which it can obtain such funds.

Krickel K. Carrick, *The Federal Reserve System* (Boston, Federal Reserve Bank, 1926), 7–31 *passim*.

CHAPTER XV — AGRICULTURE, CONSERVATION AND RECLAMATION

74. Reclamation and Conservation (1908)

BY HAROLD HOWLAND (1921)

Howland has been on the editorial staffs of the *Outlook* and *Independent*. Conservation first gained prominence when President Roosevelt in 1905 persuaded Congress to create the Forestry Service. Later, plans were worked out for the conservation of irrigation waters as well.—Bibliography: C. R. Van Hise, *Conservation of Natural Resources in the United States*.

THE first message of President Roosevelt to Congress contained these words: "The forest and water problems are perhaps the most vital internal questions of the United States." At that moment, on December 3, 1901, the impulse was given that was to add to the American vocabulary two new words, "reclamation" and "conservation," that was to create two great constructive movements for the preservation, the increase, and the utilization of natural resources, and that was to establish a new relationship on the part of the Federal Government to the nation's natural wealth.

Reclamation and conservation had this in common: the purpose of both was the intelligent and efficient utilization of the natural resources of the country for the benefit of the people of the country. But they differed in one respect, and with conspicuous practical effects. Reclamation, which meant the spending of public moneys to render fertile and usable arid lands hitherto deemed worthless, trod on no one's toes. It took from no one anything that he had; it interfered with no one's enjoyment of benefits which it was not in the public interest that he should continue to enjoy unchecked. It was therefore popular from the first, and the new policy went through Congress as though on well-oiled wheels. Only six months passed between its first statement in the Presidential message and its enactment into law. Conservation, on the other hand, had begun by withholding the natural resources from exploitation and extravagant use.

It had, first of all, to establish in the national mind the principle that the forests and mines of the nation are not an inexhaustible grab-bag into which whosoever will may thrust greedy and wasteful hands, and by this new understanding to stop the squandering of vast national resources until they could be economically developed and intelligently used. So it was inevitable that conservation should prove unpopular, while reclamation gained an easy popularity, and that those who had been feeding fat off the country's stores of forest and mineral wealth should oppose, with tooth and nail, the very suggestion of conservation. . . .

On the very day that the first Roosevelt message was read to the Congress, a committee of Western Senators and Congressmen was organized under the leadership of Senator Francis G. Newlands of Nevada, to prepare a Reclamation Bill. The only obstacle to the prompt enactment of the bill was the undue insistence upon State Rights by certain Congressmen, "who consistently fought for local and private interests as against the interests of the people as a whole." In spite of this shortsighted opposition, the bill became law on June 17, 1902, and the work of reclamation began without an instant's delay. The Reclamation Act set aside the proceeds of the sale of public lands for the purpose of reclaiming the waste areas of the arid West. Lands otherwise worthless were to be irrigated and in those new regions of agricultural productivity homes were to be established. The money so expended was to be repaid in due course by the settlers on the land and the sums repaid were to be used as a revolving fund for the continuous prosecution of the reclamation work. Nearly five million dollars was made immediately available for the work. Within four years, twenty-six "projects" had been approved by the Secretary of the Interior and work was well under way on practically all of them. They were situated in fourteen States—Arizona, Colorado, Idaho, Kansas, Montana, Nebraska, Washington, Utah, Wyoming, New Mexico, North Dakota, Oregon, California, South Dakota. The individual projects were intended to irrigate areas of from eight thousand to two hundred thousand acres each; and the grand total of arid lands to which water was thus to be brought by canals, tunnels, aqueducts, and ditches was more than a million and a half acres.

The work had to be carried out under the most difficult and adventurous conditions. The men of the Reclamation Service were in the truest sense pioneers, building great engineering works far from the railroads, where the very problem of living for the great number of workers was no simple one. On the Shoshone in Wyoming these men built the highest dam in the world, 310 feet from base to crest. They pierced a mountain range in Colorado and carried the waters of the Gunnison River nearly six miles to the Uncompahgre Valley through a tunnel in the solid rock. The great Roosevelt dam on the Salt River in Arizona with its gigantic curved wall of masonry 280 feet high, created a lake with a capacity of fifty-six billion cubic feet, and watered in 1915 an area of 750,000 acres.

The work of these bold pioneers was made possible by the fearless backing which they received from the Administration at Washington. The President demanded of them certain definite results and gave them unquestioning support. In Roosevelt's own words, "the men in charge were given to understand that they must get into the water if they would learn to swim; and, furthermore, they learned to know that if they acted honestly, and boldly and fearlessly accepted responsibility, I would stand by them to the limit. In this, as in every other case, in the end the boldness of the action fully justified itself."

The work of reclamation was first prosecuted under the United States Geological Survey; but in the spring of 1908 the United States Reclamation Service was established to carry it on, under the direction of Mr. Newell, to whom the inception of the plan was due. Roosevelt paid a fine and well-deserved tribute to the man who originated and carried through this great national achievement when he said that "Newell's single-minded devotion to this great task, the constructive imagination which enabled him to conceive it, and the executive power and high character through which he and his assistant, Arthur P. Davis, built up a model service—all these made him a model servant." . . .

. . . By 1915 reclamation had added to the arable land of the country a million and a quarter acres, of which nearly eight hundred thousand acres were already "under water," and largely under tillage, producing yearly more than eighteen million dollars' worth of crops. . . .

It had been the immemorial custom that the water powers on the navigable streams, on the public domain, and in the National Forests should be given away for nothing, and practically without question, to the first comer. This ancient custom ran right athwart the newly enunciated principle that public property should not pass into private possession without being paid for, and that permanent grants, except for home-making, should not be made. The Forest Service now began to apply this principle to the water powers in the National Forests, granting permission for the development and use of such power for limited periods only and requiring payment for the privilege. This was the beginning of a general water power policy which, in the course of time, commended itself to public approval; but it was long before it ceased to be opposed by the private interests that wanted these rich resources for their own undisputed use.

Out of the forest movement grew the conservation movement in its broader sense. In the fall of 1907 Roosevelt made a trip down the Mississippi River with the definite purpose of drawing general attention to the subject of the development of the national inland waterways. Seven months before, he had established the Inland Waterways Commission and had directed it to "consider the relations of the streams to the use of all the great permanent natural resources and their conservation for the making and maintenance of permanent homes." During the trip a letter was prepared by a group of men interested in the conservation movement and was presented to him, asking him to summon a conference on the conservation of natural resources. At a great meeting held at Memphis, Tennessee, Roosevelt publicly announced his intention of calling such a conference.

In May of the following year the conference was held in the East Room of the White House. . . . The object of the conference was stated by the President in these words: "It seems to me time for the country to take account of its natural resources, and to inquire how long they are likely to last. We are prosperous now; we should not forget that it will be just as important to our descendants to be prosperous in their time."

At the conclusion of the conference a declaration prepared by the Governors of Louisiana, New Jersey, Wisconsin, Utah, and South Carolina, was unanimously adopted. This Magna Charta of the conservation movement declared "that the great natural resources supply the material basis upon which our civilization must continue to depend and upon which the perpetuity of the nation itself rests," that "this material basis is threatened with exhaustion," and that "this conservation of our national resources is a subject of transcendent importance, which should engage unremittingly the attention of the Nation, the States, and the people in earnest coöperation." . . .

The conference urged the continuation and extension of the forest policies already established; the immediate adoption of a wise, active, and thorough waterway policy for the prompt improvement of the streams, and the conservation of water resources for irrigation, water supply, power, and navigation; and the enactment of laws for the prevention of waste in the mining and extraction of coal, oil, gas, and other minerals with a view to their wise conservation for the use of the people. The declaration closed with the timely adjuration, "Let us conserve the foundations of our prosperity."

As a result of the conference President Roosevelt created the National Conservation Commission, consisting of forty-nine men of prominence, about one-third of whom were engaged in politics, one-third in various industries, and one-third in scientific work. Gifford Pinchot was appointed chairman. The Commission proceeded to make an inventory of the natural resources of the United States. This inventory contains the only authentic statement as to the amounts of the national resources of the country, the degree to which they have already been exhausted, and their probable duration. But with this inventory there came to an end the activity of the Conservation Commission, for Congress not only refused any appropriation for its use but decreed by law that no bureau of the Government should do any work for any commission or similar body appointed by the President, without reference to the question whether such work was appropriate or not for such a bureau to undertake.

Harold Howland, *Theodore Roosevelt and His Times* [*Chronicles of America,* XLVII] (New Haven, Yale University Press, 1921), 130–149 *passim.*

75. Water on Arid Lands (1910)

BY CHIEF ENGINEER FREDERICK H. NEWELL

Newell served as chief engineer, director, and consulting engineer of the U. S. Reclamation Service, until he became president of the Research Service. Here he discusses in general terms some of the principles of irrigation farming.—Bibliography: J. L. Matthews, *Conservation of Water;* G. F. Swain, *Conservation of Water by Storage;* R. P. Teel, *Irrigation in the United States.*

RECLAMATION works have been laid out in all of the Western States and Territories and an investment of over $60,000,000 has been made. Part of the works in each State has been completed and is being operated, returning a part of the cost. About 10,000 families are being supplied with water. Most of these have come from the humid regions and have located upon tracts of land which formerly were considered valueless, and in portions of the country which were called desert. In short, by the use of a trust fund which is being returned and used over again, the waste waters of the Nation are being conserved, destructive floods prevented, apparently valueless land converted into highly productive farms, and thousands of families settled upon small tracts sufficient for their support. To this extent relief is being given to the tendency toward congestion in the industrial centers and home markets are being extended. The farmer located upon a small irrigated tract owned and cultivated by himself necessarily practices intensive farming, produces the highest crop value per acre, is a large consumer as well as producer, and becomes the most valuable citizen in the stability of the commonwealth. . . .

The object of the reclamation act, as stated in the law is the construction of irrigation works for the reclamation of arid or semi-arid lands in the States and Territories named in the act. But the purpose behind the mere reclamation of the land is the providing of opportunities for homes for an independent self-supporting citizenship. The law is not drawn for the purpose of making men rich, but for providing opportunities for citizens who have the skill, energy, and thrift sufficient to make use of the opportunities for securing a home for themselves and for their children; one in which the family may be supported; and one where with the growth of the country and increased land values, it will be possible for an increasing number of families to maintain themselves upon subdivisions of the original farms.

Thus far the wisdom of the framers of the act has been demonstrated, and it has been shown that, with wise administration, the law is proving of inestimable value to the States and to the Nation. From time to time, it is necessary to make improvements or changes in the organic law, such as are inseparable with growth, but as a whole this act has proved remarkably complete. . . .

As might be imagined, the population in the first few years is largely transitional. The same qualities which bring a man to a project tend to make him leave it. He has heard of all the good things, has read the roseate descriptions of irrigation, its benefits, but the drawbacks have never been brought to his attention. It is hardly to be wondered that many of the people who take up irrigation for the first time suddenly awake to the fact that it is not wholly a matter of sunshine and flowers, and that for success energy, skill, and thrift are required. In order to get well started on an irrigated farm a man must have not only good fortune but must be prepared to endure privations which he would not be willing to consider at home; doing this, however, with the assurance that the reward ultimately will be correspondingly great. . . .

The size of the farms obtainable from the public domain is defined by the reclamation act not by an arbitrary number of acres, as in the case of the homestead and other similar laws, but the Secretary of the Interior is required to give a "limit of area per entry, which limit shall represent the acreage which in the opinion of the Secretary may be reasonably required for the support of a family upon the lands in question." . . . .

In the extreme southern part of the arid region, where the daily sunlight and warmth is most favorable for the production of crops, it results that where the land is carefully tilled, where it has been put into high grade crops, and especially in fruit, 10 acres may be ample for the support of a family. This is because of the fact that with intensive cultivation, crop follows crop in rapid succession, there being hardly any interval for rest during the year. Alfalfa, for example, may be cut eight or ten times, while there may be three successive crops during the year of grains or vegetables.

Farther north, where the summer season is limited, and there is a long cold winter, the area required for a family is correspondingly greater. With alfalfa and sugar beets, 40 acres may be considered a fairly good sized farm, as, for example, in the more favorable parts of Montana, and elsewhere, 80 acres is usually the limit. Few men can handle successfully over 80 acres of irrigated land, especially with high-priced water. . . .

The requirement of actual settlement on the reclaimed land has been one which has led to much discussion and has been the cause of much of the hardship incident to pioneering. The theory of the law as originally passed was that the Government, investing this trust fund without profit and interest, does this for the purpose of securing settlement in the more sparsely populated western States. The prime object was not so much to enrich these localities or States as to secure resident citizens, who would not only cultivate the soil and become producers but would build up the institutions of the State, make roads, organize schools, and add to the strength of the Commonwealth. . . .

. . . From the standpoint of a man working in a store or machine shop, a teacher or professional man, the idea is extremely attractive of getting one of these homesteads from the Government, visiting it occasionally, adding improvements, and hiring a man to look after it until the community has been built up and the days of pioneering have passed. His monthly savings can be put into the little farm and provision made for the future without interfering with his daily wage-earning capacity. It seems to him a useless hardship to be compelled either to give up the farm or to go and live upon it, and he urges that if he be allowed to hold the farm and invest his savings in it he can in the end bring about a higher development than would be possible if he spent all his time on the farm itself.

There is, however, no way of distinguishing between the small investor and the large, and if the school-teacher has the right to enjoy absentee landlordism, so has the man of larger means. Thus it would soon happen that the bounty of the Government would be enjoyed by people of comparative wealth and leisure, renting their farms to the class of men who are most needed as resident owners.

The crops planted by the settlers are as varied as are the farmers themselves and the climatic surroundings. They naturally endeavor to raise the things with which they are familiar and are somewhat slow in adapting their methods to the requirements of the soil and

climate. As a rule, grain is planted first, as it is a quick crop and it
is possible to realize an early return from the new ground. The experienced irrigator endeavors to get a small part of the land into
alfalfa as quickly as possible, knowing that it enriches the soil. With
his first grain crop he sows on part of his land some alfalfa seed and
if the stand is good he leaves this small tract in alfalfa for a few years,
cultivating the remaining areas and adding each year to the alfalfa
tract until the time arrives when he can plow in the alfalfa which was
first planted, turning the plants under to enrich the soil, then cultivating it and planting to root crops.

One of the problems with the lighter and sometimes better soils
is to hold these in place until the crops are established. The desert
vegetation, the sagebrush and greasewood, while undisturbed protect
the soil from the winds, but, as has been shown by bitter experience
again and again, when these plants are removed and the ground is
plowed the winds of early spring sweeping furiously across the dry
level field blow the soil away in clouds, carrying off the seed.

It requires a few incidents of this kind to convince the newcomer
that it is wise to follow the advice given him not to clear his entire
farm at once, but to leave rows of sagebrush across the path of the
prevailing spring winds. He soon appreciates that it is little short
of wicked to burn the sagebrush, and instead of piling it for destruction
he learns to leave it in long windrows, cultivating the places between
until the ground is well shaded by the growing crop and the roots
have been firmly established, then he can remove the remaining sagebrush or windbreaks and get his entire field into crop. In a few years,
by careful handling, the light soil becomes reasonably compacted, or
held back by the roots and straw of the vegetation, or protected by the
growing trees and shrubbery, so that no further damage is incurred.

These problems of dealing with the settlers, of giving them sound
advice, and at the same time collecting from them the cost of the works,
involve the problems which are far more difficult than those of engineering construction or related business management. The difficulties of management are complicated by the fact that the irrigator frequently regards his individual interest as antagonistic to that
of the community or management, insisting upon wasting water because of the mistaken belief that the more of a good thing he has the
better. . . .

The value of the crop produced and the consequent ability of the farmers to return the cost of the investment are dependent directly upon water being received on each farm in proper quantity and at the right time. If too much water is applied the crops will be correspondingly injured, the available soluble salts in the soil will be washed out or brought to the surface, the land will depreciate in value, and large areas will be destroyed. With intensive cultivation and the crop production in the more valuable fruits, berries, or vegetables under ideal conditions, the yield may be several hundred dollars an acre. By a slight error in handling the water the crop value may be lessened by a hundred dollars an acre or more.

Although the net product per acre may appear to be large and satisfactory, and it is impossible to prove that higher values might have been reached, yet the man who thoroughly understands the situation appreciates that there has been a loss of $100 per acre, which is directly attributable to lack of good management, and that under better conditions higher values would have been attained by the farmers. This possible reduction of crop values in a highly developed agricultural area of say 10,000 acres at $100 per acre means a loss to the community of a million dollars, or, rather, under better or more successful management of the water, the net return of the community might have been $1,000,000 more during the season.

This is by no means a fanciful idea. The study of ditch management and crop production in irrigated regions shows that in many instances there has been a shortage of water at a critical time, due to lack of forethought or skill on the part of some one.

The average farmer does not appreciate what this has meant to him, as he is apt to rarely figure out these larger matters with any degree of precision, and has been accustomed to disappointments in his crops so often that he regards such matters as inseparable from agriculture. If the crop looks fairly well he frequently goes no deeper. Possibly never having seen a full-crop production under excellent conditions he has no standard by which to judge.

This matter was well illustrated by an experienced irrigation manager who examined one of the large projects in Wyoming where the farmers for several years had been what they considered fairly successful. They had raised profitable crops and had succeeded in getting along with constant temporary repairs to the main canal. He took the history of a single season's operation and the number of days that the canal was out of service through accidental but preventable breaks, and figured on a conservative basis what would have been the crop products had the works been maintained in excellent order by skilled men. He showed that had fire swept through the country and destroyed every visible improvement in the towns of the vicinity the loss to the entire community would have been less than had actually resulted from preventable failure to operate the canals properly. The spectacular view of a burning barn or storehouse, rivets public attention upon this definite loss, but the gradual and unimpressive delay in development of the crop day by day is not noticeable. While all of the neighborhood would rush to aid the owner of the burning barn, yet no one knows or apparently cares while the valuable fruits or other crops are being imperceptibly reduced in value to a far larger degree.

Frederick H. Newell, in *Annual Report of Smithsonian Institution, 1910* (Washington, Government Printing Office, 1911), 169–178 *passim.*

———◆———

76. Scientific Farming (1912)

BY DEAN EUGENE DAVENPORT

Davenport is Professor Emeritus of Thermatology at the University of Illinois, having spent a lifetime in the teaching of agricultural science in various capacities; he has been President of the Colegio Agronomica at São Paulo, Brazil, and was Dean of the College of Agriculture at the University of Illinois from 1895 to 1922.—On farmers' problems, see also No. 72 above and Nos. 77, 80, 81, 82 below.—Bibliography: *Agriculture Year Books* of the Department of Agriculture.

THE world could not long have lived under the oldtime destructive methods of agriculture, no matter how profitable they might have been temporarily to those engaged therein. The waste of fertility was too great. Lands that had been thousands of years in the making were ruined within a generation. Had those methods been continued, however temporarily profitable they may have been, the decline of the country would have been inevitable from sheer inability to wring sufficient sustenance from the soil.

Chemistry was the first of the sciences to turn its attention to agriculture, and the first two subjects studied were the scientific feeding of animals and the food requirements of crops. By the new methods of investigation devised by the scientist, it was speedily discovered that the old feeding practices, while securing results, were yet enormously wasteful in that the rations were sadly unbalanced so far as the requirements of the animals were concerned, resulting in corresponding losses in food value. The result was the devising of a "balanced ration," which very nearly corresponds in its component parts to the real needs of an animal for nourishment and thus avoids the wastage of the surplus, particularly of the more expensive nitrogenous foods.

Turning his attention to the soil, the chemist found correspondingly wasteful practices. To be sure the farmer had learned through experience generations ago that manures and other fertilizers would increase the growth of crops, though he was about as particular to apply soot and other carbonaceous material as he was to apply the really effective fertilizers. The chemist quickly discovered that of all the elements necessary to the growth of plants only three need ordinarily to concern the farmer. Of these, nitrogen is enormously expensive, costing in the markets of the world some fifteen cents a pound, and as at least four pounds are required for a bushel of wheat it was evident that the wheat supply of the world must have been produced at wholesale expense of natural nitrogen. The scientist did not rest until he discovered, through the agency of bacteriology, that the valuable nitrogen could be captured from the atmosphere, whence it originally came. This fact was probably the most notable contribution which science has ever made to the progress of agriculture and, so far as we can see, the most notable it will ever be able to make. The dependence of man upon atmospheric nitrogen brought into form for plant use is beyond the power of comprehension. . . .

An early field for scientific investigation was that of diseases, first of animals and afterwards of plants. Indeed it was while working in this territory that some of the most important discoveries have been made, particularly concerning parasitic infection. The result of all this investigation has been the saving of enormous numbers of animals and of large acreage of plants by precautionary methods, such as quarantine, disinfection, etc., though the direct treatment of individual animals is generally inadvisable for economic reasons.

It is almost needless to remark that with these developments in the domain of agriculture much that was formerly tradition and superstition has begun to pass away. How recent it has all been, however, is shown by the fact that men still live who plant their seeds and kill their meat with reference to the phases of the moon, who treat "hollow-horn" and "wolf in the tail" by incantation, who put a red-hot horseshoe into the churn to drive the witches away, and who castrate only when the sign is right. While instances of this kind can still be found, it is yet true that the great masses of farmers today, even in the remoter agricultural districts, have caught the scientific spirit; and most of the material that now goes to constitute the revised agriculture of the twentieth century rests upon well established facts. So true is this that no man in these days can get a hearing anywhere upon any matter which does not rest, or at least seem to rest, upon experimental knowledge.

We have not yet reached the end of this development. We may be said to be just now in the very beginning of sanitary science regarding the operations of the farm. A man must do more now than to produce his milk or butter; he must produce it in a way which will assure the consumer that he is not taking communicable diseases in the milk, which is a kind of universal culture medium for everything which comes its way. It is this fact which has so notably raised the cost of city milk and is so appreciably reducing the mortality of infants.

Economics is perhaps the last of the sciences to reform the practices of agriculture. In the Far West it has taken the form of mountain and desert over which fruit must be transported to reach the Eastern markets. In this way the last vestige of extreme individualism on the farm is being obliterated. What the passing of this individualism may mean so far as independence and the development of personal initiative are concerned, only time will tell; but one thing is clear—that as the facts in agriculture are developed by scientific research, the truth stands out that the business of food production, to some extent at least, must be organized and conducted around larger units than that of a single farmer and his family.

The "organization of the farm" is a scientific conception of the most recent development. So long as wild lands could be had for mere occupancy, a farmer could get nothing out of his business but the bare return for labor; his land could have no value and there could be no investment except a slight one in implements and animals. Now, however, when the public domain is practically exhausted, competition for land will raise its price, food values must go up, for the farmer must realize income on capital as well as on labor, and his business is gradually assuming the form of other capitalized industries. This puts a new economic phase on agriculture and the whole question of how to organize and conduct a farm is a new one in economic science, as it is in agricultural practice. We still await its solution. Indeed, its serious study has only just begun.

The universal extension of agricultural education may be said to be the direct result of the development of scientific agriculture. There is little in mere handicraft that can be taught; it must mostly be acquired by experience. It is only when a subject has reached the scientific stage that it becomes teachable through the elucidation of the principles involved. Because of the ease and speed with which certain of these principles can be learned, and because of their immediate and far-reaching effect, particularly upon the permanence of agriculture, the demand is universal that the subject should be taught in as many of the schools as possible. The economist readily sees that the oldtime wasteful methods cannot prevail; that if we are to have a permanent civilization we must have a permanent food supply; and this must depend not upon practices that gradually impoverish the land, but rather on those scientific procedures which leave it each generation a little better than before in order that it may meet the demands of an increasing population with a more highly developed civilization.

This then is the aim and purpose of scientific agriculture: to replace tradition with well established facts; to substitute for the irregular and uncertain purposes of the individual a systematic and well organized business of food production by the community at large; to further adapt our domesticated animals and plants to the purposes of man; and to stop forever that reckless depletion of the power of the soil to produce, which will not only fix a low limit to the population of our country, but so weaken the constitution of the people as to lay the foundation for disease. It aims, too, to establish in these early and prosperous days, through education, such standards of living as shall prevent the coming of those hard conditions which have descended upon such races as have surrendered themselves to the mere business of getting a living on worn-out soil.

Eugene Davenport, in *Annals of the American Academy of Political and Social Science* (Philadelphia, March, 1912), XL, 46–50 *passim*.

———◆———

77. The Farmer's Chance (1919)

BY PRESIDENT KENYON L. BUTTERFIELD

Butterfield has written various works of agricultural value, and has taken an active part in the Grange movement. He was President of the Massachusetts Agricultural College from 1906 to 1924, and was later at the head of Michigan State College.—Bibliography: S. J. Buck, *The Agrarian Crusade* [*Chronicles of America*, XXXXV]; *Agriculture Year Books*.

AFTER all the farmers must direct their own destinies. The best service that government can render farmers is to help them to help themselves. The paternalism of the state and the gratuitous benevolence of the city are equally futile in the building of a rural democracy. The coöperative efforts of farmers are indispensable to real rural progress. Whether in securing better farm practice, or in obtaining more satisfactory profits, or in evolving a better country life, the collective intelligence and planning of the great masses of farmers should be added to all investigation and teaching by specialists, all projects of government, all the work of school and college, all laws for regulation or control. . . .

. . . Only through association can farmers defend themselves; only so can they make their fullest contributions to the general welfare. There is danger in organization. The individual may lose himself in some big overhead attachment. Powerful combinations of farmers may exercise their power wrongfully. But the gains are far greater than the losses. The farmer has been called the most independent of men; but alone he is no longer independent. He becomes truly free, under modern conditions, only as he joins with his fellows for common ends. The dangers arising in associated activity from impulse or ignorance, selfish class interests or feeling can be met by education, time and experience.

Though it is doubtful if a farmers' political party can have any

permanent place in America, the farmers must be free to act together
to influence parties, measures and men. There should be room in the
rural program for a fighting force of farmers. The need for such
aggressive tactics may arise only occasionally; but sound policy calls
for its recognition. But rural associations do not exist for their own
sakes. They must seek to serve. They must not be narrow in their
views or in their activities. They are for the good of all, or they are
no good at all. They must be ready to coöperate heartily with one
another and with public agencies. They should become as efficient
as possible, each doing its own part in the program of rural betterment. . . .

Each agency or institution devised to assist farmers and farming
should work out a clearly marked policy and program. Its particular
task in rural improvement needs to be defined and recognized. A
particular form of organization, as yet not fully utilized in America,
is the thorough coöperation of the growers of a particular product, as
of cotton growers, wheat growers, stock-breeders, in all parts of their
business—producing, selling, and establishing relationships to other
interests or to government. Industrial solidarity seems necessary
for greatest coöperative effectiveness. The citrus-fruit growers of
California have shown the way to one of the most important and
promising methods of agricultural advancement. . . .

In some respects the most important single improvement in rural
affairs is to develop real communities of farming folk. These communities must often be created—they do not exist. The community
idea is simply that of a group of farmers and the people closely allied
with them, acting together as one man. The members of this local
group can plan as a unit in production of crops, agreeing on kinds
and amounts. They can sell together and buy together. They can
act together in school and church affairs and in matters of public
health. A community may have its own ideas and ideals, its own
church, school, farmers' exchange, library, in fine all organized activities that seem necessary or desirable. The local community is
almost essential in a real rural democracy, and indeed is the unit of
democracy.

In any program of rural reconstruction that aims to be comprehensive it would be a fatal blunder not to stress the importance of the
social or humane factor. The life is more than meat. The man is

worth more than dollars. "The farmer is of more consequence than the farm and should be first improved." The big farm question is getting and keeping the right sort of people on the land. A satisfying farm life is necessary to a permanent agriculture and consequently to the best farming. The city will always be replenished from the country-side. We must therefore omit no plan and decline no exertion that will encourage a good farm life. . . .

Kenyon L. Butterfield, *The Farmer and the New Day* (New York, Macmillan, 1919), 254–258 *passim.*

◆

78. Agricultural Extension Work (1924)

BY H. W. HOCHBAUM

Hochbaum is associated with the extension work of the Department of Agriculture. For information on local developments, county farm agents may be consulted in many communities.—Bibliography: publications of various State agricultural colleges; O. M. Kile, *The Farm Bureau Movement.*

THE county agricultural agent is the local extension representative of the State college of agriculture, the United States Department of Agriculture, and the local people wherever extension work is carried on coöperatively. He is the joint representative of these agencies in developing and carrying on in a mutual way plans for meeting the larger problems of farming and farm life. Administratively, he is responsible to the extension division of the State agricultural college, which guides and directs his work. His work is financed largely from public funds. His relationship to the people or organized groups of people of his county is that of a public official, and his work is with all the people. He works with all organizations and not for any one organization or group. He is a leader who points the way to better and more profitable farming and a more satisfying country life, and teaches how these objectives may be attained. . . .

The county extension office is a logical center and clearing house for the many movements that may be developed to aid in redirecting and improving agriculture and rural problems. The extension agent lends a sympathetic ear to the needs of the many rural organizations and gives time to causes which these may advance in the interest of public welfare. . . .

The reports of county agricultural agents show that the average agent will rarely serve effectively or long if he assumes the position of an adviser or expert on all agricultural matters. In common parlance, the successful county agricultural agent is more than a "trouble shooter" or "handy man" for individuals calling on him for help. His reports testify that he builds more soundly and permanently by working to secure definite progress and tangible accomplishment in a few well-selected and fundamental problems which are the concern of many individuals. He makes intensive studies of the farming and country-life conditions of his county so that he may be able to diagnose existing problems and ills. He selects problems to work on which fall within the scope of extension work, shows the people that such problems are important locally, and suggests that their solution be worked out jointly with the extension service. Steadfastly and consistently the agent works to arouse the attention and interest of the rural people in these problems, and to kindle enthusiasm and attract active support for their solution. Withal, he bends every effort to select and to organize rural leadership and to train the people of his county to work together in solving these problems, encouraging as far as possible a widespread adoption of the practices that may be recommended. . . .

The people are taught through community program making to recognize a community or commodity problem as their problem. The problem of the individual is submerged in the larger interest of the group. The group problem becomes the individual's problem. Moreover, the local people learn that by self-help and group action, the larger problems can be solved with the joint help of the community and the extension service. Thereby, community action and community betterment are encouraged, more people are reached, and larger interests are benefited. . . .

. . . In many cases extension agents learn that they must find or devise means by which people may adopt recommended practices.

The reports of county agricultural agents give many illustrations of these points. They show, for example, that the use of lime in a community may be held in check because of the lack of conveniences for handling the lime. Where dependence is placed upon the individual to use lime under such conditions, comparatively small amounts are used, but when through the efforts of the extension agents lime bins are established in certain communities, many more people use lime because it has been made easy for them to get lime. Often the high cost of lime may be the limiting factor. Thus when an agent devised a means of providing cheap lime the people used large quantities of it. . . .

Similarly, lack of local equipment may prevent many farmers from adopting practices which have been proved worth while and which they are ready to accept. It may be necessary for the county agricultural agent or specialist to help organize a supplementary service. The man with the home orchard is not able to produce clean fruit unless he sprays. That may be demonstrated to him. He can not, however, afford, in some cases, the type of machinery that is necessary to insure effective spraying. Therefore the county agricultural agent and specialist may develop such service associations as spray rings. In this way a few farmers can band together, own a machine coöperatively, and do effective spraying. In other localities, because of different conditions, county agricultural agents and specialists may have to devise modifications of this, as, for example, by establishing a commercial spray service to insure the production of clean fruit. . . .

Extension agents are recognizing that the teaching of improved practices may be expedited for the great mass when the improvements suggested are reduced to demonstrations of single practices of a simple nature. This principle is based on the knowledge that the great mass of people are reached through the eye and imitate what has been seen. Therefore, if such teaching can be reduced to terms of single practices these may be more likely to be adopted by the average farmer. In other words, in the past extension agents have been dealing, perhaps too much, with principles and have not realized the difficulty the average person has in applying principle to practice. . . .

A simple demonstration in liming may be used as an example. The demonstration is designed so that a strip of land is left unlimed through a field, the remainder of which has been limed according to the conditions to be met in that field. The most favorable time for comparing results is at the harvest. A number of people are invited to the field, and in their presence the crop removed from a certain area of the limed soil is weighed and compared with the crop cut from the same sized area in the unlimed part of the field. The lesson is obvious. Through liming, definite increased crop production is obtained. . . .

The employment of volunteer local leaders to assist in carrying on extension work is a feature which has been given increased attention during the year. . . .

The reports of extension agents indicate unusual interest in methods of obtaining a spread of influence from demonstration work or other extension activities. No doubt, all realize the necessity for securing the greatest amount of interest in the demonstration work. Of late the agents are more actively concerned in working to turn this interest into action on the part of a large number of people and getting them to adopt the practices which are demonstrated. . . .

The systematic methods used by some agents to secure a wider spread of adoption should be of great interest to others. Thus, extension agents in Maine are trying the plan of making a campaign for the enrollment of coöperators following a demonstration period. Coöperators in this sense mean the people who pledge themselves to adopt the practices, the results of which have been proved by demonstrations. The success of the method is worthy of further study by extension agents everywhere. The principle involved is that of following the demonstration period by, or merging with it, a definite and systematic attempt to bring to a large number of people results of the demonstrations, and then by several methods to secure pledges from such people that they will adopt the practice recommended. . . .

There is a very definite need for training courses or other work that will better prepare men for county agent work. The assistant State director of extension in Indiana emphasized this fact in his annual report:

Approximately one-fourth of the men now on the job have been appointed during the past year. This great demand for county agricultural agents emphasizes the need through the agricultural colleges to give special attention to the training of men for the extension service. This work is so well established that, though farmers are complaining about high taxes and insisting upon reduction in expenses, the demand is not to cut out the county agricultural agents as an economical movement, but to have a more efficient service through the office, if this be possible.

One of the new developments during the past year in California has been an undergraduate course in agricultural extension methods. This course was given during the second semester of the year 1921–22 to a class of more than 30 students. The course considers the history, methods, and administration of extension work. Four of the students are now employed as assistant county agricultural agents in California. It has been found that the men who took this course are more finished in extension work than other men of similar age and training who graduated from the same college, but did not take a course in extension methods.

H. W. Hochbaum, *Methods and Results of Coöperative Extension Work*, United States Department of Agriculture *Department Circular 316* (Washington, Government Printing Office, 1924), 1–34 *passim*.

———◆———

79. Relation of Geography to Timber Supply (1925)

BY CHIEF FORESTER WILLIAM B. GREELEY

Greeley entered the United States Forest Service in 1904, and has been Chief Forester since 1920. The two great purposes of the service are to prevent waste of our existing timber supply and to further the growth of timber as a crop for the use of future generations.—On timber reserves, see "Timber, Mine or Crop," in *Agriculture Year Book*, 1922. On methods of timber protection, see various publications of the Forest Service.

. . . THE stern facts of geography have largely controlled these past developments in our forest industries and in the cost of their wares to the American consumer. The true measure of timber supply is not quantity but availability. Sixty per cent of all the wood that is left in the United States and 75 per cent of its virgin timber lie west of the Great Plains, whereas two-thirds of the population and an even larger proportion of our agriculture and manufactures are east of the Great Plains. The forests bordering the Pacific Coast contain over a trillion board feet of virgin stumpage. At the most, they will not supply our present consumption very long: but already the unbalanced geographical distribution of this resource is creating well-nigh famine prices in the parts of the United States where forest products are used in the largest quantities. Dependence upon the softwood forests of Siberia as the principal source of supply would differ from our present situation only in degree.

And as geography controls the cost of the products of virgin forests when they reach the ultimate consumer in Massachusetts, Illinois, or Florida, so will geography control the substitution of other sources of timber supply. Most of the other countries have progressed from one stage to another in their source of wood more or less as single geographical units. In the United States the distances are so great and the local conditions so diverse that this transition is bound, for some time to come, to be regional rather than national. We have already seen that, owing to the concentration of the paper industry in the northeastern states, more than half of our consumption of wood fiber products is now drawn from foreign sources. And by the same token, the exigencies of the portions of the country farthest removed from the dwindling frontier of virgin forests are driving them to a new source of wood, namely the timber crop.

Forestry is the economic competitor of transportation. As long as cheap virgin stumpage available at no great distance dominated our lumber and paper markets, there was no place in the economic scheme of things for systematic timber growing. But once the cost of transporting forest products from the nearest virgin sources exceeds the cost of growing them at home, timber culture not only becomes economically feasible but sooner or later is impelled by purely commercial forces. This is just what is taking place today, to a limited degree, in New England, New York, Pennsylvania, and New Jersey; and, to a still more limited degree, in the South. Second growth white pine in New England, 30 or 40 years old, is worth from $10 to $18 per thousand board feet standing in the woods. Second growth southern pine of the same age brings from $8 to $12 on the stump. With such returns before them and with timber values constantly moving upward, hard-headed business men realize that forestry pays. One might almost plat the process by a series of geographical zones; and show that when the freight rate into any consuming region from the nearest large supply of virgin timber passes the $10 or $12 mark, an economic basis for timber cropping is afforded and forestry slowly finds a place in the use of land.

Forest conservation in the United States hitherto has been largely a matter of public ownership of timber land and public policies based not upon costs and profits but upon foresight of coming national necessities. Today it is percolating down into the counting house and the directors' board room. The illusion of inexhaustible virgin forests has spent itself. Wood-using industries recognize the alternatives which they face—*producing* their future raw material or passing out of existence. A committee of pulp and paper manufacturers is studying ways and means of perpetuating their industry on American soil. A committee of turpentine and rosin producers has visited France to learn the naval stores forestry of the Landes and how it may be applied to our southern pineries. These are signs of the times.

Like the other nations in similar plight, we must barter for all the timber we can secure from our neighbors. The prospects in this direction, however, are not encouraging. Our present exports and imports of lumber and other forest products nearly balance. The imports can undoubtedly be increased somewhat, particularly of paper from Canada and of lumber in limited quantities from certain Canadian provinces and from Mexico. The hardwood forests of South America and the softwood forests of Siberia hold out possible sources of relief. But a number of other industrially aggressive nations are in the same situation as the United States. A recent survey of the principal forest resources and wood-using countries of the world shows that the markets of the whole earth are short of raw materials for paper and construction lumber, and that the accessible supply of timber, particularly of coniferous timber, is not adequate to meet the requirements of modern civilization. The cost of transporting Asiatic or South American lumber to the United States, added to prices at the source fixed by keen international competition, would be well-nigh prohibitive for ordinary construction or industrial purposes.

Nevertheless we must get all the foreign wood that we can to tide over the lean years, and we must go after it intelligently and systematically. For one thing, a thorough study should be made of the resources available in the hardwood forests of Central and South America and their utility for the replacement of our rapidly waning supply of native hardwoods.

Undoubtedly we must and will learn to use less wood. The high cost of lumber has already decreased its per capita consumption in the United States about 40 per cent below the peak of 1906. Steel, cement and clay products have been substituted for much of the construction lumber formerly used; and coal, oil, and electricity have taken the place of much fuel wood. These substitutions are increasing, as wood becomes more dear; and it is well that they should. On the other hand, the use of wood is constantly widening as the chemist and engineer discover new methods of converting or fashioning it for modern requirements. Wood is now manufactured into grain alcohol and artificial silk, even into baking powder and electrical conduits. The field for wood fiber products is constantly enlarging. Notwithstanding the substitution of other materials and the curtailed use of wood for many of its old functions, the total drain upon our forests thus far has not materially lessened. The danger lies not in reducing the use of wood where satisfactory substitution is possible, but in growing shortage for many essential needs for which there are no substitutes. In most of the industrial countries of Europe the per capita consumption of wood is not diminishing, but increasing; and the United States cannot expect permanently to follow a different course if it is to hold its living standards and retain its industrial leadership.

One of the most essential constructive remedies is to reduce the drain upon our forests by reducing the waste in the manufacture and use of their products. The very abundance and cheapness of virgin timber in the United States has bred wasteful methods of logging, manufacture, and refabrication which are yielding but slowly to the pressure of scant supply and high costs. The general application of even our present knowledge of waste elimination in logging, milling and refabricating lumber, in timber preservation, in the conversion of wood into fiber products and the like, would reduce the current drain upon our forests by 20 or 25 per cent. And we still have much to learn before all the possibilities of economy in the use of our forests are fathomed. The elimination of preventable losses from forest fires and from destructive insects and tree diseases would save an enormous total of useful timber. A cord of wood saved is equal to a cord of wood grown. And one of the most obvious things that should be done with all possible dispatch is to conserve our existing timber supply to the last foot by research in the conversion and use of forest products on an adequate scale, accompanied by wide dissemination of its results through the forest industries and forest consumers.

After everything else has been said, no solution of our forest problem is possible without the generous growing of trees. We must come, in the last analysis, as every other country treading the same path has come, to forestry as the necessary and economic employment of much of our land. This solution is as complete as it is inevitable. Intensive timber culture on the 470 million acres of forest land in the United States, timber culture on a par with that of Germany, France and Scandinavia, can produce a yearly crop equivalent to more than all the wood which the United States now consumes. There will be a margin of 20 per cent or more to take care of the greater requirements of the future. The only question is how quickly can this be brought to pass and how much national suffering must be endured before a perpetual supply of timber is assured on our own soil. National habits in the use of land and its resources change slowly; and at best we must travel a slow and painful road before the goal is reached.

Underlying this whole question is one of the outstanding facts of the economic geography of the United States, namely, that one-fourth of her soil remains today, after three centuries of settlement and expanding agriculture, *forest land*. There is small prospect that the area available for growing trees will be reduced materially, if at all, for many years to come. While the inroads of the farm are continuing here and there, the great tide of forest clearing for cultivation seems largely to have spent itself. For many years indeed, the abandonment of farm land in forest growing regions of the older States has practically offset new clearing on the agricultural frontier.

Wholly aside from the need for timber, the problem of keeping one-fourth of the soil of the United States productively employed is one of no small urgency in the national economy. The idleness of cutover land, following the migration of the sawmills, has already been a widespread cause of depopulation, decline in taxable values, and general rural bankruptcy. In the busiest timber manufacturing regions of a few decades ago, there remain today over 80 million acres of practically unproductive and unused land. No country can afford such wastage.

Forestry not only is the only way to re-establish an adequate source of timber in the United States: it is the only way to utilize a large part of her land—to maintain a vigorous rural population with industries, communities and good roads. On both counts, forestry should become part and parcel of our program of land utilization.

William B. Greeley, in *Economic Geography* (Worcester, Clark University, 1925), I, 5–14.

————◆————

80. Sources of Mechanical Power (1925)

BY DIRECTOR GEORGE OTIS SMITH

This article by the Director of the United States Geological Survey summarizes the power resources of the country. For the famous Muscle Shoals development, see No. 157 below.—Bibliography: Chester G. Gilbert, *The Energy Resources of the United States* (1919); *Superpower*, compiled by L. T. Beman (1924); World Power Conference, 1924, *Prosperity through Power Development* (1925).

THE United States is preëminently the most generous user of mechanical energy in the world. Before summarizing this country's position in its possession of the principal sources of energy— water, coal, and oil—it will be enlightening to obtain a general idea of the magnitude of the present drafts upon our supply, as well as the relative demands made upon these three principal sources.

Tryon and Mann, in estimating the current consumption of energy in the United States, place the total at more than 25,000 trillion British thermal units and show that of this total the mineral fuels supply 87 per cent—coal 65 per cent, oil 18 per cent, natural gas 4 per cent. Water power supplies only 4 per cent, work animals 3 per cent, and the wind less than one-tenth of 1 per cent. Inasmuch as the total includes heat energy as well as mechanical energy, firewood is credited with 6 per cent, so that even in these days the forest still yields more energy than wind and water combined; but the mineral fuels now furnish more than six times as much energy as all these others with work animals added. This increasing dependence on mineral fuels is further emphasized by the facts that as late as 1880 they were subordinate to firewood and that prior to 1850 they furnished less energy than even the work animals.

As the world's largest users of mechanical energy, and indeed of most of the products of mines, smelters, mills, and factories, we need to study every available inventory that can be made of the power resources of the United States, especially in comparison with similar resources of other industrial peoples. In making this comparison we may conveniently state our national reserves of energy in terms of present population, thus translating the statistics of our material resources into per capita units.

The potential water power of the United States, only a small part of which is developed, is less than 1 horsepower per person, an allotment far below that of the peoples of Norway, Canada, and Sweden; even Switzerland has twice as large a per capita wealth in water power. The developed water power credited to the United States, though at first it seems large, becomes insignificant when it is reduced to per capita units, being less than one-tenth of 1 horsepower, far below the third of 1 horsepower per capita of Switzerland or Canada and the seven-tenths of Norway.

In per capita reserves of coal the United States possesses more than 23,000 tons, not including lignite, for every man, woman, and child of the present population. Other industrial nations rank about as follows: Great Britain has about 5,000 tons per capita, Germany probably still owns not less than 4,000 tons, Belgium perhaps 1,500 tons, France probably more than 800 tons, Spain less than 400 tons, and Japan 150 tons.

We can not state our per capita reserve of petroleum with so much assurance of quantitative accuracy as we can state reserves of coal or water, yet the best estimate available shows that considered as a future source of energy petroleum occupies a status far different from that of coal. The share of each man, woman, and child, in the unmined petroleum recoverable under present conditions and by present methods is probably less than 100 barrels, and the present annual production is a little over 6 barrels. These simple figures are full of significance. We undoubtedly have more oil than any other industrial nation, but certainly far from enough.

With this picture of the world distribution of energy resources in mind we can glance at the map of the United States and consider the facts of distribution within our own country, which we do well to keep in mind is continent-wide.

The center of energy for the United States may be determined in terms either of present production or of potential supply. Considering first the centers of gravity for the three main sources of energy, we may note that these centers are located in what most people in the United States would term the "Far West." The center of maximum potential water power is in the middle of Wyoming, about 35 miles southwest of Casper. The center of the original tonnage of coal in the United States is similarly determined as about at the crossing of 41° north latitude and 99° west longitude, or 30 miles west of Grand Island, Nebraska. In this determination the lignite regions were not included, nor the coal that lies at greater depth than 3,000 feet. The center of the remaining petroleum resources, as estimated by the oil geologists, is on the New Mexico-Colorado line, northeast of Raton.

It is not practicable to reduce these energy resources—water, coal, and oil,—to common units of weight and to fix a common center of gravity for all the potential power awaiting the use of future generations, but a glance at the map suggests the northeast corner of Colorado as the region that is nearest central for the coal fields, the oil pools, and the water powers of the United States. It is interesting to note that western Colorado is the center of the oil shale deposits of Utah, Wyoming, and Colorado, a reserve of energy far exceeding in quantity the petroleum resources that are now being so rapidly depleted.

The mention of future demand for power naturally leads to the determination of the present centers of production and the trend of the demand as indicated by comparison of these with earlier determinations. In 1924 the approximate center of coal production was in Madison County, Ohio, about 30 miles southwest of Columbus. In 1918 the corresponding center was some 50 miles farther north and west. The center of oil production is now in northeastern New Mexico, about 40 miles southeast of Raton; in 1918 it was near the Kansas-Colorado line, somewhat more than 150 miles to the northeast. The center of electric-power generation in the United States in 1924 was in Illinois, 50 miles southwest of Chicago, and the shift of this center since 1920 was somewhat west of south and amounted to less than 20 miles. Another interesting element of the geographic distribution of the demand for petroleum products is the center of automobile registration, which in 1924 was in Illinois, close to Peoria. The automobile thus leads population in its westward course, for the center of population, as last reported, was in Indiana, 50 miles southwest of Indianapolis. Indeed, the recent trend of all three centers has been to the west and south, with the exception of that for coal production, which in the year or two has felt the pull of West Virginia's marked increase of output from nonunion mines.

Franklin K. Lane, in writing of the complexity of the task of developing all our available power for the purpose of making America the home of the cheapest, the most abundant, and the most serviceable power in the world, said, "There are few who know even one sector of the great battle front of power." The fuller knowledge of the distribution of the supply of energy with which this country is blessed is an essential part of economic geography.

George Otis Smith, *A World of Power* in *Economic Geography*, July, 1925 (Worcester, Clark University), I, 139–142.

———◆———

81. The New Economics of Farming (1926)

BY EX-GOVERNOR FRANK O. LOWDEN

Lowden, a lawyer by training, was a member of Congress from 1906 to 1911, and Governor of Illinois from 1917 to 1921. Although a man of wealth, he is also a practical farmer, and has done so much in the way of solving farmers' problems that he has more than once been mentioned for the Presidency. For food-production and farm-operating costs, see articles on various crops in *Agriculture Year Book*, 1921–1925; on farm finance, see also No. 72 above.—Bibliography as in Nos. 72 and 77 above.

WE hear much these days of the inefficiency of the American farmer. How far this is from the truth let the figures attest. The Year Book of the United States Department of Agriculture for 1921 is authority for the statement that in America are found less than 4 per cent of the farmers and farm laborers of the world. And yet the American farmers produce nearly 70 per cent of the world's corn, 60 per cent of the world's cotton, 50 per cent of the world's tobacco, 25 per cent of the world's oats and hay, 20 per cent of the world's wheat and flaxseed, 13 per cent of the world's barley, 7 per cent of the world's potatoes.

In the simpler age, cost of production did not concern the farmer much. . . .

Today all is changed. The farmer is a business man bound by the laws which operate in other business fields. His cash expenditures are large. If he is to produce enough of food and clothing for the teeming millions in the industrial centers he too must employ industrial means in production. . . . . He is a producer no longer for himself mainly, but to supply the needs of this industrial age. The surplus which he produces is now the important thing.

Cost of production therefore has become as vital a question with the farmer as with the manufacturer. And yet when he complains that he is not receiving cost of production for the things he sells he is told that the prices of farm products are controlled not by cost of production but only by the law of supply and demand. It must be conceded, though, I think, that no one, farmer or manufacturer, can go on producing indefinitely in this commercial world at less than cost of production. Does it not follow that some way must be found, if we are to insure future adequate supply of food and clothing, by which the producers of these prime necessities can secure at least the cost to them of producing those necessities?

Under present conditions we have this anomaly: the farmer is not nearly so likely to suffer from a short crop as from a bumper crop. . . .

. . . Those who tire of the farmer's complaint say that he must adjust his production to the probable demand just as industry does. While no doubt progress can be made through farmer organizations to better coördinate supply with demand, he cannot avoid the occasional surplus.

To illustrate, in 1924 the corn crop amounted to 2,300,000,000 bushels. The following year, or 1925, it was 2,900,000,000 bushels. And yet the 2,900,000,000 bushels were worth less, according to the Government, by $300,000,000, than the smaller crop of the year before. Suppose now that the farmers, seeing that the 2,300,000,000 bushels were worth $300,000,000 more than 2,900,000,000 bushels, had attempted to adjust their acreage to the more profitable smaller crop. They would have cut it down 25 per cent. Did they do this? Not at all. They reduced their acreage about one-half of one per cent. And it is fortunate for the world that they pursued this course. For, according to the Government's last estimate, the yield this year will be close to 225,000,000 bushels less than last year—an amount less than the average for the five year period, and certainly no more than we will easily consume. Now if they had effected the reduction of 25 per cent which some of our theoretical friends suggest, we would have had a crop this year of about 2,000,000,000 bushels, or way below the nation's need. The result would have been very high prices for corn, and what is more important to the consumer, a very burdensome increase in the price of pork and beef products. Indeed, no one can say to what price corn would ascend with a 2,000,000,000 bushel crop when it went to $1.25 a bushel with a 2,300,000,000 bushel crop, as it did in 1924.

The fact is, the farmer must always plan to raise more than just enough if the world is to be fed and clothed. Everyone recognizes this need. That is why a reasonable carryover from season to season is regarded by the commercial world as necessary if we are to have a feeling of security for the coming year.

A surplus, therefore, of the staple products of the farm is inevitable and necessary. The nation that holds this surplus is the richer for having it. Industry can plan the better for the future if it knows in advance that we shall have enough of food and raw materials. The farmer asks why, if this occasional surplus is a good thing for everyone else, it should result in a loss to him. . . .

If there were not surpluses some years, there would be a deficiency in others, and the world would be lacking in sufficient food and clothes. If, however, the farmer alone must bear the crushing burden of a surplus, under the slow operation of economic laws, the time will come when there will be no surplus, and when therefore the world will go hungry and but half clothed. In the interest, therefore, of society as well as of the farmer, we must contrive some method by which the surpluses of the very essentials of life shall become a benefit to him who produces them and not a burden.

The problem is how to attain this object. It is clear that the individual farmer cannot do this. If the producers of any farm commodity were completely organized, it is conceivable that they might accomplish this very end.

Organization of the farmers for the purpose of marketing their crops collectively is progressing. I believe that some day it will cover the entire field. . . .

It is doubtful, however, if the coöperatives of the staple farm products are ever sufficiently organized to take care of this ever-present problem of surplus unless some way be found by which the cost of handling the surplus is borne equally by all producers of the particular commodity.

If the producers of any farm product are only partly organized and attempt to take care of the surplus, the producers of that commodity who are not members of the coöperative receive the full benefit of the improved price without bearing any of the burdens incident to the surplus. . . . It is difficult to maintain the *morale* of an organization when outsiders receive the benefits of the organization in a larger measure than do the members themselves. For this reason some of the tobacco coöperatives recently have found themselves in great difficulty.

Let us consider our cotton for a moment. We produce on an average about 60 per cent of all the cotton in the world. The next largest producer is India, but India grows an inferior quality of cotton which is used principally in the Oriental trade. Without American cotton the cotton mills of Europe would be idle and industrial chaos would come. Without American cotton England could hardly survive. And yet we have permitted the spinners of Europe largely to determine the price for this prime necessity of life. . . .

The world has long been used to the advantages of mass production. It now appears that mass selling is to be given a trial.

Some of us have thought we have seen an analogy between the occasional surplus of staple farm crops and the surplus credit resources of the banks before the adoption of the federal reserve system. The resources of the banks as a whole were adequate for the business of the country as a whole. It frequently happened, however, that an unusual demand at some particular place exceeded the resources of that community, while in other sections there were ample credit resources in excess of their need. The federal reserve system was designed, among other things, to mobilize the credit resources of those banks which had a surplus and employ them where the credit resources were deficient. It sought to do in reference to space with surplus credit resources what should be accomplished in reference to time with the occasional surpluses of the farm.

We have therefore suggested a federal farm board. We have proposed that such board should be vested with power of inquiring into certain facts. Those facts are: Is there a surplus of some basic farm product? Does this surplus depress the price below cost of production with a reasonable profit? Are the growers of that product sufficiently organized coöperatively as to be fairly representative of all the producers of that product? If the Board finds that all of these questions must be answered "yes" it is then empowered to authorize the coöperative to take control of the surplus. The only aid from the Government which the coöperative would require would be that the Government should distribute among all the producers of the particular commodity the cost to the coöperative of handling the surplus. Neither the Government nor the Government Board would determine the price. Nor would even the coöperative itself "fix" the price in any other sense than industry generally determines prices. It, like every other industry, would study all the conditions affecting the particular commodity and from time to time decide upon a price which conditions would seem to warrant. It would simply enjoy the advantages which come from organized selling. . . .

Commerce and Finance, a leading financial journal of New York, states that if the South should find itself able to hold and finance the surplus it

might easily mean a difference of 6 or 7 cents a pound in the average price of middling cotton for the season.

Is there any simpler method by which this ability could be achieved than in the program I have outlined? . . .

It is . . . objected to the program I have been discussing that it will increase the cost of living to the consumer. This may be so temporarily, though in a much less degree than is supposed. However, taking a long time view, it should have just the opposite effect, as I think I shall be able to show. . . .

Experience in other industries has shown that the producer and the consumer are both best served as prices tend to become stabilized. Progress in an industry is measured by its approach to stabilization of price. Wide fluctuations in the price of any commodity always result in a loss to the producer and consumer alike. As one able writer puts it:

Fluctuations only benefit the speculative middleman. When prices soar, the producer rarely receives the full value of the increase, but the consumer invariably has to pay it. A severe fall in wholesale prices is very rarely fully reflected in the retail price to the consumer, but is always completely felt by the producer. It would therefore seem that stable prices would benefit both the producer and the consumer.

The tendency in America for the last quarter of a century has been toward stabilized prices save in agriculture alone. In agricultural products, however, the swing of prices in recent years has been more violent than ever before. To illustrate, during the years 1923, 1924 and 1925 the price of hogs fluctuated about one hundred per cent. The fluctuation in the price of pork products to the consumer was about a third of this. During the same period the price of wheat fluctuated one hundred per cent. The fluctuation in the price of bread to the consumer was less than five per cent. It is clear that the consumer derives no benefit from the low prices at which agricultural products at times have sold.

It is evident that in the interest of the consumer as well as of the producer we should find some means for stabilizing prices of farm products. . . .

It may be that there is a better solution of the problem than the one I have suggested. I am not insisting upon any particular remedy. I only say there is a farm problem of the gravest importance and that a solution must be found if we would preserve our civilization. . . .

Frank O. Lowden, *Address before the American Farm Bureau Federation*, 1926.

---

82. The Pink Invader (1928)

BY VICTOR H. SCHOFFELMAYER

Following the destructive onslaughts of the boll weevil, has come the even more damaging advance of the pink bollworm, which threatens to be one of the most serious modern problems of the agricultural south.—For accounts of the battle against this and other pests, see *Agriculture Year Book*, 1926 and following years.

MAKING its way out of the rugged canyon country which marks the Texas-Mexican border along the Rio Grande, then crossing high mountains and some 200 miles of desert and ranching region, the pink bollworm has invaded the western edge of America's Cotton Belt. Between the recent infestation, embracing some 400,000 acres in seven West Texas counties, and the Atlantic seaboard there lies a continuous cotton field of over 40,000,000 acres.

Thus, the problem of controlling this formidable pest has assumed national importance. Cotton growers of the South, producing 60 per cent of the world's cotton crop, the entire cotton industry of the United States, representing an investment of approximately three billion dollars, the cotton oil industry, railroads and steamship lines, tens of thousands of cotton gins, all are menaced by this destructive pest. Prompt eradication of the pink bollworm is necessary, for it is extremely doubtful if the South could continue to raise cotton under the combined handicap of the boll weevil and this latest pest. The former already has cost the South hundreds of millions of dollars, although in a measure it can be checked by timely poisoning. But so far as present knowledge goes poison is ineffective against the pink bollworm since it spends the greater part of its life within the seed in the interior of the cotton boll. The worm has been known to live more than two years inside a cotton boll. It not only destroys the seed but cuts and stains the cotton fiber. In highly infested fields the cotton is scarce worth picking. Scientific investigations show the boll weevil prefers to attack the squares, as the early fruit forms of cotton are called, whereas the pink bollworm attacks the green bolls. It is obvious that what the weevil would leave would fall a prey to the worm.

The only effective method employed against the pink bollworm has been found to be eradication by depriving the insect of its essential food—cotton. It can be starved out. Some ten years ago it got into this country in both Texas and Louisiana. Prompt enforcement of non-cotton zones succeeded in wiping out the worm where these methods were applied. No cotton was permitted to be raised for three years in one case and for two years in subsequent cases.

At that time it first entered the United States in a shipment of cottonseed from Mexico to an oil mill at Hearne, in Southeast Texas, and was discovered in a cotton field adjacent to the mill on September 10, 1917, by Ivan Shiller, an inspector of the Federal Horticultural Board. A few weeks later pink bollworms were found in fields near Anahuac, on the Gulf Coast of Texas, and shortly afterward in cotton fields in Galveston, Jefferson, Liberty, Harris, Brazoria and Hardin counties, all of which are situated along the Gulf.

It was plain that there could be no connection between the initial infestation at Hearne and those on the Gulf Coast. Thorough investigation indicated that these last outbreaks were due to the Galveston hurricane of 1915, which swept several thousand bales of Mexican cotton, stored on the docks at Galveston, on to the mainland of Texas. At that time many Mexican cotton bales contained cottonseed, due to faulty ginning. It was only a matter of time and proper conditions for the worms in the seeds to develop into moths and fly to near-by cotton fields.

While Federal and state officials were busy with the Southeastern Texas outbreak the pink bollworm appeared in November, 1918, in cotton fields in the Big Bend country in extreme West Texas, in Presidio and Brewster counties. This infestation was traced to Mexican laborers who entered the state carrying infested bedding or other goods. This is one of the roughest frontiers in the Southwest. The Rio Grande meanders through deep canyons, but occasionally the valley widens to a mile or more and cotton fields exist on both sides of the stream, farmed almost entirely by Mexicans in a rather primitive manner.

In December of 1918 the pink bollworm was found in cotton fields in Ward, Reeves, and Pecos counties. In 1920 it was found in El Paso. The same year it spread to the Messilla Valley above El Paso in New Mexico and to the cotton fields along the Pecos River in the Carlsbad district.

In 1920 two outbreaks of the worm were discovered in Louisiana, one in the southwestern corner of the state and the other near Shreveport. About the same time infestation to a limited extent was discovered in the Texas black-land belt in Ellis County and another in North Texas at Marilee.

The man of the hour in this emergency proved to be Dr. W. D. Hunter, who was in charge of Southern crop insect investigations for the United States Department of Agriculture. He recognized the seriousness of the situation and organized a force which for efficiency probably has never been surpassed.

Doctor Hunter, who died two years ago, gave the remaining ten years of his life to the control and eradication of the pest. His intimate knowledge of the insect's life cycle led him to the conclusion that there is only one certain way of eradicating it—by depriving it of its essential food, cotton. He conceived the idea of non-cotton zones, although such an idea was extremely unpopular at a time when no provisions existed for compensating growers not allowed to raise cotton. Doctor Hunter's tact, generalship, knowledge of men and acquaintance with every angle of the trying situation enabled him to bring public opinion to his side after some of the stormiest mass meetings ever recorded in Texas history. In 1917 the Texas Legislature passed an act designed to prevent the establishment of the pink bollworm in the state. Under this act authority was granted to quarantine the districts in which the insect might be found and to establish zones in which the planting of cotton might be prohibited. Under this act, in January, 1918, the governor of Texas quarantined the Hearne district as well as the seven counties in the Trinity Bay section of the Gulf Coast.

A safety zone of ten miles in width was thrown around the infested areas to prevent the worm's escape. In February of 1918 the governor issued a proclamation prohibiting the planting of cotton in the quarantined areas. Then the fireworks started. Angry protest meetings were held, at one of which a rope was brought in to impress Doctor Hunter and his cohorts. These stressful years, no doubt, contributed to Doctor Hunter's death, but that his timely and energetic action prevented the infestation of the South's cotton is now generally conceded.

Later a law was enacted under which the state of Texas, in coöperation with the Federal Government, reimbursed farmers for all "just and necessary losses incurred" due to the non-cotton zones. Texas paid two-thirds of the losses and the Federal Government one-third. The Southeast Texas outbreak cost Texas about $700,000 for compensation and administration of field work. The Government's share was about $250,000 for compensation, but the total cost to it in control measures is believed to be nearly $3,000,000.

The Louisiana non-cotton zones cost that state about $400,000 and the Federal Government paid an additional one-third as much.

The idea of compensation is based upon actual loss suffered by growers. This means that wherever other crops, such as corn, oats, feed and hay, can be raised the value of these crops is taken into account in the settlement of claims. In Southeast Texas at the time the non-cotton zones were enforced cotton sold for as high as thirty-five cents a pound. Settlement was on a basis of approximately $18.50 an acre, which was considered just. The settlement in Ellis County, one of the richest cotton counties in the world, was on a basis of about $16 an acre.

In the western areas of Texas and in New Mexico it was deemed sufficient to establish regulated zones instead of non-cotton zones because this area was separated from the main Cotton Belt by a natural barrier of hundreds of miles. State and Federal road stations were established on the cardinal highways, at which all auto and truck or wagon traffic was subjected to rigid inspection.

Yet the bollworm crossed the barrier of mountains and non-cotton growing region and got into the new cotton-growing area of West Texas. R. E. McDonald, Texas chief entomologist, has advanced the view that the moth of the pink bollworm may be carried by winds. He has arrived at this conclusion by studying the prevailing wind currents in the Big Bend region, from which he believes the worm has entered the newly infested counties.

The discovery of the pink bollworm in the seven counties of West Texas last winter naturally aroused widespread alarm. The effectiveness of the methods used in combating the pest on its former appearance was recalled. Dr. Charles L. Marlatt, chairman of the Federal Horticultural Board and chief of the Bureau of Entomology, after a visit to the old and new infested areas of Texas, announced a plan of "eradication with adequate compensation." A resolution was introduced in Congress by Representative J. P. Buchanan of Texas and Senator Ransdell of Louisiana, asking for a Federal appropriation of $5,000,000 for eradication of the pest, with full compensation to growers deprived of the right to raise cotton in non-cotton zones.

This was emphatically in line with sentiment in Texas, which felt that this was a national problem. And the growers in the West Texas country, which has come into recent development as a cotton and general farming empire, naturally felt they should not bear the brunt alone. The country is new and many farms and homes are being bought out of the earnings of the land.

After a stay in Texas, Doctor Marlatt, working closely with the Texas State Pink Bollworm Commission, was assured that non-cotton zones might be made to work if the Government would properly compensate. The Pink Bollworm Commission in its report to Governor Dan Moody of Texas stated:

We have decided not to recommend a non-cotton zone in all of the area this year because of the far-reaching loss and damage that would be occasioned at a

time when it is impossible to provide prompt and adequate compensation on such
a large scale on the part of the State and National Governments.

But, recognizing the possibility—unless regulations should be shown to be
effective and this can only be done by unanimous co-operation—that such drastic
measures may be necessary, we urge that arrangements be at once begun for securing national and state aid, prior to the 1929 crop, that such a non-cotton zone
would require.

The commission recommended a non-cotton zone only for Brewster
County, which produces only about 175 bales of cotton a year, and
for the six other counties recommended regulated zones with sterilization of all cottonseed and fumigation of all lint.

Farmers in the affected areas rejoiced in the commission's report
as it left them free to raise cotton. They have promised full compli-
ance with the regulations.

Other Southern states, fearing an invasion of pink bollworms and
having quite enough to do to keep ahead of the boll weevil, sent one
hundred representatives to Memphis last March and after mildly
veiled threats of quarantines against Texas cotton adopted a resolution
indorsing the Buchanan measure in Congress for full Federal compensation in non-cotton zones. Also they urged that steps be taken to
bring about an immediate plan of coöperation between Mexico and
the United States to stamp out the pink bollworm.

At the same time that the pink bollworm spread from the Rio
Grande border into the main Texas cotton belt it also spread from
New Mexico into Arizona.

The Texas infestation, old and new, totaling fourteen counties,
embraces 472,300 acres, of which 85,300 acres became infested in 1918
and 1920. In the old area cotton is grown only under irrigation and
yields of as high as two and three bales an acre are not uncommon.
This high yield enables cotton to be grown in spite of the worm. The
farther north the territory the less the damage, since cold winters
check the pest. In the El Paso Valley, which produces the bulk of the
cotton of the border counties, the worm has done very little damage,
in the opinion of the cotton growers.

The newly infested counties of West Texas are in dry-farming territory. The average three-year yield for this area is 70,000 bales, and
for the old area about 60,000 bales.

Entomologists for a long time had feared that the worm would in some manner spread to areas farther eastward and as a precautionary measure scouts were placed in these areas five years ago. The first signs pointing to pink bollworm damage appeared in 1925, but no worms were found and none were found in 1926. But in the winter of 1927 the pink bollworm was found on the Johnson Brothers Ranch.

The worm was dead and so has been every specimen taken since that time, which means nothing from the standpoint of danger to the cotton industry. They would have been alive if a cold winter had not killed them before they had a chance to select suitable winter quarters.

By the end of March one hundred scouts had located twenty-four infested cotton fields in Ector, Andrews, Martin, Midland, Howard, Dawson and Glasscock counties.

Victor H. Schoffelmayer, in *Country Gentleman* (Philadelphia), July, 1928. 8 ss., *passim*. Copyright by the Curtis Publishing Company.

CHAPTER XVI — MONOPOLIES AND TRUSTS

83. The Northern Securities Case (1904)

BY JUSTICE JOHN MARSHALL HARLAN

After the decision in the Knight case, which seemed to leave the anti-trust laws with teeth dulled to harmlessness, business combinations flourished. In the Northern Securities case they had their first serious conflict with government authority. For Mr. Justice Harlan, see No. 101 below. For Hill, see No. 62 above.—Bibliography: Edward Dana Durand, *The Trust Problem;* Jenks and Clark, *The Trust Problem;* William H. Taft, *The Anti-Trust Act and the Supreme Court;* A. H. Walker, *History of the Sherman Law; Compilation of Anti-Trust Decisions* (Senate Docs., 62d Congress, 1 Sess., No. 111).

IS the case as presented by the pleadings and the evidence one of a combination or a conspiracy in restraint of trade or commerce among the States, or with foreign states? Is it one in which the defendants are properly chargeable with monopolizing or attempting to monopolize any part of such trade or commerce? Let us see what are the facts disclosed by the record.

The Great Northern Railway Company and the Northern Pacific Railway Company owned, controlled and operated separate lines of railway—the former road extending from Superior, and from Duluth and St. Paul, to Everett, Seattle, and Portland, with a branch line to Helena; the latter, extending from Ashland, and from Duluth and St. Paul, to Helena, Spokane, Seattle, Tacoma and Portland. The two lines, main and branches, about 9,000 miles in length, were and are parallel and competing lines across the continent through the northern tier of States between the Great Lakes and the Pacific, and the two companies were engaged in active competition for freight and passenger traffic, each road connecting at its respective terminals with lines of railway, or with lake and river steamers, or with seagoing vessels. . . .

Early in 1901 the Great Northern and Northern Pacific Railway companies, having in view the ultimate placing of their two systems under a common control, united in the purchase of the capital stock of the Chicago, Burlington and Quincy Railway Company, giving in payment, upon an agreed basis of exchange, the joint bonds of the Great Northern and Northern Pacific Railway companies, payable in twenty years from date, with interest at 4 per cent per annum. . . .

By this purchase of stock the Great Northern and Northern Pacific acquired full control of the Chicago, Burlington and Quincy main line and branches.

Prior to November 13, 1901, defendant Hill and associate stock-holders of the Great Northern Railway Company, and defendant Morgan and associate stockholders of the Northern Pacific Railway Company, entered into a combination to form, under the laws of New Jersey, a *holding* corporation, to be called the Northern Securities Company, with a capital stock of $400,000,000, and to which company, in exchange for its own capital stock upon a certain basis and at a certain rate, was to be turned over the capital stock, or a controlling interest in the capital stock, of each of the constituent railway companies, with power in the holding corporation to vote such stock and in all respects to act as the owner thereof, and to do whatever it might deem necessary in aid of such railway companies to enhance the value of their stocks. . . . Thus, as stated in Article VI of the bill, "by making the stockholders of each system jointly interested in both systems, and by practically pooling the earnings of both for the benefit of the former stockholders of each, and by vesting the selection of the directors and officers of each system in a common body, to wit, the holding corporation, with not only the power but the duty to pursue a policy which would promote the interests, not of one system at the expense of the other, but of both at the expense of the public, all inducement for competition between the two systems was to be removed, a virtual consolidation effected, and a monopoly of the interstate and foreign commerce formerly carried on by the two systems as independent competitors established."

In pursuance of this combination and to effect its objects, the defendant, the Northern Securities Company, was organized November 13, 1901, under the laws of New Jersey. . . .

This charter having been obtained, Hill and his associate stock-holders of the Great Northern Railway Company, and Morgan and associate stockholders of the Northern Pacific Railway Company, assigned to the Securities Company a controlling amount of the capital stock of the respective constituent companies upon an agreed basis of exchange of the capital stock of the Securities Company for each share of the capital stock of the other companies.

In further pursuance of the combination, the Securities Company acquired additional stock of the defendant railway companies, issuing in lieu thereof its own stock upon the above basis, and, at the time of the bringing of this suit, held, as owner and proprietor, substantially all the capital stock of the Northern Pacific Railway Company, and, it is alleged, a controlling interest in the stock of the Great Northern Railway Company, "and is voting the same and is collecting the dividends thereon, and in all respects is acting as the owner thereof, in the organization, management and operation of said railway companies and in the receipt and control of their earnings."

No consideration whatever, the bill alleges, has existed or will exist, for the transfer of the stock of the defendant railway companies to the Northern Securities Company, other than the issue of the stock of the latter company for the purpose, after the manner, and upon the basis stated. . . .

Summarizing the principal facts, it is indisputable upon this record that under the leadership of the defendants Hill and Morgan the stockholders of the Great Northern and Northern Pacific Railway corporations, having competing and substantially parallel lines from the Great Lakes and the Mississippi River to the Pacific Ocean at Puget Sound combined and conceived the scheme of organizing a corporation under the laws of New Jersey, which should *hold* the shares of the stock of the constituent companies, such shareholders, in lieu of their shares in those companies, to receive, upon an agreed basis of value, shares in the holding corporation; that pursuant to such combination the Northern Securities Company was organized as the holding corporation through which the scheme should be executed; and under that scheme such holding corporation has become the holder—more properly speaking, the custodian—of more than nine-tenths of the stock of the Northern Pacific, and more than three-fourths of the stock of the Great Northern, the stockholders of the companies who delivered their stock receiving upon the agreed basis shares of stock in the holding corporation. The stockholders of these two competing companies disappeared, as such, for the moment, but immediately reappeared as stockholders of the holding company which was thereafter to guard the interests of both sets of stockholders as a unit, and to manage, or cause to be managed, both lines of railroad as if held *in one ownership*. Necessarily by this combination or arrangement the holding company in the fullest sense dominates the situation in the interest of those who were stockholders of the constituent companies; as much so, for every practical purpose, as if it had been itself a railroad corporation which had built, owned, and operated both lines for the exclusive benefit of its stockholders. Necessarily, also, the constituent companies ceased, under such a combination, to be in active competition for trade and commerce along their respective lines, and have become practically one powerful consolidated corporation, by the name of a holding corporation the principal, if not the sole, object for the formation of which was to carry out the purpose of the original combination under which competition between the constituent companies would cease. Those who were stockholders of the Great Northern and Northern Pacific and became stockholders in the holding company are now interested in preventing all competition between the two lines, and as owners of stock or of certificates of stock in the holding company, they will see to it that no competition is tolerated. They will take care that no persons are chosen directors of the holding company who will permit competition between the constituent companies. The result of the combination is that all the earnings of the constituent companies make a common fund in the hands of the Northern Securities Company to be distributed, not upon the basis of the earnings of the respective constituent companies, each acting exclusively in its own interest, but upon the basis of the certificates of stock issued by the holding company. No scheme or device could more certainly come within the words of the act—"combination in the form of a trust or otherwise . . . in restraint of commerce among the several States or with foreign nations,"—or could more effectively and certainly suppress free competition between the constituent companies. This combination is, within the meaning of the act, a "trust"; but if not, it is a *combination in restraint of interstate* and *international commerce;* and that is enough to bring it under the condemnation of the act. The mere existence of such a combination and the power acquired by the holding company as its trustee, constitute a menace to, and a restraint upon, that freedom of commerce which Congress intended to recognize and protect, and which the public is entitled to have protected. If such combination be not destroyed, all the advantages that would naturally come to the public under the operation of the general laws of competition, as between the Great Northern and Northern Pacific Railway companies, will be lost, and the entire commerce of the immense territory in the northern part of the United States between the Great Lakes and the Pacific at Puget Sound will be at the mercy of a single holding corporation, organized in a State distant from the people of that territory. . . .

By the decree in the Circuit Court it was found and adjudged that the defendants had entered into a combination or conspiracy in restraint of trade or commerce among the several States, such as the act of Congress denounced as illegal; and that all of the stocks of the Northern Pacific Railway Company and all the stock of the Great Northern Railway Company, claimed to be owned and held by the Northern Securities Company, was acquired, and is by it held, in virtue of such combination or conspiracy, in restraint of trade and commerce among the several States. . . .

If there was a combination or conspiracy in violation of the act of Congress, between the stockholders of the Great Northern and the Northern Pacific Railway companies, whereby the Northern Securities Company was formed as a holding corporation, and whereby interstate commerce over the lines of the constituent companies was restrained, it must follow that the court, in execution of that act, and to defeat the efforts to evade it, could prohibit the parties to the combination from doing the specific things which being done would effect the result denounced by the act. To say that the court could not go so far is to say that it is powerless to enforce the act or to suppress the illegal combination, and powerless to protect the rights of the public as against that combination. . . .

The Circuit Court has done only what the actual situation demanded. Its decree has done nothing more than to meet the requirements of the statute. It could not have done less without declaring its impotency in dealing with those who have violated the law. The decree, if executed, will destroy, not the property interests of the original stockholders of the constituent companies, but the power of the holding corporation as the instrument of an illegal combination of which it was the master spirit, to do that which, if done, would restrain interstate and international commerce. The exercise of that power being restrained, the object of Congress will be accomplished; left undisturbed, the act in question will be valueless for any practical purpose.

Justice Harlan, Opinion of U. S. Supreme Court in *Northern Securities Company v. United States, 193 U. S. Reports,* 320–358 *passim.*

---

84. Government Ownership of Railroads (1906)

BY WILLIAM JENNINGS BRYAN

William Jennings Bryan, of Nebraska, member of the House of Representatives from 1891 to 1895, was three times the candidate of the Democratic Party for President of the United States; but his highest office was that of Secretary of State under President Wilson. That position he resigned in 1915 because he was unwilling to participate in a war administration. His views on government ownership are expressed in several of his public addresses. The experience of government operation of railroads during the war was enough to satisfy most citizens that its disadvantages exceeded its merits.—Bibliography, mainly on the question of government regulation: J. H. Bede, *Railroad Rate Legislation;* Felix Frankfurter, *Cases under the Interstate Commerce Act;* E. R. Johnson, *American Railway Transportation;* F. H. Spearman, *Strategy of Great Railroads;* F. H. Dixon, *Railroads and Government.*

IF you ask me whether the question of Government ownership will be an issue in the campaign of 1908, I answer, I do not know. If you ask me whether it ought to be in the platform, I reply, I cannot tell until I know what the Democratic voters think upon the subject. If the Democrats believe that the next platform should contain a plank in favor of Government ownership, then that plank ought to be included. If the Democrats think it ought not to contain such a plank, then such a plank ought not to be included. It rests with the party to make the platform, and individuals can only advise. I have spoken for myself and for myself only, and I did not know how the suggestion would be received. I am now prepared to confess to you that it has been received more favorably than I expected. It has not been treated as harshly as I thought possibly it would be treated. That it would be gravely discussed by others I hoped. There is this, however, that I do expect, namely, that those Democrats who opposed

Government ownership will accompany their declaration against it with the assertion that they will favor Government ownership whenever they are convinced that the country must choose between Government ownership of the roads and railroad ownership of the Government. I cannot conceive how a Democrat can declare, no matter to what extent the railroads carry their interference with politics and their corruption of officials, he is still opposed to Government ownership. I think I may also reasonably expect that Democrats who oppose Government ownership will say that if Government ownership must come, they prefer a system whereby the State may be preserved and the centralizing influence be reduced to a minimum. Such a plan I have proposed, and I have proposed it because I want the people to consider it and not be driven to the federal ownership of all railroads as the only alternative to private ownership. The dual plan, that is, federal ownership of trunk lines and State ownership of local lines, not only preserves the State, and even strengthens its position but it permits the gradual adoption of Government ownership as the people of different sections are ready to adopt it.

I have been slow in reaching this position and I can therefore be patient with those who now stand where I stood for years, urging strict regulation and hoping that that would be found feasible. I still advocate strict regulation and shall rejoice if experience proves that that regulation can be made effective. I will go farther than that and say that I believe we can have more efficient regulation under a Democratic administration with a Democratic Senate and House than we are likely to have under a Republican administration with a Republican Senate and House, and yet I would not be honest with you if I did not frankly admit that observation has convinced me that no such efficient regulation is possible, and that Government ownership can be undertaken on the plan outlined with less danger to the country than is involved in private ownership as we have had it or as we are likely to have it. I have been brought to regard public ownership as the ultimate remedy by railroad history which is as familiar to you as to me. Among the reasons that have led me to believe that we must, in the end, look to Government for relief, I shall mention two or three. First and foremost is the corrupting influence of the railroad in politics. There is not a State in the union that has not felt this influence to a greater or less extent. The railroads have insisted upon controlling legislatures; they have insisted upon naming executives; they have insisted upon controlling the nomination and appointment of judges; they have endeavored to put their representatives on tax boards that they might escape just taxation; they have watered their stock, raised their rates and enjoined the States whenever they have attempted to regulate rates; they have obstructed legislation when hostile to them, and advanced, by secret means, legislation favorable to them. Let me give you an illustration:

The interstate commerce law was enacted nineteen years ago. After about nine years this law was practically nullified by the Supreme Court, and for ten years the railroad influence has been sufficient in the Senate and House to prevent an amendment asked for time and again by the Interstate Commerce Commission. That railroad influence has been strong enough to keep the Republican party from adopting any platform declaration in favor of rate regulation. When the President, following three Democratic platforms, insisted upon regulation, he was met with the opposition of the railroads, and every step, every point gained in favor of the people, was gained after a strenuous fight. The bill was improved by an amendment proposed by Senator Stone, of Missouri, restoring the criminal penalty which had been taken out of the interstate commerce law by the Elkins law. The same amendment had been presented, in substance, in the House, by Congressman James, of Kentucky, and had been defeated by Republican votes. The bill was further improved by an amendment proposed by Senator Culberson, of Texas, forbidding the use of passes, and it would have been still further improved by the amendment proposed by Senator Bailey, of Texas, limiting the court review, but the railroad influence was strong enough to defeat this amendment.

I have no idea that the railroads are going to permit regulation without a struggle and I fear that their influence will be strong enough very much to delay, if it does not entirely defeat, remedial legislation. You, in this State, know something of the railroad in politics. When I visited the State and spoke for Mr. Goebel, I heard him charge upon every platform that the railroads were spending large sums in opposition to his election, and I have always believed that the railroad influence was largely responsible for the assassination of that brave defender of the rights of the people.

Another reason which has led me to favor Government ownership, is the fact that the people are annually plundered of an enormous sum by extortionate rates; that places are discriminated against and individuals driven out of business by favoritism shown by the railroads. You say that all these things can be corrected without interference with private ownership. I shall be glad if experience proves that they can be, but I no longer hope for it. President Roosevelt, although expressing himself against Government ownership, has announced that only successful regulation can prevent Government ownership. Is there any Democrat who is not willing to go as far as President Roosevelt and admit the necessity of Government ownership in case the people are convinced of the failure of regulation? I cannot believe it.

Then, while we attempt to make regulation effective, while we endeavor to make the experiment under the most favorable conditions, namely with the Democratic party in power, let us not hesitate to inform the railroads that they must keep out of politics; that they must keep their hands off of legislation; that they must abstain from interfering with the party machinery and warn them that they can only maintain their private control of the railroads by accepting such regulation as the people may see fit to apply in their own interest and for their own protection. Without this threat our cause would be hopeless. It remains to be seen whether, with this threat, we shall be able to secure justice to the shippers, to the traveling public and to the taxpayers.

Speech at Louisville, Ky., 1906.

85. The Coal Monopoly (1912)

BY JUSTICE HORACE H. LURTON

The attempt to control anthracite coal production was executed with great technical skill, but the Supreme Court looked through the apparent formalities of the scheme at its actual effect, and then acted to dissolve the combination. For Mr. Justice Lurton, see No. 101 below.—Bibliography: Chester G. Gilbert and Joseph E. Pogue, *The Energy Resources of the United States* (1919); Arthur M. Hull, *Coal Men of America; a Biographical and Historical Review of the World's Greatest Industry* (1918); *What the Coal Commission Found* (1925), based on the report of the commission in five volumes; Eliot Jones, *The Anthracite Coal Combination in the United States* (1914).

THE bill alleges that anthracite coal is an article of prime necessity as a fuel and finds its market mainly in the New England and Middle Atlantic States. The deposits of the coal, with unimportant exceptions, lie in the State of Pennsylvania, but do not occupy a continuous field, though found in certain counties adjoining in the eastern half of the State, and embrace an area of 484 square miles. . . .

From an early day it has been the settled policy of the State of Pennsylvania to encourage the development of this coal region by canal and railroad construction, which would furnish transportation to convenient shipping points at tidewater. One of the defendant carriers, the Delaware, Lackawanna & Western Company, was given the power to acquire coal lands and engage in the business of mining and selling coal in addition to the business of a common carrier, and all railroad companies were permitted to aid in the production of coal by assisting coal-mining companies through the purchase of capital stock and bonds. Thus, it has come about that the defendant carriers not only dominate the transportation of coal from this anthracite region to the great distributing ports at New York Harbor, but also through their controlled coal-producing companies, produce and sell about seventy-five per cent of the annual supply of anthracite. As a further direct consequence of the State authorized alliance between coal-producing and coal-transporting companies, it has come about that the defendant carrier companies and the coal-mining companies affiliated with the carrier companies now own or control about ninety per cent of the entire unmined area of anthracite. . . .

Thus, there exists, independently of any agreement, combination or contract between the several defendant carrier companies for the purpose of suppressing competition among them, this condition:

First. Excluding two carrier companies not made defendants which reach but a limited number of collieries, the Pennsylvania Railroad Company and the New York, Ontario & Western Railroad Company, the six carrier companies who are defendants are shown to control the only means of transportation between this great anthracite deposit and tidewater, from whence the product may be distributed by rail and water to the great consuming markets of the Atlantic Coast States.

Second. These carriers and their subsidiary coal-mining and selling companies produce and sell about seventy-five per cent of the total annual supply of anthracite coal. Of the remainder, the independent operators mentioned above produce about twenty per cent.

The chief significance of the fact that the six carrier defendants control substantially the only means for the transportation of coal from the mines to distributing points at tidewater is in the fact that they, collectively, also control nearly three-fourths of the annual supply of anthracite which there finds a market. The situation is therefore one which invites concerted action and makes exceedingly easy the accomplishment of any purpose to dominate the supply and control the prices at seaboard. The one-fourth of the total annual supply which comes from independent operators in the same region has been sold in competition with the larger supply of the defendants. If, by concert of action, the source of competition be removed, the monopoly which the defendants, acting together, may exert over the production and sale will be complete.

This bill avers that the defendants have combined for the purpose of securing their collective grip upon the anthracite coal supply by exerting their activities to shut out from the district any new line of transportation from the mines to tidewater points, and to shut out from competition at tidewater the coal of independent operators with their own coal. . . .

The theory upon which the bill is framed and upon which the case has been presented by counsel is, that there exists between the defendants a *general combination* to control the anthracite coal industry, both in respect of mining and transportation from the mines to the general consuming markets reached from shipping points at New York

Harbor, and the production and sale of coal throughout the United States.

The contention is that this *general combination* is established, first, by evidence of an agreement between the carrier defendants to apportion between themselves the total coal tonnage transported from the mines to tidewater according to a scale of percentages; second, by a combination between them, through the instrumentality of the defendant, the Temple Iron Company, to prevent the construction of a new and competing line of railroad from the mines to tidewater; third, by a combination between the defendants by means of a series of identical contracts for the control of the coal produced by independent coal operators, thereby preventing competition in the markets of other States between the coal of such independent operators and that produced by the defendants; and, finally, by certain so-called contributory combinations, already referred to, between some, but not all, of the defendants.

Aside from the particular transactions averred as "steps" or "acts in futherance" of a presupposed *general combination*, the charge of such a combination is general and indefinite. . . .

The capital stock of the Temple Iron Company, aggregating only $240,000, was all secured. That company was then operating a small iron furnace near Reading. Its assets were small, but its charter was a special legislative charter which gave it power to engage in almost any sort of business, and to increase its capital substantially at will. Control of that company having been secured, it was used as the instrument for the purpose intended. . . .

The Temple Company increased its capital stock to $2,500,000 and issued mortgage bonds aggregating $3,500,000. Simpson & Watkins agreed to sell to the Temple Company their properties for something near $5,000,000. They accordingly transferred to the Temple Company the capital shares in the several coal companies, holding the title to their eight collieries, and received in exchange $2,260,000 in the shares of the Temple Company, and $3,500,000 of its mortgage bonds. . . .

Thus, it came about that when this bill was filed the stock of the Temple Company, which, as seen, is a mere holding company for the several defendant carrier companies, was owned by the defendants. . . .

That under the law of Pennsylvania each of the defendant carrier companies has the power to acquire and hold the stock of coal-producing companies may be true. That the Temple Company may, under the same law, have the power to acquire and hold the capital stock of the Simpson & Watkins' collieries may also be conceded. But if the defendant carriers did, as we have found to be the fact, combine to restrain the freedom of interstate commerce either in the transportation or in the sale of anthracite coal in the markets of other States, and adopted as a means for that purpose the Temple Company, and through it, the control of the great Simpson & Watkins' collieries, the parts of the general scheme, however lawful considered alone, become parts of an illegal combination under the Federal statute which it is the duty of the court to dissolve, irrespective of how the legal title to the shares is held. . . .

We are in entire accord with the view of the court below in holding that the transaction involved a concerted scheme and combination for the purpose of restraining commerce among the States in plain violation of the act of Congress of July 2, 1890. . . .

The decree of the court below is affirmed as to the Temple Iron Company combination.

Justice Lurton, Opinion of U. S. Supreme Court in *United States v. Reading Company*, 226 *U. S. Reports*, 338–373 *passim*.

86. A Liberal's Protest (1912)

BY SENATOR ROBERT M. LA FOLLETTE, SR.

La Follette (1855–1925) was one of the great independent leaders of political thought in the United States. He sought first to accomplish reforms by working from within the Republican organization in Wisconsin. In that state he served several terms as Governor, and later was repeatedly elected to the United States Senate. In 1924 he was the candidate of the Progressive Party (successor of the 1912 party of that name) for the Presidency. Aggressive and sincere, though sometimes erratic, he was a genuine leader, and his proposals for Republican party platforms, though ridiculed when offered in the conventions, were usually adopted four or eight years afterward.—Bibliography as in Nos. 83 and 84 above.

THE trust problem has become so interwoven in our legal and industrial system that no single measure or group of measures can reach all of it. It must be picked off at every point where it shows its head.

Every combination of a manufacturing business with the control of transportation, including pipe lines, should be prohibited, in order that competitors may have equal facilities for reaching markets.

The control of limited sources of raw material like coal, iron ore, or timber, by a manufacturing corporation, should be broken up and these resources should be opened to all manufacturers on equal terms.

It is claimed on all sides that competition has failed. I deny it. Fair competition has not failed. It has been suppressed. When competitors are shut out from markets by discrimination, and denied either transportation, raw material or credit on equal terms, we do not have competition. We have the modern form of highway robbery. The great problem of legislation before us is first for the people to resume control of their government, and then to protect themselves against those who are throttling competition by the aid of government.

I do not say that competition does not have its evils. Labor organizations are the struggling protest against cutthroat competition. The anti-trust law was not intended or understood to apply to them. They should be exempt from its operation.

The tariff should be brought down to the difference in labor cost of the more efficient plants and the foreign competitor, and where there is no difference the tariff should be removed. Where the protective tariff is retained its advantages must be passed along to labor, for whose benefit the manufacturer contends it is necessary.

The patent laws should be so amended that the owners of patents will be compelled to develop them fully or permit their use on equal terms by others.

More vital and menacing than any other power that supports trusts is the control of credit through the control of the people's savings and deposits. When the Emergency Currency Bill was before Congress in 1908, Senator Aldrich slipped into the conference report certain provisions which he had withdrawn in the Senate, and withdrew provisions which he had first included. He eliminated protection against promotion schemes, excluded penalties for false reporting, dropped provisions for safeguarding reserves, inserted provisions for accepting railroad bonds as security. Now he comes with another plausible measure to remedy the admitted evils of our inelastic banking system.

When we realize that the control of credit and banking is the greatest power that the trusts possess to keep out competitors, we may well question their sincerity in offering a patriotic measure to dispossess themselves of that power. It is the people's money that is expected to give security to this plan and the people must and shall control it.

The proposed Aldrich Currency Plan is the product of a commission composed of men who are or have been members of the committees of the two houses of Congress, which have controlled all legislation relating to currency and banking. With such a record it behooves the public to examine with the utmost care any plan which they recommend, however plausible it may appear upon its face. A critical study of the scheme of this commission will convince any student of government finance, that under the guise of providing elasticity to our currency system, it is in reality an adroit means of further concentration and control of the money and credits of the United States under a fifty-year franchise, augmenting the power of those who already dominate the banking and insurance resources of the country.

Our National Banking Law is a patchwork of legislation. It should be thoroughly revised. And all authorities agree that a comprehensive plan for an emergency currency is vitally important. When the basic principle of such a plan is once determined, when it is settled that government controlled banks are to be, *in fact*, controlled by the government *in the public interest*, the details can easily be worked out.

An emergency currency circulation should be backed by proper reserves, issued only against commercial paper that represents actual and legitimate business transactions. No plan should be adopted which admits of control by banking interests which, under existing conditions, means, in the end, control by the great speculative banking groups.

In all our plans for progressive legislation, it must not be forgotten that we are only just beginning to get control of the railroads. The present law is an improvement, but the Interstate Commerce Commission requires to be greatly strengthened. It should have a much larger appropriation, enabling it to prosecute investigations in all parts of the country. It should make physical valuations of the railroads, eliminating watered stock, monopoly values and the unwarranted inflation of railway terminals to conceal monopoly values. And the Commerce Court should be abolished as a mere subterfuge interposed to handicap the commission.

As a first necessary step for the regulation of interstate commerce, we *must* ascertain the reasonable value of the physical property of railroads, justly inventoried, upon a sound economic basis, distinguishing *actual* values from *monopoly* values derived from violations of law, and must make such discriminating values the *base line* for determining rates. The country should know how much of the eighteen billions of capitalization was contributed by those who own the railroads, and how much by the people themselves. We should also provide for the extension of the powers and the administrative control of the Interstate Commerce Commission.

I have sketched the growth and power of the great interests that to-day control our property and our governments. I have shown how subtle and elusive, yet relentless, they are. Rising up against them is the confused voice of the people. Their heart is true but their eyes do not yet see all the intricate sources of power. Who shall show them? There are only two agencies that in any way can reach the whole people. These are the press and the platform. But the platform in no way compares with the press in its power of continuous repeated instruction.

One would think that in a democracy like ours, people seeking the truth, able to read and understand, would find the press their eager and willing instructors. Such was the press of Horace Greeley, Henry Raymond, Charles A. Dana, Joseph Medill, and Horace Rublee.

But what do we find has occurred in the past few years since the money power has gained control of our industry and government? It controls the newspaper press. The people know this. Their confidence is weakened and destroyed. No longer are the editorial columns of newspapers a potent force in educating public opinion. The newspapers, of course, are still patronized for news. But even as to news, the public is fast coming to understand that wherever news items bear in any way upon the control of government by business, the news is colored; so confidence in the newspaper as a newspaper is being undermined.

Cultured and able men are still to be found upon the editorial staffs of all great dailies, but the public understands them to be hired men who no longer express honest judgments and sincere conviction, who write what they are told to write, and whose judgments are salaried.

To the subserviency of the press to special interests in no small degree is due the power and influence and prosperity of the weekly and monthly magazines. A decade ago young men trained in journalism came to see this control of the newspapers of the country. They saw also an unoccupied field. And they went out and built up great periodicals and magazines. They were free.

Their pages were open to publicists and scholars and liberty, and justice and equal rights found a free press beyond the reach of the corrupt influence of consolidated business and machine politics. We entered upon a new era.

The periodical, reduced in price, attractive and artistic in dress, strode like a young giant into the arena of public service. Filled with this spirit, quickened with human interest, it assailed social and political evils in high places and low. It found the power of the public service corporation and the evil influences of money in the municipal government of every large city. It found franchises worth millions of dollars secured by bribery; police in partnership with thieves and crooks and prostitutes. It found juries "fixed" and an established business plying its trade between litigants and the back door of blinking justice.

It found Philadelphia giving away franchises, franchises not supposedly or estimated to be worth $2,500,000, but for which she had been openly offered and refused $2,500,000. Milwaukee they found giving franchises worth $8,000,000 against the protests of her indignant citizens. It found Chicago robbed in tax-payments of immense value by corporate owners of property through fraud and forgery on a gigantic scale; it found the aldermen of St. Louis, organized to boodle the city with a criminal compact, on file in the dark corner of a safety deposit vault.

The free and independent periodical turned her searchlight on state legislatures, and made plain as the sun at noonday the absolute control of the corrupt lobby. She opened the closed doors of the secret caucuses, the secret committee, the secret conference, behind which United States Senators and Members of Congress betrayed the public interest into the hands of railroads, the trusts, the tariff mongers, and the centralized banking power of the country. She revealed the same influences back of judicial and other appointments. She took the public through the great steel plants and into the homes of the men who toil twelve hours a day and seven days in the week. And the public heard their cry of despair. She turned her camera into the mills and shops where little children are robbed of every chance of life that nourishes vigorous bodies and sound minds, and the pinched faces and dwarfed figures told their pathetic story on her clean white pages.

The control of the newspaper press is not the simple and expensive one of ownership and investment. There is here and there a "kept sheet" owned by a man of great wealth to further his own interests. But the papers of this class are few. The control comes through that community of interests, that interdependence of investments and credits which ties the publisher up to the banks, the advertisers and the special interests.

We may expect this same kind of control, sooner or later, to reach out for the magazines. But more than this: I warn you of a subtle new peril, the centralization of advertising, that will in time seek to gag you. What has occurred on the small scale in almost every city in the country will extend to the national scale, and will ere long close in on magazines. No men ever faced graver responsibilities. None have ever been called to a more unselfish, patriotic service. I believe that when the final test comes, you will not be found wanting; you will not desert and leave the people to depend upon the public platform alone, but you will hold aloft the lamp of Truth, lighting the way for the preservation of representative government and the liberty of the American people.

Robert M. La Follette, *La Follette's Autobiography* (Robert M. La Follette Co., 1912), 789–797 *passim*.

◆

87. Regulation of Trusts (1914)

BY PRESIDENT WOODROW WILSON

The influence of President Wilson was largely responsible for the passage of the Clayton Act, intended to add to the effectiveness of the existing anti-trust legislation. For Wilson see Nos. 129–132 below.—Bibliography as in No. 83 above; see also G. C. Henderson, *Federal Trade Commission;* Herman Oliphant, *Cases on Trade Regulation;* William Z. Ripley, *Trusts, Pools, and Corporations.*

IN my report "On the State of the Union," which I had the privilege of reading to you on the 2d of December last, I ventured to reserve for discussion at a later date the subject of additional legislation regarding the very difficult and intricate matter of trusts and monopolies. The time now seems opportune to turn to that great question; not only because the currency legislation, which absorbed your attention and the attention of the country in December, is now disposed of, but also because opinion seems to be clearing about us with singular rapidity in this other great field of action. In the matter of the currency it cleared suddenly and very happily after the much-debated Act was passed; in respect of the monopolies which have multiplied about us and in regard to the various means by which they have been organized and maintained it seems to be coming to a clear and all but universal agreement in anticipation of our action, as if by way of preparation, making the way easier to see and easier to set out upon with confidence and without confusion of counsel. . . .

The great business men who organized and financed monopoly and those who administered it in actual everyday transactions have year after year, until now, either denied its existence or justified it as necessary for the effective maintenance and development of the vast business processes of the country in the modern circumstances of

trade and manufacture and finance; but all the while opinion has
made head against them. The average business man is convinced
that the ways of liberty are also the ways of peace and the ways of
success as well; and at last the masters of business on the great scale
have begun to yield their preference and purpose, perhaps their judgment also, in honorable surrender.

What we are purposing to do, therefore, is, happily, not to hamper
or interfere with business as enlightened business men prefer to do it,
or in any sense to put it under the ban. The antagonism between
business and government is over. We are now about to give expression
to the best business judgment of America, to what we know to be the
business of conscience and honor of the land. The Government and
business men are ready to meet each other halfway in a common effort
to square business methods with both public opinion and the law.
The best informed men of the business world condemn the methods
and processes and consequences of monopoly as we condemn them;
and the instinctive judgment of the vast majority of business men
everywhere goes with them. We shall now be their spokesmen. That
is the strength of our position and the sure prophecy of what will ensue
when our reasonable work is done.

When serious contest ends, when men unite in opinion and purpose,
those who are to change their ways of business joining with those who
ask for the change, it is possible to effect it in the way in which prudent
and thoughtful and patriotic men would wish to see it brought about,
with as few, as slight, as easy and simple business readjustments as
possible in the circumstances, nothing essential disturbed, nothing
torn up by the roots, no parts rent asunder which can be left in wholesome combination. Fortunately, no measures of sweeping or novel
change are necessary. It will be understood that our object is *not* to
unsettle business or anywhere seriously to break its established
courses athwart. On the contrary, we desire the laws we are now
about to pass to be the bulwarks and safeguards of industry against
the forces that have disturbed it. What we have to do can be done
in a new spirit, in thoughtful moderation, without revolution of any
untoward kind.

We are all agreed that "private monopoly is indefensible and intolerable," and our programme is founded upon that conviction. It will
be a comprehensive but not a radical or unacceptable programme

and these are its items, the changes which opinion deliberately sanctions and for which business waits:

It waits with acquiescence, in the first place, for laws which will effectually prohibit and prevent such interlockings of the *personnel* of the directorates of great corporations—banks and railroads, industrial, commercial, and public service bodies—as in effect result in making those who borrow and those who lend practically one and the same, those who sell and those who buy but the same persons trading with one another under different names and in different combinations, and those who affect to compete in fact partners and masters of some whole field of business. Sufficient time should be allowed, of course, in which to effect these changes of organization without inconvenience or confusion.

Such a prohibition will work much more than a mere negative good by correcting the serious evils which have arisen because, for example, the men who have been the directing spirits of the great investment banks have usurped the place which belongs to independent industrial management working in its own behoof. It will bring new men, new energies, a new spirit of initiative, new blood, into the management of our great business enterprises. It will open the field of industrial development and origination to scores of men who have been obliged to serve when their abilities entitled them to direct. It will immensely hearten the young men coming on and will greatly enrich the business activities of the whole country. . . .

The business of the country awaits also, has long awaited and has suffered because it could not obtain, further and more explicit legislative definition of the policy and meaning of the existing antitrust law. Nothing hampers business like uncertainty. Nothing daunts or discourages it like the necessity to take chances, to run the risk of falling under the condemnation of the law before it can make sure just what the law is. Surely we are sufficiently familiar with the actual processes and methods of monopoly and of the many hurtful restraints of trade to make definition possible, at any rate to the limits of what experience has disclosed. These practices, being now abundantly disclosed, can be explicitly and item by item forbidden by statute in such terms as will practically eliminate uncertainty, the law itself and the penalty being made equally plain.

And the business men of the country desire something more than that the menace of legal process in these matters be made explicit and intelligible. They desire the advice, the definite guidance and information which can be supplied by an administrative body, an interstate trade commission.

The opinion of the country would instantly approve of such a commission. It would not wish to see it empowered to make terms with monopoly or in any sort to assume control of business, as if the Government made itself responsible. It demands such a commission only as an indispensable instrument of information and publicity, as a clearing house for the facts by which both the public mind and the managers of great business undertakings should be guided, and as an instrumentality for doing justice to business where the processes of the courts or the natural forces of correction outside the courts are inadequate to adjust the remedy to the wrong in a way that will meet all the equities and circumstances of the case. . . .

Inasmuch as our object and the spirit of our action in these matters is to meet business halfway in its processes of self-correction and disturb its legitimate course as little as possible, we ought to see to it, and the judgment of practical and sagacious men of affairs everywhere would applaud us if we did see to it, that penalties and punishments should fall, not upon business itself, to its confusion and interruption, but upon the individuals who use the instrumentalities of business to do things which public policy and sound business practice condemn. Every act of business is done at the command or upon the initiative of some ascertainable person or group of persons. These should be held individually responsible and the punishment should fall upon them, not upon the business organization of which they make illegal use. It should be one of the main objects of our legislation to divest such persons of their corporate cloak and deal with them as with those who do not represent their corporations, but merely by deliberate intention break the law. Business men the country through would, I am sure, applaud us if we were to take effectual steps to see that the officers and directors of great business bodies were prevented from bringing them and the business of the country into disrepute and danger.

Woodrow Wilson, Address to Congress, January 20, 1914.

88. Railroad Regulation (1903–1914)

BY PROFESSOR FREDERIC AUSTIN OGG (1918)

For Ogg see No. 21 above.—Bibliography as in No. 84 above.

. . . THE carriers had been feeling the losses arising from rebating and excessive rate-cutting, and Paul Morton, president of the Santa Fé system, volunteered to aid the government in putting an end to these unlawful practices. President Roosevelt seized the opportunity by stirring to action the Interstate Commerce Commission and the Department of Justice, and by securing from Congress the needed legislation. The Elkins amendments were passed practically without opposition, and dealt solely with inequalities of rates. They forbade variations from any published tariff (whether or not involving discrimination), made liable to punishment not only the railway corporation itself, but its officers and agents, and also shippers knowingly accepting favors; abolished the penalty of imprisonment provided for by an amendment of 1889; and specially authorized injunction proceedings to restrain carriers from violating the law.

Consolidation was checked, and the power of the government to deal with all great corporations was vindicated, by a decision handed down by the Supreme Court in the Northern Securities Case, March 14, 1904, wherein it was held that a merger of two or more competing roads was contrary to the Sherman anti-trust law of 1890. This was a great triumph; and the Administration, hitherto deterred by lack of power, threw itself unreservedly into the work of railway and trust regulation. The "big stick" began to be brandished, the "square deal" to be preached.

The chief railroad problem that remained was rate-making. In his annual message of December 6, 1904, the President urged that the Interstate Commerce Commission be given power to fix exact rates; and on February 8, 1906, the House passed, by a vote of 346 to 7, a comprehensive measure introduced by Chairman Hepburn of the Interstate and Foreign Commerce Committee. The Senate wavered, and the debates were long and brilliant. But under executive pressure, and in the teeth of the most powerful railroad lobby in the history of the country, it at length fell into line, with only three dissenting votes. June 29, 1906, the bill became law.

The Hepburn Act was in form an amendment of the act of 1887; but it marked a wholly new departure. It raised the number of members of the Interstate Commerce Commission from five to seven, lengthened the term of members from five to seven years, and brought up their salary from $7,500 to $10,000. It extended the interstate commerce laws and the jurisdiction of the Commission, to interstate pipe lines, express companies, sleeping-car companies, and all incidental services at terminals. It authorized the Commission to fix the form of accounts and records used by the carriers, and to require all accounts to be submitted for inspection. It restored the penalty of imprisonment for failure to observe published tariffs, and prescribed a fine of three times the amount of the rebate for shippers or other parties knowingly accepting or profiting by unlawful favors. A new and drastic "commodity clause," intended to divorce transportation from other business, forbade interstate or foreign transportation, after May 1, 1908, of any commodity (other than timber) produced or mined by the carrier, except articles required for the carrier's own use.

Of largest importance was the section giving the Commission its first express grant of rate-making power. The grant stopped short of the desires of the radicals. It did not include authority to make interstate rates generally; but it authorized the Commission, on complaint and after a hearing, to determine and prescribe just and reasonable maximum rates, regulations, and practices. Carriers were given the right to bring suit in any circuit court to annul such actions, with appeal to the Supreme Court.

The gains for regulation were: broader jurisdiction, separation of transportation from other business, suppression of passes, uniformity and publicity of accounts, and the express grant of administrative rate-making power. Concessions to the railroads included broad and indefinite court review and the restriction of rate-making to maximum rates. The railroads came off better than they had hoped. The Commission, moreover, took up its added duties in a spirit of moderation. Many early decisions were in the carriers' favor, and for a few years the operators seemed to have accepted the situation with good grace.

It was to be expected that the new legislation would be reviewed by the courts. The "commodities" and rebating clauses were tested speedily. September 10, 1908, the Circuit Court of Appeals at Philadelphia rendered a decision in the Delaware and Hudson Case pronouncing the commodities clause unconstitutional. The case was appealed, and on May 3, 1909, the Supreme Court reversed the judgment, but construed the prohibition laid upon carriers not to be applicable to commodities manufactured, mined, or owned by corporations in which the carriers were stockholders. This emasculated the clause; practically all of the anthracite coal roads were exempted, although it was mainly to reach them that the clause had been adopted. On the other hand, in reaffirming, in the same year, a verdict imposing a fine on the New York Central Railroad for giving rebates to the American Sugar Refining Company, the Supreme Court unanimously pronounced the anti-rebating features of the law constitutional. . . .

Meanwhile, railroad regulation had been taken up earnestly in the states. At best, the jurisdiction of the national government was limited; and the country was in no mood to be satisfied with the remedy of abuses in commerce at great distances. The thing that troubled the mass of shippers and consumers was discriminations, excessive rates, and inadequate service in local traffic. A renewed appeal to state authority was stimulated by the Hepburn law; and in the early months of 1907, when the legislatures of thirty-nine states were in session, legislation was passed touching every phase of railroad organization and management. The movement was reminiscent of the grangerism of 1870–1877. But whereas the granger laws appeared in only a few western states, the present legislation was nation-wide. In all, more than three hundred railroad measures were enacted—one hundred and seventy-seven in ten states alone. . . .

In 1908 the railroads, suffering from the financial crisis of 1907 as well as from ill-advised regulation, were hard pressed; twenty-four lines, aggregating eight thousand miles, were forced into the hands of receivers, while others were saved only by rigid economy. Few legislatures were in session during the year, and little railroad legislation was enacted. By 1909 the clamor had somewhat subsided; the forty-one legislatures in session passed a total of six hundred and sixty-four railroad laws; but these measures were less harsh than those of 1907. Thereafter railroad legislation by the states seldom produced serious controversies. The principle of regulation was incontrovertibly established; and difficulties over rate-making were largely avoided by assigning that important function to a body of experts forming a state railroad commission, or, in lieu of such an agency, to the public utilities or corporations commission. In 1917 but two states were without a commission exercising powers of this kind.

Railroad regulation was little discussed in the national campaign of 1908. But President Taft felt that public sentiment demanded further action; besides, he was under pledge to follow up the policies of his predecessor. In its annual report for 1908 the Interstate Commerce Commission asked for fresh grants of power, including authority to make physical valuations, to bring proceedings without complaint, and to control issues of railway stocks and bonds. January 7, 1910, the President laid before Congress the Administration's program, in a tentative bill drawn by Attorney-General Wickersham.

The measure was introduced in the Senate by Stephen B. Elkins, chairman of the Committee on Interstate Commerce, and in the House by James R. Mann, chairman of the Committee on Interstate and Foreign Commerce. It failed to arouse either the public or the railroads, but it was debated at length in both houses and amended out of all semblance to its original form. May 10, the House passed it by a vote of 201 to 126, and on June 3 the Senate adopted it, in somewhat different form, by a vote of 50 to 12. A conference committee worked out a basis of agreement, and the measure became law June 18.

While under consideration in Congress the Hepburn Act was much weakened by amendment. The Mann-Elkins Act, on the other hand, was strengthened; so that, although a product of compromise, it turned out to be a very important piece of legislation. Its provisions were directed mainly to two ends: expediting appeals from the Interstate Commerce Commission, and increasing the Commission's powers. The congestion and delay in appeal proceedings called for remedy. At the President's suggestion, the law provided a new tribunal, composed of five circuit judges selected by the Chief Justice, and known as the Commerce Court. This court was to sit continuously at Washington for the purpose of hearing appeals from the rules and acts of the Commission. Appeals from its judgments might be carried to the Supreme Court, with precedence over all save criminal cases. . . .

Under the terms of the new law the Commerce Court was organized in December, 1910, with Martin A. Knapp, former chairman of the Interstate Commerce Commission, as presiding judge. The tribunal never gained popular confidence, and in 1912 Congress in effect abolished it by cutting off its appropriation. . . .

Judicial decisions after the passage of the Hepburn Act tended to exalt the regulative power of the federal government and of its agent, the Interstate Commerce Commission. In the Minnesota Rate Cases, decided June 9, 1913, the Supreme Court took new ground in asserting that state regulation of intrastate rates was exclusive only until Congress acted, and that Congress might regulate such rates as against state control whenever it wished, for the reason that intrastate rates indirectly determined interstate rates. In the Texas-Shreveport Case, decided June 8, 1914, the court held not only that the federal government could regulate intrastate rates, but that the Interstate Commerce Commission already had the necessary authority. The Minnesota cases were primarily a test of the rate-making powers of the states; and the court ruled that the states had full power to fix rates on railroad traffic within their borders, except where the use of such power would interfere directly with the regulation of commerce beyond their borders, or amount to confiscation. This was a disappointment to the railroads, which within ten years had developed a preference for federal, as against state, rate-making control; yet there was promise of relief in the new reaches of the federal authority.

Frederic Austin Ogg, *National Progress* [*American Nation*, XXVII] (New York, Harper, 1918), 45–56 *passim*.

PART VI

ADMINISTRATIVE METHODS AND EXPEDIENTS

CHAPTER XVII — PARTY AND POLITICAL ORGANIZATION

89. The Party Campaign Committee (1904)

BY ALBERT HALSTEAD

Halstead has been a newspaper correspondent and editor, has held various posts in the United States Consular Service, and is at present Consul General at Montreal. An essential part of the modern political organization, the party campaign committee is a creation of circumstances rather than of the intent of the founders of our government. Cortelyou was rewarded by appointment to Roosevelt's Cabinet as Secretary of the newly formed Department of Commerce and Labor; see No. 28 above.—For the various campaigns, see *American Year Book* for appropriate years, and volumes of memoirs and biography, such as A. W. Dunn, *From Harrison to Harding;* H. H. Kohlsaat, *From McKinley to Harding;* Theodore Roosevelt, *Autobiography;* Joseph Bucklin Bishop, *Notes and Anecdotes;* Champ Clark, *My Quarter Century;* Robert M. LaFollette, *Personal Narrative.*

IT has been customary for the Republican nominee for President to select his own campaign manager, the national committee electing his choice to its chairmanship. When his nomination was assured, President Roosevelt sought a manager. Senator Marcus A. Hanna, who had outlived the calumnies that characterized the policy of the opposition in his two successful campaigns to elect William McKinley, was the President's original choice. He and the Ohio Senator discussed that matter before the latter's last illness. The President urged Mr. Hanna to accept, but he was unwilling, as he knew his impaired physical resources were unequal to the task. But had he lived, though he could not have commanded the Republican forces in action, M. A. Hanna would have been the chief adviser of his successor to the national chairmanship.

Theodore Roosevelt was in no hurry to decide upon the man to whom he would intrust his political fortunes. He consulted with party leaders and patiently considered the merits of the several men mentioned. For various reasons, the name of every one whose political experience made him seem available was dismissed. But, finally, as if by inspiration, George B. Cortelyou was suggested. It was a ray of light on a vexatious problem. The President knew Cortelyou thoroughly, knew what he had been to Cleveland, and especially to McKinley. He had learned to value at their real worth his qualities and his capacity,—first, through the intimate association of President with secretary, and then as a cabinet officer. He knew Cortelyou had met every emergency and equalled every responsibility. Here was a man with the genius of organization, trained by hard experience, acquainted with every politician of prominence, in touch with political conditions in every section, who had independence and moral courage. With all the qualities required of a national chairman, except that of experience in actual political management, he was not hampered by narrow views, but was resourceful, energetic, and wholly trustworthy.

Having seen Mr. Cortelyou tried in all conditions, knowing his faithfulness and appreciating in full measure his ability, the President chose him to conduct the campaign upon which hangs his own political future, and to a large degree the destiny of the nation. A great factor was the knowledge that Mr. Cortelyou would be chairman in reality, and not a figurehead to follow Presidential dictation, or to be controlled by any other influence. . . .

Four months is the extreme limit of a Presidential campaign. The first ten weeks must be devoted to organization and preparation alone, for no matter how important the issues, the people will not take keen interest during the heated term. The organization of the two parties has been completed. Mr. Cortelyou, in whose hands are the reins of control, is responsible for the conduct of the Republican fight. Consult he does, as any general, with his lieutenants, but his is the deciding voice as much as is that of the President in his cabinet. Now comes the strenuous seven or eight weeks of active campaigning. Each party has two headquarters, one in the East and the other in the West, that the managers may be in closer touch with the several battle-grounds. While the Republicans will not concede that any of the States that were carried by McKinley in 1900 are doubtful, they must accept the battle where the enemy gives it, and concentrate their energies on the States which the Democrats attack. In the East, the Democrats are attempting to capture New York, Connecticut, New Jersey, Delaware, Maryland, and West Virginia. To fight for these, though most of them are not regarded as doubtful, is the duty of the Eastern headquarters, located in New York City. In the West, Indiana, Illinois, Wisconsin, Nebraska, Colorado, Idaho, Montana, and Utah are receiving the most Democratic attention. For the conduct of the campaign in these States the Western headquarters at Chicago is held responsible. Each headquarters is in Chairman Cortelyou's direct control. He will divide his time between the two as the exigencies of the situation require, but will at all times be in intimate touch with both.

The actual conduct of the campaign, under Chairman Cortelyou's direction, is in charge of the executive committee, appointed by him. Assigned to the Eastern headquarters are Charles F. Brooker, of Connecticut; Senator Nathan B. Scott, of West Virginia; Gov. Franklin Murphy, of New Jersey; and William L. Ward, of New York. Each is a national committeeman. Each comes from a State in which the opposition will make the most desperate fight. In the States they represent the issue will be determined. Mr. Brooker is a manufacturer, who stands high in his State, and has had previous experience in national politics. Senator Scott was one of Senator Hanna's right hand men in his two campaigns and one of his devoted friends. Governor Murphy is a manufacturer and a trained manager, to whom the Republicanism of New Jersey is largely due. William L. Ward is a political expert, and fully conversant with the New York situation. On duty at the Western headquarters are Harry S. New, of Indiana; Frank O. Lowden, of Illinois; R. B. Schneider, of Nebraska; and David W. Mulvane, of Kansas. Each of these, except Mr. Schneider, is a national committeeman. Mr. New knows Indiana thoroughly, and is a trained manager. Colonel Lowden, also an expert in politics, is in close touch with Illinois, and is a State leader. Mr. Schneider understands Nebraska and the currents that run in the West. Mr. Mulvane, in addition to his knowledge of the Kansas situation, is fully conversant with that in Colorado and the other inter-mountain States.

At the Western headquarters, Elmer Dover, of Ohio, secretary of the national committee, is stationed. In Mr. Cortelyou's absence, he is in command. Though young, he has had the benefit of training under the late Senator Hanna, whose private secretary he was. He and Senator Scott represent the old Hanna *régime*. The responsibilities imposed on Mr. Dover are because of his proved and exceptional fitness. At the Eastern headquarters is Louis A. Coolidge, of Massachusetts, director of literary and press work, who has charge of the headquarters when Mr. Cortelyou is in the West. He has proved his executive talent in places of responsibility, and his experience as a Washington newspaper correspondent, with his wide acquaintance with public men and understanding of political conditions, prepared him particularly for his new activity. More than anyone, except Mr. Cortelyou himself, is he the President's representative. Senator Scott is head of the speakers' bureau for the East, the same work he performed under Chairman M. Hanna, and Representative James A. Tawney, of Minnesota, is chief of the similar bureau in the West. Here is evidence of that coöperation between the national and Congressional committees that promises such good results, for Mr. Tawney is also in charge of speakers for the Congressional committee.

No campaign can be run without money. It is needed to meet the many heavy expenses that are not only wholly legitimate, but absolutely necessary. Rent, printing, postage, stationery, traveling, canvassing, clerical hire, literature,—these are some of the items of expense. While some money comes unasked,—as for example, Mrs. Hanna's large contribution,—most of the necessary funds must be solicited. That means a most important committee,—that on finance. The members of this committee cannot be made known, as that would embarrass and hamper their activities. It must be understood that in the solicitation of money there are no promises and no pledges to corporations or others. It is popularly supposed that there is great carelessness in the expenditure of money by a national committee. That may be so, on occasions, but in the present campaign the Republicans have a most careful system of vouchers and auditing, which prevents the waste or misuse of its funds. Each expenditure is scrutinized as carefully as if the committee were conducting a great business house, and is as strictly accounted for.

In addition to the sources of information at Chairman Cortelyou's disposal, he has a large advisory committee, composed of skilled politicians from all sections. They never meet as a body, but communicate with the chairman by letter or in person, telling him of the progress of the fight in their several States. The value of this committee is immeasurable. It was selected with great care. . . .

A campaign is organized on the plan of an army. Discipline is imperative. The conduct of each tactical unit affects the result as much as it does the fate of an army in battle. Chairman Cortelyou deals directly with the several State organizations, depending upon them for the execution of his plans. With them there is the most harmonious relation. As he relies on the State committees, so they act through their several city and county committees. He is informed of conditions in every State, and is in receipt of constant reports from all contested points. Where disaffection exists, there particular efforts are made to overcome it. Literature to enlighten voters and to destroy misconceptions is sent thither in great quantities, and speakers are dispatched to awaken the apathetic and arouse enthusiasm. As the campaign progresses new methods are developed to meet new situations. Constant vigilance is the order. While there is no hope of the Republicans carrying any Southern State, any more than the Democrats can expect to win in rock-ribbed Republican States in the North, this year Republican Congressional candidates will contest every Southern district. This will occupy Southern leaders more than usual, and tend to keep them from invading the North. Representative Babcock, of Wisconsin, who has won five consecutive campaigns for the House, is in charge of the Congressional canvass. He has the prestige of success and of experience.

Education of voters, next to organization, is most important. This is chiefly the duty of the literary bureau. It distributes documents and furnishes material, including editorial and news matter, for the country press. Much of this is distributed through the associations that provide "plate matter" to the small newspapers that cannot set up their general news. It also informs newspaper correspondents, stationed at headquarters, of each day's development. The theory that governs its work is that the average voter will be impressed more by brief, striking statements of fact that explain Republican policies, show the benefits that have followed their enforcement, and puncture Democratic pretensions. In this it appeals especially to the busy city voter. The Congressional committee also distributes documents, chiefly Republican Congressional speeches and public reports, under Congressional franks. Before the campaign is ended many millions of these, weighing tons, will have been sent out from its distributing office in Washington. The Congressional literature appeals especially to the country voter. The literary bureau does not trench upon the distributing work of the Congressional committee. It seeks to make its news service attractive, to entertain while it educates. Statistics that talk, cartoons, and striking posters are some of its best methods.

The speakers' bureaus provide "spellbinders" to gladden the hearts of cheering multitudes and awaken them to the pitch of enthusiasm that brings them to the polls. Probably more than five hundred speakers will be on the hustings under the direction of the national committee in addition to the thousands that State and local committees will dispatch into the political mission fields. A campaign book has been issued, which is an admirable history of Republican executive and legislative accomplishments in the eight years of its full control of the Government. . . .

Each member of the executive committee has his own department, and is responsible to Chairman Cortelyou. Among their duties are the winning of first voters, club organization, naturalization and the prevention of naturalization frauds, registration, detection of tricks and fraud, correction of misrepresentation, and a thousand others.

Albert Halstead, *Chairman Cortelyou and the Republican Campaign*, in *Review of Reviews* (New York, 1904), XXX, 294–298 *passim.*

90. Political Finances (1910)

BY PROFESSOR CHARLES A. BEARD

Beard has served as Professor of Politics at Columbia University, and has written several important works in the fields of history and government. The methods of collecting funds to finance political campaigns have sometimes been so successful that the large sums expended by candidates for office have given rise to national scandals. For specific instances of excessive expenditure, see periodical accounts of the Senate investigations of the cases of Newberry of Michigan (1921–1922) and Vare of Pennsylvania (1928–1929).

IT is evident that parties cannot exist without organization and that organizations of permanent workers cannot exist without funds, and that the funds must be derived from some place—either from loyal party supporters or from private persons and organizations expecting to derive monetary advantages from the victory of the organization to which they contribute. It becomes necessary, therefore, to examine the sources from which a party organization must expect to derive its sustaining funds.

1. There are, in the first place, the public offices which are to be looked forward to as the legitimate reward of party services. The adoption of the principles of civil service reform has reduced to some extent the relative number of offices to be filled by partisan workers, but nevertheless there remains an enormous number of federal, state, and local offices to be distributed. It is estimated that the political appointments within the gift of the President have an annual value of more than $12,000,000. The multiplication of the functions of state government tends to place an ever larger appointing power in the hands of the governor and the state senate or some other central authority. Every state legislature has within its gift appointments to legislative offices and positions to employ for partisan purposes, usually free from civil service control. For example, there are sergeants-at-arms and assistant sergeants-at-arms, principal doorkeepers, first and second assistant doorkeepers, journal clerks, executive-clerks, index clerks, revision clerks, librarians, messengers, post-masters, janitors, stenographers, and messengers to the various committees and assistants first and second, too numerous to mention —the legislature of New York costs the state for its mere running

expenses alone more than $800,000 a year. Then there are the city offices, high and low, steadily multiplying in number and, in spite of the civil service restrictions, to a large extent within the gift of the political party that wins at the polls. Finally there are the election officers, a vast army of inspectors, ballot clerks, and poll clerks for the primary and regular elections, who derive anywhere from $10 to $50 a year for their services. New York City spends annually more than $400,000 in paying the officials who preside at primaries and elections.

2. In the next place there are the levies on the candidates. Generally speaking, no one can hope to be elected to office to-day without being nominated by one of the political parties. The party organization wages the campaign which carries the candidate into office, and what is more natural and just than the demand that the candidate shall help to pay the legitimate expenses of the campaign? It is a regular practice, therefore, for party organizations, state and local, to levy tribute from candidates for nominations as well as from nominees to office—generally in proportion to the value of the office they seek. Mr. Wheeler Peckham testified before the Mazet Commission in 1899 as follows: "It is generally assumed that a candidate for a judicial position (New York City) pays somewhere or other, either for nomination or election, or assessment in some way, quite a large sum. Judges have spoken to me about assessment and deprecated the existence of it very strongly. I suppose the amount paid would range between $10,000 and $25,000. . . . I assume that referees are to a great degree appointed with reference to the judge's recognition of the political party or political organization that nominated or elected him, and to which he owed his nomination. Judges of the courts here recognize their obligation to the political organization which elected them, and they have a desire, and it is carried to a greater or less extent in the distribution of the patronage that belongs to them, to recognize that fact." There are in addition levies on office-holders, after election, even in spite of the laws forbidding this practice. Office-holders do not always wait to be pressed by the party in this matter. It is not expedient to wait.

3. The construction of parks, school buildings, highways, and other public works is a fruitful source of revenue to the party organization which controls the letting of contracts. High bids may be accepted

on the condition that the surplus shall go to the party war chest or to party leaders. The capitol building and grounds at Albany cost the state nearly $25,000,000, and the plunder of the public treasury in the construction of the capitol at Harrisburg is a matter of recent history.

4. Undoubtedly the most fruitful source of revenue for party organizations within recent years has been contributions from corporations (now frequently forbidden by law). Railway, insurance, banking, gas, electric, street railway, telegraph, express, telephone, and other public service corporations must receive many privileges from cities and states. They must secure franchises in the first place, and some must have permits to tear up streets and highways, and extend their operations in various forms. To secure special favors, for which they ought to pay large sums to the public, corporations too often find it cheaper and easier to contribute handsomely to party organizations and to have the organization "control" the proper officials. Very often, also, party leaders compel corporations to pay heavily for securing permits to which they are legitimately entitled, and in such instances corporations usually find it easier to pay than to go to law or argue. . . .

5. The most despicable source of party revenue is that derived from the protection of saloons, gambling, and vice in every form. The extent to which this opportunity is exploited is, of course, difficult to determine; but indisputable evidence from cities as far apart as San Francisco and New York illustrates only too painfully the way in which party war chests are sometimes augmented by stained money drawn from criminal elements to which police immunity is afforded.

Although the exact amount of money collected by various political organizations from time to time is difficult to ascertain, the total levied in any year of a general election undoubtedly reaches a fabulous sum, and this money is applied largely to the conduct of campaigns, although some portions of it frequently find their way into the private exchequers of party leaders. It is spent for printing, advertising, hiring halls, securing speakers, and paying the rank and file of party workers. Undoubtedly large sums find their way through some of the election district captains to venal voters. The extent of the purchasable vote is, of course, impossible to state; but a careful study of Rhode Island made some years ago placed it between ten

and twenty-five per cent of the total number.   Every worker in practical politics, although he may not acknowledge it, probably knows
that votes are bought, sometimes grossly by outright purchase at a
fixed price, and at other times in more subtle ways, as for example,
by paying railway fares and expenses for electors going home to vote,
paying countrymen to come out to vote, and employing party workers
with the tacit understanding that they have little or nothing to
do. . . .

The last, but by no means the least, powerful element in organized
politics is the management of the voters.   Party leaders and workers
assist the poor voters by a thousand charitable acts.   They give
outings, picnics, clam-bakes, and celebrations for them; they help
the unemployed to get work with private corporations or in governmental departments; they pay the rent of sick and unfortunate men
about to be dispossessed; they appear in court for those in trouble,
and often a word to the magistrate saves the voter from the workhouse
or even worse; they remember the children at Christmas; and, in
short, they are the ever watchful charity agents for their respective
neighborhoods.   A kind word and a little money in time of pressing
need often will go further than an eloquent tract on civic virtue.   Thus
politics as it works through party organization is a serious and desperately determined business activity; it works night and day; it is
patient; it gets what it can; it never relents.

Charles A. Beard, *American Government and Politics* (New York, Macmillan,
1910), 667–672 *passim*.

————◆————

91. Party Organization in State and County (1915)

BY PROFESSOR JAMES T. YOUNG (1923)

Young is Professor of Public Administration at the University of Pennsylvania.

THE local machinery of a party is organized on its national
model.   In each commonwealth there is a State committee, a
large body which seldom meets, most of its work being performed by
the chairman.   The State leader, who is usually one of the Senators,
controls this committee completely.   He consults with its members

and with the local leaders from each county and congressional district, but all of the committee's resolutions, decisions, and other acts are approved by the leader before being presented to the committee itself. Nevertheless the committee may be important in time of emergency or crisis or factional warfare for control of the party organization. This is clear from a glance at its chief powers, which are: (*a*) to draft the platform of the party in the State, (*b*) to fill vacancies which may occur among the party candidates shortly before election, (*c*) to conduct correspondence with the various local, county, city, and congressional district committees and with the national committee.

This latter authority is much more important than it seems—it gives the State committee power to determine which is the officially recognized party head in any local district. The local office-holders and those who want office are continually bickering for control of the local party organization. In a dispute between two rival factions the State committee makes an authoritative decision and by this means is often able to put down an insurrection in the party. (*d*) It is in the State committee, too, that the slate of delegates at large to the national presidential convention is usually prepared, and advice given to the leaders in congressional districts as to the choice of their delegates to the convention. The State committee is chosen either by the county committees—one member from each county or by direct primaries, according to the State law. These primaries also nominate candidates for State and local offices but where conventions exist the latter make the choice. (*e*) One of the less important functions of the State committee about which, however, much enthusiasm is shown, is the indorsement of the national platform in presidential and congressional elections. This is done by a series of high-sounding resolutions which are intended for "domestic consumption" among the voters of the State. (*f*) The collection and distribution of funds for the State campaigns. Many State laws now provide for the publication of receipts and their sources, and of expenses for all purposes connected with nominations and election campaigns.

Whether conventions or direct primaries are used, there are always certain important committees for control of which the rival factions struggle: (*a*) the city or county committee, (*b*) the ward committee, and (*c*) the district committee.

The city—or in the rural sections the county—committee, is a body of 40 or 50 men chosen by the ward committees or elected by the voters at the primary. Its powers correspond to those of the State committee, and it uses to the full its prerogative of recognizing and supporting local division committeemen and leaders and thereby determining who shall have the official party control in each locality. It is the city committee which "steam-rollers" all dangerous independent leaders within the party fold. Its control of the funds also is unquestioned and despite laws requiring public statements of receipts and expenses most of the city committees today are still irresponsible; they are often accused of misappropriating a part of the funds which pass through their hands.

The ward committee or, in the rural sections, the township committee, is chosen directly by the party members at the primary and is a miniature city committee. Under it come various district committees of which there are often 30 or 40 in a city ward, according to the density of the population. These are also chosen by the voters and it is to these latter that the real work of getting out the vote is delegated. Each district chairman has a certain sum of money allotted to him by the county committee; he also directs the party workers under his control. The central county or city committee is kept well informed of the conditions in every subdivision at all times. The personal interest and affairs of each voter or the means which may be used to influence him must all be familiar to the local workers in the party organization. . . .

We must understand clearly that the work of the party is after all personal in its nature. The voter must be appealed to by a personal talk and through direct influence rather than by circulars or campaign letters. The party is therefore built upon the division worker as its foundation stone. If he is active and intelligent, and if he keeps in friendly touch with the voters frequently from one election to another, the party does well in his divisions. The committee chairmen recognizing this, hold frequent meetings with the workers to keep up a spirit of watchfulness and devotion. . . .

There is a popular impression that the party takes care of its workers by giving them government positions, but this is only partly true. The advance of the civil service movement has limited the scope of party resources in this respect and the leaders find it necessary to cast about for outside positions for their subordinates. There is a rich field of opportunity in the many corporations which have city contracts or franchises or which manage public utility businesses such as lighting, street railways, and the like. . . . The men so placed have not the precarious tenure that they would have in a purely political job and it is the practice of many corporations and business concerns to deal with the leaders of *both* parties, following the principle of "safety first."

Then, too, when a party worker falls upon hard times he may go to his local leader or feudal superior and secure a loan, a new position, or a job for some member of his family. When trapped in the meshes of the law a word in season spoken to the committing magistrate by the chief will secure his discharge and later his immunity from further prosecution. This beneficent protective influence follows him even to prison, if he is so unfortunate as to be convicted; large numbers of politically befriended criminals are allowed greater privileges while in jail and often escape the full service of their terms. Nor does the party worker's special privilege stop here. When he is on the "out," that is, when the opposite party is in power, he will nevertheless be treated with greater consideration than an ordinary citizen. It is an undoubted fact that a minority party worker going into the city hall or county offices can secure favors from his political rivals which are not granted to others. Every successful leader carries on his roll of the faithful, the names of those who have fulfilled instructions. Though the popular indignation of the moment may condemn them, the policeman who commits an illegal act in the course of his party "duties," the ballot-box stuffer whose zeal for the party's success leads him to be caught, the minor henchman who, taking his instructions too literally, intimidates the voters of a rival faction—all these men may safely reckon on the leader's utmost protection and what is more important, a later reward in the shape of some suitable office when the leader returns to power. The public wrath is fleeting, the "organization's" care of its own is tireless.

But let it not be supposed that this faithful care and intense loyalty are personal in their nature; far from it. They represent the carefully thought-out policy of an intelligent self-interest. Once the leader has permanently lost his power all his subordinates must perforce flock to the new successor and tender their services like vassals to a new feudal chief. The boss is absolute while he is boss but let him lose his ability to furnish jobs and funds and he will at once realize the truth of the aphorism that "there is nothing so dead as a dead politician."

James T. Young, *The New American Government and Its Work* (New York, Macmillan, 1923), 559–564 *passim*.

———◆———

92. Voting for President (1916)

FROM THE NEW REPUBLIC

This editorial from a liberal weekly outlines the broad powers of the head of the United States government—powers which lend importance to the business of balloting for President. For some examples of the exercise of presidential power, see Nos. 23–26 on Roosevelt and Nos. 129–132 on Wilson.

ONCE every four years the American people seize the opportunity afforded by the presidential campaign to indulge in a prolonged feverish and enervating debauch. The outbreak stands alone in their political life. Ordinarily they waste very little excitement or sentiment on politics. They have to vote so frequently, for so many insignificant offices and on so many futile occasions that voting has become cheap. It has become an operation hardly more thrilling or perturbing than that of smoking a cigar. But in this exceptional instance the infusion of water into the voting privilege has not availed to diminish its value. There has been conferred upon the American voter the opportunity of casting one vote of transcendent importance. The Presidency has been increasing in size until it is now probably the most powerful political office established by any modern system of government. In seizing the occasion offered by a presidential campaign to break into an orgy of political excitement American voters are only allowing their feelings to rise and effervesce in sympathetic commotion with the tremendous hazards, temptations and doubts of casting a vote for a presidential candidate.

Although our American constitutions were framed largely for the purpose of preventing the concentration of too much power in the hands of one man or one body of men, all the precautions adopted by the fathers have not sufficed to prevent what they most feared from taking place. An American President who is large enough to cope with the opportunities of his office can do more individually to mould the political behavior of his fellow countrymen and the destinies of his country than can the Russian Czar or the German Kaiser. He is, to be sure, circumscribed by a comprehensive group of constitutional restrictions from which they are free, but the limitations upon his authority are formal and its prerogatives are substantial. During his briefer term of office he can drink deeper than they of the actual sources of political power. An absolute monarch must always be to a very considerable extent the accomplice of a permanent bureaucratic machine and the mouthpiece of an authoritative national tradition. A Kaiser is a figurehead for kaiserism. But the power of an American President is to a much larger extent personal. His cabinet is composed of clerks. Even if a permanent, independent and self-willed bureaucracy is coming, it has yet to be organized. The country is governed less by authoritative traditions than by a fluid and immediate public opinion, and all conditions are conspiring to confer on the President prodigious influence on the formation of public opinion. The American people are more than ever a newspaper democracy. The President is obliged to be a newspaper hero. Whatever he does or says is unexceptionable and incomparable news. The vague and changing national tradition permits him to mould popular ideas and guide popular impulses. He can use as an instrument the most insidious and pervasive vehicle of publicity which ever pervaded the highways of a national mind. His fellow countrymen in so far as they cannot be converted into accepting his leadership can be hypnotized into failing to oppose it.

The President's opportunity of informing and dominating American political life has been much enhanced by recent changes in the nature and relative importance of American foreign policy. In this region his legal authority is unusually extensive. The nation's official diplomatic agents are responsible to him. His position as commander-in-chief of the army and the navy has in the past been of minor importance except during war; but when the army consists of 500,000 trained soldiers and the navy is large enough to upset the balance of international maritime power, those prerogatives begin to wear a royal aspect. While he cannot declare war or make peace, the formulation of the foreign policy which may inevitably involve the country in war is being confided very largely to him. Until recently foreign policy was the phase of American politics about which there was least controversy. It was dictated by specific and authoritative instead of by a fluid and uncertain condition. But now that American isolation has passed and the situation of the United States demands rather a positive and a dangerous than a negative and safe policy, a really colossal responsibility has been imposed on the man who happens to be President. He alone has complete access to the sources of knowledge upon which action must be conditioned. He alone has the authority to act, when action is necessary. He alone can override congressional opposition and force public opinion to accept his decisions. Mr. Wilson's success in his fight with Congress over armed merchantmen is a significant demonstration of the extraordinary power which has been lodged in the President as a result of the novel problems and crises of American foreign affairs. In its relation with other countries the President incontestably and almost exclusively speaks and acts for the whole nation.

The transformation of the American President into a potentate has been the occasion of many misgivings and apprehensions. It is urged that the American people are putting too many of their political eggs in one basket. They are erecting their Chief Magistrate into a plausible imitation of a dictator. They are allowing their presidential election to assume certain characteristics of a plebiscite, which confers on the successful candidate a general license to govern the country. The system, it is said, of presidential government will not work. No one can measure up to the size of a President's job. He cannot at the same time be sufficiently capable as a leader, an administrator, a negotiator, a law-giver, and a publicity agent. He would not have the time even if he had the ability. Neither can a voter cast a discriminating vote for an office which requires of its incumbent the performance of such varied and exacting tasks. He would be turning the government largely over to one man; and in so doing he could only be gambling upon the chance of getting the kind of government in which he believed. His support could amount to nothing but an expression of general confidence.

There is much force in these misgivings and apprehensions. The President is being asked to do more than one man or many men can do properly, and the Presidency is in danger of being transformed into an overloaded and unmanageable political office—one which might become an offense in the hands of a weak man. But talk about dictatorships and plebiscites is an exaggeration. The American nation has the qualities as well as the defects of a newspaper democracy. Its Presidency is an excessively exacting office, only because it has become the indispensable mouthpiece of national public opinion. Certain essential aspects of his power are as much dependent on popular confidence as is the power of the British Cabinet dependent on the confidence of the House of Commons. Without the support derived from public opinion and renewed, if not from day to day, at least from month to month, his ability to initiate and to govern would be pared down within narrow limits. Even his express constitutional prerogatives would be sterilized by the want of public support. A dangerous or incompetent but unpopular President could do many kinds of damage; but he could not undermine American institutions. The Presidency obtained its recent accessions of power only in response to a genuine need of national leadership. Its transformation does not indicate that the American democracy is no longer capable of self-government, and it does not call for condemnation, opposition and reaction. What it does call for is analysis, understanding and an improved organization.

The real difficulties and dangers of the situation do not arise from the transformation of the Presidency into a great representative institution. They arise from the failure to transform the other political institutions, associated with the Presidency, into more serviceable associates of that high office and more effective checks upon the possible abuses of its power. A chief executive who is responsible for formulating and initiating the foreign and domestic policy of a government needs to be surrounded by advisers who are something better than clerks and who are themselves independently representative of certain phases of organized opinion. The cabinet members obtain the quality of being independently representative only by sitting in the legislative body and by securing some independence of position as a consequence of their influence on Congress. But the really formidable difficulty is Congress itself and the system of local partisan organization which Congress chiefly represents. The President, no matter how strong he is in popular confidence, is obliged to govern by means of a party and by means of a majority in Congress.

Yet these party organizations and congressional majorities are always seeking to nullify one essential phase of a successful system of presidential government. They always insist on retaining ultimate direction of the administration of the national business and the national laws. They will yield anything to a President except their control over finance and over the appointment of upper administrative officials. Thus the President can neither dispense with the congressional party machine nor depend on it for loyal service and independent counsel. It hampers him grievously in the practical work of administration which should be lodged entirely in the hands of the executive. But it does not supply an effective organ of independent or disinterested criticism and advice. Presidents, no matter how able and well meaning they are, will certainly fail to live up to the needs of the office unless they are supplied with really expert assistance and really independent counsel. And they will never get it until some President is willing to sacrifice his legislative program and his party popularity to the supremely important work of emancipating presidential government from the handicap of disloyal and defective instruments, and restoring to congressional government its proper function of independent review, criticism and discussion.

New Republic, April 5, 1916.

———————◆———————

93. The National Conventions (1924)

BY PROFESSOR WILLIAM B. MUNRO

Munro is Professor of History and Government in Harvard, and an authority in his field. The conventions of 1924 and 1928 were broadcast to the nation at large by radio, as were also many of the campaign speeches of the candidates and their partisans.

THE National Conventions of the two major parties are always held during the month of June. The leaders of each party are free to fix their own dates, but by usage the Republicans always hold their convention first. Usage has also dictated that the conventions be held in different cities. The selection of both dates and places is made by the national committees. In choosing a convention city they are influenced by a variety of considerations, such as the availability of a large auditorium, financial guarantees, the accessibility of the place, the political strategy of the choice, and so on.

The Republican Convention, which meets in Cleveland this year, will have 1109 delegates and an equal number of alternates. The Democratic Convention, which assembles in New York City, will be slightly smaller, with 1098 delegates. Hence the entire membership of a national convention, counting delegates, alternates, officials, and attendants, usually runs above 2500, in addition to which there are several hundred newspaper men who must be accommodated either on the floor, on the platform, or somewhere else within range of the speakers. All others who are fortunate enough to obtain tickets go to the galleries, and these, though they accommodate several thousand spectators, are never roomy enough to hold a small fraction of those who apply.

On the floor of the convention hall there are wooden poles set up, and attached to these are placards, each bearing the name of a state. The delegates group themselves accordingly, with the alternates directly in rear of them. The hour for the opening of the convention arrives; the chairman of the national committee calls it to order and introduces the temporary presiding officer. The latter has been selected in advance and his principal function is to make a "keynote" speech; in other words, a formal address in which the party's platform is forecast. In the old days it was necessary to choose a leather-lunged orator for this job, but amplifiers have now come to the rescue. At best the convention hall is a noisy place, even when the delegates are making an effort to be quiet and to hear what is being said. Every delegate is on edge, anxious to get to the main business and have it over with. Long speeches, no matter how excellent in quality, are unwelcome.

But the convention cannot get to its main business, which is the nominating of a presidential candidate, until some preliminaries are finished. The credentials of delegates have to be verified, rules of procedure adopted, permanent officers appointed, and a platform drafted. This work is done by committees which bring in their reports on the day after they are named, and these reports are usually adopted by the convention with equal promptness unless there is an insurrection, in which case the preliminaries may occupy several days.

Sooner or later, but commonly the third day of the convention, the work of making a nomination begins. The proceedings start by having the secretary call the roll of the states in alphabetical order, Alabama first and Wyoming last. When the name of a state is called, the chairman of its delegation may present a name, or he may yield his turn to some other state which is farther down the roll, thus permitting its delegation to name a favorite son. In this way, one after another, a half dozen or more candidates may be proposed for the favor of the convention. Then the first ballot is in order.

Printed or written ballots are never used at national conventions. All voting is oral and open. The roll of the states is called once more and each delegation, through its chairman, announces its vote. It was formerly the rule at Democratic conventions that the vote of the entire delegation from each state must be cast as a unit whenever a majority of the delegation so demanded; but this rule has now been considerably modified. The Republicans, on the other hand, have never had a "unit rule" but have permitted delegations to report a divided vote whenever there has been a failure to agree unanimously. In any event most delegations vote as a unit, especially on the first ballot, and some of them are kept so well in hand that they continue to do so throughout the convention.

At the Republican convention a majority of the delegates is sufficient to make the ballot decisive. But the Democrats require a two-thirds vote. Five hundred and fifty votes will be sufficient to settle the matter at the Cleveland convention, but it will take 732 votes to effect the choice of a Democratic standard bearer at the New York gathering. The ostensible purpose of this two-thirds rule is to keep a few large states from determining the choice of the convention, as they conceivably might do under the majority plan if they happened to be united; but the requirement of a two-thirds consensus is regarded by many Democrats as unjustifiable and there has been a growing demand for its abrogation.

Occasionally a convention settles the presidential nomination on the first ballot. More often, however, the first ballot shows a scattering of votes and proves indecisive. Then the convention proceeds to ballot a second time, a third time, and so on until a decision is reached. As successive ballots are taken there is a switching of votes from one candidate to another; the favorite sons drop out one by one;

the "dark horses" are trotted into the arena, and all manner of deals are made by the men who control various delegations. Sometimes it requires a large number of ballotings to reach a decision. In 1880 Garfield was not chosen until 36 ballots had been taken, and Woodrow Wilson did not clinch his first nomination until the 46th. Meanwhile, as ballot after ballot is being taken, the strategists and wirepullers of the convention rush madly about, holding whispered conferences amid the din of the convention floor or in some accessible place outside. Delegations march around the hall, cheering vociferously for their heroes, while bands blare forth and the galleries join in the pandemonium. It is one of the great absurdities of American government that we should expect the virtual selection of the nation's chief executive to be made by such a process and in such an environment. Nothing could be farther removed from what the Fathers of the Republic had in mind.

It is not surprising, under the circumstances, that national conventions should sometimes do strange things, for even the most coolheaded among men can hardly fail to be swept off their balance by the whirling excitement of the affair. Left to itself a national convention would act exactly like any other mob, and the leaders are well aware of this; so they do not leave the convention to itself. They take every possible means to hold it in check, to ensure its docility, and to determine its decision. They are aided in doing this by the self-evident fact that a gathering of more than a thousand excitable delegates must have leadership from some quarter; it cannot lead itself anywhere save into chaos. The ultimate action of a national convention is almost always determined, therefore, by the success with which a relatively few men can assert their mastery by direct control or by compromise. We say that the convention nominates; what we really mean is that a few leaders do it, and the convention then ratifies their action.

It is easy, of course, to pick flaws in this system of nominating candidates for the presidency. As a system it leaves much to be desired. But it is by no means so easy to devise something that would be demonstrably an improvement. Ten years ago President Wilson urged that the nominations be made by direct presidential primaries in all the states, each voter expressing his preference. This would leave the national conventions with no function but to frame the party platforms. The people would nominate their candidates for the presidency just as they now pick their candidates for the governorship in many of the states.

The idea sounds attractive, no doubt, but it would be wholly impracticable in operation. The popular vote, at a nation-wide presidential primary, would frequently be split among several candidates and no one would have a clear majority. What then? Would the nomination go to the one who obtained a plurality, or would there be a second popular primary? The former alternative would hardly be an improvement on our present system; the latter would sometimes entail the holding of a dozen primaries before a decision could be reached. When there is a general consensus upon any particular candidate the convention method of making the nomination is quite as satisfactory as any other; when there is no general agreement, but a division of support among several aspirants, there is no way of securing a majority choice except by deliberation and compromise. A primary can act, but it cannot deliberate or compromise. That is the principal reason why we keep the convention as a nominating agency, despite its serious shortcomings.

We complain that the convention plan puts too much power into the hands of a few men, and our complaint is all-too-well founded. But no matter what governmental device we may adopt we shall not avoid the gravitation of large powers into the hands of the few. Government by the whole people is a pleasing platitude, but the world has never had (and never can have) a government of that sort. Government by the whole people is a contradiction in terms. If the whole people undertook to govern by direct action they would give us something chaotic, but it would not be "government" as men commonly understand that term. The people as a whole have neither the knowledge, the time, the interest, nor the desire to exercise the actual functions of government. Nobody knows this better than the demagogues who flatter the people by assuring them that they have. Democracy has functioned best where the people have recognized the inevitability of government by the few and have seen to it that these few are wisely chosen.

William B. Munro, in *Independent* (Boston, 1924), CXII, 306–307.

CHAPTER XVIII — PUBLIC QUESTIONS IN STATES AND CITIES

94. A City Reformer (1901)

BY MAYOR TOM JOHNSON (1913)

Johnson (1854–1913) started as clerk in a street railway office, and there invented several railway devices. He afterward became an owner of street railway properties of which he disposed when he entered politics. His plans of municipal ownership attracted nation-wide attention. He was a Representative from Ohio from 1891 to 1895. As mayor of Cleveland (1901–1909) he introduced several radical reforms in the city government.—His autobiography, *My Story*, edited by E. J. Hauser, was published in 1913. On reforms of another kind, in San Francisco, see No. 95 below.

. . . ONE of the first things which engaged my attention was the selection of my cabinet, and I made a good many mistakes in my earliest appointments. It was about a year before I really succeeded in getting an efficient set of directors.

There were innumerable matters calling for immediate consideration and I acted as quickly as possible in as many directions as I could. The secret of a good executive is this—one who always acts quickly and is sometimes right.

In less than a week after taking office I ordered uniformed police-men stationed at the doors of gambling houses and houses of prosti-tution having saloons in connection, and instructed them to take the names and addresses of all persons who entered. It makes a man mighty uncomfortable to go on record in this way, even if he gives a fictitious name and address. This method proved so successful as to the gambling houses that in a short time public gambling in Cleve-land was practically abolished. I knew that we couldn't rid the city of the social evil any more than we could rid it of private gambling, but I was determined to permit no saloons in connection with houses of prostitution and to destroy the pernicious practice of the police of levying fines upon unfortunate women. It had long been the custom in Cleveland, as in other large cities, for the police to raid these houses and collect a lot of fines whenever the funds of the police court got low. This simply amounted to blackmail and hadn't the slightest effect in checking the evil, but rather stimulated it and gave rise to a horrible system of favoritism and extortion. I called my policemen together and told them that not a cent was to come into the city's hands by this method, that if the police court had to depend for revenue upon fines imposed in this manner, it would have to go without pay. Street soliciting by either sex was strictly prohibited.

You can't legislate men or women into being good, but you can remove artificial stimulants to make them bad. Cleveland's way of dealing with this problem during my administration compares very favorably, I believe, with the methods employed by any other American city. It became an established part of the policy of Chief Kohler— of whom more later—but the idea of placing a uniformed officer at the entrance to places of questionable repute did not originate with the chief or with me. It was a plan my father used while he was chief of police of Louisville, and he got it from Yankee Bly, a detective famous in Kentucky in the sixties and seventies. . . .

I refused to sign city ordinances unless they were properly engrossed. I insisted that everybody who had anything to do should do it the best that it could be done, and altogether we were a pretty busy lot of workers. So many things seemed to demand attention at once that I had my hand on every department of the city government before I had been in office a month. Of course all these activities cost money and as there wasn't sufficient available money in sight, the usual howl of "extravagance" was raised. But I knew these things had to be done if we were to keep our promise to give good government and I went ahead and did them, trusting to devise a way to get the funds afterwards.

Under what is called economy in city government there is much foolish holding back of necessary public improvements. If fraud and graft are kept out there is not apt to be much unwisdom in public expenditures; and from the business man's standpoint the return for the original outlay is very large—even where debt is created within reasonable limits. . . .

Limitation on taxes for public works is as foolish as limitation on increase in capital and plant of manufacturing enterprises. The question is not "how much do you spend?" but "how wisely do you spend it?" To economize on needed public improvements is worse than wasteful.

The generally accepted standard of values in this connection is all wrong. So obsessed have we become with the idea of property rights that we are constantly forgetting that in the last analysis we are dealing with men and women and children and not with things.

But to give "good government" in the ordinarily accepted sense of the term, wasn't the thing I was in public life for. It was a part of our policy from the beginning of our work in Cleveland, it is true, but as a side issue, merely. While we tried to give the people clean and well lighted streets, pure water, free access to their parks, public baths and comfort stations, a good police department, careful market inspection, a rigid system of weights and measures, and to make the charitable and correctional institutions aid rather than punish wrong-doers, and to do the hundred and one things that a municipality ought to do for its inhabitants—while we tried to do all these things, and even to outstrip other cities in the doing of them we never lost sight of the fact that they were not fundamental. However desirable good government or government by good men may be, nothing worth while will be accomplished unless we have sufficient wisdom to search for the causes that really corrupt government. I agree with those who say that it is big business and the kind of big business that deals in and profits from public service grants and taxation injustices that is the real evil in our cities and the country to-day. This big business furnishes the sinews of war to corrupt bosses regardless of party affiliations. This big business which profits by *bad government* must stand against all movements that seek to abolish its scheme of advantage. . . .

The constitution of Ohio says that all property shall be appraised at its true value in money and the statute carrying this provision into effect uses the same words. . . .

The local taxing board, or board of equalization, appointed by previous mayors, was in the control of tax-dodgers. While it was really vested with great power this board had exercised that power principally in correcting clerical errors or in adding to the tax duplicate the value of additions to small property like painting houses or putting in bathtubs. . . .

Small taxpayers generally were paying full rates, while the public service corporations, steam railroads and large land-owning interests were paying between ten and twenty per cent only of the amount required by law. More than half the personal property and nearly all the valuable privileges were escaping taxation.

At first our Tax School was maintained by private funds and had no legal connection with the city government, but those in charge of it were granted the use of city maps and were permitted to call upon employes of the civil engineer's department for help in connection with the maps. Witt was the first man I appointed and he objected to taking the position, but I would not take "no" for an answer.

The clerks employed first copied the records in the county auditor's office showing the assessed value of all lots and buildings in the city. From these records, on a map sixteen feet square and comprising one whole ward, we showed the inequalities in assessed values. Citizens in general and tax-payers in particular were invited to a large room in the City Hall, at one end of which this map was suspended. Pursuing this method by multiplying the number of maps the assessment of real estate block by block and ward by ward was shown. Discussion was invited, criticisms and suggestions asked for, and by means of this discussion, together with a searching investigation of the records of real estate transfers and leases, we ascertained the real value of one foot front of land by one hundred feet in depth, which method is known as the Somers unit system of taxation and without which no fair and accurate appraisal of land can be made.

When the unit values were finally agreed to they were written into the center of each block on the various maps. The members of the city board of equalization then signed the map making it thereby a public record showing the date on which the values had been agreed upon. Then a photographer made a picture of the map and negatives of this photograph were furnished the clerks who were at work in another room, and they . . . wrote into each space provided on these small maps, the actual cash value of each particular piece of land and the assessed value as well. . . .

The city board of equalization, already referred to, was a municipal institution of long standing. Its members were appointed by the mayor. It was these members who signed the map in the Tax School and it was this board which would have corrected the inequalities in taxation *had not the State legislature wiped it out by legislative enactment*, and provided in its stead a board of review appointed by State officials.

This board of review was paid from county funds for a purely municipal service. To this board we sent the names of all owners and the description of their property which was underassessed. To the people we sent the letter already mentioned and requested all those whose property was overassessed to seek their remedy from the board of review.

So far as I know this was the first intelligent and concerted effort to relieve the people of Ohio of the injustice of the privilege in taxation which had been a decennial bone of contention in the State for eighty years. . . .

The question of taxation was no less a State question than a local one. Indeed our whole Cleveland movement was more than local, more than a one city movement from the very beginning. The big lesson we started out to teach through the Tax School and in other ways was that taxation in all its forms, however designated, is merely the rule by which burdens are distributed among individuals and corporations. Farms, buildings, personal property, land, pay no taxes, yet so persistently have these inanimate objects been spoken of as being taxed that the public has all but lost sight of the fact that it is men and women who are taxed and not things. So long and so universally has taxation been regarded as a fiscal system only that comparatively few people recognize it for what it is, viz.: a human question.

Tom Johnson, *My Story* (New York, Viking Press, 1913), 121–131 *passim*.

———————◆———————

95. Purifying San Francisco Politics (1906)

BY FREMONT OLDER (1926)

This is a part of the life story of a San Francisco newspaper editor (now editor of the *San Francisco Call*) who engaged in a crusade of political reform over a period of many years. Older fought crooks vigorously with their own weapons and gained notable success, the value of which he afterward questioned. Part of the book is devoted to questions of prison reform and the reclamation of prisoners. All characters are sufficiently identified in the text except Heney, who was a special prosecuting attorney, and Burns, renowned detective. For another view of municipal government problems, see No. 94 above.

AFTER I furnished Heney with the evidence of the bribery of Ruef in the matter of the prize fight permits, there was a long interval of searching and investigation without results. Spreckels was somewhat discouraged. At length, however, the evidence secured by Burns was presented to the Oliver Grand Jury, and early in the fall of 1906 Schmitz and Ruef were both indicted for extortion in the French restaurant cases.

We all felt these cases to be a side issue. We had already suspected the bribery of the supervisors for the overhead trolley franchise, and our principal efforts were spent in trying to get at those facts. . . .

The indictment of Ruef and Schmitz were ominous danger signals to [Calhoun]. He was a very brilliant man, clever, resourceful, daring, ruthless; of a temper that stopped at nothing. He knew what we did not know at that time. He knew that he had paid $200,000 to Abraham Ruef through his attorney, Tirey L. Ford, for the purpose of bribing the supervisors to give the United Railroads the overhead trolley franchise.

He knew, when Heney was appointed and upheld by Judge Graham, that he stood in danger of being exposed. Sooner or later, the trail we were following would lead to him.

His first move was characteristically adroit and unscrupulous. He precipitated a street car strike. . . .

There was a long investigation of the claims of the carmen for more pay, a lot of testimony was taken, and some time passed before the matter was adjusted. The men were not satisfied with the terms that the United Railroads offered them. Calhoun seized upon the situation to bring on a strike among the carmen. The deal was made in Mayor Schmitz' house, with Bowling, secretary-treasurer of the Carmen's Union, acting with Calhoun and Schmitz.

Cornelius, the president of the Carmen's Union; Michael Casey, Andrew Furuseth and other labor men were anxious to prevent the carmen from striking, fearing they would lose and hoping that Heney's investigation would lead to the discovery of the bribing of the supervisors by Calhoun.

In this situation, Cornelius stood against the strike and Bowling

for it. Our plan was to try to bring about a secret ballot, reasoning
that if the men voted secretly they would vote against the strike.
Bowling was advocating an open ballot, counting on the men's fear
to vote openly against the strike. Bowling won out. . . .

Immediately the street cars were tied up. This second calamity,
following hard upon the disaster of the fire, and halting the city's
attempt at rebuilding, infuriated the business men and property
owners of San Francisco. Calhoun knew the city; he knew what would
influence the powerful men of the city. He knew that San Francisco
was in ruins and that the business men above all things wanted the
street cars to run; otherwise they would be utterly ruined.

With the entire approval of the business men of San Francisco, he
imported professional gangs of strike-breakers, headed by Farley, and
attempted to run the cars. The strikers attacked these strike-breakers
viciously. Rioting broke out on the streets, men were beaten, crippled, killed. The city was in a turmoil. In the midst of it, in the most
picturesque way, Calhoun rode up and down Market street in his
automobile, winning tremendous admiration from the business people
and property owners.

"There's a man who isn't afraid of anything! He's for San Francisco and the rebuilding of San Francisco. He'll break this strike,
and save us, if any man can," they said on every hand. Calhoun
could not have made a better move than secretly to force this strike,
and then boldly and openly to break it, by force.

It was a spectacular move, cleverly planned; endearing him to the
powerful people of San Francisco, who hated labor unions anyway,
and particularly at this time, when the hard work of rehabilitation
and the desperate task of keeping business going depended on the
street cars moving.

When the strike was in progress the men received $5 a week each
in benefits. One week the money did not come—$5,000 for a thousand
men. The international president, McMahon, was away from his
home office and had failed to send it. The Labor men who had been
with me in the fight to prevent the strike came to me and said: "If
we don't have $5,000 by one o'clock to-day, the strike will be broken.
If the men don't get their $5 apiece at one o'clock they'll give in and
go back to work, and all their efforts and suffering will come to nothing."

I had exerted every effort of which I was capable in trying to prevent the calling of the street car strike, but I did not want to see the strike lost now and the men who already had been led into so much suffering forced to lose their chance of getting something out of it all. Therefore, since it was necessary to have the $5,000 by one o'clock that afternoon if these men were to get their strike benefits and be held in line, I determined to do my utmost to provide the $5,000.

I found two friends who were willing to lend me $2,500 each. I had the money changed into $5 gold pieces, put it in a sack, and sent it out to the headquarters of the Carmen's Union. Bowling, the traitor secretary-treasurer, who had planned the strike with Calhoun, was there. The sack was given to him and he was told to distribute the money among the men. He was obliged to do so, but he kept the sack and carried it to Calhoun as evidence that I had saved the men from losing the strike at that time.

Eventually, Calhoun, through his force of imported strike-breakers, succeeded in crushing the strike he had begun, and the men went back to work—beaten; and Calhoun became the hero of the hour. Before that time came, however, we struck a trail that led us hot on his track. We were getting closer to him every day.

While we were in the midst of our investigations, Schmitz suddenly set out for Europe. The day after he had left it was announced in the newspapers that he had dismissed the president of the Board of Works, Frank Maestretti. The news came as a thunderbolt.

Could it be possible that Ruef and Schmitz dared to dismiss Frank Maestretti, a man who, we felt convinced, was in on all the city graft, or at least knew of it?

I was very much excited, and sent for Maestretti and Golden M. Roy. I knew Roy to be a close friend of Maestretti, the two men being partners in the Pavilion Skating Rink. They came to my office, and I talked with them about the removal of Maestretti. They still hoped he would be reinstated by wire from Schmitz.

I said: "Well, if he is not, perhaps you will be willing to talk with me." After some discussion, they left, saying they would know about it next day, and asking me to call on them then.

On the following day I met them in their office at Pavilion Rink. I told them that I represented powerful interests in San Francisco who were going to get the facts of the graft, and that I thought they would do well to get in on the ground floor with me. They admitted that they could tell me some very interesting things, but they put me off, saying they would see me again.

Maestretti followed me out of the office and warned me against Roy, saying he was a Ruef man and could not be trusted. When I reported this to Burns he very cleverly analyzed it as meaning that Maestretti wanted the whole thing to himself and wanted Roy shut out. . . .

Burns had many meetings with Maestretti, and he soon discovered that Roy was the man who knew all the facts, and that unless we could get Roy we would get nowhere.

"Work on Roy," he said.

In my eagerness to get information from Roy my mind went back to the days before the fire. At that time Roy owned a jewelry store on Kearney street, near the *Bulletin* office. A friend of his called on me and said that Schmitz had offered Roy a position as police commissioner. Having a wife and family whom he dearly loved, Roy did not want to take the place if I was going to attack him. . . .

I reproved Roy for having anything to do with Schmitz. I said that he was a man of family, that he ought not to risk his reputation by affiliating with such men as Ruef and Schmitz. Afterward I learned that this mild criticism worried him tremendously.

Recalling this episode gave me an idea. I had a very violent, personal attack written on Roy. It was a page article, embellished with pictures. I raked up everything in Roy's activities that could place him in a discreditable light before the community. Then I had a page proof of this article printed secretly in the *Bulletin* office. When it was ready I laid it face down on my desk and sent for Roy. Burns waited in an adjoining room.

Roy came into my office. He said: "Well, what can I do for you, Mr. Older?" in what I thought was a patronizing tone.

I was very much excited. "You can't do anything for me," I said, "but I'm going to put you in the penitentiary." I picked up the page and handed it to him to read.

He began to read it, turned pale, and reeled on his feet. "Read it all," I said.

"I'm reading it all."

He finished, laid it down, and said: "What do you want me to do?"
"I want you to tell the truth."

"All right," he said. "I'm willing to tell you the truth—everything." I pressed a button and Burns came in. I turned Roy over
to Burns and left the room.

In a little while Burns called me and said: "Roy wants to see his
friends before he talks."

I said: "I don't think we ought to let him see his friends. It's a
friend; it isn't friends. It's Ruef he wants to see." Roy sat there
without saying a word.

"No," Burns said. "I think it best to let him see his friends.

I said nothing more. After a moment Roy got up and walked out.
He was shadowed, of course. He went directly to his home, where
his wife and children were, and stayed there, sending no messages and
telephoning nobody till midnight. Then he telephoned Burns and
asked to see him. When they met he told Burns much that he knew
about the Ruef briberies. This interview led directly to the confessions of the eighteen supervisors who had taken money in the overhead trolley franchise deal. We had reached Calhoun at last.

Fremont Older, *My Own Story* (New York, Macmillan, 1926), 89–98 *passim.*

----

96. The Recall (1912)

BY PROFESSOR ARTHUR N. HOLCOMBE

For Holcombe see No. 29 above. Roosevelt's ill-advised advocacy of the recall
of judicial decisions was one of his stumbling-blocks in the election of 1912, as mentioned in No. 30 above; see also Nos. 102 and 103 below. For further developments
in the use of the recall see *American Year Book*, 1913 and following years.—Bibliography: E. P. Oberholtzer, *Initiative, Referendum and Recall.*

THE most discussed feature of popular government during 1912
has been the recall. During 1911 the recall was adopted in
California and Arizona (in the latter states, applying only to legislative and executive officers), and provision for the submission in 1912
of constitutional amendments establishing the recall was made in
Idaho, Nevada, and Washington. In the same year provision was

made for the submission of recall amendments in 1914 in North Dakota and Wisconsin, provided the legislatures of those states meeting in 1913 indorse the proposed amendments. In 1912 the Arizona legislature provided for the submission of an amendment to the people at the general election extending the recall to the judiciary and the Louisiana legislature proposed a recall amendment not applying to the judiciary. Recall amendments were also submitted upon the initiative of the requisite number of voters in Arkansas and Colorado. On the other hand, constitutional conventions in New Hampshire and Ohio declined to submit recall amendments, and in Indiana a new constitution proposed in 1911, containing a provision authorizing the legislature to establish the recall, subject to certain restrictions, was declared by the courts to have been improperly framed, and was not submitted to the people. At the November election the recall amendments were adopted in Arizona, Colorado, Idaho, Nevada, and Washington, but not in Louisiana. The Arkansas amendment was defeated in September. . . .

The chief features of the state-wide recall are (1) its scope; (2) the size of the petition required to institute a special recall election; (3) the mode of conducting the election; and (4) the provision made for acquainting the voters with the grounds of recall alleged by petitioners and with the defense of the accused.

(1) The recall may apply to all elective state officers, or to all except judicial officers. The former is the scope of the original Oregon recall (1908), of the California (1911), Arizona (1911–12), Arkansas (1912), Colorado (1912), and Nevada (1912) amendments, and of the amendment proposed for submission in 1914 in North Dakota. The Idaho, Louisiana, Washington, and Wisconsin amendments do not apply to the judiciary. . . .

(3) There are several modes in which the recall may be conducted. The name of the officer against whom the petition is filed may be placed upon the official ballot at the special election, together with those of other candidates for the office nominated by petition. If the office-holder fails to secure a plurality of all votes cast, he is thereby recalled and the candidate receiving a plurality is declared his successor. This is the method adopted in Oregon in 1908. Or the recall election proper may be preceded by a special primary, at which two candidates are selected to compete for the office in question at an

ensuing election. If the office-holder fails to be renominated at the primary he is thereby recalled. This is the method commonly used in municipal recall elections, but has not been proposed for any state-wide recall. Again, there may be a single election, but a separate vote on the question of recall. In this case the name of the office-holder does not appear as a candidate to succeed himself. Candidates for the succession may be nominated by petition, by a special primary, or by designation of any appropriate party committee recognized by law. If a majority of those voting at the election vote for the recall, the office-holder is removed from office, and the office goes to the candidate with the highest vote. A vote for a successor is void unless the voter votes also on the question of recall, and if the majority vote against recall all votes for a successor are void. This is substantially the method adopted in California in 1911, and is followed in Arkansas and Colorado. The Oregon plan is followed in Arizona, Nevada, and North Dakota. The Idaho and Wisconsin amendments are general in terms, and leave to the legislature the task of filling in details.

(4) The grounds for the recall, according to the original Oregon plan, are to be set forth at the head of the recall petition. Further official publicity for the charges is provided by reservation of space on the ballot for a statement by the petitioners in not more than 200 words. The office-holder against whom the charges are brought may set forth his defense in a similar statement on the ballot. Furthermore, the legislature is authorized to provide some compensation to the office-holder for the expense of his campaign should he not be recalled. Similar provisions are contained in most of the later recall amendments. In general the machinery of the recall adopted in California, and followed in the amendments submitted under the initiative in Arkansas and Colorado, seems an improvement over the machinery of the original plan. . . .

In Arizona the legislature of 1912 provided for the extension of the recall to United States senators, congressmen, and the United States judge for the Arizona district. As all of these officers hold their positions under the federal constitution, and as the federal judge is not even elected by the people of Arizona, the recall cannot be applied to them by the ordinary process of an amendment to the state constitution. Consequently what may be termed the advisory recall of United States senators and congressmen and the advisory resignation and appointment of federal judge were established by statute. The advisory recall of United States senators and congressmen and the advisory resignation of federal judge were doubtless suggested by corresponding constitutional provisions for the mandatory recall of state officers, including the judiciary. The advisory appointment of federal judge was apparently established upon the theory that the President, in the selection of local judicial appointees, customarily enjoys the benefit of advice from some representative of the locality concerned, generally the United States senator, if of the same party. Why not substitute the people of the state for the senator as the source of the advice? The Arizona law, therefore, provides for an advisory vote to indicate the popular choice of a candidate for a judicial appointment, as well as to indicate the popular desire for the resignation of a United States district judge. . . .

The recall of judicial decisions is a device first suggested by Theodore Roosevelt in an address before the Ohio Constitutional Convention, Feb. 21, 1912. Its purpose may best be explained in the language of its first public sponsor. In his speech to the Progressive National Convention at Chicago in August Mr. Roosevelt said:

In dealing with the fundamental law of the land, in assuming finally to interpret it, and therefore finally to make it, the acts of the courts should be subject to, and not above, the final control of the people as a whole. . . . The people themselves must be the ultimate makers of their own Constitution, and where their agents differ in their interpretations of the Constitution the people themselves should be given the chance, after full and deliberate judgment, authoritatively to settle what interpretation it is that their representatives shall thereafter adopt as binding.

Whenever in our constitutional system of government there exist general prohibitions that, as interpreted by the courts, nullify, or may be used to nullify, specific laws passed, and admittedly passed, in the interest of social justice, we are for such immediate law or amendment to the Constitution, if that be necessary, as will thereafter permit a reference to the people of the public effect of such decision under forms securing full deliberation, to the end that the specific act of the legislative branch of the government thus judicially nullified, and such amendments thereof as come within its scope and purpose, may constitutionally be excepted by vote of the people from the general prohibitions, the same as if that particular act had been expressly excepted when the prohibition was adopted. This will necessitate the establishment of machinery for making much easier of amendment both the National and the several State Constitutions, especially with the view of prompt action on certain judicial decisions—action as specific and limited as that taken by the passage of the eleventh amendment to the National Constitution.

It is pointed out by the advocates of the recall of judicial decisions that the Dred Scott decision of 1857 was, in effect, recalled by Section I of the Fourteenth Amendment, adopted in 1868, and that the income-tax decision of 1895 is now in process of recall by a pending amendment.   Mr. Roosevelt's proposal is to expedite such recalls whenever they are clearly demanded by public opinion. . . .

An amendment to the state constitution, restricting the right to declare laws unconstitutional to the supreme court, and providing a more direct process by which nullified statutes may be constitution-alized, so to say, was submitted under the initiative in November to the people of Colorado and adopted by them by a vote of 55,416 to 40,891.   This amendment virtually authorizes the people by the use of the referendum to order the enforcement of a statute which has been enacted by the legislature and approved by the governor but vetoed by the supreme court.

Arthur N. Holcombe, in *American Year Book* (New York, Appleton, 1913), 64–67 *passim*.

------◆------

97. The Planning of Cities (1912)

BY E. C. GARDNER

The discovery that growing population often made older cities unlivable, and entailed great expenditures for re-planning, has given impetus to this new science, which seeks to anticipate growth and to plan with beauty and unity in mind.   For interesting suggestions along this line see Benton MacKaye, *The New Exploration*.

MOST American cities of over 50,000 population naturally fall into commercial, manufacturing and residential sections.   The commercial is devoted to business of all kinds, excepting large manu-facturing.   The more homogeneous and compact its composition the better; and its actual requirements in different cities are almost iden-tical.   The needs of manufacturing, as regards ground plan, depend on local conditions which vary widely and are often closely related to transportation problems and to the housing of the workmen.   Even a small city may have many manufacturing districts.   Plans of the residential portions have usually been determined by local topography, by accident, and by real estate owners and promoters.

The financial value of civic esthetics is great; but the commercial portion of a city can be made beautiful in only one way—that is, by supplying in the most simple, direct and scientific maner whatever is necessary for its business prosperity. One mistake of the average layman is in beginning at the wrong end. Beauty is always willing to be won, if wisely sought, but in business development, utility is her most successful wooer. It is another error to assume that beautiful parts make a beautiful whole. That is exactly what never—almost never—happens. The most harrowing inharmonies may be composed of exquisitely lovely units.

Undoubtedly the professional adviser has his place in civic development if, in addition to professional skill, he has the moral strength and mental acumen to detect and defy the efforts of the unscrupulous who would artfully use him as a means of gaining their own selfish ends; but for the elementary features of the fit and characteristic plan of any city, the residents who are familiar with the conditions and have given the various problems long and careful study, are most likely to arrive at safe and sane conclusions, and they should at least work with him. Moreover—and this is a point of great significance, though often overlooked—every city and town, like every man, should rejoice and be glad in a personality of its own. This personality is apt to be modified, if not quite obliterated, when the planning is put into the hands of a stranger.

Facility of transportation is to the business city what the circulation of the blood is to an animal, or of the sap to a tree—the measure of its life, the source of its proper development. This means such an arrangement of alleys, streets, thoroughfares and avenues as will allow the most free, direct and economical migration and transportation from each portion to every other, from all parts of the city to the surrounding country, and *vice versa*.

Once, among the most civilized people, the market place, the forum, the cathedral square, the temple portico—in later times the "meeting house"—were in actual fact the social and political headquarters of the community. Now, to establish in the commercial portion of a great city one conspicuous "center" of civic beauty, society, education, of important affairs of all kinds—around which public interests should revolve, to which they should look for initiative, and from which all should radiate—is neither possible nor desirable, unless the city happens to be the capital of the state or nation.

Numerous central points, stations, foci, or whatever they may be called, may be useful and logical in a large and growing city, but the municipality should not provide greater size and elegance for any one than for each and all of them. To expend an undue proportion of its revenues for esthetic display, or for advertising purposes in a single locality, leaving the remainder in comparative poverty and nakedness, is unreasonable, undemocratic and unjust.

What, for instance, can be said in justification of a city which, while suffering from a lack of schools, of necessary bridges, of safe and convenient railway stations, of adequate playgrounds, of suitable hospitals, of proper police force, and from a perennial nuisance of dust in the streets and dirt in the alleys, still imposes a tax equivalent to twenty dollars each on every man, woman, child and infant in the city in order to erect a monumental building by no means indispensable, that has neither dignity of location nor suitable environment —this being a single feature of an attempt to develop a "Grand Civic Center" in a well-known city of nearly 100,000 inhabitants?

The width of main thoroughfares is a matter for careful study, too often left to the greed and caprice of real estate owners or the theories of experts. In manufacturing and residential regions they can hardly be too wide; in commercial and especially in retail districts, less so. Greater width there involves greater cost of construction and maintenance, a loss of time, much inconvenience in crossing from side to side, and, in northern latitudes, large expense for the removal of snow.

In old cities increasing the width of the main avenues to accommodate the increasing business is a difficult proposition, because the street fronts, which are the most expensive parts of the buildings, block the way. Cutting new streets through sections solidly built up is wasteful and can only be justified by imperative need. Many main streets in the old New England cities might be arcaded, throwing the entire sidewalks behind the present line of store fronts, supporting the walls above on columns and carrying glass roofs over the intersections of the cross streets. The enormous advantage on retail streets of such arcades, especially in northern cities, the cheapness of artificial light and the comparatively small loss of room are strong reasons for the adopt on of this expedient where traffic is congested on account of inadequate width of streets.

These and other features of city planning are so simple that the plain layman need not err in their application to local conditions, provided he will not forget that the commercial portion of a city is one great institution for transacting business, for which the fundamental requirements are safety, comfort and efficiency; in brief, utility; without which permanent beauty is impossible.

E. C. Gardner, *Planning the Commercial Portions of Cities* in *American City*, May, 1912 (New York), VI, 724–727.

—————◆—————

98. The Initiative and Referendum (1917)

BY DELEGATE ALBERT BUSHNELL HART

For Hart, see No. 13 above. The initiative and referendum have been adopted in many states; referendum is largely used to ascertain popular opinion with respect to the amendment of state constitutions; the initiation of laws by petition of citizens has played a very minor part.—Bibliography as in No. 96 above. Extended debates on the question in the *Debates of the Massachusetts Constitutional Convention* (1917–1919).

I NOW come to the third point, which is the apprehension felt by some members concerning the I. and R. One would suppose from the things that have been said about this measure that it had hoofs and horns. I will not burden you with quotations on this subject. The proprietor of a patent medicine in New England made a great fortune out of his wares many years ago. How did he make his fortune? Why, by a phrase. He advertised: "I won't guarantee that my Golden Discovery will cure every ill that flesh is heir to; it won't cure thunder-humor." He sold thousands and thousands of bottles to people who said: "Well, I don't know what ails I have, but I know I haven't got thunder-humor, so I know it will be good for me." The opponents of the I. and R., at intervals, when something is said about this measure, shake their heads and say: "It won't cure thunder-humor." It is not the advocates of the measure who expect it to cure everything.

I find two sets of conflicting arguments against it. One is that it is out of accord entirely with the American spirit,—a totally unknown system. Another is that it is a throw-back to a discarded method of which our ancestors grew tired. Most reliance is placed on the argument that it is an abandonment of the fundamental principles of American government. That is curious, because if it is the case, think how many of our sister states are without an American or a democratic government. Think of the awful condition of the people in these communities. Since the popular vote was introduced it appears that 350 propositions have been submitted under the initiative and referendum, of which 133 were accepted and 217 voted down. I shall never forget the remark of a friend, a banker in Portland, Oregon, a very conservative man, who had been Speaker of the House of Representatives of his State and was very much against the I. and R. "It is an awful thing, that I. and R.," he said. "Why, it has got so bad in Oregon that in the last election the people had to vote down two-thirds of the measures that were presented to them." In Oregon this immoral method is so deeply seated that people actually use it to defeat measures! It must be said that they had not before their minds the sufferings of the members of this Convention who have been able to see across the ages the Commonwealth of Massachusetts devasted by freak laws passed by the friends of the I. and R. . . .

The two charges against the initiative and referendum that seem to have most weight, that seem to stick closest, and therefore which I would like if possible to erase from your minds, are, first, that it is a minority method, under which a "mere minority" will make the decisions, thence the argument passes to the point that a majority ought not to make decisions; that is, that a minority will decide but a majority ought not to prevail. The point that I want to make here is that a proper vote under the initiative and referendum stands on precisely the same footing as the election of members of this body, as elections to the Legislature, as votes on referenda whether general or local, as votes upon constitutional amendments. . . .

In the few minutes remaining I wish first of all to summarize several points made at the previous session with regard to the general character of the I. and R.

(1) I should like to emphasize for the benefit of those in the Convention whose minds are not clear upon this question, the fact that

the I. and R. is in accordance with the previous practice of the Commonwealth of Massachusetts in most respects; and the proposed referendum in all respects. The Walker measure confers on that point no further powers than those now enjoyed by the people of Massachusetts except the right to pass upon acts of the Legislature without the consent of the Legislature.

(2) The I. and R. is not out of accord with the American principles of government, because it is in force in a considerable number of States in the Union. Much has been said about the character of those governments, because there have been disorders in Colorado and in Arizona, and upon that I should like to make two remarks. The first is: Who are the people, who own the capital in Colorado and in Arizona, engaged in those mining operations in which there have been disturbances? They are eastern capitalists to a very large degree. The labor difficulties in those States are due as much to the owners of the mines as to those who work in them. And I suppose there is nobody here who would hesitate to invest money in Colorado or in Arizona in what he thought was a good proposition lest the people by the initiative and referendum in those States should take it away. If you deny that the I. and R. is a reasonable part of the American system of government, you throw a considerable number of States in anarchy.

(3) Let us never forget that the Supreme Court of the United States, having been asked in a case arising out of the Oregon initiative and referendum to rule that the initiative and referendum was not republican government, declined to interfere, asserting that the question as to what was or was not a republican government under the Federal Constitution was a question for Congress to settle, and Congress has settled it by recognizing the authorities of the I. and R. States in every case, without any suspicion or any limitation, notwithstanding the fact that they are dependent in part upon the I. and R. . . .

I began by showing you that I myself was elected by about one-fourth of the usual voters in the Eighth Congressional District of Massachusetts; that every member, every one of the four members elected from that district, was chosen by about the same vote, and that every one of us is in a position to say that a fourth of the usual voters are unintelligent voters; that there is not a man sitting here who is not bound to admit that that fraction of the voters who voted for that entire district are intelligent. If competent to pass upon the question whether you and I shall be members of this Convention, are they not equally competent to pass upon legislative questions? . . .

A deliberate and deliberative Legislature ought to be sufficient for practical purposes, but I submit that there is not a State in the Union in which the Legislature is sufficiently free from influences which do not come directly from the voter. It is invisible government that the gentleman has left out of account. We have heard a great deal about ten men drawing up an initiative petition; about "a secret, irresponsible committee sitting in some study;" ten men, every one of whom has to sign his name and take oath to it. I should like to ask the members of this Convention if they have ever heard of ten men sitting in a study or an office or something of that kind and drafting measures for the Legislature of Massachusetts without signing their names, without any mortal man, except an intermediary between them and certain persons in the Legislature, knowing who drafted the bill? What we are asking for is a responsible initiative and not an irresponsible. . . .

The truth is that no measure on initiative is likely to get any headway unless it has the signatures of some known and responsible men who represent some definite principle. People talk here as though the action of ten men was final. For a constitutional amendment you must get fifty thousand; for an act you must get twenty-five thousand; and when you have twenty-five thousand you have a far stronger backing than most of the legislation that now comes before the General Court of Massachusetts.

Now, gentlemen, let me return to this question of the unintelligent voter. In the first place, we are constantly told that there is distinction between voting for men and voting for measures. Unfortunately for that argument there is no such difference recognized in the law of Massachusetts. The elections for this Convention, or for a Governor, are treated in precisely the same way as a constitutional amendment. The main difficulty with all this argument that the irresponsible will initiate amendments is simply that you leave out of account the fact that the final decision is made by voters, by the same voters who now vote upon constitutional amendments, who will vote upon the amendments submitted by this Convention; they are exactly the voters who will vote upon questions of the initiative.

Speech of Albert Bushnell Hart, in *Debates in the Massachusetts Constitutional Convention* (Boston, State Printers, 1918), II, 446–452 *passim*.

———————◆———————

99. Traffic Problem of Chicago (1924)

BY E. S. TAYLOR

Taylor, as Manager of the Chicago Plan Commission, took a leading part in the solving of problems arising from the congestion of the metropolis. Similar ambitious projects have been under development in other cities, among them Cleveland and Boston. The latter city has planned its through-traffic streets largely on the basis of a novel and elaborate traffic survey.—Bibliography: *The American City*, and other periodicals devoted to city planning and civic betterment; *The American Motorist*, and other periodicals concerned with motoring and traffic problems.

THE mastery of the traffic situation in Chicago is bound up with the execution of the Chicago Plan. Every Saturday night there are one thousand, one hundred and fifty more automobiles upon the streets of Chicago than there were on the preceding Saturday night. This increase goes on week in and week out. By the close of the present year there will be between sixty-five thousand and sixty-nine thousand more machines upon the streets of Chicago than there were on December 31, 1923. This gives an idea of the serious problem confronting the Chicago Plan Commission in its efforts to expedite the movement of persons and vehicles to and fro from one section of the city to another.

So far as the traffic features of the Chicago Plan are concerned, the Plan provides for three avenues of effort. The first of these is the creation of a quadrangle of wide streets around the central business district. Next is the provision of every possible channel of communication between the heart of Chicago and the north, the west, and the south sides of the city. Thirdly, there is the provision for a system of wide thoroughfares, such as are usually called "major streets," extending from one end of the city to the other. Construction work on all three of these undertakings is now going forward. . . .

Chicago, as any school child knows, is bounded on the east by the waters of Lake Michigan. Its development, therefore, ever since the days of Fort Dearborn, has had of necessity to be south, west and north. But as the frontier Indian trading post grew, developing first into a village and then into a city, it ran against obstacles in all three of these directions which forced its business growth up into the air rather than outwards. These obstacles were the Chicago River and the railroad rights of way, formidable enough to the north and west, but even more so to the south, where nearly one square mile of territory is absorbed by railroad occupancy to the extent that only one single north-and-south street connects the central business district with the south and southwest sides of the city through this district.

Thus it was that in laying out the Plan of Chicago the technicians provided for the development of a quadrangle of wide streets surrounding the heart of Chicago, for the purpose of allowing through-bound traffic to go around the congested district rather than through it; and for the further purpose of permitting the central business district to grow and expand normally, so that it should occupy several times its present restricted area of only one-quarter of a square mile.

Within Chicago's loop today there are nineteen streets. Upon fifteen of them are double-track street car lines with cars at present turning in all four directions at nearly every intersection. A new plan of traffic regulation eliminating left-hand turns in the loop is expected to better conditions somewhat, but thorough-going and permanent improvement will come only as the result of four streets comprising this quadrangle which will—it is expected—be entirely finished within the next two or three years, and once the quadrangle is in operation it will cut present loop street traffic nearly in half. Traffic counts show that upon the downtown streets of Chicago every week day there are about 175,000 vehicles, 10,000 street cars, and nearly a million pedestrians. . . .

The improvement of Michigan Avenue has been successful beyond almost all hopes. It was an object lesson that won many friends to the Chicago Plan. This is perhaps the place to say that every improvement in the Chicago Plan has its own intrinsic usefulness; yet, although each single project can stand alone on its own merits, as they dovetail together to form the whole plan, they represent the best possible physical development for the city.

The two-level Michigan Avenue improvement, separating traffic automatically by providing separate levels for different classes of vehicles, cost about $16,000,000. It was completed in 1920 and has already paid for itself six times over. Not only has it increased traffic facilities more than 700 per cent and eliminated an annual charge of $2,000,000 resulting from traffic regulations which were formerly necessary, but it has also increased surrounding property values more than $100,000,000. The cost was borne half by the city as a whole and half by the property in the benefited (specially assessed) district. . . .

Upon the northern boundary of the loop district, along South Water Street, there has been ever since the oldest Chicagoan can remember, a great produce market. So congested has this market been all day long that not only was a very important east-and-west public street entirely absorbed by private business, but also every north-and-south street, connecting the central business district with the north side of the city, was jammed to such an extent that all moving traffic was confined to the 20-foot-wide street car right of way in the middle of the streets. The widening and double-decking of South Water Street began October 1, 1924. That is to say, the wrecking of buildings to make way for the new embankment began. This work was, of course, preceded by years of technical study, by a course of judicious publicity, and by a long case in court for the condemnation of the property and the acquisition of the land. The new embankment is to be a mile and a quarter in length, from the intersection with Michigan Avenue to the bend in the river at Market Street. It is to be a two-level street all the way, the upper surface for traffic of all classes, and the lower street for heavy commercial traffic which will have a course unobstructed by any cross traffic. On January 1, 1925, this new street will, by city ordinance, be named Wacker Drive, in honor of Chairman Charles H. Wacker of the Chicago Plan Commission, in recognition of his distinguished services to the city.

This improvement gives the city two new streets where before it had none at all; for although South Water Street existed nominally, in practice it was entirely given over to the produce market, and was a thoroughfare for market vehicles only. The market is now moving to a more appropriate location, and the future development of the upper level of Wacker Drive will be of the very highest type of office buildings, hotels, theaters, etc. On the upper water side of the 110-foot-wide street will be a promenade with a handsome balustrade and steps at intervals leading to the lower level, which is to be 135 feet wide, 25 feet of which is dock space. The lower street will be used entirely by heavy commercial vehicles. It is wide enough for six lanes of trucks, three each way, at the same time. The lower level of Wacker Drive will provide a direct route along the northern edge of the loop district, unobstructed by any cross traffic, for commercial vehicles traveling between the boat and railroad terminals east of Michigan Avenue and the warehouse district on the west side of the city.

In addition to the very great benefit which the city will derive from the acquisition of two new streets through its most congested area (the central business district), the improvement of South Water Street means even more in the relief of congestion in this city. It is the last link in the quadrangle of wide streets intended to by-pass through-bound traffic around the loop.

E. S. Taylor, *The Plan of Chicago in 1924* in *Annals of the American Academy of Political and Social Science* (Philadelphia, November, 1924), CXVI, 225–228 *passim*.

---

100. State Police Problems (1926)

BY SUPERINTENDENT LYNN G. ADAMS

With the exception of the Texas Rangers, the Pennsylvania State Police Force is the oldest organization of its kind in the United States. From the time of its founding the author has had an active and important part in its work. On the resignation of Major John C. Groom, Captain Adams became major and its second superintendent. During the World War he had charge of the military police in Paris. On matters of police work his reputation and authority are great. For another view of related problems, see No. 109 below. For some account of State Police work, see Katherine Mayo, *The Standard Bearers*, *Mounted Justice*.

FOR the purpose of scientific study of crime in the United States there are very few authentic data available. As an instance, we have no record of the number of crimes committed in the state of Pennsylvania; consequently, we cannot form an accurate idea of the number of criminals that go undetected. Nor is there any effective means of collecting such information. This condition is general throughout the United States.

Between January 1, 1921, and the present date, the Pennsylvania State Police have made 480 arrests in homicide cases. In 320 there is evidence of premeditation. From this fact, I conclude that most of them believed that they had better than a gambler's chance to escape detection, apprehension and conviction. Every theft, robbery, burglary, embezzlement, forgery and swindle is the result of some person or persons believing that they could evade justice; each had conceived an idea that justice is not only blind but crippled, probably based upon their observations of the way our mills of justice have functioned in the past. Indeed, if I may be facetious, I would say that if you could see a reproduction of their conception of justice in a statue, it would probably be mistaken for the "Winged Victory of Samothrace."

Frequently in our publications we find articles saying that one thing or another is responsible for the unsatisfactory condition that exists as concerns crime. One will say that it is due to the inefficiency of the police, another that it is the courts' delays, still another that it is the economic condition of the country that permits a few to have much while many have little, or that the solution is a matter of eugenics, or that politics are responsible.

It is my opinion that conditions are a result of a combination of weaknesses in all parts of our law enforcement machinery.

There is no reason for me to cite facts or figures to show that we are having more crime in this country than is desirable. I think we may all agree that general law enforcement develops far too many failures. Therefore, I think it is best that I confine myself to stating what, in my opinion, are the causes for this undesirable condition and suggest what I consider would be some effective remedies. My opinion may or may not be correct, and my only excuse for expressing it is that it is the result of twenty years' experience in the Pennsylvania State Police Force, an organization that has handled as many as 120 murder cases and 11,000 miscellaneous crimes in a single year. . . .

The law enforcement machinery of the United States is made up of several more or less independent or disassociated units only coordinated by the fact that none can reach the full purpose for its being without the co-operation of the others. Each of these units is frequently actuated by influences which are opposed to each other, and the results are frequently unsatisfactory, or negative.

The units of law enforcement machinery consist of the police, the magistrate's court, the prosecuting attorney, grand juries, judges of the lower courts, petit juries and courts of appeal.

To facilitate the study of the problem of law enforcement, let us assume that what appears to be a crime has been committed. The person making the discovery reports the fact to the police—the first unit of the law enforcement system. The first function of the police is to investigate for the purpose of determining that a crime has been committed, and if so, by whom. Its second function is to apprehend the guilty person and deliver the prisoner and the evidence to the proper judicial officer for a preliminary hearing. The effectiveness of the police unit can only be determined by the verdict and only when the other units of the system have functioned in practice as they are expected to function in theory.

The police unit in order to do its work effectively must possess certain qualifications. The first of these is intelligence backed up by training and experience. Otherwise, it will not be able to grasp the significance of the various elements of evidence, nor will it be able to give each element thereof its proper value, nor reach the correct valuation of the sum of these elements, producing proof.

In this country the method of selection of policemen is without doubt the least likely to secure the first and most necessary qualification. The generally adopted method of selection is political, physical and mental—at a ratio of one hundred to fifty to one. Nor is there much being done in the direction of intelligent training of men for this kind of service. Comparatively recently, some of the larger cities have started training schools, as have most of the state police forces in states where such organizations exist. But as a rule, in the smaller cities, the policeman is appointed, given a uniform, a badge, a billy and a gun, and then sent out with an older policeman to learn the limits of his beat.

Methods of organization narrow the field of advancement by promotion to such limits that very few intelligent and ambitious young men will favorably consider police service as a field for their life's work. This defect of organization is also responsible for there being very few competent executive police officials. It is remarkable that in a country where the benefits of special training and organization are so effectively demonstrated in our commercial affairs, that they should be considered unnecessary in one of our most important public services.

The matter of apprehending a criminal after detection often requires not only trained intelligence but also organization and co-operation of the highest development. With our present-day means of rapid transit, it is possible for the criminal to place great distances between himself and the scene of the crime in a very short space of time. With police forces disconnected, each interested in its own problems, it is not surprising that frequently a great criminal can remain hidden and unmolested in the very shadow of a police station. The surprising thing is that so many are apprehended.

Also charge against the effectiveness of the police unit political interference with the performance of its duties and a lowering of the morale which results in taking of bribes and a spiritless performance of duty.

Taking all of these conditions into consideration, we find the real reason why the police unit of our law enforcement system must bear a large share of the responsibility for failure in law enforcement.

Let us suppose for the purpose of this examination of the subject that in this case of crime, the police have been successful and the case now passes on to the next unit—the magistrate or justice-of-the-peace.

It is the function of this unit to determine that the evidence is or is not sufficiently convincing to justify the arrest and the incarceration of the accused.

In Pennsylvania, and most of the states, this official is not required to be learned in the law, nor to have any other qualification than that he be sufficiently popular to receive a plurality at the polls; and yet failure on his part to place the proper valuation on the evidence or to perform some other of his duties may partially or wholly nullify the activities of the police force, no matter how thoroughly it has performed its work.

Let us assume, however, that the case under consideration has passed successfully on to the next unit in order—the prosecuting attorney.

It is here that the indictment is prepared and the evidence marshalled in proper order and presented to both the grand and the petit juries. It is here placed in its proper order on the calendar. It is the prosecuting attorney who must examine and cross-examine the witnesses. Thus he must uncover errors, exaggerations, omissions, deceit and prejudice, to develop the facts concerning the case. Here again we find that a special fitness to perform the work at hand has little, if anything, to do with selection. A plurality at the polls is all that is required. Indeed, the office too frequently goes to young and inexperienced attorneys who have not yet built up a paying practice. The criminal, if he has sufficient money, can avail himself of the cleverest legal talent that will devote all of its time to the one case at hand, while often an inexperienced prosecuting attorney must prepare a large number of cases for each term of court. If he err, the case may be irrevocably lost, while if the criminal loses he may appeal and often does receive a new trial. Political expediency may, and all too frequently does, interfere with the success of the case. It is also responsible for unnecessary delays which result in minor details being forgotten by witnesses or the loss of evidence through death or disappearance of witnesses. Thus we find, through lack of ability, overwork, political expediency and dishonesty, another unit that must bear its share of the responsibility for failure.

Next in order, our case comes to juries both grand and petit, and back of the juries is the juror-selection system. In many states, this consists of the commission that selects names of citizens and places them in a wheel or other mixing device and then some person who has been blindfolded draws out a sufficient number to fill the quota required. Here again, political or other improper motive frequently enters into the selection of names to be placed in the wheel. A juror is really a judge whose duty it is to weigh and give a valuation to the evidence produced by each side. He must frequently compare the statements of two or more witnesses whose testimony is directly opposed to each other. He must frequently listen to and weigh the testimony of experts in highly complicated and technical matters. In petit juries, one juror in error or prejudiced may upset the whole case and prevent justice being done. And yet in all my police experience, I have never known of a court where there was evidence of any special attempt having been made to choose jurors on account of intelligence, education or good character.

Our case having safely passed the juries and a verdict of "guilty" having been returned, it now goes to the next unit of the system— the judge. Here we have an official who in theory is impartial; yet at varying periods, in most states, he is required to stand for re-election and to be the subject of political favors. A dishonest judge may defeat justice in innumerable ways. He may grant continuances of a case with all the disastrous results of delay. He may err so that the defendant may secure a new trial. He may in some cases suspend or pass inadequate sentences. He may in other instances grant paroles, and by these devices bring to naught all the efforts that have preceded.

It would naturally be supposed, in the event of conviction and adequate sentence, that justice would stand triumphant. But not so. It is here that the pardoning power, too frequently acting upon misinformation often supplied by well-meaning persons of narrow vision, nullifies all that has been accomplished.

In twenty years of police experience, I have seen justice fail in each unit that I have mentioned, and in every manner that I have mentioned—not once, but many times.

Respect for law is based upon its effectiveness in dispensing impartial justice. Except perhaps when modified by religion, man's instincts are all on the side of expediency. And most religious persons are religious on account of expediency; as soon as a thing becomes inexpedient, it is avoided. There is an abundance of evidence to prove that effective detection, apprehension, conviction and punishment does inhibit crime; and inhibition is in the same proportion as the conviction and punishment. This is Nature's way of enforcing her laws. If man's laws could be made as effective as the law of gravitation, this would be a very law-respecting nation.

One who attempts to criticize should be prepared at least to suggest what appears to be a remedy.

The police unit of our law enforcement system is lacking in intelligence and organization and is hampered by political control. Consolidation, removal of political influence, centralizing control, and special training are the remedies.

The consolidation of the police system with centralized control creates a field of service for advancement that would attract intelligent and ambitious young men into the service. Its removal from politics would strengthen the morale and discipline.

The establishment of training schools would have the same relative purpose in the police organization that Annapolis Naval Academy and the Newport Training Station have in the Navy.

Because I have felt that twenty years' experience in police service and a study of the systems of the United States and Europe have given me some authority to express an opinion as to the police system, I have done so quite freely, but inasmuch as I know so little of the obstacles, trials and conditions in the other units of law enforcement, it would be unbecoming as well as foolish for me to attempt to say how they should be constructed or improved, and therefore I will refrain from so doing. But I may say that the first and most important step in the direction of improvement is a thorough study of all of the parts and the system as a whole, and to that end there should be a commission created that would have the power and authority to collect the material for such a study.

The statistics collected by such a commission would not only provide material for study of the question, but would serve as a measure of the effectiveness of the various units and prevent many of the evils that now exist.

Lynn G. Adams, in *Annals of the American Academy of Political and Social Science* (Philadelphia, May, 1926) CXXV, 143–147 *passim*.

CHAPTER XIX — THE COURTS AND THEIR PLACE IN GOVERNMENT

101. The Supreme Court Justices (1911)

BY ELBERT F. BALDWIN

Since 1911, Justices have been appointed as follows: McReynolds (1914), Brandeis (1916), Taft, as Chief Justice (1921), Sutherland and Butler (1922), Sanford (1923), Stone (1925). Holmes and Van Devanter alone remain of those who composed the Court in 1911.—Bibliography: Charles Warren, *The Supreme Court and Sovereign States* (1924), *Congress, the Constitution and the Supreme Court* (1925).

THE Supreme Court convenes daily at noon, adjourns for lunch from two to two-thirty, and at half-past four adjourns for the day. At noon the clerk cries, "The Honorable, the Supreme Court of the United States." Every one rises, and the Judges in their black gowns file in. When the Judges have taken their places behind the bench, the clerk calls: "Oyez, oyez, oyez! All persons having business with the Supreme Court of the United States draw near and give their attention, for the Court is now sitting. God save the United States and this honorable Court!"

For the first time in nearly two years there are no vacancies. The Chief Justice enters first, and he is the most impressive-looking of the company. Edward Douglass White, of Louisiana, is sixty-five years old. In physical appearance no man in public life, not even President Taft, better deserves the adjective "ponderous." But listen to Mr. White as, later, he speaks to Attorney General Wickersham (who is summing up the Government's side in the Tobacco Case), and you will see that the Chief Justice's voice is like velvet. Its quality is emphasized, as he bends forward to speak to the counsel below, by an expressive gesture of the hand raised slightly with the first two fingers together. Somehow this gesture suggests to your imagination the man's fairness. Mr. White is a Democrat, a Southerner, an ex-Confederate, and a Roman Catholic. After the war he

426

practiced law in Louisiana, then he was elected State Senator, and afterwards was appointed Associate Justice of the Louisiana Supreme Court. Twenty years ago he was elected United States Senator, in 1894 he was appointed Associate Justice of the Federal Supreme Court, and has just been appointed Chief Justice to succeed Chief Justice Fuller. This action breaks a precedent. No Associate Justice had ever before been elevated to the Chief Justiceship. The reason for this has doubtless been the desire to emphasize the post of Associate Justice as a finality, and to give to its occupant the feeling that no higher office can be conferred upon him, thus freeing him from any imaginary temptation to conform his decision to supposed White House wishes in order to stand well in line for succession—that is, supposing the Associate Justice to be a combination of weakness and ambition. . . .

The qualifications for office of the new Chief Justice are high. His distinction as lawyer, judge, statesman, *and man* is preëminent and indisputable. Hence the Senate acted immediately on his nomination, quite as much because of its confidence in him as a candidate for the highest judicial position as because he was at one time a member of that body. When his name was presented to the Senate by the President, it made an exception of its rule to refer the names of appointees to committee. It immediately went into executive session, and in fifteen minutes had taken favorable and unanimous action. Such a compliment would have silenced the critics of the nomination, had there been any, of a man whose name, as a synonym of intellectual integrity and impartiality, may rank with the first dozen names of members of the Supreme Court since its creation. In addition to sheer legal caliber, the Chief Justice is perhaps the only man on the Federal bench who can argue a case in French. Moreover, he has had an extensive experience in the practice of the Code Napoléon, on which the civil law of his native State of Louisiana is founded. . . .

All this time the Judges have been filing in, and the name of John Marshall comes again to mind as one looks upon the tall figure of John Marshall Harlan, of Kentucky. That poor light and air are not always fatal to health is proven by this well-preserved man, seventy-seven years old. Of the sixty-two men who have sat on this bench, he has been the associate of twenty-six. His service has been not only twice as long as that of any other member of the present Court: his term of over thirty-three years has never been exceeded save by Marshall, Story, and Field. Though oldest in years, Justice Harlan seems the keenest of the Judges to grasp a possible humor in any situation, as was shown a few days ago during the progress of the Tobacco Case in his criticisms of the chewing-tobacco market. Judge Harlan's academic and law studies were undertaken at those comparatively little-known institutions Center College and Transylvania University. He began practicing law at Frankfort, the capital of the State. As far back as 1858 he was elected County Judge, and the following year was Whig candidate for Congress. When the war came, as a Unionist he raised an infantry regiment and served in General Thomas's division. After the war Mr. Harlan practiced law in Louisville, and in 1877 was appointed Associate Justice by President Hayes. As usual, a Republican appointed a Republican.

Enter, after Judge Harlan, Mr. Justice McKenna, of California, also a Republican. Joseph McKenna is sixty-seven years old, and was appointed in 1898 by President McKinley. In appearance he somewhat resembles Senator Cullom, of Illinois, albeit more red-blooded. Chin whiskers and spare figure make both look like the typical Brother Jonathan. Judge McKenna has had long service in judicial and legislative life. He has been in the California Legislature and in no less than four Congresses. President Harrison made him a Circuit Judge, and President McKinley made him Attorney-General and later Associate Justice. The Chief Justice and Mr. Justice McKenna are the only Roman Catholics on the bench.

Enter the next in order of appointment, Mr. Justice Holmes, a Republican, of Massachusetts. He was appointed in 1902 by President Roosevelt. The Holmes face is winsome, whether that of the Autocrat of the Breakfast Table or that of his son, the present Associate Justice. The Holmes mind is notable too, whether that of father or son. "Justice Holmes can wear any one out, such is his mental pace when he gets going," said a critic to me to-day. Certain it is that his mind is one of the most remarkable on the bench, a fact specially appreciated by the Chief Justice, between whom and Justice Holmes a strong friendship exists. It is a case of "extremes meet," one man being from the far South and with a somewhat Southern temperament, while the other man is a typical Yankee from the far North. Indeed, Justice Holmes is a capital example of Massachusetts culture and patriotism. He is a Harvard man of the class of 1861. The same year he was commissioned first lieutenant of the Twentieth Massachusetts Volunteer Infantry. At Ball's Bluff he was shot through the breast, and at Antietam shot through the neck. He rose through the army grades, and when the conflict between North and South was over went through the Harvard Law School, his course having been interrupted by the war. After years of law practice in Boston he was made a member of the Massachusetts Supreme Court, and finally Chief Justice of that Court. Despite his gray hair and mustache, his still youthful countenance (like his father's at the same age) and his alert manner give little evidence of his age—sixty-nine years.

Enter the next Judge in order of appointment, William Rufus Day, of Ohio, appointed in 1903 by President Roosevelt. Justice Day seems all brain—a brain which was applied with historic result when he was chairman of the Commission which negotiated the treaty of peace with Spain. Judge Day is sixty-one years old, and comes from Canton, Ohio, President McKinley's home. He was a great friend of McKinley, who made him his Assistant Secretary of State, later Secretary of State, and still later appointed him Circuit Judge.

Enter the next Judge in order of appointment, and now we jump from 1903 to 1909. The Judge is Horace Harmon Lurton, of Tennessee, a Democrat, appointed by President Taft to succeed Justice Peckham. Judge Lurton is sixty-six years old. Despite his years, he seems as pertinacious in asking questions of counsel from the bench as if he were a very young man, and his nasal Yankee voice has in it little of the soft Southern twang one might expect. He was educated at Cumberland University, began practicing at Clarksville, Tennessee, and rose through the judicial grades to be Chief Justice of his State. President Cleveland appointed him Circuit Judge, and, as we have seen in the case of the Chief Justice, the fact that a man was a Democrat proved no bar to his judicial preferment when President Taft became convinced that, beyond any other, the man was fitted for the place. As one looks at Mr. Justice Lurton and his next-door neighbor but one, Mr. Justice Harlan, the story comes to mind of how these two men were once mortal enemies. It was half a century ago. Harlan and Lurton were on opposite sides in the Civil War. Harlan was Colonel of the Tenth Kentucky Infantry (Unionist) and Lurton was a private in the Third Kentucky Cavalry (Confederate). At Cumberland River Colonel Harlan tried to train a cannon ball on Lurton and company, but the Confederates won. At Buffington's Island, however, Trooper Lurton was taken prisoner and transferred to Johnson's Island in Lake Erie, "the best prison in the North," he says. The echoes of the Civil War are getting fainter, but the bringing together of two such men on the same bench revives a memory.

Enter the next Judge in order of appointment, Charles Evans Hughes, of New York, a Republican, appointed last summer by President Taft to succeed Justice Brewer. Mr. Hughes is forty-eight years old. He is the only Judge who wears a full beard, and this, together with a very virile manner and voice, distinguishes him somewhat from most men. They used to say of one of the Cardinals that underneath his vestments he would sometimes "kick out," as he used to during his years as a soldier. One has a little of that feeling as one regards the vigorous prosecutor of the insurance companies and the Progressive Governor of New York, now in judicial robes and judicial dignity. This has been emphasized within the past few days by Mr. Justice Hughes's opinion in the Alonzo Bailey case, an opinion likely to become historic. In any event, it brilliantly marks the entrance of a man who had shown himself a great administrator into a new field of activity, where he will doubtless show himself a great judge.

Enter the next Judge in order of appointment, Willis Van Devanter, of Wyoming, a Republican, appointed last autumn by President Taft to succeed Justice Moody. Mr. Van Devanter is fifty-one years old, and is a very human-looking document indeed. He was born in Indiana, and was educated at De Pauw University and at the Cincinnati Law School. After some years of practice in Indiana he removed to Cheyenne, Wyoming. He rose through various grades to be Chief Justice of the Supreme Court of his State. Six years ago President Roosevelt appointed him Circuit Judge. His present appointment is particularly interesting in view of the Standard Oil Case, because in the Circuit Court he had already had part in that case. The question arose whether he could take part in it on the Supreme Bench. This, however, would not differ in its essential nature from what occurred in the Nebraska Maximum Freight Rate Case, when Justice Brewer, of the Supreme Court, sat as Circuit Judge; his opinion declaring the Nebraska law unconstitutional was afterward sustained by the Supreme Court in a decision in which he shared.

Enter the next and final Judge in order of appointment, Joseph Rucker Lamar, a Democrat, but, despite that, appointed by a Republican President to succeed to the place left vacant by the promotion of Justice White. Mr. Justice Lamar is fifty-three years old. Of all the Judges, he seems the best worth looking at. Like the other Southern Judges, Chief Justice White and especially Mr. Justice Lurton, so the latest addition to the Bench interrupts counsel once in a while. Mr. Justice Lamar's voice is singularly resonant, full-toned, and bell-like in quality. He was born in Georgia and educated at the University of Georgia. He practiced law at Augusta, and for a short time was a member of the State Legislature. To his new position he brings a distinguished record of service on the Supreme Court of Georgia. . . .

The assured tenure of office and the Supreme Court's authority in determining what is law, both greater than in England, have always attracted eminent men to accept membership in the Court. Yet it is, nevertheless, evidence of American patriotism when men of the caliber of our Supreme Court Justices are willing to abandon active work as advocates—work bringing them many times the financial returns they now receive—and take their places on the Federal Bench. Of course one may say that no greater honor can come to a man than to sit on that Bench, and this is true. At the same time it is a pity that our Government should evince so little appreciation of the financial sacrifice involved as to pay the Chief Justice of the United States $13,000 a year, less than is received by a Justice of the Supreme Court of New York City, while the head of the British Bench receives no less than fifty thousand dollars.

Elbert F. Baldwin, *The Supreme Court Justices* in *Outlook*, January 28, 1911 (New York), XCVII, 156–160 *passim*.

102.   The Federal Judiciary System (1923)

BY PROFESSOR JAMES T. YOUNG

For Young, see No. 91 above.   For first-hand information on the changing attitude of the federal courts with respect to particular legislation, see certain sequences
of decisions collected in Felix Frankfurter, *Cases under the Interstate Commerce Act;*
Herman Oliphant, *Cases on Trade Regulation.*   See also No. 101 above, and Nos.
103 and 122 below.

OUR American courts are passing through an era of searching
criticism; the stock promoter and the radical agitator, alike,
are dissatisfied with judicial rulings.   It is also complained that the
judges' decisions lag too far behind public opinion, a strong current of
popular sentiment is demanding a cheaper, quicker, and simpler
method of procedure, and there are sporadic proposals for a recall
which shall place it in the power of the people by majority vote to
oust from office any judge or other official at any time.   The judicial
system is about to undergo some revision in order that it may reflect
more accurately and helpfully the business and social development of
our period.   The worth-while criticisms of our system may be divided
into two general classes; first, that the judicial process is so slow and
costly as to be a luxury for the rich.   There is much truth in this
charge and it applies not only to the Federal courts but to those of
the States as well.   England and the Continental countries have far
surpassed us in the admirable simplicity and dispatch of their court
procedure.   In America it is not uncommon for a law suit to require
from five to seven years from its inception to its final decision.   This
occurs when both sides are willing to expedite the case and where
the question is not such a close one as to require more than one argument before the final court.   When mistakes in procedure occur or
either side interposes delays, or where a re-argument is necessary,
from one to three years additional time may be required, making a
total of from six to ten years of litigation.   Numerous instances of
this latter kind are constantly recurring.

Since much of this unfortunate slowness has been due to over-
crowding of the dockets of the courts and to the immense recent growth
of litigation over Federal laws, Congress by the Act of September 14,
1922, created twenty-four additional judgeships and provided for an

annual conference of the senior judges from all the circuits, at which a report is made covering the number and kind of cases on the docket in each of the Courts and the need of additional assistance. The Chief Justice may request the conference judges to assign extra judges to districts where help is needed. A movement has also been started to simplify and hasten procedure of the Federal Courts and to give the Supreme Court power to prescribe forms and rules for all the Federal Courts. Some of the delays are unavoidable, but much must be charged to downright slowness. So, for example, in Atherton Mills v. Johnston, decided by the Supreme Court May 15, 1922, an injunction was sought to prevent the enforcement of the Child Labor Law. Johnston filed his complaint April 15, 1919, and by the time the case was decided, three years and one month later, the Supreme Court ruled that the child having reached an age in excess of 14 the case would no longer be considered! On the same day the Supreme Court handed down a decision that the Act was unconstitutional.

In Truax v. Corrigan, decided December, 1921, a still more striking case is presented. Here an employer sought an injunction to protect his business from an unlawful conspiracy, filing his complaint in 1916. He was denied protection by the State courts and appealed his case to the United States Supreme Court where it was decided in his favor in 1922. Although he thus won a legal victory by his six years' fight in the courts, his business had meanwhile been completely destroyed and himself financially ruined.

A much larger increase in judgeships is urgently needed. In some of the jurisdictions the docket is so overburdened that cases cannot be called for a year after they are filed. The abuse of "continuances" is also a serious block to quick procedure. For these both the attorneys and courts are responsible. It is now customary even in the Federal courts for the judge to grant several continuances or postponements on the application of either side, without serious question. The attorneys, knowing this, make use of it not only to enable them to conduct other cases but also to delay and harass the opposing party.

In the second place, lawyers and laymen alike agree that the procedure in most of our courts is needlessly complicated, and inordinately time-consuming. Mr. Taft both as President and as Chief Justice has showed his acquaintance with these weaknesses and made a special effort to remedy them. Pursuant to his suggestion, the Supreme Court revised and simplified the entire method of pleading and conducting equity suits in all the Federal courts; a similar revision is contemplated for the ordinary *law* cases. Most of the needless complexity in the starting of suits and in the nature of the exact pleas to be entered has descended to us from English procedure of two hundred years ago—while in the land of its origin, this same procedure has long been abandoned for simpler, more convenient forms. In this respect our Federal courts are far more advanced than those of the States. The tendency to seize on trivial detail or minute discrepancies in statement or form has been allowed to run riot through our procedure with appalling cost to the community and to the popular respect for the courts. Under the continued stimulus of Chief Justice Taft and the American Bar Association strong efforts are now being made to divest procedure of its unnecessary formalities and delays. Nothing could be done which would so effectually rehabilitate the judicial system in the trust of the people. In the last analysis we do not measure the value of our tribunals by the method of their choice, whether appointed or elected, nor by their qualifications, nor their salaries, nor by the recall, nor even alone by their erudition and knowledge of the law—rather do we believe "by their fruits ye shall know them." If the courts can give us broad, statesmanlike interpretations of the law through a quick, simple, and cheap method of procedure, it matters not whether they are appointed nor whether we can recall them or their decisions. And if on the other hand we adopt every modern device to make them sympathetic with the popular will but allow the technicalities of a by-gone age to remain, encumbering their machinery, their real work is not done.

A third and more serious criticism of our court system is that it protects the powerful against the weak, and is largely a means of maintaining and fortifying the interests of the conservative classes exclusively. This criticism while untrue in many cases has sufficient basis to require examination. The legal training of the judge from the time he starts out as a practicing lawyer is such as to attract his attention to the sacredness of property; his mind is chiefly occupied with the means of upholding property rights. In examining the historical reasons for our existing law, he is inclined to look with much greater care upon the past than upon the present growth of the law.

As a result his whole professional education makes him intensely conservative unless by temperament his natural instinct favors progressive changes. A profession whose members are trained by long environment to this view of life must naturally tend to sympathize with what is, rather than to seek new interpretations of the law in the interest of less influential classes of the people.

It is no criticism of the judge to say that his education has molded his habit of mind, since the same is true of any other professional or business class, yet the fact is a serious weakness in our judicial system, and has created a feeling in wide circles that the judiciary is under the influence of property interests. Such a control if it exists is not the result of a deeply laid plot or scheme but rather of this psychological fact of natural reaction against change, caused by the environment and training of the judge's mind. This conservative bias must be changed, not by a change in the appointing power, not by a recall, nor by any other device which may threaten the independence of the judges, but rather by a change in the method of training men for the bar. Since the judge is first a lawyer, it is the education of the lawyer which must be made to include a knowledge of the causes and nature of social and economic growth. If our law is to be progressive it must be interpreted by men trained to see the necessity of legal growth and life. Here again some foreign systems have developed more rapidly than our own. They have insisted on giving prospective attorneys and judges a thorough training in social and economic as well as legal affairs. If the members of our courts in this country were so educated there would be little reason for complaint of class partiality. If our judicial system were simplified, our court procedure curtailed and expedited, and the legal training of the attorney were made more social in character we should have a national judiciary second to none.

James T. Young, *The New American Government and Its Work* (New York, Macmillan, 1923), 324–328.

103.   Five to Four in the Supreme Court (1923)

BY FABIAN FRANKLIN

Franklin has been an editor of the Baltimore *News*, New York *Evening Post*, and *The Independent*.   He discusses a problem that has engaged many of the best legal minds.

WHEN an act of Congress, or of a State Legislature, is invalidated by a decision upon which the Supreme Court is nearly equally divided, there is naturally aroused a considerable amount of irritation and even resentment.   Proposals of various degrees of merit or plausibility are made from time to time to do away with this situation.   Perhaps the worst of these proposals was that to which Mr. Roosevelt lent the weight of his name and the impetus of his popularity, and which was generally referred to as the "recall of judicial decisions."   The peculiar vice of this scheme was that it was calculated to destroy the power of the Supreme Court as a defender of the Constitution at the very times when, of all times, the assertion of that power was most needed.   The greatest danger of enactments which override the Constitution is precisely when popular feeling is highly excited in favor of some particular measure that does so.   It is when popular clamor or the ruling sentiment of the moment is most urgent that Congress is most apt to disregard Constitutional limitations in its eagerness to please the public; and to give that very public the power to reverse the court's decision would be, in practical effect, to reduce the judgment of the court to a nullity in the very cases in which appeal to that judgment is most vitally needed.   To a more or less distinct apprehension of this we may, I think, ascribe the failure of the recall-of-decisions idea to make headway in public opinion, in spite of the prestige of its chief sponsor.

A far more plausible proposal is that which has recently gained much prominence through its advocacy by Senator Borah.   This would not impair the finality of the court's decision, but would require, for the invalidation of an act of Congress or of a State Legislature, more than a bare majority of the court; unless as many as seven of the nine justices agreed in pronouncing it unconstitutional, the act would stand.   For this proposal what looks like a pretty strong case can be made, and has been made; but I think it will appear, upon examination, that neither of the two arguments that are urged in its behalf is sound.

The chief argument by which the proposal is supported is that the deliberate act of a legislative body is entitled to a certain presumption of constitutionality; that to overthrow this presumption the infringement of the Constitution alleged against the act must be clear and palpable; that an infringement which turns upon considerations so refined, so doubtful, or so unimportant as to leave nearly half of the Justices unconvinced cannot be of this character; and that accordingly the act should not be set aside unless the court is almost unanimous in pronouncing it invalid.

I think I have put this argument in as strong terms as it is capable of; and it certainly has an appearance of great force. But let us examine the matter a little more closely. The Supreme Court is not a hostile body, eager to invalidate the acts of Congress or of the State Legislatures; there is not a member of it who takes pleasure in arraying judicial authority in opposition to legislative power. When five justices have pronounced an act unconstitutional and four have refused to do so, each one of the five and each one of the four has given to the presumption of constitutionality all the weight to which in his judgment it is entitled. The five adverse judgments have not been rendered in wantonness, but because to each of five justices the infringement *did* seem sufficiently clear, and sufficiently important, to overthrow that presumption; and likewise the four favorable judgments have been influenced, in a degree which there is no means of estimating, by this very consideration that a legislative act should not be invalidated unless the constitutional objection to it is of unmistakable force and importance. In a word, the proposal to require more than a majority vote to pronounce an act unconstitutional rests on the assumption that the court does not give due weight to considerations which are dictated by ordinary fairness and common sense; an assumption for which there is no warrant. The more self-evident it is that the court ought to give due weight to the fact of legislative action, the more we feel certain that, as a general rule, though of course with exceptions, it actually does so; and in point of fact the record of its opinions is full of evidence that such is the case. The proposal to add to the weight which is actually attached to the presumption of constitutionality by requiring a seven-to-two vote to overthrow it is really a proposal to weight the scales against the Constitution; it is a proposal to apply to legislative acts not the natural presumption which we have been discussing, but something like the rigorous presumption of innocence which protects a person accused of crime. But this presumption, it should be remembered, is based on the maxim that it is better that ninety and nine guilty men should escape than that one innocent man should suffer; a maxim that we cannot transfer to the present subject unless we are prepared to say that it is better that ninety and nine unconstitutional laws should go into effect than that one constitutional law should be nullified.

The second argument that is urged in behalf of the change rests on an altogether different ground; it is based not on the inherent merits of the procedure but on the effect of it upon the standing of the court in public estimation. The spectacle, we are told, of five-to-four decisions invalidating legislative acts is calculated to lower the repute of the Supreme Court and to lessen its authority in the eyes of the nation. Undoubtedly there is some truth in this; though the way in which the court has maintained its standing in the country, decade after decade, in the face of recurrent instances—and important instances—of such decisions seems to indicate that the damage is not so serious as might be imagined. But be this as it may, would the requirement of a seven-to-two vote tend to increase respect for the court? Would it tend to give the judgments of the court a greater authority in the public mind? I think that precisely the opposite would be the case. Every time six out of the nine justices pronounced a law unconstitutional and the law nevertheless went into effect, the country would witness a spectacle far more damaging to the court's prestige than any that is now presented. For we should be living under laws which the Supreme Court, by a two-to-one vote, had condemned as unconstitutional, and which nevertheless we should, by habit and practice, necessarily regard as constitutional. If anybody were claiming that the Supreme Court was infallible the fact of five-to-four decisions would be absolutely conclusive refutation of the claim; but no such claim is asserted. We all know that a decision of the court may be wrong; but we also know that what it has decided is the final law of the land. But under the seven-to-two plan the final law of the land may be in direct opposition to the court's emphatic decision as to its constitutionality. Respect is due some criticisms of its fallibility; it has survived them and will undoubtedly continue to survive them. But how long would it survive repeated exhibitions not of fallibility, which is a necessary attribute of all things human, but impotence, which is the one failing that a court of last resort cannot afford to exhibit?

Fabian Franklin, in *The Independent*, April 14, 1923 (Concord, N. H.) CX, 246–247.

---

104. The Work of a Juvenile Court (1925)

BY JUDGE BENJAMIN BARR LINDSEY

Lindsey was judge of a special court in Denver, dealing with juvenile and domestic relations problems. He has made both enemies and champions by his frank advocacy of new approaches to many of the difficulties with which he has had to deal.

BOYS suit my taste best when they are between twelve and fourteen, though I like them all, regardless of age, and have several of them daily as an *entrée* in my human-nature menu.

Some of them steal automobiles, some steal automobile accessories, others run away from school, still others run away from home. Some defy the cop just to see what he'll do about it; some upset some fruit stand and harvest the reddest of the apples while the owner shrieks in resounding Neapolitan what Judge Lindsey will do to them when he gets them into court. On the other hand, I regret to say that some of them wiggle their fingers at victims who threaten them with my vengeance; and angry citizens have come many times to my court bitterly reproaching me that I "stand back of the young rascals." For here, even as in the case of flappers and flippers, I am famous as an "encourager of immorality."

But I am not an encourager of immorality nor of anti-social conduct of any sort. What I understand first of all is that I must find means to keep these boys from repeating their offenses, and that any punishment which fails to get that result is likely to present society with a dangerous criminal. Reform can come about only through a change in the boy's way of thinking. He doesn't wilfully think wrong; he does it because the premises of his logic are incorrect. Change that and you change the boy; for direct, logical, free, and vigorous thinking, independent of adult conventions, is a peculiar gift of boyhood. A boy has a way of thought which is as deadly direct in its logic from an accepted premise as the path of the bullet from a rifle. If the boy misses it simply means that the rifle is sighted wrong, that's all; there is nothing wrong with the rifle itself.

It is this that makes some of my boy cases almost appallingly funny; for humor is often nothing but a form of logic so honest and remorseless that it follows through to the bitter end.

Take, for example, the case of a certain little "Mickey." Mickey was one of the most conspicuous instances of original sin that I ever had to deal with; and in his dealing with society he seemed born to trouble as the sparks fly upward. His age was eleven; and the police had long since formed the habit of arresting Mickey on general principles whenever anything went wrong in the street where he lived. Sometimes Mickey's hard little pipe-stem legs would carry him to my chambers ahead of time when he felt, as he used to say, "Judge, I dun got in trouble again; en I thought I better git here before de cops do"; and his squinty blue eyes and his shock of Irish red hair were a familiar sight in the court house.

It came to pass, therefore, that whenever there was mischief afoot, and the local cop had gone ahunting, Mickey would run the instant he spied him; and this he would do even if he was innocent, as sometimes happened. Flight naturally drew suspicion and pursuit, and Mickey would then be confronted by the difficulty of explaining why he had run if he "hadn't done nuthin'."

"Mickey," I said to him on one occasion, "when you are innocent, why not stand your ground?"

A pained expression came into his face. "Judge," he said, "don't you know that you can't tell a cop nothin'? Judge, *when a cop is after yuh, he's agin yuh;* and there's only one thing t'do—Ditch and Skidoo. If yuh don't yuh just naturally gits pinched."

"But, Mickey," I protested, "that's no reason why you should lie to the cop."

To my surprise he said, "Judge, I never lies to the cop."

"I don't know what you call it, then," I said, "when you knocked the props out from under that fruit stand, and you skedaddled with the cop after you; and when he caught you you told him you didn't do it. Just now you told me you did do it. You told me the truth, and you lied to the cop."

Again he put on the air of injured innocence that he could assume to perfection when he wished, and then came back at me with this:

"Judge, dat ain't lyin' to the cop; dat's *stringin'* de cop. For yuh see, Judge, it's like dis. Dat guy had pinched me so much when I hadn't done nothin' dat when he pinches me for somethin' I done I says I didn't do it, so as to make up fer *one* of the times when he says I done it when I didn't. Dat's stringin' de cop. An' he's still got a lot o' string comin' to 'im!"

I defy anybody to show that Mickey did not there make an effective appeal to the elemental right of self-defense, or to show that the policeman had any right to expect the truth from his lips.

The attitude of injustice and revenge on the part of the police—like the attitude of injustice and revenge on the part of parents, forced Mickey to seek an avenue of escape. He lied, not because he was a liar but because he had encountered injustice; also because he was an ingenuous and independent thinker, not afraid of himself or of his own judgments, or of a God fashioned for him, like an idol, by somebody else. . . .

When I first started my work in the Juvenile Court of Denver I began, to the wrath and consternation of all sensible and sane persons, including the sheriff, who missed numerous fat fees because of my peculiarities, to send boys, when I had to send them, to prisons or State institutions on their own responsibility. Formerly they had generally been taken to such places handcuffed to an officer, and the court officials, including the sheriff, were a unit in calling me a crackbrained fanatic, and in predicting that since it was necessary to handcuff these boys to an officer to keep them from getting away, they would obviously fly to the ends of the earth if the handcuffs and the officer were both omitted. This, said they, was the only thing that could logically happen. . . .

The boys didn't run. The minute the handcuffs and the officers were out of the way they didn't feel any desire to run. In fact they couldn't be persuaded to run. I gave them their railroad fare, explained the idea, and they always arrived. They didn't arrive only occasionally. They kept it up, in spite of a certain newspaper, which scolded, threatened, and ridiculed by turns.   If a boy didn't have any other motive for going through, he would do it in order to put one over on the newspapers and police and the district attorney's office, and show them that they didn't know what they were talking about.

So far the record is 100 per cent.   I've never lost one.   Four or five out of all those hundreds did once, at first, run away, but they returned and apologized for their lack of sense and loyalty.

Back in the days when I was beginning my work among juveniles, I had one boy who was among the first I sent to Golden. . . . Skinny was always running away from the cops.   He had served time in the reform school, and had been the terror of that institution.   He was the leader of several gangs, and had within him the imagination, the fire, the courage, and the talents for roguery that, in other walks of life, made Captains of Industry—the kind whose exploits in millions are so magnificent that nobody has the heart to put them in jail.

I shall never forget the day when two six-foot policemen, both of them breathing hard and both of them evidently more or less under a nervous strain, came into my chambers with the diminutive form of Skinny between them, each of them with a big hand firmly encircling his lean little arms.   Skinny clearly resented the familiarity, and yet I think he took a kind of pride in their evident respect for his resourcefulness.

One of these officers I knew to be very hostile to my methods; and, as I learned, he had just tipped off a reporter that the Judge was going to try sending Skinny to Golden alone, and that it was going to result in a good laugh on the Judge.

I told Skinny flat that I was going to have to send him to Golden. This brought from him a storm of tears and violent pleadings for "one more chance."   But as I had given him "one more chance" on former occasions, I now had to point out that he was at the end of his rope. I tried in vain to calm him, but he wouldn't be consoled.   And yet I just had to get hold of him somehow; and make some appeal that would win him.

I looked into the face of the policeman, who wasn't taking the trouble to conceal a sneer; and I looked at the interested and expectant face of the reporter who was there on the policeman's tip.   And the thought came to me that I might shell them with their own guns.

"Skinny," I said, "do you know what this officer has told this reporter? He has told him that there is going to be a good story in this because Skinny can't be trusted; and that when I try to send you to Golden by yourself, and you run away, it will be a fine joke on the Judge. Now what do you think of that?"

Skinny's tears dried so fast that I seemed to see them sizzle into steam; and he turned on the policeman with flashing eyes. "So dat's what yuh told de guy, did yuh! Yuh thinks yuh knows a lot; but yuh don't know nuthin' at all." Then he turned to me. "Judge, gimme that writ an' watch me fool dis cop."

I handed him the writ and some money, and the last I saw of him he was tearing across the court-house yard, regardless of keep-off-the-grass signs.

The policeman laughed as he saw him go. "Judge," he said, "that's the Grand Throw Down for you."

But at Police Headquarters there was another policeman who, even in those early days, had a faith in my methods which is common enough among our Denver police now. This man took up the cudgels in my behalf, and offered the cynic a substantial wager that Skinny would go through. The bet was made, and the stakes were placed in the hands of a stake-holder, who in due time called the Industrial School on the telephone. It appeared that Skinny was there. It appeared, moreover, that he was following a line of good behavior which was astounding to those who had had official dealings with him before.

Months later I made a trip to Golden; and out from a crowd of boys darted Skinny, his face all smiles, the pinched look gone from it, and a different expression about the eyes. "Say, Judge," he shouted the instant he was within earshot, "didn't we put one over on dat cop?"

Skinny is a prosperous Denverite today instead of an inmate of the penitentiary. He has a happy wife and a thriving family. Occasionally he drops in to watch me deal with other Skinnys; he always votes for me.

Ben B. Lindsey and Wainwright Evans, *The Revolt of Modern Youth* (New York, Boni and Liveright, 1925).

PART VII

THE HUMAN RELATIONS

CHAPTER XX — PROBLEMS OF CRIME AND MORALS

105. Piety and Playfulness (1922)

BY GLENN FRANK

Glenn Frank, essayist and editor of the *Century* magazine, was made President of the University of Wisconsin in 1925. He is also the author of No. 136 below. Besides the volume from which this extract is taken, he has written *The Politics of Industry* (1919).

AN ever increasing band of moral overseers are agitating for a playless Sunday—playless in order that it may be pious. These crusaders are animated by the belief that a perfectly definite line can be drawn between things sacred and things secular. They purpose to rid the American Sunday of things secular and make it by force of law a sacred day. They make their appeal to two powerful elements of the American population, the uncritically religious element of our population, from whom any appeal in the name of a more religious observation of the Sabbath is likely to win support, and organized laborers, who have long and rightly fought for one day of rest in seven. The general objective of the crusaders has been stated by their leader, the Reverend Harry L. Bowlby, as follows: "Our object is to defend and preserve the Lord's Day as a day of rest and worship, and to enunciate and urge one day of rest in seven for all the toiling masses."

With this general objective all right-thinking Americans are in heartiest accord. If decent, law-abiding, and essentially Christian Americans oppose the campaign—and the name of such opponents is legion—it is not because they are hostile to the protection of Sunday as a day of physical and spiritual refreshment and a day of rest for men and women who toil. It is not because they regard the general statement of the purpose of the campaign as wrong. It is because the moment the crusaders pass from a general statement of purpose to the details of their program, they fly in the face of all the elementary facts of human nature, perpetrate a travesty upon Christianity, and attempt to start the United States pell-mell back to the now happily forgotten witch-burning days when certain of our New England ancestors confused their own intolerant egotism with the purposes of God. Regardless of the loftiness of their purpose, they are attempting to loose forces that will make for a renaissance of the ugliest and most inhuman aspects of Puritanism.

Propagandists propose the outlawing of every sort of sport on Sunday. Baseball must go. Not one turn of the reel must be allowed to the movie film. The guardians of the Sabbath will not be fooled by so-called sacred concerts; they do not believe they are sacred. The Sunday newspaper must come under the ban. All public parks must be cleared of Sunday ball games. Interstate commerce must halt on Sunday. Cool waters of the sea must call in vain to anxious bathers on sweltering Sundays. All Sunday excursions must stop. The workman of a congested district must not be so sinful as to want to take his family out of the city for a breath of air and bath of sunlight on Sunday. Candy-stores must lock their doors on Sundays. The delicatessen, to which overworked housewives are wont to turn for their Sunday evening meal, must serve its public in six days a week. The great army of indoor men who depend upon the Sunday golf game for ozone and exercise must relegate cleek and brassy to the attic on Sunday and content themselves with calisthenics. The tennis-player must put aside his racket on Sunday. The Sunday schedule of street-cars, subway-cars and steam-trains must be cut to the irreducible minimum. And children must not study their Monday lessons on Sunday.

All this the self-appointed guardians of the Sabbath would enforce by law. Doesn't all this hark back the least bit to the old Puritan law, that read:

"This court, taking notice of great abuse and many misdemeanors committed by divers persons in their many ways, do therefore order that whosoever profane the Lord's day by doing unnecessary servile work, by unnecessary travailing, or by sports and recreations, he or they that so transgress shall forfeit for every such default 40 shillings or be publickly whipt; but if it clearly appear that sin was proudly and presumptiously and with a high hand committed, against the known command and the authoritie of the blessed God, such a person shall be put to death or grievously punished at the judgment of the court."

Those old Puritans never doubted that their personal notions were infallible interpretations of the "known command and authoritie of the blessed God." They had private back stairs access to the infinite. It never occurred to them that an intolerant god is the ignoblest work of man. We can smile at the assumed infallibility of our dead ancestors, but when the ghost of their narrow conceptions of God and life begins to walk again among us, reinforced by the inevitable efficiency of modern propaganda, it behooves us to realize that all the humaner conceptions of life we have slowly attained are menaced.

I am not being carried away by the usual panic over personal liberty. I realize that almost every advance step toward a better social organization has been resisted by men who cried that their personal liberties were being outraged. The fact is that the history of human progress has been one continued story, without an instalment missing, of restrictions upon personal liberty. Just as, it may be said in passing, every real advance towards a more decent administration of international relations must involve some loss of national sovereignty. The most damning indictment against the present-day advocates of blue laws is not that they purpose to interfere with the personal liberty of the citizen. I can think of many interferences with personal liberty that might prove a blessing to the country. We might, with no small benefit to the country, experiment with a few restrictions upon the personal liberty of certain profiteers in the setting of prices, not to mention the occasional landlord who sees fit to make hay while the sun shines upon an acute housing situation. If the crusaders for a saner Sunday proposed restrictions upon the personal liberty of the citizens that were economically, sociologically, or religiously sound, we might join their ranks.

But their detailed proposals haven't a leg to stand on. Their program is based upon a false notion of Christianity. It is a glaring instance of good intentions gone wrong. I want to emphasize these two fundamental errors of the playless Sunday program, the false notion of rest and the false notion of Christianity. It is upon these two counts that the blue-laws crusade will be defeated, if defeated at all. The cry of "personal liberty" will be so much wasted breath. The truth is that the average American citizen will talk more about and do less to defend his personal liberty than the citizen of almost any other free country on the globe. But if the average American fully realizes that the playless Sunday is not only a bad thing for the nation physically, but that it is essentially un-Christian, he may be immune to the propagandist's plea. This, I am convinced, is true.

There are two books—books that have been off the press for a long time—which I fear the crusaders for a playless Sunday have not read understandingly. They are the dictionary and the New Testament. I suspect that the advocates of blue laws have read the Old Testament faithfully, for their program is strangely reminiscent of many severe, unrealistic, not to say inhuman regulations recorded in the Old Testament—regulations which Jesus pronounced obsolete when he announced his more generous régime of justice and love and flung to the world his gospel of the more abundant life.

I want these crusaders to read the dictionary in order to learn the elementary fact that rest is not of necessity the calm and repressed process their program implies. After I have been at my desk for six days, it is quite possible that a brisk game of tennis on Sunday will "rest" me more than the whole day spent in an easy-chair; it is even possible that a game of tennis early on Sunday morning will clear my brain and put me in a better mood for service and sermon later in the forenoon. The advocates of a playless Sunday might suggest that a long walk would serve the same purpose. But I refuse to see the subtle spiritual distinction between the slow motion of my legs while walking and the swifter motion of my legs in a tennis game. The only chance multiplied thousands of men and women from offices, stores, and factories have to romp and play and find genuine rest from their work is in the ball games and tennis games in our parks on Sunday or in a round of golf. To deny them this would be a calamity to physical America. Blue laws are the advance agents of indigestion and flabby muscles. I do not mean that the American

Sunday should be turned into a sports carnival. I agree that the man who chases a dollar for six days of the week and a golf-ball on the seventh, with never a thought of "God or home or native land," is simply an undesirable citizen. I agree that materialistic America needs to give more time to the things of the mind and spirit. But that cannot be insured by a return to the cheerless régime of pre-Christian and Puritan days. The Puritan Sabbath was not a day of rest. I will venture the guess that the old Puritans were more tired on Monday morning than upon any other morning of the week.

Glenn Frank, *An American Looks at His World* (Newark, University of Delaware Press, 1923), 124–131.

---

106. Prohibition (1923)

BY PRESIDENT EMERITUS CHARLES W. ELIOT

Dr. Eliot, President of Harvard University from 1869 to 1909, was one of the great leaders of American thought. He did much to improve educational methods and standards in both colleges and secondary schools, and was notable for his intelligent faith in the American character. For other matter by the same author see Nos. 141 and 206 below.—Bibliography: Howard Lee McBain, *Prohibition, Legal and Illegal*.

. . . I REMEMBER well that, twenty years ago or thereabouts, I was entertained by the Harvard Club of Louisiana at a large dinner in the city of New Orleans, where I sat next to a gentleman who was generally recognized in New Orleans as the leader of their Bar. I noticed the moment we sat down that there was an extraordinary variety of things to drink on the table; and I also noticed that my neighbor took everything that was passed and in large quantity, so much so that I began to be a little anxious about his condition later. But suddenly he turned to me and said, "Mr. President, do you know that the New Orleans Bar, and I as its leader, are going in for complete prohibition in the State of Louisiana?" I could not help expressing surprise that *he* was going in for that. Whereupon he said, "Well, you don't suppose that we, the members of the Bar, expect to have the law applied to us, do you?" (*Laughter*) He was positively a vigorous advocate of complete prohibition for

Louisiana, but all the time had not the slightest notion that a pro-hibitory law could be applied to him or any of his friends, or would be.

That opened my eyes somewhat in regard to the expectation with which the sudden, unanimous support of prohibition came to pass in the Southern States. It was nearly unanimous, you remember, and remains so to this day. The Southern States are the strongest supporters in this country of prohibitory legislation.

Then, some time later, I found myself attending a Harvard Club dinner in the State of Missouri. There were many things to drink at that dinner also. I was informed that some of the leading citizens of Missouri, engaged in manufacturing operations, were going to move their plants over into the State of Kansas. I observed later that a large number of Missouri manufacturers did move their plants over into the State of Kansas, and learned, on inquiry, that those manufacturers had made up their minds that they could conduct their businesses much better in a State where a prohibitory law existed than they could in a State where the law did not exist.

I have had the delight of passing my summers for more than forty years—yes, it is fifty-two years since I first began to go to Mount Desert in summer—in the State of Maine. There I observed that the prohibitory law in Maine was not observed at all excepting in com-munities where, as one guest has said to-night, the great majority of the population was in favor of prohibition. There alone was the distribution of alcoholic drinks restrained. I lived there fifty summers, observing the fact that the prohibitory law in Maine was not generally enforced; observing that the summer residents of the State of Maine, who, as you know, live all along the shore and in several of the beautiful lake regions, paid no attention to the prohibitory law.

What inference did I draw from that experience? Simply that un-less the strong majority of any government unit in the States where prohibitory laws exist was in favor of prohibition, the law would, as a matter of fact, not be enforced.

But further: It was obvious that no single State could possibly enforce prohibition, because it had no power to prevent the manu-facture of alcoholic drinks outside the State or their importation into it. You must have national prohibition to make prohibition effective. It must be nation-wide, or it simply cannot be enforced.

So I supported for many years in Massachusetts, not prohibition, but local option; but then I learned that the sale of distilled liquors in saloons licensed to sell light wines and beer cannot be prevented. Nobody should advocate the repeal of the Volstead Act except those who believe in the unrestricted sale of alcoholic beverages. I ought perhaps to say that I took wine or beer when I was in the society of people who were using them. I never had any habit of drinking them at home; but I always took them when I was in the company of men or women who were using them. I had no feeling that alcohol was bad for everybody, or bad for me. I never knew alcohol to do me any harm; but then I never drank distilled liquors at all. When the United States in the spring of 1917 went to war, you remember that with the support of all the best civilian authorities and of the officers in the Army and Navy, our Government enacted a prohibitory law for the regions surrounding the camps and barracks where the National Army was being assembled. The Act proved to be effective and highly beneficent.

Then I said to myself, "If that is the action of my Government to protect our soldiers and sailors preparing to go to war, I think it is time for me to abstain from alcoholic drinks altogether." It is only since 1917 that I have been a total abstainer; but that is now six years ago, and I want to testify here, now, that by adopting total abstinence, after having had the opposite habit for over seventy years, one loses no joys that are worth having, and there is no joy-killing about it. On the contrary, I enjoy social life and working life more since I ceased to take any alcohol than I did before.

That talk, gentlemen, about joy-killing and pleasure-losing, and so forth, is absolute nonsense for a man who has any sense himself. . . .

We all know that our Puritan ancestors and our Pilgrim ancestors were not persons who cultivated the finer joys of life. They left behind them the great architecture of England, and its parks and its music. The Pilgrims came over from Holland, having lived there for ten or fifteen years in sight of all the glorious Dutch paintings, sculpture, and architecture. They abandoned all those things, and settled in the wilderness, where there was little possibility of cultivating the love of beauty and little power, too, of resisting the theological dogmas they had imbibed, which taught that human nature was utterly depraved, and that most of the human race were bound for a fiery hell.

Those are the people from whom the leading thinkers and doers of America sprang; and it is naturally inevitable that we, their descendants, should lack the love of beauty in nature and in art, and even in music. We do lack it. The Pilgrims and the Puritans lacked it to an extraordinary degree.

Where did they find their pleasures? Largely in drink. They drank hard at weddings, funerals, and all public festivals. We have that inheritance, but can we not resist and overcome it? Can we not grow up into a love of beauty in nature and in art? Can we not cultivate in ourselves the delight in music—in singing and in playing instruments? We are not hopeless in those respects; and those are the things we have got to learn to love, in order to escape from this wretched evil of alcoholism.

But how shall we do it? We must cultivate in ourselves the finer inspirations, the purer delights, and the greater joys in art and in work. But, more than that, we have got to practise resistance to acknowledged manifest evils in our common life.

That has always been my way of living, from day to day, in the practice of my profession. From the beginning, that was the way I lived. I attacked what seemed to me a plain, acknowledged, manifest evil, and advocated the best remedy I knew for that evil. That is just what we have got to do to-day, gentlemen, about this abominable evil of alcoholism associated with venereal disease; because that evil will kill us unless we kill it. By "us" I mean the white race, and particularly the American stock. Must we not accept the proposition that we must either destroy alcoholism and venereal disease, or those evils will destroy us? I believe that to be the plain truth; and I want to call on every lover of his kindred and of his country, hourly, daily, year after year, to contend against these evils, alcoholism and venereal disease, until they are obliterated from the world. Finally, may we not reasonably distrust the legal view that has been repeatedly presented here this evening, namely, that the rights and privileges of decent and vigorous people should not be abridged for the sake of indecent or weak people who abuse their privileges?

Charles W. Eliot, address before The Economic Club of Boston, March 6, 1923, in *A Late Harvest* (Boston, Atlantic Monthly Press, 1924), 261–267 *passim*. Copyright by Charles W. Eliot; reprinted by permission.

107.   Legislating Morals (1924)

BY CLARENCE S. DARROW

This is an extract from an article opposing the national prohibition legislation, written by one of the most widely known members of the bar. Mr. Darrow has interested himself in a variety of liberal causes and has appeared in numerous famous cases, many of them concerned with matters of social importance or humanitarian interests. He is a professed agnostic. This article is to be contrasted with No. 106 above.—Bibliography as in No. 106. *American Year Book*, Vols. 1925–1929.

. . . THE English criminal code is filled with examples of the process of getting rid of legislation by disuse. Up to the beginning of the last century more than two hundred offenses were punishable by death in England, including loitering and loafing, petty larceny and poaching. The scaffold had its thousands of victims, but crime increased. Finally juries refused to convict, judges found excuses, the laws became dead letters, and eventually they passed into the rubbish heap. They were repealed in the end because they encumbered the books and no longer had any vital force. The humanizing of the English penal code came from the fact that juries would not convict. They were too humane and decent to obey the laws.

The history of the past is carried into the present. All our codes are filled with obsolete laws. The Fugitive Slave Law was never obeyed in the North; it took more than a law to compel a humane white man to send a black man back to slavery. The Sunday laws today in many states of the Union forbid the publication of newspapers, the running of trains and street cars, riding and driving for pleasure, attending moving picture shows, playing any game, the starting out of boats on voyages, or doing of any work except works of necessity. Nearly all these laws are dead, though they still remain on the books. They are dead because they do not fit the age. They are not now a part of the customs, habits and mores of the people. They could not be enforced.

After the Civil War the Constitution was amended to abolish slavery and provide equality between whites and blacks. Congress and most of the Northern States thereupon passed explicit legislation forbidding any discrimination between the races in public places, such as hotels, theatres, railroad trains, street cars, restaurants and the like. But these laws, as everyone knows, are now openly ignored. The Negro does not go to the good hotels; he does not have good seats in the theatre; he does not enter the best restaurants; is not permitted to mingle with the whites, or to get what the whites believe belongs exclusively to them. This is not only true in the South; it is rapidly becoming a fact in the North. Custom and habit override the law because of the deep prejudice of the white against social equality with the black. Any effort to enforce these laws would bring serious consequences either North or South, and would no doubt injure the condition and standing of the black man, which can only be improved by a long process of education and growth. It cannot come from passing laws. All sorts of gambling is forbidden by the statutes of the various States. This includes betting and playing cards for money or prizes; it includes raffles even at church fairs. Yet most Americans gamble in some way or other—and are not prosecuted.

The Anti-Trust Act is a notorious example of legislation that is not enforced and cannot be enforced. Only a few prosecutions have ever been brought under it, and even when a prosecution has been successful ample means have been found to accomplish the desired ends in spite of the law. It has never kept Big Business from organizing and combining. It never can or should. Nevertheless, Big Business, through complaisant law officers and courts, has been able to enforce it against organizations of workingmen that engage in strikes. This is done in spite of the fact that it was passed in the interest of workmen and consumers and to control Big Business.

No one who has property believes in the tax laws. No one obeys them or pretends to obey them. When speaking of these laws no one shouts from the housetops the silly doctrine that a law must be enforced because it is on the books. No one even quotes the foolish statement of General Grant that the "best way to repeal a bad law is to enforce it." No doubt Grant was a good soldier, but he was never suspected of being a philosopher or an historian. The way to get rid of a bad law, which means a law obnoxious to large masses of people, is not by trying to keep it alive, but by letting it die a natural death. This is the way that society has always followed in dealing with unjust laws. The tax laws are a part of our civil and criminal codes, yet those who shout the loudest for enforcing Prohibition never pretend to obey them. When a man argues that a law must be enforced so long as it is a law, or that the best way to repeal a bad law is to enforce it, he is talking about some law he wants enforced and not about a law that he believes is tyrannical and unjust. . . .

It is much easier to pass a law than to repeal an old one. Legislation which represents special interests or is demanded by organized associations which make a great show of power before law-making bodies is seldom met by strong opposition. The force which demands the law is active and persistent; its insistence leads politicians to believe that a large mass of men is behind it. But when the statute goes into effect it may create serious oppression and violent disorder; it may come into conflict with the desires and prejudices of the majority of the people affected by it. But, once it is on the books, an active minority can easily prevent its repeal. It is only by the steady resistance of the people that it is eventually destroyed.

In spite of the common opinion, this method has always been the ruling one in getting rid of bad laws. It is Nature's way of letting the old die by opposition, neglect and disuse. If it were not in operation there could be no real progress in the law. If history were not replete with illustrations, if philosophy did not plainly show that this must be the method of society's growth, it would be easier to understand the people who so glibly argue that, whatever the cruelty of the hardship, the law must be enforced while it is on the books. A law cannot be taken off the books while it is complacently obeyed. Constant protest is the only manner that history offers the common people of having their way in the making and administration of the law.

All this, of course, does not mean that all laws are or should be habitually violated. The larger part of our criminal code represents the ideas of right and wrong of nearly all our people. But the sumptuary laws that regulate individual conduct and custom are never believed in by the great mass of the people. Men, unfortunately, are in the habit of being influenced by aphorisms and catchwords. We continually hear of "Law and Order," as if they always went together and law came first. As a matter of fact, order is the mother of law, and the law which seriously overturns habits and customs does not promote order, but interferes with it instead. The enforcement of an unpopular law by drastic threats, by increasing penalties, by more cruelty, is not the administration of justice; it is tyranny under the form of law. . . .

A great part of the misconception about the power of law comes from the assumption that the social group is held together by law. As a matter of fact, the group came into being long before the statutes. It formed itself automatically under the law of the survival of the fittest. The group is always changing in accordance with this natural law. Even statutes and courts are powerless when they stand in its way. . . .

All laws are made, altered and amended in the same way. When a large class does not respect them, but believes them to be tyrannical, unjust or oppressive, they cannot be enforced. It is a popular idea that the majority should rule. But this does not mean that the people should vote on every question affecting human life, and that the majority should then pass penal statutes to make the rest conform. No society can hold together that does not have a broad toleration for minorities. To enforce the obedience of minorities by criminal statute because a mere majority is found to have certain views is tyranny and must result in endless disorder and suffering.

When the advocates of Prohibition urge that all laws must be enforced, they really refer to the Prohibition laws. They do not refer to the numerous other laws in every State in the Union that have never been enforced. Even the drastic Volstead Act has not prevented and cannot prevent the use of alcoholic beverages. The acreage of grapes has rapidly increased since it was passed and the price gone up with the demand. The government is afraid to interfere with the farmer's cider. The fruit grower is making money. The dandelion is now the national flower. Everyone who wants alcoholic beverages is fast learning how to make them at home. In the old days the housewife's education was not complete unless she had learned how to brew. She lost the art because it became cheaper to buy beer. She has lost the art of making bread in the same way, for she can buy bread at the store. But she can learn to make bread again, for she has already learned to brew. It is evident that no law can now be passed to prevent her. Even should Congress pass such a law, it would be impossible to find enough Prohibition agents to enforce it, or to get the taxes to pay them. The folly of the attempt must soon convince even the more intelligent Prohibitionists that all this legislation is both a tragedy and a hoax.

A wise ruler studies the customs and habits of his people and tries to fit laws and institutions to their folkways, knowing perfectly well that any other method will cause violence and evil; he knows that fitting laws to men is like fitting clothes to men. The man comes first and both the laws and the clothes should be fitted to him. Instead of increasing penalties, stimulating cruelty, and redoubling the search for violators, he should take a lesson from Trajan, the Roman Emperor, as shown by his correspondence with Pliny. About the year 112, when the campaign against the Christians was in full sway in the Empire Pliny, who was the governor of a province, wrote to Trajan for instructions as to how to carry on the prosecutions. The Emperor replied: "Do not go out of your way to look for them."

Clarence S. Darrow, *The Ordeal of Prohibition*, in *The American Mercury* (New York, 1924), II, 423–427 *passim*. Reprinted by permission of the author.

---

108. Criminal Syndicalism (1925)

BY WILLIAM SEAGLE

Seagle is a New York lawyer. For related matters see Nos. 173 and 194 below.— Bibliography: Z. Chafee, Jr., *Freedom of Speech, The Inquiring Mind;* Walter Lippmann, *Liberty and the News;* J. G. Brooks, *American Syndicalism: The I. W. W.;* Victor L. Berger, *Testimony at His Trial in Illinois;* Morris Hillquit, *Socialism in the United States.*

. . . THE Criminal Syndicalism statutes in general all have a common design, with clauses as standardized as those of fire and life insurance policies. They forbid the advocacy of the duty, necessity, or propriety of committing sabotage or other violence as a means of accomplishing changes in industrial ownership or control, or of effecting political change. To attempt to justify criminal syndicalism or to publish matter advocating or justifying the same is also *verboten*. The criminal anarchy laws make it unlawful to preach the doctrine that organized government should be overthrown by force and violence. Besides, mere membership in a syndicalist or anarchistic organization is usually made criminal, and any two persons who unite to urge such doctrines are declared to be conspirators. A meeting-house used by them acquires the legal status of a house of ill-fame: to let a hall to them is prohibited.

Some special features are provided in several of the States out of an abundance of caution. For example:

1. In Massachusetts, where the act in general is mild, it is curiously specific to the effect that the accused may be arrested without a warrant.

2. The Washington act, without providing for immunity, declares that no witness in a sedition case may refuse to testify on the conventional ground that his evidence may incriminate him.

3. The Colorado act imposes the penalty of first degree murder for any death that is the result of its violation; thus, a speaker who makes a speech which is held to be seditious may receive the death penalty if a fatal riot occurs afterward.

4. The Kentucky act states as a matter of law what is elsewhere the usual rule in practice—that "in any prosecution under this act it shall not be necessary to prove any overt act on the part of the accused." . . .

In general, the penalties provided are extremely savage, running on the average to ten years. In six States, Colorado, Iowa, Louisiana, Montana, New Jersey and Pennsylvania, a sentence of twenty years may be imposed; in Kentucky, twenty-one years, and in South Dakota no less than twenty-five years. The timid law-makers seem to forget that homicide and the destruction of property are already punishable under the ordinary criminal law, and that what they make *malum prohibitum* is simply excitable or prophetic language. . . . Perhaps, the solons of Connecticut deserve the prize for the law which outlaws all persons who "before any assemblage of ten or more persons advocate in any language any measure, doctrine, proposal or propaganda intended to *injuriously affect* the government of the United States or the State of Connecticut."

Turn now to New Hampshire, a near neighbor to Connecticut. It not only has no criminal syndicalism or sedition laws, but its constitution, like that of Maryland, specifically recognizes the right of revolution, as witness:

The doctrine of non-resistance against arbitrary power and oppression is absurd, slavish and destructive of the good and happiness of mankind.

Thus in Connecticut it is a high crime to read before ten citizens the constitution of New Hampshire! . . .

Ten State Supreme Courts have formally sustained and approved these idiotic statutes. The anarchy and sedition laws have been held valid in New York, Pennsylvania, and Illinois, and the criminal syndicalist acts in Idaho, Minnesota, Oregon, Washington, Michigan, Kansas, and California. Beside, the Connecticut courts, for all practical purposes, may be said to have approved its sedition law when they decided that even if it was unconstitutional an alien could not plead its infirmity. In order to shut out aliens from the right to liberty as "persons" under the Fourteenth Amendment, the Connecticut Dogberries exhumed a case of pre-Civil War vintage in which it was held that slaves were not freed by coming upon free soil of the State. . . .

There has been developed in California a convicting machine with an almost ideal technique. Indeed, it is practically flawless. While all good Californians, including judges, know that all wobblies [members of the Industrial Workers of the World] are criminals *per se*, the ancient forms of the Common Law relating to evidence unfortunately require that in every prosecution the alleged criminal character of the organization to which the accused belongs must be established by competent testimony. In other words, one not a wobbly cannot testify as to the nature and purposes of the I. W. W. without violating the hearsay rule. The difficulty appears formidable, but it has been met in a formidable manner. The State of California at great expense ($250 a day and expenses!) has hired three patriotic men, all former members of the I. W. W., to be professional witnesses. One of them has admitted in court that he was once convicted of theft, arson, and perjury. Another, affectionately known as Three-Fingered Jack, has served a sentence for the rape of a twelve-year-old girl. The third has confessed that he has deserted from the Army and Navy eleven times. Court records, moreover, show that he has been confined in a government insane asylum. He once admitted on the witness stand that he had never told the truth before in his life. He has appeared as an "expert" against the I. W. W. nine times, testifying to his harrowing experiences while a member.

Naturally enough, an I. W. W., confronted by such professionals, seeks "expert" testimony himself to prove that his organization is innocent. But this is simply jumping out of the frying pan into the fire. For example, consider the case of two I. W. W.'s who went on trial for criminal syndicalism in Sacramento county in April, 1922. Ten witnesses, fellow I. W. W.'s were put on the stand by the heedless defence to prove that the I. W. W. organization did not advocate force and violence. There ensued a very droll episode. On the spot the ten I. W. W. witnesses were arrested, and the admission of membership which they had made on the stand was the offence with which they were charged! After two juries had disagreed, all ten were convicted of criminal syndicalism in January, 1923, and got from one to fourteen years at San Quentin! . . .

. . . But the readiest weapon for dealing with radical meetings comes from the licensing power of municipalities. The Constitution guarantees the right of free speech, but where is the citizen to exercise that right? The public streets, squares, and parks of a democracy would occur to most men as suitable places. But a joker lies in the fact that the State is held to have full control over all public places, and may therefore forbid their use in its discretion. The law requires a license to be obtained, usually from the mayor, before a meeting may be held in the streets or parks. The mayors of the United States early awoke to the use which they could make of this licensing power to curb laborites and radicals, and it is only to such scoundrels that licenses are refused. Since it is practically impossible to prove an abuse of discretion, little relief can be had from the courts. . . .

In many American cities the police have even forbidden meetings in private halls, and labor unions have been prevented from holding their regular business meetings in their own quarters. . . . The proprietors of halls are given to understand that if they insist on hiring them to dangerous citizens the police will get after them. The multitudinous regulations of the fire and health and tenement-house codes are discreetly mentioned, and it is hinted to the proprietors that if they insist they will one day find themselves with their licenses revoked upon some technicality. It is practically impossible to secure judicial review in such cases.

A lawyer can no longer advise a client as to his rights merely upon the basis of the law upon the books. He has to acquaint himself also with constabulary jurisprudence. The rules are frequently couched in very unjudicial language. Thus, the police commonly assume that a speaker who addresses a meeting in a foreign language means no good; as a jurist might put it, such a meeting is only conditionally privileged. In many places, the police regard the possession of such papers as the *New Republic* or the *Nation* as *prima facie* evidence of criminal intent. They also have their own sedition law, which forbids making speeches that are "too radical." They hold that it is criminal in all cases to resist arrest, and that all meetings are criminal which are likely to be disturbed.

It will perhaps have been noticed that I have been able to muster but little eloquence on the subject of the Constitution. The truth is that we are rapidly approaching, if we have not already reached, the bankruptcy of constitutionalism. The doctrine of fundamental and inalienable rights, after a century and a half, is in rapid decay. The cream of the jest is that, as the old rights come more and more flagrantly to be violated, precisely those States where they are most at a discount hasten forward with statutes making instruction in the Constitution compulsory in the public schools.

William Seagle, in *The American Mercury* (New York, 1926), VII, 36-42 *passim*. Reprinted by permission of the author.

------◆------

109. Politics and Crime (1926)

BY PROFESSOR RAYMOND MOLEY

Moley is Associate Professor of Government at Columbia University. He has written many books on political and sociological subjects.—For additional information on crime in its political aspects, see No. 100 above.

THE startling crime rate in the United States is probably due to the defects in the administration of justice. Certainly it seems unlikely that any of the current popular guesses as to the causes of our regrettable situation, such as "the aftermath of the war," the high tide of immigration, or the effects of the Volstead Act, are to be seriously credited. And wherein the administration of justice fails to work smoothly, it fails because it is compelled to operate under the handicap of politics. From arrest to conviction, from sentence to release, political influences are present, and wherever they are present they are pernicious. . . .

A judiciary composed of strong independent personalities with fine standards of propriety and a sense of responsibility not only for what happens in the court room, but for other related segments of the process of justice, could do much to restore the prestige of the administration of justice in every state. But such leadership, except in scattered instances, is impossible when the judiciary is so exposed to political influences. Judges must get elected, and so conduct themselves as to attain re-election. The term, in an overwhelming number of states, is six years or less, a period not long enough to permit even the newly elected judge to forget the necessity of building his following for the next election. A distinguished member of the Bar, who had served a term on a state supreme court, said this in private conversation:

I could not bring myself to run for re-election. It meant constant breaking in upon the time which a judge, sensitive to the quality of his written opinions, should give to study. It meant traveling from town to town, climbing stairways to the offices of professionally unworthy but politically powerful lawyers. It meant accepting invitations to attend meetings of every sort, to speak on topics representing every kind of irrelevance. It meant accepting familiarities from the unworthy without flinching, rejecting improper requests without administering the rebuke which they deserved. It was a hard choice, for I wanted the office, but the price was more than I could pay.

If this is the verdict when the office is so far removed from political influences as is the state's highest court, what must be the humiliation which our political system visits upon the judges of county and municipal courts! . . .

Next in importance to the Bench, in the enforcement of law, is the prosecutor. The discretionary powers of this office are so great that pressure for favors of various kinds is continuous, and often politically irresistible. The possibility of building political influence through the use of this office is so tempting that it becomes the very keystone of the county ring in most of the three thousand counties in American states. In large cities, the assistant prosecutors are often chosen with a view not to specialization in the types of cases tried, but with reference to the nationalities most common in the city. Thus, the Italians, if numerous, are represented by a member of their race who meets with those fellow-nationals who find their way into the toils of the law, or who, perhaps, are concerned with someone else who has been so unfortunate. Favors, or promises of favors, constitute a tremendous source of political power. The political leaders of that nationality operate through this representative, and each finds the other useful, while both contribute to the power of the machine.

The prosecutor's office has become, moreover, a place where careers are started. This is especially true in rural communities. The prosecutor is young. According to the Missouri Survey of Criminal Justice, just reaching completion, the median age of prosecutors in that state is from twenty-five to twenty-nine years; the median number of years of experience is from one to four. Thus the prosecutor's office is the first step in a political career. . . .

One of the results of the political nature of this office is the tendency of prosecutors to give undue attention to spectacular cases, to the neglect of that much larger class of cases, important in themselves but not likely to attract widespread attention. This means that while the prosecutor may devote tremendous energy to securing the conviction of a few notorious criminals, he is likely to permit a large proportion of cases to go to trial with only indifferent preparation. . . .

The discretionary power of the prosecutor has been mentioned. This means, in most jurisdictions, that he may refuse to permit a case to proceed from arrest to the first hearing by refusing to issue a warrant. In the Missouri Survey already cited, it was found that, in the city of St. Louis over a considerable period of time, the prosecutor refused 972 out of 2464 applications for warrants. This is only the beginning of the exercise of discretion. Most cases are disposed of before trial by a *"nolle pros";* which is in fact decided upon by the prosecutor, by dismissal in the preliminary hearing, or by a "no bill" by the grand jury. The prosecutor dominates the grand jury, and often quite effectively influences the decision in the preliminary hearing. In both of these instances he may actually dispose of the case without formally assuming responsibility. His power over the criminal case is practically decisive. He is, then, politically the key to the whole process of law enforcement. . . .

Everyone is familiar with the politics of police departments. It found a new and picturesque expression during General Butler's tenure in Philadelphia. Another chief of a very large city said in confidence: "I couldn't last ten days if I permitted my force to attack crime as they really could attack it." It is possible that this chief was overstating the case, but his statement would meet with agreement by chiefs in other cities. One city had an "unofficial" chief who managed appointments, assignments and promotions. He brought about some raids and prevented others. The official chief knew of his operations and resented them, but was powerless to prevent them. A commissioner in one of the few cities in the United States which still remains under state control, said: "How am I going to avoid politics in the police department? I am in politics." . . .

We have already indicated that politics is not always based upon political party divisions. It may be most deeply rooted in religious, racial or some other interest in the community. . . . Another form of "pull" was shown in New York during the last months of the Hylan administration. An actress appearing at two theatres was for several nights transported from one to the other with a police escort. The accounts of eyewitnesses claimed a speed for her limousine of fifty miles an hour. Traffic was held for her, and thus, with the aid of the police, she secured all of the advertising that the "White Way" could afford.

Thus the whole process of justice from arrest to pardon is colored, if not dominated, by political influences. These influences are not entirely party influences; they represent in large part those political forces which are less responsible, such as the newspaper press, economic interests, immigrant groups and others.

There are other general relationships between politics and crime which present a more immediate problem. One of these is the effect of the rising tide of liquor. In December of last year, there were convicted at one time in a Federal district court a score of defendants on a charge of conspiracy. Among them were a number of prominent politicians of St. Louis and of Cincinnati. There were office-holders, including the Harding appointee to the Internal Revenue Collectorship in St. Louis. The act out of which the charges grew was the stealing of liquor from a warehouse, to the value of nearly a million dollars, and the use of the liquor in bootlegging. The drag net of the Department of Justice caught the entire group, from the "higher ups" to those who had actually performed the criminal acts. The personnel of the group thus captured is a very interesting example of the operation of criminal groups everywhere. There are connections with politicians and office-holders high in power, with ample money drawn from the business in which they were engaged and with influence which, in a mere state case, might have prevented any successful prosecutions.

The money now available from bootlegging operations is a very important factor in the problem of crime generally. It furnishes the sinews of war when the police are engaged more actively than usual in making arrests. It buys bondsmen and the property which bondsmen pledge. It employs able lawyers for defense, and it purchases influence. This element of corruption has so affected the administration of justice that it is most certainly to be named a major cause of crime. . . .

After an experience extending to an intimate contact for several years with this question, a contact which has included participation in the two major investigations of the field made in Cleveland and in Missouri, the writer of this article is brought to the conclusion that *of all causes of the mounting tide of crime in America, the political aspect is the most important.* New laws and new scientific discoveries will not avail much. Increased severity of punishment can accomplish very little. The institutions which are charged with law enforcement are too intimately bound to political interests. The influence of the political factors suggested in the preceding paragraphs must bear the major responsibility for the "crime wave." Thirty years ago, the government of the American city was called a failure by Lord Bryce because its politics had become utterly corrupted by public contracts and public utilities. To-day, more profitable interests have found lodgment in the processes of justice.

Raymond Moley, in *Annals of the American Academy of Political and Social Science* (Philadelphia, May, 1926), CXXV, 78–84 *passim.*

CHAPTER XXI — LABOR AND INDUSTRY

110. A Laborer Meets His First Capitalist (1900)

BY SECRETARY JAMES J. DAVIS (1922)

This extract is from the autobiography of a Welsh immigrant boy who made a name and place for himself in America, lent his energies to a variety of public-spirited undertakings, and served in the cabinets of Presidents Harding, Coolidge and Hoover, as Secretary of Labor. He early saw the importance of the organization of labor and the necessity also of avoiding arbitrary power. He had good success in the pacific settlement of labor disputes.—Bibliography: Samuel Gompers, *Seventy Years of Life and Labor;* David Karsner, *Debs, his Life and Letters;* F. F. Carlton, *Problems of Organized Labor;* Selig Perlman, *Trade Unionism in the United States; American Year Book*, Vols. 1910–1919, 1925, articles on Labor.

ELWOOD, Indiana, was a small village that had been called Duck Creek Post-Office until the tin mill and other industries began making it into a city. In my capacity as president of the local union and head of the mill wage committee, I was put in personal contact with the heads of these great industrial enterprises. This was my first introduction to men of large affairs.

I approached them with the inborn thought that they must be some sort of human monsters. The communist books that Comrade Bannerman had given me taught me to believe that capitalists had no human feelings like ordinary mortals. I therefore expected to find the mill-boss as cunning as the fox and ape combined. I supposed that his word would be worthless as a pledge and would be given only for the purpose of tricking me. His manners I expected to be rude; he would shout at me and threaten me, hoping to take away my courage and send me back to my fellows beaten.

What I found, of course, was a self-possessed man, the model of courtesy and exactness. He differed from us men in one respect. His mind was complex instead of simplex. That is, he could think on two sides of a question at the same time. He had so trained his mind by much use of it that it was as nimble as the hands of a juggler who can keep several objects tossing in the air at the same time. We men were clumsy thinkers, and one thing at a time was all we could handle without fumbling it.

The great manufacturer never showed any emotion. He was never angry, domineering, sneering or insulting. He kept these emotions under control because they could do him no good, and because they would give pain to others. We fellows never hesitated to show how we felt. We would jibe one another, laugh at a fellow to his chagrin, and when we were angry bawl each other out unmercifully. For a fellow to smile when he was angry and not let the other fellow know it, was a trick we had not learned. That a bloodthirsty, cruel capitalist should be such a graceful fellow was a shock to me. I saw from the start that the communist picture of a capitalist as a bristling, snorting hog was the farthest thing from the truth. The picture was drawn by malice and not from a desire to tell the truth.

I learned that when Mr. Reid and his fellows gave their word they never broke it. It was hard to get a promise from them, but once they made a promise they always fulfilled it. If they said they would meet us at a certain hour, they were always there on the minute. They were patient, firm and reasonable, and they always treated us as their equals.

They always gave us the reasons for the stand they took. At first I doubted their sincerity, but in the end I learned that the reasons they cited were the true reasons. At first they thought that they would have to guard themselves against roguery and doubledealing on the part of the tin workers. This showed that they had had unpleasant experiences. For, men who knew their business as well as they did must surely have had some cause for their suspicion. Baseless suspicion is a trait of ignorant men, and these men were not ignorant. A burnt child dreads the fire.

I decided to take them as my models, to learn all their virtues and let them know that I was as square in my dealings with them as they were with me. I studied their business as thoroughly as I studied the case of the men. I soon got from them all the concessions we had demanded when we called the strike. It was fortunate for us that the strike was cancelled, for we kept our jobs and in due course got all the things we were going to strike for.

In fact, I got so many concessions by dickering with those bosses that I made life a burden for them at times. I knew the cost of every different kind of plate the mill put out, and so I could demand a high rate of wages and support my demands with logic. My midnight studies had not been in vain. It all came back in cash to the working man; and yet it was my own pals who had rebuked me for being too bookish. This did not make me sour. I loved the fellows just the same, and when they showed their faith in me, it more than paid me back.

But I had learned this general rule: The average working man thinks mostly of the present. He leaves to students and to capitalists the safeguarding of the future.

James J. Davis, *The Iron Puddler* (Indianapolis, Bobbs-Merrill Co., 1922), 191–194. Reprinted by special permission of the publishers.

———◆———

111.   The Courts and Labor (1908)

BY PRESIDENT THEODORE ROOSEVELT

For Roosevelt see Nos. 23–26 above.—Bibliography as in No. 110 above. See also No. 112 below.

AT the last election certain leaders of organized labor made a violent and sweeping attack upon the entire judiciary of the country, an attack couched in such terms as to include the most upright, honest, and broad-minded judges, no less than those of narrower mind and more restricted outlook. It was the kind of attack admirably fitted to prevent any successful attempt to reform abuses of the judiciary, because it gave the champions of the unjust judge their eagerly desired opportunity to shift their ground into a championship of just judges who were unjustly assailed.

Last year, before the House Committee on the Judiciary, these same labor leaders formulated their demands, specifying the bill that contained them, refusing all compromise, stating they wished the principle of that bill or nothing. They insisted on a provision that in a labor dispute no injunction should issue except to protect a property right, and specifically provided that the right to carry on business should not be construed as a property right, and in a second provision their bill made legal in a labor dispute any act or agreement by or between two or more persons that would not have been unlawful if done by a single person.

In other words, this bill legalized blacklisting and boycotting in every form—legalizing, for instance, those forms of the secondary boycott which the Anthracite Coal Strike Commission so unreservedly condemned; while the right to carry on a business was explicitly taken out from under that protection which the law throws over property. The demand was made that there should be trial by jury in contempt cases, thereby most seriously impairing the authority of the courts. All this represented a course of policy which, if carried out, would mean the enthronement of class privilege in its crudest and most brutal form, and the destruction of one of the most essential functions of the judiciary in all civilized lands.

The violence of the crusade for this legislation, and its complete failure, illustrate two truths which it is essential our people should learn. In the first place, they ought to teach the workingmen, the laborer, the wage-worker, that by demanding what is improper and impossible he plays into the hands of his foes.

Such a crude and vicious attack upon the courts, even if it were temporarily successful, would inevitably in the end cause a violent reaction and would band the great mass of citizens together, forcing them to stand by all the judges, competent and incompetent alike, rather than to see the wheels of justice stopped. A movement of this kind can ultimately result in nothing but damage to those in whose behalf it is nominally undertaken. This is a most healthy truth, which it is wise for all our people to learn.

Any movement based on that class hatred which at times assumes the name of "class consciousness" is certain ultimately to fail, and if it temporarily succeeds, to do far-reaching damage. "Class consciousness," where it is merely another name for the odious vice of class selfishness, is equally noxious whether in an employer's association or in a workingman's association.

The movement in question was one in which the appeal was made to all workingmen to vote primarily, not as American citizens, but as individuals of a certain class in society. Such an appeal in the first place revolts the more high-minded and far-sighted among the persons to whom it is addressed, and in the second place tends to arouse a strong antagonism among all other classes of citizens, whom it therefore tends to unite against the very organization on whose behalf it is issued. The result is therefore unfortunate from every standpoint. This healthy truth, by the way, will be learned by the socialists if they ever succeed in establishing in this country an important national party based on such class consciousness and selfish class interest.

The wage-workers, the workingmen, the laboring men of the country, by the way in which they repudiated the effort to get them to cast their votes in response to an appeal to class hatred, have emphasized their sound patriotism and Americanism. The whole country has cause to feel pride in this attitude of sturdy independence, in this uncompromising insistence upon acting simply as good citizens, as good Americans, without regard to fancied—and improper—class interests. Such an attitude is an object-lesson in good citizenship to the entire nation.

But the extreme reactionaries, the persons who blind themselves to the wrongs now and then committed by the courts on laboring men, should also think seriously as to what such a movement as this portends. The judges who have shown themselves able and willing effectively to check the dishonest activity of the very rich man who works iniquity by the mismanagement of corporations, who have shown themselves alert to do justice to the wage-worker, and sympathetic with the needs of the mass of our people, so that the dweller in the tenement houses, the man who practices a dangerous trade, the man who is crushed by excessive hours of labor, feel that their needs are understood by the courts—these judges are the real bulwark of the courts; these judges, the judges of the stamp of the President-elect, who have been fearless in opposing labor when it has gone wrong, but fearless also in holding to strict account corporations that work iniquity, and far-sighted in seeing that the workingman gets his rights, are the men of all others to whom we owe it that the appeal for such violent and mistaken legislation has fallen on deaf ears, that the agitation for its passage proved to be without substantial basis.

The courts are jeopardized primarily by the action of these Federal and State judges who show inability or unwillingness to put a stop to the wrongdoing of very rich men under modern industrial conditions, and inability or unwillingness to give relief to men of small means or wage-workers who are crushed down by these modern industrial conditions; who, in other words, fail to understand and apply the needed remedies for the new wrongs produced by the new and highly complex social and industrial civilization which has grown up in the last half-century.

Theodore Roosevelt, Message to Congress, December, 1908, in *Cong. Record*.

———◆———

112. The Labor Union Boycott (1915)

BY JUSTICE OLIVER WENDELL HOLMES

For Holmes see No. 101 above and No. 122 below.—Bibliography as in No. 110 above. See also No. 111 above.

. . . THIS is an action under the act of July 2, 1890, for a combination and conspiracy in restraint of commerce among the States, specifically directed against the plaintiffs, among others, and effectively carried out with the infliction of great damage. The declaration was held good on demurrer in Loewe *v.* Lawlor where it will be found set forth at length. The substance of the charge is that the plaintiffs were hat manufacturers who employed non-union labor; that the defendants were members of the United Hatters of North America and also of the American Federation of Labor; that in pursuance of a general scheme to unionize the labor employed by manufacturers of fur hats (a purpose previously made effective against all but a few manufacturers), the defendants and other members of the United Hatters caused the American Federation of Labor to declare a boycott against the plaintiffs and against all hats sold by the plaintiffs to dealers in other States and against dealers who should deal in them; and that they carried out their plan with such success that they have restrained or destroyed the plaintiff's commerce with other States. The case now has been tried, the plaintiffs have got a verdict, and the judgment of the District Court has been affirmed by the Circuit Court of Appeals.

The grounds for discussion under the statute that were not cut away by the decision upon the demurrer have been narrowed still further since the trial by the case of Eastern States Retail Lumber

Dealers' Association *v.* United States. Whatever may be the law otherwise, that case establishes that, irrespective of compulsion or even agreement to observe its intimation, the circulation of a list of "unfair dealers," manifestly intended to put the ban upon those whose names appear therein, among an important body of possible customers combined with a view to joint action and in anticipation of such reports, is within the prohibitions of the Sherman Act if it is intended to restrain and restrains commerce among the States.

It requires more than the blindness of justice not to see that many branches of the United Hatters and the Federation of Labor, to both of which the defendants belonged, in pursuance of a plan emanating from headquarters made use of such lists, and of the primary and secondary boycott in their effort to subdue the plaintiffs to their demands. The union label was used and a strike of the plaintiffs' employés was ordered and carried out to the same end, and the purpose to break up the plaintiffs' commerce affected the quality of the acts. We agree with the Circuit Court of Appeals that a combination and conspiracy forbidden by the statutes were proved, and that the question is narrowed to the responsibility of the defendants for what was done by the sanction and procurement of the societies above named.

The court in substance instructed the jury that if these members paid their dues and continued to delegate authority to their officers unlawfully to interfere with the plaintiffs' interstate commerce in such circumstances that they knew or ought to have known, and such officers were warranted in the belief that they were acting in the matters within their delegated authority, then such members were jointly liable, and no others. It seems to us that this instruction sufficiently guarded the defendants' rights and that the defendants got all that they were entitled to ask in not being held chargeable with knowledge as matter of law. It is a tax on credulity to ask anyone to believe that members of labor unions at that time did not know that the primary and secondary boycott and the use of the "We don't patronize" or "Unfair" list were means expected to be employed in the effort to unionize shops. Very possibly they were thought to be lawful. By the constitution of the United Hatters the directors are to use "all the means in their power" to bring shops "not under our jurisdiction" "into the trade." The by-laws provide a separate fund to be kept for strikes, lockouts, and agitation for the union label. Members are forbidden to sell non-union hats. The Federation of Labor with which the Hatters were affiliated had organization of labor for one of its objects, helped affiliated unions in trade disputes, and to that end, before the present trouble, had provided in its constitution for prosecuting and had prosecuted many what it called legal boycotts. Their conduct in this and former cases was made public especially among the members in every possible way. If the words of the documents on their face and without explanation did not authorize what was done, the evidence of what was done publicly and habitually showed their meaning and how they were interpreted. The jury could not but find that by the usage of the unions the acts complained of were authorized, and authorized without regard to their interference with commerce among the States. We think it unnecessary to repeat the evidence of the publicity of this particular struggle in the common newspapers and union prints, evidence that made it almost inconceivable that the defendants, all living in the neighborhood of the plaintiffs, did not know what was done in the specific case. If they did not know that, they were bound to know the constitutions of their societies, and at least well might be found to have known how the words of those constitutions had been constructed in the act.

It is suggested that injustice was done by the judge speaking of "proof" that in carrying out the object of the associations unlawful means had been used with their approval. The judge cautioned the jury with special care not to take their view of what had been proved from him, going even further than he need have gone. But the context showed plainly that proof was used here in a popular way for evidence and must have been understood in that sense.

Damages accruing since the action began were allowed, but only such as were the consequence of acts done before and constituting part of the cause of action declared on. This was correct. We shall not discuss the objections to evidence separately and in detail as we find no error requiring it. The introduction of newspapers, etc., was proper in large part to show publicity in places and directions where the facts were likely to be brought home to the defendants, and also to prove an intended and detrimental consequence of the principal acts, not to speak of other grounds. The reason given by customers for ceasing to deal with sellers of the Loewe hats, including letters from dealers to Loewe & Co., were admissible. We need not repeat or add to what was said by the Circuit Court of Appeals with regard to evidence of the payment of dues after this suit was begun. And in short neither the argument nor the perusal of the voluminous brief for the plaintiffs in error shows that they suffered any injustice or that there was any error requiring the judgment to be reversed.

Justice Holmes, *Opinion of the United States Supreme Court* in *Lawlor v. Loewe*, *235 U. S. Reports*, 533–537.

---

113. The Age of Big Business (1919)

BY BURTON J. HENDRICK

Hendrick is widely known as a journalist and editor. He edited the *Life and Letters* of Walter H. Page. For Ford's account of his automobile manufacturing methods, see No. 154 below.—Bibliography: Garet Garrett, *The American Omen;* Harold U. Faulkner, *American Economic History*. See also bibliography of No. 83 above.

SUPERLATIVES come naturally to mind in discussing American progress, but hardly any extravagant phrases could do justice to the development of American automobiles. In 1909 the United States produced 3700 motor vehicles; in 1916 we made 1,500,000. The man who now makes a personal profit of not far from $50,000,000 a year in this industry was a puttering mechanic when the twentieth century came in. If we capitalized Henry Ford's income, he is probably a richer man than Rockefeller; yet, as recently as 1905 his possessions consisted of a little shed of a factory which employed a dozen workmen. Dazzling as is this personal success, its really important aspects are the things for which it stands. The American automobile has had its wild-cat days; for the larger part, however, its leaders have paid little attention to Wall Street, but have limited their activities exclusively to manufacturing. Moreover, the automobile illustrates more completely than any other industry the technical qualities that so largely explain our industrial progress. Above all, American manufacturing has developed three characteristics. These are quantity production, standardization, and the use of labor-saving machinery. It is because Ford and other manufacturers adapted these principles to making the automobile that the American motor industry has reached such gigantic proportions.

A few years ago an English manufacturer, seeking the explanation of America's ability to produce an excellent car so cheaply, made an interesting experiment. He obtained three American automobiles, all of the same "standardized" make, and gave them a long and racking tour over English highways. Workmen then took apart the three cars and threw the disjointed remains into a promiscuous heap. Every bolt, bar, gas tank, motor, wheel, and tire was taken from its accustomed place and piled up, a hideous mass of rubbish. Workmen then painstakingly put together three cars from these disordered elements. Three chauffeurs jumped on these cars, and they immediately started down the road and made a long journey just as acceptably as before. The Englishman had learned the secret of American success with automobiles. The one word "standardization" explained the mystery.

Yet when, a few years before, the English referred to the American automobile as a "glorified perambulator," the characterization was not unjust. This new method of transportation was slow in finding favor on our side of the Atlantic. America was sentimentally and practically devoted to the horse as the motive power for vehicles; and the fact that we had so few good roads also worked against the introduction of the automobile. Yet here, as in Europe, the mechanically propelled wagon made its appearance in early times. This vehicle, like the bicycle, is not essentially a modern invention; the reason any one can manufacture it is that practically all the basic ideas antedate 1840. Indeed, the automobile is really older than the railroad. . . . The French and English machines created an entirely different reaction in the mind of an imaginative mechanic in Detroit. Probably American annals contain no finer story than that of this simple American workman. Yet from the beginning it seemed inevitable that Henry Ford should play this appointed part in the world. Born in Michigan in 1863, the son of an English farmer who had emigrated to Michigan and a Dutch mother, Ford had always demonstrated an interest in things far removed from his farm. Only mechanical devices interested him. He liked getting in the crops, because McCormick harvesters did most of the work; it was only the machinery of the dairy that held him enthralled. He developed destructive tendencies as a boy; he had to take everything to pieces. He horrified a rich playmate by resolving his new watch into its component parts—and promptly quieted him by putting it together again. "Every clock in the house shuddered when it saw me coming," he recently said. He constructed a small working forge in his school-yard, and built a small steam engine that could make ten miles an hour. He spent his winter evenings reading mechanical and scientific journals; he cared little for general literature, but machinery in any form was almost a pathological obsession. Some boys run away from the farm to join the circus or to go to sea; Henry Ford at the age of sixteen ran away to get a job in a machine shop. Here one anomaly immediately impressed him. No two machines were made exactly alike; each was regarded as a separate job. With his savings from his weekly wage of $2.50, young Ford purchased a three dollar watch, and immediately dissected it. If several thousand of these watches could be made, each one exactly alike, they would cost only thirty-seven cents apiece. "Then," said Ford to himself, "everybody could have one." He had fairly elaborated his plans to start a factory on this basis when his father's illness called him back to the farm.

This was about 1880; Ford's next conspicuous appearance in Detroit was about 1892. This appearance was not only conspicuous; it was exceedingly noisy. Detroit now knew him as the pilot of a queer affair that whirled and lurched through her thoroughfares, making as much disturbance as a freight train. In reading his technical journals Ford had met many descriptions of horseless carriages; the consequence was that he had again broken away from the farm, taken a job at $45 a month in a Detroit machine shop, and devoted his evenings to the production of a gasoline engine. His young wife was exceedingly concerned about his health; the neighbors' snap judgment was that he was insane. Only two other Americans, Charles B. Duryea and Ellwood Haynes, were attempting to construct an automobile at that time. Long before Ford was ready with his machine, others had begun to appear. Duryea turned out his first one in 1892; and foreign makes began to appear in considerable numbers. But the Detroit mechanic had a more comprehensive inspiration. He was not working to make one of the finely upholstered and beautifully painted vehicles that came from overseas. "Anything that isn't good for everybody is no good at all," he said. Precisely as it was Vail's ambition to make every American a user of the telephone and McCormick's to make every farmer a user of his harvester, so it was Ford's determination that every family should have an automobile. He was apparently the only man in those times who saw that this new machine was not primarily a luxury but a convenience. Yet all the manufacturers, here and in Europe, laughed at his idea. Why not give every poor man a Fifth Avenue house? Frenchmen and Englishmen scouted the idea that any one could make a cheap automobile. Its machinery was particularly refined and called for the highest grade of steel; the clever Americans might use their labor-saving devices on many products, but only skillful hand work could turn out a motor car. European manufacturers regarded each car as a separate problem; they individualized its manufacture almost as scrupulously as a painter paints his portrait or a poet writes his poem. The result was that only a man with several thousand dollars could purchase one. But Henry Ford—and afterward other American makers—had quite a different conception.

Henry Ford's earliest banker was the proprietor of a quick-lunch wagon at which the inventor used to eat his midnight meal after his hard evening's work in the shed. "Coffee Jim," to whom Ford confided his hopes and aspirations on these occasions, was the only man with available cash who had any faith in his ideas. Capital in more substantial form, however, came in about 1902. With money advanced by "Coffee Jim," Ford had built a machine which he entered in the Grosse Point races that year. It was a hideous-looking affair, but it ran like the wind and outdistanced all competitors. From that day Ford's career has been an uninterrupted triumph. But he rejected the earliest offers of capital because the millionaires would not agree to his terms. They were looking for high prices and quick profits, while Ford's plans were for low prices, large sales, and use of profits to extend the business and reduce the cost of his machine. Henry Ford's greatness as a manufacturer consists in the tenacity with which he has clung to this conception. Contrary to general belief in the automobile industry he maintained that a high sale price was not necessary for large profits; indeed he declared that the lower the price, the larger the net earnings would be. Nor did he believe that low wages meant prosperity. The most efficient labor, no matter what the nominal cost might be, was the most economical. The secret of success was the rapid production of a serviceable article in large quantities. When Ford first talked of turning out 10,000 automobiles a year, his associates asked him where he was going to sell them. Ford's answer was that that was no problem at all; the machines would sell themselves. He called attention to the fact that there were millions of people in this country whose incomes exceeded $1800 a year; all in that class would become prospective purchasers of a low-priced automobile. There were 6,000,000 farmers; what more receptive market could one ask? His only problem was the technical one— how to produce his machine in sufficient quantities.

Burton J. Hendrick, *The Age of Big Business* [*Chronicles of America Series,* XXXIX] (New Haven, Yale University Press, 1919), 171–181 *passim.*

---

114. Prohibiting Child Labor (1919)

BY OWEN R. LOVEJOY

Lovejoy, a sociologist by vocation, was General Secretary of the National Child Labor Commission from 1907 to 1926, and has been Secretary of the Children's Aid Society of New York, since that time. He is also editor of *The American Child.* See also No. 118 below.

HITHERTO we have more or less unconsciously employed the sliding scale in relation to child-labor standards. We put prohibition of night work in one State, which had an extremely low all-round standard, on very much the same plane of achievement as establishing an eight- instead of a ten-hour day in another State, which had relatively high standards. That is, it has been natural to work with almost equal enthusiasm for high standards in States where the demand for them was strong and for much lower standards where the demand was less or where it was lacking. Then when those standards were established we worked for still higher ones. We used the sliding scale in accordance with the age-old theory of demand and supply. This theory in economics is fallacious. It is time to discard it in social work. It is time to consider solely the individual, for what is right for the individual is right for industry and society and the world at large.

Arguments have been used to prove that child labor is not economical; that it is fatal to labor because it lowers wages; that it is not in harmony with efficiency for the manufacturer; that it is not conducive to the education or to the physical health and vigor of the nation. Now it is time to talk of the child, and in turning to the child it is evident that really very little account has been taken of him. We know that work cannot be good for his health, but we do not know scientifically how bad it is for him, nor what are the effects of different kinds of work upon his development, nor at what age it is, physically speaking, permissible for him to enter industry in general.

A few States require by law a physical examination of children when they leave school and apply for work permits, but the fact that these children have not been subject to systematic physical examinations during their school life makes this examination of almost negligible value. Furthermore, up to date not a single one of the 48 commonwealths requires systematic physical examination of children between 14 and 16 years of age who are at work. America has not even had the intellectual curiosity to try to find out what industry does to her children.

Furthermore, though certain studies have been made of child nature, of child psychology, and of adolescence, we really do not know what the child needs mentally and spiritually. I think it is time we applied ourselves to this task. We know that nearly half the children who leave school in order to go to work do so because they are tired of school, because they dislike the teacher, "did not get on," or prefer to work. Why does this common phenomenon of revolt against school appear so regularly at the age of 13 or 14? Is it the fault of the child or of the school? Are we willing frankly to face the fact that the elaborate and formal school system built up by us adults on behalf of children is not acceptable to the beneficiaries? That perhaps they could point a way to its improvement? What in short are the needs of children? It is evident that in order to fix our standards, this question must first be answered. But until the studies can be made—and they never can be finished, for as science advances new light will continually be thrown upon one of its most interesting and baffling problems—certain minimum legislative requirements should be set up, to be established as soon as possible in the more advanced communities, and to be approached for the present as a limit in States whose citizens demand less protection.

A reasonable minimum age for entrance into industry would be 16 years. This should apply to all common work, such as that offered by factories, mills, canneries, offices, stores, laundries, restaurants, and to all the miscellaneous occupations entered by children. It should be a flat minimum, that is, for all gainful occupations with the one exception of agriculture. Eighteen years should be the minimum age for work in mines and other especially dangerous industries, and 21 the age for morally dangerous work such as falls to the lot of night messengers in our cities. There should be periodic examination of all working children to see that they are not being broken down in health, and means should be adopted for their transfer, if advisable, to less harmful industries or their removal from industry altogether. Such an examination, made not less than once a year, would in a short time show just what are the industries and operations which induce excessive fatigue, predispose to disease, or lead to stunted growth.

As to hours of employment the regulations recently proposed by the Commission on International Labor Legislation for insertion in the Peace Treaty and adopted by the Peace Conference in Paris, April 28, 1919, offer a suggestive basis. The Sixth Article proposes "the abolition of child labor and the imposition of such limitations on the labor of young persons as shall permit the continuation of their education and assure their proper physical development." The term "abolition of child labor" is so indefinite that unless light were thrown upon it by other portions of the statement, it would have little more effect than similar declarations in our own national political party platforms. Fortunately, however, the commission speaks with a definiteness that leaves no room for doubt. The Fourth Article proposes "the adoption of an eight-hour day or a 48-hour week as the standard to be aimed at where it has not already been obtained." This limitation of hours does not relate to child labor, which, according to Article Six, is to be entirely abolished. This eight-hour day and 48-hour week refers to labor in general—to the protection of men and women—to those of mature physical development.

The corollary is obvious, and it has already been recognized under existing conditions by the adoption of an eight-hour day for children in States where the limitations of hours for men and women were 10,

11, or 12 hours, or where, perhaps, no limitation existed. The principle underlying this discrimination in the interest of children assumes that the growing, developing child subjected to industry should have the burden laid on gradually rather than all at once, and that if men and women need protection, children need more protection. But now we face a new condition, for certainly America with its natural resources and abundance of enterprise cannot afford to stand on a lower plane than the one proposed in this international labor compact. If an eight-hour day measures a desirable social limitation for the labor of men and women, then an eight-hour day is too long for the labor of children. For the first two years at least—namely from 16 to 18 years of age—no child engaged in ordinary industrial processes should be employed to exceed six hours a day. Therefore we should propose as the maximum industrial burden that restriction of hours to six per day and prohibition of night work [for those] under 18 years of age should of course form part of the program.

Obviously this program cannot be put into immediate effect so long as excessive industrial burdens are laid on the shoulders of half-starved mothers, and so long as our schools persist in "teaching" instead of educating our children. It would be absurd to force law-making ahead of standards that public opinion can maintain. But these standards are suggested as the ones that in our educational and legislative work should undoubtedly be our object. How soon we may hope to approach them under existing conditions I leave to our statistical experts. Since 1890 our population has increased 60 per cent and our net annual production of wealth has increased 700 per cent. Obviously, therefore, if people were able to exist in 1890 they should be able to exist on a very much higher plane and a more comfortable plane in 1918; and during this period we have produced millionaires more prolifically than anything else except paupers.

Although approximately three-fourths of our working children are employed in agriculture, this is one of the most difficult of all occupations to regulate. Farm work is undoubtedly harmful when accompanied by exploitation as in the Colorado beet fields and the Southern cotton fields, and yet work about the home farm on a variety of occupations, or work for a neighbor, may be highly healthful and instructive. The most serious objection to this form of work is that it almost invariably tends to keep the child out of school for more or less of the short period that rural schools are in session. The child gradually falls behind his normal grade, one year, two years, or three years. He is both ashamed and bored at being forced to study with younger children on matters that are too elementary to hold his attention. Retardation leads to further retardation and to early dropping out altogether.

The trouble suggests the cure. While it might be unfair and would undoubtedly be quite impossible to enforce a law directed against the employment of children on farms, we can raise the educational standard in rural communities, and we must do so at once if we wish to retain our rural population and our agricultural soundness. The condition of our rural communities not only affects our social and civic institutions; it strikes at the very foundation of economic prosperity. Ten per cent of the rural population cannot read an agricultural bulletin, a farm journal, a thrift appeal, a newspaper, the Constitution, or their Bibles; answer an income tax questionnaire; or keep business accounts. Secretary Lane says: "We spent millions of dollars in presenting to the country the reasons why we were at war, and more than ten per cent of the money that was spent was spent fruitlessly, because the people who got the literature, who got the speeches, who got the appeals, could not understand one word that was written."

One thing that draws our boys to the city is the call of life and human intercourse and better facilities for knowledge. If we can in some manner endow our country schools with vitality, man them with teachers earning and getting living wages, introduce the spirit of community effort, and give scope for the instinct of workmanship, and if we can then create and enforce adequate compulsory education laws, we shall have eliminated the worst evil of children's employment in agriculture. We shall at the same time be building up an educationally equipped and consciously effective agricultural and land-minded population.

Continuation schools and laws compelling employers to allow time for attendance by their employees under 18 years of age should be the reverse side of our child-labor laws. But it is very difficult to confine oneself to legislative prohibitions when the whole trend of child-labor effort and education work in this country is in the direction of construction rather than prohibition. Our enforced laws, however good, however effective in keeping children out of industry and in school, will avail very little unless we provide a better substitute than work, and a better school system and curriculum than the one in vogue. And here we return to the question of children's needs. Let us by all means work for the minimum standards which common sense and our industrial experience justify, but let us at once begin the campaign for the scientific determination of the physical effects of work, through regular physical examination of school and working children. Let us by all means encourage educational experiments, especially those which seek in some way to satisfy the craving of youth and adolescence for real work, for learning through doing, and for wage-earning. If we can finally eliminate the two evils of being taught on the one hand and being exploited on the other, we shall have touched the heart of the problem. It is possible that this may be done by bringing work into the schools or taking the schools out into the world of adult endeavor and labor; by substituting for our industrial training, education through responsibility and initiative in different kinds of hand and brain work. Such experiments will inevitably lead to a better understanding of child nature and to an interpretation of its unexpressed demands.

Owen R. Lovejoy, in *Standards of Child Welfare: Report of Children's Bureau Conferences* (Washington, Government Printing Office, 1919), 81–85.

---

115. Workmen's Compensation (1923)

BY EZEKIEL HENRY DOWNEY

Downey (1879–1922) was compensation actuary of the Insurance Department of Pennsylvania and the Pennsylvania Compensation Rating and Inspection Bureau.—Bibliography: *American Year Book; Monthly Labor Review* of the Department of Labor.

THE awakening of public conscience to the social problem of work injuries led, near the end of the first decade of the present century, to the appointment of many official commissions and legislative committees to investigate the subject of employers' liability and workmen's compensation. These commissions held public hearings, took volumes of testimony, gathered much original material on the working of employers' liability and recommended legislation designed to sweep away the common-law system. In consequence of all this agitation sixteen compensation laws were enacted before the close of the legislative year 1912. The less progressive states gradually fell into line until at the end of 1921 only six commonwealths and the District of Columbia retained the outworn system of employers' liability. Seldom has a legislative movement of equal social significance spread more rapidly over the land.

Territorially speaking, the American compensation system is almost complete. Save only Missouri, every industrially important commonwealth in the United States, and every manufacturing or mining province in the Dominion of Canada has embodied the principle of compensation in statute law. Industrially the new system is much less comprehensive. Congress has failed to enact laws for the protection of seamen and of railway workers engaged in interstate commerce and the Federal Supreme Court, by a most unfortunate decision, removed longshoremen from the jurisdiction of the several states.

Congress passed an act, on June 10, 1922, amending the Judicial Code, which undertook to give to the states jurisdiction over maritime workers, except members of the crews of vessels. This act was declared unconstitutional by the Federal Court of the Southern District of Alabama. Most of the state laws except agricultural and domestic employments, many exempt establishments which employ fewer then four, five or even ten persons, some few leave public employees without the pale. Certain acts are limited to enumerated "extra-hazardous" employments but the list of such employments is usually so comprehensive as to belie the designation. Some workers and casual employees not in the regular course of the employer's business are everywhere excluded. In respect to injuries covered a majority of the jurisdictions still exclude occupational disease and nearly all require that the injury shall both arise out of and occur in the course of the employment. Having regard to all these limitations it is perhaps within the mark to say that some two-thirds of the work injuries which annually occur in the United States are covered by the compensation scheme.

Taking the country as a whole and disregarding injuries not subject to compensation, the temporary disability benefit is not more than one-fourth the wage loss.

For permanent disabilities compensation bears a still smaller proportion to economic loss. Only nine states—New York, Ohio,

West Virginia, Colorado, Oregon, Washington, North Dakota, Nebraska and Nevada—pay a straight life pension for permanent total disability. Even these pensions in no case exceed two-thirds of wages and all are subject to arbitrary weekly maxima. California, Idaho, Illinois, Montana and Utah, provide that payments shall continue during total disability but shall be reduced to $12, $10, or even $5 weekly after five, six or ten years, if the injured is so unfortunate as to survive beyond that period. In other states payment for total disability is limited to six, eight or ten years, and often to a total amount of $4,000 or $5,000. Since the average age of persons permanently incapacitated by injuries is little more than forty years the typical American compensation act provides only partial support for about one-third of the remaining life expectancy.

Still more curious, inadequate and indefensible are the benefits for permanent partial disability. For loss of a hand, foot, leg or eye the *rate* of compensation is usually the same as for total disability but the *duration* thereof is limited to a stated number of weeks: 200 weeks for the loss of an arm or leg, 150 weeks for the loss of a hand or foot, 100 weeks for the loss of an eye. No attempt is made in these specific indemnity schedules to apportion the amount of compensation to the degree of disability or even to preserve any relativity as among the several injuries enumerated. One state allows more for an arm than for a leg, another reverses these proportions; one accounts a hand the same as an arm, another distinguishes shoulder, elbow, wrist and palm. Wholly apart from these haphazard inequalities, the schedules are fundamentally unscientific and inequitable in that they provide compensation for a limited term on account of disability which is permanent in character. . . .

In case of death seven states—Minnesota, New York, West Virginia, Washington, Oregon, North Dakota and Nevada—and the Federal government provide a pension to the widow during widowhood and to children up to the age at which they may legally be employed. In Pennsylvania, Delaware, Idaho and Wyoming payments to children continue through the period of compulsory school attendance although the widow's pension terminates six or eight years after the husband's death. But in quite three-fourths of all the states the death benefit ceases after a stated number of weeks—commonly six years—irrespective of the number, ages or status of dependents.

Even this short period often is further curtailed by the device of a maximum total amount. In two-thirds of the states, again, compensation is the same to a widow and seven children as to a widow alone. The pensions usually are very small. Under most of the statutes the rate is the same as for disability and is subject to the same weekly maximum: $12, $15, or $18. In eighteen commonwealths the allowance varies with the number and relationship of dependents. The widow's pension in a majority of these states is nominally thirty or forty per cent of wages with ten per cent additional for each child, but the maximum weekly payment to the largest family is $12 in Pennsylvania, $15 in Alabama and only $20 in New York. By a singular perversion of common sense the allowance to orphaned children is usually less (where any distinction is made) than to an able-bodied widow. But neither the inadequate weekly payment rate nor the limited total amount is as indefensible as the fore-shortened duration of payments. A majority of children orphaned by industrial accidents are under eight years of age, more than a third are under five and nearly a sixth are under two. Compensation to these children, is, in most states, cut off before they have finished the grammar grades or even before they have entered the public schools. To the childless widow of thirty the time limit of three hundred weeks may not be particularly unjust, but to the mother of several young children or to the woman of fifty who has been a housekeeper for twenty-five years, the restricted period of compensation merely postpones the day of pauperism.

For inadequate death and disability benefits there is at least the excuse of low cost to employers, but for insufficient medical, surgical and hospital care even this pretext fails. The cost of unlimited therapeutic relief is, in per cent of payroll, a bagatelle. Yet it is in their medical provisions that the American compensation laws are most absurdly deficient. One state requires no medical, surgical or hospital treatment of injured workmen, five states demand such treatment for no more than two weeks after the injury, seven limit statutory care to thirty days, seven to sixty days and six to ninety days. Many states impose, besides, a monetary limit of $100, $150 or $200. These limits are to be read in the light of surgical records and surgical charges. The cost at regular rates of reducing a simple fracture of the arm or leg is not less than $200 and the cost of a major amputation—to say nothing of open operations or of orthopædic surgery—is at least $500. A badly infected wound, a deep burn, a fracture of any long bone or a dislocation of any major joint will commonly require attention for more than sixty days and operative procedure to relieve ankylosis, adhesions or malformations is frequently needed a year or more after the injury. The effect of the niggardly medical limitations in our compensation acts is to deprive thousands of injured workmen of that therapeutic care which would prevent permanent disability and to throw tens of thousands into charity wards and free clinics.

In fine, the American benefit scales are grossly inadequate whether measured by the economic cost of industrial injuries or by the needs of injured workmen and their families. All the acts profess to be based upon the principle of occupation risk but all fall much short of realizing that principle in practice. Even under the most liberal of our compensation laws, industry bears less than half of the direct monetary cost of work injuries.

Ezekiel Henry Downey, *Workmen's Compensation* (New York, Macmillan, 1924), 146–153 *passim*.

CHAPTER XXII — CONCERNS OF WOMEN

116. Education of Jane Addams (1900)

BY MARY H. PARKMAN (1917)

Jane Addams has been a prominent figure in social reform and betterment, especially in Chicago. She recounts something of her own work in No. 120 below. —For bibliography, see No. 120.

THIS is the story of a girl who early learned to see with the "inward eye"; she "felt the witchery of the soft blue sky" and all the wonder of the changing earth, and something of the life about her melted into her heart and became a part of herself. So it was that she came to have a "belonging feeling" for all that she saw—fields, pine woods, mill-stream, birds, trees, and people.

Perhaps little Jane Addams loved trees and people best of all. Trees were so big and true, with roots ever seeking a firmer hold on the good brown earth, and branches growing up and ever up, year by year, turning sunbeams into strength. And people she loved, because they had in them something of all kinds of life.

There was one special tree that had the friendliest nooks where she could nestle and dream and plan plays as long as the summer afternoon. Perhaps one reason that Jane loved this tree was that it reminded her of her tall, splendid father.

"You are so big and beautiful, and yet you always have a place for a little girl—even one who can never be straight and strong," Jane whispered, as she put her arms about her tree friend. And when she crept into the shelter of her father's arms, she forgot her poor back, that made her always carry her head weakly on one side when she longed to fling it back and look the world in the face squarely, exultingly, as her father's daughter should.

"There is no one so fine or so noble as my father," Jane would say to herself as she saw him standing before his Bible-class on Sundays. Then her cheeks paled, and her big eyes grew wistful. It would be too bad if people discovered that this frail, crooked child belonged to him. They would be surprised and pity him, and one must never pity Father. So it came about that, though it was her dearest joy to walk by his side clinging to his hand, she stepped over to her uncle, saying timidly, "May I walk with you, Uncle James?"

This happened again and again, to the mild astonishment of the good uncle. At last a day came that made everything different. Jane, who had gone to town unexpectedly, chanced to meet her father coming out of a bank on the main street. Smiling gaily and raising his shining silk hat, he bowed low, as if he were greeting a princess; and as the shy child smiled back she knew that she had been a very foolish little girl indeed. Why, of course! Her father made everything that belonged to him all right just because it *did* belong. He had strength and power enough for them both. As she walked by his side after that, it seemed as if the big grasp of the hand that held hers enfolded all the little tremblings of her days. . . .

Years afterward, when Jane Addams spoke of her childhood, she said that all her early experiences were directly connected with her father, and that two incidents stood out with the distinctness of vivid pictures.

She stood one Sunday morning, in proud possession of a beautiful new cloak, waiting for her father's approval. He looked at her a moment quietly, and then patted her on the shoulder.

"Thy cloak is very pretty, Jane," said the Quaker father, gravely; "so much prettier, indeed, than that of the other little girls that I think thee had better wear thy old one." Then he added, as he looked into her puzzled, disappointed eyes, "We can never, perhaps, make such things as clothes quite fair and right in this hill-and-valley world; but it is wrong and stupid to let the differences crop out in things that mean so much more; in school and church, at least, people should be able to feel that they belong to one family."

Another day she had gone with her father on an errand into the poorest quarter of the town. Always before, it had seemed to her country eyes that the city was a dazzling place of toy- and candy-shops, smooth streets, and contented houses with sleek lawns. Now she caught a glimpse of quite another city, with ugly, dingy houses huddled together, and thin, dirty children standing miserably about without place or spirit to play.

"It is dreadful the way all the comfortable, happy people stay off to themselves," said Jane. "When I grow up, I shall, of course, have a big house, but it is not going to be set apart with all the other big homes; it is going to be right down among the poor, horrid little houses like these."

Always after that, when Jane roamed over her prairie playground or sat dreaming under the Norway pines which had grown from seeds that her father had scattered in his early, pioneer days, she seemed to hear something of "the still, sad music of humanity" in the voice of the wind in the tree-tops and in the harmony of her life of varied interests. For she saw with the inward eye of the heart, and felt the throb of all life in each vital experience that was hers. It would be impossible to live apart in pleasant places, enjoying beauty which others might not share. She must live in the midst of the crowded ways, and bring to the poor, stifled little homes an ideal of healthier living. She would study medicine and go as a doctor to the forlorn, dirty children; but first there would be many things to learn.

It was her dream to go to Smith College, but her father believed that a small college near her home better fitted one for the life to which she belonged. . . .

After receiving from her Alma Mater the degree of B. A., she entered the Woman's Medical College in Philadelphia to prepare for real work in a real world, but the old spinal trouble soon brought that chapter to a close. After some months spent in Dr. Weir Mitchell's hospital, and a longer time of invalidism, she agreed to follow her doctor's pleasant prescription of two years in Europe.

"When I returned I decided to give up my medical course," said Jane Addams, "partly because I had no real aptitude for scientific work, and partly because I discovered that there were other genuine reasons for living among the poor than that of practising medicine upon them."

While in London Miss Addams saw much of the life of the great city from the top of an omnibus. Once she was taken with a number of tourists to see the spectacle of the Saturday-night auction of fruits and vegetables to the poor of the East End, and the lurid picture blotted out all the picturesque impressions, full of pleasant human interest and historic association, that she had been eagerly enjoying during this first visit to London town. Always afterward, when she closed her eyes, she could see the scene; it seemed as if it would never leave her. In the flare of the gas-light, which made weird and spectral the motley, jostling crowd and touched the black shadows it created into a grotesque semblance of life, she saw wrinkled women, desperate-looking men, and pale children vying with each other to secure with their farthings and ha'pennies the vegetables held up by a hoarse, red-faced auctioneer.

One haggard youth sat on the curb, hungrily devouring the cabbage that he had succeeded in bidding in. Her sensation-loving companions on the bus stared with mingled pity and disgust; but the girl who saw what she looked on with the inward eye of the heart turned away her face. The poverty that she had before seen had not prepared her for wretchedness like this.

Mary H. Parkman, *The Heart of Hull-House: Jane Addams*, in *St. Nicholas*, January, 1917 (New York, Century Co.), XLIV, 202–204 *passim*.

---

117. Technical Education for Women (1906)

BY PRESIDENT HENRY S. PRITCHETT

Pritchett was President of the Massachusetts Institute of Technology from 1900 to 1906; President of the Carnegie Foundation for the Advancement of Teaching since 1906. The cases which he instances here were merely forerunners of the more modern movement in which women have invaded, in greater or less numbers, almost every field of endeavor formerly supposed to be open only to men.

SOME years ago the head of the chemical department in one of our best-known schools of technology received a letter from a large firm engaged in a chemical industry in a Western city. The letter stated—it is a very common form of letter to be received at educational institutions—that the firm would be glad to secure for its chemical laboratory "the best man in the class of this year." The reply of the professor was, "The best man is a woman." "Very well," answered the firm, "we will try your woman."

The outcome of this correspondence was a very successful career on the part of the young woman who was the "best man" in her class. . . .

The word technical education is used in our country loosely—sometimes to mean the training of a man or woman for any calling which requires skill. In this sense a cook, a dressmaker or a laundrywoman is a technically trained person as truly as a chemist, an architect, a librarian or a trained secretary.

In the more strict sense of the term, however, technical education is applied to the training of men and women for those professions or callings which require a fairly good general education as the basis of preparation for them and for success in them. . . .

I shall try to point out briefly some of the directions in which women now have opportunities for technical education quite comparable to those which men receive. In some cases this education is received in the same institution and side by side with men; and distinct efforts are being made in some women's colleges to fit women for professional work in special directions for which it is believed they have particular ability.

Ever since our Civil War women have been fitting themselves in increasing numbers for the work of the teacher. This fact the general public and the women themselves thoroughly understand, but it is not so well understood that for nearly the same time the way has been equally free to a woman who desires to fit herself for any of the technological callings—such as architecture, the various branches of engineering, chemistry and biology. The great state universities which were founded immediately after the war threw open their courses to women on the same terms as men. . . .

I know one young woman who had the hardihood to go through a course in naval architecture and marine engineering, including all the work in the foundry. On graduation she found a good place in a large shipyard.

Taking into consideration the fact that such professions as architecture and chemistry have for so long a time been available to women, it is a little singular that more women have not been attracted to them. I cannot but think that this is partly due to the greater ease of preparation for the teacher's life. To be a chemist or an architect means first of all a good general education as a foundation, with the technical training added. This means not only longer and harder work, but greater expense, and up to the present time these or some other reasons have served to keep the number of women who enter technical callings—save in the one calling of the librarian—insignificant in comparison with those who seek to be teachers.

Even in the exception noted there is a distinction, for the number of places available to librarians is, after all, limited, and one who becomes a librarian does not enter into competition with the whole world in quite the same way as when entering upon architecture or chemistry—pursuits in which there is practically no limit to the number of those who may succeed. . . .

A few technical schools are being developed at the present time for the training of women in technical callings which are supposed to appeal more directly to womanly qualities and tastes, and which shall still require a foundation of general education similar to that expected of the engineer or the chemist. . . .

Here are found not only technical courses for educated women in chemistry, biology and library work, but four-year courses in such subjects as household economics, including the economics of house-building, house sanitation and decoration; a secretarial school intended to fit educated women for the place of secretary to an administrative officer, whether in public office or in business, and other courses intended to prepare educated and highly trained experts in certain departments of our domestic economy which have heretofore been left to find their experts by chance.

The idea is an interesting and suggestive one. Why should there not be developed in our highly organized life a class of experts trained to deal with the problems of household economics, let us say, whether this is considered from the standpoint of house-building and maintenance, or from the standpoint of the efficiency and wholesomeness of the food supply? . . .

The technical part of the course of four years includes the economics of house-building and of architecture, the chemistry of food and of cooking, something of the biology and of the engineering of household sanitation, and a thorough study of the matter of household values, dietetics and marketing, including, of course, the ordinary keeping of accounts.

What sort of a career will such an expert find open to her? One of the most obvious and important will be the place of an institutional manager, the manager of a hospital, school or other large institution in which the domestic interests of a number of persons enter. If women achieve success in such employment, they will find constantly widening opportunities as managers of the large and complicated administration of the houses of the rich.

Another path open to those who undertake such courses will be found in the teacher's profession. Still another will be found in the investigation and improvement of the methods of our domestic economy, which methods are today crude, wasteful, and but little affected by the immense progress of modern science.

Henry S. Pritchett, *American Women in Industry*, in *Youth's Companion*, June 21, 1906 (Boston), 307.

---

118. Night Work for Women (1910)

BY FLORENCE LUCAS SANVILLE

Miss Sanville, at the time of writing, was Executive Secretary of the Consumers' League of Philadelphia. She took an active and important part in securing the passage of labor legislation to protect women and children in Pennsylvania. As appears from this account, her recommendations were based on personal experience.—Bibliography as in No. 115 above.

THE length of a factory girl's work-day varies from a legal limit of eight hours in one or two advanced States to ten, eleven, or twelve in less enlightened communities; and in some States where the law still fails to protect its women from industrial exploitation the hours are regulated only by the needs of the industry.

In Pennsylvania, the State which I have studied most closely, the law prescribes a limit of twelve hours daily and sixty hours weekly for women over eighteen; for girls under that age the law since January 1, 1910, restricts this further to fifty-eight hours a week and an average of ten hours a day. In the larger cities of this State the tendency has been toward a ten-hour day in industries where there is a sufficient organized demand among the workers to make itself felt. But in the factories scattered through the villages and small mining-towns, in which great numbers of young girls are employed—such as are established by the silk industry—I found in a period of industrial depression that over half of the mills were working ten and a half to eleven hours a day. It was especially interesting to discover that,

with one or two exceptions, all the ten-hour mills were situated in the
zone which had been affected by a successful strike in 1907; and in
many of these factories we were told jubilantly by the girls that
"they used to work sixty hours, but it had been shortened to fifty-
five."

Eleven hours of work a day means entering the factory at 6.45 in
the morning and leaving it at 6.15 at night, with a half-hour at midday. During a large part of the year it means that for day after day
the sun does not shine upon these hosts of working women and children, as they come in the chill of the early morning and return in the
dusk of the evening.

The work which fills these crawling minutes is not absorbing—is
not even interesting; but the few people who are disposed to consider
the dismal tone which covers a life made up of such days, generally
recover their equanimity by the comfortable thought, "But, after all,
they don't mind it—they're used to it."

Now, if my two summers as a silk-mill worker have taught me anything, it has taught me the fallacy of this statement. The appalling
monotony of the day was not the subject of conversation—it was not
even directly referred to that I can recall. But countless little incidents were significant of the attitude of the workers. One of these
occurred on my first day of work. As the minutes of the morning
wore interminably on, a young girl came up to me, her face beaming
its good news. "Eleven o'clock—only an hour more! " Then, a
few minutes later, crestfallen and downcast, she returned to say "Aw—
I looked wrong—it's only ten!" The disappointment in her voice cut
painfully; all the dull fatigue, the sickening weariness of her unspoken
revolt, were in it.

In fact, I found that the passage of the time becomes the most
absorbing question of the day about an hour after work has commenced. In mills where the employer failed to provide a clock I
quickly found that, as the discovered possessor of a watch, my life
became a burden. If I passed down the room for a drink of water
at the sink, I ran the gauntlet of a continuous volley of questions—
"What's the time, please?" "Let's see your watch"; while the
operation of drinking from the broken glass was made more difficult
by the little group of questioners who besieged me. The second day
I found it hard not to be impatient, despite the wistful questions and

answering expressions of pleasure or disappointment at my reply; the third day in self-defence I left my watch at home—although my penalty was to share the prevailing ignorance of how the day was passing.

The evils of prolonged hours of labor for girls are intensified when this labor is performed at night. Night work after a given hour is prohibited by law for all women in certain industries in a few States; Massachusetts, for instance, requires that no woman shall work in a textile factory after 6 P. M. Other States protect all girls up to a certain age from any night employment—as in Ohio, where no girl under eighteen years of age is allowed to work after 6 P. M. Many States have no restrictive legislation on this subject. Pennsylvania, four years ago, forbade all children under sixteen, with the exception of boys in certain kinds of occupation to work for wages after 9 P. M., and the Legislature of 1909 has included all girls below eighteen years in this protected class. But this law, which sounds so well on paper, has up to the present proved but a lame one on account of the loose requirements of the age certificates; how lame, Miss Cochran and I saw most clearly when we first applied for work on the night shift.

As we went into the factory our passage was blocked by a return stream of girls, and the announcement that "the boiler was burst, and there was no work that night." In the outpouring throng, jubilant at their release, were so many short skirts that it might well have been a group of schoolgirls, dismissed late by their teacher. We naturally fell in with the girls whose way led in the same direction as ours, and we walked down the railroad track together.

"Yer never worked nights, did yer?" was the first question put to us. We confessed not. "Y'll git more fer it—but it's terrible hard." I asked about the hours and found that they were from 6.30 in the evening until 6 in the morning, with a half-hour at midnight. "They keep the doors locked so that no one can't git out—they didn't used ter."

A few of the girls left the track to cut across a near-by lot. "We're goin' to git some blueberries afore it gits dark," they called out as they went away. . . .

Finally all our escort had dispersed except Lena R——, a thin-shoul-dered, anæmic-looking girl, with a sweet, bright face. She looked so young that I asked her age. "I'll be fourteen in the winter," she replied, and added that she had been doing night work since she was eleven.

"Gee—but I didn't think I'd be so lucky tonight; Monday's always the worst night to keep awake.

"I hate—*hate* the mill," the child exclaimed, hotly. "I never did no work till my pa got killed in the mine three years ago."

In Pennsylvania the factories which employ women at night have, with the growth of public sentiment in the matter, become comparatively rare; and with the more stringent new law, which is already in operation, the young girls will be more carefully protected. But many States have neither public sentiment nor legislation on the subject; and in them the cases of disaster and ruin worked to human life would, were the toll ever taken, prove appalling.

One of the most striking evils in the physical environment of women in the factories is the lack of seats, due sometimes to a simple oversight, at other times to a definite and most erring—as well as inhuman—policy of the employer, begotten by an idea that the right to sit down encourages slow work and laziness. As a result of one of these two reasons, so very few mills as to be an almost negligible quantity provide the seats which are required by the Pennsylvania law. In other factories, while no seats of any kind are visible, there is no rule against sitting down if anything to sit on can be improvised. . . . There are many mills, however, in which sitting was absolutely forbidden; in which a rest in the course of an eleven-hour day could be obtained only at the risk of being caught by the foreman and told roughly to "get up and watch out for ends."

The harmful effect of continuous standing upon young and growing girls, is too well established a fact to require any elaboration. In addition to the permanent ill effects, much immediate and unnecessary suffering, especially in hot weather, is inflicted by the prohibition of sitting. I could always detect the existence of this rule by a glance at the stocking-feet of the workers, and at the rows of discarded shoes beneath the frames. For after a few hours the strain upon the swollen feet becomes intolerable, and one girl after another discards her shoes. . . .

Another harsh and very common practice of employers is to cover the lower sashes of the windows with paint, and to fasten them so that they cannot be raised in hot weather. This is done so that the girls "don't waste time looking out." The utter fallacy of this policy was made as clearly evident to me as was the rule against sitting down. In the factories of my acquaintance where these rules are not imposed, I have never seen their absence taken advantage of. On the contrary, I have noticed that the girls have an object in getting their work under way—so that they may win the reward of a few minutes' rest. And the keen consciousness which the workers possess of their employer's attitude toward them, as expressed in occasional seats and raised windows, works wholly for his interests—not against them. . . .

I have implied that the eating of the midday meal is a very haphazard operation. Only in the rarest cases is a separate lunch-room provided—in a study of thirty-two factories in a single industry we found just two that did so. The dinner "hour" is almost universally a half-hour, so that only the few girls who live practically at the factory door are enabled to go home. Those who are left have at their disposal within the mill a seat on the oily floor, or on a bobbin-tray, in a room which often reeks of ill-smelling raw material. In the summer it is possible to go out-of-doors—and where the location of the factory makes it practicable, this is the general rule. But sometimes this wholesome alternative is not offered.

I recall one factory, situated on a bed of fine coal-dust between two railroad tracks. The sole choice lay between a seat on the coal-heap in the blaze of the sun or on the oily floor of the mill, in an atmosphere where the noise of the machinery gave no possibility of rest. Some of my most vivid and painful recollections of the noon hour call up pictures of weary figures crouched on a heap of spools, their heads sunk between their hands, as if to shut out the clatter of the machinery—on account of the short lunch period, some factories keep their machinery in motion, instead of shutting it down—their shoeless feet on a floor strewn with the remains of their own and other luncheons.

It would be grossly unfair were I to indicate that every mill in which we worked, or with which we came in contact, was characterized by such brutal indifference on the part of the management. In some factories the girls spoke with enthusiasm of the generosity and consideration of their employers. And one mill which we visited in an effort to obtain work was not only spotlessly clean, but was even brightened by pots of growing plants and great bunches of mountain laurel placed throughout the work-rooms.

Florence Lucas Sanville, *A Woman in the Pennsylvania Silk-Mills*, in *Harper's Monthly Magazine*, April, 1910 (New York), 651–662 *passim*. Reprinted by permission of the author.

———————◆———————

119. Is Woman Suffrage Important? (1911)

BY MAX EASTMAN

Eastman is a widely known journalist, and a frequent contributor to liberal publications. Women were admitted to vote in federal elections by the Nineteenth Amendment to the Constitution, which became effective in 1920. For an account of the progress of the campaign by women for the right to vote in various states, see *American Year Book*, years 1910–1919, 1923–1929.

THEODORE ROOSEVELT, in a cautious reference to the movement for equal suffrage, recently delivered this opinion:

We hear much about women's rights. Well, as to that, decent men should be thinking about women's rights all the time, and while the men are doing that—the women should be attending to their duties.

As evading a political issue with a moral platitude, we might pass that statement by, were it not for what it reveals by implication. It reveals that Mr. Roosevelt, with probably most of the men of his profession, still regards the equal-suffrage movement as a clamor for rights. I believe that not one-fiftieth of the women engaged in that movement are actuated by a desire to get rights. Probably none of the men so engaged are actuated by a desire to give them rights. It may appear true to these men that if any adult woman, with the established qualifications, desires to vote, it is not their business why she desires to vote, it is unjust to deny her the opportunity. They may believe that as an ambitious republic we can ill afford, either for what we call practical reasons or for reasons of romantic sentiment, to deny a direct justice to a number of hundred thousand people who vehemently ask for it. They may be unable—even as politicians—to refrain from thinking about women's rights. But such thoughts are not the heart of their enthusiasm. The heart of their enthusiasm is not an acknowledgment that equal suffrage is abstractly right or just, but a conviction that it is important. . . .

Let me say at the start that we do not look to women's votes for the purification and moral elevation of the body politic. That is a lovely hope, transmitted to us in its classic form, I believe, by George William Curtis. "I am asked," he exclaims, "would you drag women down into the mire of politics? No, sir, I would have them lift us out of it."

But we are not much stirred by the hope of such miracles in this day. We are more scientific than to judge women in general by the one we have in our romantic eye. We look round in the city and the country, and we see who the men are and who the women are; and we conclude that neither sex has exclusive hold of the reins, or spurs, of morality. . . .

The sexes are more idealistic in what they do together than in what they do apart. For this reason the coming of women—or the coming, let us say, of families—into politics, will perhaps bring a certain benefit other than what you might estimate by counting the wise or virtuous women's votes. It will make impossible, for instance, that state of conscience prevalent among male politicians, who go into the service of the State with the happy feeling that they have left their virtues at home in the safe-keeping of their wives and daughters. Men throw the innocence of their women folk as a sop to God, and go about the devil's business. But it may be doubted whether God or any one else was ever satisfied with innocence as a substitute for virtue active in the world. I could never see the value of preserved innocence. It is perfectly possible that our republic will be damned to moral destruction, men and women together, and it is possible that it will be saved to great usefulness, but certainly if it is saved it will be saved not because of the number of cloistered innocents it contains within its boundaries, but because of the number of effective human beings who save it. Any measure, therefore, will do well, which tends to reduce the number of those males who think that an ineffectual wife can do the being good for the whole family.

Especially it will do well if it reduces the number of such men in public affairs, where the lack of those high standards that we set for ourselves in our homes is lamentably apparent. "He is such a good man in his family!" we say of our disgraced representative. Perhaps, if we do not waste our time trying to make him good outside his family, but allow his family and its acquaintance with him to extend into the sphere of his political activity, he will be good there too, or else no-where, and there will be no doubt about it. He will at least realize the importance of honor in public service, and no longer be able to return home and think he is better than his acts. . . .

The relegating of women to a life of futile or neurotic sainthood, with exclusive charge of the goodness of the community and nothing to do with the community's behavior, has been a great foolishness at the bottom of our social habits. Of this ancient practice and the quite recent idealization of it, of the damage it has done to men and women and children, no history can give the account. Nor is it easy to estab-lish a sense of it in an age which is permeated by the sentiments of a degenerate feudalism. It may awake the sane and the heroic in us, however, to recall the pagan ideal of Plato. He says, in the seventh book of the laws:

The legislator ought to be whole and perfect, and not half a man only. He ought not to let the female sex live softly and waste money and have no order of life, while he takes the utmost care of the male sex, and leaves half of life only blessed with happiness when he might have made the whole state happy.

Two truths that will be news to many after two thousand years, are contained in that sentence. First, that it is just as important for women to be happy as for men; and, second, that true happiness for the best spirits of either sex, does not consist in living softly and wast-ing money and having no order of life, but in regulated purpose and achievement. . . .

. . . The purpose of life is that it be greatly lived, and it can be greatly lived only by great characters. Yet it can be shown, upon a practical demand, for what special purposes we need women of great spirit.

We need them, first, for the cultivation of a certain gentle humility and good sense in their husbands. . . . To idolize that which is held inferior in power and wisdom, because it excels in innocence of the actual world, is to commit the characteristic folly of decadence. Surely if man as a lover of women is to become an equable union of the tender and heroic, he will need to be both subdued and elevated by his love. He will not be brought to such perfection by the constant purveyal of privileges to a supposedly inferior being; nor will he be brought there by the discipline of a woman who wields her privilege with cunning or thunder, and under a system of "female subjection" rules the household. No, he will come into that perfection, if at all, in the company of a woman so developed as naturally to believe that she will be treated as an equal.

. . . Who can think that intellectual divergence, disagreement upon a great public question, could disrupt a family worth holding together? On the contrary, nothing save a community of great interests, agreeing and disagreeing, can revive a fading romance. When we have made matrimony synonymous with a high and equal comradeship, we shall have done the one thing that we can do to rescue those families which are the tottering corner-stones of society. And that we cannot do until men and women are both grown up.

A greater service of the developed woman, however, will be her service in motherhood. For we are in extreme need of mothers that have the wisdom of experience. . . . Keep your mothers in a state of invalid remoteness from genuine life, and who is to arm the young with wise virtue? Are their mothers only to suckle them, and then for their education pass them over to some one who knows life? For to educate a child is to lead him out into the world of his experience; it is not to propel him with ignorant admonitions from the door. A million lives wrecked at the off-go can bear witness to the failure of that method. I think that the best thing you could add to the mothers of posterity is a little of the rough sagacity and humor of public affairs.

Such are the great reasons for making the sexes equal in politics; such have been the reasons ever since the question was broached in the age of Pericles. It is not an issue to be answered by an appeal to chivalry, which is but a perfection of manners among the people of noble leisure; the need is deeper and more universal than that. Nor is it at its best a demand for justice upon the part of citizens unrecognized. Nor is it a plan to prevent corrupt practices in politics, or instil into the people's representatives any virtue other than the virtue of representing the whole people. That is the aim of those who advocate that we extend the suffrage to women. It is an act demanded by the ideal principle to the proof of which our government is devoted. It is, moreover, a heroic step that we can take with nature in the evolution of a symmetrical race.

Max Eastman, in *North American Review* (New York, 1911), CXCIII, 60–71 *passim*. Reprinted by permission of the author.

120. Larger Aspects of the Woman's Movement (1914)

BY JANE ADDAMS

For Jane Addams, see No. 116 above.—Her published books include *Twenty Years at Hull House* (1910); *Women at The Hague* (1915); *Spirit of Youth and The City Streets* (1917); *Peace and Bread in Time of War* (1922); *The Long Road of Woman's Memory* (1917); *Democracy and Social Ethics* (1902).

PERHAPS no presentation of history is so difficult as that which treats of the growth of a new consciousness; but assuming that the historic review, now so universal in the field of social judgment and investigation, is applicable to any current development, I have ventured to apply it to that disturbing manifestation called the "votes-for-women" movement, which at the present moment is not only the centre of hot debate but, unhappily, also of conduct which in the minds of many is most unseemly. . . .

To begin then with the world-wide aspect of the votes-for-women movement—that there may be nothing more petty about us than the theme itself imposes—it is possible to make certain classifications of underlying trends, which, while not always clear, and sometimes overlapping, are yet international in their manifestations.

First: the movement is obviously a part of that evolutionary conception of self-government which has been slowly developing through the centuries. For the simple reason that self-government must ever be built up anew in relation to changing experiences, its history is largely a record of new human interests which have become the object of governmental action, and of the incorporation into the body politic of the classes representing those interests. As the governing classes have been enlarged by the enfranchisement of one body of men after another, government itself has not only become enriched through new human interests, but at the same time it has become further democratized through the accession of the new classes representing those interests. The two propositions are complementary. . . .

In certain respects the insistence of women for political expression, which characterizes the opening years of the twentieth century, bears an analogy to their industrial experiences in the early part of the nineteenth century, when the textile industries were taken out of private houses and organized as factory enterprises. . . . It is hard to see now how the basic industry of England could have been developed without the thousands of women and girls who in spite of public opprobrium followed their old occupations.

But is it not obvious that, as industrial changes took spinning out of private houses, so political changes are taking out of the home humanitarian activities, not to mention the teaching of children? The aged poor of a community who were formerly cared for in the houses of distant relatives or old neighbors, the sick who were nursed night and day by kindly friends and acquaintances taking turn and turn about, are now housed in large infirmaries and in hospitals built and supported by the taxpayers' money. The woman who wishes to be a teacher or a nurse takes her training in public institutions, as she formerly went to the factory to spin, not because she wishes primarily to leave home but because her work has been transferred. . . .

Studied from a second aspect, the "votes-for-women" movement is doubtless one result of the fundamental change which is taking place in the conception of politics analogous to the changes in the basic notions in education, criminology, and political economy. Graham Wallas, in his very interesting book *Human Nature in Politics*, points out that, while educators have learned to study child psychology so that teachers understand children rather than manage schools, and that while jurists are ceasing to classify offenders solely on the basis of their crimes and are beginning to regard them as human beings, politicians have not yet learned to apply social psychology to the field of political action. The individual voter is still regarded as a party adjunct, a useful unit for party organization exactly as the old economist long considered the "economic man" as a sort of lone wolf impelled by no other motive than the desire for food. Quite as the science of political economy made little progress until it got rid of that fiction and looked at men as they really exist, each a bundle of complicated and overlapping motives, so politicians are making many blunders because their action is not founded upon the genuine facts of human existence. They have failed to observe how rapidly the materials and methods of political life are changing, that the law courts and legislature are struggling desperately to meet modern demands with conceptions of property and authority and duty founded upon the rude compromises made centuries ago, that there is obvious need for bolder arrangements and interactions in the distribution of employment, education, invention. Such changes can only come about if they are carried on with that same spirit of free thinking and outspoken publication that has won in the field of natural science.

An able man long ago pointed out that the qualities most valuable in an electorate are social sympathies and a sense of justice, then openness and plainness of character, lastly habits of action and a practical knowledge of social misery. Woman's value to the modern states, which constantly are forced to consider social reforms, lies in the fact that statesmen at the present moment are attempting to translate the new social sympathy into political action.

The contemporary efforts to extend the principles of social insurance to illness in several European states, and to control unemployment through national labor exchanges, are not so much social reforms as titanic pieces of social engineering in which the judgment of women is most necessary. Governmental commissions everywhere take woman's testimony as to legislation for better housing, for public health and education, for the care of dependents, and many other remedial measures, because it is obviously a perilous business to turn over delicate social experiments to men who have remained quite untouched by social compunctions and who have been elected to their legislative positions solely upon the old political issues. Certainly under this new conception of politics it is much easier to legislate for those human beings of whose condition the electorate are "vividly aware," to use a favorite phrase of Professor James. . . .

Women have discovered that the unrepresented are always liable to be given what they do not need by legislators who wish merely to placate them; a child labor law exempts street trades, the most dangerous of all trades to a child's morals; a law releasing mothers from petty industry that they may rear worthy children provides a pension so inadequate that over-burdened women must continue to neglect their young in order to feed them.

More than one woman, while waiting in the lobby for an opportunity to persuade recalcitrant law-makers in regard to a legislative measure, has had ample time to regret that she had no vote by which to select the men upon whom her social reform had become so absolutely dependent. Such a woman can even recall some cherished project which has been so modified by uninformed legislation during the process of legal enactment that the law finally passed injured the very people it was meant to protect. . . .

The third trend in the feminist movement might be called evolutionary rather than historic, if indeed the two may be separated. In this trend the very earliest stage is doubtless represented by those women of Asia who are making their first struggle against the traditional bondages and customs whose roots creep back into primitive times, and whose efforts are yet in that incipient and unorganized state which characterized the efforts of western women a hundred years ago.   As a whole, this trend is connected with contemporary revolutions carried on by men demanding a direct representation in governments which at present ignore them.   The most striking example, perhaps, is Russia, where women have taken an active part in the recently established constitutional government.   Twenty-one of them at the present moment are sitting as members in the Finnish Parliament.   Due to that inveterate tendency of revolutionists to incorporate into their program the most advanced features of existing governments, the demand for woman's political representation has reached even Mohammedan countries, such as Persia and Turkey, where it is directly opposed to their religious teaching.   Both China and Siam, in spite of eastern customs, have given women a political status in their new constitutions by extending to certain classes of them the right of suffrage. . . .

The final impression of a review of this movement we have ventured to consider is of a cause growing, pushing, and developing in all the nations upon the face of the earth, representing new experiences and untrammeled hopes.   It is everywhere surprisingly spontaneous and universal.   It not only appears simultaneously in various nations in both hemispheres, but manifests itself in widely separated groups within the same nation, embracing the smart set and the hard driven working woman; sometimes the movement is sectarian and dogmatic, at others philosophic and grandiloquent; it may be amorphous and sporadic, or carefully organized and consciously directed; but it is always vital and is constantly becoming more widespread.

Jane Addams, in *Annals of the American Academy of Political and Social Science* (Philadelphia, November, 1914), LVI, 1–8 *passim*.

PART VIII

NATIONAL LEADERS

CHAPTER XXIII — AMERICAN PUBLIC MEN

121. John Hay, a Great Secretary of State (1900)

BY HENRY MACFARLAND

See also No. 24 above, taken from Hay's *Diary*.—Bibliography: William Roscoe Thayer, *The Life and Letters of John Hay*. For brief sketches of the personalities of national political figures, see C. W. Gilbert, *The Mirrors of Washington, Behind the Mirrors;* E. G. Lowry, *Washington Close-Ups;* William Allen White, *Masks in a Pageant.*

UNTIL President McKinley, at the beginning of his administration, appointed Colonel Hay ambassador to Great Britain, he had not been conspicuous in public life for fifteen years. But that was because, always unostentatious, and indeed retiring, he had avoided prominence, declined public office, and kept out of the newspapers. For during all those years, besides working in literature and meeting all social demands especially with a gracious hospitality, Colonel Hay was a power in politics, more, rather than less, important because he worked chiefly behind the scenes. He appeared from time to time on the Republican stump to make speeches notable for their cleverness, clearness, and cogency, but he was never conspicuous in conventions or hotel lobbies, at the White House, the Capitol, or at the Cabinet offices. But in the inner councils of the Republican party his influence was potent, and the party managers knew how freely he gave his time, his efforts, and his money for the success of his principles and candidates. President McKinley was long his candidate for the Presidency, and he thoroughly appreciated all that Colonel

Hay did for him, and also the unusual fitness of Colonel Hay for public service. He would have made Colonel Hay Secretary of State at the beginning of his administration if he had not been constrained by circumstances to transfer Senator Sherman to the State Department. It was well, however, both for Colonel Hay and the administration, that he was sent just at that time as ambassador to Great Britain, for his public and private services there were of high order and great importance. In that propitious hour, when the interests of both countries drew them closer together to their mutual advantage, he did all that the American ambassador could do to promote the friendliest relations and to secure our share of the benefits. The policy of benevolent neutrality which England followed to our advantage in the Spanish war was promoted by his efforts, and he utilized its influence in every possible way. Colonel and Mrs. Hay, blessed with fine social gifts and the means to make them effective, made the best impression on English society. Colonel Hay's public addresses were models of their kind and examples of propriety which might well be followed by all our ambassadors. Colonel Hay made personal friends of most of the leading men of England, and through the opportunities of the embassy gained the friendship of many continental statesmen. When he returned to become Secretary of State, after less than eighteen months' service, he left behind him a shining reputation, and he brought back invaluable knowledge of the statecraft of every court in Europe.

Beginning his service as Secretary of State with this wealth of information, which many of his predecessors did not have after four years' service at the head of the Department and having a perfect acquaintance with the methods, traditions, and archives of the Department, and a thorough knowledge of the diplomatic corps in Washington, as well as of our leading public men, Colonel Hay came fully equipped to his latest and greatest opportunity and did not have to lose time in preparing to work. . . . The new Secretary of State was (and is) a firm believer in Washington's teaching against entangling foreign alliances. . . . He is equally a believer in the Monroe Doctrine and has repeatedly made this thoroughly understood in the European capitals. But while he has been careful to keep this country out of the quarrels of Europe and to keep Europe from interfering politically with the affairs of this continent, he has not hesitated to utilize, in temporary conference and coöperation, the advice and assistance of any nation in the promotion of our interests, now spread world-wide. He has considered these interests as interrelated, and therefore the diplomacy of the State Department under his direction has treated our foreign affairs as a whole. There has been marked unity as well as unusual skillfulness, vigor, and tactfulness in it, but its chief characteristic has been its sagacious foresight.

His great achievement will appear in history as the maintenance of the "open door" in China and the consequent postponement, if not prevention, of the threatened dismemberment of that empire, which will probably be considered one of the greatest achievements ever won by our diplomacy. It has already made a great impression upon all the governments of the world and has already had important results. When Colonel Hay took the portfolio of State, fifteen months ago, the peace commission had not begun the treaty of Paris with Spain, and all Europe was wondering what the United States would do with its new influence in the affairs of nations, then fully recognized as a result of its unexpected demonstration of power in the Spanish war. The ablest English and continental statesmen then regarded the retention of the Philippines by the United States as inevitable, which most American statesmen did not see, and, looking beyond, faced the larger question, also hidden from most American statesmen, of what this would mean in the future of China and all the Orient. . . . He early took steps toward securing from the great powers, who had already mapped out a division of the Chinese coast among themselves, a formal recognition of our right to the "open door" under our commercial treaties with China. They realized, of course, that this meant that they could not appropriate to themselves the markets of China as they had already planned to do. Russia, France, and Germany, who were the most aggressive in these designs, also realized that they could not afford to ignore or to offend the United States, the new power of the world, with sovereignty over the Philippines, especially as Great Britain's interest in the matter lay rather with the United States than with them, and Japan, the new power of the Orient, ambitious to control in China and Korea, was ready to lend her aid to the United States. So verbal assurances that the "open door" should be maintained in China were given by all the powers interested. This did not content Secretary Hay, and he asked for similar assurances in writing. Some of the powers demurred, and so showed that the written assurances were needed. They intimated that instead of them they would like to give the United States an equal slice of the territory of China. Secretary Hay made them understand that the United States would not participate in the division of China and must have the written guarantees of the "open door." When they realized that he meant just what he said they promised to send the assurances in writing. The United States, acting simply for herself and the conservation of her rights under treaties with China, has not only fully protected them, to the incalculable advantage of the United States and her commerce, but has preserved the integrity of China's territory. Secretary Hay's diplomacy maintained the peace of nations by preventing any concerted attack upon Great Britain during her Transvaal trouble, and, indirectly, promoted the new understanding between Great Britain and Germany which works powerfully to the same end and also to the advancement of our interests in the East. . . .

Secretary Hay is not a club man, although he belongs to fashionable clubs in Washington and elsewhere, but finds his chief happiness in his home. He is a great pedestrian and a familiar figure on the streets of Washington, rather short and sturdy in build, walking briskly with the swing of youth, and always perfectly dressed. He has a fine, strong face with keen, dark eyes, which demand eyeglasses, and black hair and bushy beard turning gray.

He is so young for his years, so agile and virile in mind and body that his friends feel that he may be elected President after President McKinley finishes his second term, if he does not become President before.

Henry Macfarland, *Secretary John Hay*, in *Review of Reviews* (January, 1900), XXI, 38–41 *passim*.

122. Oliver Wendell Holmes, Eminent Jurist (1916)

BY PROFESSOR FELIX FRANKFURTER

Frankfurter, a leader of liberal thought, is a professor in the Harvard Law School. He is especially concerned with matters of constitutional interpretation and federal control of business and transportation. On Holmes, see also No. 101 above. For an extract from a characteristic opinion by Holmes, see No. 112 above.

MR. JUSTICE HOLMES'S influence has been steady and consistent and growing. His opinions form a coherent body of constitutional law, and their effect upon the development of the law is the outstanding characteristic of constitutional history in the last decade. . . .

Mr. Justice Holmes has recalled us to the traditions of Marshall, that it *is* a Constitution we are expounding, and not a detached document inviting scholastic dialectics. To him the Constitution is a means of ordering the life of a young nation, having its roots in the past— "continuity with the past is not a duty but a necessity"—and intended for the unknown future. Intentionally, therefore, it was bounded with outlines not sharp and contemporary, but permitting of increasing definiteness through experience. . . .

He has ever been keenly conscious of the delicacy involved in reviewing other men's judgment not as to its wisdom but as to their right to entertain the reasonableness of its wisdom. We touch here the most sensitive spot in our constitutional system: that its successful working calls for minds of extraordinary intellectual disinterestedness and penetration lest limitations in personal experience and imagination be interpreted, however conscientiously or unconsciously, as constitutional limitation. . . .

We are in a field where general principles are recognized but settle few controversies. Claim or denial of governmental power, of "individual rights," reveal themselves not as logical antitheses, but as demands of clashing "rights," of matters of more or less, of questions of degree. . . .

Thus, while Mr. Justice Holmes has expounded the philosophy of differences of degree and applied it in a variety of cases, he has been alert to demand a telling difference upon which a distinction can be predicated. A neat instance is his dissenting opinion in Haddock *v.* Haddock.

> I am the last man in the world to quarrel with a distinction simply because it is one of degree. Most distinctions, in my opinion, are of that sort, and none are the worse for it. But the line which is drawn must be justified by the fact that it is a little nearer than the nearest opposing case to one pole of an admitted antithesis. When a crime is made burglary by the fact that it was committed thirty seconds after one hour after sunset, ascertained according to mean time in the place of the act, to take an example from Massachusetts, the act is a little nearer to midnight than if it had been committed one minute earlier, and no one denies that there is a difference between night and day. The fixing of a point when day ends is made inevitable by the admission of that difference. But I can find no basis for giving a greater jurisdiction to the courts of the husband's domicile when the married pair happens to have resided there a month, even if with intent to make it a permanent abode, than if they had not lived there at all.

This, in brief, is the attitude in which and the technique with which Mr. Justice Holmes approaches the solution of specific questions in the two great active fields of constitutional law: the Commerce Clause and the Fourteenth Amendment.

Just as the needs of commerce among the several states furnished the great centripetal force in the establishment of the Nation, so the Commerce Clause has now become the most important nationalizing agency of the Federal Government. Mr. Justice Holmes has at once applied this power with unimpaired depth and breadth, and affirmed the true basis of its need to-day no less than in 1789.

> I do not think the United States would come to an end if we lost our power to declare an Act of Congress void. I do think the Union would be imperiled if we could not make that declaration as to the laws of the several States. For one in my place sees how often a local policy prevails with those who are not trained to national views, and how often action is taken that embodies what the Commerce Clause was meant to end.

The extension of interstate commerce through modern inventions, the overwhelming field which it has absorbed, are obvious. Logically, there is no limit to the interrelation of national commerce and the activities of men in the separate States. But the main ends of our dual system of States and Nation here, too, call for adjustment, and logic cannot hold sterile sway.

> In modern societies every part is related so organically to every other, that what affects any portion must be felt more or less by all the rest. Therefore, unless everything is to be forbidden and legislation is to come to a stop, it is not enough

to show that, in the working of a statute, there is some tendency, logically discernible, to interfere with commerce or existing contracts.

Therefore distinctions have to be made and "even nice distinctions are to be expected." But the Federal power must be dominantly left unimpaired and a State cannot defeat the withdrawal of national commerce from State tampering "by invoking the convenient apologetics of the police power." . . .

His general attitude towards the Fourteenth Amendment at once reflects his whole point of view towards constitutional interpretation and is a clue to the hundreds of opinions in which it is applied. In all the variety of cases the opinions of Mr. Justice Holmes show the same realism, the same refusal to defeat life by formal logic, the same regard for local needs and local habits, the same deference to local knowledge. He recognizes that government necessarily means experimentation; and while the very essence of constitutional limitations is to confine the area of experimentation, the limitations are not self-defining, and they were intended to permit government. Necessarily, therefore, the door was not meant to be closed to trial and error. "Constitutional law, like any other mortal contrivance, has to take some chances." . . .

In industrial and social legislation the fighting, of course, has been around the conception of "liberty." Mr. Justice Holmes has been unswerving in his resistance to any doctrinaire interpretation. The effectiveness of his fight lies mostly in the acuteness with which he has disclosed when a claim is doctrinaire. Perception of the forces of modern society and persistent study of economics have enabled him to translate large words in terms of the realities of existence. . . .

What makes these opinions significant beyond their immediate expression is that they come from a man who, as a judge, enforces statutes based upon economic theories which he does not share, and of whose efficacy in action he is sceptical. The judicial function here finds its highest exercise.

In the regulation of utilities we have an excellent illustration of the need of balancing interests and the delicacy of the task. Mr. Justice Holmes has both laid down the general consideration and illustrated their application. . . .

Only the shallow would attempt to put Mr. Justice Holmes in the shallow pigeonholes of classification. He has been imaginatively regardful of the sensibilities of the States, particularly in State controversies, and he has shown every deference, even as a matter of "equitable fitness or propriety," to agencies of the States. In thus manifesting every rightful regard for self-reliant individual States, he to that extent only the more sought to maintain, so far as the judiciary plays a part, the full vigor of our dual system. From his opinions there emerges a conception of a Nation adequate to its great national duties and consisting of confederate States, in their turn possessed of dignity and power available for the diverse uses of civilized people.

In their impact and sweep and fertile freshness, the opinions have been a superbly harmonious vehicle for the views which they embody. It all seems so easy,—brilliant birds pulled from the magician's sleeve. It is the delusive ease of great effort and great art. He has told us that in deciding cases "one has to try to strike the jugular," and his aim is sure. He has attained it, as only superlative work, no matter how great the genius, can be attained. "The eternal effort of an art, even the art of writing legal decisions, is to omit all but the essentials. 'The point of contact' is the formula, the place where the boy got his finger pinched; the rest of the machinery doesn't matter." So we see nothing of the detailed draughtsmanship. We get, like Corot's pictures, "magisterial summaries."

We get more: we get the man. Law ever has been for him one of the forces of life, a part of it and contributing to it. Back of his approach to an obscure statute from Oklahoma or Maine we catch a glimpse of his approach to life. That glimpse each must get and treasure for his own.

Felix Frankfurter, *Constitutional Opinions of Justice Holmes*, in *Harvard Law Review* (April, 1916), XXIX, 684–699 *passim*.

123. Joseph H. Choate, Counsellor and Ambassador (1917)

BY EX-SECRETARY ELIHU ROOT

See No. 51 above. For one aspect of Root's work, see Joseph H. Choate, *The Two Hague Conferences*.

MR. CHOATE'S service in the foreign affairs of the country was of the highest value. When he was appointed Ambassador from the United States to Great Britain at the age of sixty-seven, there were several very serious and difficult questions between the two countries, which required to be treated with great skill and judgment if serious controversy was to be prevented. The very positive defiance of Great Britain in Mr. Cleveland's Venezuela message of December, 1895, and the general expression of American feeling in support of that defiance, had created an atmosphere not altogether favorable to mutual concessions. This had been modified, but not wholly dispelled, by Great Britain's discouragement of European intervention during our war with Spain, and by the wisdom and good sense of Mr. Hay and President McKinley on the one side and Lord Salisbury on the other during the first two years of the McKinley Administration. . . .

When Mr. Choate was appointed, the United States had just reached a full realization of the necessity of a canal across the Central American Isthmus under American control. We were forced to that realization by the result of the war with Spain, the cession of Porto Rico, and the responsibility for the protection of Cuba; by the growth of population and commerce on the Pacific Coast; by the acquisition of Hawaii and the Philippines; by the appearance on the horizon of grave questions of international policy toward the Far East. It was necessary for our internal commerce and our naval protection that our Atlantic and Pacific coasts should be united by a ship canal under control; but the way was blocked by the Clayton-Bulwer Treaty of 1850, under which the United States and Great Britain had agreed that any such canal should be practically under a partnership of the two nations. The object could not be attained while that Treaty stood. Under the wise and highly competent diplomacy of Mr. Choate in London and Mr. Hay in Washington the partnership was abandoned, and the obstacle of the Clayton-Bulwer Treaty was removed upon the sole condition of equal treatment to the commerce of the world in the canal to be built and controlled by the United States.

When Mr. Choate went to London, China seemed to be on the verge of partition by the great Powers, who had established naval and military stations and spheres of influence in Chinese territory, and who, mutually suspicious, were reaching out, each for more control, in order to prevent other powers from acquiring it. There was no escape from partition, except by stopping that process. With partition the door for American trade with China would be closed, and the opportunity of China for liberty and self-government would disappear. America alone was free from suspicion, and from the vantage-ground Mr. Hay undertook to stop the process of partition by proposing a universal agreement on the principle of the open door. Without the agreement of Great Britain effort would have been useless. It fell to Mr. Choate to secure that agreement from the British Government, and it was given cheerfully and ungrudgingly, and the principle of the open door was established in China. . . .

. . . There were many other important things done—and well done —during his six years of service. Let no one suppose that results in the negotiation of such affairs come of themselves. They require long and patient labor, quick perception, judgment of character, tact, skill, and wisdom. Incompetency is fatal.

His service in direct relation to the people of Great Britain was perhaps even greater than his service in negotiation with the British Government. The most important thing in the relations between modern democracies is the feeling of two peoples toward each other. If they like each other and trust each other, any question can be settled. He carried to Great Britain the same readiness for service, the same social unselfishness, the same cheerful, brilliant, and interesting qualities as a public speaker, which had made him so admired and beloved at home. He accepted countless invitations to attend countless banquets and corner-stone layings, and openings of institutions, and unveilings, and celebrations, and meetings of all kinds, and to make countless speeches.

Ambassadorial dignity did not injure him in the slightest degree. He must have been wearied often, but he was never bored, for he really interested himself in the affairs and the characters of the people. He talked to them in a sympathetic way about their affairs, and he told them simply and interestingly about the great men of our history and what Americans were doing, and thinking, and feeling. He was clever and stimulating, and enveloped his serious thought there as he did here with a mantle of humor and fun. He must have kept our British cousins guessing for a while at first, but they soon came to know him, and to understand him with undiluted enjoyment. . . .

The selection of Mr. Choate as an Ambassador Extraordinary at the head of the American Delegation to the Second Hague Conference in 1907 followed naturally upon his career at home and in Great Britain. No other man in the United States had shown himself possessed in so high a degree of so many of the qualities necessary for that service. He had learning without pedantry, power of expression which never sacrificed accuracy to rhetoric, or sense to sound, courage saved from rashness by quick perception and long experience, the lawyer's point of view and the statesman's point of view, the technique of forensic debate, and the technique of diplomatic intercourse. His brilliant success in the Embassy to Great Britain and the high position which he had acquired there had made his great reputation known to the public men of Europe, who at that time ordinarily knew little and cared less about American lawyers, so that he was able to perform his duties at The Hague with great personal prestige and authority.

His work at The Hague fully met the expectations of his Government, and fully justified his selection, for he became one of the great leaders of the Conference and held a commanding position in its deliberations, and under him the whole American delegation worked together with admirable team play. . . .

But the greatest of all the services which Mr. Choate rendered to his country in his long and useful life was at the close, when he realized —as he did very soon after the beginning of the war—that the independence and liberty of the United States were threatened less immediately but no less certainly than those of England and France, by the German grasp for military dominion. With all the vigor and strong conviction of youth he abandoned the comfortable leisure to which the ninth decade of his life entitled him, and threw himself with enthusiasm into the task of making his countrymen see as he saw the certain dangers that lay before them, and the duty that confronted them to rouse themselves and act, for the preservation of their own liberties and the liberties of the world. With voice and pen he pressed his appeal with all the authority of his great reputation, with the wisdom of his experience, the power of an intellect undimmed, of a heart still warm, with the intensity of a great and living patriotism.

When that appeal and the appeal of others who thought and felt with him were answered, and the great decision was made that committed a slowly awakening people to struggle and sacrifice for the preservation of the institutions which he had defended all his life, a great relief and joy possessed him. He was made Chairman of the New York Committee for the reception of the Commissions from England and France under Balfour and Viviani and Marshal Joffre, who came to America after the declaration of war to confirm and help to make immediately practical and effective the new league of Democracy for the war against autocracy. It was his part to lead the people of his own City in a reception of our new allies, so generous and warm-hearted as to strike the imagination of the people of all three countries.

He met the French Commission and then the British Commission. He welcomed them in our behalf with gracious and impressive hospitality. He rode with them through the streets thronged with cheering crowds, and shared with them the respect and homage accorded to the significant and represented figures of that great and unique occasion. He attended all the receptions and banquets, and public and private entertainments, by day and by night, which attended their visits. Daily, and sometimes twice and sometimes three times a day, he made public addresses, appropriate and dignified, and full of interest and deep feeling. His adequate representation filled his own people with pride, and aroused their patriotism and their noblest qualities, and he impressed our guests with confidence and satisfaction.

When the final service of the crowded week was finished, at the Cathedral of St. John the Divine, on Sunday, the thirteenth of May, he bade Mr. Balfour good-bye with the words "Remember, we meet again to celebrate the victory"; and with stout and cheerful heart he bore the burden of his years to his home, to meet the physical reaction that he had been warned was inevitable; and in a few hours the great heart filled with the impulses of noble service and with love of country, and liberty, and justice, ceased to beat. He had given his life for his country.

Elihu Root, *Address before the New York City Bar Association*, Dec. 20, 1917, in *Men and Policies* (Cambridge, Harvard University Press, 1924), 35–43 *passim.*

124. William S. Sims, Earnest Admiral (1921)

BY EDWARD G. LOWRY

Lowry is a Washington journalist and correspondent. For accounts of some naval affairs in which Sims played a part, see bibliography with No. 187 below.

. . . LIKE some of Admiral Sims's close associates in the navy, I do not take much stock in his so-called "indiscretions." To me they have always seemed more like maturely deliberated utterances. I do not think he goes off at half-cock. He knows very well what he is doing. He exercises when he sees fit, and thinks a need exists, his quality of being unafraid. He has grown in his own stature and in public esteem through these "indiscretions." Another thing he has that makes for confidence and poise and a quick willingness to back his own play, and that is, perfect health. To-day at sixty-three he is a better man physically than the average man of forty-five. He functions easily. He keeps in the pink. That perfect good health would make him chipper and gay, even without his eager, dancing spirit.

Once upon a time, not in the long ago, I went to an East Side ball in New York. Word had come to my newspaper office that there might be trouble there. It turned out to be a decorous and sedate party until a lad took his little flat derby hat, shaped precisely like the half of a Rocky Ford melon, and shied it out into the middle of the floor. "Hooray for Hell," he said. Then it began. I think Admiral Sims has a little something of that spirit in him. There is a certain gayety and joyousness of spirit about him that likes a shindy. It is a quality the Irish have. It made Donnybrook Fair famous. Admiral Sims has enjoyed his controversies. He has carried them on in a spirit of high good humor. They have stimulated him. He is always a gay companion when he is under fire and engaged in a cut and thrust enterprise.

In sharp contrast with this carefree aspect of his personality is his methodicalness of method. He has a remarkably retentive memory, really one of these of-course-I-place-you-Mr.-Addison-Sims-of-Seattle minds. But he does not depend on this memory alone. He reënforces and documents it. His books, papers, records, maps, etc., are kept in a precisely ordered, cross-indexed filing system with a place for every-thing and everything in its place. One of his aides once told me:

"I recall one day in Newport when the Admiral was laid up in bed with a slight cold (I never knew him to have anything more serious than this) receiving a note from him asking me to send him a certain paper that was in his office. The memo which I received from him was a sketch of his office bookcase with all of the books on the two upper shelves indicated by name and the location of the paper he wanted indicated with reference to one of these books. I found the paper exactly where he said it was and sent it to him forthwith. That bookcase, like everything else he has ever seen, was photographed on his mind and the negative filed away for future reference."

This is not to say that Admiral Sims is a man who loves details and buries himself in them. He knows how to keep subordinates busy, and to distribute work as well as any man I have ever known. I only seek to indicate that he can be carefree and joyous when he is in a row because he has carefully and thoroughly prepared his position before he begins to fight; to support my contention that he does not go off at half-cock.

He does not play for his own hand, either, his own personal, selfish reward, aggrandizement, and preferment. He is bound up in the navy. He has been honest with himself and the country he serves so conspicuously. I frankly confess that I was not wholly and per-fectly sure of his disinterestedness until the World War. In some of his other enterprises that brought him into the public eye and notice there was a possibility that a yearning for personal acclaim and a de-sire to lift himself to become a figure in the world might have been one of his motives. There were never lacking persons to whisper this charge.

But the great war was the searching test. Admiral Sims could have so managed his affairs and the affairs of the navy abroad, so conducted himself toward the Navy Department and the powers at home in Washington, could have been so smooth, so pliant, so dis-creet, so accommodating, and complaisant, so adroit in taking the easiest way, that he might have returned full of honors—which he would not have deserved. I think there is no doubt he could have so contrived his business that he would have been made a full Admiral for life with the thanks of Congress, and mayhap a sword or some additional token. But he was never tempted to advance his personal interests at the expense of the public interest or an efficient prosecution of the war to an early and unimpeded conclusion. He might have taken to the water and paraded himself before a gaping continent had he so chosen, and only a handful of people in all the world would have known that he was play-acting. To the others he would have been a hero.

Instead, as was his duty and obligation, he kept a careful, orderly record of all that was done and all that was not done that affected our participation in the war at sea. Then when the war ended he came home and had it out with Mr. Josephus Daniels and the Navy Department. He submitted a piece of constructive, documented, supported, and attested criticism of naval administration. He pressed it boldly and fearlessly. He forced a controversy. He got a Senate investigation and the whole naval conduct of the war thoroughly aired and investigated. He was sustained in his contentions and his criticisms. It was a public service. It was not the first nor the second time he had stood up against the Navy Department and won. It was the third time.

In 1901, after trying in vain over a long period through official channels to get action and remedy, Admiral Sims wrote directly to President Roosevelt over the head of the Navy Department and charged that the navy couldn't shoot for beans. He proved it by the target practice records. It was a disillusioning and disconcerting revelation. It raised a rumpus. Roosevelt brought Sims home from China and put him in charge of the navy's target practice.

"Do exactly as he says for eighteen months," said Roosevelt. "If he does not accomplish something in that time, fire him."

Sims was inspector of target practice for six and one-half years, until our naval gunners became the best shots in the world. Whether they have retained that eminence, I do not know. There was some good shooting in the North Sea a little while ago in which we did not participate. But if we are not still the best naval gunners in the world, we have not fallen back to the humiliating inefficiency that was ours prior to Sims's criticism. That was a piece of effective constructive criticism in naval gunnery.

His second notable encounter with the Navy Department grew out of his first. He brought about a radical change and improvement in naval construction. Roosevelt helped him in this, too. From 1900 to 1907 Sims constantly poured into the Department a flood of reports in which he repeatedly charged gross errors of construction in our fighting ships. They weren't properly protected, they weren't properly designed, there was virtually nothing about them that was not wrong; they were armored under water but not above, the guns lay so low that in a sea they were awash; the gun apertures in the turret were too large and offered no protection to the gun crews, the magazines were exposed and badly placed.

"The Kentucky is not a battleship, at all. She is the worst crime in naval construction ever perpetrated by the white race," was one descriptive comment.

By the beginning of 1908 these charges and assertions were appearing in public print. Sims was threatened with court-martial. Secretary Metcalfe, who didn't know or even suspect that President Roosevelt was privy to all that was going on, wrote Sims a formidable letter. But Roosevelt quietly squelched all that. The present design and construction of American battleships dates from those criticisms and that issue forced by Sims.

Twice it was thought the part of "discretion" by the President or the Navy Department to administer Pickwickian reprimands to Admiral Sims for his "indiscretions." At the Guildhall in London in 1910 he said: "If the time ever comes when Great Britain is menaced by a European coalition she can count upon every ship, every dollar, and every drop of blood of her kindred beyond the sea." Of course, this was a great "indiscretion," doubly so because of the fact that it was true. Sims was reprimanded, and then when his prophecy came true was dispatched to London to give the aid he had promised; that he had stepped outside his jurisdiction to promise.

His latest "indiscretion" was a frank public expression of his views about a faction or an element of the Irish people. It inevitably caused a commotion and Sims was duly reprimanded by the Secretary of the Navy—and then went across the street and spent a pleasant social hour by invitation with the Commander-in-Chief of the Army and Navy, the President of the United States. The next three months he spent in endeavoring to answer all the letters, telegrams, and messages of warm commendation he received. The flood of these came to be so great that he had to have a form letter of reply printed.

Sims is a keen professional. The navy is his be all and end all. He thinks ahead. He tries to peer into the future. He has a clear professional vision and a working imagination. He has never become a "shellback" in the navy.

In the present rivalry between the surface craft and the aircraft at sea his mind is veering toward the aircraft as something new and full of undeveloped possibilities. He has been urgent before committees of Congress in asking for airplane carriers. These carriers may prove to be the capital ship of the immediate and imminent future. This eager, almost boyish, quality of his mind that makes him quick to receive new ideas, new things, is a thing that makes him likable as a companion.

Young officers in the navy are his warmest and most enthusiastic admirers. One of them told me: "There has always been a team whenever we were at sea with Admiral Sims as the captain, elected to this position by the team because he has always been the best member on it. His has been a discipline of appreciation rather than a discipline of fear."

A fine, gay, upstanding sailor man. That he is unafraid is the thing to know and remember about him.

Edward G. Lowry, *Washington Close-Ups* (Boston, Houghton Mifflin, 1921), 246–253.

* * *

125. Elihu Root, Public Servant (1921)

BY ANDREW TEN EYCK

For matter by Root see Nos. 51 ana 123 above.

A CERTAIN lawyer, who had often met Elihu Root in the practice of his profession, interested me one evening in the smoking-room of a transatlantic liner by the remark that Mr. Root took hold of the case when the papers were ready. "Let me have all the papers." Then in the quiet of his office he evolved the solution that should win in court. This man said that Mr. Root works like a mathematician with intricate problems: he detaches the situation first, then solves it; that his legal acumen is something more than business ability or legal knowledge.

The success Mr. Root achieved twenty years ago as a lawyer in handling difficult problems of big business is remembered. At the age when most men of the first caliber have either made or unmade a public career through previous service in politics he obtained the Government of the United States, as it were, for his client. Then great constructive accomplishments began to appear. He reorganized the United States Army; created the General Staff; devised and drafted the Platt Amendment for Cuba; wrote every word of the organic law of the Philippines; inaugurated a foreign policy toward Latin America —a thing which had not existed since the days of Blaine. It was Mr. Root who prevented Japan from reaping the full fruits of victory over Russia, just as he had prevented England from remaining in China after the Boxer crisis by accepting the Czar's proposal to withdraw. Mr. Roosevelt's appraisement of these things, which in the heat of a partisan campaign he did not amend, was: "The greatest man that has arisen on either side of the Atlantic in my lifetime."

The words which my fellow-counselor and traveler spoke of Mr. Root's *modus operandi* have some pertinency as he joins the Washington Conference on limitation of armaments and the threatening problems of the Pacific and Far East. "Let me see all the papers. Let us get these difficulties out where we can look at them. This is the first thing to do." When Mr. Root came over to London a year ago last July from The Hague, I spent part of an afternoon with him. It was in his suite at Claridge's. Henry White was there. Mr. Root was fresh from The Hague, where he had been sitting for a month in conference. He remarked how hard it was in international conference to get the papers out where one can work at them. "The difficulty is not with principles," he said, "but with understanding each other through the barriers to communication which different ways of thinking and feeling present. It is another country, another language, another literature, another custom, and sometimes a great many, that you have to deal with. One learns quickly there that respect for the feelings and prejudices of others is the condition for having one's own feelings and prejudices respected. That is the problem of diplomacy."

We had known in London of Mr. Root's conference with Lord Phillimore when he first arrived in England on his way to The Hague. Mr. Root believes in having a plan—not a too comprehensive plan, but a working plan. He points to one cause of the failure of Paris as the lack of a plan. When he walked down the gangplank at Plymouth, he carried in his pocket a scheme for the Permanent Court of Justice. He conferred with Lord Phillimore. The merit of the Root plan which was adopted was its avoidances of the pitfall of the Hague Tribunal for Arbitration in the manner of selecting judges. The testimony of its merits is the now complete panel of judges for the International Court of Justice selected by the Assembly of the League of Nations.

The Root psychology has, perhaps, the inherent limitation of the defects of its virtue. Detachment of view for solution of problems in politics creates suspicion. It does not produce the conviction of impartiality that it should. "There must be something behind or hidden in this ideal Constitution," said a great enough number of people to defeat the adoption of the proposed Constitution in New York in 1915. "He is not one of us," said emissaries in Russia in 1917 before the Root mission arrived. "He would make the best President, but Taft is the best candidate," said Mr. Roosevelt.

And yet he enjoys a position in England not unlike that of Bryce in America. He declined the proffered headship of the International Court of Justice. He is spoken of throughout Europe in the equivalent of the phrase of Roosevelt: "The greatest man on either side of the Atlantic." Lord Bryce said to me: "Your greatest Secretary of State since Webster, the greatest brain you have."

It has been said of Mr. Root that he is aloof and unimaginative. I do not agree. The manner in which he goes about the solution of problems may suggest aloofness. But he will talk to you and intimate what is going on in his mind—more than you may advisedly repeat. He seeks your view-point. He is sociable. His imagination is that of the mathematician rather than the poet. It is the vision of a constructive worker. He has always followed the lure of great problems in business and in public office. Of the possibilities in statesmanship that have come to him he has selected to wrestle with those that appealed to the imagination: a code judicial for the Philippines, an ideal Constitution for the State of New York, a mission to aid a limitless country like Russia, the scheme for the International Court of Justice. Now that the Court is in being, the routine work of its headship would waste and dull the strength of his remaining years. There is not allurement in such work for Mr. Root's constructive imagination. But there is in the part he is to take in the Washington Conference. That is why he has taken it.

I talked with Mr. Root on the eve of his journey to Washington to see Mr. Harding. He was impressed with what Lord Bryce had said to him at Williamstown about the people in America having more interest in foreign affairs than those in England. He said to me that he believed it was a true observation, and asked my opinion. "I do not suppose," said Mr. Root, "that until recent years foreign affairs have enlisted the slightest interest on the part of the people of the United States. We must get rid of that feeling which exists so widely throughout the world and that Bret Harte describes in one of his books—the feeling that exists in a village to which a stranger comes, and the people look upon him as having the defect of being a foreigner. We need a certain international-mindedness."

I asked Mr. Root if it was sound to say that questions of armament can be considered only in connection with those issues because of which nations take up arms, and that therefore it follows that the coming Conference should first vitally concern itself with such issues. "Decidedly yes," was the answer that he made. "That is fundamental, more fundamental than is apparent."

The significance of Mr. Root's observation is best appreciated in reading the reports which were recently handed to the League of Nations at Geneva on the status of armaments in each country. One year ago the Powers agreed to a continuous armament reduction. Nothing was said about those problems that make for war. The records are now in, and prove the direct method of Geneva a confessed failure. The great signatory Powers—Great Britain, France, Japan, Italy—refused not only to reduce armament but even to report on existing status. On one pretext or another the burden of armament has constantly increased. Let us see if Washington will do better. At least it deserves credit for the frankness of addressing itself not only to technical questions of armament but to those persistent problems that threaten the peace of the world.

Mr. Root believes the coming Conference will be our way into a working world co-operative arrangement. I think I may say that it is his hope that there will grow out of the Washington Conference a permanent Association of Nations for conference which will include the United States and all other civilized Powers. Perhaps there is some intimation of the weight he gives to technical disarmament in what he once said of the provisions of the League Covenant bearing on the limitation of armaments: "The success of these provisions is vital. If they are not effective, the whole effort to secure future peace goes for nothing. There must be a permanent commission to inspect the carrying out of disarmament. Every country should consent, just as every trustee is willing to have an independent audit of his accounts." Geneva has just shown that such consent is not forthcoming.

Mr. Root is in excellent health. There are the same quick step, alert and erect carriage, glow of health in his cheeks, that there were six years ago in the Constitutional Convention at Albany, where I saw him daily. He looks by less than twenty years the seventy-six that he is. He is enjoying life. He spent the winter in California and the summer at his boyhood home at Clinton, New York. There is in his reappearance in Washington something contradictory to what Englishmen say of our public men: "They do not come back. Ten years is the length of their careers."

Washington will see the unchanged Root. It will find him asking for all the papers overnight. He comes from another generation, familiar because of his part in a former day with the supreme efforts then made to regulate and secure the peace of the world. In this he stands uniquely serviceable to his country and the Conference as a whole. He knows the rocks on which the ships have foundered. Mr. Root has the solemn sense that there is about to be a drama which means life or death in its ultimate *dénouement*—that the Washington Conference is not to deal with the late war, which was done ill or well at Paris, but to prevent the next war, to make peace before war comes.

Andrew Ten Eyck, *Elihu Root: A Study of the Man and His Ways* in *Outlook* (New York, 1921), CXXIX, 429-430.

126. Henry Cabot Lodge, a Massachusetts Institution
(1924)

BY SENATOR JAMES W. WADSWORTH, JR.

This address by a Senator from New York characterizes one of the most scholarly
of our national statesmen. Lodge supported the Wilson administration during the
World War, but steadfastly opposed the President's plan for American participation in the League of Nations. On this, as on other controversial subjects, he sustained his convictions with great warmth and astuteness. For Lodge, see also No.
202 below; and for a speech by him, see No. 171 below.

MR. PRESIDENT: I am glad of this opportunity to express
my appreciation of HENRY CABOT LODGE. I shall not attempt to review his remarkable achievements in public life or in the
field of literature, but shall confine myself to one or two comments as
to his personal characteristics as I found them to be.

At the outset, Mr. President, I may be pardoned a personal reference. Ten years ago or thereabouts I came to the Senate, comparatively speaking, pretty much a youngster both in years and experience,
and conscious of that fact, sought advice from those who could give
it. It was with some trepidation that I went to Senator LODGE
and with what boldness I could summon asked him for help. I shall
never forget the generosity of his response. Not only at that time but
during all our service together in the Senate he extended to me, as
he did no doubt to many others, that friendly hand and generous
slap on the back which is so encouraging, especially when coming from
an older to a younger man. I learned, therefore, early in my contact
with Mr. LODGE of his innate kindliness and generosity.

It has been said or thought of him, perhaps, by some people that
he was not very approachable. I have a different conception of him
in that respect. Mr. LODGE had a sensitive regard for the privacy
of others. One can not visualize him, or one finds it difficult
to visualize him, "scraping acquaintance" with a total stranger.
He might be well-nigh overcome with desire to know a man and discuss some topic of interest with him, but he could not bring himself
to invade that man's privacy. This may have been shyness; it may
have come from the old New England habit of thought—and it should
be remembered that in his blood flowed the essence of old New Eng-

land—but whatever gave rise to that habit in him it had a most profound effect upon his relations with his fellows. He wanted friendship; he could not go out and demand it; but when he formed a friendship or when friendship came to him, he was proud of it and cherished it in a manner difficult to describe.

There was much of the poet in him. He loved beauty in art and literature, and one could have no more delightful experience than to hear Mr. LODGE discourse about great authors, great books, great paintings, and great statues. To the most ill informed on matters of that sort, Mr. LODGE could describe works of art and literature in a manner to capture the imagination of his listeners.

He could clothe an author or a book in his description in such a fashion as to excite the interest of his hearers and bring them to a better comprehension of the classics in these fields. I say it was a delight, as well as an education, to hear him discourse on things of that sort. Sometimes I thought that he was at his very best when, surrounded by a group of friends, he found an opportunity thus to converse.

I say he loved beauty in nature. Perhaps it is not generally known to the public that Mr. LODGE loved a good horse. In all of his life he loved horses. Nothing gave him more of a thrill, I am led to believe, than galloping across country, across fields, out in the open, on an intelligent and high-spirited horse. He loved to exchange reminiscences with lovers of the horse, and he did it in such fashion as to display his affection for that noble animal and also his liking for the outdoors; and, Mr. President, if I may be pardoned the suggestion, it is very seldom that a man who loves an intelligent and high-spirited horse fails to be a good sportsman in all of life's contentions.

His patriotism has been mentioned here this afternoon and full justice has been done to it. I might make this observation: It seemed to me as I heard him talk with his friends on both sides of the Chamber during the days when great debates were going on in the Senate in relation to the future of our country and its contact with other nations, that his patriotism had a certain element of fierceness in it. I am sure that all of you can remember the intensity with which he would express his convictions concerning the destiny of the United States, whether he was expressing them upon the floor of the Senate or in private conferences. There was an element of fierceness in it, and this may be regarded as somewhat unusual in a scholar and historian. All too often, in my humble judgment, scholars extend their national affections a little too liberally and are lacking in that very intensity of love for their own country which, after all, is so essential to a nation if it is to survive in a crisis. But Mr. LODGE's reading, his study of the history of nations and the habits of human beings, apparently led him to that kind of patriotism which I have endeavored to describe. He was proud of his country, always proud of it. No matter whether the administration here at Washington was Democratic or Republican, he was proud of the United States. He could not bear to think that it was taking second place in any of its international contacts. I have often thought, as we have talked with him in the Committee on Foreign Relations, that his consistent support of the Diplomatic and Consular Service was due in large measure to this feeling. He wanted to be sure that the American ambassador or the American minister or the American consular officer was holding his own against all comers at his foreign post.

The Senator from Utah [Mr. Smoot], in referring to Mr. LODGE's patriotism, has mentioned his support of an administration of an opposite party when the country was facing a great crisis. That was perfectly typical of him. He was not without ambition. What good man is without ambition? But his ambition was to serve. He might have led a much happier life had he not been in public service. He had many resources at his command—financial, social, literary— which would have engaged his time and delighted his mind; but he wanted to serve, to serve his country. He wanted to serve her well; and at times he was conscious, I think, of the fact that he had served his country well, and that made him happy. His pride in service was not confined to his own service. He was happy and glad to see others serving well; and, I think, nothing in all his life made him quite so happy and quite so proud as the service rendered to his country by his son-in-law, Augustus P. Gardner. Many of you, no doubt, have heard him mention Mr. Gardner with a very evident thrill of pride.

Mr. LODGE was devoted to his home; and his home was in Massachusetts, never in Washington. Whenever he got the chance he went back to Nahant, which had been his home from early boyhood, the home of all his family, and in some measure the home of his grandchildren. His heart was there, and there was much of deep and rich sentiment in his heart. As I recollect him now, I feel that he would have been even happier had he been able to express his tender sentiments to his fellows as freely as he would have liked. His inability to do so—if I may use that expression—was due to that quality or habit of thought which I tried to describe a few moments ago.

Mr. President, contact with a man like Mr. LODGE is inspiring; it is helpful, and, I say frankly, especially helpful to those of younger years. We are all better men for his having been here, and this country is a better country.

James W. Wadsworth, Jr., Address in the United States Senate, January 19, 1925; *Henry Cabot Lodge: Memorial Addresses Delivered in Congress* (Washington, Government Printing Office, 1925), 52–56.

---

127. Eugene Debs, Social Leader (1926)

FROM THE NATION

Eugene Victor Debs (1855–1926) was a sincere socialist and pacifist, and a great leader of men of his faith.—Bibliography: David Karsner, *Debs, his Life and Letters.*

"'GENE DEBS was the only Jesus Christ I ever knew." So Sam Moore, an embittered Negro convict faced with lifelong imprisonment, explained to the warden of Atlanta Penitentiary the extraordinary effect upon him of 'Gene Debs's friendship. 'Gene Debs was a man who evoked that extravagant, almost unbelievable, type of affection in thousands upon thousands of his fellow-men. He evoked it because he gave it. At his funeral services in Terre Haute Victor Berger said that Debs went beyond the Biblical command to love thy neighbor as thyself, for he loved his neighbor better than himself, and the vast crowd with tear-stained faces solemnly nodded assent.

To this love for human beings Debs added a love for humanity. The two are not always combined. The concern for humanity, the vision, the dauntless courage, the uncompromising spirit of the prophet and pioneer may be consistent with a ruthless disregard for the immediate interests of individual human beings. It was not so with Debs. His courage was born of love. His passion for mankind, his hope for the workers grew out of the love of comrades, not only as they might become but as they were with all their faults and weak- nesses. In this combination of dauntless prophet, far-seeing idealist, and simple lover of men lay the man's greatness.

Debs embraced the cause of the workers from choice and not ne- cessity. The outward circumstances of his early life and his own gifts were of a sort that would have led him naturally to political and financial success. Indeed, while he was still a very young man, he made a successful beginning in local politics. But his sympathies, long before he was a Socialist, were with the workers. Our generation has almost forgotten that Debs began as an unusually successful labor organizer. He was the founder of the present Brotherhood of Railway Trainmen. When he became convinced that this form of craft organization was not adequate to the needs of the railway workers he resigned his $4,000-a-year position to become president of the American Railway Union at $900 a year. The world still remembers that union and its part in the Pullman strike. The strike and the union were both broken by Grover Cleveland's use of United States troops against the protest of Governor Altgeld of Illinois. This strike, too, was marked by the beginning of government by injunction, and Debs was sent to jail for six months on a charge of contempt— the forerunner of a series of similar acts of judicial tyranny.

In prison Debs first learned of Socialism and became a Socialist, although not until after the first Bryan campaign did he irrevocably tie his fortunes to that movement. Following his release from prison Debs undertook to raise and pay off $40,000 of debts accumulated by the American Railway Union. This obligation he fulfilled at great cost to himself at a time when not even the creditors of the union held him responsible.

From 1897 on, Debs's life and fortunes were inextricably mingled with those of the Socialist movement. Five times he was its candidate for President. He was not primarily a builder of policies, nor in his later years an organizer. He was a flaming spirit, a living incarnation of an ideal. That ideal was an ideal of uncompromising struggle, but of struggle by non-violent methods. The victory he wanted was a victory of peace. It was impossible that Debs could believe the European war a war for democracy, or that any war could end war. So he made himself the spokesman of the Socialist ideal of peace through an understanding between the workers of the world. For his devotion to liberty and peace he was sentenced to ten years of penal servitude. Today it seems almost unthinkable that on the basis of his famous Canton speech any man could have been convicted. In no sense were his words pro-German. They did not ask American troops to lay down their arms. They were a plea for the end of war, for the recognition of Russia, for the preservation of liberty at home. Yet that speech, during a "war for democracy," sent a man past sixty years of age, suffering from the heart disease which finally resulted in his death, to jail with common felons. Worse still, after the armistice Debs was kept in jail by the personal vindictiveness of a President who had himself acknowledged the economic causes of the war as plainly as the man whom he held prisoner. It was left to President Harding, in response to public demand, to restore Debs to freedom. Neither he nor President Coolidge gave him back his citizenship.

Of Debs's permanent place in the history of the labor movement and of social progress it is too early to speak. Philosophically, in spite of the Communist attempt to claim him, he was an extreme democrat, a convinced believer in freedom. However much he might admire the achievements of Russia, he never could identify himself with any sort of dictatorship. Our generation with its little faith in the common man may find his philosophy old-fashioned. Temporarily, at least, it has lost much of its appeal. Yet Debs himself was the sort of man who gives one new confidence in men and their possibilities. That he was what he was, that he loved as he loved, is reason for hope. He belongs to the republic of the immortals whose memory is a living inspiration to mankind.

Nation, November 3, 1926 (New York), 443.

128. William E. Borah, Free Lance (1926)

BY RAY T. TUCKER

Senator Borah has represented his state of Idaho at Washington for twenty years. Nominally a Republican, he has defied precise classification because of his independent views on nearly all subjects and his determination to defend them. He succeeded Henry Cabot Lodge (see No. 126 above) as Chairman of the Foreign Relations Committee of the Senate. For a speech by Borah, see No. 193 below.

WILLIAM EDGAR BORAH'S first noteworthy appearance on the American scene, as brilliant prosecutor of three Western mining leaders who had found dynamite more effective than collective bargaining, was contemporaneous with the homicidal outbreak of Harry Thaw and the evolution of a type of newspaper which seized upon both men as equally good copy. Borah's forensic feats in that remote Idaho court-room were pictured in great and colorful detail by a swarm of metropolitan reporters, and so his star was high in the firmament when he hung his black wide-awake hat on a Senate office peg on March 4, 1907, combed back his shaggy brown mane, and looked around for new worlds to astound, if not to conquer.

His part in prosecuting Big Bill Haywood, Moyer and Pettibone had made a deep impression upon the Old Guard leaders of the Senate. They rubbed their hands at the accession of this solid and serious Republican from the Mormon State of Idaho, for their ranks were in sore need of recruits in those muck-raking, panicky days of 1907. The Old Guard envisaged Borah as a stalwart reinforcement in the holy work of resisting the new movement for reform, and stifling the awakening class-consciousness of the American working man. He was immediately made chairman of the Committee on Labor and Education, an unheard-of trust for a first-termer, for any attempt to translate the rising clamor of the down-trodden into legislative reality would have to have its beginnings in that committee. To certain cynical colleagues who expressed alarm at the bestowal of such a key post on an untried man, Senator Aldrich, the Republican boss, replied with a cloak-room wink: "It's all right. I've looked him up. He's an anti-labor man and a corporation attorney."

But Aldrich, for once, was wrong. He was the first of the long line of Senators to grapple unsuccessfully with the enigma of Borah.

For almost immediately the newcomer took to disconcerting, and, in the view of the Old Guard, grossly immoral practises. Far from guarding valiantly the Senate citadel of capitalism, he proceeded, with full steam, to make a wreck of it. Soon his committee was reporting out, and getting passed, the most radical proposals an astonished and horrified Senate had ever been asked to consider on the labor question. There were bills establishing the eight-hour day on government contracts, bills for the creation of a new and highly dubious Department of Labor, and subversive resolutions for the investigation of the twelve-hour day and the seven-day week in the sacrosanct iron and steel industries. Borah and labor became articulate together, and began to sing the same appalling tune. It was good business for a young Senator trying to get upon the first pages, but in Aldrich's view it was sheer spoils and treason. His protégé was striking mighty blows at everything the Aldriches held to be sacred. No more disastrous treachery had ever been heard of on Capitol Hill.

From that painful perfidy dates the conviction of all the Republican stalwarts that Borah is an untrustworthy fellow. His doings since then, stretching over a score of years, have only confirmed this judgment. To the Old Guard of to-day, as to that of 1907, he is a puzzle and a plague. As the years have rolled on, indeed, he has puzzled the safe and sane men more and more, for sometimes he has been violently against them and at other times he has been amazingly with them. There are many facets, it appears, to his character. At times he has stood forth as a soaring Liberal; at times he has been more conservative than Mr. Coolidge. The public, long since despairing of understanding him, or reconciling the conflicting manifestations of his personality, now views him, it would seem, as *sui generis*—a courageous but incomprehensible figure, one who voices his convictions unexpectedly and boldly, no matter how adversely they may affect his party standing or his political security.

His enemies call him an obstructionist, a dreamer, a prima donna, and say he prefers the fame which flows from strutting the political peaks in solitary grandeur and obstinacy to solid accomplishments shared with his peers. When his Senate colleagues discuss him among themselves, they use very plain English: he is a faker, a trimmer, a false alarm. His admirers are just as intemperate; to them he is the foremost exponent of practical idealism in American public life to-day and the perennially prospective messiah of a third party dedicated to righteousness. Meanwhile, Mr. Borah himself appears to know precisely what he believes, and why. His one and constant boast is that he is an old-fashioned American who patterns his beliefs and conduct after the Constitution and the—to him—obvious purposes of the Founding Fathers. He can justify—to himself at least—every act of his mystifying career by constitutional precedents. Before the heroes who founded this best of all governments his abasement is absolute.

But necessity often compels him to resort to curious personal interpretations and a species of revelation to satisfy this passion for following in the Fathers' footsteps. As the social and political order has grown more complex his divinations have had to become more numerous and arduous, and to many it now seems that his divining-rod has been overworked and warped. But to all entreaties that he discard it, or lay it up for repairs, he remains deaf, for he believes that he cannot go wrong if he clings to the Constitution, or to his understanding of it. With the thunderous assertion that "the Fathers understood the science of government as no other single group of men ever understood it," he annihilates his opponents, and he will continue to do so as long as his colleagues in the Senate let pass without challenge his highly dubious citations of precedent, and his clairvoyant glimpses into the minds of Washington, Hamilton and Jefferson. . . .

Mr. Borah's views on Prohibition will probably not affect the eventual settlement of this problem. The chief harm he will do will be to help defer the day when it can be disposed of without prejudice and without bigotry. Meanwhile, his speeches will fan the flame of fanatic passion, whether he means them to or not, and he himself will depart further and further from the record. For once he has attacked a subject, he has a tendency to neglect the facts, so lured is he by the magic of his own voice. It is a common failing, but in him it amounts to a disease. He is a great believer in oratory. Perhaps no other man in American public life to-day would so sincerely deplore the passing of the spoken word as a political and parliamentary weapon. Fortunately for him, he believes that this will come "only after selfishness and sensuality shall have imbruted or destroyed all the nobler faculties of the mind."

The conventional method of describing a Senate combat in which Mr. Borah takes a hand is to liken it to a bullfight. Borah, as the careless and imaginative pen records it, leans back easily in his seat, seemingly taking no interest in the subject under discussion. A faintly cynical smile occasionally appears on his lips. Finally he climbs to his feet, still smiling and leaning slightly forward. And then, urbanely, effortlessly, he becomes the picador, hurling jibing darts into the hide of the poor Senator who has aroused him. The victim, squirming, eventually flings back with an angry retort. Then Borah becomes the mighty matador. His dimpled chin juts out, the vertical lines in his forehead deepen into a frown, his eyes flash, he tosses his tremendous mane, and his words pour forth torrentially. They become rapier thrusts, seeking straight the heart of his antagonist, who presently falls. Borah then tosses aside his rapier lightly and resumes his seat. His colleagues stare in admiration; the galleries rock with applause.

What the correspondents fail to see is that Borah's rapier is sometimes tipped with poison. He often bests an opponent because the poor fellow is not sufficiently versed in history to controvert some of his most devastating and inaccurate assertions and allusions. A checkup reveals a Borah mistaken in his facts, but unless the error is detected while the combatants are on their feet, he gets the headlines, and his rival gets the ha-ha. During a debate, for example, on the French debt Senator Bruce of Maryland essayed to defend France by citing its generosity to the struggling colonies, while Mr. Borah contended that France had assisted the colonies merely to embarrass England. A sneer was Mr. Borah's retort to the Maryland Senator's assertion that France had given Benjamin Franklin 6,000,000 livres for which no repayment was asked. But as the debate continued, the plodding Bruce seemed to have the better of it in his authorities and facts. The great matador was about to be worsted. But no! Out flashed that famous rapier.

"Mr. President," appealed Borah, "I object to the Senator putting incorrect history into my speech!"

The galleries shook with applause and Senators chuckled at the discomfiture of the pedestrian Mr. Bruce. It was another Borah triumph. But meanwhile it is a fact that France *did* advance the 6,000,000 livres as a gift.

In much the same way, Mr. Borah has gained certain strategic victories in his demand for a more liberal policy toward Russia. As precedent, he cites the Washington Administration's recognition of a France as bloody and disorganized as Russia is supposed to be to-day. Washington's Cabinet faced the same problem, he declares, and *unanimously* decided to accord recognition. The Senator apparently forgets, or slurs over the fact, that his hero, Alexander Hamilton, proposed to so hedge around recognition that it would have been a meaningless gesture. Nor does he point out that it was Jefferson's honest mind which prevailed over views of Hamilton and his clique in the Cabinet.

These seem trifling things, and they are, as politics go. They are done almost daily by Mr. Borah's more obscure fellows. But in the great Idaho seer they seem somehow incongruous and discreditable. His many failures, though sometimes more magnificent than his lesser colleagues' successes, loom large because of the high expectations he arouses. If he has come to be regarded throughout the country as the foremost trimmer in American public life to-day he has only himself to blame.

Ray T. Tucker, *Borah of Idaho*, in *American Mercury* (December, 1926), IX, 385–393 *passim*. Reprinted by permission of the author.

CHAPTER XXIV — PRESIDENT WOODROW WILSON

129. A Breaker of Precedents (1912)

BY EX-SECRETARY JOSEPHUS DANIELS (1924)

Daniels served as Secretary of the Navy under Wilson from 1913 to 1921. He was a southern newspaper editor, with no special preparation for governmental administration. He was an earnest and prodigious worker, but roused opposition.— Bibliography on Wilson: W. E. Dodd, *Woodrow Wilson;* H. J. Ford, *Woodrow Wilson;* H. W. Harris, *Woodrow Wilson from the English Point of View;* A. M. Low, *Woodrow Wilson;* David F. Houston, *Eight Years with Wilson's Cabinet;* Charles Seymour, editor, *The Intimate Papers of Colonel House;* J. P. Tumulty, *Woodrow Wilson as I Knew Him;* William Allen White, *Woodrow Wilson;* Woodrow Wilson, *Speeches and Public Papers,* collected by various editors.

IN December, 1912, shortly after Governor Wilson had been elected President, a friend visited him at the executive offices, in Trenton. This gentleman, who afterwards became a member of his Cabinet, had called to secure the influence of the President-elect to adjust differences in Delaware which threatened to defeat the election of a Democratic Senator in that State. A Senate in sympathy was important to the working together to carry out party pledges. Governor Wilson was keen to do anything proper in the matter, but the threatened division was adjusted without the necessity of his intervention.

"Did you ever hear the reading of a President's message at the joint session of Congress?" he asked the visitor, apropos of nothing. His friend had.

"Did anybody pay attention to the reading?" he asked, and his visitor told him that usually the members chatted or read papers while the clerks read the message. Many of them went out, and it was out of the ordinary for anybody to listen to it, the Congressmen preferring to read it for themselves later. That was all, but later when President Wilson stood in Congress to deliver his message in person, the conversation was recalled.

Jefferson had discontinued delivering the messages in person because he thought it savored too much of an "address from the throne." When Wilson announced his intention to return to the practice begun by Washington, old-timers thought it looked too much like possible executive dictation. But after his first appearance, when not only Congress but the diplomats and all who could gain admittance to the House of Representatives listened intently, applauding what they approved, there was none to doubt the wisdom of restoring the Washington practice. This breaking of a precedent an hundred years old was an innovation which demonstrated its wisdom. He prefaced the message by saying: "I am very glad indeed to have this opportunity to address the two Houses directly and to verify for myself the impression that the President of the United States is a person, not a mere department of Government hailing Congress from some isolated island of jealous power, sending messages, not speaking naturally and with his own voice—that he is a human being trying to coöperate with other human beings in a common service." He added: "After this pleasant experience, I shall feel quite normal, in all our dealings with one another." Both President Harding and President Coolidge followed the example of their precedent-breaking and precedent-making predecessor. Wilson ended recommendations to Congress. The delivering of the message is now an impressive occasion and the views of the executive receive greater consideration than when the clerks hurried or droned through their messages.

Readers of "The State," written many years before he broke the precedent of a century by delivering his message in person, might have known he would do that very thing. He had said in his book, "Washington and John Adams addressed Congress in person on public affairs, but Jefferson, the third President, was not an easy speaker and preferred to send a written message." Here is his scorn of the way precedents control: "Subsequent Presidents followed his example, of course. Hence, a sacred rule of constitutional action."

"You do not mean to tell me that Wilson is thinking of doing so revolutionary a thing as that?" exclaimed an old-time Senator to a friend of Wilson's shortly before the inauguration in 1913. "The Senators would resent it. It would be a fatal mistake. I hope you will dissuade him if he has such a thing in mind."

The friend of Wilson had just returned from Princeton and was talking to the Senator about his visit. The President-elect had asked him: "Is there not a room in the Capitol set apart for the President?" "Yes." "Does the President ever occupy it?" The answer was that it was occupied by the chief executive only at the close of Congress when he signed measures passed in the rush hours. At other times, it was explained, it was used by the Senators to see favored visitors.

"What would you think," asked Wilson of his visitor, "if I should make use of it now and then when it was desirable to hold conferences with Senators?" The friend, himself lacking reverence for outworn precedents, said that the builders of the Capitol having constructed a room called "The President's Room," he could see no reason why it should not be used by the officer for whom it was set apart, but added, "If you use it, there will be the cry that you are trying to control legislative action. It has not been used since the time whereof the memory of man runneth not to the contrary."

Later, when President Wilson for the first time occupied the President's room and held conferences there with a number of Senators on important policies, this happened: the old-time Senator, who had been shocked at the very thought of the innovation, in an interview published next morning, expressed his gratification that, instead of sending for Senators to make a trip to the White House, the new President did them the courtesy to call at the Capitol for conferences. Nevertheless, though this Senator was converted, President Wilson never occupied his room at the Capitol that there was not talk of "executive dictation" and of the attempt "to relegate the Senate to a subordinate position." Most Senators, however, did not indulge in such criticism, for while they found Mr. Wilson earnestly advocating his measures, they found he was seeking a common ground of agreement. Adamant for the principle at stake he was, but reasonable and ready for every helpful concession. Often his open-minded conferences with Senators and Representatives caused him to adopt gladly the methods their experience showed were an improvement on his own. But once the line of battle had been drawn, once the opponents of the principle involved were seeking compromise that would impair the idea aimed at, in the Federal Reserve contest and others, he adopted the motto of Grant: "I purpose to fight it out on this line if it takes all summer."

It has been a precedent time out of mind in the White House that no one must sit down while the President is standing. There is a story that years and years ago, a lady of fifty took a seat while waiting for her husband at the close of a brilliant reception. A White House visitor reminded her of the rule and told her it was regarded as lèse majesté. President Wilson upon all formal occasions made no change in rules. One evening when the receiving party were gathered in the library upstairs awaiting the signal to descend the stairs in the "grand march" as it is called, a member of the Cabinet and a lady house guest drew up their chairs by the fireplace for a cozy chat, all unmindful that the President was standing. The wife of the Cabinet officer, who was standing and engaged in conversation with the President, gave the wifely command by her eyes to her husband. He obeyed it and came to his feet immediately. Seeing this pantomime, the President walked over to the Cabinet member, placed a hand on each shoulder, pressed him back into the chair, saying with a smile, "Sit down and behave yourself," and, turning to the wife, added that no matter what the policy at formal occasions, no office could make him forget his right to be a gentleman at his own fireside.

"Mr. Bryan was saying to me," said President Wilson at an early meeting of the Cabinet—he repeated the remark that the Secretary of State had made, in a low tone of voice, before the Cabinet session had actually begun. Other members were talking and Mr. Bryan had chosen the moment when the others were so engaged to speak of a state department matter which was not important enough for discussion. "I am repeating this whispered message," President Wilson went on to say, "solely because when I read the 'Diary of Gideon Welles' I was impressed by the resentment felt by the other members of the Cabinet when Seward would take the President aside and talk with him alone, while the other members sat by wondering why they could not be let in on the conversation between the President and the Secretary of State." That precedent of private conferences obtaining in Lincoln days was not followed.

One precedent which had been established from the beginning was that the President of the United States should not go beyond the borders of his country. Some indeed had an idea that it was prohibited by the Constitution or the laws. Therefore, when Wilson decided to go himself to Paris to take part in framing the peace treaty, there was a great outcry that he was not only smashing tradition and breaking precedent, but he was also violating the proprieties. So fierce was the criticism that an outsider would have supposed that Wilson was breaking all the Ten Commandments at once. Mr. Lansing, Secretary of State, whose mind was not open to departures from custom, says in his book, "I felt it to be my duty, as his official adviser in foreign affairs, and as one desirous to have him adopt a wise course, to tell him frankly that I thought the plan for him to attend was unwise and would be a mistake." The assumption that it was Lansing's duty "as official adviser in foreign affairs" to protest against Wilson's going received no rebuke from the President, showing he was often a patient and long-suffering man. "The President listened to my remarks without comment and turned the conversation into other channels" was the entry Lansing made in his diary after the interview, and again in his diary Lansing says he wrote at the time: "I prophesy trouble in Paris and worse than trouble here."

On the other hand, the New York *Times* succinctly said Wilson's going to Paris was "one of four times when Wilson fell up stairs." At the Conference of Governors held in Annapolis, December 18, 1918, Secretary Lane gave this effective answer to the criticisms of Wilson's going to Paris:

"I have seen criticisms of the President and so have you for going across the water at this time. The spirit which animates him in going is the spirit of the new day. It is the spirit of giving your hand to your neighbor. It is the spirit that would make this war the end of wars.

"The man who stands as the representative of the foremost democracy of the world goes to Europe, not that he may march down the Champs Élysées, not that he may receive the plaudits of the French multitudes. But he goes to Europe as the champion of American ideals because he wants to see that out of the war comes something worth while. He would have been derelict, he would have been negligent, he would have been false to our ideas of him, if he had not stood in Paris in person as the champion of that principle which we love and those institutions which we hope to see spread around the world.

"To me, Woodrow Wilson in Paris represents not the ambitions of Napoleon, striving to master the world by force, but of the greater Pasteur, the healer of the nation who comes to bring peace, happiness, and to secure gratitude from those whose lives and homes he makes secure."

Every reader of Wilson's "Congressional Government" should have known he would go to Paris to the Peace Conference. "When foreign affairs play a prominent part in the politics of a nation, its executive must of necessity be its guide; must utter every initial judgment, take every first step of action, supply the information upon which it is to act, suggest and, in a large measure, control its conduct," and he added: "He must always stand at the front of our affairs, and the office will be as big and as influential as the man who occupies it."

"After all," he said to the Englishmen in the Mansion House at London, when he visited there in December, 1918—"after all, the breaking of precedents, though this may sound strange doctrine in England, is the most sensible thing to do. The harness of precedent is sometimes a very sad and harassing trammel. In this case the breaking of precedent is sensible for a reason that is very prettily illustrated in a remark attributed to Charles Lamb.

"One evening, in a company of his friends, they were discussing a person who was not present and Lamb said, in his hesitating manner.

"'I h-hate that fellow.'

"'Why, Charles,' one of his friends said, 'I did not know that you knew him.'

"'Oh,' he said, 'I-I-I d-don't. I can't h-hate a man I know.'

"And perhaps that simple and attractive remark may furnish a secret for cordial international relationship. When we know one another we cannot hate one another."

He walked the groove of change.

Josephus Daniels, *The Life of Woodrow Wilson* (Philadelphia, John C. Winston, 1924), 220–227. Reprinted by special permission of the publishers.

130. "Too Proud to Fight" (1915)

BY SIR A. MAURICE LOW (1918)

Low was the chief American correspondent of the London *Morning Post*.—Bibliography as in No. 129 above.

ON the seventh of May, 1915, the *Lusitania* was torpedoed. Before that Germany had committed more atrocious crimes, since then the atrocities of which Germany has been guilty make the sinking of the *Lusitania* trivial, but nothing that Germany has done so profoundly affected the moral sense of the entire world. In America there went up a cry for vengeance; many persons who had conscientiously obeyed the President's injunction to be neutral in thought and action now openly proclaimed their detestation of Germany and felt that the United States must, to preserve her own self-respect and dignity and in vindication of the rights of humanity, declare war on Germany. But the President remained unmoved. He sat in the White House a solitary and lonely figure (Mrs. Wilson had died two days after England declared war), listening to the growing storm; listening and pondering and waiting. He knew of the mounting excitement, he knew that nothing would be more gratifying to the men who had been the partisans of England from the first than the uniting of their country with England and France in the war against Germany; he knew that the torpedo fired by a German submarine commander had become a powerful agent in bringing the moral issue home to the nation; he knew he had but to speak, and the indifferent and the apathetic would be quickened and they would join in the demand for war; but he also knew, and perhaps no man knew it so well as he, that the destruction of the *Lusitania* had not united his people. There were still two camps, the partisans of Germany had not been converted; Americans who believed the war was none of their affair were shaken, but not convinced. And he knew that to go to war with a divided country was impossible. Moreover he had not abandoned hope that the United States could be kept out of the war; and while from the depths of the Atlantic the dead of the *Lusitania* besought him that they be not forgotten, and he was resolved that never should they be forgotten and in the fullness of time their murder should be expiated, he still cherished the faith that policy might so shape events that the toll of American life would not have to be increased.

Some days before the *Lusitania* had been sent to the bottom Mr. Wilson had accepted an invitation to address a meeting of newly naturalized citizens in Philadelphia on the evening of May 10. It was known of course that the Government of the United States could not permit such a gross violation of international law as the sinking of the *Lusitania* and the murder of its citizens to go unnoticed, and the public eagerly awaited the President's action, speculating whether it would be such a vigorous demand on Germany for reparation and assurances that the crime would not be repeated that, virtually, it would be an ultimatum and force the United States into the war on the side of the Allies, or whether Mr. Wilson would be content to engage in a diplomatic duel with Germany. Mr. Wilson gave no sign. In accordance with his custom at a time of crisis he withdrew from practically all contact with his official advisers or public men; isolated and aloof, perhaps seeking spiritual guidance,— as Lincoln did more than once and Robert E. Lee is known to have spent the night in prayer before his duty was revealed to him that his allegiance was to his State and not to his Government,—Mr. Wilson took counsel of himself but none other, and the people believed he would reveal himself in the forthcoming speech. . . .

Mr. Wilson prepared his speech before the news of the sinking of the *Lusitania* reached him; segregated, he still had means of knowing the temper of the country, and he must have known with what intense anxiety the world awaited his deliverance and the construction that would be put on his every word. The speech as written was not changed. He repeated what he had said many times since his election; he dwelt upon the mission of America to humanize the world, its duty to set an example of peace to the world; he pictured America created to unite men and to elevate mankind, dwelling especially, as applicable to his audience, on the obligation of every man to dedicate himself to America and to leave all other countries behind, and then he astonished every one and amazed the country no less than the entire world by saying:

"The example of American must be a special example. The example of America must be the example not merely of peace because it will not fight, but of peace because peace is the healing and elevating influence of the world and strife is not. There is such a thing as a man being too proud to fight. There is such a thing as a nation being so right that it does not need to convince others by force that it is right."

That was the only reference to the thing that engrossed all men. The President's speech was published in full in the leading newspapers, but that sentence—"there is such a thing as a man being too proud to fight"—stripped of its context, was singled out; it was flung on the telegraph wires and cables to the far corners of the earth, and it was accepted by the world as the President's reply to Germany. Germany had sunk the *Lusitania*, Germany had murdered American men and women and little children, and America, speaking through her President, could find no word of scorn or condemnation for the guilty, no pity for the dead, no promise they should be avenged; it could feel no generous prompting of passion, but was content proudly to glory in her cowardice.

Bitterly attacked in his own country, lampooned satirized and jeered at abroad, any other man temperamentally different would have offered explanation or defense, or at least through his friends sought to soften the harsh judgment of the world and make it plain that what he said and the interpretation given to it did him an injustice. Mr. Wilson did nothing. With what might very well have been thought the superb indifferency of disdain, with what the public might very well believe was utter contempt for what it said or thought or believed,—but which, in fact, was an extraordinary exhibition of courage and self-control,—Mr. Wilson dismissed the matter as if it were too trivial to require further attention. He had unlimited confidence, it was a confidence almost fatalistic, in the ultimate triumph of right and reason and the victory of morality in the long struggle. Lincoln, we are told, as an advocate of the abolition of slavery and prohibition saw that they could not be hastened, that they could be safely agitated but must not be prematurely pressed, and it was wisdom to wait until "in God's own time they will be organized into law and thus be woven into the fabric of our institutions." Mr. Wilson had the more difficult task not to crystallize moral sentiment into law, which is the foundation on which all law rests, for in a free country law is simply the concrete expression of morality, but to weld passion, prejudice and self-interest into a great moral renunciation.

There is a curious thing in connection with the President's use of the phrase "too proud to fight" which is worth mention and is of interest to the psychologist. Mr. Wilson is a Southerner by birth, descent and tradition, and although all his life from early manhood has been lived in the North, heredity is ineradicable. To the Southerner, especially the Southerner of the generation of Mr. Wilson's childhood, "proud" has a different meaning and is used in a different sense than it is by the Northerner. Men of the North seldom talk about their pride; men of the South frequently do, and they mean not pride in the Shaksperian sense, but in the same sense that the American of the North or the Englishman does self-respect. A Southerner will say, "I am too proud to do it," a Northerner or an Englishman would say, "My self-respect will not allow it." It was undoubtedly in that sense that Mr. Wilson, subconsciously reacting to his Southern heritage, used "proud," meaning that there are occasions when a nation, no matter how great the temptation, must not fight, just as an individual, to save his own self-respect, must not engage in a brawl.

It will not be necessary critically to consider the long correspondence that passed between the American and German Governments, but the sinking of the *Lusitania* brought the first break in Mr. Wilson's Cabinet and led to the resignation of Mr. Bryan on the following eighth of June.

A. Maurice Low, *Woodrow Wilson: An Interpretation* (Boston, Little, Brown, 1918), 165–172 *passim*.

131.   Leadership of Woodrow Wilson (1917)

BY EDGAR E. ROBINSON AND VICTOR J. WEST

Robinson is Professor of American History at Stanford University. West (1880–1927) was at the time of writing Professor of Political Science at Northwestern University.—Bibliography: Ray S. Baker, *World War and World Settlement* (1923); John Spencer Bassett, *Our War with Germany* (1919); J. B. Brown Scott, *A Survey of International Relations Between the United States and Germany, August 1, 1914, to April 6, 1917* (1917); William E. Dodd, *Woodrow Wilson and His Work* (1920); Robert Lansing, *The Big Four and Others of the Peace Conference* (1921); Lansing, *The Peace Negotiations* (1921); Charles Seymour, editor, *The Intimate Papers of Colonel House* (1926).

IT is now possible to state definitely the several elements of which President Wilson's foreign policy was compounded. There were in the first place the fundamental beliefs of the man himself—the unshakable convictions which had become his after years of study of the efforts of the peoples of the world to govern themselves. The primary and basic principle was a faith in democracy, both as an ideal and as a practice. Upon the soundness of the democratic principle he rested all his other beliefs.

Because he believed in democracy he believed that every nation should regard every other nation as its equal; that fair dealing was the best means of preserving friendship and peace between nations; that the guidance of established law was essential to international justice and fair dealing; and that, if unhappily disputes should arise between nations, the proper means for settling them was a reasoned consideration before a court of arbitration of the controversies in the light of the law. Finally, he believed not that force should never be used by nations against each other, but that it should be relied upon only to combat criminal aggression and to further great humanitarian purposes.

Principles alone, however, did not make the Wilson foreign policy. His beliefs and his own actions based thereon the President could control; there were also external modifying circumstances for the most part outside of his direction. Chief of these were obviously the events in international relations having their origin in other governments or nations,—events which could not possibly be foreseen or controlled by the President, and which thus constituted the chief danger to the successful application of principles. Only slightly less difficult to control were the acts and speeches of United States officers at home and abroad and the activities of the governments of the various members of the American union. There were, moreover, the constitution and laws of this country, the treaties, the obligations incurred by previous administrations, and the accepted rules of international law,—in brief the whole body of public law which set the boundaries to the exercise of power by the President.

There was still another element conditioning the direction of foreign affairs by President Wilson. That was the public opinion of the nation, with its almost imperceptible and sometimes incomprehensible shifts. It was true of course that, in the performance of duties imposed upon him by the Constitution, the chief executive of the United States might by the direction of diplomacy and otherwise have brought his country to a pass where it was dangerous to go forward and dishonourable to withdraw,—all without reference to the attitude of the public mind. But President Wilson's faith in democracy was too deep to permit the exclusion of foreign affairs from as much popular control as was possible. When he moved he wished to move in accord with the desires of the people, and he was quick to realize what moves in international relations the people would approve. He was not unmindful, however, of the unrivalled opportunity for great leadership which the presidency offered its incumbent, and he did not neglect this opportunity. His speeches and even his formal state papers, his messages and proclamations, seem to have been directed toward informing and moulding public opinion.

A careful and unbiased study of the record of President Wilson reveals convincingly the sincerity with which he held the principles he affirmed. It was not mere facility of expression which made it possible for him to restate in so many ways and with such telling effect the time-honoured ideals of a great democratic people. No charlatan of politics, however facile, however adroit, could have maintained his hold upon public opinion through four such trying years. The profound convictions of a scientist as to the fundamentals of political philosophy, wrought into his thinking in the years when there was no thought of his entering public life, were the guides President Wilson followed as leader and servant of his people.

It is important to know that President Wilson sincerely believed in what he professed to believe. But the true significance attaches to his rigid adherence to his beliefs in practice. Others have held the same principles, and quite as sincerely. If they have rarely applied them as practical guides in foreign relations it is because there was lacking either the intellectual ability to perceive the necessity for so applying them or the moral courage to follow the difficult road that must be travelled in so applying them. It remains to be shown how President Wilson consistently and faithfully lived up to his professions at a time when the opportunity for service was so great and failure to serve would have been so disastrous.

His faith in the democratic principle led him habitually to submit his foreign policy to the test of public opinion in the United States; if public opinion did not support him, his policy must be modified or the public mind educated; and his way of educating public opinion was to announce a general policy and allow it to be discussed among the people. His belief in democracy impelled him to insist on granting to the Filipino people a great measure of self-government and to promise them a still wider participation as they learned to use their new powers. It impelled him likewise to leave the Mexican people free as far as possible to work out their own solution—as the European nations had for centuries been doing—of their own problems. And finally it impelled him to make that important distinction between the German people and the German Imperial government on which he based his declaration that German guarantees of peace could be accepted only when supported by the unmistakable will of the German people.

His belief in the equality of nations led him to feel as much pride in the fact that the first of the "Bryan peace treaties" to be ratified was with Salvador, as he would have felt had it been with Great Britain. It inevitably impelled him to refuse to permit the United States to assume such responsibilities toward its own citizens that it must incur the risk of interfering with the political life of another people; better it was that the less advanced peoples of the world should do without the help of America than that the United States in order to give its aid should seem to take a mortgage on their future independence and integrity.

His reliance on justice and fair dealing between nations moved him to be scrupulously punctilious in the observance of treaty obligations, as when he insisted upon the repeal of the tolls exemption clause of the Panama Canal Act. It led him, even in the absence of treaties and when the right of the United States was unquestioned, to deal with other nations according to principles of equity, as, for example, in trying to meet the complaint of the Japanese against the laws of California and of the United States. It obliged him while professing friendship for a nation to actually act toward it in a friendly manner; it was impossible for him while trying to conduct the case of the United States against Germany in 1915 by diplomatic means to have been all the time preparing and strengthening and mobilizing the military and naval power of the United States.

His adherence to established law led him to insist that the "orderly processes" of constitutional method be followed in changing administrations in the states of the new world; appearance of intrigue and assassination in the elevation of Huerta to the presidency of Mexico could not be condoned by recognition of him. The same principle obliged him to insist on the strict observance by all belligerents in the Great War of the rights of neutrals under the sacred agreements and customs of international law, and that those rules should not be altered in any respect by any one belligerent nor to the detriment of neutral rights by all the belligerents.

His conviction that arbitration was the most desirable means of composing international disagreements led his administration not only to renew the arbitration treaties concluded by previous administrations, but to take a step forward by negotiating a series of treaties providing for "commissions of inquiry." It led him, and would have done so had there been no agreement to arbitrate, to defer the settlement of disputes with Great Britain until after the war when matters at issue could be decided on a basis of justice. It impelled him to propose mediation between the warring powers of Europe and to accept without hesitation the mediation of Latin America in the dispute with Mexico.

Finally, his belief that war should not be resorted to until other means of resolving differences between nations had been exhausted, and then only for purposes which were bound up with the welfare of mankind, led him to use every diplomatic method for bringing the German government to realize the gravity of its offence against civilization and humanity, and to defer actual warfare until the American people could assure themselves that they were really to fight for a great world-wide and age-old human purpose.

The moves in Wilson's foreign policy, with few and justified exceptions, were consistent with each other. Had he not taken for the United States the ground he did take in 1913 and held it during four years in spite of enormous difficulties, the United States could not have stood on that ground and fought from that vantage point in 1917. Had he not yielded to Great Britain the utmost of its rights under treaty with the United States he could not have later honestly demanded from Great Britain and from Germany the observance of all neutral rights under international obligations. Had he cynically ignored the results of official iniquity in Mexico in the first weeks of his administration he could not four years later convincingly have condemned—as he did in his note to Pope Benedict XV—the gross iniquity of officialdom in Germany. Had his government ever infringed upon the sovereignty of less powerful peoples he could not, without exciting derision, have ever championed the rights of Poland and Belgium and the Balkan states. Had the United States, under his presidency, demanded indemnities of Mexico or attempted by conquest to annex Mexican territory, the United States could not have admonished the world that there should be no conquests as the result of the Great War. Had this administration not dealt fairly with the Mexicans, the Chinese, the Filipinos in the first years of his responsibilities, he could not have expected the English, the Russians, the French, least of all the Germans, to rely with confidence on his assurance of intent to deal fairly with them in the later years. In short, had he not, during his entire incumbency, conducted himself as the first servant of a democracy should, he could not have expected to carry conviction when, on April 2, 1917, he asked the United States to go to war to make the world "safe for democracy."

If President Wilson's foreign policy had led immediately to the restoration of order in Mexico and had secured from European nations the demands of the United States without involving it in the conflict, it would have been hailed as tremendously successful. But it would have merited praise no more than it did deserve it, those results not having been accomplished. The motives which actuated it, the ends which it tried to achieve, the principles which guided it and the means which it used would have been precisely the same. There are so many variables in the facts of national and international affairs and their relationships are so complex, that the same principles applied by the same methods in two apparently precisely similar sets of circumstances may work to a happy result in the one case, and by the merest accident, to an unhappy one in the other. The principles and methods alone are under true control of statesmen, and they ought to be judged, not primarily by immediate results, but with reference to their permanent value to serve the desirable permanent purposes they are calculated to serve.

But the results of the Wilson policy themselves justify the policy. It was a result of that policy that the American people finally saw the imperative necessity for their participation in the Great War. It was a result of that policy that the war, a European quarrel originating obscurely in petty dynastic ambition, in greedy economic rivalry, and in base national hatred, was transformed, by the entrance of the United States, into a world conflict with the united forces of democracy and international peace ranged squarely against autocracy and continued world struggle. It was a result of that policy that the United States,—not England, not France, not even new Russia,— became the leader, the bearer of the "great light for the guidance of the nations," in the magnificent new venture of democracy to league the peoples of the world together to serve the ends of peace and justice.

Edgar E. Robinson and Victor J. West, *The Foreign Policy of Woodrow Wilson* (New York, Macmillan, 1917), 149–157.

———◆———

132. An Estimate of Woodrow Wilson (1918)

BY EX-SECRETARY DAVID F. HOUSTON (1926)

Houston was Secretary of Agriculture 1913–1920, and of the Treasury, 1920–1921, in Wilson's Cabinet.—Bibliography as in No. 129 above.

I SAID that Woodrow Wilson was a Scotch-Presbyterian Christian. With him God was an immanent presence. He was with him in the White House, and if he could discover what He wanted, he gave no heed to what anybody else or everybody else wanted or thought.

Reference has been made to the meeting of the Cabinet before our forces took Vera Cruz, when he startled the Cabinet by asking those who still believed in prayer to pray over the matter. That he did so constantly admits of no doubt. Mr. Wilson believed in an Over-ruling Providence. This is revealed in many of his addresses, and there is abundant evidence of his solemn reliance on Its guidance. . . .

It follows that Mr. Wilson had a strong belief in the might of right. In all my contacts with him, in everything I heard him say, I was impressed by this more than by anything else, viz: That he was interested above all things in discovering what was right: what was the right thing to say and the right course to pursue. He was nervous only about the possibility of being wrong. The only real appeal one could make to him was on the right or wrong of a matter. He had little stomach for compromises of any sort, and none for compromises which had a shade of the compromising in them. He was content when he felt that he had arrived at the heart of a matter and had the right of it. He was then prepared to go ahead regardless of consequences. In his assessment of measures, personalities, personal equations, personal ambitions, and self-seeking were ruthlessly brushed aside. He had, in his processes and actions, in very high degree, the element of objectivity. In all his thinking and actions in the field of government and economics, his mind directed itself to the merit of the question, and he assumed that others were equally unselfish and devoted. . . .

Mr. Wilson had something more than this objectivity in all public matters. He was strikingly selfless, or unselfish. He had no personal ends to serve and no thought of attempting to serve them. It was difficult to get him to take any interest in himself; and in my eight years of contact with him, it never occurred to me at any time to raise a question as to how a proposed course of action might affect him or his fortunes. I knew that he would resent it. On a few occasions, when someone ventured a suggestion of the kind, he met with a very prompt and stern rebuke. Mr. Wilson worked for the approval of his own conscience and for that of mankind, or as he expressed it, for the verdict of history.

He was utterly sincere when he asserted that he had never been interested in fighting for himself, but that he was always intensely interested in fighting for the things he believed in. He was speaking naturally when he said that it was a matter of personal indifference to him what the verdict of the people was in 1916.

Never at any time did he attempt to make personal capital out of his high position. He was humbled rather than exalted by it, and his keen wits penetrated quickly the atmosphere with which lesser spirits surrounded themselves when they descended upon Washington in their official dignity. . . .

Wilson could not stoop to employ the arts which many men use to gain favour and popularity. He had little aptitude for the game of practical politics and resented its practices. He was weak in the technique of managing and manipulating men, and he had no desire to gain strength in this art. He relied on the strength of the cause in which he was interested.

Wilson was sensitive, shy, and reserved. He was a gentleman and could not and would not try to capitalize his personal advantages. There were intimacies to which he, like other true gentlemen, would not admit the public, and he naturally assumed that right-minded men would not seek to be admitted to them. These were inhibitions resulting from temperament and generations of good breeding. He could only with difficulty attempt to reveal himself, and when he did so, he had only moderate success. . . .

The difficulty Wilson had in freely meeting people, aside from his temperament, was reinforced by a certain philosophy he entertained, by the stress under which he worked and by his physical state. He would not seek out men to consult with, but, within the limits of his time and strength, he did see people who sought him on business. He would play no favourites; and I think the fact that he could not see certain individuals, whom he might have liked to confer with more frequently without seeming to play favourites and creating ill feeling, caused him to limit his contacts; and on account of the fact that he was never very robust and that the demands on him were terrific, he felt it imperative to limit his social contacts to the minimum.

Wilson was undoubtedly aware of the popular impression that he was not approachable. In his address to the Press Club in New York in June, 1916, he touched upon this matter, saying:

"I have heard some say that I was not accessible to them, and when I inquired into it, I found they meant that I did not personally invite them. They did not know how to come without being invited, and they did not care to come if they came on the same terms with every-body else, knowing that everybody else was welcome whom I had time to confer with." . . .

Wilson belonged to the aristocracy of brains. He was an intel-lectual thoroughbred. His mind, which was of high quality, had been refined and disciplined by years of hard study and by years of teaching. His faculties were always thoroughly at his command. He did not have to labour and strain for results. He was quick to grasp the essential points in a complex problem or set of facts, to get to the heart of the matter under discussion, to see facts in their proper relation, and to arrive at a sound conclusion; and long and careful training, combined with natural talent, gave him the ability to express his thoughts tersely, artistically, and eloquently, with-out apparent effort and without prolonged preparation. In all the years in which I listened to him talking, informally, in Cabinet meet-ings, or elsewhere, I never detected a word or phrase out of place, or heard him use a bungling sentence. He was one of three men I have known whose conversation or address, taken down and reported by an intelligent stenographer, could be published without any real need of editing. The other two were his uncle, Dr. James Woodrow, and President Eliot. What this means, even the average well-trained man well knows. Most of them probably experience a feeling of humiliation when their spontaneous utterances are taken by stenog-raphers and returned to them. They find more difficulty in straighten-ing out their expressions than they would in rewriting the state-ment. . . .

Certainly, in point of formal education, Wilson was the best trained man who ever occupied the White House. He had received the best training that American universities could furnish, and he had supplemented this by long years of study as a professor and as a lecturer. He was a student of history. He saw things in their perspec-tive in systematic, orderly fashion. He knew the limitations of things. He had been a profound student of American institutions and prob-lems, and had developed knowledge of foreign governments and his-tory. Mr. Wilson was a pioneer among Americans in the study of foreign arrangements and governmental policies. His book, "The State," dealing with comparative governments, was the first in the field; and Wilson was instructing America about foreign matters before most of his critics had escaped from the bondage of provincial-ism.

It was a genuine pleasure to talk with Wilson, to engage in confer-ence with him and to discuss light or serious, simple or complex matters with him. He could be light and gay. Nobody could or did tell so many good or apt stories as he; and yet he did not manufacture stories or lug them in by the ears. They appeared naturally, and they came quickly; and his sallies, while seldom biting and never bitter, were keen and enlightening. He was witty rather than humorous, in this characteristic resembling the best English and New England thinkers and speakers rather than the typical American. His wit never verged on the doubtful or the vulgar. He naturally resented vulgarity and irreverence.

One reason why it was a pleasure to discuss matters with Wilson is that he was quick and did not have to be educated. One could assume more with him than with almost any other person I have known. And he was patient, very patient, patient even of dullness. He was much more patient than I would dream of being, or ever desired to be. I saw him many a time sit and listen with courtesy to long-drawn-out statements by men of mediocre capacity and little information, who had had scant opportunity to form useful judgments, and who usually obscured the subject at every turn. Not infre-quently I almost writhed in agony and ill-concealed irritation, but Mr. Wilson never gave a sign. I have, therefore, always been greatly amused by representations that he would not take counsel or listen to advice. Some of those, including one or more members of his Cabinet, who gave currency to this view, could only mean that he did not frequently take their advice or heed their views; and he was wise, because their views, as a rule, were of little assistance, their knowledge was scanty and impressionistic, and their judgment bad, and yet they desired to seem to be in the President's intimate counsel and to be in the limelight.

It is not true that Wilson did not consult his Cabinet on new de-partures and policy, or on important matters. He did; and he would have done so more freely had he not known that the very ones—and they were few in number—who criticized him for failure to do so made it difficult for him to do so by their persistent practice of herald-ing everything to the public, whether it was wise or timely or not.

And, Mr. Wilson was not what I would call obstinate. He was slow in arriving at conclusions. He took pains to get light and all the facts; and then, when he thought he had all he could get or needed, he made up his mind. Then he was difficult to move. This was as it should have been. I admired him for this trait. He was difficult to move because it was not easy to give him better reasons for a different course than he had for the one he proposed to take, but he was not immovable. Better reasons and sound reasoning would alter his views, and changed conditions would modify them. A number of times I witnessed him change his views quickly, views which he strongly entertained. He altered his views on preparedness. He altered his views on proposed statements, such as notes to Germany; and he swung round completely on the proposal for a tariff commission. . . .

But, as a writer for the untrained and undiscriminating reader and as a speaker, Wilson was not without a marked defect. He said too much in too few words and, when he had finished a thought, he let it drop. Several times I have heard him laughingly remark in Cabinet meetings that he did not care how much anyone said provided he said it in a few words. He studied his subject carefully, digested all the facts he could assemble, and then painted his picture with as few strokes as possible. His statements were based on wide knowledge and were the result of prolonged reflection. He uttered conclusions and did not take the trouble to reveal the steps he had taken or his mental processes. He wrote from a broad background of history and literature, and, not infrequently, his forms of expression were unconventional and not familiar to the average man, expressions whose origin and implication few of his half-educated audiences knew or could grasp. He habitually paid his audiences the compliment of appealing to their intelligence and of assuming that they knew more than they did.

Wilson coined very few phrases. Only a few of them struck the popular mind. Some of them were unfortunate. Some of them it would have been better if he had not used. Two of them, "Too proud to fight" and "Peace without victory," were the causes of violent criticisms, as was the sentence, "The objects which the statesmen of the belligerents on both sides have in mind are virtually the same, as stated in general terms to their own people." . . .

It was particularly unfortunate that he used the phrase, "Too proud to fight" just when he did. At the time he was being criticized for timidity and lack of understanding of the issues of the struggle. It was used in an address in Philadelphia, May 10, 1915, only three days after the sinking of the *Lusitania*, and three days before the first *Lusitania* note was sent. . . .

Of course, Wilson, when he was speaking, did not have the *Lusitania* controversy in mind. With his customary single-track habit of thought, he was dealing, before foreign-born citizens after a naturalization ceremony, with the meaning of America and with their responsibilities. His mind easily dropped into an expression, a close parallel to which he was familiar with because of his long residence in the South. At the time he lived in the South duelling was still practiced. . . . I had frequently heard men say that they had too much self-respect to be insulted by persons of a certain sort or to notice a challenge from them—they were too proud to notice or to fight such persons. Wilson's full thought he expressed as follows: "The example of America must be a special example. The example of America must be the example, not merely of peace because it will not fight, but of peace because peace is the healing and elevating influence of the world and strife. Is not there such a thing as a man being too proud to fight? There is such a thing as a nation being so right that it does not need to convince others by force that it is right." Very little of this utterance, except the phrase itself, was ever referred to or published. Partisans used the phrase out of its context for their own purposes. Neither was the trouble taken to point out that this same thought was not new with Wilson, and that he had employed it at least twice before. . . .

The use of the phrase "Peace without victory" also was unfortunate. . . . What Wilson, of course, had in mind was that the peace which should follow victory should be a just peace and, therefore, a permanent peace, and that it was of the utmost importance that when the victory was won the victors should be reasonable. He, of course, apprehended that they would not be reasonable; and what occurred in Paris and what has occurred since have demonstrated that his apprehensions were well grounded. . . .

It was pure tragedy that a man like Wilson, who knew what war means, who had witnessed the horrors of its aftermath, who detested it as a method of settling difficulties and thought it stupid, should have been called upon to lead this nation into war. He spoke from his heart and experience when he said to Congress, in his War Message: "It is a fearful thing to lead this great nation into war"; and he held back for more than two and a half years for many reasons. I thought at the time, and still think, that he was right in his thinking and his action at each stage of the developments. . . .

Naturally, the situation became tense when the *Lusitania* was sunk. Many citizens, especially in Eastern cities, were for immediate action. . . . I was in the West for five weeks following this tragedy. I realized clearly then that the majority of the people were not even thinking of this nation's entering the struggle. I was in most parts of the Union several times between 1915 and the spring of 1917, and at no stage, up to that time, were the masses of the people ready for this nation's participation. Wilson, too, had full knowledge of the state of mind of the great majority of the people. . . .

Wilson led the nation into war at the right moment—the moment when Germany abandoned all pretences, broke her promises, declared her intention to resume unrestricted submarine warfare, and undertook to dictate the course we should follow. Then Uncle Sam rolled up his sleeves and made it plain that he was "free, white, and twenty-one" and would see whether anybody could tell him what he could or could not do. From this moment, Wilson had back of him a united and determined people, and he knew it.

Wilson hated the thought of war. He knew what it meant, but he accepted the challenge with the same poise and calm courage that he had manifested in the more difficult former trial of maintaining peace.

Wilson's knowledge of the meaning of war and what the new task involved and his boldness were made manifest at the outset and were evident at each stage of the development, from first to last. There was no hesitating. He did not waver for an instant, and he had at no time any doubt as to the issue. With him it was a foregone conclusion. There was in him the spirit of the Crusader and of the Roundhead. He would have immediate and good execution of the enemy, for the good of their souls and for the glory of God. . . .

Wilson's determination and success in keeping the hands of the politicians off the army and the navy will be rated one of his great contributions to the nation in this time of stress. For it, Wilson is entitled to the gratitude of all the people.   It is to be hoped that the precedent he set will be followed for all time.

Wilson habitually took the long view.   He preferred to go down to defeat fighting for a cause which he knew some day would triumph than to gain a victory of an issue which he was confident would in time be shown to be false.   He played for the verdict of history.

What history will say of Wilson, I do not know.   That he will figure largely in it is obvious.   It is unavoidable that he should.   He was a central figure in this nation, and one of the central figures of the world in the period of its most colossal tragedy.   Quoting him, I may say:

"We find every truly great mind identified with some special cause. His purposes are steadfastly set in some definite direction.   The career which he works out for himself constitutes so important a part of the history of his times that to dissociate him from his surroundings were as impossible as it would be undesirable."

From *Eight Years with Wilson's Cabinet*, by David F. Houston (copyright 1926, Doubleday, Page and Company), II, 159–254 *passim*.

PART IX

THE ARTS AND SCIENCES

CHAPTER XXV — PHILANTHROPY AND CULTURAL ADVANCE

133. The Pan-American Exposition (1901)

BY WALTER HINES PAGE

Page was a journalist and writer; editor at one time of the *Forum;* later of the *Atlantic*. He was a member of the publishing firm of Doubleday, Page & Company. He was made Ambassador to Great Britain by President Wilson, and incurred criticism by his failure to observe strict personal neutrality during the period before American entry into the World War. For his account of his problems at the outbreak of war, see No. 166 below. For an adverse criticism of his conduct as Ambassador, see No. 167 below.—Bibliography on expositions: *American Year Book* and contemporary periodicals.

" WHATEVER else we may do," said one of the directors of the Pan-American Exposition, at Buffalo, when the plans for it were under discussion, "we must make a beautiful spectacle." This purpose was never for a moment forgotten; it became the dominant purpose; and it is as an outdoor spectacle that the Exposition is most novel and noteworthy. It is its spectacular features that will be longest remembered and that will have the greatest effect on the popular mind. And it is a sight worth traveling across the continent to see—a sight such as nobody ever saw before. . . .

The most impressive view—the view that one ought to take first in order to get the full effect of the whole scene—is from the Triumphal Bridge just at dusk when the lights are first turned on. The great towers of the bridge make a dignified, stately approach to the court with its play-day effect—its domes and pinnacles and warm colors, the fountains, and the great electric tower as the climax of it all. You have hardly realized the scene as it appears in the dusk, when on the rows of posts tiny dots of light appear in clusters, like little pink buds in a nosegay. You become gently aware of similar pink points on the tower—apparently millions of them; and on either side they outline all the buildings—in rows about the panels on the domes, under arches, over windows, everywhere. The buildings themselves seem for an instant to become invisible, and you see only their outlines marked in these tiny dots of fire. And the court seems larger than it was by sunlight, for you seem to see a whole city of towers and domes, and eaves and doors, outlined in sparks. Then the pink points grow brighter and change their hue, and in another moment the full illumination bursts forth, and the whole great court becomes luminous with a soft brilliancy that does not tire the eye. And it is a new kind of brilliancy. You are face to face with the most magnificent and artistic nocturnal scene that man has ever made. It is an effect so novel and so gentle in its glow that you think of fairy-land, not a fairy-land of tinsel, but the fairy-land that you once believed in.

I had the pleasure to see this illumination first in the company of a child of ten years. She stood for a minute in speechless wonder. Then she cried "Oh, isn't it beautiful!" And she danced in forgetfulness of herself and asked "Is it really real?" For the sensation is of an optical illusion. You ask yourself if it be not a trick played on you with mirrors and lenses. But, when you turn your eyes away from the brilliancy of the electric tower and look down the long court of buildings in the soft glow, the colors are more beautiful than they are by sunlight. Nor do you forget that the chromatic note of green of Niagara, and that the beautiful world of light is the illuminating power of the great cataract. If you could forget this fact, there is just enough noise of fountains to remind you of it, and symbolical representations of the falls in sculpture greet you as you gaze at the tower. It is the Great Cataract silently expressing its power in a soft, fairy-like, nocturnal, outdoor scene of wonderful illumination.

This spectacle is all the more worth seeing because no satisfactory notion either of the color or of the illumination can be conveyed by picture or by description. It must be seen or it will be missed. It gives an impression that one is likely to carry always in one's memory. And it is this nocturnal spectacle that is the peculiar triumph of the Exposition.

The builders of the Exposition planned one spectacle to which everything converges, and the means by which they have produced it are
architecture, illumination, fountain-effects, statuary, color and horticultural and floral adornment. The freedom from precedent with
which they have worked is remarkable.

. . . A visitor would do well, whatever gate he enters, to go first
to the statue of Washington, which is at the southern end of the
grounds. From this statue an avenue leads over the Triumphal
Bridge into the main court and to the Electric Tower.

Starting at the statue of Washington, the avenue leads northward
up a gentle incline between rows of columns and between the four
great towers of the bridge. These towers are crowned with equestrian
figures of a standard bearer, and are ornamented with symbolical
groups of statuary. One great pillar by its sculpture and its inscription
stands for Patriotism, another for Liberty, and so on.

The canal on either side of the bridge broadens into a lake, and
symbolical figures of great beauty by Mr. Martiny represent the
Atlantic Ocean and the Pacific Ocean. By this approach over the
bridge to the main court a single view takes in the whole scene, and
the unity and simplicity of the ground plan become obvious. There
is one long court running from south to north from the Triumphal
Bridge to the Electric Tower. With its approach, and with the plaza
behind the tower, this court is very much longer than the central
court of any preceding exposition. Its width admits the lakes and
fountains in the centre, and broad ways on either side, which give the
buildings and the tower room enough for effective display.

The transverse court (east and west) intersects the main court just
north of the bridge. Their intersection makes the great area of the
esplanade, which will hold a quarter of a million spectators. The
transverse courts end in curved groups of buildings, the Government
group on the east, and on the west the buildings given to Horticulture,
Mines and the Graphic Arts; and at each curved end of this transverse court are a lake, a sunken garden and groups of statuary.

Along the main court towards the tower are the six other principal
buildings—first the two octagonal domed buildings, the Temple of
Music, and facing it the Ethnology buildings; then facing each other
across the main court, the building for Machinery and Manufactures
and the Liberal Arts building; next the Electricity building, and

facing it the Agricultural building. The great Electric Tower stands in the space between these. Beyond and on either side are restaurant buildings, and back of all the great gates and the connecting colonnade.

This is the general plan. And you can see it all from one point in front of the Triumphal Bridge. Outside these courts lie many buildings and the greater part of the area covered by the Exposition. But it were better at first to ignore these; for standing anywhere in the court the buildings outside it are properly shut from view. You are aware only of this one spectacle, and all the buildings and all their accessories—lakes, fountains, statuary, colonnades—are a unit. They have been treated as a unit by engineers, architects, sculptors, decorators, electricians.

And it is necessary to realize how large this area is which has had this unified treatment. The space in the Court of Honor at Chicago was 563,000 square feet; the court area at Paris was 720,000; and the court space at Buffalo is 1,400,000—nearly three times as great as the Court of Honor at Chicago. By daylight it seems smaller than it is; and by the electric light it seems very much larger.

Walter H. Page, *The Pan-American Exposition*, in *World's Work*, August, 1901 (New York), II, 1015–1024 *passim*.

———◆———

134. Theodore Thomas, Orchestral Conductor (1905)

BY CHARLES EDWARD RUSSELL (1927)

Russell is a journalist, and author of many books on political and sociological subjects. Theodore Thomas (1835–1905) was the first really great American conductor—an eminent musician, a brilliant leader. He was responsible, among other innovations, for the now common custom of having the players of stringed instruments in the orchestra move their bows in unison.

MOST of my time from 1900 to 1905 being cast upon Chicago, I was enabled to renew my acquaintance with Mr. Thomas there and to follow his work. He was then giving regular concerts on the Friday afternoon and Saturday evening of each week through a season of twenty-four weeks. Monday, Tuesday, Wednesday and

Thursday mornings were spent in rehearsal, ten o'clock to noon. The concerts were in the great Chicago Auditorium; the rehearsals upon its stage.

As a rule, outsiders were not admitted to these practising bouts, but by hard petitioning I won an exception in my favor and formed a habit of attending at least one rehearsal every week. In that vast space I sat the one auditor of a deeply interesting procedure. In many ways, it had profit; for one, it made me better acquainted with the peculiar mind and methods of Theodore Thomas than I could have become from a hundred mere conversations.

I was not long in discovering one of the secrets of that extraordinary command over his players so many observers had talked about. Aside from the recondite psychology of a dominant nature, which never will be revealed to us, the thing was simple enough. He never once assumed the attitude that he wanted anything done only because he wanted it done.

"Do this because I tell you to do it," was never once suggested or hinted. His attitude was always, "We shall do this a certain way because we all know it is the best way and we are equally interested in having this work perfect." He did not say these words, you will understand, but conveyed always the sense of them: an odd illustration of spiritual democracy, if I may use that phrase, for nothing else can express it. From reading Stephen Fiske and others I had been led to expect a Termagant; a kind of shouting, brow-beating, fault-finding, foot-stamping mogul of the baton. I was astonished to find that ordinarily he was the gentlest and most lovable old autocrat that ever went in shoe leather. At the same time, he was absolutely businesslike, absolutely certain of himself, firm, rigorous, insatiable of effort, but even when he called an individual player to task for error, I think he never aroused resentment in the wandering one. There was no humiliation in his corrective ardor, and that made the difference. After this I hardly have need to say that he never raved up and down the stage tearing his hair and cursing, as conductors of the old time were pictured, perhaps libelously. The Thomasian idea of venting wrath upon one that had forfeited his esteem was the sentence of excommunication. "Let him never speak to me again."

He displayed one attribute in his rehearsals that I have not heard of in other conductors, though it may not be so uncommon as I think.

He seemed to know by an infallible instinct when the players were becoming weary and needed relaxation. It was remarkable to see how completely and quickly he changed his bearing at such a time. The moment before he had been urging them forward, repeating passages, softening shadows, bringing intensities into proper relations, polishing a phrase until it glittered. Now he dropped the baton, leaned over his stand and told a funny story or cracked a joke. When everybody had laughed and stretched out and known a moment's ease, he resumed the work as before. It struck me as strange that he could divine so surely when these periods of rest were needed, and much more wonderful that he could at will throw off the austere dignity supposed to pertain to his position, throw it off, put it on, throw it off, and never for a moment impair discipline or lose in any degree the respect and confidence of the men he commanded. . . .

Walter Unger, who for many years sat at the first violoncello stand, and was a 'cellest of great distinction, used to be fond of telling this instance of Thomas's acuteness of hearing:

Unger had broken his violoncello and must have it repaired. The workman changed the position of the sound post. Next rehearsal, Unger had a short obbligato to play. When the rehearsal was over, Thomas said to him: "Is that a new instrument you have there, Mr. Unger?"

He had detected the slight change in its tone.

Everything to the Thomas mind must be exactly thus and so, and above all, the audience was not to be distracted with any interruption, even the slightest, of the regular and smoothly working machine. . . .

He was then spending his summers at Felsengarten, returning to Chicago early in September. He told me once that the next four weeks after his return were to him the hardest of the year. They comprised what he called his "fighting rehearsals." Through the long summer vacation the members of the orchestra were playing helter-skelter, in summer gardens, theaters, for dances, under any chance leadership or none at all. In that time they drifted so far away from the symphony form that four weeks of drill were required to get them back to standard. This will seem wonderful only to those that have not glimpsed the peculiarly and unreasonably sensitive elements in the orchestral equation. Why, it is a fact that even from Saturday night to Monday morning, while the season was in full swing, the men would fall off, so that the Monday morning rehearsal was always the hardest. . . .

I once asked him to tell me the story of the American Opera Company. He told it. He said:

"Good intentions, bad management, no money."

His terminology was not only terse but satisfying. The question has often been raised in late years what he would have thought of modern music if it had appeared in his time. I think I can contribute an indication of his probable attitude. In the years that I have now in mind I had often to go to New York and so utilized the chance to observe how and what the Eastern orchestras were doing. On one such visit a famous organization brought out with press trumpetings a new symphony by a budding German composer. . . . The composition with which he had favored us just then was a forerunner and most admirable specimen of what later developed into the cubist or ultramodern school. So nearly as I could make out, it depicted life in a madhouse, a large, teeming madhouse, situated somewhere on the East Side of New York, near the elevated railroad, and in a street where there was much trucking on bad pavements. The first two movements seemed devoted to hysteria, the third to an interesting study of the pathology of acute mania, while the last, in which the elevated railroad fell down while all the inmates of the asylum screamed at once in different keys over a background of fish horns was one of the most remarkable things I had ever heard.

A considerable part of the audience received this contraption with ecstacy, a sure-enough sign of the antiquity of a well-known affectation. I understood in New York that a copy of the work had been sent to Mr. Thomas with the expectation that he would give it a Chicago premier, and his judgment on it was awaited with interest. When I returned I mentioned to him casually that I had heard the composition in New York and it had seemed to be viewed with favor. He said:

"Musical mud." . . .

He had much to do with the furthering of orchestral music in America but nothing with the singular superstition that the conductor produces all the music, causing it to flow at his will out of the small end of his baton. I think he would have been much amazed if he could have looked ahead and seen the extent to which the public he was tutoring was to be ensnared with this childlike belief. Since it is the fact that the conductor's real work is done at rehearsals and not before the public, and since he was so hard set against all affectations, he never pretended anything to the contrary. With patient labor he drilled his players to play each composition as he desired to have it played. When the public performance came on he gave them the time and with his left hand conveyed intelligencies to them, but he never did a sand dance about the platform and his every movement was not only graceful, as I have said, but usually restrained. . . .

Yet he had his own affluent means of communicating his purposes to the men that played before him. So far as the audience could see, he was doing little more than to beat the time with his right hand and baton, a thing that always caused grumbling among the superficial, if they had been used to directorial gymnastics. What the audience could not see was his face and eyes, eloquent with feeling and command, and the all-controlling movements of his left hand. This he held so that only the players could see it and to them it was never inarticulate. When he desired increasing emphasis he beckoned with it, palm toward himself; when he wished restraint he turned the palm the other way and made a repressing gesture. In the crescendo passages it rose; in diminuendo it was lowered. In all this as in so many other devices of his, the thought was to offer to the listener no distracting suggestions, but allow him to concentrate his mind on the music and nothing else. . . .

He was an iron-willed autocrat while he was rehearsing and an easygoing democrat about everything else. He believed in giving everybody a chance, and otherwise than as artists all men looked about alike to him. Once in Cincinnati there had been, after the last evening Festival performance, one of the celebrations that the orchestra was accustomed to hold on gala occasions. This lasted late. As usual, Thomas led all the fun. It was daybreak when they emerged upon the street. At that hour there were neither cabs nor street cars to be found, and Thomas was a long distance from home. Someone commiserated him upon the dismal walk ahead of him.

"Walk!" says Thomas. "I'm not going to walk. See that milk cart? That goes up my way. I'm going home on that."

He summoned the astonished driver, hopped into the narrow seat, put a cigar into his own mouth and another into the driver's, and went off, gently humming "The Evening Star."

I have not known of another conductor that pursued so resolutely the practice of affording his men a chance to appear as soloists. Since soloists were necessary, why not pick them from our own ranks? seemed to be his idea. At one time he had, if I remember rightly, four in his first violin choir that had been thus distinguished. Solo performances by 'cellists, harpists, viola players, clarinetists, flutists, oboists, the organist, and even by bass violinists are scattered through his programs. Some of the men had been with him for years and looked upon him as a father. Dear old Mr. Beckel, for instance, so many years his principal in the bass violin group. I suppose that if he had become convinced that Theodore Thomas's plans and the welfare of music in America required his death, he would have asked for two glasses of beer and then sent for the hemlock. . . .

One reason for his potent influence upon his men was the deep respect they had for his musicianship, first, and then for his transparent integrity. The world at large is easily fooled by pretentious incompetence, but two bodies here below are not fooled at all. A ship captain may fool his passengers, his owners, his underwriters, the press, and the public; he cannot fool his crew. With them, either he knows his business or he does not. It is so with the members of a grand orchestra and their leader. Conductors have been known in orchestral annals that lived and had honor and grew fat and died renowned, whose men would crouch behind their stands that they might not see the baton's eccentric gyrations. Some there have been that were the subject of their players' everlasting mirth, and some whose players ran habitually half a beat behind. No such filigrees adorn the story of Theodore Thomas. Baton and men proceeded in faultless harmony and at the end all sound of all instruments seemed cut off as if with one huge knife, sharp and clean.

At one of the last rehearsals I attended everything went well, the difficult points were smoothed out easily, the tonality seemed perfect. About half-past eleven Thomas laid down his baton, made his little bow, and said, "Well done, children, well done! We can all go home now. Thank you, children!" He turned on them his big, kindly, genial smile. I had heard him say that before, and never thought that day I should not hear him say it again.

From *The American Orchestra and Theodore Thomas*, by Charles Edward Russell (copyright 1927, Doubleday, Page and Company), 263–285 *passim*.

135. Beautifying the Nation (1906)

BY EDWARD BOK (1920)

Bok was a Dutch immigrant boy, who came to the United States at the age of six and has become one of the outstanding self-made men of the country.   Starting as a stenographer, he went into journalistic work, and at length became associated in the management of the *Ladies' Home Journal*, which he helped to bring to great popularity and success.   Bok has written *America, Give me a chance!; The Americanization of Edward Bok; Twice Thirty; The Young Man in Business*.

. . . BOK now turned to *The Ladies Home Journal* as his medium for making the small-house architecture of America better. He realized the limitation of space, but decided to do the best he could under the circumstances. He believed he might serve thousands of his readers if he could made it possible for them to secure, at moderate cost, plans for well-designed houses by the leading domestic architects in the country. He consulted a number of architects, only to find them unalterably opposed to the idea. They disliked the publicity of magazine presentation; prices differed too much in various parts of the country; and they did not care to risk the criticism of their contemporaries. It was "cheapening" their profession!

Bok saw that he should have to blaze the way and demonstrate the futility of these arguments. At last he persuaded one architect to co-operate with him, and in 1895 began the publication of a series of houses which could be built, approximately, for from one thousand five hundred dollars to five thousand dollars. The idea attracted attention at once, and the architect-author was swamped with letters and inquiries regarding his plans.

This proved Bok's instinct to be correct as to the public willingness to accept such designs; upon this proof he succeeded in winning over two additional architects to make plans. He offered his reader full building specifications and plans to scale of the houses with estimates from four builders in different parts of the United States for five dollars a set. The plans and specifications were so complete in every detail that any builder could build the house from them.

A storm of criticism now arose from architects and builders all over the country, the architects claiming that Bok was taking "the bread out of their mouths" by the sale of plans, and local builders vigorously questioned the accuracy of the estimates. But Bok knew he was right.

Slowly but surely he won the approval of the leading architects, who saw that he was appealing to a class of house-builders who could not afford to pay an architect's fee, and that, with his wide circulation, he might become an influence for better architecture through these small houses. The sets of plans and specifications sold by the thousands. It was not long before the magazine was able to present small-house plans by the foremost architects of the country, whose services the average householder could otherwise never have dreamed of securing.

Bok not only saw an opportunity to better the exterior of the small houses, but he determined that each plan published should provide for two essentials: every servant's room should have two windows to insure cross-ventilation, and contain twice the number of cubic feet usually given to such rooms; and in place of the American parlor, which he considered a useless room, should be substituted either a living-room or a library. He did not point to these improvements; every plan simply presented the larger servant's room and did not present a parlor. It is a singular fact that of the tens of thousands of plans sold, not a purchaser ever noticed the absence of a parlor except one woman in Brookline, Mass., who, in erecting a group of twenty-five "*Journal* houses," discovered after she had built ten that not one contained a parlor! . . .

For nearly twenty-five years Bok continued to publish pictures of houses and plans. Entire colonies of "*Ladies' Home Journal houses*" have sprung up, and building promoters have built complete suburban developments with them. How many of these homes have been erected it is, of course, impossible to say; the number certainly runs into the thousands.

It was one of the most constructive and far-reaching pieces of work that Bok did during his editorial career—a fact now recognized by all architects. Shortly before Stanford White passed away, he wrote: "I firmly believe that Edward Bok has more completely influenced American domestic architecture for the better than any man in this generation. When he began, I was short-sighted enough to discourage him, and refused to coöperate with him. If Bok came to me now, I would not only make plans for him, but I would waive any fee for them in retribution for my early mistake."

Bok then turned to the subject of the garden for the small house, and the development of the grounds around the homes which he had been instrumental in putting on the earth. He encountered no opposition here. The publication of small gardens for small houses finally ran into hundreds of pages, the magazine supplying planting plans and full directions as to when and how to plant—this time without cost.

Next the editor decided to see what he could do for the better and simpler furnishing of the small American home. Here was a field almost limitless in possible improvement, but he wanted to approach it in a new way. . . .

Bok realized that he had found the method of presentation for his interior-furnishing plan if he could secure photographs of the most carefully furnished homes in America. He immediately employed the best available expert, and within six months there came to him an assorted collection of over a thousand photographs of well-furnished rooms. The best were selected, and a series of photographic pages called "Inside of 100 Homes" was begun. . . .

The editor followed this up with another successful series, again pictorial. He realized that to explain good taste in furnishing by text was almost impossible. So he started a series of all-picture pages called "Good Taste and Bad Taste." He presented a chair that was bad in lines and either useless or uncomfortable to sit in, and explained where and why it was bad; and then put a good chair next to it, and explained where and why it was good.

The lesson to the eye was simply and directly effective; the pictures told their story as no printed word could have done, and furniture manufacturers and dealers all over the country, feeling the pressure from their customers, began to put on the market the tables, chairs, divans, bedsteads, and dressing-tables which the magazine was portraying as examples of good taste. It was amazing that, within five years, the physical appearance of domestic furniture in the stores completely changed.

The next undertaking was a systematic plan for improving the pictures on the walls of the American home. Bok was employing the best artists of the day: Edwin A. Abbey, Howard Pyle, Charles Dana Gibson, W. L. Taylor, Albert Lynch, Will H. Low, W. T. Smedley,

Irving R. Wiles, and others. As his magazine was rolled to go through the mails, the pictures naturally suffered; Bok therefore decided to print a special edition of each important picture that he published, an edition on plate-paper, without text, and offered to his readers at ten cents a copy. Within a year he had sold nearly one hundred thousand copies, such pictures as W. L. Taylor's "The Hanging of the Crane" and "Home-Making Hearts" being particularly popular.

Pictures were difficult to advertise successfully; it was before the full-color press had become practicable for rapid magazine work; and even the large-page black-and-white reproductions which Bok could give in his magazine did not, of course, show the beauty of the original paintings, the majority of which were in full color. He accordingly made arrangements with art publishers to print his pictures in their original colors; then he determined to give the public an opportunity to see what the pictures themselves looked like.

He asked his art editor to select the two hundred and fifty best pictures and frame them. Then he engaged the art gallery of the Philadelphia Art Club, and advertised an exhibition of the original paintings. No admission was charged. The gallery was put into gala attire, and the pictures were well hung. The exhibition, which was continued for two weeks, was visited by over fifteen thousand persons. . . .

But all this was simply to lead up to the realization of Bok's cherished dream: the reproduction, in enormous numbers, of the greatest pictures in the world in their original colors. The plan, however, was not for the moment feasible: the cost of the four-color process was at that time prohibitive, and Bok had to abandon it. But he never lost sight of it. He knew the hour would come when he could carry it out, and he bided his time.

It was not until years later that his opportunity came, when he immediately made up his mind to seize it. The magazine had installed a battery of four-color presses; the color-work in the periodical was attracting universal attention, and after all stages of experimentation had been passed, Bok decided to make his dream a reality. He sought the co-operation of the owners of the greatest private art galleries in the country: J. Pierpont Morgan, Henry C. Frick, Joseph E. Widener, George W. Elkins, John G. Johnson, Charles P. Taft, Mrs. John L. Gardner, Charles L. Freer, Mrs. Havemeyer, and the owners of the

Benjamin Altman Collection, and sought permission to reproduce their greatest paintings.

Although each felt doubtful of the ability of any process adequately to reproduce their masterpieces, the owners heartily co-operated with Bok. But Bok's co-editors discouraged his plan, since it would involve endless labor, the exclusive services of a corps of photographers and engravers, and the employment of the most careful pressmen available in the United States. The editor realized that the obstacles were numerous and that the expense would be enormous; but he felt sure that the American public was ready for his idea. And early in 1912 he announced his series and began its publication.

The most wonderful Rembrandt, Velasquez, Turner, Hobbema, Van Dyck, Raphael, Frans Hals, Romney, Gainsborough, Whistler, Corot, Mauve, Vermeer, Fragonard, Botticelli, and Titian reproductions followed in such rapid succession as fairly to daze the magazine readers. Four pictures were given in each number, and the faithfulness of the reproductions astonished even their owners. The success of the series was beyond Bok's own best hopes. He was printing and selling one and three-quarter million copies of each issue of his magazine; and before he was through he had presented to American homes throughout the breadth of the country over seventy million reproductions of forty separate masterpieces of art.

The dream of years had come true.

Bok had begun with the exterior of the small American house and made an impression upon it; he had brought the love of flowers into the hearts of thousands of small householders who had never thought they could have an artistic garden within a small area; he had changed the lines of furniture, and he had put better art on the walls of these homes. He had conceived a full-rounded scheme, and he had carried it out.

It was a peculiar satisfaction to Bok that Theodore Roosevelt once summed up this piece of work in these words: "Bok is the only man I ever heard of who changed, for the better, the architecture of an entire nation, and he did it so quickly and yet so effectively that we didn't know it was begun before it was finished. That is a mighty big job for one man to have done."

Edward Bok, *The Americanization of Edward Bok* (New York, Charles Scribner, 1920), 240–250 *passim*.

136.   The Problem of Spending (1919)

BY GLENN FRANK

For Glenn Frank, see No. 105 above.

I HAVE just had one of the most exhilarating intellectual experiences of my life.   One of our distinguished rich men discussed with me the dilemma he faces in attempting to decide how he should dispose of his fortune in order to make it contribute to the largest possible public good of this and future generations.   The man in question is a refreshing contrast to the type of gray-minded executive who has amassed a fortune by that mysterious sixth sense—the money sense. He is essentially an inventor, a social inventor.   He has always been animated by the pioneer's restless itch for exploration of new and undeveloped areas of business.   His highly successful business has been the product of a mind keenly sensitive to the social implications and public responsibilities of business.   He is, in the best sense of that much abused and weather-beaten word, a liberal.

To his credit, let it be said that he has no one pet idea, social, political, religious, or economic, that he desires to foist upon future generations by putting behind it an adequately financed and astutely organized propaganda.   He is concerned that future generations think in a liberal fashion upon the problems they have to face at the time rather than that future generations agree with ideas which he today regards as liberal.   In other words, he is more concerned that after his death his fortune shall minister to liberal purposes, whatever they may happen to be at the time, than to any liberal program now in existence.   He is more interested in the creed-maker than in the creed-keeper.

All this is, I think, commendable.   It marks a definite advance over the plutocratic, paternalistic philosophy which animates a certain type of rich man who at the moment of will-making thinks in the conventional terms of endowments and foundations alone.

I am not attempting to suggest a wholesale condemnation of foundations and endowments.   Most of us agree, I think, that the endowment of scientific research, of the war against disease, and of education are salutary forms of endowment.   But even in these instances there is a vast and relatively untouched opportunity for men and money, saturated with scientific imagination, to stimulate the people to do these things for themselves instead of having these things done for them by endowments and foundations. The man who could use his imagination, his leadership, and his money to influence the medical profession and the masses of men and women throughout the country toward the working out of a program that would make of the medical profession a national health army instead of the physical rescue crew of private practitioners it now is, and that would inject sanity into our daily habits of living, would go further toward making us a physically fine people than any foundation studying this or that disease can possibly do. We need foundations for the study of cancer and hookworm and yellow fever and typhus. I am not attempting to send even a breath of criticism in their direction. I am only concerned to suggest that throwing several million dollars at a group of scientists and saying to them, "Study cancer," is a relatively easy thing to do. The world is waiting for the rich man who will undergo the intolerable fatigue of thought in addition to the gracious gesture of benevolence, and furnish the imaginative impulse that will awaken medical statesmanship in the medical profession, and convince the masses of our citizens that they should be as fanatically propagandist about health as about prohibition. . . .

As L. P. Jacks has suggested, it is one thing to know what to do with several million dollars when one does not have them; it is a different thing when they stand to one's credit in the bank. The first is as easy as talking; the second, as difficult as martyrdom. I should like, however, to set down certain observations regarding rich men and their money both during their lifetime, when their living will dictates its use, and after their death, when their documentary will dictates its use.

First, taken by and large, the rich man's greatest opportunity for public service lies inside his private business. That is to say, statesmanship in business is of greater social value than philanthropy outside of business. I have often thought of the case of Carnegie. Mr. Carnegie, when he reached the zenith of his industrial and financial power, sold out and spent the rest of his life in so-called "public work." He endowed libraries, built peace palaces, and enjoyed a wide-spread reputation as a distinguished servant of the common good. I wish

Mr. Carnegie had possessed the requisite imagination and statesmanship to see that in his steel industry he possessed a remarkable social laboratory in which he might have helped the nation to experiment its way toward some solution of the vexed problem of industrial relations. I cannot but feel that had he spent his energy and his money in this fashion there would now stand to his credit something far more satisfying than the cobwebs that have been spun across the entrance to his peace palace at The Hague. In other words, Mr. Carnegie had the opportunity to be a statesman in business; he chose to be a philanthropist outside business.

Second, there is something fundamentally ineffective in the final working out of virtually all endowed efforts. I believe that normal human beings basically dislike having things done for them. It may be that some day we shall discover that the only uplift that really uplifts is the doing of some creative thing, the example of which will be contagious, and doing it so successfully that it pays its own way.

Third, it is a dangerous thing for the American people to permit rich, conservative, old men to endow for future generations their own old and conservative ideas.

Fourth, the only thing any man of sincere and disinterested public spirit has any right to project across future generations is the spirit, the purpose, and the general direction of his mind. Even this right must be hedged about by the proviso that the spirit, the purpose, and the general direction of his mind be dynamic, liberal and headed toward the future. . . .

Fifth, no one has yet devised a technic for endowing the endower's impulse in distinction from his ideas.

As I stated in an earlier paragraph, it is refreshing to find a rich man who in the main is willing to subscribe to at least the first four of these statements. I have said that my rich friend is animated with the pioneer's instinct, and possesses a creative mind. He may yet render my fifth statement obsolete by devising a technic for endowing that elusive thing, the liberal spirit. If he does, he will be the world's greatest benefactor.

I doubt that he will. I do not believe that it is possible to express the liberal spirit generation after generation through any organization or piece of machinery that any man can devise and endow. The spirit of the inventor, of the pioneer, of the progressive is constantly in conflict with established institutions. If the first group selected by the rich man to administer his fortune for liberal purposes is to be self-perpetuating, the obvious fact is that the members of this group will select their successors at a time more conservative. This means that the second generation of administrators will be more conservative than the first, and so on. . . .

How, then, is a rich man to provide for the continuous functioning of his fortune after his death? The answer is, I think, that he cannot and should not. There are of course all sorts of qualifications to this dogmatic statement. I think it is possible and desirable for certain fortunes to be left intact as endowments to scientific research and the like. My statement applies only to the rich man who desires that his fortune shall, generation after generation, promote political, social, and industrial liberalism. I have my own notion of what I should do if I were a multimillionaire facing the problem of making my will, and wanted to be as certain as it is humanly possible to be that my fortune would minister to liberal and progressive social policies. My notion clusters around the endowment of living genius, and would mean that my fortune would disappear as an entity or single fund at the end of one generation. But that is another story for another time.

Glenn Frank, *A Perplexed Millionaire*, in *An American Looks at His World* (Newark, University of Delaware Press, 1923), 1–10 *passim*.

———————◆———————

137. The Architecture of Expediency (1924)

BY LEWIS MUMFORD

Mumford is an author, concerned largely with cultural and esthetic subjects. He has been connected with a number of professional publications for architects, which will satisfy seekers after more exact knowledge of what is being done in the way of modern building.

THE provinces in which mechanical architecture has been genuinely successful are those in which there have been no conventional precedents, and in which the structure has achieved a sense of absolute form by following sympathetically the limitations of material and function. Just as the bridge summed up what was best in early industrialism, so the modern subway station, the modern lunch room, the modern factory, and its educational counterpart, the modern school, have often been cast in molds which make them conspicuous esthetic achievements. In the Aristotelian sense, every purpose contains an inherent form; and it is only natural that a factory or lunch room or grain elevator, intelligently conceived, should become a structure quite different in every aspect from the precedents that are upheld in the schools.

It would be a piece of brash esthetic bigotry to deny the esthetic values that derive from machinery: the clean surfaces, the hard lines, the calibrated perfection that the machine has made possible carry with them a beauty that is quite different from that of handicraft—but often it is a beauty. Our new sensitiveness to the forms of useful objects and purely utilitarian structures is an excellent sign; and it is not surprising that this sensitiveness has arisen first among artists. Many of our power-plants are majestic; many of our modern factories are clean and lithe and smart, designed with unerring logic and skill. Put alongside buildings in which the architect has glorified his own idiosyncrasy or pandered to the ritual of conspicuous waste, our industrial plants at least have honesty and sincerity and an inner harmony of form and function. There is nothing peculiar to machine-technology in these virtues, however, for the modern factory shares them with the old New England mill, the modern grain elevator with the Pennsylvania barn, the steamship with the clipper, and the airplane hangar with the castle.

The error with regard to these new forms of building is the attempt to universalize the mere process or form, instead of attempting to universalize the scientific spirit in which they have been conceived. The design for a dwelling house which ignores everything but the physical necessities of the occupants is the product of a limited conception of science which stops short at physics and mechanics, and neglects biology, psychology, and sociology. If it was bad esthetics to design steel frames decorated with iron cornucopias and flowers, it is equally bad esthetics to design homes as if babies were hatched from incubators, and as if wheels, rather than love and hunger, made the world go round. During the first movement of industrialism it was the pathetic fallacy that crippled and warped the new achievements of technology, which turns all living things it touches into metal.

In strict justice to our better sort of mechanical architecture, I must point out that the error of the mechanolators is precisely the opposite error to that of the academies. The weakness of conventional architecture in the schools of the nineteenth century was the fact that it applied only to a limited province: we knew what an orthodox palace or post office would be like, and we had even seen their guilty simulacra in tenement-houses and shopfronts; but no one had ever dared to imagine what a Beaux Arts factory would be like; and such approaches to it as the pottery works in Lambeth only made the personality more dubious. The weakness of our conventional styles of architecture was that they stopped short at a province called building—which meant the province where the ordinary rules of esthetic decency and politeness were completely abandoned, for lack of a precedent. . . .

So much of the detail of a building is established by factory standards and patterns that even the patron himself has precious little scope for giving vent to his impulses in the design or execution of the work; for every divergence from a standardized design represents an additional expense. In fact, the only opportunity for expressing his taste and personality is in choosing the mode in which the house is to be built: he must find his requirements in Italy, Colonial America, France, Tudor England, or Spain—woe to him if he wants to find them in twentieth-century America! Thus the machine process has created a standardized conception of style: of itself it can no more invent a new style than a mummy can beget children. If one wishes a house of red brick it will be Georgian or Colonial; that is to say, the trimming will be white, the woodwork will have classic moldings, and the electric-light fixtures will be pseudo-candlesticks in silvered metal. If one builds a stucco house, one is doomed by similar mechanical canons to rather heavy furniture in the early Renaissance forms, properly duplicated by the furniture makers of Grand Rapids—and so on. The notion of an American stucco house is so foreign to the conception of the machine mode that only the very poor, and the very rich, can afford it. Need I add that Colonial or Italian, when it falls from the mouth of the "realtor" has nothing to do with authentic Colonial or Italian work?

Commercial concentration and the national market waste resources by neglect, as in the case of the Appalachian forests they squandered them by pillage. Standardized materials and patterns and plans and elevations—here are the ingredients of the architecture of the machine age: by escaping it we get our superficially vivacious suburbs; by accepting it, those vast acres of nondescript monotony that, call them West Philadelphia or Long Island City or what you will, are but the anonymous districts of Coketown. The chief thing needful for the full enjoyment of this architecture is a standardized people. Here our various educational institutions, from the advertising columns of the five-cent magazine to the higher centers of learning, from the movie to the radio, have not perhaps altogether failed the architect.

The manufactured house is set in the midst of a manufactured environment. The quality of this environment calls for satire rather than description; and yet a mere catalog of its details, such as Mr. Sinclair Lewis gave in Babbitt, is almost satire in itself. In this environment the home tends more and more to take last place: Mr. Henry Wright has in fact humorously suggested that at the present increasing ratio of site-costs—roads, sewers, and so forth—to house-costs, the house itself will disappear in favor of the first item by 1970. The prophetic symbol of this event is the tendency of the motor-car and the temple-garage to take precedence over the house. Already these incubi have begun to occupy the last remaining patch of space about the suburban house, where up to a generation ago there was a bit of garden, a swing for the children, a sandpile, and perhaps a few fruit trees.

The end of a civilization that considers buildings as mere machines is that it considers human beings as mere machine-tenders: it therefore frustrates or diverts the more vital impulses which would lead to the culture of the earth or the intelligent care of the young. Blindly rebellious, men take revenge upon themselves for their own mistakes: hence the modern mechanized house, with its luminous bathroom, its elegant furnace, its dainty garbage-disposal system, has become more and more a thing to get away from. The real excuse for the omnipresent garage is that in a mechanized environment of subways and house machines some avenue of escape must be left open. Distressing as a Sunday automobile ride may be on the crowded highways that lead out of the great city, it is one degree better than remaining in a neighborhood unsuited to permanent human habitation. So intense is the demand for some saving grace, among all these frigid commercial perfections, that handicraft is being patronized once more, . . . and the more audacious sort of interior decorator is fast restoring the sentimentalities in glass and wax flowers that marked the Victorian Age. This is a pretty comment upon the grand achievements of modern industry and science; but it is better, perhaps, that men should be foolish than that they should be completely dehumanized.

The architecture of other civilizations has sometimes been the brutal emblem of the warrior, like that of the Assyrians: it has remained for the architecture of our own day in America to be fixed and stereotyped and blank, like the mind of a Robot. The age of the machine has produced an architecture fit only for lathes and dynamos to dwell in: incomplete and partial in our applications of science, we have forgotten that there is a science of humanity, as well as a science of material things. Buildings which do not answer to this general description are either aristocratic relics of the age of handicraft, enjoyed only by the rich, or they are fugitive attempts to imitate cheaply the ways and gestures of handicraft.

We have attempted to live off machinery, and the host has devoured us. It is time that we ceased to play the parasite: time that we looked about us, to see what means we have for once more becoming men. The prospects of architecture are not divorced from the prospects of the community. If man is created, as the legends say, in the image of the gods, his buildings are done in the image of his own mind and institutions.

Lewis Mumford, *Sticks and Stones* (New York, Boni and Liveright, 1924), 177–189 *passim*.

138. The New York Legal Aid Society (1925)

BY LEONARD MCGEE

The Legal Aid Societies in several large cities are organized to help secure justice for persons who are too poor to incur the expense of the usual lawyer's fees.   In large part their staffs are composed of law school students of exceptional standing, who are eager to take this means of gaining an early knowledge of the practical side of the law.

THE Legal Aid Society of New York conducts its business along the same lines as any private law office having a general practice of the law. We endeavor to assist in all branches of the law and with several exceptions will represent our clients in litigated matters in any of the courts of the state. It must be borne in mind that our first aim is to give *legal* aid. . . . Secondly: This legal aid is given gratuitously, *if necessary*, which means that no person because of his inability to pay our small retainer charge of twenty-five cents shall be refused assistance. The Society is not strictly a charitable institution, for we do not feel that the getting or the securing of something to which an individual is legally entitled is charity but justice. . . . Thirdly: Our assistance is given *to all who may appear worthy thereof*. Where it appears either from the admission of the client or from some other reliable source that the client has been guilty of theft or dishonesty or further misconduct in immediate connection with the transaction out of which his claim arises, or in relation to the defendant, then the claim of such applicant may be refused. . . .

I know of no better opportunity to study human nature and to get an insight into the mode of living and the conditions under which our poor labor than to sit at a desk in any of our offices and listen to the complaints of those who seek legal aid. There come the wage earners who have been deprived of the only thing of value they possess, their time and the work of their hands; abandoned or mistreated wives who are desirous of procuring a divorce, a separation or an annulment; unfortunate children whose small inheritances are tied up in court with endless bands of red tape; childless parents who are desirous of adopting some little boy or girl; victims of various swindling schemes; improvident borrowers who have become involved with usurious money lenders; the widow who has been left perhaps an industrial policy of insurance but cannot realize on the same until Letters of Administration have been granted; sea-faring men who have gotten into the hands of the crimp, etc.

Our Society carried all the way from the Municipal Court to the Court of Appeals in the state of New York a case involving the sum of $24, in which the defendant was what is commonly known as a loan shark. The decision of the Court of Appeals confirmed our contention, and while the original claim involved only $24, the final decision affected claims totalling over $100,000 held by the various loan companies in New York City against the poor. . . .

Although our clients fall into certain classes, one must not forget that each is a living, feeling individual. No matter how ignorant or hardened, each feels the sting of injustice; each nurses a wrong which to him seems the most cruel in the world; each is discouraged and embittered by his helplessness to right the wrong. Among such as these seeds of anarchy fall on fertile soil. . . .

. . . We still have the spectacle of the rich man with his staff of well paid lawyers doing with impunity what a poor man would be put in jail for doing. Laws do not execute themselves. The most benevolent legislation put upon our statute books is utterly useless unless one has the means to set the wheels of justice in motion.

The less one has the more it hurts to have that little taken away. . . . It is those unfortunates who cherish rights they have not the means to protect and enforce, we long to serve.

Suppose you had come to New York on an immigrant ship. Suppose you had entered through Ellis Island where the gentlest treatment is none too polite and had lost all of your personal effects through some irresponsible baggage agent. Suppose you had been set adrift in a strange city and had been obliged to find a home in the slums of our city when only a dollar or so stood between you and starvation; suppose you found work in some sweatshop where you toiled for a week, only to be turned away without a cent for your time and labor and the fruits of your labor had gone to the enrichment of some parasite of the community whose whole life is aimed at reaping where he has not sown. What then would you think of New York? What feeling would you entertain for one who is able to compel the proprietor of that sweatshop to pay you what was justly your due?

But viewed even in that light, you cannot have a sympathetic understanding of our work until you become familiar with particular cases and acquainted with individual clients.

A woman hobbled into the offices one day, all bent and broken with rheumatism. She told of the struggle she and her husband had had to keep their little family together and a roof over their heads. But they had found a way and with it a little happiness, until the husband unexpectedly inherited $10,000 from relatives in Germany. Then his crippled wife and his old friends were not good enough for him. He took nine of the ten thousand dollars and disappeared. Not, however, without some thought for his family, as he deposited $1000 in a savings bank and left the bankbook where his wife would find it after his departure. But he had not reckoned with certain legal difficulties. The money was deposited in his name and could not be drawn by the wife and with that $1000 dangling there in plain sight, the wife and children were being fed out of the poor basket.

. . . We obtained a decree of legal separation for the woman with an allowance for support. The Court appointed a receiver of the husband's property who was authorized to draw the $1000 from the bank and use it for the needs of the family. While that lasts the woman and the children are provided for. . . .

For several years past, numerous complaints have been filed in the various offices of The Legal Aid Society against certain furniture concerns, concerns conducting their business, or part of it, on what might be termed the "club-plan." This "club-plan" was a scheme whereby certain agents of the companies induced the purchaser to sign a contract agreeing to pay twenty-five cents a week until he had paid the sum of $17.50, at which time he was to be entitled to select certain articles supposed to be of the value of $17.50. These contracts contained a peculiar feature to the effect that each week a drawing was had, and the one who held what might be termed a lucky number was entitled to receive an article worth $17.50, without the making of any further payments. This drawing feature was a means of advertising, but it was also a lottery, and lotteries are prohibited under our existing laws.

The contract-holders who applied to us for assistance complained, and justly so, because the articles selected by them, and the articles delivered, were hardly ever the same. Another bad feature of the business was that of offering to a contract-holder, after the full purchase price had been paid, an article of such inferior value that the customer in many cases refused to accept it, and upon the earnest solicitation of one of the salesmen, was induced to pay several dollars more for an article of excellent value. There were seven or eight of these concerns in New York City.

Thanks to the activity on the part of the District Attorney's office in New York County, warrants were issued for the arrest of all the proprietors upon the charge of running a lottery. The defendants waived examination in the Magistrate's Court, and their cases came on to be heard in Sessions, and just prior to their arraignment in Sessions a request was made by the various proprietors and by the District Attorney's office that The Legal Aid Society suggest ways and means whereby the holders of these "club-plan" contracts would receive something on their contracts. . . . I prepared and submitted a plan of adjustment which proved acceptable to the defendants, the District Attorney's office, and the Court, so that when the cases came on for trial, the defendants all pleaded guilty, sentence being suspended that an opportunity be given to the defendants to make restitution in accordance with the terms of my plan. . . .

Little can one appreciate the difficulties encountered in dealing with a proposition of this size. Our sole idea in this undertaking was to see that the poor received something for their money, receiving that something at a time when it would be most needed, instead of running the chance of having the business of these concerns tied up for indefinite periods, and, in the end, the possibility of receiving nothing. While I feel perfectly sure that all of the customers whose claims were adjusted were not wholly satisfied with the adjustment, I have the consolation of knowing that they received something for what they paid in, whereas if no such plan as I devised had been accepted, their chances of recovering anything would have been lost.

Leonard McGee, in *Annals of the American Academy of Political and Social Science* (Philadelphia, March, 1926), CXXIV, 28–32 *passim*.

CHAPTER XXVI — EDUCATION

139. Public School Ideals (1916)

BY SUPERINTENDENT WILLIAM WIRT

Wirt is Superintendent of Schools at Gary, Indiana; he is the author of the famous Gary System of practical education, and has been the initiator of several other highly successful and widely imitated innovations in public-school teaching.

PUBLIC–SCHOOL ideals have changed during the past ten years. This change has been sudden and, in a sense, inspiring. Many educational leaders, who as radical progressives were instrumental in promoting the new view-point, are now considered conservatives because they are not able at once to realize completely these new ideals of the school. For a long time the doctrine has been preached that the school should train the heart and the hand as well as the head, that the school should develop industrial efficiency as well as scholarship, that the school should teach the art of right living as well as arithmetic, reading, and writing. But when the public has at last been converted and demands that the whole child be sent to school, and that the needs of all the children be met, the school is overwhelmed with its responsibility. The traditional school organization and equipment are found to be inadequate.

The first business of the school is to get the child into a condition to be taught what the school has to teach: the child must have good health, intelligence, reliability, and industry in order to succeed either in the school or out of the school. He must have real life experiences to supplement the book study, and must have a chance to use the knowledge gained from books not only to master the knowledge but also to understand why he should study the books. The traditional school, with children strapped to fixed school seats for nine hundred hours a year, and loafing in the streets three hours for one spent in school, is not prepared to develop good health, intelligence, industry, or reliability. The public and the teachers now see that the tremendous current of energy expended for the education of the city child is being short-circuited through the wasted life of the city street. The principal reason for the great change in the ideals of the school to-day is that our city thought is now being dominated by men and women who were themselves city boys and girls and understand their needs and handicaps. They know that the average city home cannot provide a sufficient quantity of wholesome activity at work and play any more than it can provide adequate opportunities for study and academic instruction.

It was the industrial training of children in the home and small shop that made children of the past generation reliable, industrious, physically strong, and contributed much to their general intelligence. The school plus the home and the small shop educated the child. To-day the small shop has been eliminated and the home has lost many of its former opportunities. A much greater part of the education of the child must be assumed by the school of the present generation. It is true we have in the schools a little manual training and are now talking about prevocational and vocational training. But the school still considers the problem entirely from the standpoint of how to do a little of the industrial training with the least disturbance to the traditional programme. What we really need is a complete reorganization of the entire elementary-school system to meet changed social and industrial conditions. Patchwork will not do, and, besides, it is expensive. The school must do what the school, home, and small shop formerly did together.

I am in favor of an elementary-school system that really trains all of its children, and educates the whole child, while it keeps him in school until sixteen years of age. We desire a public institution that will be a study, work, and play school. We want the school to continue to develop culture and scholarship. We believe that when the wasted time of the street is used for wholesome work and play, supplementing the study hours, the school will be more successful in developing culture and scholarship and also able to fit boys and girls for life.

Not only must the wasted street time of the child be eliminated, but the time and energy of the teacher must be conserved. It is the business of the administration of the school to develop and keep the teacher in the best condition to teach, the child in the best condition to learn, and both in the best possible environment for teaching and learning. A successful work, study, and play school provides the best environment for teaching and learning, and develops in the child the right attitude of mind toward the school. It has been demonstrated that such a school conserves the energy and time of the teacher. When the children want to know what the school has to teach, the teacher's work is comparatively light. In fact, no teacher can by any expenditure of energy educate the child. Each child must educate himself. When children are busy educating themselves, and the teacher is only a wise director of their efforts, the nervous drain of the traditional school disappears.

Financing an ideal school is not a problem. Well-equipped work-shops, supervised playgrounds, fine auditoriums, gymnasia, labora-tories, and swimming-pools are not extravagant luxuries. These additions to the school plant actually reduce the total cost of the school to the taxpayers. Schools with abundant provision for work and play activities as well as study are extravagant only in the oppor-tunities offered the children. The great problem is to know what kind of a school will meet the children's needs and how to run such a school when you have secured it. You can afford any kind of a school desired if ordinary economic public-service principles are applied to public-school management. The first principle in turning waste into profit in school management is to use every facility all the time for all the people. The modern city is largely the result of the application of the principle of the common use of public facilities that we need for personal use only part of the time. Ample accommodations may be provided in all facilities in the schools, if they are in use constantly by alternating groups. And this may be done at less cost than regular classrooms provided on the basis of the exclusive private possession of a desk and one-fortieth of a classroom by each pupil.

The public now understands clearly that the successful rearing of children is as much of a social and economic problem as it is a peda-gogical problem. No longer is the public going to permit the peda-gogue to dictate school conditions regardless of social and economic needs.

William Wirt, *Introductory Note* to *The Gary Public Schools* by Randolph S. Bourne, in *Scribner's Magazine*, September, 1916 (New York), 371–380.

140. Employment of Disabled Service Men (1918)

BY FREDERIC W. KEOUGH

Able specialists studied the problem of the rehabilitation of disabled soldiers with more interest and thoroughness during the World War than ever before. Even with an elaborate scheme of reëducation, many veterans were not adequately equipped to support themselves after their discharge. See also No. 155 below.

ILLUSTRATED feature stories on the re-education of the wounded soldiers and sailors usually describe mechanical and human miracles. Such presentations of the subject cause us to think that there is an enormous task ahead of us in making, by mechanical means, whole men out of little more than remnants. To accept this as indicative of the problem of re-education is to warp the judgment and misdirect the general endeavor. At the outset, let it be understood that the causes of military disability are, to the extent of at least fifty per cent, of a medical nature. A disabled soldier or sailor is not necessarily a man without legs or arms.

Ninety per cent of all returned wounded men go back to their old jobs. With them the employment problem is simple. Only ten per cent have to be re-educated. Undoubtedly many more men are injured annually in American industries than we may expect in a year's war. Consequently the teaching of any trade or any kind of machine operations to this seventy per cent gives them better incomes and easier work than their former occupations. To the extent of over ninety per cent re-education is nothing more than common, ordinary industrial education—in established industrial schools, in day, continuation, and night classes, and in factories when the crippled man is so nearly competent to do the proposed work that the employer can properly put him to work, supervised by some one in the establishment. . . .

Bringing the physically unfit and disabled man to an irreducible minimum is a national obligation. In caring for disabled soldiers and sailors, no source of possible benefit to their condition should be left unexhausted. If disabilities make it inadvisable for a man to follow his former employment, he should be fitted for a new occupation by appropriate training.

But of what avail is all this if the injured man is not afforded opportunity adapted to his capabilities? The number and character of industrial opportunities are the determining factor in the success of any effort to rehabilitate disabled men. Unless manufacturers are willing to employ restored and re-educated men; unless it is known how many and what kind can be taken into industrial establishments, the workers will stand idle in the market place.

The problem of the handicapped man is not a new one, for he has been with us for a long time and our records of industrial accidents, even for a year, ought to supply us with enough material for the problem of what to do with them. The matter of rehabilitation of the men disabled in the present war will be a matter of national concern for at least fifty years. It should be approached soberly, therefore, and with none of the hysteria that attaches to the home-coming of the military hero. It is one thing to welcome back a soldier in uniform and if he is suffering from the effects of wounds to overload him with attentions. When he lays aside the military garb and pursues the path of the civilian, the honors and attentions that have been showered on him are likely to cease.

The United States has resolved that every returned soldier shall have a full opportunity to succeed. When necessary, war cripples must be thoroughly trained in schools and industry, and industrial opportunities must be disclosed for those who need occupation. Jobs must be adapted to them, in order that they may become competitors in every sense with the workers who are whole. Occupations that do not exist must be brought into being. Certain work must be reserved for cripples, and devices must be discovered and adapted that will fit the victims of war back into all the ordinary activities of life. . . .

In the clerical field are undoubtedly the greatest number of openings. Unlimited places are offered in the shipping, receiving and bookkeeping departments of almost every factory. Stenography and typewriting likewise hold possibilities, particularly for the blind. In France, numerous blind soldiers have been trained to take dictation on a special machine, and they transcribe their notes rapidly and accurately. Clerical work, of course, requires that the injured man possess a certain grade of intelligence and general education, and when either is lacking, the task of placing him in industry becomes more difficult. Obviously we cannot turn all our injured soldiers into the clerical field. The great majority will by natural inclination and training return to factory work.

Machinery building firms state that they have numerous opportunities, and almost all the prominent automobile manufacturers make similar expressions. One great automobile plant has stated that at present it has in its employ 1,500 more or less disabled men, and out of these, almost 300 are suffering from the loss of either hands or legs; these crippled men, when placed in work that is properly adapted to them are found just as efficient as the other workers, showing that the crippled worker can hold his own with his fellowmen, if placed in the right surroundings. This may almost be taken as a general rule for all industries in which the crippled worker is to be utilized. . . .

It is the general opinion that on account of the heavy nature of the iron and steel industry, few openings are possible for the crippled worker; but a large steel corporation in Chester, Pa., announces that it will be willing to take from eighteen to twenty disabled men, and a New Jersey iron worker makes the same offer. A Detroit steel casting company announces that in the core room a considerable number of these workers could be employed, as all the materials are brought to and taken away from the men. A large stove manufacturer in Milwaukee is confident that he can utilize at least 100 such workers in his business.

The printing industry undoubtedly holds many opportunities, for many of the smaller machines, particularly in the composing room, can be operated while the worker is sitting. A man familiar with linotype composition work, who might be blinded, may easily manage the keyboard by the touch system.

In the list of industries holding opportunities for the men crippled in their lower limbs, the positions named are almost entirely in the regular processes of the work; but it must be remembered that in almost every factory, no matter in what line, there are numerous odd jobs requiring both intelligence and skill which are particularly suitable for disabled men. These include such positions as gatemen, carpenters, watchmen, inspectors, shipping and receiving clerks, elevator men, etc., and one factory announces that it is particularly ready to co-operate in this work because its employment manager and safety engineer are both cripples. Any factory preparing to give employment on a large scale to crippled men who would have to be taught in the plant, could do no better than to have a crippled man as teacher of the various processes, because his knowledge of the worker's limitations, as well as of the work to be taught, will give him a peculiar sympathy and tact in dealing with a difficult subject.

In the foregoing, the opportunities have been noted principally for men who have the use of both arms, yet many men suffering from the loss of arms will have to be replaced in industry. At first sight the task seems hopeless, but correspondence with various firms who either employ or are willing to employ such cripples, shows that the places are much more numerous than would at first be expected.

A manufacturer of band saw machinery in Michigan announces that one of his employes who lost an arm some years ago earns as good wages as if he had two. A silicate book slate company which employs only eighteen men is willing to take three or four who lost either an arm or a leg, while a furniture company offers to take twenty-five similarly crippled. The lumber industry seems to offer numerous possibilities in this line, and many firms, notable among them a Chicago company, offered to take a number of workers who have one good arm.

For men so disabled, the chemical industry is particularly inviting, for the large number of processes which require little manual labor but careful watching, make it possible to employ a man lacking both arms, and one chemical firm in Maryland has offered to take fifteen such men and train them to watch processes. An Ohio chemical firm makes a similar offer, and I believe that these replies may be taken as an index of the general condition of the industry. Another offer for men with one arm gone comes from a wheel manufacturer, and is followed by one from a maker of wire nails, who says that he could use the crippled men to pack the nails in small boxes. . . .

It has been the experience of firms already employing disabled men that they are so keenly appreciative of the opportunity offered, that their spirit of willingness more than makes up for the disability. Several of our correspondents who have cripples in their employ have stated this. But it has been most aptly summed up by a New England firm which says that the crippled workers in its employ are so satisfactory, that the writer has often wished that he had more such men.

It is essential that it be impressed upon our disabled men that their spirit and attitude toward their work are the biggest factors in their success. Manufacturers on the whole are ready to give them every opportunity, but the will to make good must be strong in the workers. One firm summed it up by saying that there is always something a cripple can do, even in the way of pure manual labor; but his value to himself and to his employer depends very largely on his own attitude towards the work. . . .

The need of employing every available worker will be with us not only this year and next but for far in the future. Employers are glad to take disabled soldiers and sailors into their establishments, and give them training that will enable them to put out a first class product, but they have to keep in mind at all times the necessity of production. Therefore, they do not wish to give disabled men work that, in the language of the day, will "hold them for a while." Many of the physically handicapped who cannot work at the bench and earn the old rates of pay, can, however, apply their proficiency in receiving instructions and imparting them in the supervision of other workers.

In the consideration of the crippled soldier problem, it must be kept in mind that there is little, if any, sentiment in business any more than there is any patriotism in politics. Employers are not in business for their health or for philanthropic motives; they are merely middlemen who sell their products for their real worth, and neither the employer nor the employe can get more out of anything than he puts into it. The reward of the workman, therefore, is in accordance with the proficiency and skill which he expends.

The fact that a man is a disabled soldier or sailor is not enough to place him in any systematic manufacturing plant. He must be productive. If he displays any aptitude for training he will be taken in, instructed and paid while learning, and he will be shown that merely average production is expected of him.

Many of the wounded men who return will require no special training, and these naturally will be the first to find their way back into industry. They will be welcomed, for war is teaching us the necessity of conserving and utilizing every ounce of our labor strength. The returned soldier can always find work, for mature men are teachable, and the returned soldier will be so thoroughly in earnest that the instructor will not only be surprised with the rapidity with which he picks up the work, but the accuracy which he can command.

The disabled service man looks forward with joy and anticipation to the day when he will get back to work. There need be no thought of coercion in restoring such men to industry. The suggestion of the surgeon of the early possibility of a wounded soldier taking up his old-time vocation is always gladly accepted. . . .

Every American soldier on the firing line ought to be buoyed up by the consciousness that if he suffers injury, his wounds will be healed, his return home will be expedited, his special occupational ability will be analyzed, his ambition stimulated and every effort will be made to enable him to gain a position of economic independence. He can feel in his heart that the hardships he undergoes are appreciated, and know that a sincere effort is being made for him.

The men interested in the work of rehabilitating injured soldiers are not restricting their imagination to the present. They are looking forward to a period after the war, when hospital reconstruction and trade re-education will continue, reducing the wastage of civil life and adding to the new spirit of co-operation between capital and labor.

Frederic W. Keough, in *Annals of the American Academy of Political and Social Science* (Philadelphia, November, 1918), LXXX, 84–94 *passim.*

———◆———

141. Education Since the World War (1921)

BY PRESIDENT EMERITUS CHARLES W. ELIOT

For Eliot, see No. 106 above.

. . . IT remains to consider the improvements in American education which have taken place, or are in near view, since the United States went to war with Germany in April, 1917, that is, during the four most pregnant years in American history. Congress and the Administration united in a strenuous endeavor to create a huge national army quickly by draft. The examinations which drafted men were required to undergo revealed two facts about the mass of the population included in the draft, which took the people of the United States and its Government by surprise, and made them both eager for remedies. The first was the amount of illiteracy. The second was the amount of venereal disease. Two prompt conclusions were arrived at. First, that the education of the entire people could not be left exclusively in the hands of the States and the municipalities, but must be treated as a fundamental national interest. Secondly, that the entire army and navy must be instructed, in their camps and cantonments, in the means of avoiding and preventing venereal diseases, in order that the army in France might be kept fit to fight. Some guidance to this latter resolution had come earlier from the official reports from Henry L. Stimson, Secretary of War in President Taft's Cabinet, who had published the fact that the American regular army of that day suffered more from venereal diseases than any other army in the world; and from the action of Commanders of the National Guard which made part of the force that in 1912 guarded the Mexican boundary, these commanders having shown how to protect their men from the portable villages of prostitutes which were promptly established in the immediate vicinity of the camps, and with which the officers of the regular army had no disposition to interfere. The instruction administered to the army was of the crudest sort; for it was given to the men through a dictation by young officers from small hastily prepared manuals, which, however, were written by competent persons. The camps and cantonments in this country were energetically defended against both brothel and saloon, on the ground that each fed victims to the other. These measures proved remarkably effective; and the American people drew the conclusion that it was not only desirable but feasible to prevent venereal diseases in the mass of the population on a great scale. Hence a resolution on their part that the needed instruction on this subject should be given thereafter in all American schools, as part of a universal course on biology and public health. The accomplishment of this purpose is well under way, though by no means completed.

At the same time many non-governmental agencies set to work to contend against the evil of illiteracy. The Young Men's Christian Association became active in the work of teaching recent immigrants from alien races the English language and the elements of civics, winning to their classes both young men and adults. Numerous cosmopolitan clubs were organized in factory towns in the eastern part of the country, which devoted themselves to similar kinds of teaching. The chief emphasis was placed on the teaching of the

English language, and during the years which have elapsed since the Armistice, much success has attended these efforts.

This success is a strong encouragement to the idea dawning among thinking Americans that popular education should by no means be confined to children under fourteen or under eighteen, or to young people under twenty-four, but should be carried forward by evening schools, Saturday classes, and vacation schools, after regular attendance at school or college has ceased. Immediate results appear in the raising of the age of compulsory attendance at school; in the creation of the junior high school; of the evening classes in technical institutes, for boys and young men who are already at work in trades; and in the many offerings by universities of short courses in medicine, business administration, teaching, and engineering specialties for men who have already entered on the practice of their professions. The national government, the states, and various institutions of higher education are already offering numerous courses of this nature for adults. Progress in this direction is greatly stimulated by the new dangers that threaten democracy. The labor troubles, for example, proceed from a lack of intelligence and reasoning power in large bodies of voters, who may be consumers, employers, or employees. The recent enactments about the tariff have similar sources in the ignorance and lack of reasoning power among millions of our people. The only way to overcome these evils which result from the general lack of trained senses, practice in reasoning, and trustworthy information, is to strengthen the education of both the young and the adult.

A small amount of schooling was enough for the voters of town meetings in the New England of two hundred years ago, or one hundred years ago. It is not enough for the voters of continental United States to-day, who are called upon to act by their votes, or by the votes of the representatives they select, on national and international problems which are both strange and vast—too vast indeed for experienced statesmen as well as for the populace. Even in the comparatively simple field of military and naval operations, the Great War produced no military or naval commander competent to deal with the vast extensions of area and extraordinary novelties in modern warfare. In the same way no religion, Confucian, Buddhist, Brahman, Mohammedan, or Christian, has developed during the past seven years any new strong hold, either on its own people or the other peoples. At this moment all the Christian churches, denominations, or sects are wondering how they can recover their former hold on their several bodies or groups. Every secular or religious organization and every state or nation seems to need more intelligence, more vision, and more sense of duty toward the high calls of honor and conscience. There is but one road upward—more education, and wiser.

The national government has for many years maintained scientific establishments for national uses, such as the United States Coast Survey, the Naval Observatory, the Boards for maintaining a national quarantine, and the various bureaus in the Departments of Agriculture, the Interior, and the Treasury, which deal with conservation, forestry, parks, and irrigation. The war added greatly to the number of applied-science commissions in the government service, such as the commissions on explosive engines, aëroplanes, and poison gas. Some of these scientific activities have survived the Armistice, particularly those which affect the education of the people and the public health. Besides the national government, several states have taken on new functions in support of popular education. For example, Massachusetts has passed a carefully considered law which helps the schools of rural communities practically at the expense of the urban. Large appropriations have already been made by Congress, to be distributed by a national health board or commission among the states which are prepared to coöperate with the government in treating and preventing diseases. Although national aid to universal physical training is not yet consummated, it is plain that before long the national government will distribute such aid, and the states carry the beneficent plan into execution. This great improvement, though suggested by the experience of the nation at war, is really a great step forward toward national health and happiness, and industrial efficiency.

The national efficiency in time of war called for the service of experts in great variety, chemists, physicists, biologists, psychologists, and engineers; and the whole people acquired a new sense of the value of experts, and of the institutions which train them. There have resulted extensive improvements in those institutions. A curious case of carrying over into peace times a war invention, is the use of the psychological tests applied to the classification of recruits for the army and navy in the classification of school children.

Since 1914 financial and manufacturing corporations have manifested an increasing desire for graduates of colleges or technical
schools as managers, superintendents, and employment agents. Many
of these corporations affirm that the kind of managers and superintendents now needed cannot be brought up in the works, but must
have received an appropriate training in good secondary schools,
colleges, technical schools, or the graduate departments of universities.

Seeing these things, intelligent parents keep their children at school
as long as they can, instead of putting them to earn money for the
family as soon as the law allows, or before. Hence the extraordinary
resort to colleges and technical schools since the Armistice, and the
vigorous efforts to raise new endowments for these institutions, many
of which have been highly successful.

These achievements and tendencies loudly proclaim the secondary
schools and all the institutions of higher education have made great
gains since the twentieth century opened, and are going to make
many more as the twentieth century advances.

It remains to mention the remarkable educational enterprise on
which the democratic government of the United States has embarked
since it went to war with the autocratic government of Germany—
the Prohibition enterprise. Prohibitory legislation began in the
States, first in Maine, later in Kansas, and later still in some Southern
States. The national movement began with the war; and national
scope and purpose were necessary to its success. It rests solidly on a
Constitutional Amendment adopted by large majorities, and on Acts
of Congress which commended themselves to both political parties,
and secured strong majorities. It is a hopeful effort to teach the
entire people that alcoholic drinks never do any good, usually do harm,
often destroy family happiness, and as a rule impair productive
efficiency in the industries of the country. This teaching, to be effectual, must ultimately be based on prolonged experience with prohibitive legislation. It involves continuous and universal instruction in the schools and homes of the rising generation—instruction
both scientific and ethical. It also involves a considerable advance
in the ethics of the medical and legal professions, and in their sense of
responsibility to the community. No other national government,
democratic or autocratic, has ever attempted such a vast philanthropic and educational enterprise.

All men and women who believe that education is the best safeguard of democracy may rest content with the progress of education in the United States since the Civil War.

———◆———

142. The University of Today (1921)

BY EDWIN E. SLOSSON

Slosson has been Professor of Chemistry at the University of Wyoming, and literary editor of *The Independent;* at present he is known as a popular writer on scientific subjects.

THE era of splendid generosity that set in during the later eighties transformed the older institutions and added such new ones as Clark University of Worcester, Massachusetts, founded by Jonas G. Clark; the University of Chicago, founded by John D. Rockefeller; and Leland Stanford, Jr., University, founded by Senator Leland Stanford of California. These three universities, opened between 1889 and 1892, were so well endowed by their founders that from the start they took equal rank with institutions a century or more older.

As patrons of the universities usually preferred to have their donations take the tangible form of buildings, there soon arose new classrooms, laboratories, chapels, libraries, and dormitories that quite outshone the more primitive and utilitarian structures of earlier days. Formerly buildings had been put up one by one at long intervals as the needs of the institution and its funds permitted. The campus of an old college thus became a sort of architectural museum with specimens of the changing·fashions of a century. But when gifts of millions came in at one time it was possible to plan harmonious groups. The University of Chicago adopted for all its buildings the English collegiate Gothic in gray limestone and Stanford University an Hispanic Romanesque style in red and yellow with mosaic inlays. Harvard erected a unified group of five marble buildings for its medical school, and the Massachusetts Institute of Technology in 1916 removed to a new site on the Cambridge bank of the Charles River, where a group of buildings in classic style has been erected.

The imitation of Oxford and Cambridge models as shown in the new buildings of Princeton, Chicago, Pennsylvania, and elsewhere is indicative of a tendency to turn again to England for educational ideals. Residential halls and common rooms were established in many places in order to get something of the English college atmosphere, and Princeton introduced a preceptorial system of personal instruction in small groups suggested by the tutorial system of the older British universities.

With increasing wealth and luxury on the part of the universities came a desire for ceremonial display. Commencement ceremonies which had been dropped into desuetude were revived and elaborated. Academic costumes of the medieval style were introduced or invented. The fashion spread like wildfire from East to West, and in a few years mortar-board caps and gorgeous gowns were to be seen on almost every campus in the country.

Coincident and connected with the rise of ceremonial was the development of athletics. In the early days colleges were disposed to frown upon student sports and in some cases, as at Princeton, tried to prohibit them; but in the latter part of the nineteenth century public games became recognized by the college authorities as the most effective form of advertising and by the students as the quickest road to fame. A gymnasium came to be considered as necessary as a library, and more money was spent on a single football game or boat race than would formerly have sufficed to run the college for a year. In the modern American university the stadium has assumed an importance and popularity such as it has not enjoyed since the fall of Rome and Byzantium.

The dominant power in undergraduate social life of today is the fraternity, a unique feature of the American college, though it corresponds in a way to the corps of the German universities. We have already noted the founding, at old William and Mary in the Year of Independence, of the first Greek letter society, Phi Beta Kappa, as a philosophical organization. In consequence of the anti-masonic agitation of 1826 Phi Beta Kappa abandoned its ritualism and secrecy and is now simply an honorary fraternity admitting about a tenth of the seniors, men and women alike, on the ground of scholarship. But in 1826–27, even when the popular opposition to secret societies was most fierce, three fraternities—Kappa Alpha, Sigma Phi, and Delta Phi—were founded at Union College, and from this center the movement spread rapidly though secretly to the New York and New England colleges. Since then the fraternities have continued to thrive and multiply, although at times college authorities, State Legislatures, and "Barbarian" students have tried to suppress them. At the present time there are over two hundred fraternities and sororities, some academic and some professional, some local and some national, certain of which have as many as seventy-five local chapters. These societies which were once outlaws now receive practically official status in the college organization and, instead of meeting in woods and cellars, are allowed to have their handsome chapter-houses on the campus. A few institutions like Princeton retain the old prohibition, but at Princeton upper-class dining clubs have grown up which have a strong resemblance to the Greek-letter fraternities. During the last quarter of a century the membership of the national fraternities has risen from 72,000 to about 270,000, of whom 30,000 are women. They own or rent 1100 chapter-houses valued at $8,000,000.

The chief characteristics of the recent period of American education are expansion and diversification. Higher education has burst through the four walls and four years that formerly confined it and has overflowed the land. The number of students studying the classics increases year by year, but the number studying new subjects increases much more rapidly. The older colleges in the country are thriving and doing better work than ever, but the city institutions have expanded more rapidly.

The rigid requirements for entrance to college and the prescribed course afterwards were broken down, and the elective system provided a place for new studies. The efforts of Jefferson to introduce election into Virginia and of George Ticknor to do the same for Harvard had been, as we have seen, unsuccessful; but, when Charles William Eliot, a chemist with radical ideas in education, became President of Harvard in 1869, he was able in the course of the next twenty-five years to provide for a completely elective system. The example of Harvard was followed somewhat hesitatingly by almost all the others.

Another university president of similar initiative, William Rainey

Harper, had the opportunity in the University of Chicago of creating a new institution instead of reforming an old one and was thus able to introduce many innovations that have been generally adopted. One of these, the continuation of college work throughout the summer, enables the ambitious to complete a four years' course in three and gives teachers from other institutions an opportunity to carry on graduate work. The University of Chicago imported the idea of extension courses from Oxford and also established correspondence courses. Other agencies for making education accessible to the largest possible number of students Harper derived from the Chautauqua Institution, in which he had long been active. The Chautauqua movement started in a camp-meeting of Sunday School teachers at Chautauqua Lake, New York, in 1874. Similar assemblies were established in other States and not only served to stimulate interest in systematic reading but afforded a platform for the free discussion of public questions that has had as great an influence over politics as the earlier lyceum movement. From the platform of the Chautauqua assemblies held every year it is possible to speak to five million people.

It is usual now for the city universities to give public lecture courses, provide evening classes, and otherwise extend their privileges to those not enrolled as regular students. Through the initiative of the late Dr. Henry M. Leipziger, the City of New York has established a system in the school buildings of free evening lectures which are attended by a million adult auditors a year.

Besides stimulating and satisfying the educational demands of the American people, the universities have extended their influence to foreigners, both by drawing them to this country and by establishing schools in other lands. As the home missionary movement started most of the colleges west of the Alleghenies, so the foreign missionaries carried the American college around the world. In China there are eighteen colleges and universities established by American missionaries. In Turkey the American schools accommodate five thousand collegiate students. Such institutions as Robert College and the American College for Girls at Constantinople and the Syrian Protestant College at Beirut have trained the leaders of the new nationalities emerging from the chaos of the Great War.

Edwin E. Slosson, *The American Spirit in Education* [*Chronicles of America*, XXXIII] (New Haven, Yale University Press, 1921), 275–282.

143.   A Workaday College (1925)

BY JOHN PALMER GAVIT

Gavit has been a newspaper reporter, editor, and manager. Antioch is the fore-most college experimenting with the aim of combining practical experience and academic training. Almost all of its students work half of each year, in practical lines, as part of their education.

TWO distinctive things about Antioch College attract most attention. One is its half-and-half division of the students' time between "book-learning" in the college itself, and a job—a job in the ordinary sense of the word at regular current rate wages—outside, in the near-by city of Dayton or one of the other neighboring communities; a few as far away as Cleveland or even Philadelphia. The other is the fact that the full college course at Antioch takes six years instead of the four usually required. Exceptionally able and industrious students can finish in five; and there is a provision for a few "full-time" students who do not take jobs and finish in four years; but this is rather deprecated and penalized by a higher tuition fee.

Antioch believes that that sort of education, even under its own curriculum, is inadequate. It is the belief that after six years of the combination of "cultural" study and "coöperative" work, as they call it, the student will be substantially farther along in his life progress than he would be two years after graduation under the conventional four-year system.

Each job is held ordinarily by two students, constituting a "coöperating" pair, who jointly and severally contract to hold it for a year, including the summer vacation, which they divide between themselves. One works while the other studies in the college; the job is thus continuous. A feature of the system is the conference about the ins-and-outs of the job as the partners periodically exchange places. While on the job the students live where, after the fashion and at the expense they can afford, as other workaday folk do; though in Dayton, where the majority of the jobs are located, Antioch clubs have been established.

The jobs are found and assigned by the personnel department of the college and there is no difficulty about finding them; employers are glad to have these intelligent, serious-intentioned young people. And, obviously, the system enables the college to take care of twice as many students as it could if the whole student body were continuously at college.

Now the primary purpose of this system is not "vocational" in any narrow sense of the word. It is not that the student may learn a trade, business, or profession; though in many cases doubtless it contrives toward that result. Neither is it that the student may earn his or her way through college; though unquestionably it does assist materially in that regard. It is inherent and coherent in the vitals of the Antioch theory of what constitutes education—real culture.

Antioch is not the only educational institution in which study and outside occupation are combined. The University of Cincinnati, for example, has long used that method, and it is a commonplace of college life all over the country to have students in occupations of many kinds earning their way. The big difference is this—it is a crucial difference: that the University of Cincinnati, so far at least as this feature is concerned, is primarily vocational, technological; and that the self-support in the ordinary college is regarded as an outside and more or less incongruous and interfering factor—a necessary, but rather regrettable evil.

Modern education lays and will lay increasingly its stress upon *development through real activities;* upon experience as superior for educational purposes to instruction; upon living as a primary means to learning; upon doing as equal and complementary to reading, talking, and listening. The direct aim of Antioch College is to send forth roundly developed men and women with a running start in all the ensemble of life; trained not exclusively by reading of books and hearing the expounding of books, but also by first-hand experience with living; developed by what they have done and learned for themselves in the doing of it—in self-reliance, initiative, sound judgment, and the actual practice of responsibility in activities valuable for their own sake.

The outside jobs are of almost every conceivable kind, from farming to stenography, from common labor in a foundry to translating advertising matter from English to Chinese. Several students have organized and operated business enterprises of their own—even a farm. . . .

During a pilgrimage among a score or more of American colleges I have heard almost *ad nauseam* about a sacred and awesome thing called scholarship. I have found it very difficult to get a definition of it. Of many attempts no two were alike. The only one that seemed worth the breath that uttered it was this:

The possession of a practically adequate but ever growing body of general information, with special and detailed knowledge in one's particular field; and no less the capacity for usefully applying that knowledge in the relationships of real life.

It will do. Antioch seems to have that idea of "scholarship." Its course of study and activity embodies and presupposes both aspects of it. . . .

It is not easy to get into Antioch College; but the principal prerequisites are not scholastic. Entrance examinations of the ordinary sort cut very little figure. It is more or less assumed, to be sure, that "failure to complete a high school course . . . raises doubt as to the student's fitness for college work, and definite evidence of such fitness is necessary to remove that doubt," but much more weight attaches to what you *are* than to what you have studied.

Not, what have you studied? But what have you got out of what you did study? And what kind of person are you? For "only young men and women of high personal character, receptive intellect, and power of application can hope to complete the course, and those who are not impelled by serious and earnest motives are not encouraged to apply for admission."

So you have to submit convincing testimony about yourself, from responsible persons who think they know you as regards a rather searching list of personal qualities; you have to undergo a psychological test and file a statement of physical condition leaving little to the imagination or faith. But to top all that, you must write a letter giving not only somewhat detailed biographical facts about yourself, but as searching a self-analysis as you know how to make, and a photograph ("preferably a 'snapshot' taken of you without a hat"). Who are you, what do you think you are, and how did you get to be that way? Why do you want to come to Antioch, and what makes you suppose you can succeed here? What do you want to be and do in the world, and why?

The examination of this material is searching, and wherever practicable it is supplemented by an exhaustive personal conference. And there is a dropping all along the way of those who, having got in, fail to show affirmatively that they understand what Antioch is all about. Flunking in examinations is the least of it.

Experience thus far shows that an average working student must bring with him from home between $200 and $400; correspondingly more if he is not to earn part of his expense. Last year the highest actual expenditure—this was by a woman—was $873; the lowest, $330. The average weekly earnings of the men were $17.50; of the women, $15. The highest among the men was $36; among the women $18; the lowest was $10.

Antioch students know what it costs them. They have to. Every student in his freshman year must "get the habit" of keeping track of income and expense. For one of the most interesting and valuable features of this college is a required freshman course—three hours a week for the first half year, in what you might call personal financial hygiene. "F-1," they call it—"Personal Accounting and Finance."

In this course every mother's son and daughter of them is obliged to make at the outset as a matter of required class work a personal budget of expected expense and income, and to keep books, in a standard form, and audited by the professor. The books must balance, too;—else no credit! To come out at the end with a deficit is to flunk the course. And, by the way, while there is a column for "miscellaneous"—if you put anything in that column you must pass on to the next column and elucidate.

Another required freshman course which tends to start the student off with an appreciation of what he is about, is that known as "College Aims," leading him as it were to "budget" his purposes in life and to focus his effort.

Is the "Antioch Plan" really functioning? It is—no doubt about it. It has still far to go; some of its program is still to a certain extent a plan rather than an accomplishment; some important things are barely under way. But remember that the "New Antioch" has been in existence only three years. The progress in that short time is astonishing.

John Palmer Gavit, in *The New York Evening Post*.

CHAPTER XXVII — AMERICAN LITERATURE

144. Nature and John Burroughs (1900)

BY GEORGE GLADDEN

John Burroughs was a keen observer of wild life, a lover of animals, and a charming writer on nature subjects. Any of his books will convey intimate pictures of life in the woods and fields. For a nature writer of another sort, see No. 162 below.

"YES, sir," said the small boy, promptly. Then he hesitated, and gazed intently down the shaded road. The pause was so long that it suggested a resumption of the interrupted reverie, but the nodding head indicated a more definite mental activity; and when the reply came, it was explicit. "It's the fifth house on the other side of the road."

A curving driveway disappearing into a grove of maple, oak, and spruce trees hinted at the whereabouts of the "fifth house on the other side of the road." Half-way down the drive there was suddenly revealed to the pedestrian the figure of a man of rather less than medium height, with a long, snowy-white beard, and hair in which there was only a little of the earlier gray. He was standing at the edge of the drive, motionless, and gazing upward into the foliage of a maple tree within a few steps of the front porch of the "fifth house." At the sound of the pedestrian's step he turned, acknowledged his identity, and added a quiet and courteous greeting. Then almost immediately his gaze went back to the bough of the maple-tree, and he said:

"I have been watching that wood thrush. I think she is trying to turn her eggs; she seems to be moving about in the nest. I have never happened to see a bird in the act of turning her eggs; it would be interesting to observe how she manages it."

A sympathetic reader of John Burroughs's books could not have asked a meeting with him more appropriate than this. It seemed to express perfectly the genius of the man; the spirit of loving interest in his subject which breathes from his every page, and this simply because it is the very essence of his being. During the afternoon and evening that followed, his talk was mainly of birds, and always in that manner in which one speaks of friends who are loved and admired and understood. These recollections of that afternoon and evening will reflect, as faithfully as the writer may, some glimpses of the atmosphere in which "Locusts and Wild Honey," and "Signs and Seasons," and "Wake Robin," and all of the other pictures which bear the name of the same artist, came into being.

"Riverby," the "fifth house," almost over the door of which the wood thrush has built her nest, is in the beautiful little village of West Park, on the west bank of the Hudson, and a few miles above Poughkeepsie. Back of the house, and at the edge of the hillside that overlooks the river, Mr. Burroughs has a little villa—a sort of embryonic "Slabsides." On the way thither through the orchard he showed me a ruby-throated humming-bird's nest, scarcely larger than a good-sized English walnut. The little mother darted away as we approached, and sped nervously about the orchard, but her every movement was promptly reported by my keen-eyed host. Such eyes could keep half a dozen pens busy.

In the villa on the hillside Mr. Burroughs has done much of his writing. There is a little summer-house a few steps away, and here we lingered for a while, listening to the bubbling song of a house-wren and gazing at the great shining stream and the gliding steam yachts and the creeping sails. A remark about the view from his visitor led Mr. Burroughs to say: "Yes, it is a beautiful sweep of water, but I grow tired of it. It has got to be too cosmopolitan; there are too many yachts and steamboats and other suggestions of wealth and commercialism. Over at "Slabsides" I have a little river that I love. It is a real river, with trees hanging over it, and birds in the trees, and beautiful nature on every side—and no steamboats."

By the lovely, winding wood-road, "Slabsides," the picturesque and interesting retreat of Mr. Burroughs, is about a mile from "Riverby"; by the path over the wooded hillside it is rather less distant. Up this path Mr. Burroughs led the way, at a pace that gave plenty of exercise to a pair of lungs barely half as old as his. "I am a pretty good walker yet," he remarked, "except in the city. When I was last in New York, I walked from Fourteenth Street up to the American Museum of Natural History (about three miles), and I was quite tired when I got there. It was partly the unyielding sidewalks that wearied me, I suppose; though the roar of the city wears on my nerves. My ears are very sensitive, and the clatter and crash of the street always affects me. Three or four days in the city is about all I can stand at a time."

"Slabsides" we found in possession of a large and very complacent-looking cat, with fur, both in texture and marking, singularly like that of a lynx. It was a curious animal for a bird-lover to have as pet, and Mr. Burroughs expressed misgivings about "Sally" as she greeted him with many little caressing "pur-r-r-me-ows" and much sidling about and rubbing against his legs. "I am afraid she catches birds sometimes, though I have never known her to," he said. "This morning she captured a chipmunk and brought him in here and devoured him. I was very sorry about that, and I told her so, for the chipmunk is an interesting little fellow, and quite harmless. About an hour afterward she appeared with a full-grown red squirrel; and I praised her for that, for you know what a murderous wretch the red squirrel is in bird-land. If I could teach her to catch red squirrels and let the birds and chipmunks alone, I would be glad to have her about. She came to me as a waif, and I haven't had the heart to turn her away. I take care to see that she has all the milk she can drink, but I am afraid, nevertheless, that she catches birds when she can." And a few minutes later Mistress Sally showed that she would if she could, by trying, under our very eyes, to stalk a black-and-white creeping warbler that had flown into the vine curtain which shades the porch. The campaign was cut short, gently but firmly, and with admonitions as to the sin of such designs; but for several minutes Sally's eyes continued to show felonious intent. . . .

Mr. Burroughs is not quite alone in his wilderness-framed garden, so far as human neighbors are concerned. Mr. Ernest Ingersoll found him out there a year or more ago, and immediately decided to make for himself a workshop and retreat after the fashion of "Slabsides." So he built a lodge on the hillside just above the spring. And further along on the same hillside a Poughkeepsie gentleman has perched a commodious little villa with broad piazzas which command the superb views up and down the valley of the Hudson. Under the eaves of this villa, and within arm's reach as one stands on the piazza, a phœbe has built her nest, and was quietly hatching her eggs, undisturbed by the proximity of her human neighbors.

"I saw her building her nest," said Mr. Burroughs, "and noticed that she did not seem to have any bump of locality. She would come flying up here with her beak loaded with mud, and drop it on the beam beside one of the rafters. But she seemed to forget each time where she had deposited her load, and the result was that she soon had the building of four or five houses on her hands. I thought that was rather more than one small bird ought to undertake, so I interrupted the building operations by putting stones or blocks of wood on the foundations of all except one of the nests, and in that way concentrated the attention of Phœbe upon a single site. This set her right, and she went ahead and finished up one house—the one she is using now." It seemed to me that this story illustrated more than merely a bird idiosyncrasy.

In a tree at the edge of the little plateau on which Mr. Ingersoll has built his lodge, I was shown a turtle-dove sitting patiently upon her roughly built nest, over the edges of which, on either side, appeared the head and tail feathers of a young bird, evidently almost fully fledged, and altogether too large for the mother to cover any longer. And further down the hillside I was privileged to peep into a yellow-billed cuckoo's nest—a small handful of loosely laid sticks and twigs. My report of the condition of this home caused Mr. Burroughs a good deal of concern. Neither of the parents was in sight, and there was only one egg in the nest. A day or two before, he said, there had been a young bird and an egg there. "I fear that means another tragedy," he said; and those who have read the chapter on the "Tragedies of the Nests," in "Signs and Seasons," will understand his meaning.

If these bits of news from "Slabsides" have served to suggest the genius of the place, their purpose has been accomplished. It is hardly an exaggeration to say that every form of life, animate or inanimate, has some definite significance for Mr. Burroughs. That phœbe has become a personality, an individual, to him, not alone because of her rather pathetic absent-mindedness, but because she has let her friend into the secrets of her home up there under the eaves. And it is so with the turtle-dove of exaggerated maternal instinct; while the disappearance of the infant cuckoo suggests a domestic calamity none the less dire because its exact nature can only be conjectured. I do not

believe that Mr. Burroughs ever loses an opportunity to add to knowledge of bird personality by observation of this kind; and his physical
vision, which is well-nigh infallible even now when he has passed the
threescore milestone, keeps him constantly supplied with such opportunities. If I mistake not, much of the charm of what he writes is
the result of the expression of this personal familiarity with the birds,
this tendency to write definitely and always sympathetically about
some one bird.

George Gladden, *John Burroughs*, in *Outlook*, October, 1900 (New York), LXVI,
351-355 *passim*.

------◆------

145. Our Mark Twain (1914)

BY HILDEGARDE HAWTHORNE

Hildegarde Hawthorne, grand-daughter of Nathaniel Hawthorne, is the author
of a number of books, most of them for younger readers.—Bibliography: Mark
Twain, *Autobiography*.

SAMUEL LANGHORNE CLEMENS was of pure southern
blood. His father, John Marshall Clemens, was a Virginian.
His mother, a Miss Lambdon, came from Kentucky, and Sam was
born November 30, 1835, in Florida, Missouri.

But there was nothing sectional about Twain. He belonged to the
whole of America, not only by sympathy and understanding, but
through actual experience. Half his young manhood was passed in
the wild west. When he was city editor for the "Territorial Enterprise," of Virginia City, Nevada, he was kept busy writing up stage
robberies, shooting affairs, lucky strikes, raids, all the thrilling incidents of life on the border. He had himself been a prospector, and
an unlucky one, missing millions more than once by a hair's-breadth.
It was just as well for him and for the world, because if he had struck
it rich, then "The Adventures of Tom Sawyer" and the other immortal
books would probably never have been written. . . .

It isn't only that Mark Twain lived all over America. He lived
through all the different phases of the country's growth. His family
was slave-holding. He went through the war of the Union, fighting

a little, getting captured twice, breaking parole the second time, and escaping to the west. He had been a printer, a writer, a river pilot, and a prospector. In California, he began to make his mark as a humorist. While on the "Territorial Enterprise," he had begun to sign his articles and stories "Mark Twain," a pseudonym about which there have been several stories. Clemens himself said that he took the name from a Captain Isaiah Sellers, who wrote the river news for the New Orleans "Picayune," signing it Mark Twain, and who died in 1863. The origin of the name is well known, coming from the man at the bow of the river steamer who heaves the lead—"By the mark, three. By the mark, twain," etc.

Next in line for young Sam Clemens was the fame accruing from his story of "The Jumping Frog." He had heard this story, or its suggestion, told by Coon Drayton, an ex-Mississippi pilot, at Angel's Camp. Mark Twain loved this story, and later on he wrote it up. He also told it, and Bret Harte used to say that no one knew how funny the story was who hadn't heard it told in that inimitable drawl by Sam himself.

This story brought him world-wide fame. But as for money, Clemens still had precious little of that. He kept at his journalistic work, and in 1866 was sent to the Sandwich Islands, from which place he sent in his great scoop of the *Hornet* disaster. You can read all about it in Twain's "My Début as a Literary Person," and also how "Harpers" accepted the story for the magazine, and how the delighted author was going to give a banquet to celebrate the event. But he had not written his signature clearly, and when the story appeared it was under the name "Mike Swain."

After this, Twain began to lecture, making a great hit all along the Pacific coast, and in December, 1866, he came to New York on the first leg of his tour around the world, the tour that resulted in "The Innocents Abroad," though it did not go all round the proposed circle. From that time, Clemens' standing was assured. The profits of the book were $70,000. After this the east was Clemens' home. He married Miss Olivia L. Langdon in 1870, and made his residence in Hartford for many years. In 1875, he wrote the great book about *Tom Sawyer*, which is largely autobiographical. Sam was a good deal like the inimitable *Huck Finn* in his boyhood, "Do what we would, we could not make him go to school," his mother said. One day, when his father, doubting whether the boy really was going to the school for which he had set out, followed him, Sam got behind a huge tree-stump on the way to the school, slowly circling it to keep out of sight as his father walked on. This father was a stern, severe man, and poor Sam had many an uncomfortable encounter with him.

Twain was sixty years old when he started to repay the debts of his failure as a publisher. He made a tour round the world, lecturing everywhere, besides writing several books, among them the splendid "Pudd'nhead Wilson." Every cent was paid off, and, before he died, he had made a new fortune.

What a man he was! Beginning as a barefoot boy in a sleepy Mississippi river town, a journeyman printer with little education and no promise of a future, a river pilot, an unlucky prospector, he became a man of world-wide fame and immense influence. His books have gone everywhere, have made generations laugh and weep. He was not only a great humorist, he was a man of high courage and fine ideals, a man who hated shams and lies, and struck at them fiercely. He knew human nature, laughed at its queer contradictions, admired and respected its goodness and kindness. Always he is intensely American, without being provincial. Not only did he have a genius for writing. He had a genius for being a man. If, as a young man, he was inclined to be too extravagant, too irreverent, he conquered that tendency. He grew in wisdom and in perception, and he loved people, loved men and women and children. That is why we all love him. There is a glow to him. You can warm your heart at his books, much as you warm your hands at a fire. . . .

To the whole world of youth Mark Twain is *Tom Sawyer*, the Immortal Boy, the greatest boy of fiction, the American boy, and yet the essential boy that links all boys of whatever nationality together. *Tom* and *Huck*—what more do you want?

What impressed you perhaps most about Mark Twain was that he seemed to have met everybody. There wasn't a type of human nature he hadn't personally known. And this was very near the truth, for his years on the Mississippi and in the west, coupled with his long life in the east and his knowledge of Europe and the Orient, had brought him into contact with all sorts and kinds of "humans."

Read, if you haven't read, "Tom Sawyer," "Huck Finn," and "Life on the Mississippi." And then sit down and be thankful that America produced Mark Twain. You can hardly imagine one of them without the other.

Hildegarde Hawthorne, *Mark Twain and the Immortal Tom*, in *St. Nicholas*, December, 1914 (New York, Century Co.), XLII, 164–166 *passim*.

---

146. Review of Book Reviews (1916)

BY EDMUND LESTER PEARSON

Pearson has been associated with the New York Public Library, and has been an editor of *The Outlook* and the author of several books. For examples of book reviews, see Sunday editions of the New York *Times* or *Herald-Tribune*, *The Bookman*, and other periodicals devoting more or less space to literary subjects. And see, as one type of literary criticism, No. 148 below.

. . . LET us discuss these two charges against American book-reviewing. First, there is the commercialism, the control of the literary page by the business manager; the muzzle placed upon a free expression of honest opinion by the power of the dollar. There can be little doubt that it exists. The testimony of men who ought to know is so strong; the antecedent probability is so much in its favor, that it cannot wholly be denied.

From personal experience I am unable to relate a single thrilling encounter with Mammon. During five or six years I have intermittently written reviews of various books for a newspaper which devotes to reviewing probably more space than any other journal in the country. It also carries a large amount of book-advertising. For a much shorter time I wrote reviews for one of the periodicals. Whether the editors were so impressed by my appearance of honesty that they thought it hopeless to tempt me, or whether they are not accustomed to try to tempt anyone, I will let you decide. But they never conveyed to me, directly or indirectly, that I should praise this book, or "go easy" on that book, because its publisher was a big advertiser with them. Nor was one line, nor one word, of adverse criticism, condemnation or ridicule ever deleted or altered in my reviews by the editorial "blue-pencil,"—that mythical implement which all editors are supposed to keep handy. Perhaps my experiences were lucky: in fact, I know they were.

But it would be wrong to argue from this instance that there is no such thing as commercial influence on book-reviewing. In certain places it undoubtedly exists,—the testimony of experienced and widely-informed men is almost invariably in the affirmative. The man who buys space in newspapers and magazines, whether to advertise books, or patent medicines, or a department store, or a theatre, or a railroad, holds a weapon over the heads of the publishers. His power can be used—it frequently is used—as a subtle and effective kind of bribery, one of the new and refined forms of sin which our civilization has developed.

So this evil which affects us, is only a small manifestation of a very large national evil: the power which the advertiser holds to corrupt the press, and through the press to mislead public opinion. It is bad; it bothers us and troubles us to find that there are book-reviewing publications which can be muzzled or bought. But as we are citizens first, and librarians afterwards, it is absurd to lose the sense of proportion. It is foolish to explode with wrath over this matter and not to save any indignation for the larger damages which can be wrought. It would be ridiculous to think merely of venal book-reviews and to forget the children who are drugged and the wretched invalids, who are humbugged because many publications do not dare to tell the truth about patent medicines; or to forget the railroads and corporations which, by purchasing advertising space can and do buy editorial opinion, color the news, and poison at its source the information upon which we depend to govern our acts and votes.

Some of the persons who find fault with reviewing as it exists today, seem to imply that the all-important thing is that bad books should be blamed. They forget that it is equally important that good books should be praised and their authors encouraged.

In our every-day speech we have almost lost the primary meaning of the word "criticism." We seldom think of it in its real sense,—a "judgment." Almost invariably we use it in its third or fourth meaning: "harsh or unfavorable judgment." . . .

Has it ever occurred to you to wonder what might happen to some of the greatest classics of literature if they could suddenly appear to us unattended by their reputations? Suppose that the mighty name of Shakespeare was totally unknown, that the world had never seen nor heard of his plays. Then suppose that somebody discovered the plays and published them. I think I can see, in my mind's eye, some of the comments they would provoke in certain cautious publications. How the "sensationalism" of the last act of "Hamlet" would be deplored! Do you fancy that our Library Association's *Book-List* would approve "Othello"?

In regard to the other comment of Mr. Perry, about American book-reviewing—that it lacks candor, trained intelligence, and distinction—that is true, but not novel. Many of the attacks upon book-reviewing are unduly severe. Mr. Thompson, in the article in the *Atlantic Monthly* which I have quoted, was inclined to be rather strict with the book-reviewers, as well as with authors, who do not maintain the dignity of literature and keep small personalities about themselves out of print. A number of years ago, Professor Brander Matthews wrote an essay called "Literary Criticism and Book-Reviewing." He speaks of those who make ". . . a three-fold assumption:—first, that it is the chief duty of the critic to tear the mask from impostors and to rid the earth of the incompetent; second, that the critics of the past accepted this obligation and were successful in its accomplishment; and third, that there is to-day, at the beginning of the twentieth century, a special need for this corrective criticism."

Mr. Matthews denies the truth of all these assumptions. His article is extremely sensible, and valuable to read in connection with Bliss Perry's indictments of book-reviewing. Although written some years before Mr. Perry's articles, it is in the nature of an answer to them, stating, as it does, the other side. He wrote in reply to a British author of a volume of "Ephemera Critica," and at the beginning makes the distinction, which I have already quoted between book-reviews and literary criticism:

"The aim of book-reviewing is to engage in discussion of our contemporaries, and this is why book-reviewing, which is a department of journalism, must be carefully distinguished from criticism, which is a department of literature. This is why also we need not worry ourselves overmuch about the present condition of book-reviewing, since it has not all the importance which the British author of "Ephemera Critica" has claimed for it and since it can really have very little influence upon the future of the literature. As a fact, the condition of book-reviewing is not now so lamentable as the British author has declared, and it is not indeed really worse than it was in earlier years;

but it might be very much worse than it is, and very much worse than it ever was, without its having any unfortunate influence on the development of a single man of genius. Indeed, genius never more surely reveals itself as genius than in its ability to withstand the pressure of contemporary fashion and go on doing its own work in its own way."

In regard to the notion that there were so many great book-reviewers in the golden past, Mr. Matthews relates this experience:

"In my leisurely youth, when I had all the time there was, I bought a forty-year file of a London weekly of lofty pretensions and of a certain antiquity, since it has now existed for more than threescore years and ten; and in the course of a twelvemonth I turned every page of those solid tomes, not reading every line, of course, but not neglecting a single number. The book-reviewing was painfully uninspired, with little brilliancy in expression and with little insight in appreciation; it was disfigured by a certain smug complacency which I find to be still a characteristic of the paper whenever I chance now to glance at its pages. But as I worked through this contemporary record of the unrolling of British literature from 1830 to 1870, what was most surprising was the fact that only infrequently indeed did the book-reviewers bestow full praise on the successive publications which we now hold to be among the chief glories of the Victorian reign, and that the books most lavishly eulogized were often those that have now sunk into oblivion."

Edmund Lester Pearson, in *Bulletin of the New York Public Library*, December, 1916. Reprinted by permission.

---

147. The Modern Drama (1919)

BY PERCY H. BOYNTON

Boynton is Professor of English at the University of Chicago. In his *History of American Literature*, Chapter XXVII, he gives a much more extended account of this subject. Many contemporary plays are now being published in book form, and are helpful to persons who have no opportunity to see them performed.

FROM 1865 to 1900 the American drama occupied a place of so little artistic importance in American life that the literary historians have ignored it. . . .

With the last decade of the nineteenth century, however, a new generation of playwrights began to win recognition—men who knew literature in its relation to the other arts and who wrote plays out of the fullness of their experience and the depth of their convictions, hoping to reach the public with their plays but not concerned chiefly with immediate "box-office" returns. The movement started in England and on the Continent and—as we can now see—in America as well, but the traditional American neglect of American literature led the first alert critics on this side the Atlantic to lay all their emphasis on writers of other nationalities. . . . But by 1910 the drift of things was suggested by the contents of Walter Pritchard Eaton's "At the New Theatre and Others." In this book, of twenty-three plays reviewed, ten were by American authors, and in the third section, composed of essays related to the theater, two of the chief units were discussions of Clyde Fitch and William Winter. And the dedication of Eaton's book is perhaps the single item of greatest historical significance, for it gives due credit to Professor George P. Baker of Harvard as "Founder in that institution of a pioneer course for the study of dramatic composition" and as "inspiring leader in the movement for a better appreciation among educated men of the art of the practical theater." . . .

"The movement for a better appreciation among educated men of the art of the practical theater," although led by one college professor, was itself a symptom of fresh developments in the art to which he addressed himself. Omitting—but not ignoring—the rise of the modern school of European dramatists in the 1890's, we must be content for the moment to note that this decade brought into view in America several men who were more than show-makers, even though they were honestly employed in making plays that the public would care to spend their money for. The significant facts about these playwrights are that they gave over the imitation and adaptation of French plays, returned to American dramatic material, and achieved results that are readable as well as actable. Their immediate forerunners were Steele MacKaye (1842–1894) and James A. Herne (1840–1901)—the former devotedly active as a teacher of budding players and as a student of stage technique, the latter the quiet realist of "Shore Acres" and other less-known plays of the simple American life. Coming into their first prom-

inence at this time were Augustus Thomas (1859) and Clyde Fitch
(1865–1909). . . .

Clyde Fitch in twenty years wrote and produced on the stage thirty-
three plays and staged twenty-three more—an immense output. . . .
Fitch was never profound, never sought to be; but he was deservedly
popular, for he combined no little skill with an alert sense of human
values in everyday life, and he brought an artistic conscience to his
work. Because he was so successful his influence on other dramatists
has been far-reaching; and those who have been neither too small
nor too great to learn from him have learned no little on how to write
a play.

Mr. Augustus Thomas has lived in the atmosphere of the theater
from boyhood. He began writing plays at fourteen, was directing
an amateur company at seventeen, and had his first New York success
in his twenty-eighth year. Since 1887 he has been a professional play-
wright; he has nearly fifty productions to his credit, and he is now
art director of the Charles Frohman interests. . . .

In a short chapter it is impossible to discuss in detail any other of the
playwriters who have done with less applause but with no less devotion the kind of writing represented by the best of Fitch and Thomas;
and it would be invidious to attempt a mere list of the others, as if a
mention of their names would be a sop to their pride. The case must
rest here with the statement that these two men were the leaders of
an increasing group and that the desire to compose more skillful and
more worthy plays was paralleled by a revival of respect for the modern
drama and the modern stage. . . .

Professor Baker at Harvard and Professor Matthews at Columbia
were looked at by some with wonder and by others with amused doubt
when they began as teachers to divide their attention between the
ancient and the modern stage. Yet as the study progressed their
students became not only intelligent theatergoers but constructive
contributors, as critics and creators, to the literature of the stage;
and then in the natural order of events the whole student body came
to realize that the older drama should be reduced to its proper place
and restored to it; that it was an interesting chapter in a literary and
social history because it was not a closed chapter, but a preliminary
to the events of the present. . . .

The first really great attempt to ask anything less of the modern

drama in America, to demand no more of the play than is demanded
of the opera or the symphony, was the founding of the celebrated and
short-lived New Theater in New York (1910–1911). That it failed
within two years is not half so important as that it was founded, that
others on smaller scales have since been founded and have failed,
that municipal theaters have sprung up here and there and are being
supported according to various plans, that scores upon scores of little
theaters, neighborhood playhouses, and people's country theaters
have been founded, that producers like Winthrop Ames and Stuart
Walker are established in public favor, that the Drama League of
America is a genuine national organization, and that the printing of
plays for the reading public is many fold its proportions of twenty
years ago. The Napoleonic theatrical managers are still in the saddle
in America, and the commercial stage of the country is still managed
from Broadway, but the uncommercial stage is coming to be more
considerable every season. The leaven of popular intelligence is at
work. . . .

Percy MacKaye (1875) embodies the meeting of the older traditions—his father was Steele MacKaye—and the most recent development in American drama, the rise of pageantry and the civic
festival. As a professional dramatist he has been prolific to the extent
of some twenty-five plays, pageants and operas. His acted plays
have varied in range and subject from contemporary social satire to an
interesting succession of echoes from the literary past—plays like
"The Canterbury Pilgrims" (1903), "Jeanne D'Arc" (1906), and
"Sappho and Phaon" (1907), which he seems to have undertaken, in
contrast to Hovey, for their picturesque and poetic value alone. His
special contribution, however, has been to the movement for an un-
commercialized and national theater through the preparation of a
number of community celebrations. These include the Saint Gaudens
Pageant at Cornish, New Hampshire (1905), the Gloucester Pageant
(1903), "Sanctuary, a Bird Masque" (1913), "St. Louis, a Civic
Masque" (1914), and "Caliban, a Community Masque" (New York,
1916, and Boston, 1917). The fusing interest in a common artistic
undertaking has brought together whole cities in the finest kind of
democratic enthusiasm, and the effects have not been merely temporary, for in a community such as St. Louis the permanent benefits
are still evident in the community chorus and in the beautiful civic

theater which is the annual scene of memorable productions witnessed by scores of thousands of spectators.

Percy H. Boynton, *A History of American Literature* (Boston, Ginn & Co., 1919), 437–447 *passim*.

---◆---

148. Two Eminent Novelists: Cabell and Hergesheimer (1922)

BY CARL VAN DOREN

Van Doren has been associate in English at Columbia University since 1923; has been literary editor of *The Nation* and *Century* magazines; is now an editor of the *Literary Guild;* and author of many books. For material on contemporary authors see such periodicals as *The Bookman* and *The Saturday Review of Literature*.

ALTHOUGH most novelists with any historical or scholarly hankerings are satisfied to invent here a scene and there a plot and elsewhere an authority, James Branch Cabell has invented a whole province for his imagination to dwell in. He calls it Poictesme and sets it on the map of medieval Europe, but it has no more unity of time and place than has the multitudinous land of *The Faërie Queene*.

Nothing but remarkable erudition in the antiquities of Cockaigne and Faery could possibly suffice for such adventures as Mr. Cabell's, and he has very remarkable erudition in all that concerns the regions which delight him. And where no authorities exist he merrily invents them, as in the case of his Nicolas of Caen, poet of Normandy, whose tales *Dizain des Reines* are said to furnish the source for the ten stories collected in *Chivalry*, and whose largely lost masterpiece *Le Roman de Lusignan* serves as the basis for *Domnei*. One British critic and rival of Mr. Cabell has lately fretted over the unblushing anachronisms and confused geography of this parti-colored world. For less dull-witted scholars these are the very cream of the Cabellian jest.

The cream but not the substance, for Mr. Cabell has a profound creed of comedy rooted in that romance which is his regular habit. Romance, indeed, first exercised his imagination, in the early years of the century when in many minds he was associated with the decorative Howard Pyle and allowed his pen to move at the languid gait then characteristic of a dozen inferior romancers. Only gradually did his gaiety strengthen into irony. Although that irony was the progenitor of the comic spirit which now in his maturity dominates him, it has never shaken off the romantic elements which originally nourished it. Rather, romance and irony have grown up in his work side by side. His Poictesme is no less beautiful for having come to be a country of disillusion; nor has his increasing sense of the futility of desire robbed him of his old sense that desire is a glory while it lasts.

The difference between Mr. Cabell and the popular romancers who in all ages clutter the scene and for whom he has nothing but amused contempt is that they are unconscious dupes of the demiurge whereas he, aware of its ways and its devices, employs it almost as if it were some hippogriff bridled by him in Elysian pastures and respectfully entertained in a snug Virginian stable. His attitude toward romance suggests a cheerful despair: he despairs of ever finding anything truer than romance and so contents himself with Poictesme and its tributaries. The favorite themes of romance being relatively few, he has not troubled greatly to increase them; war and love in the main he finds enough.

Besides these, however, he has already been deeply occupied with one other theme—the plight of the poet in the world. . . .

Of all the fine places in the world where beautiful happenings come together, Mr. Cabell argues, incomparably the richest is in the consciousness of a poet who is also a scholar. There are to be found the precious hoarded memories of some thousands of years: high deeds and burning loves and eloquent words and surpassing tears and laughter. There, consequently, the romancer may well take his stand, distilling bright new dreams out of ancient beauty. And if he adds the heady tonic of an irony springing from a critical intelligence, so much the better. When Mr. Cabell wishes to represent several different epochs in *The Certain Hour* he chooses to tell ten stories of poets—real or imagined—as the persons in whom, by reason of their superior susceptibility, the color of their epochs may be most truthfully discovered; and when he wishes to decant his own wit and wisdom most genuinely the vessel he normally employs is a poet. . . .

Joseph Hergesheimer employs his creative strategy over the precarious terrain of the decorative arts, some of his work lying on each side of the dim line which separates the most consummate artifice of which the hands of talent are capable from the essential art which springs naturally from the instincts of genius. On the side of artifice, certainly, lie several of the shorter stories in *Gold and Iron* and *The Happy End*, for which, he declares, his grocer is as responsible as any one; and on the side of art, no less certainly, lie at least *Java Head*, in which artifice, though apparent now and then, repeatedly surrenders the field to an art which is admirably authentic, and *Linda Condon*, nearly the most beautiful American novel since Hawthorne and Henry James.

Standing thus in a middle ground between art and artifice Mr. Hergesheimer stands also in a middle ground between the unrelieved realism of the new school of American fiction and the genteel moralism of the older. "I had been spared," he says with regard to moralism, "the dreary and impertinent duty of improving the world; the whole discharge of my responsibility was contained in the imperative obligation to see with relative truth, to put down the colors and scents and emotions of existence." And with regard to realism: "If I could put on paper an apple tree rosy with blossom, someone else might discuss the economy of the apples."

Mr. Hergesheimer does not, of course, merely blunder into beauty; his methods are far from being accidental; by deliberate aims and principles he holds himself close to the regions of the decorative. He likes the rococo and the Victorian, ornament without any obvious utility, grace without any busy function. . . .

To borrow an antithesis remarked by a brilliant critic in the work of Amy Lowell, Mr. Hergesheimer seems at times as much concerned with the stuffs as with the stuff of life. His landscapes, his interiors, his costumes he sets forth with a profusion of exquisite details which gives his texture the semblance of brocade—always gorgeous but now and then a little stiff with its splendors of silk and gold. An admitted personal inclination to "the extremes of luxury" struggles in Mr. Hergesheimer with an artistic passion for "words as disarmingly simple as the leaves of spring—as simple and as lovely in pure color— about the common experience of life and death"; and more than anything else this conflict explains the presence in all but his finest work of occasional heavy elements which weight it down and the presence in his most popular narratives of a constant lift of beauty and lucidity which will not let them sag into the average.

One comes tolerably close to the secret of Mr. Hergesheimer's career by perceiving that, with an admirable style of which he is both conscious and—very properly—proud, he has looked luxuriously through the world for subjects which his style will fit. Particularly has he emancipated himself from bondage to nook and corner. The small inland towns of *The Lay Anthony*, the blue Virginia valleys of *Mountain Blood*, the evolving Pennsylvania iron districts of *The Three Black Pennys*, the antique Massachusetts of *Java Head*, the fashionable hotels and houses of *Linda Condon*, the scattered exotic localities of the short stories—in all these Mr. Hergesheimer is at home with the cool insouciance of genius, at home as he could not be without an erudition founded in the keenest observation and research.

Without question the particular triumph of these novels is the women who appear in them. Decorative art in fiction has perhaps never gone farther than with Taou Yuen, the marvelous Manchu woman brought home from Shanghai to Salem as wife of a Yankee skipper in *Java Head*. She may be taken as focus and symbol of Mr. Hergesheimer's luxurious inclinations.

Only at intervals does some glimpse or other come of the tender flesh shut up in her magnificent garments or of the tender spirit schooled by flawless, immemorial discipline to an absolute decorum. That such glimpses come just preserves her from appearing a mere figure of tapestry, a fine mechanical toy. The Salem which before her arrival seems quaintly formal enough immediately thereafter seems by contrast raw and new, and her beauty glitters like a precious gem in some plain man's house.

The Lay Anthony ends in accident, *Mountain Blood* in melodrama; *The Three Black Pennys*, more successful than its predecessors, fades out like the Penny line; *Java Head* turns sharply away from its central theme, almost as if *Hamlet* should concern itself during a final scene with Horatio's personal perplexities. Now the conclusions of a novelist are on the whole the test of his judgment and his honesty; and it promises much for fiction that Mr. Hergesheimer has advanced so steadily in this respect through his seven books.

Carl Van Doren, *Contemporary American Novelists* (New York, Macmillan, 1922), 104–130 *passim*.

149.   A Poet Questions Progress (1923)

BY VACHEL LINDSAY

Vachel Lindsay (he says the name is pronounced "Vachel, like Rachel; not Vachel, like satchel") contends that poetry should be sung. The songs may be improvised as one reads, but the author provides marginal suggestions by way of help in the interpretation. Carl Sandburg is another modern American poet with similar ideas. "The Sante Fé Trail" sounds the raucous horns of progress against the quiet background of the prairies.

THE SANTA FÉ TRAIL

I. In Which a Racing Auto Comes from the East

THIS is the order of the music of the morning:—
    First, from the far East comes but a crooning.
The crooning turns to a sunrise singing.
Hark to the *calm*-horn, *balm*-horn, *psalm*-horn.
Hark to the *faint*-horn, *quaint*-horn, *saint*-horn. . . .

To be sung delicately, to an improvised tune.

Hark to the *pace*-horn, *chase*-horn, *race*-horn.
And the holy veil of the dawn has gone.
Swiftly the brazen car comes on.
It burns in the East as the sunrise burns.
I see great flashes where the far trail turns.
Its eyes are lamps like the eyes of dragons.
It drinks gasoline from big red flagons.
Butting through the delicate mists of the morning.
It comes like lightning, goes past roaring.
It will hail all the windmills, taunting, ringing,
Dodge the cyclones,
Count the milestones,
On through the ranges the prairie-dog tills—
Scooting past the cattle on the thousand hills. . . .
Ho for the *tear*-horn, *scare*-horn, *dare*-horn,
Ho for the *gay*-horn, *bark*-horn, *bay*-horn.
Ho for *Kansas, land that restores us*
When houses choke us, and great books bore us!

To be sung or read with great speed.

To be read or sung in a rolling bass, with some deliberation.

Sunrise Kansas, harvesters' Kansas,
A million men have found you before us.
A million men have found you before us.

II. In Which Many Autos Pass Westward

I want live things in their pride to remain.
I will not kill one grasshopper vain
Though he eats a hole in my shirt like a door.
I let him out, give him one chance more.
Perhaps, while he gnaws my hat in his whim,
Grasshopper lyrics occur to him.

In an even, deliberate,
narrative manner.

I am a tramp by the long trail's border,
Given to squalor, rags and disorder.
I nap and amble and yawn and look,
Write fool-thoughts in my grubby book,
Recite to the children, explore at my ease,
Work when I work, beg when I please,
Give crank-drawings, that make folks stare
To the half-grown boys in the sunset glare,
And get me a place to sleep in the hay
At the end of a live-and-let-live day.

I find in the stubble of the new-cut weeds
A whisper and a feasting, all one needs:
The whisper of the strawberries, white and red
Here where the new-cut weeds lie dead.

But I would not walk all alone till I die
Without some life-drunk horns going by.
And up round this apple-earth they come
Blasting the whispers of the morning dumb:—
Cars in a plain realistic row.
And fair dreams fade
When the raw horns blow.

On each snapping pennant
A big black name:—
The careering city

Whence each car came.
They tour from Memphis, Atlanta, Savannah,
Tallahassee and Texarkana.
They tour from St. Louis, Columbus, Manistee,   *Like a train-caller in*
They tour from Peoria, Davenport, Kankakee.   *a Union Depot.*
Cars from Concord, Niagara, Boston,
Cars from Topeka, Emporia, and Austin.
Cars from Chicago, Hannibal, Cairo.
Cars from Alton, Oswego, Toledo.
Cars from Buffalo, Kokomo, Delphi,
Cars from Lodi, Carmi, Loami.
Ho for Kansas, land that restores us
When houses choke us, and great books bore us!
While I watch the highroad
And look at the sky,
While I watch the clouds in amazing grandeur
Roll their legions without rain
Over the blistering Kansas plain—
While I sit by the milestone
And watch the sky,
The United States
Goes by.

Listen to the iron-horns, ripping, racking.   *To be given very*
Listen to the quack-horns, slack and clacking.   *harshly, with a snap-*
Way down the road, trilling like a toad,   *ping explosiveness.*
Here come the *dice*-horn, here comes the *vice*-horn,
Here comes the *snarl*-horn, *brawl*-horn, *lewd*-horn,
Followed by the *prude*-horn, bleak and squeaking:—
(Some of them from Kansas, some of them from
    Kansas.)
Here come the *hod*-horn, *plod*-horn, *sod*-horn,
Never-more-to-*roam*-horn, *loam*-horn, *home*-horn.
(Some of them from Kansas, some of them from
    Kansas.)
            Far away the Rachel-Jane   *To be read or sung,*
            Not defeated by the horns   *well-nigh in a whis-*
            Sings amid a hedge of thorns:—   *per.*

"Love and life,
Eternal youth—
Sweet, sweet, sweet, sweet,
Dew and glory,
Love and truth,
Sweet, sweet, sweet, sweet."

WHILE SMOKE-BLACK FREIGHTS ON THE DOUBLE-
    TRACKED RAILROAD,
DRIVEN AS THOUGH BY THE FOUL FIEND'S OX-GOAD,
SCREAMING TO THE WEST COAST, SCREAMING TO
    THE EAST,
CARRY OFF A HARVEST, BRING BACK A FEAST,
AND HARVESTING MACHINERY AND HARNESS FOR
    THE BEAST,
THE HAND-CARS WHIZ, AND RATTLE ON THE RAILS,
THE SUNLIGHT FLASHES ON THE TIN DINNER-PAILS.

Louder and louder, faster and faster.

And then, in an instant, ye modern men,
Behold the procession once again,
The United States goes by!
Listen to the iron horns, ripping, racking,
Listen to the *wise*-horn, desperate-to-*advise*-horn,
Listen to the *fast*-horn, *kill*-horn, *blast*-horn. . . .

In a rolling bass, with increasing deliberation.

With a snapping explosiveness.

    Far away the Rachel-Jane
    Not defeated by the horns
    Sings amid a hedge of thorns:—
    "Love and life,
    Eternal youth,
    Sweet, sweet, sweet, sweet,
    Dew and glory,
    Love and truth.
    Sweet, sweet, sweet, sweet."

To be sung or read well-nigh in a whisper.

The mufflers open on a score of cars
With wonderful thunder,
CRACK, CRACK, CRACK,
CRACK-CRACK, CRACK-CRACK,
CRACK, CRACK, CRACK,
Listen to the gold-horn. . . .
Old-horn. . . .

To be brawled in the beginning with a snapping explosiveness, ending in a langourous chant.

Cold-horn. . . .
And all of the tunes, till the night comes down
On hay-stack, and ant-hill, and wind-bitten town.
Then far in the west, as in the beginning,
Dim in the distance, sweet in retreating,
Hark to the faint-horn, quaint-horn, saint-horn,
Hark to the calm-horn, balm-horn, psalm-horn. . . .

To be sung to exactly the same whispered tune as the first five lines.

They are hunting the goals that they understand:—
San-Francisco and the brown sea-sand.
My goal is the mystery the beggars win.
I am caught in the web the night-winds spin.
The edge of the wheat-ridge speaks to me.
I talk with the leaves of the mulberry tree.
And now I hear, as I sit all alone
In the dusk, by another big Santa-Fé stone,
The souls of the tall corn gathering round
And the gay little souls of the grass in the ground.
Listen to the tale the cottonwood tells.
Listen to the windmills, singing o'er the wells.
Listen to the whistling flutes without price
Of myriad prophets out of paradise.
Harken to the wonder
That the night-air carries. . . .
Listen . . . to . . . the . . . whisper . . .
Of . . . the . . . prairie . . . fairies

This section beginning sonorously, ending in a languorous whisper.

    Singing o'er the fairy plain:—
    "Sweet, sweet, sweet, sweet.
    Love and glory,
    Stars and rain,
    Sweet, sweet, sweet, sweet. . . ."

To the same whispered tune as the Rachel-Jane song— but very slowly.

Vachel Lindsay, *Collected Poems* (New York, Macmillan, rev. ed., 1925), 152–158.

150. Tabloid Journalism (1926)

BY RICHARD G. DE ROCHEMONT

De Rochemont is a Boston journalist. The tabloid newspapers, so named because of their condensation of size and content, have become a symbol of the low intellectual standard of their readers, and a synonym for sensationalism. See also No. 151.

WHEN the New York *Daily News* sprang into being, in June, 1919, there was considerable speculation and no little scorn in newspaper offices throughout the country. Many editors predicted that the new paper, which was half the usual size and broke not a few of the other conventions of American newspaper production, would disappear in two months. Others saw alarming possibilities in the very brazenness of the new creation, knowing its promoters to be hard-boiled and successful publishers. After a time reports drifted in of the paper's gains in circulation and advertising, and converts began to speak of the small-sized picture daily as the newspaper of the future. Rumors that journals long established were soon to be reduced to tabloid size passed freely. Every new publication would be tabloid, it was said. The little papers could be sold at a low price, and yet meet expenses with the money received from circulation alone. All their revenue from advertising would be clear profit. The traditionally imperturbable Fourth Estate began to get excited. Now seven years have passed, and the subject is still full of interest to newspaper workers. The first tabloid has succeeded, and in greater measure than even its sponsors dreamed. Other tabloids have entered the field, in cities much unlike New York. What has been their success? What is their future?

At the beginning of this year fifteen daily tabloids were being published in the United States, and many weekly and bi-weekly papers in the smaller towns had adopted the tabloid form. The daily tabloids all have the same size. Without exception, their width is about twelve inches and their depth sixteen to eighteen inches. From four to six columns, of about 200 agate lines in length, take the place of the normal eight-column page.

They are of two distinct orders. There are those which attempt to present principally news, and a smaller number which feature pictures. . . .

The news tabloid originated in New York City in 1891, when two attempts were made to operate a compact daily paper providing predigested news for the hurried reader. Colonel John A. Cockerill, early in that year, brought out the *Morning Advertiser*, with four pages of four columns each, and proclaimed it to be "The Ideal Paper for Busy People." It was an immediate failure. On February 1 the late Frank A. Munsey brought out the *Star*, which he had acquired a short time before, in a new tabloid form under the name of the *Daily Continent*. The *Continent* carried a considerable amount of advertising, and received a great deal of favorable comment at the time, but, like the *Morning Advertiser*, it was not a commercial success. Munsey discontinued its publication on June 30 of the same year, and did not experiment further with tabloid journalism.

The genealogy of the picture tabloid goes no farther back than 1903, when Lord Northcliffe began to experiment with little papers in London. In America the archetypal tabloid is the New York *News*, which at present has a clientele of over a million patrons. All the other papers of the same class have been brought out in an attempt to duplicate the success of its owners, Col. R. R. McCormick and J. M. Patterson, of the Chicago *Tribune*, who first proved conclusively that only a sharp lowering of the IQ [Intelligence Quotient] of a newspaper was necessary to make it attractive to a hitherto unexploited portion of the great metropolitan rank and file. These gentlemen, operating the *Tribune* with unbounded energy and great success, visited London after the war, and were greatly impressed by the tabloids of that city, and notably by the London *Mirror*. So plans were made to start a similar enterprise in New York. Two considerations prompted the launching of the venture in New York rather than in Chicago. In the first place, the Eastern city's population is by far the more cosmopolitan, and was therefore thought to be more susceptible to the benefits about to be offered it. In the second, it was feared that in case the *News* should not prove successful, its failure would reflect on the *Tribune*, if both papers were published in Chicago.

The original intention had been to make the *News* an evening paper, since the old-time yellow journals had been most successful in the afternoon field. But a careful survey of the situation showed a chang-

ing trend toward the morning papers, and the new paper was established as one of them. In June, 1919, the first issue went on the
streets. Its popularity was immediate. It was backed by plenty of
money, but as the event proved, less than $250,000 was needed to
start it on its way, and it began to yield enormous profits after a little
more than a year. Bull-dog editions, dated as of the next day and
put on the street as soon as the afternoon papers' sale slowed down,
helped to swell the circulation. . . . The close of 1923 saw the *News*,
after a little more than three years, with a daily sale of 633,578 copies,
with 569,381 on Sunday. During the following year these totals rose
to 786,398 and 807,279, respectively. The daily circulation for 1925
went over a million, while the Sunday edition reached 1,122,065.

In a recent issue of the weekly magazine published by the Chicago
Tribune organization, Mr. William H. Field, general manager of the
News, related in detail the history of the paper, with particular emphasis on the benefits Moronia has received at its hands. Two of
these boons are its red-hot pictures of great news events and its inspiring prize contests. In the matter of the news pictures Mr. Field
is somewhat romantic, for they were printed years ago by many very
conservative papers, including even the Boston *Transcript*. Rhap-
sodizing over the contests, he argues feelingly that "no one can deny
that they bring a bit of sunshine into otherwise dull lives." As many
as two million replies have been received in a single contest, he
says.

The tabloids that have arisen in the wake of the *News* have all
shown steady, but much slower growth. They at once adopted the
principal features of the *News*, and have continued to copy them
almost exactly. The habitual tabloid reader knows just where to
find them, no matter what paper he happens to pick up. Diagrams,
with the arrow showing the way the slayer fled or the suicide fell;
strips of pictures, not too cleverly faked by the "art" department to
"tell the story"; dismal cartoons, making absolutely no sense except
to a constant reader, for they all tell continued stories; beauty,
fashion, household and health hints; the stimulating and philanthropic
prize contests; the Voice of the People, the Inquiring Photographer,
the advice to the moron smitten with the tender emotion, the sporting
department, the editorial page or half-page, and the daily instalment
of a novel dealing with the difficulties of a gay but moral stenographer

in eluding the lubricous embraces of her wealthy employer—all these things are in every one of them.

The pictures, of course, are the very backbone of the tabloid. Editors differ as to what gives a picture appeal, some declaring for sex interest, some for news value, and others for a vague "human" interest. In all truth it does not seem to matter greatly, so long as there is some attack upon a simple emotion. The true tabloid reader will gape at any picture, whether it means anything or not. The front page, except for a headline in 96-point Gothic, is entirely given up to pictures, as the two center pages also often are. The latter are known as the double truck, and are usually turned over for editing to a caption writer with an alleged knack of composing puns and nifties agreeable to the lightweight reader. News, with the exception of a few featured stories, is cut down to a point where it often becomes unintelligible. The whole concoction is spiced with half-column portraits of undistinguished and unbeautiful persons. But in the *News* itself, the news matter is often very competently handled.

The other party in tabloid journalism, cleaving to the pure and the dull, has not fared as well as its more sensational competitors. Its papers have shown gains in advertising and circulation, but in no instance more than might have been expected from any newspaper, regardless of its format, which had contentedly steered a middle and uneventful course. These more saintly tabloids employ many ancient dodges to lure circulation, and as the cost of producing them is less than that of a full-size paper, the majority of them have kept above water. The exception is provided by the Vanderbilt chain. Its collapse came in the early months of this year. . . .

The future of the tabloid press in America is a matter of dispute. It has been predicted recently by Carr V. Van Anda, of the New York *Times*, that in a few years all the daily newspapers will be forced to adopt the tabloid form. Undoubtedly the increase in the cost of newsprint and the convenience of the new size in production and distribution point to its further proliferation. But many advertisers do not believe that it affords sufficient room on its pages for effective display advertising, and say that they thus find its space more expensive than the results justify. Careless make-up and slipshod printing have been deterrents to profitable advertising accounts in many cases.

The news tabloids, as differentiated from the picture variety, have done but indifferently well. Their gains have been slow, and the public has shown no great enthusiasm for the benefits of the new size. It is doubtful if it makes any great difference to the average reader whether his paper is bulky or compact in his pocket, or whether it obscures the view of his neighbor in the street-car more or less. The curious dullness of these tabloids has reduced them to the dead level of the greater part of the American press. Neither do they make any appeal to the more ingenious newspaper mind. The story of the old-timer who quit his reporter's job on a tabloid "to go back to newspaper work" is typical. No aspiring reporter cares to work on a paper which allows no space for presenting a colorful, reasonably complete story. When given a free choice, such men head for the full-size papers. Thus the tabloids, in the main, are staffed by old hands in a state of disillusionment, beginners who are glad to get any sort of job, and a few smart boys and girls who have mastered the trick of writing cheap slush. If these are to be the journalists of the future little can be expected from the tabloids in the nature of sound newspaper work.

Richard G. de Rochemont, *The Tabloids*, in *American Mercury* (New York, 1926), IX, 187–192 *passim*. Reprinted by permission of the author.

———————◆———————

151. The News in Brief (1926)

BY "NERI" AND "WAMP"

A successful newspaper columnist—and "F. P. A." is one—gets a large part of his work done by admiring readers who contribute their own more brilliant literary by-products. These two satires in verse exaggerate very little the nature and methods of sensational journalism. For a serious account of the tabloids, see No. 150 above.

A. A Tabloid Reporter to His City Editor

LORD of assignments, where to-day
    Do I turn my steps in search of prey
For the presses, slumbering now,
Below?

Do I go where guarded scabs peer down
On strikers in some Jersey town.
Or follow a murder, a suicide,
Walter Ward missing or Browning's bride,
Rum boat captured, awash with booze,
Peggy Joyce wed?—but *that's* not news.

Do I brave some patrician family's hauteur,
Seeking a photo of its runaway daughter,
Or do my stuff on the seamy east side—
Some girl a mother, but nobody's bride?

Love nest or baby farm,
Block ablaze, a four alarm,
Broker sued by lady's maid,
City scandal or a dog parade?
Do I cover a wedding, a Communist fight
Or stay inside on dull rewrite?

Lord of assignments, blue is the day
And white are the sails, creeping down the bay;
Where do I go, O Gene,
Oh say?

                                              "NERI"

B. The Tabloid City Editor to His Reporter

Slave of assignments, on your way!
But keep in mind these facts to-day.
CHECK UP ON PICTURES. Get a report.
Cover the story but KEEP IT SHORT.
Slice it and Boil it. Keep it Down.
Get every angle that breaks in town.
Make it snappy and make a dead-line
(The presses begin at quarter to nine).
Here's your assignment—that's enough—
Do your stuff.

GET ME A PICTURE—don't forget.
I've one photographer waiting yet.
Call me up if he can crash
In for a flashlight—then we'll smash
It for the Pink—do all your tricks.
Get me a story and GET ME PIX.
Get the facts for a first-class staff,
Then write half.

Write me half, but all those facts
Got to get in or you get the ax.
Get me facts and PICTURES, too.
GET ME PICTURES, whatever you do.
Pix of dogs and of bathing girls,
Walter Ward's home and Peaches' curls,
That rum boat you spoke of, awash with booze,
Peg Joyce's next one—although not news;
Blue-blooded heiress, children's tricks,
GET ME PIX.

Slave of assignments—lucky wight—
I'm desk-tied here for half the night.
Out in the open, you should fret!
All in the world that you have to get
Is—no wonder your job attracts—
PIX and facts.

"WAMP"

Anonymous contributions to *The New York World*, collected in Franklin P.
Adams, *The Second Conning Tower Book* (New York, Macy-Masius, 1927), 49–51.

CHAPTER XXVIII — SCIENCE AND INVENTION

152. Early Flying Experiments (1909)

BY OCTAVE CHANUTE

The Langley plane was subsequently removed from the Smithsonian Museum, and demonstrated in successful flight, through the efforts of persons desirous of vindicating Langley as designer of the first man-carrying, heavier-than-air machine. In July, 1929, a plane remained in continuous flight for nearly three weeks.

. . . AS your president has said, on the 20th of October, 1897, I had the honor of presenting to you an account of some gliding experiments that were carried on at Dune Park, near this city. Those experiments were made solely to study the question of equilibrium and to determine if it was reasonably safe to experiment. We had the good fortune to make about 2,000 flights without any accidents—not even a single sprained ankle. The only thing we had to deplore was the fact that my son, in making one flight, tore his trousers. An account of these experiments was published in the journal of this society for October, 1897, and subsequently an account was also published in the *Aëronautical Annual*, Boston, in 1897. That publication contained the statement that it was thought that these experiments were promising, and I gave an invitation to other experimenters to improve upon our practice. The invitation remained unaccepted until March, 1900, when Wilbur Wright wrote to me, making inquiries as to the construction of the machine, materials to be used, the best place to experiment, etc. He said that he had notions of his own that he wanted to try, and knew of no better way of spending his vacation. All that information was gladly furnished. Mr. Wright wrote me an account, subsequently, of his experiments in 1900, which gave such encouraging results that each year thereafter the brothers carried on further experiments in North Carolina and at Dayton, Ohio.

On the 18th of September, 1901, Wilbur Wright read a paper before this society, in which he gave an account of what he had done up to that time.

Again, on the 24th of June, 1903, Mr. Wright read a second paper before this society, giving an account of his progress since 1901. Late in the year 1903 the Wrights applied a motor to their gliding machine, which by that time they had under perfect control, and they made their first flights on the 17th of December, 1903. . . .

Of the early flying experiments which had been made previous to that time I will mention but two.

Mr. Maxim built an enormous apparatus, weighing 8,000 pounds and spreading 4,000 feet of surface, moved by a steam engine of 360 horsepower. . . .

The next experiments were made in 1896 by Prof. S. P. Langley. After devoting some years to experimenting, he devised a working model which he started from a launching scow. The model machine flew perfectly on the 6th of May, 1896, in the presence of Alexander Graham Bell. This machine flew about three-quarters of a mile, alighted safely in the Potomac River, and was ready to fly again.

On the 28th of November, with a similar model, Langley made another successful flight, and further launches were privately made subsequently.

He was then urged by the United States Government to build a full-sized machine, capable of carrying a man, and he spent three or more years in doing so. That man-carrying machine was completed in 1903, and on the 7th of October of that year the launch was attempted. The machine, however, caught a projecting pin of the launching rail and was cast down into the Potomac. The operator, Mr. Manly, was upset, carried down into the river, and came very near drowning. Another effort was made December 8 and the same mishap occurred. Part of the launching ways caught the machine, and it never entered upon flight. There is no doubt, however, that if the machine had been properly launched it would have flown. The machine is still in existence. It was broken when alighting, and in picking it up afterwards, but has been repaired. It is most unfortunate that further effort was not then made to launch that machine, and that Langley was so severely criticized in Congress and by the newspapers. He was grievously balked of deserved success, and he died of apoplexy two years afterward.

The next attempt to fly with a man-carrying machine was in North Carolina on the 17th of December, 1903, when the Wright brothers effected three successful flights, the first to alight safely in history. The longest flight covered 852 feet and occupied 59 seconds, in the face of a 20-mile wind. . . . In 1904 they operated in a field about 8 miles from Dayton, Ohio, and it took them most of that year to learn how to turn a corner. The machine was slightly broken a number of times, repaired, and finally, in October, 1905, they got their apparatus under perfect control, and succeeded in making a flight of 24 miles in 38 minutes. They made 105 flights in 1904 and 49 flights in 1905. . . . The machine is placed on a single rail, weights are hoisted on a derrick, and a rope is carried from the derrick with a return pulley to the machine. Upon the dropping of the weights the machine is given an impulse, this method being found to be preferable to the catapult which Mr. Langley had devised and which failed him on two occasions when trying to launch his machine. . . . The launching rail is 60 feet long, and with the aid of the falling weights the machine quickly acquired the necessary velocity for rising in the air.

The years 1906 and 1907 were spent by the Wright brothers in an effort to sell their machines to various Governments. They had taken out patents in eight different countries, and they hoped to sell flying machines to war departments, together with the secrets, the tables of resistance, and all the elaborate calculations which they had made, but in each and every case the Government wanted to be shown the apparatus before buying. The Wrights refused to exhibit the machine until such time as they had a contract contingent upon their performing certain feats—notably, to fly with two passengers and with enough fuel to carry it 125 miles; that it must attain a speed of at least 36 miles an hour, maintained over a distance of 5 miles, and must fly continuously for one hour.

None of the Governments would thus contract with them. They were offered at one time $120,000 by the French Government, but they refused. They were then offered $200,000 if they would perform their feats 1,000 feet in the air. To this they said that they had no doubt that they could get up 1,000 feet but they had never done so and would not agree to the proposition.

In 1908 they changed completely their plan of operation and decided to show their machine with the risk of its being copied and getting themselves into litigation. . . . There is at the front a double-decked horizontal rudder. It will be noticed that these inventors have modified the make-up of a bird by putting the tail in front. Behind are placed vertical rudders, but it is the front rudder which elevates and gives horizontal direction to the machine. The rear rudder guides the machine to the right or left. Back of the main surfaces are the two screws revolving in opposite directions.

The machine is equipped with a pair of skids for alighting, while the French people have equipped their machines with wheels. The wheels weigh more, catch more air, and are not as safe as the skids, but the skids require a rail and a starting weight in order to get the machine into the air, unless there is a brisk head wind. . . .

Mr. Wright had extraordinarily good fortune in carrying on the experiments in France, his machine falling only once. One other accident occurred in the breaking of one of the sprocket chains in mid-air; but he then operated the machine as a glider and came down safely. The French people at first made all sorts of comments, criticisms, and caricatures of Wilbur Wright, and even published a number of amusing songs, but finally he triumphed, won their esteem and admiration, and they acknowledged that he was the master of all the aviators. . . .

Meanwhile we may go back to September, 1908, and note some of Orville Wright's performances. He had at Washington the same general arrangement, consisting of a launching rail, launching derrick, and an apparatus for hoisting up the weights, in order to give the machine impetus. This aëroplane is 40 feet across and has a breadth of 6½ feet. The front rudder is 16 feet long, 2½ feet broad, and is equipped with skids. . . . The propeller is of peculiar and original construction, and the motor is in every way the Wrights', for, in 1902, they made a canvass of the different makers of gasoline motors in this country, asking them to furnish a motor according to specifications which they presented. None of them at that time could do so, and the Wrights went to work themselves, designed a motor, and built it with their own hands. This design has proven more reliable than the motors built in France, which are unduly light. The Wright motor, originally of 15 pounds to the horsepower, was reduced to 7 or 8 pounds to the horsepower, while the French people are building motors weighing 4½ to 5 pounds, but they do not prove as reliable, while the Wright motor has never given any trouble and has proven reliable in every respect.

Orville Wright made a number of unofficial tests in 1908. On the 8th of September he rose to a height of 100 feet and flew 40 miles; on the 12th he made a little higher ascension, estimated by the Army officers at 200 feet, and flew 50 miles in 1 hour and 15 minutes. Altogether that year he made 14 flights. On the morning of the 17th of September he made several short flights. In the afternoon of that same day he met with a terrible accident; his propeller broke while he and Lieut. Selfridge were in mid-air, the machine falling to the earth, when Orville was seriously injured and Lieut. Selfridge was killed. This ended the tests of that year. The Government granted an extension of time and the trials were not resumed until July of this year (1909). The results this year, as you know, have been very successful. The official time test shows that on the 27th of July the machine remained in the air for 1 hour and 13 minutes, with two persons on board.

On the 30th of July the machine traveled 5 miles and back crosscountry in 14 minutes, with two persons on board, at a speed which averaged over 42 miles an hour. Therefore, the machine was accepted by the Government and a premium was given the Wrights of $5,000 for the extra 2 miles of speed. Wilbur Wright is now engaged in teaching the Army officers how to use the machine. Immediately after the acceptance of the machine, Orville Wright went to Berlin, and there he has been accomplishing some remarkable feats. On the 29th of August last he made his first exhibition there, flying 15 minutes. On the 8th of September he went up with Capt. Hildebrandt; on the 18th of September he went up with Capt. Englehardt, and on the 27th of September he made a demonstration before the court. On the 2d of October he took up into the air the Crown Prince, who gave him a handsome present, and on the 4th of October he made a flight of 21 miles, reaching a height estimated at 1,600 feet. This is the latest performance which he has made, although there is no telling what another day will bring forth. He is now in Paris. In London he may make some demonstrations with his machine in the course of a week or two.

Octave Chanute, *Recent Progress in Aviation*, in *Annual Report of the Smithsonian Institution, 1910* (Washington, Government Printing Office, 1911), 145–151 *passim.*

153. Steinmetz: Immigrant, Scientist and Teacher (1889-1912)

BY JOHN WINTHROP HAMMOND (1924)

Hammond, a student of electrical history, is publicity writer for the General Electric Corporation. He wrote the first popular account of the experiments with laboratory lightning. Steinmetz (1865-1923) exemplified the finest type of pure scientist—a man devoted to the solving of difficult problems, charming in his avocations, interesting to a great variety of friends. Though he might have accumulated a large fortune, he never took more than enough money to satisfy his very simple needs. In his later years he directed the great General Electric laboratory at Schenectady, where his only obligation was to investigate whatever problems challenged his insatiable scientific curiosity. A somewhat similar life story is Michael Pupin's *From Immigrant to Inventor*.

. . . IT was a Saturday afternoon when the vessel docked. The cabin passengers were put ashore at once. But those in the steerage, Steinmetz and Asmussen among them, were held on board until Monday. Saturday and Sunday were warm, pleasant days; but on Sunday night the wind changed, blowing damp and cold through an open port upon Steinmetz's head as he slept.

This sudden veering of the breeze, his first experience with the fickle North American climate, complicated his landing experience most uncomfortably, for he awoke with a very bad cold, which caused one side of his face to become swollen, and made him feel miserable generally.

Yet he hopefully confronted the immigration officers, accompanied by his loyal friend. Together they landed at Old Castle Garden, now the Aquarium, forerunner of Ellis Island.

If Steinmetz had been alone that day, his dream of coming to America might have ended abruptly right there at Castle Garden. His forlorn appearance, swollen face, empty purse, and stumbling English caused the immigration authorities to shake their heads. His knowledge of English was so scant that when the officials asked him if he knew the language he could only reply, "A few." After some minutes of searching questions and puzzled answers the official decision was reached and made known to him. He could not land! He must go back to Europe!

The tremendous disappointment that leaped into his eyes when he understood this decree did not alter the official attitude. With disconcerting briskness they sent him to the detention pen.

But his traveling companion saved the situation. Asmussen explained to the officers that Steinmetz and he were together. He stoutly declared they would stick together after landing and that he would personally see that Steinmetz did not become destitute in a strange land. Asmussen spoke English fluently. Moreover he showed a fairly substantial sum of money, which, he declared, belonged to them both. He was willing to make himself responsible for the welfare of his friend; and, upon his representations, Charles P. Steinmetz was finally admitted to America, which was to be for him the land of friends, fame, and fortune.

Yet, as already revealed, Steinmetz had not a penny in his pocket when he first set foot upon American soil. His traveling companion was his financier. He owed his friend money for paying his way over from Europe; he owed him also for any expenses that came up from day to day. He himself was destitute.

Thus it was that the two young friends found themselves in New York with both funds and prospects uncertain. Yet those few weeks were weeks of happiness for them. Asmussen had relatives in Brooklyn, and there they obtained lodgings until they could hunt up work. . . .

The next day Steinmetz went to Yonkers and called upon Rudolf Eickemeyer, who conducted a prominent manufacturing establishment near the railroad station, having succeeded the original firm of Eickemeyer & Osterheld. What happened when he entered the office is told by Walter S. Emerson, a nephew of Eickemeyer's, who was at that time an office clerk, in addition to other duties.

"He had come directly from the railroad station," Mr. Emerson relates. "He wore plain, rather rough clothes and a cap. I got the idea, from looking at him, that he was some chap who had knocked his way from place to place, looking for a job.

"I asked him whom he wanted to see. He replied: 'Mr. Eickemeyer,' speaking in a quick manner.

"I went up-stairs and found Mr. Eickemeyer. 'Uncle,' I said, 'there's a man to see you down in the office. I don't know his name; he might be a fellow who has come off a freight-train. I'll follow you down.'

"I went down behind Mr. Eickemeyer and stood in the door as the two met. Then I heard the visitor's name. I heard him say; 'I'm Mr. Steinmetz' ; and then they began to talk German and sat down together at Mr. Eickemeyer's desk.

"I stayed a little while, then left. A little later I glanced into the office. They were still talking together, Mr. Eickemeyer sitting at his desk and Steinmetz in a chair alongside. They talked for a couple of hours." . . .

This interesting interview did not produce a position for Steinmetz, however. All that Eickemeyer could do was to take the young man's name and address, promising to inform him if an opening occurred.

But Carl Steinmetz was not the sort of fellow to sit down and wait for opportunity to seek him out. A week later he again presented himself at Eickemeyer's plant, to see if there was a chance for him. His persistence was rewarded. He was told to report for work the following Monday morning.

His job was to be that of a draftsman at two dollars a day, or twelve dollars a week. And that was his start in America, secured principally by his persistent effort, within two weeks after he landed at Castle Garden. . . .

Promptly upon finding employment, Steinmetz took steps to establish himself in the western republic in another respect. Unwavering in his decision that America would be his home and his country thenceforth, he had speedily appeared before a naturalization court and taken out his first papers. He wanted to become a citizen of the new land to which he had come. This purpose was consummated in due time, for five years later he returned to Yonkers and received his second papers, which raised him to the status of a fully naturalized citizen of the United States. . . .

Long before Steinmetz had witnessed the universal adoption of his symbolic method, indeed, only a few months after his final paper on the law of hysteresis losses, the Eickemeyer & Osterheld Company passed out of existence as a separate business establishment. The interests of the company were purchased by a recently formed concern, which had come into existence on April 12, 1892, the General Electric Company. . . .

Primarily the General Electric Company bought Eickemeyer's business because of the latter's patents and valuable electrical applications. Secondarily, it is quite evident that the General Electric Company wanted the services of the youthful mathematical master, Steinmetz.

The news of the whole transaction was imparted to Steinmetz by Eickemeyer, who told him that it had been arranged for him to be transferred to the General Electric Company. Steinmetz appears to have consented without the slightest hesitation.

A few days later, Steinmetz met some of the General Electric officials, who came to Yonkers to see what they had bought and to confirm the understanding that Eickemeyer's brainy engineer was to enter the new organization. . . . [D]uring this period Steinmetz met for the first time E. W. Rice, Jr., later president of the General Electric Company and now honorary chairman of its board of directors. . . .

Mr. Rice in particular was the representative of the General Electric Company who interviewed Steinmetz on the question of entering the employ of the General Electric. He describes his visit to Eickemeyer's plant, and his first meeting with young Steinmetz, as follows:

"I was then in charge of the manufacturing and engineering of our company, and my views were sought as to the desirability of acquiring Eickemeyer's work. I remember giving hearty approval, with the understanding that we should thereby secure the services for our company of a young engineer named Steinmetz. I had read articles by him which impressed me with his originality and intellectual power, and believed that he would prove a valuable addition to our engineering force.

"I shall never forget our first meeting at Eickemeyer's workshop in Yonkers. I was startled, and somewhat disappointed, by the strange sight of a small, frail body, surmounted by a large head, with long hair hanging to the shoulders, clothed in an old cardigan jacket, cigar in mouth, sitting cross-legged on a laboratory work table.

"My disappointment was but momentary, and completely disappeared the moment he began to talk. I instantly felt the strange power of his piercing but kindly eyes, and as he continued, his enthusiasm, his earnestness, his clear conceptions and marvelous grasp of engineering problems convinced me that we had indeed made a great find. It needed no prophetic insight to realize that here was a great man, who spoke with the authority of accurate and profound knowledge, and one who, if given the opportunity, was destined to render great service to our industry.

"I was delighted when, without a moment's hesitation, he accepted my suggestion that he come with us."

As revealed by Mr. Rice, Steinmetz did most of his work on the calculation of alternating current phenomena after going with the General Electric Company. His mastery of this problem did much to enable the General Electric Company to forge ahead until it commanded a position of leadership in the world of electrical affairs. As Mr. Rice has expressed it, "Steinmetz brought order out of chaos" in the matter of alternating current calculations.

"He abolished the mystery and obscurity surrounding alternating current apparatus, and soon taught our engineers how to design such machines with as much ease and certainty as those employing the old familiar direct current. . . .

"It is not too much to say that his genius and creative ability was largely responsible for the rapid progress made in the commercial introduction of alternating current apparatus."

In the late winter of 1902–03 Dr. Steinmetz entered upon his duties as professor of electrical engineering at Union College. It was the beginning of a ten-year period in his life devoted to a unique leadership among young men, a period which left its impress upon the slowly shaping destinies of numerous fresh young lives and simultaneously stirred in Dr. Steinmetz's own life his ever-sensitive social instincts, appealing directly to the fraternal side of his nature. . . .

He could hardly be called a strict disciplinarian in the class-room. Yet his lectures were usually so well worth while, so original, and so lucid as to hold the interest of his students through an entire course. If any situation arose in which he was moved to comment on some laxity of procedure in his classes, he invariably did so in characteristic quiet fashion. His manner was mild; but it was always evident that he was perfectly aware of what was going on, knew instantly when he was taken advantage of by the thoughtless or the drone, and was too discerning to be deceived, no matter what the occasion. . . .

He possessed a remarkably clear diction; and he invariably unfolded his subject in a spirited and entertaining manner, so that even a technical lecture, as he handled it, was decidedly effective.

As a result, his classes gained a vivid impression of the broad back-

ground of the subject, securing a sound conception of the fundamentals. Even though sometimes left floundering by the ultra-
technical exposition to which they had listened, the students of Dr.
Steinmetz carried away with them a realization that electrical engineering was a vast and tremendous field, a profession of unimagin-
able possibilities, in which no man with ambition and opportunity
could feel restricted. . . .

Other educational institutions realized that under Dr. Steinmetz
the students at Union were getting a conception of fundamentals
which was bound to fire them to unusual endeavors. Dr. Steinmetz's
contagious faith in his subject, an overpowering personal enthusiasm,
and a manner of presentation that was fascinating to all except the
utterly indifferent were responsible for this result, almost as much as
his utter mastery of the course. . . .

Dr. Steinmetz lost no opportunity, while he was a college professor,
of urging his theory of a broad general education for technical men.
He always insisted that no student could fully understand electrical
engineering in just four years. That, he contended, was merely long
enough to enable him to lay a foundation, upon which he must per-
severingly build as time went on.

John Winthrop Hammond, *Charles Proteus Steinmetz* (New York, Century Co.,
1924), 129–290, *passim.* Reprinted by permission of the author.

------◆------

154. Ingenuity in Motor Manufacturing (1914)

BY HENRY FORD (1922)

For Ford, see No. 113 above; and see also J. M. Miller, *The Amazing Story of
Henry Ford.* For an elaborately illustrated account of quantity production of
automobiles, see *National Geographic Magazine*, October, 1923.

. . . IT is self-evident that a majority of the people in the world
are not mentally—even if they are physically—capable of
making a good living. That is, they are not capable of furnishing
with their own hands a sufficient quantity of the goods which this
world needs to be able to exchange their unaided product for the
goods which they need. I have heard it said, in fact I believe it is

quite a current thought, that we have taken skill out of work. We have not. We have put in skill. We have put a higher skill into planning, management, and tool building, and the results of that skill are enjoyed by the man who is not skilled. This I shall later enlarge on.

We have to recognize the unevenness in human mental equipments. If every job in our place required skill the place would never have existed. Sufficiently skilled men to the number needed could not have been trained in a hundred years. A million men working by hand could not even approximate our present daily output. No one could manage a million men. But more important than that, the product of the unaided hands of those million men could not be sold at a price in consonance with buying power. And even if it were possible to imagine such an aggregation and imagine its management and correlation, just think of the area that it would have to occupy! How many of the men would be engaged, not in producing, but in merely carrying from place to place what the other men had produced? I cannot see how under such conditions the men could possibly be paid more than ten or twenty cents a day—for of course it is not the employer who pays wages. He only handles the money. It is the product that pays the wages and it is the management that arranges the production so that the product may pay the wages.

The more economical methods of production did not begin all at once. They began gradually—just as we began gradually to make our own parts. "Model T" was the first motor that we made ourselves. The great economies began in assembling and then extended to other sections so that, while to-day we have skilled mechanics in plenty, they do not produce automobiles—they make it easy for others to produce them. Our skilled men are the tool makers, the experimental workmen, the machinists, and the pattern makers. They are as good as any men in the world—so good, indeed, that they should not be wasted in doing that which the machines they contrive can do better. The rank and file of men come to us unskilled; they learn their jobs within a few hours or a few days. If they do not learn within that time they will never be of any use to us. These men are, many of them, foreigners, and all that is required before they are taken on is that they should be potentially able to do enough work to pay the overhead charges on the floor space they occupy. They do not have to be able-bodied men. We have jobs that require great physical strength—although they are rapidly lessening; we have other jobs that require no strength whatsoever—jobs which, as far as strength is concerned, might be attended to by a child of three. . . .

A Ford car contains about five thousand parts—that is counting screws, nuts, and all. Some of the parts are fairly bulky and others are almost the size of watch parts. In our first assembling we simply started to put a car together at a spot on the floor and workmen brought to it the parts as they were needed in exactly the same way that one builds a house. When we started to make parts it was natural to create a single department of the factory to make that part, but usually one workman performed all of the operations necessary on a small part. The rapid press of production made it necessary to devise plans of production that would avoid having the workers falling over one another. The undirected worker spends more of his time walking about for materials and tools than he does in working; he gets small pay because pedestrianism is not a highly paid line.

The first step forward in assembly came when we began taking the work to the men instead of the men to the work. We now have two general principles in all operations—that a man shall never have to take more than one step, if possibly it can be avoided, and that no man need ever stoop over.

The principles of assembly are these:

(1) Place the tools and the men in the sequence of the operation so that each component part shall travel the least possible distance while in the process of finishing.

(2) Use work slides or some other form of carrier so that when a workman completes his operation, he drops the part always in the same place—which place must always be the most convenient place to his hand—and if possible have gravity carry the part to the next workman for his operation.

(3) Use sliding assembling lines by which the parts to be assembled are delivered at convenient distances.

The net result of the application of these principles is the reduction of the necessity for thought on the part of the worker and the reduction of his movements to a minimum. He does as nearly as possible only one thing with only one movement. . . .

Along about April 1, 1913, we first tried the experiment of an assembly line. We tried it on assembling the fly-wheel magneto. We try everything in a little way first—we will rip out anything once we discover a better way, but we have to know absolutely that the new way is going to be better than the old before we do anything drastic.

I believe that this was the first moving line ever installed. The idea came in a general way from the overhead trolley that the Chicago packers use in dressing beef. We had previously assembled the fly-wheel magneto in the usual method. With one workman doing a complete job he could turn out from thirty-five to forty pieces in a nine-hour day, or about twenty minutes to an assembly. What he did alone was then spread into twenty-nine operations; that cut down the assembly time to thirteen minutes, ten seconds. Then we raised the height of the line eight inches—this was in 1914—and cut the time to seven minutes. Further experimenting with the speed that the work should move at cut the time down to five minutes. In short, the result is this: by the aid of scientific study one man is now able to do somewhat more than four did only a comparatively few years ago. That line established the efficiency of the method and we now use it everywhere. The assembling of the motor, formerly done by one man, is now divided into eighty-four operations—those men do the work that three times their number formerly did. In a short time we tried out the plan on the chassis.

About the best we had done in stationary chassis assembling was an average of twelve hours and twenty-eight minutes per chassis. We tried the experiment of drawing the chassis with a rope and windlass down a line two hundred fifty feet long. Six assemblers travelled with the chassis and picked up the parts from piles placed along the line. This rough experiment reduced the time to five hours fifty minutes per chassis. In the early part of 1914 we elevated the assembly line. We had adopted the policy of "man-high" work; we had one line twenty-six and three quarter inches and another twenty-four and one half inches from the floor—to suit squads of different heights. The waist-high arrangement and a further subdivision of work so that each man had fewer movements cut down the labour time per chassis to one hour thirty-three minutes. Only the chassis was then assembled in the line. The body was placed on in "John R. Street"—

the famous street that runs through our Highland Park factories. Now the line assembles the whole car.

It must not be imagined, however, that all this worked out as quickly as it sounds. The speed of the moving work had to be carefully tried out; in the fly-wheel magneto we first had a speed of sixty inches per minute. That was too fast. Then we tried eighteen inches per minute. That was too slow. Finally we settled on forty-four inches per minute. The idea is that a man must not be hurried in his work—he must have every second necessary but not a single unnecessary second. We have worked out speeds for each assembly, for the success of the chassis assembly caused us gradually to overhaul our entire method of manufacturing and to put all assembling in mechanically driven lines. The chassis assembling line, for instance, goes at a pace of six feet per minute; the front axle assembly line goes at one hundred eighty-nine inches per minute. In the chassis assembling are forty-five separate operations or stations. The first men fasten four mudguard brackets to the chassis frame; the motor arrives on the tenth operation and so on in detail. Some men do only one or two small operations, others do more. The man who places a part does not fasten it—the part may not be fully in place until after several operations later. The man who puts in a bolt does not put on the nut; the man who puts on the nut does not tighten it. On operation number thirty-four the budding motor gets its gasoline; it has previously received lubrication; on operation forty-four the radiator is filled with water, and on operation number forty-five the car drives out on to John R. Street.

Essentially the same ideas have been applied to the assembling of the motor. In October, 1913, it required nine hours and fifty-four minutes of labour time to assemble one motor; six months later, by the moving assembly method, this time had been reduced to five hours and fifty-six minutes. Every piece of work in the shops moves; it may move on hooks on overhead chains going to assembly in the exact order in which the parts are required; it may travel on a moving platform, or it may go by gravity, but the point is that there is no lifting or trucking of anything other than materials. Materials are brought in on small trucks or trailers operated by cut-down Ford chassis, which are sufficiently mobile and quick to get in and out of any aisle where they may be required to go. No workman has any-

thing to do with moving or lifting anything.   That is all in a separate
department—the department of transportation.

From *My Life and Work*, by Henry Ford (Garden City, copyright 1922, Doubleday, Page and Company), 77–85 *passim*.

───────◆───────

155. War Surgery (1918)

FROM THE NEW YORK TIMES CURRENT HISTORY

New weapons, in the form of high explosives and poison gas, created fresh med-
ical and surgical problems, and gave opportunity for the development, during the
World War, of treatments that have since proved of immense value in peace time.
On the efficiency of crippled soldiers, see also No. 140 above.

MODERN medicine and surgery have made the present war
the least destructive to human life, in proportion to the numbers engaged, of any in the history of the world.   That is what the
most eminent physicians and surgeons assert.   This statement, considered in conjunction with the length of allied casualty lists, at first
seems incredible, but it must be borne in mind that in other wars we
reckoned the number engaged in thousands, while in this one the
figures run well up in millions, and aside from actual soldiers, in no
other conflict have there been within the firing line so many people
who were not fighting, but erecting hospitals, barracks and officers'
quarters, treating and nursing wounded, engineering the construction
of railroads, storehouses, bridges, and all the means by which a modern
army is provisioned, cared for, and transported.

In the Civil War 7 per cent. of the soldiers perished yearly.   Dr.
Woods Hutchinson is authority for the statement that the annual
death rate in the allied armies is 3 per cent., while an official survey
made for Congress places the French mortality for 1917 as low as
1.375 per cent.   Again, during the Civil War from 20 to 50 per cent.
of those injured in battle never recovered; but now from 70 to 80 per
cent. of the wounded are returned to the front within forty days.   Of
the men who live six hours after being injured 90 per cent. recover,
and 95 per cent. of those who reach the casualty clearing houses are
saved.

Five-sixths of the deaths in the Civil War resulted from what are now known as preventable diseases. The medical catastrophes of the Spanish-American war are still fresh in the recollection of this generation. The havoc which typhoid and other diseases of intestinal origin wrought among the troops who were never engaged in battle is a memory filled with shame. Those diseases were preventable then as now, but medical science had not progressed as it has in the present day. Modern methods of inoculation and sanitation have triumphed over disease and modern surgeons have accomplished results almost beyond belief. . . .

Cholera is under control by disinfecting drinking water and vaccinating against it. Dysentery is being held down to a low rate by water sterilization and latrine sanitation. Preventive measures have robbed spinal meningitis—at one time one of the most baffling and cruel of plagues—of its terrors. Epidemic meningitis, which in earlier wars was dreaded under the name of "spotted fever," is now successfully treated by means of a curative serum. "Trench fever," a sickness which rarely kills, but which is the most prolific source of disability with which our armies have to contend, has not been done away with, but at least its source—the body louse—has been determined, and the question now becomes one of prevention and sanitation.

The most frightful scourges of former wars have been tetanus (lockjaw) and gaseous gangrene. Soil highly fertilized with animal excrement, like that of France, contains in large numbers the spores of tetanus and gaseous gangrene bacilli. From the earth they gain access to the clothing of men. When particles of cloth or dirt, as frequently happens, are carried into wounds by bullets or shell fragments, tetanus or gaseous gangrene, or both, frequently develop. To Dr. C. G. Bull of the Rockefeller Institute belongs the discovery of the antitoxin for the gas bacillus. Recent experiments have proved that a single serum injection may be made carrying the antitoxins for both tetanus and gaseous gangrene. As soon as possible after a wounded man is picked up he is inoculated, and both of these diseases are now practically under control. . . .

The greatest addition to the modern knowledge of antisepsis came through the discoveries of Dr. Dakin in experimenting with chlorine preparations. It remained for Dr. Alexis Carrel to develop a way to use the solution compounded by Dr. Dakin. He worked with Dr. Dakin, and they experimented with 200 antiseptics before the hypochlorite solution was perfected. Dr. Carrel then invented a method of application which made it practical. His work was done in New York, at the Experimental Hospital, built for studying the diseases of the war and treatment of the wounded, and located just below the Rockefeller Institute on Sixty-fourth Street and the East River.

Dr. Carrel's invention is a unique mode of wound irrigation. It consists of a system of little rubber tubes, pierced here and there for the liquid to flow out. The wound is cleansed, the tubes are laid in and fed from a glass container which hangs above the bed. The flow is regulated by stopcocks. Of the wounded treated at Compiègne by this method, 99 per cent. were healed by first intention. Whereas formerly amputations frequently resulted in painful stumps, and the healing process consumed from six to eighteen months, now, when treated with the Dakin solution they heal quickly, and artificial legs can almost always be fitted within from four to six weeks after the treatment is first given. The latest method of treating wounds includes the excision of all contaminated tissue, muscle, and even bone. This is on the theory that it is better and more economical to do the thing well at first than to risk a spreading of the infection and a second amputation. The use of the knife as a vital factor in cleansing wounds was the discovery of Dr. Pierre Duval of the French Army. Every bit of infected or suspected tissue is removed. When the wound may be declared "mechanically clean" it is usually closed. That is a matter of surgical technique. Under this treatment many severe wounds heal in two weeks. This means an enormous saving in man power, bandages, nursing, and surgical attention.

In connection with this treatment the transfusion of blood taken from slightly wounded but healthy men, who are willing to make the sacrifice, is freely used. It has been discovered that blood for transfusion can be kept for several weeks without deteriorating. Every casualty clearing station now endeavors to have in its icebox in readiness for emergencies about thirty pints of blood.

To another French surgeon, Dr. de Villeon, is due the discovery of a method of operating on the lungs for the successful removal of foreign matter. To expedite the examination of the wounded, the American Army Medical Department has developed a mobile X-ray outfit which may be taken to the front line trenches. A very important phase of surgery is the restoration of faces of persons supposed to be permanently disfigured. To reach the desired effect a photograph of the man, taken before his injury, is studied by a skillful French sculptor who has given three years to this work. He makes a careful model of the face in plaster, which is used by the surgeon as a guide. By transplanting bits of cartilage and bone from the man's ribs or legs, holding them in place by paraffin or the plastic material used by dentists, and then bringing over them portions of skin lifted from the forehead or cheek or neck—skin which is left with some natural attachment to aid its nutrition—a new face is actually built up, and one which is not only agreeable in appearance, but which resembles the man's former likeness. This work is being done in England, where twelve surgeons are working in collaboration with the sculptor. A reconstruction clinic has been established in New York.

In this war, as in no other in history, careful consideration has been given to the future of individuals who have been crippled in battle. For years in this country more men have annually been totally or partially disabled by industrial accidents than have been incapacitated by the war in Europe. These injured men left to fend for themselves have, in many cases, lost their grip on their self-respect, taken to drink, and, slowly deteriorating, have become either a menace to life and property or wards of the State. Comparatively little of a constructive nature has been done to aid them. There has been no scientific concerted effort in their behalf, and, paradoxically enough, it has remained for war, that great destructive power, to arouse intelligent employers from their apathy toward this enormous economic waste. The application of methods of reclamation to the injured in battle will be bound to have its reaction for good toward those disabled in industrial life. . . .

To aid the appearance and efficiency of the crippled, many new and valuable types of artificial arms and legs have been invented. An artificial leg adopted by the Government is the invention of Major David Silver, Medical Corps, U. S. A. It is said that a cripple, after he has become accustomed to it, may learn to walk with almost natural movements. No crutch or support is necessary. The foot movement is simulated by a jointed instep. The invention has been tried successfully by a soldier who has lost both legs. When it is properly clad and booted it is difficult for a casual observer to detect its artificiality.

The Red Cross Institute for Crippled and Disabled Men at 311 Fourth Avenue, New York City, maintains a training school and acts as a clearing house for men who have been taught. The institute has a room fully equipped with facilities for enabling the cripple to make his own limbs. Here plaster casts of stumps are taken and finished limbs are adjusted. Here, too, are displayed not only artificial feet and legs, but arms and hands almost perfect in their imitation of nature. But the latter are for dress only. At work an armless man uses the devices which will best aid him to fulfill his task. His working arms are fitted not with hands, but with tools, chucks and hooks, which may be interchangeably adjusted—whatever will most adequately take the place of the hand which he has lost. . . .

Pennsylvania is the pioneer State, as such, in enabling injured soldiers to get on their feet again. The Bureau of Employment of the Pennsylvania Department of Labor and Industry maintains card files, which, compiled from a Statewide questionnaire to employers of all kinds of labor, contain a list of 42,111 jobs open to crippled soldiers and sailors. Many of them are skilled tasks which may be performed by men who have lost one or both legs or an arm.

Staff article in *New York Times Current History*, October, 1918 (New York), 120–125 *passim*.

———————◆———————

156. The First Continuous Trans-Atlantic Flight (1919)

FROM THE NEW YORK TIMES CURRENT HISTORY

Previous to the flight of Alcock and Brown, other aircraft had crossed the ocean, but only by breaking the trip, as, for example, at the Azores. Hawker and Grieve, in their attempt to make the flight in one hop, were picked up by a Norwegian tramp steamer off the coast of Ireland. Many other attempts, both successful and disastrous, followed. For Lindbergh's widely acclaimed New York-to-Paris flight, see No. 68 above.

THE great achievement of flying across the Atlantic Ocean without a single stop was accomplished for the first time June 14–15, 1919, by Captain John Alcock and Lieutenant Arthur W. Brown, one an Englishman, the other an American, when they covered the

1,980 miles between Newfoundland and Ireland in 16 hours and 12 minutes at a speed of 120 miles an hour. The night of June 14–15 thus became a permanent landmark in the history of the conquest of the air.

After the disastrous ending to the desperate attempt of Harry Hawker and his companion, Grieve, to cross the ocean in a single-engined heavier-than-air machine, the contest for the $50,000 prize offered by Lord Northcliffe's paper, The Daily Mail, centered about three ventures. First in public knowledge was Captain Raynham and his Martynside machine, which came to grief in an attempt to take the air one hour after Harry Hawker. Raynham had sent for a new engine for his badly damaged machine, and was seeking a new pilot to replace his former associate, who had been seriously injured. A big Handley-Page plane was being assembled at St. John's and tried out by Admiral Mark Kerr in keen rivalry with a third new contestant, a Vickers-Vimy machine piloted and navigated by Captain John Alcock, a British air officer, and Lieutenant Arthur W. Brown, an American aviator.

The Vickers-Vimy plane got away first. It took the air on June 14 at 4:28 P. M., Greenwich mean time. On June 15, 1919, at 8:40 A. M., Greenwich mean time, the ultimate goal of all the ambitions which flying men have cherished since the Wright brothers first rose from the earth in a heavier-than-air machine was realized when Captain Alcock and Lieutenant Brown landed near the centre of the Irish coast after a nonstop flight of 1,980 miles from Newfoundland and across the Atlantic Ocean.

One feature of the record-breaking flight was its unexpectedness. Plans for receiving Alcock and Brown were hurriedly formulated by the British Aëro Club and the Air Ministry. It had not been believed that the aviators would be able to leave Newfoundland for another week. But, spurred on by a trial trip of the big Handley-Page machine, Alcock and Brown had determined to be the first to depart. With a very small running space they managed only by the most dexterous handling to get their machine to rise. After the big biplane got under way, its wireless aërials were soon carried away by the gale, and therefore the aviators could send back no message to indicate their progress. The following day they landed at Clifden, Ireland, in a bog near the wireless station. The aviators were dazed by the force of the impact on striking the ground.

When the officers, operators, and soldiers from the wireless plant rushed toward the machine after it landed, Alcock said: "This is the Vickers-Vimy machine. We have just come from Newfoundland." The little crowd gasped, and then sent up a rousing cheer. The brief message sent by the successful aviators from Clifden to the Aëro Club read as follows:

Landed at Clifden at 8:40 A. M., Greenwich mean time, June 15, Vickers-Vimy Atlantic machine leaving Newfoundland coast at 4:28 P. M., Greenwich mean time, June 14. Total time, 16 hours 12 minutes.

A modest description that came from the airmen at Clifden told of an adventurous and amazingly hazardous enterprise. Fogs and mists hung over the North Atlantic, and the Vickers-Vimy biplane climbed and dived, struggling to extricate herself from the folds of these worst enemies of aërial flight. Rising to a height of 11,000 feet and swooping down almost to the surface of the ocean, the two aviators at times found themselves flying upside down only ten feet above the water. Mists robbed the night of the advantage of the full moon, the wireless apparatus was torn away by the wind, and the two young aviators were thrown upon their own resources almost from the start. The skillful navigation which brought the machine near to the centre of the Irish coast line was one of the finest features of the flight.

The account given by Captain Alcock to the reporter of The Daily Mail was as follows:

At Signal Hill, Newfoundland, Lieutenant Brown set our course for the ocean on 124 degrees of the compass. We kept that course until well on in the night. I had the engine throttled down nicely and I let her do her own climbing.

At dark we were about 4,000 feet up. We found it very cloudy and misty. We were between layers of cloud and could see neither the sea nor the sky. After the first hour we had got into these clouds, one lot 2,000 feet up and the other 6,000 feet. It was impossible to see the sea to get our bearings.

Drift clouds above obscured the sun, and when the night came we could see neither stars nor moon, so we flew on our original course until we struck a patch about 3 A. M. where we could see a few stars.

Brown gave me a new course of 110 degrees compass points, and we went on steadily until the weather started to get very thick again. About 4 A. M. or 5 A. M. we could see nothing. The bank of fog was extremely thick, and we began to have a very rough time.

The air speed indicator jammed. It stood at 90, and I knew not exactly what I was doing. It jammed through the sleet freezing in it, and it smelt smoky.

We did some comic stunts then. I believe we looped the loop and by accident we did a deep spiral. It was very alarming. We had no sense of the horizon. We came down quickly from 4,000 feet until we saw water very clearly. That gave me my horizon again and I was all right. That period only lasted a few seconds, but it seemed ages.

It came to an end when we were within fifty feet of the water, with the machine practically on its back.

The air speed indicator again began to work as a result of the swift dive.

We climbed after that and got on fairly well until we got to 6,000 feet, and the fog was there again. I climbed twice on top of it, only to find banks of clouds. We went higher and saw the moon and one or two stars. We "carried on" until dawn.

We never saw the sun rise. There was a bank of fog also on top of the lower cloud. We climbed up to 11,000 feet. It was hailing and snowing. The machine was covered with ice. That was about 6 o'clock in the morning, and it remained like that until the hour before we landed.

My radiator shutter and water temperature indicator were covered with ice for four or five hours. Lieutenant Brown had continually climbed up to chip off the ice with a knife.

The speed indicator was full of frozen particles and gave trouble again. They came out when we got lower an hour before we landed. We came down and flew over the sea at 300 feet. It was still cloudy, but we could see the sun as it tried to break through.

It was a terrible trip. We never saw a boat, and we got no wireless messages at all. We flew along the water and we had doubts as to our position, although we believed we were "there or thereabouts." We looked out for land, expecting to find it any time.

We saw land about 9:15 A. M. when we suddenly discovered the coast. It was great to do that. We saw two little islands, which must have been East-Sal and Turbot Islands. We came along and got to Ardbear Bay, an inlet of Clifden Bay, and when we saw the wireless mast we knew where we were exactly.

When still over Clifden village I saw after a few minutes what I took to be a nice field—a lovely meadow. We came down and made a perfect landing, but it was a bog. The wheels sank axle deep in the field. The Vimy toppled over on her nose.

The lower plane is badly damaged and broken and both propellers are deeply sunk in the bog, but I think they are not broken. The engines are all right.

The successful Vimy machine was built largely of steel. It had multiple steel tanks for fuel storage, and was equipped with double engines. Alcock, whose name was almost unknown to England before his flight, was described by his friends as a man of reticent personality. He had been an instructor and passenger carrier at Brooklands, the flying centre outside London, since 1911. His chief adventure in aviation had been in bombing expeditions against the Turks during the war; a forced descent due to engine failure had led to his imprisonment for two years. Brown had been an aviator since the age of 17, and at one time had conducted a military school of aërial navigation. The absolute correctness of his calculations during the trip, which guided the Vimy machine with scientific precision to its exact goal, the Clifden Wireless Station, was one of the most striking features of the flight.

Staff article in *New York Times Current History*, July, 1919 (New York), 112–114.

---

157. The Project at Muscle Shoals (1922)

BY JUDSON C. WELLIVER

Welliver is a newspaper man connected with western and Frank A. Munsey papers, who was selected by President Roosevelt to gather data in Europe in 1907, and has been attached to the White House organization since March 4, 1921. The long conflict of public and private interests to determine the ultimate utilization of the power site at Muscle Shoals has found expression in much debate but little action. A strong opposition has prevented its transfer to private hands at a fraction of its cost, and the government has continued unwilling to make a further large investment in the development.—Bibliography as in No. 79.

. . . THE House Committee on Military Affairs has gone into the whole question of water-powers, recovery of nitrogen from the air, manufacture and sale of fertilizers, electrification of railroads, electro-chemistry and electro-metallurgy—and, generally, into the whole fascinating realm of the impending hydro-electric revolution in industrial life.

The basis of the whole project is the great water power in the Tennessee. To develop this three dams are proposed. Dam No. 2, the most important, is 4446 feet long, at the foot of the rapids' steepest section. On both sides the river's banks are high walls of solid rock, and its bed is of the same material. The dam is keyed deep into the bed- and bank-rocks. The dam will be 135 feet high, from foundation footing to the roadway at the top; about 100 feet from the natural low water to the roadway level. This dam will back the stream up seventeen miles and will give the water a useful fall of ninety-five feet to the eighteen great turbines that will turn generators to convert its flow into electricity. According to the water supply, as many as are desired of these turbines can be used. At the high-water stages, with all working, 540,000 horsepower will be produced.

Seventeen miles upstream is the site of Dam No. 3, whose construction is not yet begun. It is considerably longer—6725 feet, but only fifty feet high, giving the water a useful fall of thirty-eight feet to its turbines. At full flow, it will develop about 216,000 horsepower. This dam will back water seventy-five miles upstream.

Dam No. 1 is a minor affair, to carry out the navigation improvement. It will be only fifteen feet high, and its site is two miles below No. 2.

The Tennessee's flow varies, according to measurements covering fifty years, from 7800 to 500,000 cubic feet per second. That means, of course, a very wide variance between its highest and lowest power potentialities. At the lowest stage ever recorded it would produce, with the installation planned, about 100,000 horsepower; at the highest, 756,000, and still leave water capable of developing 1,000,000 horsepower to run unused over the spillways. This is sheer waste; and to prevent it, so far as possible, Mr. Ford proposes to go back to the upper Tennessee, and to some of its tributaries, and build other dams to store this water at times of heavy flow, and free it in periods of low water to enlarge the flow at the power dams. Some of these storage dams would themselves be equipped with turbines and produce additional power.

This wide variability of flow represents the greatest economic difficulty in harnessing "flashy" rivers for power. The power that can be relied on absolutely all the year round is called "primary"; the varying amounts in excess of this are "secondary" power. Muscle Shoals is planned to produce 100,000 primary or minimum constant horsepower. But this minimum would be touched only a few days each year; the rest of the year, the power would be much greater, depending on the water's stage, and reaching a maximum of 756,000 horsepower. Add 120,000 supplemental steam, and include minor water powers which it is proposed to develop and link up, and a round one million maximum is in sight. . . .

The Tennessee is rated sixth among American rivers. Rising in Virginia, eastern Kentucky, eastern Tennessee and North Carolina, it flows generally southwesterly, into northern Alabama, where it bends northwest, crosses Tennessee and Kentucky, and flows into the Ohio at Paducah. . . .

If you will look at a map of the southern Appalachian region, you will observe that the rivers contain falls or long rapids where they come down from the mountains to the coastal plain. The geologists say that a long time before Adam and Eve flourished, the coastal plain at some period dropped a varying distance, and that these falls and rapids mark the line of the fault. Muscle Shoals offers the greatest water power merely because the Tennessee is the greatest of these rivers. It presents a drop of 136 feet in 37 miles; at the steepest section, a fall of 100 feet in 17 miles. The Wilson Dam is at the foot of this 17 miles of steepest fall. . . .

With the era of hydro-electric development, about the beginning of this century, Muscle Shoals began to be regarded as one of the greatest water-power opportunities, combined with the possibility of at last making navigation practicable between the upper and lower reaches of the Tennessee River. The Tennessee has at all times been one of the most navigated streams; if it were improved and the industrial possibilities of its basin developed, it would be among the world's most used rivers of commerce. It drains 44,000 square miles, having a rainfall of 50 to 70 inches, the largest of any equal area in the country except the Gulf coast of Louisiana. The importance of navigation improvement is greater because the Tennessee Valley's riches are largely in mineral, metal, and agricultural products which run to large tonnages. In 1918 the value of the metal and mineral products produced in the area tributary to the Tennessee River was about $78,000,000, the agricultural products amounted to $470,000,000 and the basic or semi-manufactured products were valued at more than $12,000,000—a total of $560,000,000 for the region. No other power than that developed from water and used as electricity could bring full utilization of the undeveloped mineral riches, because they require very great and very cheap power.

For that matter, the development of most of the latent riches in the earth's crust must depend on power in such immense units and tremendous quantities as can be possible only through the use of water power. The truth is that industry is near the end of its coal age. . . .

The other day I stood on a high point on the south bank of the Tennessee, at a point where the roaring stream is nearly two miles wide, and suggests the Amazon or Yukon. My engineering friend pointed to the stream and said:

At today's stage of the river there is 800,000 horsepower passing us. It is the power which we must harness, here and in hundreds of other places, if we are to maintain our national position industrially. For power derived from steam and coal is utterly inadequate to the demands of industrial chemistry and the electric furnace. Power from coal and steam has been found to be utterly too expensive, save in the most favorable circumstances. . . .

Both South America and Africa far surpass North America and Europe in water powers. We think of Niagara, where there is already a commercial development approaching a million horsepower, and imagine that our continent leads the world. But we have only one Niagara, and our water powers in general will prove far more expensive to develop.

This is the condition we have to look in the face. Our continent is less rich in water power, and we have not made a great advance in developing what we have. . . .

He proceeded to explain the difference between powers like Muscle Shoals, and those produced by falls. At Niagara, which is ideal, a substantially uniform volume of water goes over the falls the year round. Nature has provided her own storage reservoir. Development requires little more than the installation of the machinery. On the other hand, at Muscle Shoals, it is necessary first to build a great dam or series of dams to create your fall. These dams cost vast sums on which interest must come out of the price of power. . . .

Immense capital is required for hydro-electric developments; and, further, after the power is ready, industries must be brought to consume it. So the operation must be spread over a long period. For this reason the Government has enacted that water-power leases may be made up to fifty years. . . .

When it became apparent that the United States was being drawn into the European War, the Government entered upon a plan to develop the Muscle Shoals power to take nitrogen from the air for use in explosives. . . . Prime emphasis was laid, in favor of Muscle Shoals, on the water power and the fact that it was far inland and safe from enemy attack. Under the army engineers, plans were made and construction begun. The program fell into two parts: first, the construction of dams and electric power houses; second, the construction of great plants to produce nitrates from the air, and to be operated by the water power, with supplemental steam power.

Under this program there has been expended something over $100,-000,000 by the Government. On the side of power development, roughly $17,000,000 has gone into the Wilson Dam at the foot of Muscle Shoals. This is now about 30 per cent. finished, and various authorities estimate that from eighteen to thirty-six months will be required to complete it. . . .

The fact that $105,000,000 had been invested without a dollar's worth of product having been secured during the war (though due to the fact that the plant was completed just as the fighting ended) inevitably caused criticism. When, therefore, further appropriations were asked, in peace-time, to continue the development, and to complete the entire project, there was so much opposition that Congress, in 1920, refused. From that time on the disposition of the Government's interests was the subject of much consideration, but no action.

Shortly after the present Administration came in, the War Department sought interests that might buy the property. For a time it actually looked as if nobody was going to want, at any price, properties on which more than $100,000,000 had been spent. Whoever might take them over would be compelled to put in immense additional capital. . . .

On the face of it, Ford offers $5,000,000 for properties that cost $85,000,000. But this must be reduced by $13,000,000, which went into Nitrate Plant No. 1, which has been a failure in operation, leaving about $72,000,000. This again can be scaled easily one-half, to get at something like present cost to reproduce. Yet, assuming that Mr. Ford offers $5,000,000 for properties that to-day could be reproduced for $35,000,000, it still looks like a fine bargain.

The other side is that Mr. Ford is binding himself to produce the equivalent of 110,000 tons of ammonium nitrate annually—about one-fourth the present national fertilizer consumption of inorganic nitrogen; and to sell a finished, concentrated, high-grade fertilizer at an advance of only 8 per cent. over cost of production. This makes the appeal to the farmers; while the advocates of war preparedness insist that the Government can well afford to be liberal in view of the offer to keep the nitrate plant always ready to manufacture explosives. For the Government to do this would cost, it is estimated by the Ordnance Department, some $2,475,000 annually. . . .

Advocates of Muscle Shoals point to the varied riches of the Tennessee Valley and the Southern Appalachian region. Here, they say, is an ideal place to demonstrate a water-power program big enough to serve as a model for the whole nation. Here are railways to be electrified, and enough power to do it and still leave a vast surplus for industrial requirements. Industrial development here would diffuse the national industries, carrying many new enterprises into the South, where industrial development has been retarded. This would help solve the transportation question by moving large manufacturing interests nearer to the consumers. . . . The Tennessee Basin has not only water powers, but coal for supplementary steam power.

The availability of this area for producing munitions of war and fertilizers, is particularly dwelt upon. The salt and sulphur of Louisiana and Texas, both necessary in electro-chemical and explosive processes, can be brought by water. The greatest fluorspar deposits are in western Kentucky, with water transport handy. Fluorspar is used in chemical operations, manufacture of glass, high-grade steels, aluminum production, etc. Great deposits of iron and copper are tributary to Muscle Shoals. Phosphate rock occurs in enormous quantities immediately adjacent. Bauxite, from which aluminum is most easily recovered, exists in great deposits, the richest in Arkansas, transportable by either rail or water. . . .

Not least of the war-time arguments for Muscle Shoals was its interior location, safe from attack. . . .

From the point of view, then, of industry, fertilizers, national defense, or more widely diffused manufacturing, or of railroad electrification, Muscle Shoals appears peculiarly available. . . .

Judson C. Welliver, *The Muscle Shoals Power and Industrial Project*, in *American Review of Reviews*, April, 1922 (New York), LXV, 382–391 *passim*.

---------◆---------

158. A Broadcasting Studio (1925)

BY GRAHAM McNAMEE

McNamee is one of the first to gain individual recognition as a radio announcer, his distinction being based mainly on his graphic, extemporaneous descriptions of public events—political conventions, boxing matches, and the like.

AFTER the political conventions, I was more often at our studio on Broadway, and perhaps some description of our business operations may not be amiss before we go further afield.

Gradually the work had increased so that our two small rooms took over other offices; and at this present writing we cover a whole floor of this giant skyscraper, with a staff of a hundred, divided between the program, commercial, plant, financial, and publicity departments, including twenty-four stenographers much of whose time is taken up with the mail received from the fans.

And, as in all other houses that have something to sell, we have a staff of salesmen under the direction of a sales manager. The commodity they have to offer is not tangible and does not come in cans or packages; by the quarter, half-hour, or full hour they sell it—nothing less than time, "time on the air." Here again distinction must be drawn between the stations which like ours, WEAF, broadcast entertainment, and those which send messages from person to person, usually, these days, out to sea. Most entertainment stations have their "time" divided between entertainment they themselves arrange, and that broadcast for their clients for publicity purposes. I should say they run roughly about fifty-fifty, that is, that half of the programs are "sustaining," as we call our own, and half "commercial," as we term those programs which are paid for by outsiders. . . .

There is an art, of course, in the selection of the entertainment. A fisheries association, for example, broadcasts weekly talks on fish, and has engaged a woman to tell how to cook and serve them. She also gives new recipes—and all in an interesting way. A life insurance concern conducts setting-up exercises in the early morning. This campaign not only emphasizes the name of the client and so keeps it before the public, but it has a valuable by-product, since it improves the average health of the hosts who each morning go through these genuflections and roll so energetically on the floor, and thus conserves the treasury of the life insurance company. So a program may be double and triple shotted and much care must be taken in devising it. It would be unprofitable, obviously, for an undertaker's association to get up a program of health-giving exercises. . . .

The rates paid for "time on the air" depend on the number of stations which take the program of the client. One station alone costs from $150 to $600 an hour, varying with the estimated density of population of the region to which the station broadcasts, the more thinly settled areas costing $150, and the metropolitan district $600. In setting this last rate, WEAF is very conservative, reckoning on a radius of only one hundred miles, when actually our programs have been picked up from every state in the union, from as far south as the Argentine, and from such far-off places as Cape Town, South Africa, and the northern part of Scandinavia.

Each additional station the advertiser buys, of course, adds to the expense. In broadcasting political events, we have as many as twenty-seven stations; but fourteen is at present the largest number used for the commercial programs.

An obscure tenor I remember once drifted into our studio when radio was new and asked for and received a hearing. This, of course, did not go out on the air; as at rehearsals he simply sang before the microphone, and some of the management listened in another room as his voice came over the loud-speaker. He made good; we gave him a date; and these engagements increased in frequency. Finally we hit on a picturesque name involving a play on words which caught the fancy of the fans and also appealed to the sense of mystery. Now he is one of the best-known singers not only on the radio program but in large halls in the greatest cities.

Out of the west came another singer and composer, with little reputation—only his voice and ukelele. We usually give an audition to anyone who asks for it, if the candidate shows any symptoms of talent, and we listened to him, later placing him on the program. The fame here gained soon brought him to the attention of one of our clients, and before long he was appearing each week in a commercial hour for which he was very well paid, then sent by this same firm on a tour abroad, to appear not only in concerts but before the microphones in the capitals of Europe, New Zealand, and Australia.

So it can readily be seen that there are chances for the unknown, particularly since in our programs we aim for variety and are ever on the lookout for something new and original. . . .

In those days at the studio I met quite as many famous people as I had in the big jobs outside. And one and all I found badly smitten, on their first appearance, with that nervousness which we of the staff call "mike fever." Sometimes it is almost pathetic, the way well-known figures—men of great power, too, who have held spell-bound vast audiences—follow us around the studios, like little children seeking moral support when they are to visit the dentist.

At the joint radio début of John McCormack and Lucrezia Bori, those two famous singers were almost dead with fright, though each showed it in a different manner.

McCormack, after the rehearsal, and while waiting to begin, simply could not sit still; he paced the floor; then sat down, then stood up, sat down again, then took to his caged-animal pacing up and down once more, while all the time the perspiration ran off his face in streams.

Bori, on the other hand, was still, and apparently composed, but ice-cold. I knew it, for recognizing this strange symptom, too, she asked me to touch her arms.

"Just feel them," she said, "they're like ice—it's almost as if I were going to die." . . .

The American baritone, Reinald Werrenrath, on his first broadcasting, paced wildly up and down the floor, the coat tails of his dress suit flying—though he didn't need to wear that, he had overlooked the fact that his audience couldn't see him—and kept exclaiming humorously yet seriously enough: "I may be the worst baritone in the world; but for a concert hall this is a darn sight worse than I am!"

Louise Homer's sweet, gracious personality did not allow her to show her fear in any excitable way. Instead she seemed to be thinking of all the people to whom that night she might bring happiness. Indeed, after the experience, she confessed with tears in her eyes: "I was overwhelmed; the thought of all those dear people all over the country listening to me, in little farmhouses and, maybe, tenements, was overpowering!"

What seemed to puzzle Schumann-Heink most was that we didn't find fault. "You don't scold enough," she said to me.

"But Madame," I replied, "how could we? You follow suggestions so easily. What is there to say?"

Again she shook her head. "Maybe; but I'm afraid it isn't right. You don't scold enough. And when a teacher doesn't scold enough his pupils do very badly."

It was so with Emilio de Gogorza, too. "What would you have me do?" All the really great were like that, admitting in their well-proportioned modesty that they knew their own business, but also that others knew theirs.

Quite different, however, were a few artists whose temperament exceeded their ability—that 'cellist, for instance, who refused to play on carpet and sent us hustling through the studios for an empty cigar box on which to rest the 'cello point. A certain vice-president doesn't yet know how his choice cigars came to be dumped all over his desk. . . .

There was an artist, too, who was troublesome, though not in the studio. After the rehearsals he went out, as he said, to get something to eat. Then later he telephoned that he was sick and couldn't appear; yet someone connected with the staff saw him that evening enjoying himself in a café on upper Broadway. The truth was that he was almost paralyzed with stage fright; no illness that you can find in a medical dictionary had hit him—just "mike fever"—the fear of that little instrument of wires and springs.

It wasn't nervousness that afflicted Will Rogers so much as the lack of an audience, at least of one that could be seen. It seemed to worry him, facing that dead wall near which the microphone stood. As he went on, I noticed him turning around again and again to look inquiringly at me. And suddenly it struck me what was the matter—the typical actor's need of audible applause, at least of response he could sense and feel. Leaving my seat in the monitor's booth, from which I had been observing him, I came out and sat on the edge of the table not far from the "mike," and smiled or grinned at each thing he said. From that time on he did not turn around; he had that response which the actor always needs. . . .

Of all those we assisted, Lloyd George, perhaps, caused us the greatest worry, though innocently enough. Engrossed in his speech and gathering fire and speed as he went, he just wouldn't stand, as, say, President Coolidge does, within reasonable reach of the microphone. He stamped up and down the platform, now speaking to the boxes, then to this side of the audience, then to that, and sometimes to those on the stage behind him. One such experience taught us a lesson, and for his second speech, at the Metropolitan Opera House, we came forearmed, stationing a microphone at almost every three feet of the platform to allow for his marathon. . . .

There are many things, however, that make up for the all worries and troubles with our artists. It is a privilege to become acquainted with them; and, it must be remembered, that, once in action, all these great personalities we have just been chatting about lost all their nervousness. Their power and the reasons for their success were then abundantly evident to any observer.

Graham McNamee, *You're on the Air* (New York, Harpers, 1926), 96–113 *passim*.

---------◆---------

159. The Telephone Idea (1926)

BY ARTHUR POUND

Pound has been an editorial writer for various newspapers, and later an editor of *The Independent*.—Catherine Mackenzie, in *Alexander Graham Bell*, tells something of the degree to which the inventor of the telephone envisioned its potentialities.

WE have seen, each with his or her own eyes, but perhaps without reflecting upon its social consequences, the growth of quick communication through some part of the fifty years since Bell invented the telephone. We have witnessed this country of magnificent distances gradually binding itself together, dwelling with dwelling, town with country, village with city, across the whole area served by the exchanges and long lines of the connected companies. We who are still young have beheld millions of farm families emerge from isolation, the tucked away mountain hamlet and prairie village brought into touch with the busy currents of trade and social intercourse. Many new tools and systems originated by science and organized by business have contributed to this result; but the telephone has done as much as any other factor to make America strong and united; and, what is even more important, to make America aware of her strength and unity. One can note this tying-in of interests and sentiments in almost any corner of the vast panorama of America.

The countryside where I live, one of the first areas colonized, is dotted thickly with small villages and hamlets. Once they had no communications swifter than horse and foot; now, each is in continuous touch with the other and with the metropolis of the district. Each used to be self-sufficient, a Jack-of-all-Trades village, where practically all the necessities of life were made in crude, laborious ways by men and women held there by the sheer difficulty of getting away. Now, over this whole district, labor is fluid; village carpenters and mechanics follow their jobs over a wide range and motor home at night. Men come from the cities to work in the villages, and from the villages to work in the city. The result, economically, is a more efficient distribution of labor power, less unemployment, greater wealth production. City delivery wagons frequent country roads; the merchandising of many essentials of village and rural life proceeds from a center, with many incidental economies and satisfactions. If the villages tend to become satellites of the cities in the process, I can see no possible harm in that great enough to offset the compensating advantages. Both cities and villages are of value only as they provide shelter and opportunity for human beings, and if the inhabitants of both win through the setting up of closer relationships, why quibble over local jealousies? If the villages lose trade in certain lines to the city, they gain in other lines, through the expanding wants of the old settlers and the advent of new residents. The functions of both city and countryside, of villages and farms change somewhat in this readjustment; but the net result seems to me economically and socially good. In estimating these trends fairly, we must put littleness from our minds and consider, instead, the well-being of the masses and the general effectiveness of the nation.

Not the least of the telephone's influence on our times has been to give managers wider scope for their undertakings. Just as the huge modern office building, with tens of thousands of occupants by day and only scores of occupants at night, or the equally imposing modern apartment house which gains population while the office building is losing it, would be impossible places for work or residence without telephone service, so it is difficult to picture a large industrial enterprise of the present functioning without means of vocal communication.

In New York City sits the president of a corporation engaged in making quantities of highly intricate goods, perhaps the most intricate goods manufactured in quantity and distributed to the general public —automobiles. The long lines system puts his desk on Broadway into prompt communication with the company's plants in a dozen states. He can talk to a factory manager in Michigan as easily as he can talk to his secretary in the next room. If he desires to talk directly to any foreman in company employ, the connection can be established during the time I have been writing this paragraph;

thousands of telephone stations, in hundreds of separate buildings, are at the disposal of this executive. His personal touch carries, in the twinkling of an eye, across tremendous areas; he can gather information, give orders and hold others responsible man to man, voice to voice. And this corporation's entire telephone equipment, of course, is interconnected, so that any plant can talk directly with any other plant, and within each plant every key man has a telephone at his elbow. Back and forth across this corporate web fly endlessly the messages which direct capital and labor in the production and marketing of automobiles. Furthermore, this web of corporate communications is tied into a far greater whole; the corporation can reach out, as it were, almost instantly, to its banks, agents, dealers, supply firms and customers. Probably this executive soon will be talking in the same easy fashion to his London agents.

A single unit in this vast manufacturing system may comprise a hundred buildings scattered over two hundred acres. It would take a week to explore the area thoroughly on foot. Communicating the information necessary to effective production in such a plant would be immensely more difficult if the telephone were crossed off the slate. Other systems of interplant and interoffice communication could be arranged, no doubt, but none of them would combine the telephone's speed with the telephone's simplicity of operation, whereby every employee becomes, or at least can become at need, part of the communication's circle. From the standpoint of works management, the telephone has become indispensable to a degree that suggests that industrial expansion to the present extent, if it could have come about at all without the telephone, would have resulted in plant arrangements far different than those existing today. In that case street layouts, street car lines and city maps, the geographical settings which condition millions of lives, would be quite otherwise than they are.

One reason big business is big is because modern communications permit growth. The keen, aggressive manager can extend his control of men and things further than his predecessors could. Business enterprises expand as improved communications broaden the market into which trade may be effectively pushed.

Another reason big business is big is because consumers are becoming more alike in their tastes, and hence buy standardized goods in larger quantities. Advertising hastens this standardization of wants, but even without advertising there would be a general drift in that direction, owing to the tendency of a nation with free trade, rapid transport and quick communications to slough off its sectional peculiarities and to reduce itself to a more distinct national type. In this process the telephone, along with many other factors, plays its part. The telephone stimulates trade by making buying and selling more convenient; in addition, it furnishes a medium for an incalculable but staggeringly large amount of mouth-to-mouth advertising, assuredly the most effective of all want-stimulants.

All business, big and little, uses the telephone to good purpose. Day after day for many years Bell's invention has been saving the time of more and more millions. The tremendous growth in the national wealth, which has been a striking feature of the last half century, could not have occurred if processes had remained stationary. Wages have been raised, hours shortened, and the standard of living raised because many time saving systems and machines made those advances economically possible. The most extensive free trade area on earth, equipped with a network of superior communications, has been buying the output of plants constantly improving in efficiency—result, a trade so vast and an increase in wealth so prodigious that Europeans accustomed to another scale of values stand astonished at our statistics of production and consumption.

There remains to be considered the fact that communications have leaped ahead so swiftly that a comfortable margin of safety now exists between practice and possibility. American business has not reached, or even approached, the economic limits of safety, when all the new factors in communications are considered. The United States is, indeed, a land of ample margins in coal, food and natural resources of many sorts, but the available margin in communications is wider still, thanks to the alertness of communications engineers and the taut efficiency of communications organizations.

American telephone methods, transplanted to France in 1917, achieved remarkable results over hastily built lines, some of which even had to be improvised from unfamiliar and below standard equipment. Certain innovations, tested overseas, have since become standard practice at home after being refined to meet the needs of peaceful traffic. Since the war, also, an accelerated construction program has more than offset the lag resulting from the necessarily reduced programs of 1917–18. These two factors create an impressive margin of safety, indicating that the expansion of American trade and commerce is not likely to be slowed down by congestion in wire communications.

Certainly this expansion can never be halted as long as the telephone business continues to build for the future. No single year in the fifty of telephone history has recorded a shrinkage in telephone use. Telephones in the United States have multiplied from Bell's lone instrument to more than 17,000,000, or one to every seven persons in the United States; and the average number of telephone conversations daily has risen from less than 8,000,000 in 1900 to 70,000,000 in 1926. Nevertheless, there is no saturation point in sight; the public appetite for telephone service grows with every extension and improvement of that service. Apparently, the telephone industry is destined to grow as long as the United States grows; certainly it will continue to grow as long as individuals and groups through improved communications find it possible to increase production and sales, leisure and wages, profits and the pleasantries of life.

Arthur Pound, *Of Mills and Markets*, in *The Telephone Idea* (New York, Greenberg, 1926), 40–46. Copyright by the author.

CHAPTER XXIX — RECREATION AND TRAVEL

160. Complexities of Hotel Operation (1903)

BY ALBERT BIGELOW PAINE

Paine is famous as the biographer of several eminent Americans. Hotels have become even more elaborate since 1903, until they are incomplete without such ul-tra-modern services as radio entertainment in each room, libraries, gymnasia and swimming pools for the use of guests. Only by watching hotel advertisements in current periodicals is it possible to keep abreast of contemporary innovations in luxury.

AMONG all our institutions of progress there is none more amaz-ing than the modern hotel in immensity, in complex activities, in social significance. With a width of 200 feet and a length of nearly 400 feet, and approximately 300 feet in height—these are the dimen-sions of one of these great machines for convenient living, while within its vast walls are more than a thousand rooms—its capacity is more than twelve hundred guests per day, and it employs eighteen hundred servants to attend to their needs.

In a sub-basement, forty-two and one-half feet below the street level, is the motive power of this vast machine. Here is one of the largest private electric plants in the world. Its power drives the screws of nineteen elevators and supplies the illuminating energy of twenty-five thousand electric lights. One hundred and fifty men are employed in these power rooms, though the seven great boilers are self-stoking, and one hundred tons of coal a day are supplied to them in seven automatic and never-ending streams. In the sub-base basement, too, is the private ice-machine, which freezes fifty tons of ice and forty dozen carafes of drinking water daily, besides refrigerating the four thousand pounds of meat, fish and game necessary to feed the huge and gorgeous army of guests and servitors above stairs. It requires six skilled butchers to handle this meat item, and five men are em-ployed to open the twelve barrels of oysters that are served daily. These things are bought in open market by men whose sole business it is to buy well at whatever price is necessary to secure the quality desired.

The kitchen arrangements of the "modern hotel" are on the first basement floor. I think I had a very dim idea about such things until we went there. I believe I pictured to myself a properly attired chef with several assistants before a rather large kitchen range and in a good deal of a hurry during the rush hours, perhaps forgetting his pan of hot rolls in the oven now and then, or letting the eggs get over-done.

My mental picture was not a good one. There is a chef, to be sure, but so far as I could see he does not cook. He is simply a captain of the seventy-five other cooks who work in three relays of twenty-five each. There is no range, but a solid bank of broilers—immense grid-irons, beneath which are the fires that never die. As for the four hundred loaves of bread and eight thousand rolls required daily, the chef does not worry his mind over the patent cutters and mixers and ovens and staff of bakers needed to supply the simple item of bread; or concern himself with the quality of the eleven hundred pounds of butter that are each day required to go with it. Neither does he trouble himself with the pastry, where marvelous things are con-structed of candies and creams and fruits—works of art, some of them entitled to "honorable mention" in an academy of design. The patrons of the modern hotel are fond of deserts, and the daily item of two hundred and fifty large pies convinces me that a fair percentage of them are native born.

I must not forget the item of eggs. Eighteen thousand are required every twenty-four hours. Boiled eggs do not get overdone; they are boiled by clock-work. A perforated dipper containing the eggs drops down into boiling water. The dipper's clock-work is set to the second, and when that final second has expired the little dipper jumps up out of the water and the eggs are ready for delivery. There are men who do nothing else but fill and watch and empty these dancing dippers, and it seemed to me great fun.

On another part of this floor is the dish-washing, where great galvanized baskets lower the pieces into various solutions of potash and clean rinsing water—all so burning hot that the dishes dry in-stantly without wiping. Sixty-five thousand pieces of chinaware are cleansed in a day, and an almost equal quantity of silver. All told, there are three hundred employees in the kitchen departments of this huge living machine.

On another part of the first basement floor is the laundry. Every day is washday in the modern hotel. Eleven great revolving washers are here, four centrifugal dryers, almost exactly like the centrifugal bleachers in a sugar refinery, and six ten-foot mangles that take in a full-width sheet, smoothing as well as drying it. But the ironing of shirts and collars is done in the good old-fashioned way—by hand, only that the irons are always hot, for they are electric irons, and a perfect evenness of temperature is maintained. They are handled by a staff of sturdy-armed men and women, and an ironer's wages are considered good. . . .

There are four dining-rooms and two cafés upstairs, and perhaps a thousand people are being served at one time. They are the most brilliantly dressed, best groomed people in the world. They are also the richest. . . .

Besides dining-rooms and cafés on the first floor, there are splendid foyers, or rest rooms, fitted with every luxury in the shape of easy chairs, divans and desks, though perhaps the most striking feature of this mezzanine floor of the modern hotel may be its wonderful corridors running its length and breadth, luxuriously seated and carpeted throughout, including a gorgeous avenue of Oriental fabrics, lapis lazuli and gold. Then there are the luxurious Turkish smoking-parlor, the ample reading-rooms, and the vast billiard parlors.

The splendid office of the modern hotel is in the centre of this floor. Here is a force of men, trained for a special service, each with his knowledge and his ability ready for instant use, each with a judgment of men and conditions and emergencies that enables him to decide whether a case presented is a matter for instant action or for managerial consideration. At one corner of the office is a young man whose only duty is to supply information and guides to visitors. . . .

Near the office there is a battery of pneumatic tubes connecting with the upper floors. A bell-boy no longer carries up a visitor's card. The card is put into an air-cartridge and is fired straight to the floor where it belongs. An attendant at a little desk there sends it to the proper room. By and by the cartridge goes back to the office, and the visitor learns whether the guest he wishes to see is in his room, whether he will see him and if not, why, or, perhaps, when.

. . . The ballroom is used for dramatic performances and for balls and other social events. A card-party had just ended when I went through, and a bushel of playing-cards, once used and thrown away, were flung into the corner. Everything is luxurious, lavish and prodigal in the modern hotel.

There are five splendid banquet and reception rooms in all, and they are rarely unoccupied. Lectures, readings, musicales, grand opera performances, art auctions, mighty social affairs, that fill corridors and stairways with a dazzling and humming overflow—there is no end to these things. Night is like day, only, if anything, more brilliant. Even the casual visitor feels somehow caught in an endless whirl of gaiety and recalls certain old allegorical pictures wherein the festivities of life were meant to be thrown in high relief. . . .

It is said that a guest may spend a profitable week in the hotel without once going on the street. Entertainments are on every hand, businesses of almost every sort are represented on the ground floor, and when at a loss for other amusement the visitor may ascend to the fifteenth floor and sit for his photograph, or spend an hour in a gay roof-garden. . . .

The hotel dweller's problem is to furnish the money—the rest is easy. It is true that there may be a certain lack of individuality in his home life, and he must put up with rather narrow quarters as compared to what he might have in his own household. But he has many advantages. His meals are always ready. His servants are always at hand. He has a telephone in his room that connects not only with the office but with the systems of the outer world. He is a living embodiment of human irresponsibilities. . . .

Albert Bigelow Paine, *The Workings of a Modern Hotel*, in *World's Work*, March, 1903 (New York), V, 3171–3187 *passim*.

161.   Our Great American Game (1906)

BY DOCTOR J. P. CASEY

Dr. Casey equipped himself for the two professions of baseball and dentistry. He gives a graphic description of a thrilling game, and explains something of the tremendous popular appeal of baseball. For an excellent account of sports in America, see Rollin Lynde Hartt, *People at Play*.

. . . THERE'S no delay in a game of baseball. Its march is inevitable. A man's stay at the bat is limited. He can receive only five balls from the pitcher (not counting fouls) before the arrival of his batting crisis. If the sixth ball comes straight and he misses it, off goes his head; he's out and another reigns in his stead. . . .

And what a game it is to watch! There's work for two or three pairs of the sharpest eyes to see all that is going on. There's the man that is trying to steal from first base to second, lying far out from first base, with a spring in his body like a hickory bow, ready to dart for second base and hurtle thru dust to immortal glory if he sees the smallest sign of weakening in catcher or pitcher. He is brave, but not rash; he is far out, but not too far; for the pitcher is watching him with half an eye and stands ready to launch a Jovian thunderbolt that will dash him to pieces if he is off base.

Tense thousands watch. The fate of empires hangs on Kelly's slide.

But this is only one little detail. At the same time there is to be seen the great battle between pitcher and batter and also the runner trying to steal home from third base. A good game is a three-ringed circus with a tingle of excitement for every moment. When a base hit is made, with two men on bases in a close game, lightning looks slow and poky in comparison with the way things happen out on the diamond; the ball sizzles about, burning the air, the men on the field dart like streaks, while on the stands twenty thousand madmen worship their gods with a great outcry.

Such is baseball, our baseball! A game that clutches spectators and squeezes them till they yell; a game that makes centenarians dance and howl and throw peanut shells at the umpire. There's nothing like it in the way of games. Maybe the Spanish bull-fight comes next—when you get the real thing. But even in that there's only one thing to watch—the bull—and he isn't working all the time. We'd have to go back to Nero's times, when Rome flowed into the Coliseum, sixty thousand strong, to watch the gladiators and the beasts, in order to match the excitement of a first-class game of ball.

Take that triple play made by our boys in Cincinnati recently. It was the sixth inning and the score was a tie. Cincinnati was at the bat, with nobody out, a man on first base and another on second. Kelly, the batsman, hits the ball to Alperman, who throws to Lewis, on second base, Lewis returns the ball to first base, Hummell, who throws it to Bergen, the catcher, just in time to catch Huggins, at the end of a desperate slide. There was action—three men out—in an eye-winking—a perfect triple play by our boys, a thing only seen once in five years or more. . . .

When American baseball was first played in England—thirty years ago—the only extraordinary thing the Englishmen saw in it was the sliding. They were willing to admit that that was wonderful; the Prince of Wales, who is now King, was especially interested, tho I doubt that he ever tried it. . . .

Sometimes an outfielder chasing a high fly that is going over his head runs forty yards and reaching out his hands catches the ball with his back turned to the direction from which it came. It is not uncommon to see a fielder run a hundred feet, launch himself like a spear along the ground with one hand far outstretched and seize the ball, that has come a hundred and fifty yards, before it can touch the earth.

There is great science in throwing in from the outfield, because of the force and accuracy necessary; there is science in base-running and sliding. The "hook slide," for instance, where a man comes to the home plate on his hip, presenting only his foot for the possible touch of the ball in the catcher's hands—that is a work of thought and erudition.

But baseball science reaches its climax in the pitching. There's nothing in any other game comparable with the wonders accomplished there. The pitcher takes a sphere, makes it travel in a right line for fifty feet and then make a violent curve outward or inward, according to the twist he puts upon it. This is the thing that the scientists declared to be impossible, because of the nature of the sphere and the constitution of the air.   Yet the pitchers are doing it every day, with every ball they deliver, and the scientists have to guess again.

From the pitcher's box to the batter's stand is sixty feet; the pitcher can send the ball so that it travels fifty-seven feet straight, then shoots aside or drops at so sharp an angle that in the remaining three feet it drops or turns aside two feet.

. . . The players number millions, when all the schoolboys, little and big, are counted in, and even if all except the professional and semi-professional are excluded from the reckoning there is still a great army left. . . .

Players come into the big leagues after a long, hard apprenticeship. All the way from the schoolboy at the bottom to the expert at the top the process of elimination is going on—the struggle for the survival of the fittest.   It is probable that 500,000 boys today have the ambition to rise to the top in professional baseball and blaze upon the world another Rusie or Roger Conner, "Buck" Ewing or Pop Anson. Some lose the notion at sight of higher prizes, some weaken and are found wanting; only a few get thru and they are the pick of the pick. . . .

Some men like Pop Anson, of the Chicago team, can stay at the top in baseball for twenty years.   I've been a professional ball player for fifteen years, tho I'm a doctor of dentistry.   Daly has been a long time in the big leagues; Pat Donovan has been at the top for fifteen years; Clark Griffith, the pitcher, twelve or fourteen years, and many others from ten to twenty years.

But when the old ball player has done with the game that does not mean that he has done with the world.   When I have fielded my last ball I will practice dentistry.

The old players who have long retired are in all sorts of business. Some are lawyers, like Johnny Ward and Dave Fultz; some physicians, like Dr. Gunning; Amos Rusie is working in a lumber yard in Vincennes, Indiana; Mike Sullivan was on the Governor's staff in Boston till he died; Charley Ganzell, the Boston's old catcher, is a traveling salesman; Jim O'Rourke, formerly of the New Yorks, is playing ball today.   He owns his own club and grounds, and has a son playing on the same team with him—Connecticut State League. Roger Conner, the New York's old catcher, is a large property owner in Cincinnati; "Buck" Ewing is in business in Cincinnati.   People who remember Arlie Latham will be glad to learn his fate. Arlie was one of the greatest kickers ever seen, the leader of riots and plague of umpires. So they've made him an umpire, and crowds daily heap contumely upon him.

I think interest in baseball is going up. We get crowds of 25,000 on great occasions, tho the crowds are limited by the fact that all the seats must be back of the foul lines, while the Romans circled them all the way round the Hippodrome.

And it is a good thing for the country that baseball has such a grip. Its influence is all for good. A ball player must be an athlete and an athlete must be temperate.

J. P. Casey, in *The Independent* (August 16, 1906), LXI, 375–378 *passim*.

---

162. Racing an Avalanche (1912)

BY ENOS A. MILLS

Mills was a remarkable nature writer, his field of study mainly in the West. Similar adventures will be found related in a number of travel books.

I HAD gone into the San Juan Mountains during the first week in March to learn something of the laws which govern snow slides, to get a fuller idea of their power and destructiveness, and also with the hope of seeing them in wild, magnificent action. Everywhere, except on wind-swept points, the winter's snows lay deep. Conditions for slide movement were so favorable it seemed probable that, during the next few days at least, one would "run" or chute down every gulch that led from the summit. I climbed on skees well to the top of the range. By waiting on spurs and ridges I saw several thrilling exhibitions.

It was an exciting experience, but at the close of one great day the clear weather that had prevailed came to an end. From the table-like summit I watched hundreds of splendid clouds slowly advance, take their places, mass, and form fluffy seas in valley and canyons just below my level. They submerged the low places in the plateau, and torn, silver-gray masses of mists surrounded crags and headlands.

The sunset promised to be wonderful, but suddenly the mists came surging past my feet and threatened to shut out the view. Hurriedly climbing a promontory, I watched from it a many-colored sunset change and fade over mist-wreathed spires, and swelling, peak-torn seas. But the cloud-masses were rising, and suddenly points and peaks began to settle out of sight; then a dash of frosty mists, and my promontory sank into the sea. The light vanished from the heights, and I was caught in dense, frosty clouds, and winter snows without a star.

I had left my skees at the foot of the promontory, and climbed up by my fingers and toes over the rocks without great difficulty. But on starting to return I could see only a few inches into the frosty, sheep's-wool clouds, and quickly found that trying to get down would be a perilous pastime. The side of the promontory stood over the steep walls of the plateau, and, not caring to be tumbled overboard by a slip, I concluded that sunrise from this point would probably be worth while.

It was not bitter cold, and I was comfortably dressed; however, it was necessary to do much dancing and arm-swinging to keep warm. Snow began to fall just after the clouds closed in, and it fell rapidly without a pause until near morning. Early in the evening I began a mental review of a number of subjects, mingling with these, from time to time, vigorous practice of gymnastics or calisthenics to help pass the night and to aid in keeping warm. The first subject I thought through was Arctic exploration; then I recalled all that my mind had retained of countless stories of mountain-climbing experiences; the contents of Tyndall's "Hours of Exercise in the Alps" was most clearly recalled. I was enjoying the poetry of Burns, when broken clouds and a glowing eastern sky claimed all attention until it was light enough to get off the promontory.

Planning to go down the west side, I crossed the table-like top, found, after many trials, a break in the enormous snow-cornice, and started down the steep slope. It was a dangerous descent, for the rock was steep and smooth as a wall, and was overladen with snow which might slip at any moment. I descended slowly and with great caution, so as not to start the snow, as well as to guard against slipping and losing control of myself. It was like descending a mile of steep, snow-covered barn roof,—nothing to lay hold of and omnipresent opportunity for slipping. A short distance below the summit the clouds again were around me, and I could see only a short distance. I went sideways, with my long skees, which I had now regained, at right angles to the slope; slowly, a few inches at a time, I eased myself down, planting one free skee firmly before I moved the other.

At last I reached a point where the wall was sufficiently tilted to be called a slope, though it was still too steep for safe coasting. The clouds lifted and were floating away, while the sun made the mountains of snow still whiter. I paused to look back and up, to where the wall ended in the blue sky, and could not understand how I had come safely down, even with the long tacks I had made, which showed clearly up to the snow-corniced, mist-shrouded crags at the summit. I had come down the side of a precipitous amphitheatre which rose a thousand feet or more above me. A short distance down the mountain, the slopes of this amphitheatre concentrated in a narrow gulch that extended two miles or more. Altogether it was like being in an enormous frying-pan laying face up. I was in the pan just above the place where the gulch handle joined.

It was a bad place to get out of, and thousands of tons of snow clinging to the steeps and sagging from corniced crests ready to slip, plunge down, and sweep the very spot on which I stood, showed most impressively that it was a perilous place to be in.

As I stood gazing upward and wondering how the snow ever could have held while I came down over it, there suddenly appeared on the upper steeps an upburst as from an explosion. Along several hundred feet of cornice, sprays and clouds of snow dashed and filled the air. An upward breeze curled and swept the top of this cloud over the crest in an inverted cascade.

All this showed for a few seconds until the snowy spray began to separate and vanish in the air. The snow-cloud settled downward and began to roll forward. Then monsters of massed snow appeared beneath the front of the cloud and plunged down the slopes. Wildly, grandly they dragged the entire snow-cloud in their wake. At the same instant the remainder of the snow-cornice was suddenly enveloped in another explosive snow-cloud effect.

A general slide had started. I whirled to escape, pointed my skees down the slope,—and went. In less than half a minute a tremendous snow avalanche, one hundred or perhaps two hundred feet deep and

five or six hundred feet long, thundered over the spot where I had
stood.

There was no chance to dodge, no time to climb out of the way.
The only hope of escape lay in outrunning the magnificent monster.
It came crashing and thundering after me as swift as a gale and more
all-sweeping and destructive than an earthquake tidal wave.

I made a desperate start. Friction almost ceases to be a factor
with skees on a snowy steep, and in less than a hundred yards I was
going like the wind. For the first quarter of a mile, to the upper end
of the gulch, was smooth coasting, and down this I shot, with the
avalanche, comet-tailed with snow-dust in, close pursuit. A race for
life was on.

The gulch down which I must go began with a rocky gorge and
continued downward, an enormous U-shaped depression between high
mountain-ridges. Here and there it expanded and then contracted,
and it was broken with granite crags and ribs. It was piled and bris-
tled with ten thousand fire-killed trees. To coast through all these
snow-clad obstructions at breakneck speed would be taking the maximum number of life-and-death chances in the minimum amount of
time. The worst of it all was that I had never been through the place.
And bad enough, too, was the fact that a ridge thrust in from the left
and completely hid the beginning of the gulch.

As I shot across the lower point of the ridge, about to plunge blindly
into the gorge, I thought of the possibility of becoming entangled in
the hedge-like thickets of dwarfed, gnarled timberline trees. I also
realized that I might dash against a cliff or plunge into a deep canyon.
Of course I might strike an open way, but certain it was that I could
not stop, nor see the beginning of the gorge, nor tell what I should
strike when I shot over the ridge.

It was a second of most intense concern as I cleared the ridge blindly
to go into what lay below and beyond. It was like leaping into the
dark, and with the leap turning on the all-revealing light. As I
cleared the ridge, there was just time to pull myself together for a
forty-odd-foot leap across one arm of the horseshoe-shaped end of the
gorge. In all my wild mountainside coasts on skees, never have I
sped as swiftly as when I made this mad flight. As I shot through the
air, I had a glimpse down into the pointed, snow-laden tops of a few
tall fir trees that were firmly rooted among the rocks in the bottom

of the gorge. Luckily I cleared the gorge and landed in a good place; but so narrowly did I miss the corner of a cliff that my shadow collided with it.

There was no time to bid farewell to fears when the slide started, nor to entertain them while running away from it. Instinct put me to flight; the situation set my wits working at their best, and, once started, I could neither stop nor look back; and so thick and fast did obstructions and dangers rise before me that only dimly and incidentally did I think of the oncoming danger behind.

I came down on the farther side of the gorge, to glance forward like an arrow. There was only an instant to shape my course and direct my flight across the second arm of the gorge, over which I leaped from a high place, sailing far above the snow-mantled trees and boulders in the bottom. My senses were keenly alert, and I remember noticing the shadows of the fir trees on the white snow and hearing while still in the air the brave, cheery notes of a chickadee; then the snowslide on my trail, less than an eighth of a mile behind, plunged into the gorge with a thundering crash. I came back to the snow on the lower side, and went skimming down the slope with the slide only a few seconds behind.

Fortunately most of the fallen masses of trees were buried, though a few broken limbs peeped through the snow to snag or trip me. How I ever dodged my way through the thickly standing tree growths is one feature of the experience that was too swift for recollection. Numerous factors presented themselves which should have done much to dispel mental procrastination and develop decision. There were scores of progressive propositions to decide within a few seconds; should I dodge that tree on the left side and duck under low limbs just beyond, or dodge to the right and scrape that pile of rocks? These, with my speed, required instant decision and action.

With almost uncontrollable rapidity I shot out into a small, nearly level glacier meadow, and had a brief rest from swift decisions and oncoming dangers. How relieved my weary brain felt, with nothing to decide about dodging! As though starved for thought material, I wondered if there were willows buried beneath the snow. Sharp pains in my left hand compelled attention, and showed my left arm drawn tightly against my breast, with fingers and thumb spread to the fullest, and all their muscles tense.

The lower edge of the meadow was almost blockaded with a dense growth of fire-killed trees. Fortunately the easy slope here had so checked my speed that I was able to dodge safely through, but the heavy slide swept across the meadow after me with undiminished speed, and came crashing into the dead trees so close to me that broken limbs were flung flying past as I shot down off a steep moraine less than one hundred feet ahead.

All the way down I had hoped to find a side canyon into which I might dodge. I was going too rapidly to enter the one I had seen. As I coasted off the moraine it flashed through my mind that I had once heard a prospector say it was only a quarter of a mile from Aspen Gulch up to the meadows. Aspen Gulch came in on the right, as the now widening track seemed to indicate.

At the bottom of the moraine I was forced between two trees that stood close together, and a broken limb of one pierced my open coat just beneath the left armhole, and slit the coat to the bottom. My momentum and the resistance of the strong material gave me such a shock that I was flung off my balance, and my left skee smashed against a tree. Two feet of the heel was broken off and the remainder split. I managed to avoid falling, but had to check my speed with my staff for fear of a worse accident.

Battling breakers with a broken oar or racing with a broken skee are struggles of short duration. The slide did not slow down, and so closely did it crowd me that, through the crashing of trees as it struck them down, I could hear the rocks and splintered timbers in its mass grinding together and thudding gainst obstructions over which it swept. These sounds, and flying, broken limbs cried to me "Faster!" and as I started to descend another steep moraine, I threw away my staff and "let go." I simply flashed down the slope, dodged and rounded a cliff, turned awkwardly into Aspen Gulch, and tumbled heels over head—into safety.

Then I picked myself up, to see the slide go by within twenty feet, with great broken trees sticking out of its side, and a snow-cloud dragging above.

Enos A. Mills, *The Spell of the Rockies* (Boston, Houghton Mifflin Co., 1912), 3–14 *passim*. Reprinted by special permission of the publishers.

163. Waters of the Yosemite (1917)

BY EX-PRESIDENT CAROLINE HAZARD

Miss Hazard was President of Wellesley College from 1899 to 1910. On the national parks, see publications of the National Park Service and Geological Survey.

I

SUCH a stupendous leap! The mighty stream
　　Aghast with that achievement staggers in distress,
Becomes a shadowy thing of dream
　　Upon the brink of nothingness.
Some giant archipelago of air
　　Obtruding from the clouds descends.
With wavering outline, and a flare
　　Of iridescent color, trembles, blends,
　　Discloses dewy slopes, Titania's emerald grass,
　　Chasm and precipice Behemoth could not pass.
Rolling empurpled on the cloudless day
　　Tumultuous reveller, foaming, seething
With billows pearly as the driven spray
　　Of ocean wave, subsiding, heaving,
It floats between the earth and sky,
For sky too low, for earth too high,
　　A marvel and a wonder
　　Of color and of thunder

II

For it has life of sound.
　　The strong vibrations of the primal note
That shakes the solid ground,
　　That finds its echo in the song-bird's throat,
That shapes the life of man—
　　Reverberations shouting to the spheres
　　Atune with Saturn, and the Milky Way,
The sound that o'er creation ran
　　The gamut of its loves and fears
　　Night and day

Roars and riots in the ears
A deafening, stunning buffet of noise,
A strong, tumultuous draft of joys,
With rhythmic rise and fall,
    A bugle call
That stoops to a caress
    Of tenderness.

III

Blue and pink and amethyst
The sun-transfigured mist
Drop by drop is reassembled, caught
    Upon the giant crags. The thing of dream
Is still of crystal beauty, taught
    Once more the use of earth; a limpid stream
Rolls through lush meadows, emerald green,
    Green as the moon in Oriental night,
    Blooming with flowers, starry bright,
    The heaven above transposed, unrolled
    For that clear stream to water, to enfold
With all the beauty it could glean
From that stupendous flight
    From out the quiver
Of God's delight
    To be a river.

Caroline Hazard, *The Yosemite and Other Verse* (Boston, Houghton Mifflin Co., 1917), 7-10. Reprinted by permission of the author.

164. On Moving Pictures (1926)

BY MICHAEL GROSS AND "P. W."

On the source of these poems, see note to No. 151 above. They satirize a favorite subject of the news reels, and the flowery and melodramatic language of the moving picture sub-titles, becoming rarer with the advent of talking pictures.

A. A BALLADE OF THE NEWS REEL STANDBY

TRAINS catch fire in head-on crash;
　Earthquake buries town from view;
Steeple falls at lightning flash;
Cat greets hen, who calls to woo.
Prince bids old New York adieu;
Holland Town has jubilee;
Then, as sure as two and two—
Fighting fleet puts out to sea.

Thousands cheer as net stars clash;
Boat leaves port with one-man crew;
Planes all set for polar dash;
Dress styles on Fifth Avenue.
Horse enjoys tobacco chew;
Mayor hears the Girl Scouts' plea;
Then, Good Lord! It can't be true—
Fighting fleet puts out to sea.

East side kids enjoy a splash;
Lion leaves cage as cops pursue;
Guards protect ten million cash;
Burbank shows how yenhocks grew;
Mouse brought up on kidney stew;
Jersey girl gives birth to three;
Just a moment! They're not through—
Fighting fleet puts out to sea.

L'ENVOI

Prince! It mustn't *all* be new;
Alter one detail; 'twill do;
Please omit, if just for me,
"*Fighting fleet puts out to sea.*"

MICHAEL GROSS

B. IF THE MOVIE WRITERS TAKE UP POETRY

Athwart the rock-girt isle of life
Hate, like a lusty fungus, spread
To burgeon forth revenge and strife
And raise up passion's flaming head.

Atop the gleaming hills the sun,
Blest heavenly orb of warmth and light,
Recks not that foulest deeds are done
Beneath its iridescence bright.
Hard by a peaceful verdant vale,
Afar from strife and war's alarms,
The little town of Lilydale
Nestled like a babe in arms.

And yet beside its purling streams
Men dwelt whose passions oft ran hot,
Disturbing peaceful holy dreams
Of others who dwelt near the spot.

John Vedder (played by Colwell Sward)
Weaves most dishonest plots to gain
The fortune of May Gloam, his ward
(Played by Minerva Fenton Fane).

Tense and distressed Van Diemen stands
(Van Diemen—Oswald Chester Blake),
Imprinting kisses on May's hands
As though love's frenzied thirst to slake.

Anon Vanilla Rinderpest
(Played by Elaine Mimosa Krell)
Withdraws the papers from her breast
As Vedder loudly hisses: "Hell!"

And in the village church we see
Those twain made one as Fate foretold—
The maid as virtuous as can be,
The lad of brawn with heart of gold.

.   .   .   .

The villain's foiled; life's gall he tastes;
Defeat has stalked the things he prized;
Crime's banished to the desert wastes
While love's dear dream is realized.

P. W.

Contributions to *The New York World*, collected in Franklin P. Adams, *The Second Conning Tower Book* (New York, Macy-Masius, 1927), 73–74, 127–128.

PART X

THE WORLD WAR

CHAPTER XXX — THE UNITED STATES AS A NEUTRAL

165. The United States as a Neutral (1914)

BY PROFESSOR CHARLES CHENEY HYDE

Hyde has been in the service of the State Department, and is now Professor of International Law and Diplomacy in Columbia University. This article summarizes some of the burdens of neutrality in war time.

UPON the outbreak of the European war the United States finds itself placed in a new relation to each belligerent Power, and suddenly subjected to a variety of duties, and possessed of certain rights that accrue only in such abnormal times. With a merchant marine shrunken to insignificance, with a vast export trade threatened with paralysis by the lack of neutral bottoms, and with American citizens stranded by tens of thousands on European soil, we nevertheless face a situation that Washington would have rejoiced to substitute for that which confronted him in 1793, for to-day the United States as a neutral enjoys rights that were not dreamed of at the close of the eighteenth century; and those rights are in large degree codified.

To The Hague Conventions of 1907, concerning the rights and duties of neutral powers in naval war, and the rights and duties of neutral powers and persons in case of war on land, the United States is, happily, a party. It has also accepted the Declaration of London of 1909, concerning the laws of naval war. The purpose of that agreement was to make clear the law to be applied by the proposed International Prize Court, the arrangement for the establishment of which was

formulated at The Hague in 1907. Though the powers have not established the Prize Court or accepted generally the Declaration of
London, the United States has formally ratified both agreements.
By so doing it has recorded its approval of the rules enunciated in the
latter document. It cannot, therefore, complain of the conduct of any
belligerent which may seek to conform to or rely upon them. Although
the Parliament of Great Britain has acted adversely upon the Declaration of London, that country is, nevertheless, free to change its position and to make that arrangement the guide of its own prize courts.
Deriving their law from that source, their decisions cannot be denounced by us as unjust. For these several codifications the United
States has had to pay a price the extent of which is hardly yet appreciated. However useful may be the knowledge at the very commencement of hostilities of what a neutral may reasonably expect, the rules
themselves are in certain respects so adverse to interests of such a state
that it is only through the grim experience of a general European war
that the United States can fairly estimate how well it has conserved
its vital interests in accepting as law principles that may be relentlessly
applied.

According to the Hague Conventions, the United States as a government is obliged to refrain from taking any part in the war. Impartial participation does not suffice. We could not excuse the sale
of arms to Germany by pleading readiness to supply likewise France
or Russia. The scope of the duty of abstention is broad. The government must not furnish a belligerent with anything that will serve to
increase its fighting power, such as ammunition or other war material,
or warships. Incidental to this general duty to abstain from participation, the neutral finds itself burdened with a still more onerous duty to
prevent its territory and resources from being employed to strengthen
the military or naval power of a belligerent. The diligence required
of a neutral is measured by the "means at its disposal." Those means
must be used to prevent the commission of war-like acts within its
waters, or the passage of belligerent troops over its territory. The
neutral is obviously not responsible for what it is powerless to prevent.

From the rules of the Treaty of Washington of 1871, which made
possible the Geneva Arbitration of the so-called Alabama Claims, has
been derived the well-known principle expressed in happier terms in
1907, that "a neutral Government is bound to employ the means at

its disposal to prevent the fitting out or arming of any vessel within its jurisdiction which it has reason to believe is intended to cruise, or engage in hostile operations, against a Power with which that Government is at peace." The same vigilance is required of a neutral to prevent the departure from its territory of a vessel there adapted entirely or partly for warlike use, and intended to cruise or engage in hostile operations. Pursuant to this obligation the United States has already taken extraordinary precautions to prevent the departure from Atlantic ports of merchant vessels sailing under belligerent flags if equipped in such a way as to fight for their own countries, and under contract for public service in case of war. . . .

Whether war is waged on land or sea, neutral territory is deemed inviolable. As to this requirement The Hague Conventions are explicit. Acts of war in neutral waters are forbidden. Thus if the *Kronprinzessin Cecilie* had been captured by any enemy cruiser just as she entered Frenchman's Bay on August 4th, the United States would have had good cause to demand reparation from the government of the captor, and would also have found itself compelled to demand the release of the vessel. A prize court can not be set up on neutral territory or in neutral waters. Nor can belligerent warships make use of such waters for the purpose of increasing supplies of war material or of completing their crews, or as a base of operations against the enemy.

For numerous purposes a belligerent warship may endeavor to make use of neutral waters. The Hague Convention of 1907 indicates the scope of the privileges that such a vessel may be permitted to enjoy, and thereby enables the neutral to follow with certainty a course that shall not expose it to the charge of unneutral conduct. Let us consider a situation that might arise. A French cruiser, short of coal and provisions, and in an unseaworthy condition, is pursued by the enemy, and puts into Portland harbor to escape capture and to rehabilitate herself generally. Just inside of Cushing's Island she finds herself in the unwelcome company of a German warship that made the same port a few hours earlier. The Hague Convention has marked out the general course which the United States should follow; and by his Proclamation of Neutrality, President Wilson has indicated with precision what we would permit. Accordingly, the French ship would be allowed fuel sufficient to enable her to reach her nearest home port, or half of that amount if she were rigged to go under sail and also be propelled by steam. Although the United States could, without impropriety, if it had adopted that method of determining the amount of fuel to be supplied, allow the vessel to fill its bunkers built to carry fuel, and thereby greatly increase her efficiency, the President has announced a rule that is consistent with our previous policy and in harmony with what was, prior to 1907, generally regarded as sound practice. The latitude accorded the neutral in 1907 was not sought by the United States, was vigorously opposed by Great Britain, and was the result of a compromise to satisfy the far-reaching demands of Germany. With respect to provisions, the French ship could supply herself with garlic and Aroostook County potatoes *ad libitum*, so long as the revictualing did not exceed the so-called "peace standard."

If it were in a seaworthy condition the German cruiser would be obliged to depart within twenty-four hours after its arrival. The French vessel might, however, be allowed additional time if needed for recoaling or repairs. The latter might necessarily consume a few days. Repairs would not be permitted that would serve to do more than place the ship in a seaworthy condition, and even such repairs would not be allowed if they necessitated a long sojourn. If, as in the case of the Russian ship *Lena*, that entered San Francisco harbor in September, 1904, during the Russian-Japanese war, necessary repairs would require a stay of several weeks or months, the vessel would be promptly interned by the United States. By interning the ship the United States would be taking measures to render her incapable of putting to sea during the war.

It was declared in 1907 that the citizens of a state which is not taking part in the war are considered as neutrals. To the Americans that are now in belligerent European countries that status is precious. It enables the possessor to escape numerous burdens which the state that is engaged in war justly and of necessity imposes upon its own citizens. One cannot, however, avail himself of his neutrality if he commits acts against a belligerent, or if he voluntarily enlists in the ranks of a party to the conflict. There are, nevertheless, services which the neutral citizen on belligerent soil may render without losing his distinctive character. Americans in Paris or Berlin might, for example, organize for the purpose of assisting in matters of police or civil administration. They might also furnish loans (if their means permitted) to one of the belligerents in whose territory they did not reside. . . .

To the people of the United States as a whole the war presents no graver aspect than in its bearing upon our right to export and transport to the belligerent countries food, clothing, fuel, and other things known as conditional contraband. To make clear the problem now confronting us a brief explanation of the law is necessary. "Contraband" is the term employed to describe an article which is liable to capture because of its hostile destination. Contraband is subject to capture on a neutral vessel and is liable to condemnation. Goods which belong to the owner of the contraband and which are on board the same vessel are also liable to condemnation. Moreover, according to the Declaration of London, the vessel carrying such articles may be confiscated if the contraband forms "by value, by weight, by volume, or by freight, more than half the cargo." Maritime states have long been aware of the importance of the distinction between articles adapted solely for use in war, such as guns and projectiles, and those susceptible of use in the pursuit of peace as well as in that of war, such as food and coal. Articles of the former class have come to be known as absolute contraband, those of the latter as conditional contraband. The purpose of the distinction is to limit the right to capture articles of the latter kind to occasions when they are destined for an essentially hostile end, and to permit the capture of those of the former kind whenever they are bound for the territory of a state engaged in war. In order to protect neutral commerce from interference, the United States has struggled hard for recognition of the principle that what is capable of feeding and clothing, and otherwise ministering to the sustenance of the people of a belligerent state, should not be subject to capture and condemnation, unless shown to be not only capable of use in war, but also destined for that use. Though maritime states are not indisposed to accept this principle, there has been diversity of opinion respecting, first, what articles should be treated as conditional contraband, and secondly, under what circumstances articles recognized as such should be subject to capture. The Declaration of London appears to have solved the first difficulty by specifying in appropriate and careful lists certain articles as absolute, and others as conditional contraband (and still others as not contraband at all). Thus arms of all kinds, gun-mountings, clothing and harness of a distinctively military character, animals suitable for use in war, and armor-plate are among the articles placed in the first category. They are subject to capture if destined to territory belonging to or occupied by the enemy. This is true whether the carriage of the goods is direct, or entails transshipment or subsequent transport by land. What is decisive is the destination, not of the vessel but of the goods. Thus a consignment of uniforms, shipped from New York on an American vessel bound for Naples or any other neutral European port, would be subject to capture, even within sight of Nantucket, if it were shown that the ultimate destination of the goods was Trieste.

Articles in the second category, and described by the Declaration of London as conditional contraband, include foodstuffs, gold and silver, paper money, boots and shoes, vehicles, material for telephones and telegraph, fuel, lubricants, and harness. These articles furnish a substantial portion of the export trade of the United States.

The second difficulty already noted—concerning when conditional contraband is subject to capture—is the all-important question before the United States to-day. In more concrete and simpler form the question is: When is such contraband to be deemed to be intended for a hostile use so as to justify its capture? The vital significance of the answer that the belligerents may give is hardly yet appreciated. Thus far popular attention in this country has been focussed on the lack of American and other neutral ships available for our foreign trade. Relying upon the assurance that "free ships make free goods," we have concerned ourselves about vehicles of transportation rather than with the safety of our produce. It is important to note what assurance the Declaration of London affords. It is there provided that conditional contraband is liable to capture if shown to be destined for the use of the armed forces of a belligerent, or for a department of its Government unless, in the latter case, circumstances show that the goods cannot in fact be used for the purposes of the war. (This exception is not, however, applicable to a consignment of gold or silver, or paper money.) It is further provided that a hostile destination is presumed to exist in case the goods are consigned, not only to enemy authorities, but also to a contractor in the enemy country who as a matter of common knowledge supplies articles of the same kind to the enemy. Again, a similar presumption arises if the goods are consigned to a fortified place belonging to the enemy or to another place serving as base for its forces.

In the meantime American exporters must face the fact that, if propriety of conduct is to be tested by the Declaration of London, the belligerent Powers are in a position to capture and condemn food-stuffs, coal, and other articles within the same category, with an ease that renders shadowy and dangerously vague the distinction between what is conditional and what is absolute contraband.

Charles Cheney Hyde, in *World's Work*, September, 1914 (Garden City, Double-day, Page, 1914), 126–128 *passim*.

---◆---

166. An Ambassador on Duty (1914)

BY AMBASSADOR WALTER HINES PAGE

For Page, see No 133 above. See also, for a criticism of his conduct as Ambas-sador, No. 167 below. This is one of his letters to President Wilson, to whom he was accustomed to make elaborate personal reports. For another account of dip-lomatic problems at the outbreak of the war, see James W. Gerard, *My Four Years in Germany*.

To the President

London, Sunday, Aug. 9, 1914.

DEAR MR. PRESIDENT:
God save us! What a week it has been! Last Sunday I was down here at the cottage I have taken for the summer—an hour out of London—uneasy because of the apparent danger and of what Sir Edward Grey had told me. During the day people began to go to the Embassy, but not in great numbers—merely to ask what they should do in case of war. The Secretary whom I had left in charge on Sunday telephoned me every few hours and laughingly told funny experiences with nervous women who came in and asked absurd questions. Of course, we all knew the grave danger that war might come but nobody could by the wildest imagination guess at what awaited us. On Mon-day I was at the Embassy earlier than I think I had ever been there before and every member of the staff was already on duty. Before breakfast time the place was filled—packed like sardines. This was

two days before war was declared. There was no chance to talk to individuals, such was the jam. I got on a chair and explained that I had already telegraphed to Washington—on Saturday—suggesting the sending of money and ships, and asking them to be patient. I made a speech to them several times during the day, and kept the Secretaries doing so at intervals. More than 2,000 Americans crowded into those offices (which are not large) that day. We were kept there till two o'clock in the morning. The Embassy has not been closed since.

Mr. Kent of the Bankers' Trust Company in New York volunteered to form an American Citizens' Relief Committee. He and other men of experience and influence organized themselves at the Savoy Hotel. The hotel gave the use of nearly a whole floor. They organized themselves quickly and admirably and got information about steamships and currency, etc. We began to send callers at the Embassy to this Committee for such information. The banks were all closed for four days. These men got money enough—put it up themselves and used their English banking friends for help—to relieve all cases of actual want of cash that came to them. Tuesday the crowd at the Embassy was still great but smaller. The big space at the Savoy Hotel gave them room to talk to one another and to get relief for immediate needs. By that time I had accepted the volunteer services of five or six men to help us explain to the people—and they have all worked manfully day and night. We now have an orderly organization at four places: The Embassy, the Consul-General's Office, the Savoy, and the American Society in London, and everything is going well. Those two first days, there was, of course, great confusion. Crazy men and weeping women were imploring and cursing and demanding—God knows it was bedlam turned loose. I have been called a man of the greatest genius for an emergency by some, by others a damned fool, by others every epithet between these extremes. Men shook English banknotes in my face and demanded United States money and swore our Government and its agents ought all to be shot. Women expected me to hand them steamship tickets home. When some found out that they could not get tickets on the transports (which they assumed would sail the next day) they accused me of favouritism. These absurd experiences will give you a hint of the panic. But now it has worked out all right, thanks to the Savoy Committee and other helpers.

Meantime, of course, our telegrams and mail increased almost as much as our callers. I have filled the place with stenographers, I have got the Savoy people to answer certain classes of letters, and we have caught up. My own time and the time of two of the secretaries has been almost wholly taken with governmental problems; hundreds of questions have come in from every quarter that were never asked before. But even with them we have now practically caught up—it has been a wonderful week!

Then the Austrian Ambassador came to give up his Embassy—to have me take over his business. Every detail was arranged. The next morning I called on him to assume charge and to say good-bye, when he told me that he was not yet going! That was a stroke of genius by Sir Edward Grey, who informed him that Austria had not given England cause for war. That *may* work out, or it may not. Pray Heaven it may! Poor Mensdorff, the Austrian Ambassador, does not know where he is. He is practically shut up in his guarded Embassy, weeping and waiting the decree of fate.

Then came the declaration of war, most dramatically. Tuesday night, five minutes after the ultimatum had expired, the Admiralty telegraphed to the fleet "Go." In a few minutes the answer came back "Off." Soldiers began to march through the city going to the railway stations. An indescribable crowd so blocked the streets about the Admiralty, the War Office, and the Foreign Office, that at one o'clock in the morning I had to drive in my car by other streets to get home.

The next day the German Embassy was turned over to me. I went to see the German Ambassador at three o'clock in the afternoon. He came down in his pajamas, a crazy man. I feared he might literally go mad. He is of the anti-war party and he had done his best and utterly failed. This interview was one of the most pathetic experiences of my life. The poor man had not slept for several nights. Then came the crowds of frightened Germans, afraid they would be arrested. They besieged the German Embassy and our Embassy. I put one of our naval officers in the German Embassy, put the United States seal on the door to protect it, and we began business there, too. Our naval officer has moved in—sleeps there. He has an assistant, a stenographer, a messenger: and I gave him the German automobile and chauffeur and two English servants that were left there. He has the job well in hand now, under my and Laughlin's supervision. But this has brought still another new lot of diplomatic and governmental problems—a lot of them. Three enormous German banks in London have, of course, been closed. Their managers pray for my aid. Howling women come and say their innocent German husbands have been arrested as spies. English, Germans, Americans—everybody has daughters and wives and invalid grandmothers alone in Germany. In God's name, they ask, what can I do for them? Here come stacks of letters sent under the impression that I can send them to Germany. But the German business is already well in hand and I think that that will take little of my own time and will give little trouble. I shall send a report about it in detail to the Department the very first day I can find time to write it. In spite of the effort of the English Government to remain at peace with Austria, I fear I shall yet have the Austrian Embassy too. But I can attend to it.

Now, however, comes the financial job of wisely using the $300,000 which I shall have to-morrow. I am using Mr. Chandler Anderson as counsel, of course; I have appointed a Committee—Skinner, the Consul-General, Lieut. Commander McCrary of our Navy, Kent of the Bankers' Trust Company, New York, and one other man yet to be chosen—to advise, after investigation, about every proposed expenditure. . . .

. . . I find it hard to get about much. People stop me on the street, follow me to luncheon, grab me as I come out of any committee meeting—to know my opinion of this or that—how can they get home? Will such-and-such a boat fly the American flag? Why did I take the German Embassy? I have to fight my way about and rush to an automobile. I have had to buy me a second one to keep up the racket. Buy?—no—only bargain for it, for I have not any money. But everybody is considerate, and that makes no matter for the moment. This little cottage is in an out-of-the-way place, twenty-five miles from London, where I am trying to write and sleep, has been found by people to-day, who come in automobiles to know how they may reach their sick kinspeople in Germany. I have not had a bath for three days: as soon as I got in the tub, the telephone rang an "urgent" call!

Upon my word, if one could forget the awful tragedy, all this experience would be worth a lifetime of commonplace. One surprise follows another so rapidly that one loses all sense of time: it seems an age since last Sunday.

I shall never forget Sir Edward Grey's telling me of the ultimatum—while he wept; nor the poor German Ambassador who has lost in his high game—almost a demented man; nor the King as he declaimed at me for half-an-hour and threw up his hands and said, "My God, Mr. Page, what else could we do?" Nor the Austrian Ambassador's wringing his hands and weeping and crying out, "My dear Colleague, my dear Colleague." . . .

. . . Everybody has forgotten what war means—forgotten that folks get hurt. But they are coming around to it now. A United States Senator telegraphs me: "Send my wife and daughter home on the first ship." Ladies and gentlemen filled the steerage of that ship—not a bunk left; and his wife and daughter are found three days later sitting in a swell hotel waiting for me to bring them stateroom tickets on a silver tray! One of my young fellows in the Embassy rushes into my office saying that a man from Boston, with letters of introduction from Senators and Governors and Secretaries, et al., was demanding tickets of admission to a picture gallery, and a secretary to escort him there.

"What shall I do with him?"

"Put his proposal to a vote of the 200 Americans in the room and see them draw and quarter him."

I have not yet heard what happened. . . .

And this awful tragedy moves on to—what? We do not know what is really happening, so strict is the censorship. But it seems inevitable to me that Germany will be beaten, that the horrid period of alliances and armaments will not come again, that England will gain even more of the earth's surface, that Russia may next play the menace; that all Europe (as much as survives) will be bankrupt; that relatively we shall be immensely stronger financially and politically—there must surely come many great changes—very many, yet undreamed of. Be ready; for you will be called on to compose this huge quarrel. I thank Heaven for many things—first, the Atlantic Ocean; second, that you refrained from war in Mexico; third, that we kept our treaty—the canal tolls victory, I mean. Now, when all this half of the world will suffer the unspeakable brutalization of war, we shall preserve our moral strength, our political powers, and our ideals.

God save us!

W. H. P.

From *The Life and Letters of Walter H. Page*, edited by Burton J. Hendrick (Garden City, copyright 1922, Doubleday, Page and Company), 303–310 *passim*.

---

167. An Impressionable Diplomat (1915)

BY C. HARTLEY GRATTAN (1925)

For Page, see No. 133 above. One of his letters describing his own work is given in No. 166 above.—Bibliography: Burton J. Hendrick, *Life and Letters of Walter H. Page.*

PAGE had been born in a North Carolina hamlet; the gaudy trappings of royalty naturally máde a powerful impression upon him. Things went on swimmingly, almost deliriously, for a year. He went everywhere, got to know everybody, was soon on familiar terms with dukes, princesses and members of the Cabinet. Then, of a sudden, came the colossal shock of the war—and the era of dinners and dances gave way to an era of bitter struggle. Page's job, up to this time, had been largely ornamental. Now he was confronted by serious business. It was his job to safeguard the interests of the United States in a world at strife—in particular, to safeguard such rights as had been wrung from Great Britain, the country to which he was accredited, after more than a century of diplomatic and military combat. On August 11, 1914, President Wilson issued his neutrality proclamation. In it were these sentences:

We must be impartial in thought as well as in action; we must put a curb on our sentiments as well as upon every transaction that might be construed as a preference of one party to the struggle before another. . . . Every man who really loves America will act and speak in the true spirit of neutrality, which is the spirit of impartiality and fairness and friendliness to all concerned.

Here is a plain definition of "one who really loves America." To what extent did Mr. Page meet it?

"Mr. Page had one fine qualification for his post," a British statesman once remarked to B. J. Hendrick. "From the beginning he saw
that there was a right and a wrong to the matter. He did not believe
that Great Britain and Germany were equally to blame. He believed
that Great Britain was right and that Germany was wrong." Page,
in fact, swallowed the whole of the British propaganda, hook, bait
and sinker. On September 11, 1914, he wrote to President Wilson:
"Can anyone longer disbelieve the completely barbarous behavior
of Prussians?" Thus early was he convinced. From that time onward his letters become little better than powerful arguments for the
British case, and hysterical pleas for the United States to back up
England, regardless of all disputes regarding English violations of
American rights. On September 22, he wrote to Colonel House:
"If Germany should win, our Monroe Doctrine would at once be shot
in two, and we should have to get 'out of the sun.' . . . If England
wins . . . England will not need our friendship as much as she now
needs it." . . . He made no effort to conceal his violently pro-
English attitude. He even arrogated to himself, public servant
though he was, the right to pass upon the legitimacy of American
neutrality. President Wilson had proclaimed that "we must be
impartial in thought as well as action." Page made little attempt
to be either and he afterward wrote: "The President and the government in their insistence upon the moral quality of neutrality, missed
the larger meaning of the war. It is at bottom nothing but the effort
of the Berlin absolute monarch and his group to impose their will on
as large a part of the world as they can overrun. The President
started out with the idea that it was a war brought on by many obscure causes—economic and the like, and he thus missed its whole
meaning."

But did he? Didn't Mr. Page, rather, give merely a succinct
summary of what the British propaganda service said the war was
about? He never seemed for a minute to realize that the English as
well as their enemies resorted to propaganda. He even swallowed
the Belgian atrocity stories, for he wrote to Colonel House on November 12, 1915, that but for the British fleet London would be ruined
and plundered . . . and thousands of English women would be
violated—"just as dead French girls are found in many German
trenches that have been taken in France." He continually denounced

alleged German opinions as propaganda, but supported English opinions, no matter how wild and absurd, as the truth. "The Allied propaganda," says Bertrand Russell, "through British control of the cables secured wider publicity than that of Germany, and achieved, a notable success in winning the sympathy, and ultimately the co-operation of the United States." This propaganda, in fact, achieved the amazing *coup* of writing, to all intents and purposes, the official communications of the American ambassador to England!

But Page's love affair did not run quite smoothly. In December, 1914, Colonel House wrote to him: "The President wished me to ask you to please be more careful not to express any unneutral feeling. . . . He said that both Mr. Bryan and Mr. Lansing had remarked upon your leaning in that direction." . . . That warning, however, did not deter Page, and even a casual reading of his letters reveals how thoroughly unneutral and pro-Ally he was during all the period of American neutrality. A constant complaint of his was that the demands of the American State Department, and the pronouncements of Wilson, were bringing the United States into official and popular disfavor in England. He seems to have deliberately disobeyed his instructions intimating to Grey that the American notes of protest against English acts upon the high seas were mere matters of form, and not intended to be taken seriously. He thus weakened his own government, and greatly strengthened England, and so encouraged her violation of the rights of neutrals, and particularly of the rights of the United States. What Page worried about most was the possibility that any effort to safeguard the latter would make the English angry, and thus imperil his Anglo-American alliance. He shared precisely the English attitude toward their violation, and did his best to minimize their significance. His railings against Lansing and Polk and the other international lawyers at Washington were so vociferous and prolonged that Mr. Hendrick devotes a chapter of the biography to the quarrel. His pro-English attitude completely blinded him to the significance of England's extensive violations of American neutrality and made him a consistent apologist for her. By his attitude he completely obstructed the State Department's effort to hold England to international law. . . .

. . . Many people whom the ambassador met in the course of this visit still retain memories of his fervor in "*what had now become with him a sacred cause.*" The sacred cause was to align the United States on the side of the Allies. It was Mr. Page's official, if not sacred, duty to help the State Department to hold England to international law, and so protect the rights of Americans. Instead of doing that he threw all his strength upon the other side.

When, at last, his high services to England came to fruition and the United States entered the war, Mr. Hendrick tells us that "a well-known Englishman happened to meet Page leaving his house in Grosvenor Square the day after the declaration. He stopped and shook the ambassador's hand. 'Thank God,' the Englishman said, 'that there is one hypocrite less in London today.' 'What do you mean?' asked Page. 'I mean you. Pretending all this time that you were neutral: That isn't necessary any longer.' 'You are right!' the ambassador answered as he walked on with a laugh and wave of the hand." The King of England said to him in reviewing the situation: "Ah—Ah!—we knew where *you* stood all the time."

But now we are grandly told that Englishmen "didn't know anyone could be as American as Page!"

But by far the most amazing act of Page's ambassadorship occured in connection with the *Dacia*. Mr. Hendrick embeds this incident in approving comment, and characterizes it thus: "This suggestion from Page was one of the great inspirations of the war. It amounted to little less than genius." The *Dacia* had been transferred to American registry under a law passed in the early days of the war, admitting foreign ships to American registry. The vessel was loaded with cotton, at that time (1915) not contraband. She was American-owned at the time of her sailing (her previous owners had been Germans), American-manned, flew the American flag, and had American registry according to the laws of the United States. Before the sailing England notified the State Department that the boat was considered as subject to capture, as "enemy property," implying in this notification her total disregard of the American law of registry. Mr. Page, being an American, was interested in this matter. The *Dacia* sailed. . . . To quote Mr. Hendrick, who tells the incident better than it can be paraphrased:

When matters had reached this pass Page one day dropped into the Foreign Office.

"Have you ever heard of the British fleet, Sir Edward?" he asked.

Grey admitted that he had, though the question obviously puzzled him.

"Yes," Page went on musingly. "We've all heard of the British fleet. Perhaps we have heard too much about it. Don't you think it's had too much advertising?"

The Foreign Secretary looked at Page with an expression that implied a lack of confidence in his sanity.

"But have you ever heard of the French fleet?" the American went on. "France has a fleet, too, I believe."

Sir Edward granted that.

"Don't you think that the French fleet ought to have a little advertising?"

"What on earth are you talking about?"

"Well," said Page, "There's the *Dacia*. Why not let the French fleet seize it and get some advertising?"

A gleam of understanding immediately shot across Grey's face.

. . . So the French fleet captured and condemned the *Dacia*. The American ambassador had conspired with the government to which he was accredited to bring about the seizure of an American vessel by a foreign government. No wonder his suggestion staggered even Sir Edward. Truly it was "one of the great inspirations of the war." But whose war? Certainly not America's, for all this took place in 1915, over two years before the United States entered the conflict.

Ranking perhaps next to the *Dacia* case in the forwarding of astonishing violations of international law and diplomatic usage was Page's unprecedented consent to a British request for permission to intercept and search the baggage of all American diplomatic officials below the rank of minister who happened to be taken by the British while traveling to and from their posts in Europe. The British guards at Kirkwall admitted the illegality of the procedure, but demonstrated Page's acquiescence in the practice. A number of American representatives appear to have been subjected to this amazing indignity; in one case known to the writer the British were held at bay only at the point of an impressively manipulated revolver.

In all this Mr. Page's conduct cannot be excused, as some have tried to excuse it, on the ground that he meant well and had uppermost in his mind only the promotion of a great cause—Anglo-American unity. That was likewise the obsession of Benedict Arnold in the later days of the American Revolution, and he worked for it in a more direct and courageous fashion.

C. Hartley Grattan, *The Walter Hines Page Legend*, in *American Mercury* (New York, 1925), VI, 41–50 *passim*.   Reprinted by permission of the author.

———◆———

168.   The *Lusitania* Note (1915)

BY PRESIDENT WOODROW WILSON

President Wilson was really his own Secretary of State.   Bryan, who was appointed to that position, was opposed to the participation of the United States in the World War on any terms drafted by the President.   When Wilson insisted on the sending of this note in the customary manner over the signature of the Secretary of State, Bryan resigned.

TO AMBASSADOR GERARD:
Please call on the Minister of Foreign Affairs and after reading to him this communication leave with him a copy.

In view of recent acts of the German authorities in violation of American rights on the high seas which culminated in the torpedoing and sinking of the British steamship *Lusitania* on May 7, 1915, by which over 100 American citizens lost their lives, it is clearly wise and desirable that the Government of the United States and the Imperial German Government should come to a clear and full understanding as to the grave situation which has resulted.

The sinking of the British passenger steamer *Falaba* by a German submarine on March 28, through which Leon C. Thrasher, an American citizen, was drowned; the attack on April 28 on the American vessel *Cushing* by a German aëroplane; the torpedoing on May 1 of the American vessel *Gulflight* by a German submarine, as a result of which two or more American citizens met their deaths; and, finally, the torpedoing and sinking of the steamship *Lusitania*, constitute a series of events which the Government of the United States has observed with growing concern, distress, and amazement.

Recalling the humane and enlightened attitude hitherto assumed by the Imperial German Government in matters of international right, and particularly with regard to the freedom of the seas; having learned to recognize the German views and the German influence in the field of international obligation as always engaged upon the side of justice and humanity; and having understood the instructions of the Imperial German Government to its naval commanders to be upon the same plane of humane action prescribed by the naval codes of other nations, the Government of the United States was loath to believe—it cannot now bring itself to believe—that these acts, so absolutely contrary to the rules, the practices, and the spirit of modern warfare, could have the countenance or sanction of that great Government. It feels it to be its duty, therefore, to address the Imperial German Government concerning them with the utmost frankness and in the earnest hope that it is not mistaken in expecting action on the part of the Imperial German Government which will correct the unfortunate impressions which have been created and vindicate once more the position of that Government with regard to the sacred freedom of the seas.

The Government of the United States has been apprised that the Imperial German Government considered themselves to be obliged by the extraordinary circumstances of the present war and the measures adopted by their adversaries in seeking to cut Germany off from all commerce, to adopt methods of retaliation which go much beyond the ordinary methods of warfare at sea, in the proclamation of a war zone from which they have warned neutral ships to keep away. This Government has already taken occasion to inform the Imperial German Government that it cannot admit the adoption of such measures or such a warning of danger to operate as in any degree an abbreviation of the rights of American shipmasters or of American citizens bound on lawful errands as passengers on merchant ships of belligerent nationality; and that it must hold the Imperial German Government to a strict accountability for any infringement of those rights, intentional or incidental. It does not understand the Imperial German Government to question those rights. It assumes, on the contrary, that the Imperial Government accept, as of course, the rule that the lives of noncombatants, whether they be of neutral citizenship or citizens of one of the nations at war, cannot lawfully or rightfully be put in jeopardy by the capture or destruction of an unarmed merchantman, and recognize also, as all other nations do, the obligation to take the usual precaution of visit and search to ascertain whether a suspected merchantman is in fact of belligerent nationality or is in fact carrying contraband of war under a neutral flag.

The Government of the United States, therefore, desires to call the attention of the Imperial German Government with the utmost earnestness to the fact that the objection to their present method of attack against the trade of their enemies lies in the practical impossibility of employing submarines in the destruction of commerce without disregarding those rules of fairness, reason, justice, and humanity, which all modern opinion regards as imperative. It is practically impossible for the officers of a submarine to visit a merchantman at sea and examine her papers and cargo. It is practically impossible for them to make a prize of her; and, if they cannot put a prize crew on board of her, they cannot sink her without leaving her crew and all on board of her to the mercy of the sea in her small boats. These facts it is understood the Imperial German Government frankly admit. We are informed that in the instances of which we have spoken time enough for even that poor measure of safety was not given, and in at least two cases cited not so much as a warning was received. Manifestly submarines cannot be used against merchantmen, as the last few weeks have shown, without an inevitable violation of many sacred principles of justice and humanity.

American citizens act within their indisputable rights in taking their ships and in traveling wherever their legitimate business calls them upon the high seas, and exercise those rights in what should be the well-justified confidence that their lives will not be endangered by acts done in clear violation of universally acknowledged international obligations, and certainly in the confidence that their own Government will sustain them in the exercise of their rights.

There was recently published in the newspapers of the United States, I regret to inform the Imperial German Government, a formal warning, purporting to come from the Imperial German Embassy at Washington, addressed to the people of the United States, and stating, in effect, that any citizen of the United States who exercised his right of free travel upon the seas would do so at his peril if his journey should take him within the zones of waters within which the Imperial German Navy was using submarines against the commerce of Great Britain and France, notwithstanding the respectful but very earnest protest of his Government, the Government of the United States.

I do not refer to this for the purpose of calling the attention of the Imperial German Government at this time to the surprising irregularity of a communication from the Imperial German Embassy at Washington addressed to the people of the United States through the newspapers, but only for the purpose of pointing out that no warning that an unlawful and inhumane act will be committed can possibly be accepted as an excuse or palliation for that act or as an abatement of the responsibility for its commission.

Long acquainted as the Government has been with the character of the Imperial German Government and with the high principles of equity by which they have in the past been actuated and guided, the Government of the United States cannot believe that the commanders of the vessels which committed these acts of lawlessness did so except under a misapprehension of the orders issued by the Imperial German naval authorities. It takes it for granted that, at least within the practical possibilities of every such case, the commanders even of submarines were expected to do nothing that would involve the lives of noncombatants or the safety of neutral ships, even at the cost of failing of their object of capture or destruction. It confidently expects, therefore, that the Imperial German Government will disavow the acts of which the Government of the United States complains, that they will make reparation so far as reparation is possible for injuries which are without measure, and that they will take immediate steps to prevent the recurrence of anything so obviously subversive of the principles of warfare for which the Imperial German Government have in the past so wisely and so firmly contended.

The Government and the people of the United States look to the Imperial German Government for just, prompt, and enlightened action in this vital matter with the greater confidence because the United States and Germany are bound together not only by special ties of friendship but also by the explicit stipulations of the treaty of 1828 between the United States and the Kingdom of Prussia.

Expressions of regret and offers of reparation in case of the destruction of neutral ships sunk by mistake, while they may satisfy international obligations, if no loss of life results, cannot justify, or excuse a practice, the natural and necessary effect of which is to subject neutral nations and neutral persons to new and immeasurable risks.

The Imperial German Government will not expect the Government of the United States to omit any word or any act necessary to the performance of its sacred duty of maintaining the rights of the United States and its citizens and of safeguarding their free exercise and enjoyment.

Note dated May 13, 1915, and sent over signature of the Secretary of State.

————◆————

169.   A Message to America (1915)

BY ALAN SEEGER

Alan Seeger (1888–1916) enlisted in the Foreign Legion of the French Army, and was killed in an attack on Belloy-en-Santree in the World War. Of him John Hall Wheelock said that "for some spirits the every-day pressure of life is not sufficient, and every-day demands of life not large nor heroic enough in their claim." His letters, as well as his poems, should be used for an understanding of his fatalistic philosophy.

YOU have the grit and the guts, I know;
  You are ready to answer blow for blow.
You are virile, combative, stubborn, hard,
But your honor ends with your own back-yard;
Each man intent on his private goal,
You have no feeling for the whole;
What singly none would tolerate
You let unpunished hit the state,
Unmindful that each man must share
The stain he lets his country wear,
And (what no traveller ignores)
That her good name is often yours..

You are proud in the pride that feels its might;
From your imaginary height
Men of another race or hue
Are men of a lesser breed to you:
The neighbor at your southern gate
You treat with the scorn that has bred his hate.
To lend a spice to your disrespect
You call him the "greaser."   But reflect!

The greaser has spat on you more than once;
He has handed you multiple affronts;
He has robbed you, banished you, burned and killed;
He has gone untrounced for the blood he spilled;
He has jeering used for his bootblack's rag
The stars and stripes of the gringo's flag;

And you, in the depths of your easy-chair—
What did you do, what did you care?
Did you find the season too cold and damp
To change the counter for the camp?
Were you frightened by fevers in Mexico?
I can't imagine, but this I know—
You are impassioned vastly more
By the news of the daily baseball score
Than to hear that a dozen countrymen
Have perished somewhere in Darien,
That greasers have taken their innocent lives
And robbed their holdings and raped their wives.

Not by rough tongues and ready fists
Can you hope to tilt in the modern lists.
The armies of a littler folk
Shall pass you under the victor's yoke,
Sobeit a nation that trains her sons
To ride their horses and point their guns—
Sobeit a people that comprehends
The limit where private pleasure ends
And where their public dues begin,
A people made strong by discipline
Who are willing to give—what you've no mind to—
And understand—what you are blind to—
The things that the individual
Must sacrifice for the good of all.

You have a leader who knows—the man
Most fit to be called American,
A prophet that once in generations

Is given to point to erring nations
Brighter ideals toward which to press
And lead them out of the wilderness.
Will you turn your back on him once again?
Will you give the tiller once more to men
Who have made your country the laughing-stock
For the older peoples to scorn and mock,
Who would make you servile, despised, and weak,
A country that turns the other cheek,
Who care not how bravely your flag may float,
Who answer an insult with a note,
Whose way is the easy way in all,
And, seeing that polished arms appal
Their marrow of milk-fed pacifist,
Would tell you menace does not exist?
Are these, in the world's great parliament,
The men you would choose to represent
Your honor, your manhood, and your pride,
And the virtues your fathers dignified?
Oh, bury them deeper than the sea
In universal obloquy;
Forget the ground where they lie, or write
For epitaph: "Too proud to fight."

I have been too long from my country's shores
To reckon what state of mind is yours,
But as for myself I know right well
I would go through fire and shot and shell
And face new perils, and make my bed
In new privations, if ROOSEVELT led;
But I have given my heart and hand
To serve, in serving another land,
Ideals kept bright that with you are dim;
Here men can thrill to their country's hymn,
For the passion that wells in the Marseillaise
Is the same that fires the French these days,
And, when the flag that they love goes by,
With swelling bosom and moistened eye

They can look, for they know that it floats there still
By the might of their hands and the strength of their will,
And through perils countless and trials unknown
Its honor each man has made his own.
They wanted the war no more than you,
But they saw how the certain menace grew,
And they gave two years of their youth or three
The more to insure their liberty
When the wrath of rifles and pennoned spears
Should roll like a flood on their wrecked frontiers.
They wanted the war no more than you,
But when the dreadful summons blew
And the time to settle the quarrel came
They sprang to their guns, each man was game;
And mark if they fight not to the last
For their hearths, their altars, and their past;
Yea, fight till their veins have been bled dry
For love of the country that *will* not die.

O friends, in your fortunate present ease
(Yet faced by the self-same facts as these),
If you would see how a race can soar
That has no love, but no fear, of war,
How each can turn from his private rôle
That all may act as a perfect whole,
How men can live up to the place they claim
And a nation, jealous of its good name,
Be true to its proud inheritance,
Oh, look over here and learn from FRANCE!

Alan Seeger, *Poems* (New York, Scribner's, 1916), 162–165.

CHAPTER XXXI — BUCKLING ON THE ARMOR

170. The International Food Problem (1917)

BY ROBERT W. BRUÈRE

Bruère is a New York journalist. Food administration in the United States was less a matter of mandatory regulation than one of educating the people to voluntary coöperation in saving—a task so well performed by Herbert Hoover as Food Administrator, that to economize in this patriotic fashion became to "Hooverize." —Bibliography: C. R. Van Hise, *Conservation and Regulation during the War*.

IN terms of practical administration, how was this common table served; through what instrumentalities did we divide with our Allies our wheat loaf?

As early as August, 1914, France, with the co-operation of Great Britain, established the *Commission Internationale de Ravitaillement*, which was soon extended to co-ordinate the purchases not only of Great Britain and France, but of all the Allies, so as to prevent competition among them and to facilitate the satisfaction of their several and joint needs. In December, 1915, the British, French, and Italian governments initiated a system of joint purchases of wheat, flour, and corn which was later developed into the Wheat Executive, consisting of one representative of each country, "to purchase, allocate, and arrange for the transport of wheat, flour, and other cereal products for the three countries." This Wheat Executive proved so useful in welding the co-operative unity of these Allies that it led to the establishment of other similar bodies to deal with the garnering throughout the world of other necessities—meat, animal fats, oil seeds, sugar, nitrate of soda, hides, wool and wool products, explosives, and the raw material for the manufacture of explosives, lead, copper, coal. And, of necessity, the Allied governments established an international executive through which to pool and allocate their shipping tonnage.

These were the instrumentalities—not a legalistic court of arbitration—through which the common table was supplied, through which harmony and effective co-operation were made possible among the nations associated against the individualistic autocracies of the Central Powers—through which the military triumph of the armed democracies was guaranteed.

What was America's contribution to the common table? In the five years preceding our entrance into the war the average per capita consumption of wheat in the United States was five and three-tenths bushels. For the year 1917–18 we reduced our per capita consumption to a little less than four bushels. We had no bumper crop that year; we produced less than with care and disciplined intelligence we could have produced. We ourselves did not go hungry. Never before had so large a percentage of our own people been decently fed. And yet, according to the British Food Ministry, the United States, from July, 1917, to April, 1918, exported to the Allies 80,000,000 bushels of *wheat products*, of which 50,000,000 represented the voluntary gift of the American people. On September 24, 1918, the United States Food Administration made the following announcement:

"Under the agreement entered into by the Food Administration with the food-controllers of the Allied nations, our breadstuffs export program for the coming year will be, wheat, rye, barley, and corn, or flour, calculated as grain for breadstuffs, 409,320,000 bushels, of which from 100,000,000 to 165,000,000 may be cereals other than wheat."

The reference here to the agreement with the food-controllers of the Allies invites special notice. The Allies, like ourselves, were looking upon the bread-supply of the entire world, not as the plaything of the so-called law of supply and demand—and incidentally of profiteering middlemen—but as the common stock of all those who sat at the common table, to be consciously and deliberately apportioned to each of the co-operating nations according to their several mathematically determined needs. More than this. The computation went beyond the requirements of the individual nations as aggregates, to the needs of the individual men and women and children within each national group. At its first meeting, held in Paris in March, 1918, the Inter-Allied Scientific Food Commission succeeded in doing what until then had been regarded as a fantastic impossibility—it arrived at an agreement on the minimum food requirements of the average man. As reported in *The Survey* for August 3, 1918, the commission, at its second meeting, held in Rome, worked out the food requirements of each of the Allied countries on the basis of the *average man* and in the light of population statistics; setting against these requirements the home production, actual and potential, of each nation in order to determine how much food would have to be served to each at the common table. Thus the Inter-Allied Scientific Food Commission, acting in co-operation with the Allied food-controllers and the international Wheat Executive, brought "the vision of a world organization for the feeding of mankind an appreciable step nearer."

Without this international economic organization for the co-operative apportionment of the world's supply of food, harmony among the nations associated against imperialistic militarism would have been impossible. Revolution within the nations whose domestic supplies were inadequate to feed their people would have forced other nations than Russia to capitulate—to make a separate peace.

And as with wheat, so with all other basic commodities. What America did with her wheat loaf she did also with her sugar, meat fats, steel, cotton, coal, timber, and whatever things of value to the common cause she had. On July 17, 1918, the Food Administration announced that if the people of the United States continued to abate their normal consumption of sugar as they had done during the preceding year, their saving, and thus their contribution to the common table, measured by the price of sugar then prevailing in Canada, France, the United Kingdom, and Italy, would total for the coming year alone about $600,000,000. During the year 1916–17 the United States exported 2,000,000,000 pounds of meats and fats; during 1917–18, 3,000,000,000—1,000,000,000 pounds of meats and fats was one of America's contributions to the common table. About one-half our output of more than 1,000,000,000 pounds of copper from January to June, 1918, went to the Allies. We packed our dry groceries in paper containers instead of tin because the Allies needed the metal. We stopped building houses for ourselves in order that ships might be built to carry our contributions across the sea. We stopped wearing all-wool in order that not only our own soldiers, but the soldiers and civilians of England, France, Belgium, Italy, might be warmly clad. Before the war the United States had never loaned money to any foreign state. In September, 1918, the Bulletin of the Paris Chamber of Commerce noted with admiration that the total of America's advances to the Allies then exceeded $6,000,000,000. In addition to this vast sum, America had, during the first four years of the war alone, freely given more than $4,000,000,000 to war charities. And what the United States did, it is important to remember, is but an illustration of what all the Allies did to serve the common purpose.

The common table, not a court of arbitration, became the symbol of a new nationalism and a new internationalism.

Robert W. Bruère, *Changing America*, in *Harper's Magazine*, February, 1919, 289–294.

---

171. War with Germany (1917)

BY SENATOR HENRY CABOT LODGE

On Lodge, see No. 126 above and No. 202 below. The speech reprinted here presents the unusual spectacle of an ardent Republican lending his full support to an administration with which he was not in sympathy, and which he opposed quite as vigorously when the war-time need for unanimity was past.—General bibliography of the war: John Spencer Bassett, *Our War with Germany;* H. C. Brown, *The A. E. F. with General Pershing;* Charles G. Dawes, *Journal of the Great War;* Hunter Liggett, *Commanding an American Army;* R. R. McCormick, *The Army of 1918;* A. W. Page, *Our 110 Days' Fighting;* John B. McMaster, *The United States and the World War;* Shipley Thomas, *History of the A. E. F.* On the war at sea, see bibliography in No. 187 below. On industrial participation in the war, see G. B. Clarkson, *Industrial America in the World War;* Samuel Gompers, *American Labor and the War;* F. F. Kelley, *What America Did;* E. A. Powell, *The Army behind the Army.* See also letters and biographies of statesmen and other war-time leaders.

NO one is more conscious than I that this is a moment for action and not for debate. But, as a member of the Committee on Foreign Relations, and having taken part in framing this resolution, I wish briefly to state why I support it with the greatest earnestness of which I am capable.

The most momentous power entrusted to Congress by the Constitution is the authority to declare war, and never has Congress been called to a more solemn exercise of this great function than at this moment. We have submitted to wrongs and outrages from the Central

Powers of Europe—wrongs which involve not only injury to property, but the destruction of American lives—with a long patience. We have borne and forborne to the very limit of endurance. Now the inevitable end is here and we are about to declare war against Germany.

Speaking for myself and, I hope, for my associates generally on this side of the Chamber, I desire to say that in this crisis, and when the country is at war, party lines will disappear, and this disappearance of the party line will, I am confident, not be confined to the minority. Both Democrats and Republicans must forget party in the presence of the common danger. This is not, and cannot be, a party war. It is a war in which all Americans must be united, and no one must ask a loyal citizen, high or low, who seeks to serve his country in the field or in civil life to what party he belongs, any more than it would be possible to ask his religion or his race. As Americans we shall all, I am sure, be prepared to give to the Executive money, men, and all the necessary powers for waging war with energy and driving it forward to a successful conclusion. The President has made recommendations as to the action which he hopes Congress will take, with which I for one am in most thorough accord.

We have only a very small army and we must proceed at once and as rapidly as possible to build up a large one fit to defend the country in any emergency. We must provide for the future and for the supply of men for the Army by a system of universal military training. I agree with the President that this new army should be chosen upon the "principle of universal liability to service." Our Navy is strong in certain branches and very weak in others. It must be our business to supply the deficiencies as rapidly as possible. Fortunately those deficiencies are, as a rule, of the kind which can be most quickly supplied. It is our duty to see to it that all the money and all the legislation necessary for both the Army and the Navy are given at once.

The President has said that war

will involve the utmost practicable coöperation in counsel and action with the Governments now at war with Germany and, as incident to that, the extension to those Governments of the most liberal financial credits, in order that our resources may so far as possible be added to theirs.

I am not only in full agreement with this policy advised by the President, but it seems to me that nothing is more important than to follow it out. I am as thorough a believer as ever in the general policy laid down by Washington when he advised the people of the United States not to enter into permanent alliances; but the man who won the American Revolution through the alliance with France would have been the last to lay down a hard-and-fast rule that under no circumstances and for no purposes were we ever to ally ourselves with other nations. He covers this point completely in the Farewell Address, where he says:—

Taking care always to keep ourselves by suitable establishments on a respectable defensive posture, we may safely trust to temporary alliances for extraordinary emergencies.

Farseeing and wise, he knew very well that dangers might come which would make a temporary alliance or agreement with foreign nations imperative. That time has arrived. It would be madness for us to attempt to make war alone upon Germany, and find ourselves, perhaps, at the end left isolated, at war with that power, when all the other nations had made peace, because we had not associated ourselves with them. The Allies of the Entente, as they are called, are fighting a common foe, and their foe is now ours. We cannot send a great army across the ocean, for we have no army to send. Yet I should be glad for one if we could send ten thousand men of our regular troops, so that the flag of the United States might at least be unfurled in the fields of France. I believe that the mere sight of our flag in that region made so desolate by war would stimulate the courage and help the success of those who have the same aim that we have and who seek the same victory. We can also help the Allies, as the President recommends, with large credits and with those supplies which we can furnish and which they lack. We cannot do more in any direction to bring this war to a speedy end than to give those credits and furnish those supplies.

The President has told us that German spies

were here even before the war began, and it is, unhappily, not a matter of conjecture, but a fact proved in our courts of justice, that the intrigues which have more than once come perilously near to disturbing the peace and dislocating the industries of the country have been carried on at the instigation, with the support, and even under the personal direction of official agents of the Imperial German Government accredited to the Government of the United States.

I believe myself that the overwhelming mass of our citizens of German descent are just as loyal to the United States as any citizens could possibly be. But there is this class of agents of the Imperial German Government who are ready to engage in plots and crimes to the injury of the people of this country. "Disloyalty," if I may again borrow the words of the President, "must be put down with a firm hand."

The purpose of the German submarine campaign is the absolute destruction of the world's mercantile tonnage, something wholly new in warfare. In the old days, in previous wars, the ships of warring nations were captured, frequently in large numbers, as was the case when our privateers ranged the English Channel in the War of 1812. But it must not be forgotten that, with few exceptions, these vessels, when captured, were sent into port, condemned as prizes, and again put afloat. The total tonnage of the world was not materially reduced. But the German submarine war, ruthlessly carried on, is directed toward the complete destruction of the tonnage of the whole world. Forced into war, as we now are, our first action should be to repair in some measure this loss to our own tonnage and to that of the world by seizing the ships of Germany now in our ports and putting that additional tonnage into the world's service.

Mr. President, we have never been a military nation; we are not prepared for war in the modern sense; but we have vast resources and unbounded energies, and the day when war is declared we should devote ourselves to calling out those resources and organizing those energies so that they can be used with the utmost effect in hastening the complete victory. The worst of all wars is a feeble war. War is too awful to be entered upon half-heartedly. If we fight at all, we must fight for all we are worth. It must be no weak, hesitating war. The most merciful war is that which is most vigorously waged and which comes most quickly to an end.

Mr. President, no one feels the horrors of war more than I. It is with no light heart, but with profound sadness, although with hope and courage, that I see my country compelled to enter the great field of conflict. But there are, in my opinion, some things worse for a nation than war. National degeneracy is worse; national cowardice is worse. The division of our people into race groups, striving to direct the course of the United States in the interest of some other country when we should have but one allegiance, one hope, and one tradition, is far worse. All these dangers have been gathering about us and darkening the horizon during the last three years. Whatever suffering and misery war may bring, it will at least sweep these foul things away. Instead of division into race groups, it will unify us into one nation, and national degeneracy and national cowardice will slink back into the darkness from which they should never have emerged.

I also believe that on our entrance into this war, under the conditions which it has assumed, our future peace, our independence as a proud and high-spirited nation, our very security, are at stake. There is no other way, as I see it, except by war, to save those things without which national existence is a mockery and a sham. But there is a still higher purpose here as I look upon it. The President has said with great justice that Germany is making war upon all nations. We do not enter upon this war to secure victory for one nation as against another. We enter this war to unite with those who are fighting the common foe in order to preserve human freedom, democracy, and modern civilization. They are all in grievous peril; they are all threatened. This war is a war, as I see it, against barbarism; not the anarchical barbarism of what are know as the Dark Ages, but organized barbarism panoplied in all the devices for the destruction of human life which science, beneficent science, can bring forth. We are resisting an effort to thrust mankind back to forms of government, to political creeds and methods of conquest which we had hoped had disappeared forever from the world. We are fighting against a nation which, in the fashion of centuries ago, drags the inhabitants of conquered lands into slavery; which carries off women and girls for even worse purposes; which in its mad desire to conquer mankind and trample them under foot has stopped at no wrong, has regarded no treaty. The work that we are called upon to do when we enter this war is to preserve the principles of human liberty; the principles of democracy, and the light of modern civilization; all that we most love, all that we hold dearer than life itself, is at stake. In such a battle we cannot fail to win. I am glad that my country is to share in this preservation of human freedom. I wish to see my country gathered with the other nations who are fighting for the same end when the time for peace comes. We seek no conquests, we desire no territory and no new dominions. We wish simply to preserve our own peace and our own security, to uphold the great doctrine which guards the American hemisphere, and to see the disappearance of all wars or rumors of wars from the East, if any dangers there exist. What we want most of all by this victory which we shall help to win is to secure the world's peace, broad-based on freedom and democracy, a world not controlled by a Prussian military autocracy, by Hohenzollerns and Hapsburgs, but by the will of the free people of the earth. We shall achieve this result, and when we achieve it, we shall be able to say that we have not fought in vain.

Henry Cabot Lodge, Speech in United States Senate, April 4, 1917, in *Cong. Record.*

---

172. Insurance for Soldiers (1917)

FROM THE LITERARY DIGEST

Unhappy experience with pension plans after our previous wars was the basis of the insurance plans adopted at the outset of our participation in the World War.

PESTIFEROUS Pension Graft will become a thing of the past through the Treasury's indemnity-insurance plan for our soldiers and sailors. This prospect is visioned by certain observers who hold, as the Louisville *Courier-Journal* puts it, that the existing pension system has been "one of the greatest grafts that has been fastened upon the Federal Treasury during the history of the country." The insurance of the lives and the physical ability of our fighting men is a straightforward, business means of providing indemnity and a means of avoiding all payment of huge sums in the aggregate. The *Courier-Journal* says further that the insurance plan will work as check to persons whose claims for pensions are wholly fraudulent, "yet succeed because neither political party has the temerity to tackle graft in pensions and cast it out."

The Topeka *State Journal* considers the insurance of our soldiers and sailors only a new application of the well-known principle of employees' insurance, especially for those engaged in hazardous employment, and it adds that the wisdom and justice of a great Government in applying the principle to its citizens who for their country's sake engage in the extra hazardous employment of war are apparent to all. The Baltimore *Sun* hopes that the Government's plan will be put in shape as soon as possible, and the Omaha *News* thinks the Administration should have no trouble with Congress when it presents a finished plan, for Congress will be responsive because it will hear from millions of American homes. In the announcement of the project given to the press by the Treasury Department, we read:

"The whole proposition is based on the fundamental idea that the Government should, as a matter of justice and humanity, adequately protect its fighting men on land and sea and their dependent families. It aims to hearten the families of the men who go to the front and at the same time to give to our soldiers and sailors the comforting assurance that whatever may be their fate, their loved ones at home will not be left dependent upon charity. It is proposed to impose on the public treasury the obligation of indemnifying justly the men who have entered, or are about to enter, the American Army and Navy to fight in the cause of liberty. With our men on the soil of France and hundreds of thousands of others about to enter the service of their country, the question is one of justice and fairness and the plan should be as liberal as it is possible for a just and generous republic to make.

"Under the plan discussed it is suggested that provision be made for the support of dependents of soldiers and sailors by giving them an allotment out of the pay of the men; and also an allowance by the Government; that officers and men be indemnified against death or total or partial disability; that a system of rehabilitation and re-education of disabled men be inaugurated; and that the Government insure the lives of sailors and soldiers on their application at rates of premium based upon ordinary risks."

The new system would be administered, it is further stated, by the Bureau of War-Risk Insurance of the Treasury Department, which is already writing war-risk insurance on masters, officers, and crews of American merchant vessels and on American hulls and cargoes. In the August *Public Bulletin* of the Equitable Life Insurance Society, as quoted by the New York *Times*, we learn that it was at first suggested that the insurance companies themselves insure the fighters, but because the wishes of the Government were in the direction of indemnity insurance rather than life insurance, the company officials advised Secretary McAdoo that it would be more economical for the Government to insure the men. The Equitable asks the public to insist upon these things in connection with the insurance plan:

"1. Immediately to urge a law providing protection for the soldier's dependents during his absence.

"2. To prepare to establish reëducation schools to teach him a new trade if, through injury or sickness, he is prevented from following his usual occupation.

"3. To provide a monthly cash indemnity (heretofore misnamed a pension), which the people shall pay through their Government to compensate him for loss of earning-power due to personal injury or impaired health resulting from military service.

"4. To give his dependents, if he loses his life, a monthly cash indemnity to guard them against want until they are able to take care of themselves."

Instead of the old pension system with "its opening for extravagance, scandal, and fraud," the Equitable favors a plan which will in effect extend the workmen's compensation or indemnity idea from other Government employees to the fighting men of our Army and Navy, and we read:

"Inasmuch as this is a direct obligation and the money is rightfully due, the word pension, which smacks of charity, should be abandoned.

"Let Congress establish at once a Soldiers' Indemnity Fund and prepare an indemnity certificate or contract to be given every soldier when he enters the service. Let this indemnity contract state specifically, as similar private contracts do, the various contingencies for which the Government promises to pay the indemnity. This contract will give the soldier tangible evidence that the Government will take care of him and his family in case of need. To him it will be an asset as safe and secure and certain of performance as a Government bond. The claims under these soldiers' indemnity certificates should be investigated and adjusted by the Government as they are now by insurance companies. The operation of the entire plan can be carried on in a simple, inexpensive way.

"If you agree that our soldiers should have such a scientific and businesslike indemnity plan in place of the present wasteful, and in some ways disgraceful, pension system, write your Senator and

Congressman accordingly. Life-insurance officials responded to the request of the Government to give their views upon this subject of providing a substitute for the present pension system. At the conference it was made clear to the Government authorities that it was unwise to go to the expense of putting this plan into operation through the life-insurance companies, for the Government could itself handle it directly at less cost. The companies were ready to undertake it if the Government so desired.

"It seems perfectly clear that if a workmen's compensation law is a good thing for Government employees (and we now have it), a Soldiers' Indemnity Fund on a similar plan would be a good thing for our soldiers and sailors. Why not let these men have the comfort of knowing when they enter this war that a grateful people have already provided financial protection for them and the loved ones whom they have left to go to the defense of the nation?"

The proposed Federal insurance for America's fighting men marks a new day, according to the Chicago *Herald*, which points out that—

"The plan has been tested by the sundry belligerent countries. Canada, perhaps, has the most to teach the world, but Germany began the elaboration of a similar method of compensating war-sufferers within two weeks of the outbreak of hostilities."

The Literary Digest, August 11, 1917 (New York), 12–13.

---

173. War-Time Hysteria (1917)

COMMISSIONER FREDERIC C. HOWE (1925)

For Howe, see No. 12 above. For related matter, see No. 108 above and No. 194 below.—Bibliography: Z. Chafee, Jr., *Freedom of Speech;* L. F. Post, *The Deportation Delirium of 1920.*

HYSTERIA over the immoral alien was followed by a two-year panic over the "Hun." Again inspectors, particularly civilian secret-service agents, were given carte blanche to make arrests on suspicion. Again Ellis Island was turned into a prison, and I had to protect men and women from a hue and cry that was but little concerned over guilt or innocence. During these years thousands of

Germans, Austrians, and Hungarians were taken without trial from their homes and brought to Ellis Island. Nearly two thousand officers and seamen from sequestered German ships were placed in my care. Many of them had married American wives. They conducted themselves decently and well. They were obedient to discipline. They accepted the situation and they gave practically no trouble. They were typical of the alien enemies the country over that were arrested under the hysteria that was organized and developed into a hate that lingers on to this day.

Again I had either to drift with the tide or assume the burden of seeing that as little injustice as possible was done. I realized that under war conditions convincing evidence could not be demanded. I accepted that fact, but not the assumption that "the Hun should be put against the wall and shot." From our entrance into the war until after the armistice my life was a nightmare. My telephone rang constantly with inquiries from persons seeking news of husbands and fathers who had been arrested. On my return home in the evening I would often find awaiting me women in a state of nervous collapse whose husbands had mysteriously disappeared, and who feared that they had been done away with. I furnished them with such information as was possible. On the island I had to stand between the official insistence that the German should be treated as a criminal and the admitted fact that the great majority of them had been arrested by persons with little concern about their innocence or guilt and with but little if any evidence to support the detention.

Within a short time I was branded as pro-German. I had to war with the local staff to secure decent treatment for the aliens, and with the army of secret-service agents to prevent the island from being filled with persons against whom some one or other had filed a suspicious inquiry.

It is a marvellous tribute to the millions of Germans, Austrians, and Hungarians in this country that, despite the injustices to which they were subjected and the espionage under which they lived, scarcely an Americanized alien of these races was found guilty of any act of disloyalty of which the entire German-American population was suspected or accused.

The final outbreak of hysteria was directed against the "Reds" the winter of 1918–19. It started in the State of Washington in the lumber camps, and was directed against members of the I. W. W. organizations which had superseded the more conservative craft unions affiliated with the American Federation of Labor. There was a concerted determination on the part of employers to bring wages back to the pre-war conditions and to break the power of organized labor. The movement against alien labor leaders had the support of the Department of Justice. Private detective agencies and strike-breakers acted with assurance that in any outrages they would be supported by the government itself. The press joined in the cry of "Red revolution," and frightened the country with scare head-lines of an army of organized terrorists who were determined to usher in revolution by force. The government borrowed the agent provocateur from old Russia; it turned loose innumerable private spies. For two years we were in a panic of fear over the Red revolutionists, anarchists, and enemies of the Republic who were said to be ready to overthrow the government.

For a third time I had to stand against the current. Men and women were herded into Ellis Island. They were brought under guards and in special trains with instructions to get them away from the country with as little delay as possible. Most of the aliens had been picked up in raids on labor headquarters; they had been given a drum-head trial by an inspector with no chance for the defense; they were held incommunicado and often were not permitted to see either friends or attorneys, before being shipped to Ellis Island. In these proceedings the inspector who made the arrest was prosecutor, witness, judge, jailer, and executioner. He was clerk and interpreter as well. This was all the trial the alien could demand under the law. In many instances the inspector hoped that he would be put in charge of his victim for a trip to New York and possibly to Europe at the expense of the government. Backed by the press of his city and by the hue and cry of the pack, he had every inducement to find the alien guilty and arrange for his speedy deportation.

I was advised by the Commissioner-General to mind my own business and carry out orders, no matter what they might be. Yet such obvious injustice was being done that I could not sit quiet. Moreover, I was an appointee of the President, and felt that I owed responsibility to him whose words at least I was exemplifying in my actions. My words carried no weight with my superior officials, who were intoxicated with the prominence they enjoyed and the publicity which they received from the press. The bureaucratic organization at the island was happy in the punishing powers which all jailers enjoy, and resented any interference on behalf of its victims. Members of Congress were swept from their moorings by an organized business propaganda, and demanded that I be dismissed because I refused to railroad aliens to boats made ready for their deportation. I took the position from which I would not be driven, that the alien should not be held incommunicado and should enjoy the right of a writ of habeas corpus in the United States courts, which was the only semblance of legal proceedings open to him under the law.

In maintaining this position I had to quarrel with my superiors and the official force at the island. I faced a continuous barrage from members of Congress, from the press, from business organizations, and prosecuting attorneys. Yet day by day aliens, many of whom had been held in prison for months, came before the court; and the judge, after examining the testimony, unwillingly informed the immigration authorities that there was not a scintilla of evidence to support the arrest. For in deportation cases it is not necessary to provide a preponderance of testimony, or to convince the court of the justice of the charge; all that the government needs to support its case is a "scintilla" of evidence, which may be any kind of evidence at all. If there is a bit of evidence, no matter how negligible it may be, the order of deportation must be affirmed.

Again the pack was unleashed. No one took the trouble to ascertain the facts. The press carried stories to the effect that I had released hundreds of persons ordered deported. I had released aliens, but in each case I had been ordered to do so by the courts or the bureau. I had observed the law when organized hysteria demanded that it be swept aside. I had seen to it that men and women enjoyed their legal rights, but evidently this was the worst offense I could have committed. A congressional committee came to Ellis Island and held protracted hearings. It listened to disaffected officials, it created scare head-lines for the press, it did everything in its power to convince the country that we were on the verge of a nation-wide revolution, of which the most hard-boiled inspectors sent out by the bureau had reported they could not find a trace. When I went to the hearings and demanded the right to be present, to cross-examine witnesses and see the records, when I demanded that I be put on the witness-stand myself, the committee ordered the sergeant-at-arms to eject me from the rooms.

As I look back over these years, my outstanding memories are not of the immigrants. They are rather of my own people. Things that were done forced one almost to despair of the mind, to distrust the political state. Shreds were left of our courage, our reverence. The Department of Justice, the Department of Labor, and Congress not only failed to protest against hysteria, they encouraged these excesses; the state not only abandoned the liberty which it should have protected, it lent itself to the stamping out of individualism and freedom. It used the agent provocateur, it permitted private agencies to usurp government powers, turned over the administration of justice to detective agencies, card-indexed liberals and progressives. It became frankly an agency of employing and business interests at a time when humanity—the masses, the poor—were making the supreme sacrifice of their lives.

I had fondly imagined that we prized individual liberty; I had believed that to Anglo-Saxons human rights were sacred and they would be protected at any cost.

Latin peoples might be temperamental, given to hysteria; but we were hard-headed, we stood for individuality. But I found that we were lawless, emotional, given to mob action. We cared little for freedom of conscience, for the rights of men to their opinions. Government was a convenience of business. Discussion of war profiteers was not to be permitted. The Department of Justice lent itself to the suppression of those who felt that war should involve equal sacrifice. Civil liberties were under the ban. Their subversion was not, however, an isolated thing; it was an incident in the ascendancy of business privileges and profits acquired during the war—an ascendancy that did not bear scrutiny or brook the free discussion which is the only safe basis of orderly popular government.

Frederic C. Howe, *Confessions of a Reformer* (New York, Scribner's, 1925), 272–277.

174.   Foreigners in the Army (1918)

BY FRED H. RINDGE, JR.

Rindge at the time of writing was Secretary of the International Committee of the Young Men's Christian Association. The names on war memorials and community honor rolls all over the country attest the patriotic service of men of foreign birth or ancestry.

"BOSS, me no lika dis job. Give me my money. I goin' home." The speaker was an Italian member of America's new National Army. "And," said his captain to me, "that's all the conception a lot of them have of why they are here."

I went to the great cantonments expecting to see a great body of Americans. I found thousands of Italians, Poles, Russians, Rumanians, Greeks, and others—all potential Americans, to be sure, but with a long way to travel yet! In each of several camps of 30,000 to 40,000 men I found 4,000 to 5,000 who understand little English and speak still less. Of course this proportion would be determined in each cantonment by the districts from which the men came.

I talked with scores of colonels and other officers, and all agreed that this was one of their greatest problems. One regiment had about eighty per cent "foreigners." Many had fifty per cent. Whole companies were made up mostly of Poles or some other foreign nationality. Imagine these fellows from the slums of Chicago, Milwaukee, Detroit, Cleveland, New York, getting off their trains, being taken to camp, marched to their quarters, given instructions which they could little understand, and beginning immediately a life as new and strange to them as aëroplaning would be for you and me! . . .

To build real soldiers out of this material is a slow process, requiring infinite patience. One captain told me this as a joke on himself:

"To-day when drilling my men I was provoked so many times by one fellow who refused to listen or obey orders that I sailed into him before the whole company. After I had completed what I thought was a rather impressive speech one of the non-commissioned officers saluted and said, 'Excuse me, Captain, but that man doesn't understand a word you're saying!'"

When a new crowd of men comes to camp it is no uncommon sight to find men wandering aimlessly around in their off hours, hopelessly lost. They do not know the number of their regiment, company, or barracks, and in a camp of five thousand acres and more all barracks look alike. One of these huge cantonments is a maze for any new-comer, even for the educated American who does not hesitate to in-quire his way.

Fancy some of these foreigners, many of whom have not even their "first papers," grasping quickly the fundamentals of our government, the real meaning of our war, and the bewildering nomenclature and courtesies of the army camp! It all seems so impossible. One after-noon I had the privilege of being in one of the barracks while a colonel was explaining to his captains the exact way everything should be arranged. "Exact" hardly describes it. Of course the bed had to be made just so, the poncho had to be folded exactly right at the foot, the mess-kit had to be hung on a certain nail, a few things were per-mitted to be visible, the rest "under the mattress," etc. There by the door stood a dozen foreigners, just arrived, who could hardly speak a word of English, and my thoughts went beyond them to the boarding-houses and industrial plants whence they had come. Yet to-morrow these same foreigners would be following out these same strict orders, making their own beds with a precision that would dismay the tidiest housekeeper. Talk about raising the standard of living—in the army camps it is done with one stroke of the pen, overnight! A few days later I saw those same "rookies," in army garb, drilling, and I could barely recognize them. There is something profoundly in-spiring about it all. At the same time there is something very pathetic about the ignorance of these men. The officers, on the whole, are showing splendid patience and a fine spirit in the face of great diffi-culties.

There are humorous as well as pathetic stories. Joe came in after hours one night and was greeted by the guard in the usual manner: "Halt! Advance and be recognized!" In answer to the question, "What's your name?" Joe replied, "Ah, you no guess it in a thou-sand years." He probably went to the guard-house, and, as one colonel said, "There are many there because of ignorance rather than vicious-ness."

At Camp Upton one evening a major was stopped by a "Halt!" from the sentry. The major stopped, the sentry advanced and again said, "Halt." "Well, what do you want?" inquired the major, with rising anger. "Halt! Now I think about time you run—I shoot!" Of course the sentry was taken to task, and it was discovered that he had misunderstood the order to shoot if any man refused to halt after being ordered to do so three times. The major however, sympathized with the foreign sentry and admitted that he was a good sport in at least telling him to run! . . .

The Roberts method, as it has been called, takes a group of foreigners absolutely ignorant of the English language and teaches them all equally well, even though there may be a dozen nationalities in the class at the same time. There are three fundamental principles of the method: First, that the ear and not the eye is the organ of language. That is to say, we learned our native tongue by hearing it spoken by our parents and others. We did not learn from books until long after we had learned to speak. The Association experts, therefore, realize that they must first teach the foreigners (who, as far as English is concerned, are really children) how to speak. The reading and writing come later in the lesson.

Second, that each lesson must deal with a common experience of every-day life.

Third, that each sentence must suggest what the next sentence shall be. That is, the sentences must be logically arranged and all bear on the main theme.

A teacher, therefore, proceeds as follows: He says to his men, "You say this after me—Awake." The class in unison then repeats the word, which as yet they do not understand the meaning of, and the teacher corrects their pronunciation. He then gives them a second word—"open." They repeat this. He follows with "look," "find," "see." Very quickly the men memorize these five words in the order given, until they say them without the teacher's help. Incidentally, you will note that the men have been learning verbs, the vitally active part of each sentence. The teacher then uses these verbs in sentences, acting each sentence slowly and with dramatic precision: "I awake from sleep." "I open my eyes." "I look for my watch." "I find my watch." "I see what time it is."

In from five to ten minutes the men memorize perfectly these five sentences. They understand the meaning, because the teacher carefully enacts each word and sentence. The teacher then has his pupils memorize the second set of sentences: "It is six o'clock." "I must get up." "I throw back the bedclothes." "I get out of bed." "I put on my pants." "I put on my socks and shoes."

And so on through the process of getting up in the morning. If an hour to an hour and a half is allowed for the lesson, about half of the time is well spent in this acting out of the lesson and memorizing. It is amazing how quickly men really understand and can repeat the lesson without the teacher's help. When that point is reached the teacher exhibits a large chart upon which the lesson is printed. The men then connect what they have seen dramatized and what they have memorized with what they now see in print. Thus they say the lesson from memory while looking at the printed words with the result that they very quickly learn to recognize the printed forms of the words already learned. Then each student is given a lesson sheet to keep—on one side the lesson in print and the reverse side in script. They then read in unison both sides of the sheet many times until they are actually, in spite of themselves, learning to read. . . .

After a class the other night I heard a young Italian say to his teacher: "Teacher, I want thank you. Before I came here I no have chance to learn any much English. Now I learn whole lot, I be better soldier." . . .

Most people do not recognize that there are over 40,000 native illiterates in the camps, many of them from the southern mountains. . . . An Association secretary discovered one of these men crying himself to sleep in his barracks. When asked what was the matter he replied, "I don't like it here in France." It took considerable time for the secretary to convince the man that he was not in France, but in reality only a few hundred miles from home. The secretary did everything he could for the man. He saw he was surrounded with helpful associates, and in a few days he was in a much happier frame of mind. . . .

There are in America to-day approximately 15,000,000 foreign-born and 20,000,000 more of foreign parentage. There are only about 5,000,000 foreign-born voters, and fully 5,000,000 who speak very little English. More than 3,000,000 aliens of military age are exempt from draft because not naturalized. In the face of facts like these let us see to it that every agency in every city in America be commandeered to help educate and inspire with loyalty these men from other lands, whether aliens or citizens and whether or not they are to be drafted!

Fred H. Rindge, Jr., *Uncle Sam's Adopted Nephews*, in *Harper's Magazine*, July, 1918 (New York), 281–289 *passim*.

------◆------

175. Training Camp Activities (1918)

BY RAYMOND B. FOSDICK

Fosdick, a lawyer by profession, was Chairman of the Commission on Training Camp Activities of the War and Navy Departments; and, later, civilian aide to Gen. Pershing in France, 1919. Beyond all experience in previous wars, plans were organized to care for the social side of the soldiers' life. See also No. 186 below.

BY a comprehensive recreational and educational program, the commissions have surrounded our fighters with such clean and wholesome influences as they conceived a democracy to owe to its fighting men. The undertaking was experimental. It was perhaps the largest social program ever undertaken. It was the first time a government had ever combined educational and ethical elements with disciplinary forces, in the production of a fighting organism. . . .

Broadly, the work of the commissions has fallen under two general heads. The first embraces a vast positive program set up to compete with the twin evils of alcohol and prostitution. The more perfect its development, the less the necessity for the other phase of the organization—the suppressive work. Working together to assist in supplying the former are the agencies that, already in existence, have been accorded official recognition and placed under the direction of the commissions.

The club life of the cantonment, for instance, is in the capable hands of the Young Men's Christian Association, the Knights of Columbus, and the Jewish Welfare Board. . . .

The buildings brought into the camps by these organizations are so distributed, as to be easily available to the greatest numbers of men. A typical hut or bungalow presents a reassuring picture for those who have fears as to the social well-being of the uniformed men. Groups of men will always be found there occupying the rocking chairs and big arm chairs, smoking, playing games, or reading. A victrola and a piano are included in the equipment of each building and the men make full use of them. Around the entire wall space writing desks are built in, and these are never entirely deserted. It is estimated that more than a million and a half letters daily are written by the soldiers and sailors on the stationery that is furnished free by the Y. M. C. A. alone. The men soon learn that the building secretary is available day or night, and is not only willing but anxious to serve them as counsellor or friend. . . .

Another important agency coöperating in this work within the camps, is the American Library Association, to which has been delegated the task of solving the problem of the soldiers' and sailors' reading matter. This organization has undertaken the seemingly impossible task of seeing that there is always a good book within reach of the fighting man. A special library building has been erected or is in the course of being erected in each of the army cantonments. These are in charge of trained librarians. The entire work is carried on under the general supervision of Dr. Herbert Putnam, Librarian of Congress, who has been appointed General Director of the Library War Service. . . .

The library work in camp is linked up definitely with the educational program being carried on direct by the commissions. In many divisions gathered in by the first draft, the percentage of men who could not speak a word of English was appalling. In the Syracuse camp, there was one regiment who could not understand the commands given them. Men from the Kentucky and Tennessee mountains could not read or write. In every camp in the United States classes in English, French, spelling, reading, writing and primary arithmetic were started, and are now being conducted. Two hundred thousand men are studying the French language at the present time, in classes run under the direction of the Commissions on Training Camp Activities. Vocational training classes are being carried forward; in fact, in every camp there are classes on certain evenings of every week representing all subjects from first lessons in spoken French to lessons in electrical engineering. In this connection, the educational machinery of the Y. M. C. A. is being largely utilized. . . .

The Young Women's Christian Association, by establishing the hostess houses in camp, has solved one of the biggest problems with which military authorities have had to contend,—that of women visitors to camp. In the old days they had to stand on windy corners, or parade the often wet and muddy streets: there was no place for them to go. Now they can go to this homelike spot and talk with their men friends or relatives amid pleasant surroundings. There have already been seventy-six hostess houses erected within the army and navy camps, and more are in the course of construction. . . .

On visiting days, the hostess house is filled with groups of soldiers and civilians. Some of the old army officers did not like the idea of the hostess house at first. "Send along anything you want to," they told the commissions, "but keep these women away." However, no personal hardship or discomforts can keep them away, so long as there is a chance of their seeing their men who are soon to go to the front. They come by the thousands. They come penniless, oftentimes. They come with stories of misery and want. The hostess house is a recognition of their right to come and the hostess house is playing a large part in conserving the camp morale. The officers no less than the men are coming to look upon it as indispensable. Often now we hear from those who were loudest in objecting to the idea. They say that they are being discriminated against; that some other camp is getting a second hostess house or a special house for taking care of colored women visitors while they have only one. . . .

The civilian public comes into contact with the soldier and the sailor for the most part when they are on leave. It is this phase of their soldiering in which the commissions take the greatest interest, for their reactions to the removal of restraint are apt to be the antithesis of those under the restrictions of camp life. Discipline, character, and ideals must stand the strain of an afternoon or a week-end away from the cantonment, for on those largely depend the physical welfare of the army and navy. Thus, it is obvious that the men must have "somewhere to go." There has been a gratifying response to the demand made on the civilian population in their behalf. The towns and cities adjacent to the camps have assimilated the soldier and sailor population in a remarkably effective manner. Instead of patronage, the men have been given genuine hospitality, and they have responded in kind. That this has been brought about by a national society working along almost scientifically exact lines, is a striking commentary on the personality that may go with the efficient organization of social work. Their well-tested theories and principles had to be applied to an entirely new set of conditions.

The personal hospitality of those who have entertained the soldiers and sailors, is one of the most heartening results of the work of the commissions, for it has developed closer ties between the men and the communities and acted as a conservator of home ideals. The war camp community workers as well as the workers back of the hostess house idea have found that one of the greatest sociological needs in training camp life, is the opportunity to see and talk with women. The boys want the feminine society they were used to back home; many of them want a bit of mothering; and the people of this country are doing a great work in seeing that they get this feminine society of the right kind. . . .

Nearly all of the sports known to American life are carried on in the camps, and all of the men are not only permitted, but are encouraged to participate freely. A continually-growing emphasis is being placed especially in the army upon the semi-military sports. Trench-rushing, wall-scaling, grenade-throwing and boxing are all being promoted. Boxing is conducted under the advisory direction of the most eminent exponents of the art,—men calculated to arouse the enthusiasm of our fighters in the making. . . .

Besides the better known sports, such as baseball and football, there is a great variety of games such as volley ball, push ball, medicine ball, cross-country running, tennis, fencing and swimming. Laughter-provoking games are played regularly by great numbers of soldiers and sailors. This is important, for good humor is one of the vital elements of discipline. . . .

Supplying the means for theatrical entertainments is an obvious part of the program which has undertaken to create a rational social life for the men. Every army camp now has its well-equipped modern liberty theatre building, and the best Broadway attractions are being booked throughout the circuit so that the men have all they would get in New York. . . .

The young American's instinctive preference for sound and healthy occupations and recreations, has been met on every side by all this positive, constructive work. Strict repressive measures have at the same time been taken against alcohol and prostitution, and vice and the opportunities for intemperance—those factors deadly to military efficiency have been reduced to a minimum. . . .

The war is going to be won by manpower. We have profited by the experience of other nations and have reduced to that small inescapable minimum, the percentage of men placed on the ineffective list through immorality. It is no longer news that eighty-nine red light districts have been closed and the venereal disease rate of our army and navy has been reduced more than fifty per cent since the beginning of the war. These are the most obvious achievements in the conservation of manhood and manpower. In the last analysis, the whole suppressive program but prepares the way for the building up of a fighting force with such ideals as will stand the strain of the great encounter on the other side and bring them back better citizens for the experience. To make men fit for fighting—and after—is just plain efficiency plus.

Raymond B. Fosdick, in *Annals of the American Academy of Political and Social Science* (Philadelphia, September, 1918), LXXIX, 131–142 *passim*.

———◆———

176. Broomstick Preparedness (1918)

BY EX-PRESIDENT THEODORE ROOSEVELT

Roosevelt's own military and administrative career demonstrated the expediency of being prepared for emergencies. Inefficiency he would not tolerate. General Wood came near being the Republican candidate for the Presidency in 1920, and was subsequently appointed Governor of the Philippines.—See No. 111 above.

A STUDY of the American army for the year succeeding our entry into the war is a study of the effects of broomstick preparedness. All who defend this type of preparedness are themselves, however amicable and well-meaning, broomstick apologists.

Over eighteen months have now passed since we admitted that we were at war, and over twenty months since the Germans frankly began war upon us. With our immense manpower, wealth, and resources, the natural fighting qualities of our men and the business energy and the mechanical efficiency of our people, we have now developed a force that has made us a highly important factor in the war. Seventeen months after we entered the war we at last had a sufficiency of well-trained troops to enable General Pershing for the first time to take part in the war with a separate army, an army such as the French and the English had. But this army was still very small in size, compared to either the French or British armies. Moreover it was able to act only because it had obtained from our allies the cannon, airplanes, tanks, machine-guns, and the gas necessary in modern warfare. Without what we have thus obtained from our allies we would have been absolutely helpless. But the gallantry and fighting efficiency of our men, and the fact that several hundred thousand are now fit for use at the front, have made us already of very real weight against the Germans, for when the scales are almost trembling in the balance a relatively small weight of effort will determine the outcome. Therefore, the large number of well-meaning persons who are very forgetful, and who like to tickle their vanity by refusing to face what is unpleasant, tend already to say that our unpreparedness did not amount to anything after all, and that all things are all right, and that nobody must speak about the wrongs of the past. For this reason it is essential that our people should know just what our shortcomings were.

We cannot learn about these shortcomings from military officers. The administration by its treatment of General Wood has rendered it a work of the highest danger for any American army officer to tell the truth that ought to be told. General Wood, two years before we went into the war, and again one year before we went into the war, appeared before the Congressional Military Committees and set forth our needs. When at the end of last winter he returned from his stay in France, he told us what ought at once to be done. The administration in every case refused to profit by what he had testified, and yet in every case the events have made good everything he said. It is to General Wood that we owe primarily the Plattsburg officers' training-camps in 1915 and 1916. These Plattsburg training-camps did a work that cannot be overestimated, in providing officers; and it was the one really effective bit of preparation on our part. All that General Wood thus advised and thus did was of the very highest value to the country. Instead of rewarding him for it, the administration has punished him in the way hardest to bear for a gallant and patriotic soldier. This has represented not only a cruel injustice to him, but a deeply unpatriotic refusal to meet the country's needs.

Therefore, I am not at liberty to quote the first-hand testimony I have had as to some of the vital shortcomings in the administration of the War Department and the army during the first eighteen months of the war.

But in the camps I visited I saw some things so evident that no harm can come to any officer from my speaking of them; and there are some things which are now matters of common knowledge, although the War Department did everything it could to keep them from the knowledge of the people.

In the fall of 1917 the enormous majority of our men in the encampments were drilling with broomsticks or else with rudely whittled guns. As late as the beginning of December they had in the camps almost only wooden machine-guns and wooden field-cannon. In the camps I saw barrels mounted on sticks on which zealous captains were endeavoring to teach their men how to ride a horse. At that time we had one or two divisions of well-trained infantry in France— which would have been simply lapped up if placed against the army of any formidable military power. At that time, eight months after we had gone to war, the army we had gathered in the cantonments had neither the rifles, the machine-guns, the cannon, the tanks, nor the airplanes which would have enabled them to make any fight at all against any army of any military power that could have landed on our shores. It would have been as helpless against an invading army as so many savages armed with stone-headed axes. We were wholly unable to defend ourselves a year after we had gone to war. We owed our safety only to the English, French, and Italian fleets and armies.

The cause was our refusal to prepare in advance. President Wilson's message of December, 1914, in which he ridiculed those who advocated preparedness, was part of the cause. We paid the price later with broomstick rifles, log-wood cannon, soldiers without shoes, and epidemics of pneumonia in the camps. We are paying the price now in shortage of coal and congestion of transportation, and in the double cost of necessary war-supplies. We are paying the price and shall pay the price in the shape of taxes and a national debt at least twice as large as would have been the case if with forethought and

wisdom we had prepared in advance.   We have paid the price in the
blood of tens of thousands of gallant men.   The refusal to prepare,
and the price we now pay because of the refusal, stand in the relation
of cause and effect. . . .

The attitude of the War Department during the first months of the
war was shown by the remark of one of the high officials to the effect
that the delay of a few months was "a perfectly endurable delay."
This remark was made with all the complacency of the butterfly on
the fence to the toad under the harrow.   Others paid with their blood
for our delay.   The German submarine note came on January 31,
1917; and within the next two months an alert and efficient War Department would have had every particle of its programme minutely
mapped out and well on the way to execution.   As a matter of fact,
nothing was really begun until late in August. . . .

Every American worth his salt feels exultant pride in the splendid
courage and high efficiency of our soldiers in France.   From General
Pershing down they have made our country, and us who dwell therein,
forever their debtors.

It is well to pay these men the homage of words, but what really
counts is the homage of deeds.   It is a dreadful thing to send our fine
and gallant boys to battle, and yet to deny them the formidable
weapons and machines of war, the lack of which must be paid for by
pouring out their blood like water.

As a nation we cannot be acquitted of this wrong to our fighting
men whom we have sent to the front.   No finer fighting men were
ever known, and their deeds are deeds of deathless honor.   But our
government, by its failure to prepare in advance and by its delay,
waste, and mismanagement after the war began, has made a record
that is not pleasant for Americans to contemplate.   Let our people
never forget that if we had chosen to prepare in advance we would
probably have ended the war in ninety days after we entered it in 1917;
and that if when General Leonard Wood returned from France at the
close of last winter the administration had heeded his report and had
done as he then advised and as every patriotic man of knowledge
and insight then hoped, we would have been further advanced at the
beginning of the summer than we are now at the end of the fall.   Nine-
tenths of wisdom is being wise in time.

When, on February 3, we broke off diplomatic relations with Germany the war really began. From that moment avoidable, unwarranted delay was as inexcusable as it is now. The day before Mr. Elon Hooker had laid before the authorities at Washington an offer to turn over his entire plant to the service of the government, this being the plant better fitted than any other in the United States to undertake the manufacture of war gas and the development of new and more formidable kinds of gas on a gigantic scale. His request was refused. A year elasped before any serious effort was made to undo any of the effects of the error. At the same time we had the means for building enormous quantities of excellent machine-guns. The War Department refused to avail itself of the opportunity and dallied for about eighteen months in developing a new type of gun, leaving us meanwhile without any. We dawdled in similar fashion over the tanks. We have not yet built any field-guns, and are still dependent upon what the French can give us. It is necessary merely to refer to the appalling delay in the air service where $640,000,000 were appropriated and largely expended without securing any tangible result whatever on the field of battle until we had been at war nearly a year and a half.

. . . After a year of war, when the great German drive began, our fighting army able to take part in the active work at the front was actually smaller than that of Belgium. In the next six months we were able to place in the field an army respectable in numbers and admirable in quality; and we were able to do this only because, in view of the breakdown of our shipping programme, the British furnished their ships, so that 60 per cent of the tonnage used in ferrying our soldiers across was British. But we were able to furnish only the men. We had only the field-artillery the French furnished us. We got uniforms from the English. We did not have a single fighting-plane of American make, and naturally the French did not give us their best planes. We had very few American machine-guns or auto rifles. We had almost no gas. We had almost no tanks, and those we did have were furnished by our allies. We now have a few admirable naval guns, admirably handled, and a number of excellent bombing airplanes of our own manufacture.

The business efficiency of our people is great. Its manpower is great. Its resources are enormous. Had the administration, with an eye single to our country's needs, devoted its whole energy to speeding up the war, and abandoned all thought of politics during the war, the peace of overwhelming victory would by this time have been won. But this was not done. Never before in our history has the administration in power during a war drawn party lines as sharply as in the present war. No one but an active partisan adherent of the administration has been given any position of the slightest political responsibility; and the test in the appointment of even these, as established by President Wilson, in his messages concerning the election or reelection of congressmen, is loyalty to the administration rather than loyalty to the country. . . .

Theodore Roosevelt, *The Great Adventure* (New York, Scribner's, 1918), 143–157 *passim*.

CHAPTER XXXII — OVER THERE

177. An Embattled Press Correspondent (1914)

BY RICHARD HARDING DAVIS

Davis, a famous correspondent, had followed many armies, reported many wars, before this one. His employment was perhaps as risky as any in which a neutral could be engaged.—General bibliography on the war, for all articles in this chapter, is given with No. 171 above.

. . . I HAD started with the column at seven o'clock, and at noon an automobile, with flags flying and the black eagle of the staff enamelled on the door, came speeding back from the front. In it was a very blond and distinguished-looking officer of high rank and many decorations. He used a single eye-glass, and his politeness and his English were faultless. He invited me to accompany him to the general staff.

That was the first intimation I had that I was in danger. I saw they were giving me far too much attention. I began instantly to work to set myself free, and there was not a minute for the next twenty-four hours that I was not working. Before I stepped into the car I had decided upon my line of defence. . . . The blond officer smiled uneasily and with his single glass studied the sky. When we reached the staff he escaped from me with the alacrity of one released from a disagreeable and humiliating duty. The staff were at luncheon, seated in their luxurious motor-cars or on the grass by the side of the road. On the other side of the road the column of dust-covered gray ghosts were being rushed past us. The staff, in dress uniforms, flowing cloaks, and gloves, belonged to a different race. They knew that. Among themselves they were like priests breathing incense. Whenever one of them spoke to another they saluted, their heels clicked, their bodies bent at the belt line.

One of them came to where, in the middle of the road, I was stranded and trying not to feel as lonely as I looked. He was much younger than myself and dark and handsome. His face was smooth-shaven, his figure tall, lithe, and alert. He wore a uniform of light blue and silver that clung to him and high boots of patent leather. His waist was like a girl's and, as though to show how supple he was, he kept continually bowing and shrugging his shoulders and in elegant protest gesticulating with his gloved hands. He should have been a moving-picture actor. He reminded me of Anthony Hope's fascinating but wicked Rupert of Hentzau. He certainly was wicked, and I got to hate him as I never imagined it possible to hate anybody. He had been told off to dispose of my case, and he delighted in it. He enjoyed it as a cat enjoys playing with a mouse. As actors say, he saw himself in the part. He "ate" it.

"You are an English officer out of uniform," he began. "You have been taken inside our lines." He pointed his forefinger at my stomach and wiggled his thumb. "And you know what *that* means!"

I saw playing the fool with him would be waste of time.

"I followed your army," I told him, "because it's my business to follow armies and because yours is the best-looking army I ever saw." He made me one of his mocking bows.

"We thank you," he said, grinning. "But you have seen too much."

"I haven't seen anything," I said, "that everybody in Brussels hasn't seen for three days."

He shook his head reproachfully and with a gesture signified the group of officers.

"You have seen enough in this road," he said, "to justify us in shooting you now." . . .

When Rupert of Hentzau returned the other officers were with him, and, fortunately for me, they spoke or understood English. For the rest of the day what followed was like a legal argument. It was as cold-blooded as a game of bridge. Rupert of Hentzau wanted an English spy shot for his supper; just as he might have desired a grilled bone. He showed no personal animus, and, I must say for him, that he conducted the case for the prosecution without heat or anger. He mocked me, grilled and taunted me, but he was always charmingly polite. . . .

. . . The points he made against me were that my German pass was signed neither by General Jarotsky nor by Lieutenant Geyer, but only stamped, and that any rubber stamp could be forged; that my American passport had not been issued at Washington, but in London, where an Englishman might have imposed upon our embassy; and that in the photograph pasted on the passport I was wearing the uniform of a British officer. I explained that the photograph was taken eight years ago, and that the uniform was one I had seen on the west coast of Africa, worn by the West African Field Force. Because it was unlike any known military uniform, and as cool and comfortable as a golf jacket, I had had it copied. But since that time it had been adopted by the English Brigade of Guards and the Territorials. I knew it sounded like fiction; but it was quite true.

Rupert of Hentzau smiled delightedly.

"Do you expect us to believe that?" he protested.

"Listen," I said, "If you could invent an explanation for that uniform as quickly as I told you that one, standing in a road with eight officers trying to shoot you, you would be the greatest general in Germany."

That made the others laugh; and Rupert retorted: "Very well, then, we will concede that the entire British army has changed its uniform to suit your photograph. But if you are *not* an officer, why, in the photograph, are you wearing war ribbons?"

I said the war ribbons were in my favor, and I pointed out that no officer of any one country could have been in the different campaigns for which the ribbons were issued.

"They prove," I argued, "that I *am* a correspondent, for only a correspondent could have been in wars in which his own country was not engaged."

I thought I had scored; but Rupert instantly turned my own witness against me.

"Or a military attaché," he said. At that they all smiled and nodded knowingly.

He followed this up by saying, accusingly, that the hat and clothes I was then wearing were English. The clothes were English, but I knew he did not know that, and was only guessing; and there were no marks on them. About my hat I was not certain. It was a felt Alpine hat, and whether I had bought it in London or New York I could not remember. Whether it was evidence for or against I could not be sure. So I took it off and began to fan myself with it, hoping to get a look at the name of the maker. But with the eyes of the young prosecuting attorney fixed upon me, I did not dare take a chance. Then, to aid me, a German aëroplane passed overhead, and those who were giving me the third degree looked up. I stopped fanning myself and cast a swift glance inside the hat. To my intense satisfaction I read, stamped on the leather lining: "Knox, New York."

I put the hat back on my head and a few minutes later pulled it off and said: "Now, for instance, my hat. If I were an Englishman would I cross the ocean to New York to buy a hat?"

It was all like that. They would move away and whisper together, and I would try to guess what questions they were preparing. I had to arrange my defence without knowing in what way they would try to trip me, and I had to think faster than I ever have thought before. I had no more time to be scared, or to regret my past sins, than had a man in a quicksand. So far as I could make out, they were divided in opinion concerning me. Rupert of Hentzau, who was the adjutant or the chief of staff, had only one simple thought, which was to shoot me. Others considered me a damn fool; I could hear them laughing and saying: "*Er ist ein dummer Mensch.*" And others thought that whether I was a fool or not, or an American or an Englishman, was not the question; I had seen too much and should be put away. I felt if, instead of having Rupert act as my interpreter, I could personally speak to the general I might talk my way out of it, but Rupert assured me that to set me free the Count de Schwerin lacked authority, and that my papers, which were all against me, must be submitted to the general of the army corps, and we would not reach him until midnight.

"And *then!*—" he would exclaim, and he would repeat his pantomime of pointing his forefinger at my stomach and wiggling his thumb. He was very popular with me. . . .

As it grew later I persuaded myself they did not mean to act until morning, and I stretched out on the straw and tried to sleep. At midnight I was startled by the light of an electric torch. It was strapped to the chest of an officer, who ordered me to get up and come with him. He spoke only German and he seemed very angry. The owner of the house and the old cook had shown him to my room, but they stood in the shadow without speaking. Nor, fearing I might compromise them—for I could not see why, except for one purpose, they were taking me out into the night—did I speak to them. We got into another motor-car and in silence drove north from Ligne down a country road to a great château that stood in a magnificent park. Something had gone wrong with the lights of the château, and its hall was lit only by candles that showed soldiers sleeping like dead men on bundles of wheat and others leaping up and down the marble stairs. They put me in a huge armchair of silk and gilt, with two of the gray ghosts to guard me, and from the hall, when the doors of the drawing-room opened, I could see a long table on which were candles in silver candle-sticks or set on plates, and many maps and half-empty bottles of champagne. Around the table, standing or seated, and leaning across the maps, were staff-officers in brilliant uniforms. They were much older men and of higher rank than any I had yet seen. They were eating, drinking, gesticulating. In spite of the tumult, some, in utter weariness, were asleep. It was like a picture of 1870 by Detaille or De Neuville. Apparently, at last I had reached the headquarters of the mysterious general. I had arrived at what, for a suspected spy, was an inopportune moment. The Germans themselves had been surprised, or somewhere south of us had met with a reverse, and the air was vibrating with excitement and something very like panic. Outside, at great speed and with sirens shrieking, automobiles were arriving, and I could hear the officers shouting: "*Die Englischen kommen!*"

To make their reports they flung themselves up the steps, the electric torches, like bull's-eye lanterns, burning holes in the night. Seeing a civilian under guard, they would stare and ask questions. Even when they came close, owing to the light in my eyes, I could not see them. Sometimes, in a half circle, there would be six or eight of the electric torches blinding me, and from behind them voices barking at me with strange, guttural noises. Much they said I could not understand, but they made it quite clear it was no fit place for an Englishman.

When the door from the drawing-room opened and Rupert of Hentzau appeared, I was almost glad to see him.

Whenever he spoke to me he always began or ended his sentence with "*Mr. Davis.*" He gave it emphasis and meaning which was intended to show that he knew it was *not* my name. I would not have thought it possible to put so much insolence into two innocent words.

It was as though he said: "Mr. Davis, *alias* Jimmy Valentine." He certainly would have made a great actor.

"*Mr. Davis*," he said, "you are free."

Richard Harding Davis, *With the Allies* (New York, Scribner's, 1914), 45–68 *passim.*

———————◆———————

178. The Cathedral of Rheims (1915)

TRANSLATED FROM THE FRENCH OF ÉMILE VERHAUREN

BY JOYCE KILMER

Joyce Kilmer (1886–1918) was a graduate of Columbia University. He was on the staff of the *New York Times Sunday Magazine and Review of Books* from 1913, and contributed regularly to various periodicals.   In 1917 he enlisted in the 165th U. S. Infantry, and was killed in action on August 1, 1918.   He had published three volumes of verse, and *Literature in the Making* (1917).   Rheims cathedral, like many other ancient architectural treasures of France and Belgium, was irreparably damaged by German artillery fire.

HE who walks through the meadows of Champagne
  At noon in Fall, when leaves like gold appear,
    Sees it draw near
Like some great mountain set upon the plain,
From radiant dawn until the close of day,
    Nearer it grows
    To him who goes
Across the country.   When tall towers lay
    Their shadowy pall
    Upon his way,
    He enters, where
The solid stone is hollowed deep by all
Its centuries of beauty and of prayer.

Ancient French temple! thou whose hundred kings
Watch over thee, emblazoned on thy walls,
Tell me, within thy memory-hallowed halls
What chant of triumph, or what war-song rings?
Thou hast known Clovis and his Frankish train,

Whose mighty hand Saint Remy's hand did keep.
And in thy spacious vault perhaps may sleep
An echo of the voice of Charlemagne.
For God thou hast known fear, when from His side
Men wandered, seeking alien shrines and new,
But still the sky was bountiful and blue
And thou wast crowned with France's love and pride.

Sacred thou art, from pinnacle to base;
And in thy panes of gold and scarlet glass
The setting sun sees thousandfold his face;
Sorrow and joy, in stately silence pass
Across thy walls, the shadow and the light;
Around thy lofty pillars, tapers white
Illuminate, with delicate sharp flames,
The brows of saints with venerable names,
And in the night erect a fiery wall.
A great but silent fervour burns in all
Those simple folk who kneel, pathetic, dumb,
And know that down below, beside the Rhine—
Cannon, horses, soldiers, flags in line—
With blare of trumpets, mighty armies come.

Suddenly, each knows fear;
Swift rumours pass, that every one must hear,
The hostile banners blaze against the sky
And by the embassies mobs rage and cry,
Now war has come, and peace is at an end.
On Paris town the German troops descend.
They are turned back, and driven to Champagne.
And now, as to so many weary men,
The glorious temple gives them welcome, when
It meets them at the bottom of the plain.

At once, they set their cannon in its way.
    There is no gable now, nor wall
That does not suffer, night and day,
    As shot and shell in crushing torrents fall.

The stricken tocsin quivers through the tower;
  The triple nave, the apse, the lonely choir
Are circled, hour by hour,
  With thundering bands of fire
And Death is scattered broadcast among men.

And then
That which was splendid with baptismal grace;
The stately arches soaring into space,
The transepts, columns, windows gray and gold,
The organ, in whose tones the ocean rolled,
The crypts, of mighty shades the dwelling places,
The Virgin's gentle hands, the Saints' pure faces,
All, even the pardoning hands of Christ the Lord
Were struck and broken by the wanton sword
Of sacrilegious lust.
O beauty slain, O glory in the dust!

Strong walls of faith, most basely overthrown!
The crawling flames, like adders glistening
Ate the white fabric of this lovely thing.
Now from its soul arose a piteous moan,
The soul that always loved the just and fair.
Granite and marble loud their woe confessed,
The silver monstrances that Popes had blessed,
The chalices and lamps and crosiers rare
Were seared and twisted by a flaming breath;
The horror everywhere did range and swell,
The guardian Saints into this furnace fell,
Their bitter tears and screams were stilled in death.

Around the flames armed hosts are skirmishing,
The burning sun reflects the lurid scene;
The German army, fighting for its life,
Rallies its torn and terrified left wing;
    And, as they near this place
    The imperial eagles see
    Before them in their flight,

Here, in the solemn night,
The old cathedral, to the years to be
    Showing, with wounded arms, their own disgrace.

Joyce Kilmer, *Poems, Essays and Letters* (copyright 1918, George H. Doran Co. Publishers), 165–168.

———————◆———————

179. American Ambulance Field Service (1916)

BY JOHN MASEFIELD

Here a famous English poet reports a service in which many young Americans offered their help to the Allies, as non-combatants, prior to the entry of the United States into the war.

. . . THE real work of the section begins with darkness, when the roads can no longer be seen by observers in the sky. After supper, in the last of the light, the ambulance-cars are made ready; the two drivers in each car put on their steel helmets and take their gas masks, and the convoy (or a part of it, according to the need of the service and the severity of the fighting) moves out, car by car, toward the Postes de Secours, where they will find the wounded. Some camps are so far from the front that the first part of the journey up can be done with headlights. All roads leading to the front are crowded with men or wagons going up or coming down. In a little while after leaving camp the ambulances run into the full stream of the relief and revictualing. It is the rule upon all roads in France that troops and vehicles shall keep well to the right, so that there shall be room for the column going as well as for the column return-ing. The day is busy enough upon the roads well back from the front, though those farther up are quiet. But at night this changes, and in the darkness the life on the real roads begins. It is difficult to describe this night life on the roads, since so little of it can be seen; yet on first moving out with the cars, before darkness has fallen and the headlights are doused, enough is caught to show that in modern war there is no splendor of movement or of position, as in the old wars, when divisions of cavalry charged and the front of a battle advanced as one man, but that there is still something distinctive about it by which it will be remembered. Old wars are remembered, perhaps, for their glitter or their crash, for something big in their commanders or fatal in their results. This war will perhaps be remembered for the monotony and the patience behind the lines. There alone is the imagination struck. There, on the midnight roads, is the visible struggle; there the nations are passing and repassing to the defense of the gates, and, to many, the image of this war will be not, as before, a spangled man or anything splendid, but simply the convoy of many wagons, driven by tired men, going on and on along the darkness of a road, in a cloud of dust or in the welter of a swill of mud, each man seeing no more of the war than the tail-board of the wagon in front, or the flash of faces where men light their pipes by the roadside, or the glow of some lantern where there is a guard to pass.

So, in moving out of the camp into this life upon the roads, a man passes into the heart of modern war, which is, in the main, a war of supply. Twilight and the dust together make the wagons and the soldiers the color of a far horizon. Dust wavers and settles on the moving things, the smell of dust is in the breath, and the taste of it on the lips. The old men who work by the roadside night and day, cracking stones for road metal, disappear, as each wagon passes, in a smoke of dust.

Soon the light dies. In open parts of the road, where things passing show against the sky, the convoys of wagons, twenty in a section, move and are black. The road is noisy with their rumble. Some of them, driven by men who are perhaps asleep, sway out of line into the middle of the road. Then the ambulance-drivers, trying to get past, sound their klaxons and shout, "*À droit!*" till the sleeper wakes and turns his wagon aside. Sometimes, as the ambulance shoots ahead of a string of wagons, there is an empty stretch of road running through empty fields and the night is as in peace time. Then something big, black, and flopping shows ahead, making the darkness darker; there comes a jingling and the snort of horses, and out of the night comes, perhaps, a battery going down, gun after gun, some quickening, some staying, or empty horse-wagons with spare horses tied to the tail-board and the chains rattling on the slats and the drivers riding. They pass and drop down into the night like ships gone hull down; but others and others come, some walking, some with their men walking, calling to their horses, some rattling quick and empty, some slipping or shying or kicking at the passers. At times, as the ambulances go, something like a caterpillar appears ahead, moving slowly with a caterpillar's humping wriggle, and filling one half of the road. This blackness is lower than the other blacknesses, and unlike anything met with hitherto. At the sound of the klaxon it shogs a little to one side, stray blacknesses break from it, and the humping wriggle pauses in some disorder. It is a column of the *relève* going up to the front. It is a company of foot-soldiers marching in column of twos, each man bent under his load, which makes him twice the size of a man, and all walking slowly, many of them with walking-staffs, like pilgrims. . . .

All the way, at odd times, far off, with neither sense nor sequence, the guns have sounded almost like the noises of peace—blasting or pile-driving. Now, outside the village, as the ambulance comes out upon the hill, they sound for the first time like the noise of battle, much nearer and much more terrible. Now, too, far off, as the car runs in the open, the drivers see the star-shells going up and up, and bursting into white stars, and pausing and drifting slowly down, very, very slowly, pausing as they come, far apart, yet so many that there are always more than one aloft. They are the most beautiful things in modern war and almost the most terrible. Often they pause so long before dying that they look like the lights of peace in lighthouse and city beacon, or like planets in the sky.

In this open space the drivers can see for some miles over the battle-field. Over it all, as far as the eye can see, the lights are rising and falling. There is not much noise, but a sort of mutter of battle with explosions now and then. Very far away, perhaps ten miles away, there is fighting, for in that quarter the sky glimmers as though with summer lightning; the winks and flashes of the guns shake and die across the heaven.

One side of the road is here screened with burlap stretched upon posts for half a mile together; otherwise daytime traffic on it would be seen by the enemy. Some of the burlap is in rags and some of the posts are broken; the wreck of a cart lies beside the road, and in the road itself are roundish patches of new stones where shell-holes have been mended, perhaps a few minutes before.

Just overhead as the car passes comes a blasting, shattering crash which is like sudden death. Then another and another follow, one on the other, right overhead. On the ground above, the slope of the little hill, a battery of soixante-quinze guns has just opened fire. On the tail of each crash comes the crying of the shell, passing overhead like a screech-owl, till it is far away in the enemy lines, where it bursts. Another round follows, but by this time the ambulance is a hundred yards away, and now, on the heels of the affront, comes the answer. Rather to the right and very near in the stillness of the moonlight an enemy battery replies, one, two, three guns in as many seconds, a fourth gun a little late, and the shells come with a scream across and burst behind the ambulances, somewhere near the battery. Then a starlight goes up near enough to dazzle the eyes, and near enough, one would think, to show the ambulance to the world; and as the starlight goes down a second round comes from the battery aimed God knows at what, but so as to *arroser* the district. The noise of the engine stifles the noise of the shells, but above the engines one shell's noise is heard; the screech of its rush comes very near, there is a flash ahead, a burst, and the patter of falling fragments. Long afterward, perhaps six seconds afterward, a tiny piece of shell drops upon the ambulance. Another shell bursts behind the car, and another on the road in front; the car goes round the new shell-hole and passes on.

This is "the front." Two hundred and fifty yards away, a seventh part of a mile, two minutes' walk, are the enemy lines. Dead ahead, in what looks like a big rubbish-heap, such as one may see in suburbs where builders have been putting up a row of villas, is the Poste de Secours. The rubbish-heap was once a farm, though no man, not even the farmer, could now say where his buildings lay.

The drivers go down the sloping path into the cellars. The cellar roof has been propped and heaped with layers of timber balks interspersed with sand-bags, and the cellar itself, shored up, is like a mine. It is a vast place with several rooms in it, from one of which, strongly lighted, comes the sound of voices and of people moving. Looking round near at hand, as the eye becomes accustomed to the darkness, one sees some loaded stretchers on the floor near the doorway. Three dead men, who were alive an hour ago, lie there awaiting burial. They were all hit by one torpedo, says the stretcher-bearer, these and five others, but these three died on their way to the Poste. Some say that the dead look as though they were asleep, but no sleep ever looked like death.

Presently the sick arrive, haggard and white, but able to walk, and the gathering breaks up and the ambulances are free to go. The moon is blotted by this time; it is darker and beginning to rain, the men say. On leaving the operating-room, one hears again as a real thing the scream of the rush of the big shells, the thump of the bursts, and the crash of the great guns. The stretchers are passed into the ambulances, the sick are helped on to seats, they are covered with blankets, and the doors are closed. It is much darker now and the rain has already made the ground sticky; and with the rain the smell of corruption has become heavier, and the ruin is like what it is—a graveyard laid bare. Shells from the enemy rush overhead and burst in a village which lies on the road home. They are strafing the village; the cars have a fair chance of being blown to pieces; it is as dark as pitch and the road will be full of new shell-holes. The drivers start their engines and turn the cars for home; the rain drives in their faces as they go, and along the road in front of them the shells flash at intervals, lighting the tree-stumps.

These drivers (there are now, and have been, some hundreds of them) are men of education. They are the very pick and flower of American life, some of them professional men, but the greater number of them young men on the threshold of life, lads just down from college or in their last student years. All life lies before them in their own country, but they have put that aside for an idea, and have come to help France in her hour of need. Two of them have died and many of them have been maimed for France, and all live a life of danger and risk death nightly. To this company of splendid and gentle and chivalrous Americans be all thanks and greetings from the friends and allies of sacred France.

John Masefield, *The Harvest of the Night*, in *Harper's Magazine* (New York, 1917), CXXXIV, 801a–810b *passim*.

180. In Memory of the American Volunteers (1916)

BY ALAN SEEGER

For Seeger, see No. 169 above.

I

AY, it is fitting on this holiday,
    Commemorative of our soldier dead,
When—with sweet flowers of our New England May
Hiding the lichened stones by fifty years made gray—
Their graves in every town are garlanded,
That pious tribute should be given too
To our intrepid few
Obscurely fallen here beyond the seas,
Those to preserve their country's greatness died;
But by the death of these
Something that we can look upon with pride
Has been achieved, nor wholly unreplied
Can sneers triumph in the charge they make
That from a war where Freedom was at stake
America withheld and, daunted stood aside.

II

Be they remembered here with each reviving spring,
Not only that in May, when life is loveliest,
Around Neuville-Saint-Vaast and the disputed crest
Of Vimy, they, superb, unfaltering,
In that fine onslaught that no fire could halt,
Parted impetuous to their first assault;
But that they brought fresh hearts and springlike too
To that high mission, and 'tis meet to strew
With twigs of lilac and spring's earliest rose
The cenotaph of those
Who in the cause that history most endears
Fell in the sunny morn and flower of their young years.

III

Yet sought they neither recompense nor praise,
Nor to be mentioned in another breath
Than their blue-coated comrades whose great days
It was their pride to share—ay, share even to the death!
Nay, rather, France, to you they rendered thanks
(Seeing they came for honor, not for gain),
Who, opening to them your glorious ranks,
Gave them that great occasion to excel,
That chance to live the life most free from stain
And that rare privilege of dying well.

IV

O friends! I know not since that war began
From which no people nobly stands aloof
If in all moments we have given proof
Of virtues that were thought American.
I know not if in all things done and said
All has been well and good,
Or if each one of us can hold his head
As proudly as he should,
Or, from the pattern of those mighty dead
Whose shades our country venerates to-day,
If we've not somewhat fallen and somewhat gone astray.
But you to whom our land's good name is dear,
If there be any here
Who wonder if her manhood be decreased,
Relaxed its sinews and its blood less red
Than that at Shiloh and Antietam shed,
Be proud of these, have joy in this at least,
And cry: "Now heaven be praised
That in that hour that most imperilled her,
Menaced her liberty who foremost raised
Europe's bright flag of freedom, some there were
Who, not unmindful of the antique debt,
Came back the generous path of Lafayette;
And when of a most formidable foe

She checked each onset, arduous to stem—
Foiled and frustrated them—
On those red fields where blow with furious blow
Was countered, whether the gigantic fray
Rolled by the Meuse or at the Bois Sabot,
Accents of ours were in the fierce mêlée;
And on those furthest rims of hallowed ground
Where the forlorn, the gallant charge expires,
When the slain bugler has long ceased to sound,
And on the tangled wires
The last wild rally staggers, crumbles, stops,
Withered beneath the shrapnel's iron showers:—
Now heaven be thanked, we gave a few brave drops;
Now heaven be thanked, a few brave drops were ours."

V

There, holding still, in frozen steadfastness,
Their bayonets toward the beckoning frontiers,
They lie—our comrades—lie among their peers,
Clad in the glory of fallen warriors,
Grim clusters under thorny trellises.
Dry, furthest foam upon disastrous shores,
Leaves that made last year beautiful, still strewn
Even as they fell, unchanged, beneath the changing moon;
And earth in her divine indifference
Rolls on, and many paltry things and mean
Prate to be heard and caper to be seen.
But they are silent, calm; their eloquence
Is that incomparable attitude;
No human presences their witness are,
But summer clouds and sunset crimson-hued,
And showers and night winds and the northern star.
Nay, even our salutations seem profane,
Opposed to their Elysian quietude;
Our salutations calling from afar,
From our ignobler plane
And undistinction of our lesser parts:

Hail, brothers, and farewell; you are twice blest, brave hearts.
Double your glory is who perished thus,
For you died for France and vindicated us.

Alan Seeger, *Poems* (New York, Scribner's, 1916), 170–174.

------◆------

181.   A Lesson from the Tanks (1917)

BY HENRY SEIDEL CANBY

Canby has lectured on literary subjects at Yale, and is the author of several volumes relating to the short story; he is also editor of the *Saturday Review of Literature*. During the war he devoted himself to liaison work for the British Ministry of Information. This brought him into contact with various aspects of the war, one of which he discusses here in a charmingly whimsical way. Tanks were among the new offensive weapons developed by the World War; their first use by the English caught the Germans wholly unprepared.

. . . ARE Tanks conscious? If you should meet one sauntering along a *route nationale* or sliding down a side hill for a drink of petrol, you would not swear to the contrary. Do Tanks think? Feel a Whippet twirl under your feet, right and left, as she picks her road across trench bays, or watch a Mark V mount and jog the length of a train of flat cars until he finds one that suits him, and you can almost believe it. Do Tanks breed? Well, at least there are male Tanks and female Tanks, and to all appearances offspring seem quite as probable as with elephants. Have Tanks a sense of humor? Perhaps not, but like Falstaff they are a cause of humor in others. Five new Whippet Tanks, with their machine guns jammed, chased a fat German major down a long hill in France one morning in May, their eight miles an hour just equal to his perspiring best, while a regiment of Australians at the top collapsed in laughter and forgot to fire. I should like to ask that German (who may be still running) whether Tanks are mere machines.

The Mark IV Tank is a slow and sullen dinosaur. Four miles an hour is his limit. Frequently, with sponsons taken off, and armament removed, he mounts a platform on his back and carries a sixty-pounder gun; or hauls a sledge, like an ox team, to pull big howitzers over shell craters. The Mark V is the next step upward in evolution. He is good for five miles an hour, has made nine, and one man can drive him. "Him" is not accurate, for if his weapons are machine guns instead of two-inch cannon, "her" is the proper designation. When I climbed down into the hot and whirring middle of a Mark V, heard the gears squeal and roar, and saw through the eye-slits the ground swinging under us, I knew how a steam roller might feel in a briar patch. Nothing could stop our many ton, hundred and fifty horse power. We came to a trench, swung up, so easily, and down with scarcely a quiver, and so on about our business. And if the trench had been wider? Why then, there are "tadpole tails" provided, which hook behind and serve for leverage.

But the Mark V is a ponderous invention. It was with the Whippet that imagination touched the Tanks. The Whippet—so named I suppose from the speedy dog which chases rabbits to earth—is the pacing dromedary of Tankdom. She is light—only a few tons I should guess—and instead of accommodating man Jonah-like in her entrails, carries a cab like a camel's hump, from which one can look, sometimes perpendicularly, behind. The Whippet has two engines, one for each of her paw series, and that accounts for her eccentric motion. As she runs her eight, ten, up to a conceivable twenty miles, an hour, she squeals raucously. At a rock or a stump—both bad for Tanks, which can be "hung up" on their "bellies"—she whirls with unbelievable rapidity till your eyes are looking one way and your stomach another. Then she rumbles gaily over the field seeking for trees under twelve inches through to practise on, sees a trench, rises on her hind quarters, drops below sky-line with a teeth-shaking bump, grips the further bank, rolls up screaming, and charges off for more.

A bank attracts her. She noses it until she finds an angle not quite, but almost perpendicular, and sticking her nails in the sod, worms up, while you cling to the machine-gun, and look at grass which is both back of and below you. And as she goes she spits oil, blows dust, and flattens the world behind her. If an enemy, you may escape her by lying on the bottom of a trench; you can smash her with a shell if you can catch her on the wing, which is not easy; but the preferable place with a Whippet is on top. Never was devised a more dangerous, humorous, human engine of warfare than this. Indeed, it is not Tank tactics, which are not yet publishable, but Tank humanity, that is the subject of this writing.

I was several times a guest at "Tanks," the name applied not only to the great repair station and depot, headquarters of the Tank Corps, but also to the quiet chateau with its admirable seventeenth-century porch where the young general of Tanks and his active staff are quartered. Our talk ranged through and about and above Tank tactics and on into England and the psychology of the races at war; but it came back and back to the *raison d'etre* of the Tank. "The business of the Tank," he said, "is to meet and master the machine gun so that infantry can carry on further; and in this its use has but just begun. Its object is to save men." . . .

The truth must already be apparent. The Tank is our first real approach to the mechanical soldier—the soldier without blood to spill and nerves to tear, who can nevertheless perform the inevitable business of physical collision which must come if human will set against human will finds no better means of settling the conflict. . . . Here is a mechanical substitute for warring man. In the period of the Italian Renaissance warfare reached such a pitch of science that the mercenary generals who fought for Venice or Florence could sometimes calculate the probable outcome, and save their troops the hardships of battle. . . . Are we coming to an age when mechanisms will be sent from our fortresses to fight it out under scientific control, the best machines, best made, best handled, to win? War will scarcely be ended that way. . . . But the Tank is a first step toward substituting steel for bodies in a war where muscles have given place to high explosives, eyes to range finders, ears to microphones, noses to gas signals, legs to petrol, and skulls to "tin helmets."

It is hard not to be whimsical in mood when writing of Tanks, and yet I do not desire to be whimsical. Tanks were no joke for the Germans. Their own clumsy contrivance, built in imitation, proved how anxious and how unable they were to retort effectively in kind. And that we should be building machines to take the place of men is no mere romance of science or expedient of a warfare where "cannon fodder" has risen in price. For if the Tank takes the place of many common soldiers, then many common soldiers need no longer stay common!

The Germans recognized this principle in their later methods of attack. Roughly speaking, and in exact accord with their idea of the value of life where the state and its ambitions are concerned, they divided their infantry into two sorts. There were the regiments of inferior material, true cannon fodder, which could be pushed in masses against the enemy, succeeding often by sheer momentum, in spite of frightful losses; and there were the picked men, of "storm troop" grade, armed with machine guns, able to hold what was taken, and each worth a score of the rifle-armed rabble. This was the scheme of Prussian evolution toward super-war, a less humane and ultimately a less effective method than the British invention. Furthermore, a method which looked toward a Prussian future merely. For note that men and machines in Prussian eyes had the same value, or rather, that men by proper discipline could be made as valuable as machines. The Prussian mind conceived a battering-ram of plebeian, second-rate flesh (preferably Social Democrats, unskilled laborers, and the like) which could be crushed in assault without material loss. The Western mind imagined the Tank, a super-Tommy without his precious vital spark. . . .

If it is possible—and who will deny it—that in future wars, if we permit them, machines will serve as infantry and cavalry; that guns will be laid and fixed by mechanical means from some safe place in the rear; that submarines and monitors will operate by wave lengths sent from shore; if it is probable that the coming world, whether in war or in peace, will be as full of machinery, of appliances, electrical, chemical, mathematical, as the inside of a submarine, why then what shall we do with our Tommy in the meantime? Shall we keep him an automaton, whose humor, like the Tanks' is pathetic precisely because he does understand so little of the vast forces around him, forces as far as the moon beyond his control? Shall we make him more of a machine, or more of a man? For after the shaking-up this war has given him, neither he nor his children will stand still.

If it is more of a man that we wish to make him, a man competent to control machinery because he can think out how and where and why it is to be used, then we must educate him. Not half-heartedly as we have done, but as the Greeks would have educated him, as seemingly they did educate even their slaves, by contact and practice with the best of the technical processes he will have to follow; by absorption of the best ideas as to the relation of his work to his life. The first means technical education raised to an excellence which we have not yet given it, and broadened to cover all the processes necessary or use-

ful for the preservation of life.   There will be less and less place for
unskilled labor and unskilled fighters among civilized men; machines
will be the unskilled laborers; and if your common soldier of to-day
is left technically illiterate, he will sink to their level. . . .

We have invented machinery without learning to control it.   Let
us not invent (or suffer) new distributions of power without providing
an effective education in its use and enjoyment.

We devised the Tank and sent it upon its way rejoicing to the discomfiture of our enemies.   It is harder to devise a new and improved
man, but quite as possible.   We cannot give him religion, which he
clearly is seeking, we cannot give him a loving heart, we cannot give
him courage if he does not possess it, we cannot give him strength of
intellect, we cannot give him instinctive morality.   But a well-trained
mind, and well-trained muscles, and a fairly sound body we can give
him in nine cases out of ten—even the Chinese coolies on the British
front have been taught to build complex machinery; and a sense of
his place in the world, economic, social, ethical, historical we can give
him; and also in some measure the power of independent thought.
The object of the Tank and all mechanical contrivances is to save life,
to save life in order that in future men shall be men and not machines.

Henry Seidel Canby, *Education by Violence* (New York, Harcourt Brace &
Company, 1919), 130–151 *passim*.

---◆---

182.   An American in the British Air Service (1918)

ANONYMOUS

This impetuous young American joined the British Air Service early in the war
and recorded in vivid style a daily account of his experiences.   The extract printed
here gives a thrilling picture of combat in the air.   The author was subsequently
killed in action.

June 22nd— I GOT up this morning feeling like a week-end in the
city though I had no reason to.   I drank too much
coffee before going up and I'm as nervous as a kitten now.   Must be
getting the Woofits.

I had rather a surprise yesterday.   I was some distance back of the patrol and saw a Hun two-seater about three miles across the lines so went for him. I expected about thirty seconds at close quarters under his tail and then to watch him go down in flames. It looked like cold meat. I started my final dive about one thousand feet above him and opened fire at one hundred yards.

Then I got a surprise. I picked the wrong Hun. Just as I opened fire, he turned sharply to the left and I was doing about two hundred so couldn't turn but had to overshoot and half roll back. As I half rolled on top of him, he half rolled to and when I did an Immelman, he turned to the right and forced me on the outside arc and gave his observer a good shot at me as I turned back the other way to cut him off from the other side. I fired a burst from my turn but my shots went wild so pulled up and half rolled on top of him again and opened fire from immediately above and behind. He stalled before I could get a burst in and side-slipped away from me but gave me a no-deflection shot at him when he straightened out. I didn't have to make any allowance for his speed or direction and his observer was shooting at me. The observer dropped down in his cockpit so I suppose I killed him. But I couldn't get the pilot. He put the plane in a tight spiral and I couldn't seem to get in position properly. Cal and Tiny Dixon came in about that time and everybody was shooting at him from all angles. I know he didn't have any motor because he came down very slowly and didn't attempt to maneuver. We were firing from every conceivable angle but we couldn't seem to hit the tank or the pilot and every now and then he'd take a crack at me with his front gun when I'd try him head on.

He was a stout fellow, a good fighter and I hope he is still alive. If his observer had been any good I wouldn't be writing this now. He hit one of my front spars and that was all. I left him at one hundred feet as my engine was overheating and was sputtering and I've had enough machine gun fire from the ground to last me for a while and I don't like field guns from directly in the rear. Accidents will happen. So I started back and joined the patrol. . . .

June 24th—We found nine Hun scouts yesterday and dove on them but they wouldn't fight and ran for home. We chased them but couldn't catch them. Something funny about that. It must be a new type of plane and they were just practicing. They were fast whatever they were. My motor got to acting funny and the water began to

boil. It cut out a few times and I just did get back and landed between Kemmel and Popheringhe in a big field that was mostly shell
holes. There were some American troops up there of the 30th Division
and they helped me to get some water and get going when it cooled
off. It got me home but didn't run any too well. They have retimed
it but unless it turns up better I am going to ask for a new one. These
Hispano Vipers are fine when they are all right but the slightest
trouble bawls them all up. Springs was messing around over by
Messines and flushed a two-seater out of the clouds and got him.
Tiny Dixon was firing at him too, so they halved him. Randall
knocked down a high two-seater and Hall is missing.

We have a new pilot to take Thompson's place, Capt. Webster, a
quiet, reserved fellow. He's not a captain in the flying corps but in
his infantry regiment. When any one transfers from their regiment
to the flying corps they come in as second lieutenants but keep their
honorary rank in their regiment and draw the pay of that rank.
Then after they transfer, if they prove they're good and get a flight,
then they become temporary captains and rank as captains in the
flying corps and draw a captain's pay but keep their old regimental
rank. We have seven captains now but only three of them rank as
such and those are all lieutenants in their regiments. There's one
man who is known in the gazette as, "Lieutenant, temporary brigadier
general." He must be good. That's the right system. In our army,
if a major transfers to the aviation corps he comes in as a major and
bosses men who have been flying for years and know more about it
than he will ever know. I don't know who's going to do our fighting
but I know who's going to get all the rank and all the medals.

June 25th—Springs and I flew up to Dunkirk to get some champagne yesterday. We landed at Petit Snythe and found an American
squadron was being organized there, the 17th. Sam Eckert is C. O.
and Tipton and Hamilton and Newhall are the flight commanders.
They've got Le Rhone Camels and may the Lord make His face to
smile upon them because they are going to need more than mortal
guidance.

There was a brand new American major up there in a new Cadillac
named Fowler. We turned our nose up at him but he insisted on
being nice. His brother, who was killed at Issoudon, went to Princeton
with Springs so they got to chewing the rag. He was so new the tags

were still on his gold leaves and he didn't know how to salute,—saluted like an Englishman. When he heard why we'd come up he insisted on driving us into Dunkirk in his Cadillac. We got the champagne and he insisted on taking us into the Chapeau Rouge for a drink. We shot down a couple of bottles of champagne and he was all right, we thought, even for a new Kiwi. He kept on asking such simple questions. He wanted to know all about how our patrols were led and if we led any ourselves and how we got along with the British. He acted awfully simple, just like an ordinary U. S. major, and we did the best we could to enlighten him as to the proper method of picking cold meat and bringing most of our men back. His ideas were all wrong and we concluded that he must have been reading some of the books by the boys at home. We got a snoutful and he brought us back to the field and we invited him down to dinner at 85 and then he left. We asked Sam what Fowler had done to get a gold leaf and he told us that Fowler had been out with the British since 1914 and had the Military Cross and had done about five hundred hours flying over the lines. The joke is certainly on us. But he ought to know better than to fill a pilot full of champagne and then ask him how good he is. To tell the truth I think we were very modest. And why doesn't he wear wings or his decorations? If I had the M. C. all the rules that Pershing can make couldn't keep it off my chest. . . .

We went down to have dinner with Nigger's brother at the 2nd A. D. . . .

I heard a funny story down there. The Germans took Lille and the Allies held Armentières. For a long time they continued to run the factories in Armentières on electricity that came from Lille. A Frenchman was kept to run the power plant by the Germans and he didn't cut Armentières off. It was several months before he was caught.

June 27th—Springs is missing. He and MacGregor and Inglis were out this morning on the dawn patrol. Mac was leading and spotted a two-seater over Armentières. They went after him and had to chase him a bit further. Mac got to him first and missed his dive. Springs got under him and stayed there. The Hun stalled up and the observer was shooting down at Springs when Mac got back in position and got him. That was the last seen of Springs. Inglis says he saw some smoke coming out of his fusilage when the observer was shooting at him. It's afternoon now and no word has come from him so I guess he's cooked. Requiescat in pace, as he would say! I've got to go on a balloon straff now.

June 29th—Springs is back. He brought back a school of pink porpoises and a couple of funny stories. His guns jammed when he went under the two-seater and he was trying to clear the stoppages when the observer hit his oil pipe. His motor didn't stop at once but brought him back a little way before the bearings melted. He glided back just across the lines and crashed down wind in a machine gun emplacement. His face is a mess where the butt of his Vickers gun knocked a hole in his chin and he got a crack on the top of his head and a pair of black eyes. One of the longerons tore his flying suit right up the back and just grazed his skin and removed his helmet. Some Tommies fished him out and sorted the ruins. He says the first thing he thought of when he came to was his teeth on account of Mac. He ran his tongue around his mouth and couldn't find any front teeth. He let out a yell. "What's the matter, sir?" a Tommy asked him. "My teeth," sobs Springs, "they're all gone!" "Oh, no they ain't, sir," says the obliging Tommy, "here they are, sir!" and with that he reaches down and pulls his lips off his teeth. His teeth were all right, they were just on the outside of his face.

There wasn't any anesthetic up there but somebody brought a bottle of cognac. Every time he'd try to take a drink of it, it would all run out of the hole in his chin. So he spent the morning with his head tilted back and his mouth open while an Irish padre poured the cognac down his throat for him. He said after a little while the pain let up but they brought him another bottle so he kept up the treatment. He got back into the Forest of Nieppe and telephoned back to the wing that afternoon for a tender to come and get him. Then some doc up there gave him a shot of antitetanus serum. The tender came up after him and they started back, stopping at every estaminet on the way. He didn't have on a uniform, just his pajamas under his flying suit but had two or three hundred francs in his suit so they would stop and he'd buy champagne for the mechanics to pour down his throat. They got back here about dark, all of them tight as sausage skins. We had a celebration and made some strawberry julep to pour down his throat and we all managed to light up. Then some one noticed that his face needed a bit of hemstitching so we took him down to the Duchess of Sutherland's hospital in the woods below here. The doctor down there seemed to think the crack on his head was serious. We were in a hot room and none of us felt too good. The doc told him to stand up and close his eyes and then open them. Of course he couldn't focus his eyes. I could have told the doc that. Then he told him to close them again and keep them closed. He swayed a couple of times and then keeled over on the floor and passed out of the picture. "Ah, ha," says the doc, "I thought so! Concussion of the brain! We'll have to keep him in bed for a while." So they sewed up his face and he didn't know a thing about it next day. The doc says we can't see him for a few days as he must be kept absolutely quiet. I'd like to see them do it.

June 30th. . . .—We went to see Springs this afternoon and he seems to be doing all right. He's got lips like a nigger minstrel's and a mouthful of thread and a couple of black eyes. We took him a couple of bottles of champagne but he didn't need it as they serve it to him there. Things have been sort of quiet at the front lately in the sector and there were only three of them in there. One is a brigadier general who had been wounded seven times before this last shot in his leg.

There are about eighteen nurses there and it is the custom for all the nurses from the Duchess down to walk by and ask each patient how he feels each morning. The general says if they just had short skirts on and would whistle he'd applaud and join the chorus. Springs's face is going to be all right because they sewed it up from the inside.

War Birds: Diary of an Unknown Aviator (copyright 1926, George H. Doran Company), 206–223 *passim*.

183. Training American Aviators in France (1918)

BY COLONEL HIRAM BINGHAM (1920)

Bingham was an explorer in South America, a Professor at Yale, and a writer
on Latin-American conditions. He was Governor of Connecticut, and was elected
in 1924 to the Senate of the United States. The extract here is taken from his
account of his work as commanding officer of the Allies' largest flying school, the
Aviation Instruction Center, at Issoudun, France.—For general bibliography on
America in the war, see No. 171 above. On air service, see also No. 182 above.

THE plan for Issoudun was that it should be used chiefly as a
place where pilots already fully trained in the United States
should have a "refresher course" before being sent to the Front. Due
to the lack of advanced training planes in the United States and the
fact that it was practically impossible during the continuance of the
war for our pilots to do much more than get their preliminary training
and "acquire their wings" before coming to France, it became necessary to develop at Issoudun a complete course in advanced flying
and in aërial tactics. This was also made necessary because so many
hundreds of cadets had been sent to France without flying training at
all, and could secure only preliminary instruction at the French schools
or at our own Second Aviation Instruction Centre at Tours. . . .

At the beginning no definite course of instruction was laid out.
Most of the teachers were French pilots, who naturally used the ideas
then in vogue at the French schools which they had attended. Their
methods were better adapted for French than American aviators.
The course at Issoudun was not thought out on paper beforehand by
a theorist, but was gradually evolved under the most strenuous conditions imaginable and contained ideas derived from a very considerable number of the best American pilots in France. With a true sense
of the importance of having the best possible teachers and a keen
realization of the old adage that "a stream cannot rise higher than
its source," it was early determined to retain only the very best
American pilots for teachers and instructors. Each man that went
through the school was jealously watched by those in charge of the
work at the different fields, and if they saw unusual qualities in him,
he was promptly requisitioned as a member of the staff. . . .

With true American devotion to high ideals, the great majority of
the first class pilots selected as instructors cheerfully gave up the

chance of becoming aces themselves in order to perfect the output of the school and thus to help increase the total number of American aces at the Front. In order to prevent our self-sacrificing instructors from getting stale, a few were allowed to take turns in going to the Front for a month at a time. This gave them new ideas and new experiences. When they came back to the school they had the advantage in every case of having successfully brought down one or more Huns. This increased their prestige with their students and let them feel that they had their chance at a little real action. . . .

With such a splendid staff as was gradually built up by following this policy, it was only necessary to show each man that his ideas would be welcomed and to allow him to put into practice his own theories of teaching in order to develop a very thorough course of study. . . .

At some of the French schools the Rouleurs were especially built "penguins," which were guaranteed not to fly. At Issoudun, however, we were accustomed to use what we could get. In this case the best thing available was a Morane monoplane from which the ailerons had been taken, and which was equipped with a 40 to 50 H. P. Gnome motor.

Many of the boys who had learned to fly in the States could not understand why they were put on non-flying Rouleurs before being sent up in the air. Some of them, in fact, managed to get by Field 1 without really learning what the work there had to teach them. Later they had to be sent back from one of the advance fields because they were unable to make proper use of the rudder when taking off, taxying, or landing. They were finally ready to admit that the rudders of small fast planes, designed for successful use in the air when travelling at more than one hundred and twenty miles and hour, are not large enough when the plane is going over the ground at only twenty-five to thirty miles an hour. The pilot must use his rudder very gently in the air, but very roughly on the ground. If he does not thoroughly understand handling the small rudder of the fast scout planes, it will be almost impossible for him to make them roll straight on the ground. Most of our advanced planes were short-bodied Nieuports equipped with rotary motors. As I have already said in speaking of the troubles of our cadets, the Nieuports were extremely fond of making a violent and unexpected turn on the ground—the *cheval de bois*.

The lower left wing of the Nieuport has a slightly greater angle of incidence than the corresponding wing on the other side. This is in order to aid the pilot in overcoming the effect of the torque of the rotary motor. It causes the left wing to drag a bit, and this makes it more difficult to roll straight on the ground. This tendency is still further increased in landing on a field that is not quite level (and few French fields were really level). If in landing you happen to light on one wheel with greater force than on the other, the tendency of the Nieuport to turn abruptly and unexpectedly is very marked. It will readily be seen that it was very necessary for the student to understand thoroughly the use of a small rudder when operating on the ground. We found the cranky, non-flying "clipped" monoplanes very useful for this purpose.

Students were also encouraged to study the action of the motor before starting on their first ride, and to keep the application of power as steady as possible, since the slip stream of air from the propeller acting on the rudder is the force that causes the latter to become effective.

The student's first trip was straight across the field, towards a soldier who was stationed at the far end, whose duty it was to help him turn round and to start his motor in case he stalled it, as frequently happened. The student was not accompanied by a teacher in his wild ride. It was the duty of the teacher to watch carefully the cause of any difficulties and observe whether the student was avoiding trouble by going too slow, or was really learning to make proper use of the rudder. The second trip was made at a higher rate of speed, but with the control stick pulled well back and the tail held firmly on the ground. When the pilot had succeeded in making a good round trip with the tail skid helping to keep him straight by plowing through the field, he was told to get the tail off the ground for a few rods and then "make a landing." . . .

After having satisfied the instructors at Field 1 of their ability to use the rudder, the students walked over to Field 2, where dual control machines, operated by experienced instructors, were ready to give them their first experience in actual flying in France. . . .

The length of time which a student had to spend on Field 2 depended entirely on himself and his ability to learn rapidly and to demonstrate his efficiency not only to the instructor to whom he was assigned, but also to another first-class pilot known as the tester, who gave him his final examination. If he failed to satisfy the tester that he had mastered the intricacies of flying the 23-meter Nieuport, he was sent back to his instructor for further lessons. Each instructor was allowed to follow his own ideas to a very considerable extent, although all were obliged to ride in the front seat. Some used the telephone and some found that the students did better when left alone, and when they were not trying to listen to the telephone and "feel" the ship at the same time. . . .

Since most of our students had received their preliminary training with a stationary motor, they found it difficult to understand the gyroscopic action of the rotary motor, which inclines to pull the nose of the plane down into a spin if it is not held level on a turn. In flying the JN-4 we used to be told to nose down on the turns so as to avoid losing flying speed. This tendency of the Curtiss trained pilots had to be overcome before it was safe to let them fly with a rotary motor. American trained pilots were also inclined to fly with too little rudder. . . .

I mention these matters in some detail because many people found it difficult to understand why, after a pilot had earned his wings in the United States, it was necessary to give him instruction in a dual control machine in France. At times considerable pressure was brought to bear upon us to let the American trained pilots go directly into the fastest and smallest scout planes without giving them the instruction just described. We felt that this would be in some cases inexcusable homicide. On the other hand, some of the men who were "born pilots" needed less than an hour's instruction on Fields 1 and 2 before they were able to go on to Field 3. . . .

At Field 3 he found a 23-meter Nieuport not fitted with dual controls, but intended for solo flying. The absence of the instructor in the front seat not only made the machine lighter and enabled it to leave the ground more quickly and climb faster, but also had a psychological effect in making the pilot realize that he had no one but himself to depend upon. This ship is an excellent machine to use in carrying single passengers and landing in small fields. . . .

The work at Field 3 consisted in making the student as familiar as possible with the Nieuport 23 and giving him plenty of confidence. He was required to make a sufficient number of landings to overcome his dread of unexpected turns. His air work was carefully watched to make sure that he was equally good on both left-hand and right-hand turns. He was required to make spiral turns of more than 45° to determine whether he was able to use his elevators as a rudder and his rudders as an elevator when banking over to that extent.

His instruction in cross-country flying depended to a certain extent on what kind of planes we had. . . . The course was designed to familiarize the pilot with the difference between flying over France and flying over the United States. Most of our fields in America were so located that any one with average intelligence could find his way back to the field without the use of a map, or, if required to use a map, would be left in no doubt whatever as to his whereabouts. In France, however, with its large number of small towns and villages that looked very much alike from the air, its great number of straight, white roads leading in every direction, its crazy-quilt design of small cultivated fields, bewildering in their similarity and complexity, the chance of getting lost in the air even while using one of the excellent French maps was very considerable. The shape of the forested areas was the most important thing to learn. Our pilots were fond of telling the story of a champion cross-country flyer from the United States who had never had any difficulty with map reading and who scoffed at the idea that it was necessary for him to learn anything additional in this subject at Issoudun, getting totally lost on his first cross-country flight. He flew until obliged to land because he was out of gas. He finally had to telephone from some distant point to have somebody come and rescue him. In the United States he had flown by roads and large rivers. In France there were too many of the first and too few of the second.

In addition to this cross-country work at Field 3, students were given an hour or so with an acrobacy instructor in one of our few Avros. The student was put into all sorts of strange positions in the air to test his air sense, to give him confidence in the ability of a plane to right itself when certain definite rules were followed, and to determine whether there was anything radically wrong with his power to overcome dizziness and keep his head level under trying circumstances. If the instructor found a pilot deficient at this point, he was sent over to the hospital to consult the Medical Research Board. Advanced physical tests sometimes showed that the pilot was not fully competent and should never have been passed for training as an aviator.

Hiram Bingham, *An Explorer in the Air Service* (New Haven, Yale University Press, 1920), 126–140 *passim*.

———◆———

184. The St. Mihiel Operation (1918)

BY GENERAL JOHN J. PERSHING

The operation here described was the first in which American troops played a large independent part. Gen. Pershing's account gives some idea of the problems confronting military commanders and the considerations to be weighed in planning military operations. The author was given the official title of General of the Armies.—For general bibliography on America in the war, see No. 171 above.

AT Bombon on July 24 there was a conference of all the Commanders-in-Chief for the purpose of considering Allied operations. Each presented proposals for the employment of the armies under his command and these formed the basis of future co-operation of the Allies. It was emphatically determined that the Allied attitude should be to maintain the offensive. As the first operation of the American Army, the reduction of the salient of St. Mihiel was to be undertaken as soon as the necessary troops and material could be made available. On account of the swampy nature of the country it was especially important that the movement be undertaken and finished before the fall rains should begin, which was usually about the middle of September. . . .

The reduction of the St. Mihiel salient was important, as it would prevent the enemy from interrupting traffic on the Paris-Nancy Railroad by artillery fire and would free the railroad leading north through St. Mihiel to Verdun. It would also provide us with an advantageous base of departure for an attack against the Metz-Sedan Railroad system which was vital to the German armies west of Verdun, and against the Briey Iron Basin which was necessary for the production of German armament and munitions.

The general plan was to make simultaneous attacks against the flanks of the salient. The ultimate objective was tentatively fixed as the general line Marieulles (east of the Moselle)—heights south of Gorze-Mars la Tout-Étain. The operation contemplated the use on the western face of 3 or 4 American divisions, supported by the attack of 6 divisions of the Second French Army on their left, while 7 American divisions would attack on the southern face, and 3 French divisions would press the enemy at the tip of the salient. As the part to be taken by the Second French Army would be closely related to the . attack of the First American Army, Gen. Pétain placed all the French troops involved under my personal command.

By August 30, the concentration of the scattered divisions, corps, and army troops, of the quantities of supplies and munitions required, and the necessary construction of light railways and roads, were well under way.

In accordance with the previous general consideration of operations at Bombon on July 24, an allied offensive extending practically along the entire active front was eventually to be carried out. After the reduction of the St. Mihiel sector the Americans were to coöperate in the concentrated effort of the Allied armies. . . .

The plan suggested for the American participation in these operations was not acceptable to me because it would require the immediate separation of the recently formed First American Army into several groups, mainly to assist French armies. This was directly contrary to the principle of forming a distinct American Army, for which my contention had been insistent. An enormous amount of preparation had already been made in construction of roads, railroads, regulating stations, and other installations looking to the use and supply of our armies on a particular front. The inherent disinclination of our troops to serve under allied commanders would have grown and American morale would have suffered. My position was stated quite clearly that the strategical employment of the First Army as a unit would be undertaken where desired, but its disruption to carry out these proposals would not be entertained.

A further conference at Marshal Foch's headquarters was held on September 2, at which Gen. Pétain was present. After discussion the question of employing the American Army as a unit was conceded. The essentials of the strategical decision previously arrived at provided that the advantageous situation of the Allies should be exploited to the utmost by vigorously continuing the general battle and extending it eastward to the Meuse. All the Allied armies were to be employed in a converging action. The British armies, supported by the left of the French armies, were to pursue the attack in the direction of Cambrai; the center of the French armies, west of Rheims, would continue the actions, already begun, to drive the enemy beyond the Aisne; and the American Army, supported by the right of the French armies, would direct its attack on Sedan and Mézières.

It should be recorded that although this general offensive was fully outlined at the conference no one present expressed the opinion that the final victory could be won in 1918. In fact, it was believed by the French high command that the Meuse-Argonne attack could not be pushed much beyond Montfaucon before the arrival of winter would force a cessation of operations.

The choice between the two sectors, that east of the Aisne including the Argonne Forest, or the Champagne sector, was left to me. In my opinion, no other Allied troops had the morale or the offensive spirit to overcome successfully the difficulties to be met in the Meuse-Argonne sector and our plans and installations had been prepared for an expansion of operations in that direction. So the Meuse-Argonne front was chosen. The entire sector of 150 kilometers of front, extending from Port-sur-Seille, east of the Moselle, west to include the Argonne Forest, was accordingly placed under my command, including all French divisions then in that zone. The First American Army was to proceed with the St. Mihiel operation, after which the operation between the Meuse and the western edge of the Argonne Forest was to be prepared and launched not later than September 25.

As a result of these decisions, the depth of the St. Mihiel operation was limited to the line Vigneulles-Thiaucourt-Regnieville. The number of divisions to be used was reduced and the time shortened; 18 to 19 divisions were to be in the front line. There were 4 French and 15 American divisions available, 6 of which would be in reserve, while the two flank divisions of the front line were not to advance. Furthermore, 2 Army Corps headquarters, with their corps troops, practically all the Army Artillery and Aviation, and the First, Second, and Fourth Divisions, the first two destined to take a leading part in the St. Mihiel attack, were all due to be withdrawn and started for the Meuse-Argonne by the fourth day of the battle.

The salient had been held by the Germans since September, 1914. It covered the most sensitive section of the enemy's position on the Western Front; namely, the Mézières-Sedan-Metz Railroad and the Briey Iron Basin; it threatened the entire region between Verdun and Nancy, and interrupted the main rail line from Paris to the east. Its primary strength lay in the natural defensive features of the terrain itself. The western face of the salient extended along the rugged, heavily wooded eastern heights of the Meuse; the southern face followed the heights of the Meuse for 8 kilometers to the east and then crossed the plain of the Woevre, including within the German lines the detached heights of Loupmont and Montsec which dominated the plain and afforded the enemy unusual facilities for observation. The enemy had reinforced the positions by every artificial means during a period of four years.

On the night of September 11, the troops of the First Army were deployed in position. On the southern face of the salient was the First Corps, Maj. Gen. Liggett, commanding, with the Eighty-second, Ninetieth, Fifth, and Second Divisions in line, extending from the Moselle eastward. On its left was the Fourth Corps, Maj. Gen. Joseph T. Dickman, commanding, with the Eighty-ninth, Forty-second, and First Divisions, the left of this corps being opposite Montsec. These two Army Corps were to deliver the principal attack, the line pivoting on the center division of the First Corps. The First Division on the left of the Fourth Corps was charged with the double mission of covering its own flank while advancing some 20 kilometers due north toward the heart of the salient, where it was to make contact with the troops of the Fifth Corps. On the western face of the salient lay the Fifth Corps, Maj. Gen. George H. Cameron, commanding, with the Twenty-sixth Division, Fifteenth French Colonial Division, and the Fourth Division in line, from Mouilly west to Les Éparges and north to Watronville. Of these three divisions, the Twenty-sixth alone was to make a deep advance directed southeast toward Vigneulles. The French Division was to make a short progression to the edge of the heights in order to cover the left of the Twenty-sixth. The Fourth Division was not to advance. In the center, between our Fourth and Fifth Army Corps, was the Second

French Colonial Corps, Maj. Gen. E. J. Blondlat, commanding, covering a front of 40 kilometers with 3 small French divisions. These troops were to follow up the retirement of the enemy from the tip of the salient.

The French independent air force was at my disposal which, together with the British bombing squadrons and our own air forces, gave us the largest assembly of aviation that had ever been engaged in one operation. Our heavy guns were able to reach Metz and to interfere seriously with German rail movements.

At dawn on September 12, after four hours of violent artillery fire of preparation, and accompanied by small tanks, the Infantry of the First and Fourth Corps advanced. The infantry of the Fifth Corps commenced its advance at 8 a. m. The operation was carried out with entire precision. Just after daylight on September 13, elements of the First and Twenty-sixth Divisions made a junction near Hattonchatel and Vigneulles, 18 kilometers northeast of St. Mihiel. The rapidity with which our divisions advanced overwhelmed the enemy, and all objectives were reached by the afternoon of September 13. The enemy had apparently started to withdraw some of his troops from the tip of the salient on the eve of our attack, but had been unable to carry it through. We captured nearly 16,000 prisoners, 443 guns, and large stores of material and supplies. The energy and swiftness with which the operation was carried out enabled us to smother opposition to such an extent that we suffered less than 7,000 casualties during the actual period of the advance.

During the next two days the right of our line west of the Moselle River was advanced beyond the objectives laid down in the original orders. This completed the operation for the time being and the line was stablized to be held by the smallest practicable force.

The material results of the victory achieved were very important. An American Army was an accomplished fact, and the enemy had felt its power. No form of propaganda could overcome the depressing effect on the morale of the enemy of this demonstration of our ability to organize a large American force and drive it successfully through his defenses. It gave our troops implicit confidence in their superiority and raised their morale to the highest pitch. . . . Our divisions concluded the attack with such small losses and in such high spirits that without the usual rest they were immediately available for employment in heavy fighting in a new theater of operations. The strength of the First Army in this battle totaled approximately 300,000 men, of whom about 70,000 were French.

Final Report of Gen. John J. Pershing (Washington, Government Printing Office, 1919), 38–43 *passim*.

◆

185. The Doughboys Over the Top (1918)

BY EDWIN L. JAMES

This is a first-hand account of the work of the infantry—the men in the trenches. —For general bibliography on America in the war, see No. 171 above.

July 18, 1918.— ON a front of forty kilometers, from Fontenoy to Château-Thierry, the Americans and French this morning launched an offensive drive against the German positions. It was the first allied offensive of moment for more than a year. The Americans are playing a large rôle. They are fighting in the Soissons region, the Château-Thierry region, and other points along the big front.

When the German high command started its drive Monday morning [July 15] it started more than the Kaiser planned for. The French and Americans were entirely successful in guarding their secret and the attack at 4:45 o'clock this morning, without one gun of artillery preparation, took the Germans completely by surprise.

The Americans and French had an early breakfast and started out. Then with rolling barrages ahead of them they went on. A big piece of military work, very recent in conception, but of Foch planning, was shown when, at the precise minute, 4:45 o'clock, the French and Americans along nearly thirty miles of front went over the top and against the invaders. As in halting the German drive, the Americans were at two vital points of the allied drive—Soissons and Château-Thierry—and elsewhere as well. On what was done to the ends of the line depended the success of the whole movement.

I was present at the fighting this morning in the Château-Thierry region, where our boys had done so much to aid the allied cause already. Just as the whistle was blown for the doughboys to start, our gunners started barrages with their seventy-fives. Our troops swept down the hill north of the Bois de Belleau toward Torcy. Shouting as they went, the American soldiers advanced on Torcy, and at precisely 5:30 the commander reported that they had captured the town.

A little to the south other Americans swept around Belleau and closed up. Belleau was captured at 8:20 o'clock, and by that time German prisoners began coming back. Captured officers admitted that the coming of the Americans had been a complete surprise. Sweeping north the Americans charged into the Bois de Givry, and, after a short fight with Germans, went on down Hill 193 and into the village of Givry. Two hours later these troops had taken the town of Montairs.

In the meanwhile other American detachments with the French had charged the German positions in front of Courchamps and, while held up temporarily, brought up reinforcements, chased the Germans out of the woods, captured eighteen guns, and took possession of Courchamps. . . .

A general review of this operation shows that one reason why the Germans suffered such heavy losses in the woods forming the triangle from Fossoy, to Mézy, to Crezancy, was that the Americans were overwhelmed by such large numbers that the line could not hold, but nevertheless refused to retreat where it could possibly hold a place in the woods. This sent the German advance sweeping over large numbers of nests which sheltered ten, five, or two Americans, and sometimes one, who stuck while the boches passed by and then opened up on them.

Last night tales of heroism of these men were being told. I believe that of all of them the story of Sergeant J. F. Brown was most notable. Brown commanded a detachment of eleven men when the German onslaught came. They had shelter, which saved them under the heavy German bombardment, and when the advancing boche came along they let him pass, and then got ready to turn their machine gun loose. But just then a hundred or more Germans came along. Brown ordered his men to scatter quickly. He ducked into the woods, and saw the Huns put his beloved machine gun out of the war. The Germans passed on. Brown looked around and seemed to be alone. He started toward the Marne, away from his own lines, and met his Captain, also alone.

These two Americans, out there in the woods in the dark, the Captain with an automatic pistol and Brown with an automatic rifle, saw that the boche barrage kept them from getting to their own lines, and so decided to kill all the Germans they could before they themselves were killed. They lay in the thicket while the Germans passed by in large numbers. According to Brown's report, they heard two machine guns going back of them, and decided to go and get them. The two crept close and charged one of the machine guns, which killed the American Captain. Brown got the lone German gunner with his rifle. Then up came an American Corporal, also left alone in the woods, and Brown and the Corporal started after the second German machine gun, behind a clump of bushes.

They got close, and Brown with his automatic rifle killed three Germans, the crew of the gun. Then attracted by the shooting close at hand, up came the eleven men Brown had commanded, each looking for Germans. Brown resumed command, and led the party to where they could see more Germans in a sector of trench taken from the Americans.

These thirteen Americans performed a feat never to be forgotten. The Germans evidently were left in the trenches with machine guns to meet a counter-attack should the Americans make one. Brown posted his twelve men about the Hun position in twelve directions. He took a position where he could rake the trench with his automatic rifle. At a signal the twelve Americans opened up with their rifles from twelve points, and Brown started working his automatic rifle. Brown said he didn't know how many Germans he killed, but fired his rifle until it got so hot he couldn't hold it, and had to rest it across a stump. The Germans then, thinking they were attacked by a large party, decided to surrender. A German Major stepped out of the trench with his hands high, yelling "Kamerad!" Brown laid down his heated rifle, and while three of the hidden Americans guarded him, advanced toward the Major. Then all thirteen Americans moved in and disarmed the Germans. Brown said he didn't know how many there were, but it was more than 100.

Then, with Brown and the Corporal at the head, and the other eleven Americans in the rear, the procession started through the woods, guided by a doughboy's compass, toward the American lines. It wasn't plain sailing. They were behind the German advance, and

had to pass it and a space between the fighting Germans and the
Americans. On the way through the woods several parties of Germans
saw the advancing column, with Brown and the Corporal at its head,
and hurriedly surrendered.

Beating through the thicket, Brown led his party to a place where
the German advance line was broken. Just as he started over the
American lines the Germans laid down a barrage. This got four of
the Germans, but didn't touch an American. Brown and his twelve
comrades got back with 155 prisoners. The four killed made a total
for the thirteen Americans of 159.

American officers were almost dumfounded at the strange tale
Brown brought back, but doubt vanished when, soon after he reached
regimental headquarters, a military policeman showed up with a large
Bundle of maps and plans Brown had taken from dead German officers
killed by his automatic rifle, and, handing them to Brown, said:
" Gimme my receipt."

Brown, who is 23 years old, and last year was a shipping clerk, had
met this man on the way back, and, turning over the maps, which
made a heavy bundle, had stopped while he scribbled out the receipt
he demanded. Meanwhile barrage shells were falling all around.
This receipt is part of the records of the American army. . . .

July 21.—What a week this has been in the world's history! A week
ago, while the French were celebrating Bastille Day, the Germans,
strong in hope because of two preceding drives, were making ready
for another great effort. On the 15th they launched an attack from
Château-Thierry to north of Châlons on a 100-kilometer front. They
crossed the Marne and moved a short distance toward their objectives.
Then, out of a clear sky, July 18, came Foch's blow from Soissons to
Château-Thierry. On Thursday and Friday French and Americans
fought ahead, and then today they hit Ludendorff a body blow south
of the Marne. The week started with a formidable German offensive.
The week ends with a great allied offensive.

Americans, French, English—all the Allies—now face the fury of
the German high command, with its great military machine. That
machine is big and powerful, but it is not the machine it used to be.
The morale of the German Army is weakening from day to day.
The size of the German Army is growing surely less day by day.

The morale of the allied armies is getting better every day, and because of America the size of the allied armies is growing day by day. The defeat of Germany is but a matter of time. How much time no one can say. America should rejoice, but America should not be over-confident. But for what France has to be thankful for America has a just right to be thankful for, too.

South of Soissons, where the bitterest fighting of the week took place, it was the Americans who had the good fortune to push the line furthest ahead. Northwest of Château-Thierry, the closest point to Paris, it fell to the Americans to push the Germans back. East of Château-Thierry the Americans drove the enemy back the same day he crossed the Marne. South of Dormans the Americans held the German advance and helped drive the foe back. North of Châlons, the grand objective of the Crown Prince, the Americans stood on the plains and the boche could not pass.

It was the lot of American soldiers to be at vital points, and they made good. It is not to be supposed that Americans were at those points through accident. Perhaps Foch felt that the ultimate, complete victory depended on what the American fighting man could do, and perhaps he thought it best to know now. It seems but fair for America to know and believe that after all the greatest allied gain of this glorious week is the assurance that the American fighting man has no superior. What tens of thousands of them have done in the last week hundreds of thousands will do. The week has changed the nature of the war from an allied defensive to an allied offensive. For the first time in more than a year the Germans are on the defensive.

Edwin L. James, *The Americans in the Second Battle of the Marne*, in *New York Times Current History* (September, 1918), 399–402 *passim.*

186. Women with the Y. M. C. A. (1918)

BY KATHERINE MAYO

Miss Mayo is perhaps best known as the historian of the Pennsylvania State Police. She wrote the book from which this excerpt is taken, in part with a view to counteracting unfavorable and inaccurate reports of the work of the Y. M. C. A. in France. For other of her writing, see note with No. 100.

IN the early times, Mrs. Fitzgerald and her running mate, Miss Heermance, had turned a wretched little tavern in the village of Andelot into one of the most individual, charming, and successful Y's in France. Incidentally, they had come into long and close relationship there with the Eighty-Ninth Division—Kansas and Missouri boys. And although Andelot Y served as roadhouse for troops of many commands, the Eighty-Ninth in particular had left its warm and living impress there.

So when the underground brought word from Toul that the Eighty-Ninth was about to move forward for the Saint-Mihiel attack, the two ladies at Andelot, desperate, simply committed their daily job into the hands of a pair of sympathetic doughboys and beat their way to Toul, eighty-five kilometres distant, to tell their cherished friends good-bye.

Days passed, each one bringing eighteen hours of work apiece to the ladies of Andelot, till the day that brought the news: "This morning the Eighty-Ninth went over the top."

Then the two women looked each other square in the eye. Neither had to phrase the question in her heart.

"*You* go," said Miss Heermance at last. "You worked for them even in their home camp. It's your right."

"Beside," she added to herself, "it would kill her to keep her back now."

So Mrs. Fitzgerald, with her snow-white hair and her motherly face—a woman who would have been called "on in middle life" before people learned what life means—so Mrs. Fitzgerald once more started out, this time alone, and to beat her way far beyond Toul, through to the battle line.

It took her five days to get there. It was well over a hundred kilometres, and you remember the state of the roads. Also, she carried with her a hundred cartons of cigarettes, a big boiler full of chocolate powder, a lot of tinned milk, sugar, and a little stove. Her personal luggage did not count, being all contained in her *musette*.

Theoretically, the thing was both irregular and impossible. But the A. E. F. on that road knew Mother Fitzgerald well. Every second man remembered the kindly word and smile he had got from her in the gay little Andelot Y—remembered her dry canteen, with its rows of canned peaches, its cookies and candy, its chewing-gum and smokes—remembered her hearty "Go take what you want, and make your own change. The cash box is there on the shelf before you. It's your own money and your own home, dear—go ahead."

Never did the Andelot Y lose as much as one package of Bull Durham by that policy.

And now not a camion driver that could possibly make shift to give a lift to Mother Fitzgerald on her way to the fight, would pass her by. Not one.

Sometimes they could only take her to the next cross-road. Then they would dump her—her and her tower of cartons, her big tin boiler and her boxes and her stove. And there in the road, sitting on and among her treasures, she would eagerly watch till the next truck came along that could bring her still a bit farther on her journey.

It was on the fifth day that she overtook her children—the Three Hundred Fifty-Third Infantry as it chanced—a Kansas outfit. In Bouillonville, or, rather, where Bouillonville had been.

And Kansas, with the gaunt stare of battle still blank in its eyes, yet stood among the ruins when Mother Fitzgerald dropped into its arms.

They had loved her before. They had told her good-bye—told life and home and all they loved good-bye, through her one person. They had left her and descended into hell.

And now—she—had followed after—she with her white hair, casting safety away as a thing of no value without them.

For no one could tell how the fight would break next. Kansas, anyway, could not guess. It simply knew that these ruins were still bombarded; that gas came flooding through; that masks must be always at alert. And here was Mother Fitzgerald come to keep house!

If they loved her before, they adored her now. But—she scared them.

"My dears, don't you worry!" she purred. "Nothing that can possibly happen now is a quarter as bad to me as staying back in Andelot and knowing you boys are up here alone, with no one at all to take care of you."

And although they knew she might lose her life within the hour, they also knew she spoke the truth.

Kansas sought out the soundest fragment of building in the town to lodge her. It consisted of one room perhaps sixteen by twelve feet square, more or less intact; of a second room, adjoining, possessing three walls and a chimney; of a fairly steady stairway; and of one chamber above. All the rest was raw, fresh ruin.

In no time, after they lodged her, Mrs. Fitzgerald was busy cooking, in the room with the chimney. Boys clung around her like swarming bees. And mess-cups were filling with chocolate as fast as the line could move.

"Come and see the billet we've got for her to sleep in."

It was the room across the hall. They had swept it out as best they could. They had salvaged an Army cot and set it up at the rear. Then they had stretched a big blanket screen-fashion.

"And the top-sergeant will sleep right here, right outside her curtain, so nothing gets her at night."

"But her real bedroom's going to be upstairs. We're fixing it nice, in case they leave us here for a while. We aren't letting *her* see it till it's done, though. Want to look?"

So eager are they to show it that only a stone could refuse.

Up the rickety stairs, then through a roofless hall, and so to "the" room, where as many young Kansans as the space can hold are scraping walls and floors and slapping on what looks like whitewash.

"Why, you *are* making a job of it!"

One operating on the ceiling from a table-top looks down with an abstracted frown:

"Well, this here was a Boche town. This was a Boche house. *Does anybody think we're going to have Boche cooties eating Mother?*"

Below stairs, the top-sergeant stands waiting.

"Do you think we do right in letting her stay here?" he asks anxiously. "You know, it *is* dangerous. Anything might happen. But—just look at her in there now, and what she's doing for the boys— oh, Lord! I don't mean just the *cooking!* And—look here, will you?"

Leading the way back into the second room, he points to something green and yellow, drooping over the top of a half-smashed vase.

"See that?—Well—Mother brought it to us. God knows how she got through herself—her and all the stuff she packed. God knows where she found this. But—see?—*it's a sunflower!* And we—are Kansas!—Now, could anybody else alive have done just that, but only Mother?"

Katherine Mayo, "*That Damn Y*" (Boston, Houghton Mifflin, 1920), 130–134.

CHAPTER XXXIII — WAR ON THE SEAS

187. The American Transports (1917)

BY CAPTAIN THOMAS G. FROTHINGHAM (1926)

Capt. Frothingham is an Army officer, distinguished as a naval and military historian.—Bibliography: Albert Gleaves, *History of the Transport Service*. See also, on our part in the war at sea: R. W. Kauffman, *Our Navy at Work;* T. B. Kittredge, *Naval Lessons;* Sims and Hendrick, *Victory at Sea.*

THIS vital question, as to the possibility of transportation overseas on a large scale, was a problem for which the United States must be the one nation to provide the answer. The need came at the time when shipping had been so reduced, through losses inflicted by the U-boats, that it was impossible for Allied shipping to furnish anywhere near the amount of this transportation. Allied shipping, and of course this meant for the most part British shipping, eventually provided the greater share of the ships which carried overseas the troops of the American Expeditionary Forces, as will be narrated. But it must be stated at once, as an absolute condition of the naval situation, that, if the United States had not also been able to provide a large part of this transportation, the whole great operation must have failed, with fatal effect upon the war.

It seemed a desperate situation, and was in truth one of great difficulties. That the Transport Service was hard put to charter ships for the first expedition was evident from the list of ships given in a preceding chapter. Yet these were the best that could be gathered from American shipping by experts who went over the registry. The Army transports, controlled by the Transport Service, had the fatal defects of being slow with small bunker capacity. They were used for other purposes, but had to be discarded for transportation of troops over the Atlantic.

Consequently, the ships in the first expedition became the nucleus of the fleet of American troopships and cargo carriers of our great undertaking. It should be stated here that, before these ships of the first groups had returned to America, one great drawback in this service had been obviated. For the first expedition, there had been much delay and confusion in getting the troops and their belongings on board ship, and there had been a hectic experience at the piers. But this was not to be repeated, as, from that time, the Army Transportation Service, perfected a system for the increasing volume of transportation which loaded ships from the piers as fast as the troops arrived at the water-fronts.

But this first beginning of a fleet could only carry some 15,000 troops and 40,000 tons of freight, which was a small percentage of what was needed. It will give a measure of this to state the fact that in one month of 1918 over twenty times 15,000 troops were transported across the Atlantic. But, strangely enough, the element which meant the turning point from failure to success was provided by the enemy. Again, this was an example of the extraordinary overturns of the World War. The German merchant marine, so enthusiastically developed by the controlling German régime, became the decisive weight thrown into the balance which turned the scale against Germany.

On April 6, 1917, when the United States declared war against Germany, there were lying in the harbors of the United States and its colonies 104 ships of German ownership. Of these twenty were German liners, passenger ships, best adapted to be used as troopships, and many of them built with the idea of eventual use as German transports.

Upon our declaration of war, all these German ships were seized by the United States, following the proper precedents of international law. After inspection, it was found that the engines of these German ships had been wrecked, in the opinion of the Germans, beyond repair.

The United States Government had received ample warning, as early as the *Lusitania* crisis in 1915, that the Germans would attempt to disable these ships. But the status of these interned German steamships was all in favor of damage by their own crews. An interned ship remains in the possession of its owners and crew. Possession is not taken by the authorities of the nation in whose port the ship has been interned. It was a parallel to what occurred after the Armistice. Under the terms of this preliminary treaty of peace, the

German warships were not surrendered, but were interned at Scapa to await their disposition under the terms of the final treaty. They were thus in the possession of their German crews, and, upon the news of the final disposition of the warships of the German Fleet, the German crews sank all these ships in Scapa Flow.

The damage done to the German steamships interned in America in 1917 had been a definite part of the German naval program, as stated in the memorandum of the Chief of the German Admiralty of December 22, 1916. In this memorandum Admiral Holtzendorff expressed absolute confidence that the German steamships interned in American ports could not be used for transportation during the decisive months of the war, and they were thus eliminated from the German calculations as a means of sending American troops to Germany. But here, as often in the World War, German calculations did not take into account any factor outside of the German calculations.

All of these German steamships had cylinder engines, except the *Vaterland*, which had turbine engines. The German efforts were mainly directed toward wrecking the cylinders, as the greatest harm that could be done to a marine engine, following the idea that the one thing impossible was to run with defective cylinders. To their minds, this meant so extensive a need of replacement that it would involve a delay beyond the decisive period of the war. That these cylinders could be repaired in a short time, to be as good as new, was outside their calculations.

Yet this was what actually happened. At first inspection the Shipping Board experts had taken the pessimistic view that it was a long replacement job before the German ships could be put into operation. But the United States Navy, in the case of the two German auxiliary cruisers, had recommended that the cylinders be mended by electric welding. Upon this, the Navy Bureau of Steam Engineering was asked to examine all the German steamships, and, after examination, recommendation was made that all should be repaired by electric welding.

As a result, on July 11, 1917, the unprecedented task of repairing sixteen damaged German steamships was turned over to the United States Navy, and the Navy accomplished this task in an astonishingly short time, and with an efficiency that made the job complete once and for all. It is no wonder that at first it had been considered a hopeless case. Cylinders had been smashed, and in many cases great pieces had been knocked out of them. The German crews had done everything to the machinery that their minds could conceive. There was something almost pathetic in the amount of strenuous work put in by the Germans, and their assured complacency as to the result—only to find that a new element, outside of the German mind, was to upset all their calculations, and the very ships they had deemed useless were destined to transport over 550,000 troops to fight against the Germans at the crisis of the World War.

The success of the new process was never in doubt. The following quotations from Admiral Gleaves' book will give the reader at a glance the picture of what can only be called one of the most remarkable feats in the history of marine engineer work.

"The biggest job, of course, was the work of repairing the main engines. This was most successfully accomplished by electro-welding large cast steel pieces or patches on the parts of the castings which remained intact. This was completed in a few months, whereas to make new cylinders would have taken over a year.

"This electric welding was an engineering feat which the Germans had not calculated on. The enemy had broken out large irregular pieces of cylinders by means of hydraulic jacks. Where these parts had been left in the engine room they were welded back into place, and in cases where the pieces had been thrown overboard new castings were made.

"Electric welding is a slow and difficult process and was carried on day and night, Sundays and holidays, to the full capacity of the available skilled mechanics. After each casting had been welded, the cylinders were machined in place,—special cutting apparatus being rigged for the purpose. Finally each cylinder and valve chest was thoroughly tested under hydrostatic pressure. The repairs to the cylinders were perfectly successful. In actual trial they held up perfectly under hard operating conditions and there was not an instance of the welded portion breaking away."

This last is the true measure of this most successful exploit. It was not a temporary makeshift job of repairs, but one that made the machinery as good as new. In fact in many cases these steamships did better with their repaired engines than with the original engines. The other damages to these ships, to machinery, piping, valves, wiring, &c., were repaired with the same ingenuity and dispatch. All were ready in six months, some in a few weeks—and in many cases the damage wrought by the Germans was repaired before the working gang had completed the alterations necessary to change the ships into transports for troops.

This acquisition of the German ships was the most important factor in the solution of our great problem of transporting troops overseas. For they were available at the very time when troops were to be sent over in increased numbers, and afterwards for the ensuing crisis when the maximum of numbers must be sent. The astonishing totals of 557,788 American troops transported overseas by means of these German ships tell the whole story. This acquisition put the whole matter of troopships on a different basis.

But the work was not yet done, as the demand for cargo ships was growing out of all proportion to prewar ideas. This will be appreciated when the figures are compared. At the time of the Armistice, 500,000 dead-weight tons of American shipping were engaged in carrying supplies for the American Expeditionary Forces—that is, for every ton carrying troops four tons were needed to carry supplies. The public has thought of this operation too much in terms of ships carrying troops. The great fleet of cargo carriers has not been taken into consideration, but, after the gain of the German ships had thus helped the troopship situation, the most difficult part of the operation was to get hold of enough cargo carriers.

As a first step toward an increase of American shipping for this purpose, the United States Shipping Board, on August 3, 1917, requisitioned at the shipyards all steel vessels of 2,500 deadweight tons or over, which were then under construction. This assertion of eminent domain, though ultimately of great effect, was not the only official act which immediately added the most tonnage to the Government's merchant fleet. On October 15, 1917, the Shipping Board commandeered all commissioned and going American steel cargo steamers of 2,500 deadweight tons or over, and also all American passenger vessels of more than 2,500 gross tons that were suitable for foreign service. "This action added instantly to the federal marine 408 merchant vessels, of more than 2,600,000 deadweight tons."

Every effort was also made to acquire foreign tonnage, by seizure of enemy ships, by charter of enemy ships seized by others in the war, by purchase and charter from neutrals, by granting privileges for export in exchange for chartered tonnage, and by seizure of neutral tonnage in our ports. But it should be frankly stated that things were going very badly in respect to cargo carriers in the first six months of our participation in the war, not only from the scarcity of ships, but also from the confused situation as to allocating the available tonnage among the demands of the various industrial activities and the needs of the armed forces.

Thomas G. Frothingham, *The Naval History of The World War* (Cambridge, Harvard University Press, 1926), III, 149–158 *passim.*

———————◆———————

188. How it Feels to Be Torpedoed (1917)

BY ALBERT KINROSS

Bibliography as in No. 187 above.

THE first torpedo struck us at a few minutes past ten o'clock in the morning. I was down below in the saloon with E. We had both kept a boat-watch during the night and were the last officers to come to breakfast.

The saloon was a fine, large place, with lots of glass and tables and white-jacketed stewards. Above, on the decks, the men and most of the officers had fallen in at dawn and were to remain alert during our passage through the danger zone. A couple of Japanese destroyers, one to port and one to starboard, formed our escort. Our course was a series of zigzags at fourteen knots per hour by day and rather more at night.

E. and I ate our bacon and eggs and drank our coffee. The steward waiting on us was a clean-shaven little fellow who looked much like a low comedian. When the torpedo struck, there was no mistaking it for anything else. E. and I laughed, as much as to say: "Here she is!" Then I put on my cork belt, asked myself whether any part of me had suffered in the explosion, and received a confident answer, and next I leaped up the three flights of stairs that led to the liner's deck and my own boat-station.

E. raced with me. I have never seen him since. He had a lovable habit of mothering people. I dare say it cost him his life. There is something specially tragical about this officer's disappearance. He was the last of three brothers. Two had died gallantly in France, and so that one of her boys might be spared to the bereaved mother, E. had been taken out of the trenches and given a "safe" job at the base; yet even so the Fates had followed him.

The stewards and cooks raced with us too. There was something theatrical and cinema-ish about that picture—so many white jackets and blue uniform trousers and white overalls.

All this time—it might have been a couple of minutes—the greater part of me was so active that I have no recollection of any instant devoted to fear. Crude and horrible as it may sound, there was a large portion of my consciousness which was most vividly and delightedly enjoying itself. . . .

Just picture us, on a great liner, cosey as a grand hotel. Everything was remote from war and death, as I have seen them so constantly on land these last three years. No mud, no dirt, no continuity. And we were all at ease and leading civilian lives, with bathrooms, linen sheets, and even an American bar! I don't know why, but I had imagined it all quite differently.

As one rushed up-stairs one thought of things one had valued yesterday—two brand-new pairs of boots, one's field-glasses, some money—they seemed now so utterly of no account. Providence must have been with me, for, arrived on deck, I stood flush before my boat, Number 13. I stood there and took charge. To left of me the right people were busy with our sixty-six sisters. These ladies were part of the staff of a new hospital unit. Safely they were put into their boats, safely lowered, and safely rowed away from us. We cheered them as they left, and they cheered back. Then Tommy, lined on deck, struck up a song. He always does in moments of emotion.

I had filled my boat as full as it would go. All was ready. I stepped on board and gave the signal. Then slowly we descended. Above our heads one of the ship's officers was seeing to it that we went down all right. Immediately below us was another boat. It pushed off at last, and now we were free to hit the water. Before we pushed off I took on five of the crew who had helped to lower us. They swarmed down the ropes and reached us safely. Then I refused to take anybody else and we got the oars out and rowed away. Only then did

I notice that the ship had stopped dead. She looked perfectly steady, like a ship anchored. . . .

So we floated, one of many little units, on those waters; and for a long time we were kept passionately interested by what we saw. Speaking for myself, I have never lived through moments so tense, so big, so charged with all extremes and textures of emotion.

The big ship—she was near to 15,000 tons—stood like an island, and as if she could stand forever. While one of our destroyers went away on an unknown quest, the other drew alongside. We saw the little khaki figures swarm into her, and, to be frank, we envied them. Then the destroyer manœuvred, and there was a flash and an explosion. A second torpedo had struck and the Japanese commander had just dodged it. We now saw that his mast was broken and his wireless installation was sagging. But still the great ship stood there like an island. . . .

That moment passed, as did many another. I remember especially seeing another boat with only five men on board, four rowing gayly past us, the fifth baling. It seemed to us a horrible injustice, and several of my men said so aloud. I negatived the proposition, however, that we should get alongside and in part transfer. We seemed all right, and it struck me as best to leave well enough alone.

There followed next the most dramatic period of that spectacle. So far the great ship had stood firm, as if anchored. We noticed now that she had a definite list to starboard. The angle grew steeper, and then suddenly her bow dropped, her stern lifted, and next she slid to the bottom like a diver. It was as though a living thing had disappeared beneath the waves. We watched her, open-mouthed, a tightness at our hearts. We missed the comfort of her presence, we felt the tragedy of her surrender. In her death and engulfment there was a something more than human. So might a city built by countless hands and quick with life pass suddenly away. From somewhere in the middle of her bled a great puff of smoke, and I noticed that her deck as she stood on end, one half of her submerged, was bare and naked. It might have been a ballroom floor. . . .

Albert Kinross in *Atlantic Monthly*, December, 1917. (Boston.)

189. The Destroyers (1918)

BY ENOS B. COMSTOCK

Destroyer squadrons were largely used for convoy work; this poem celebrates their performance. On destroyers, see also No. 55 above.

GOD gathered the salt sea waters
  And wrapped them around the world;
    The gales broke free,
    And they swept the sea,
And the giant waves unfurled.

Then man made friends with the waters,
As the ages took their flight,
    For the sullen deep
    Was a friend to keep
In its wild, unfettered might.

But it isn't the wrath of the ocean,
When a nation wages war—
    When he steeps the sea
    In his treachery—
Then it is something more.

Beneath us the great ship pounded
In ceaseless monotone,
    Driving her way
    Through the lashing spray—
On to the danger zone.

They said the destroyers would meet us—
The men of the transport's crew;
    They told us, then,
    Just where and when—
The men of the transport knew.

For out of the gray of the morning,
Where the cold waves climbed the sky,
    What magical force
    Had guided their course?
When will that picturce die!

Now lost in a trough of the ocean,
Now poised on a foaming crest,
    Now driving the prow
    Of a steel-clad bow
Deep in a great wave's breast.

And we, who were new to the water,
We wondered that this could be;
    This, then, was their play,
    And they seemed to say,
These terriers of the sea:

"We'll see you safe, big brother,
Where the foul sea-demons wait;
    We'll stay with you
    And we'll see you through,
With your load of human freight."

Then here's to the sailors that met us,
And here's to their crafts of steel!
    With the grace of a gull
    In their shapely hull,
And forty knots in their keel!

Enos B. Comstock, in *St. Nicholas*, October, 1918 (New York, Century Co.), 1061.

190. U-Boat Raids off the American Coast (1918)

BY CAPTAIN THOMAS G. FROTHINGHAM

For Frothingham and for bibliography, see No. 187 above.

ON the American side of the Atlantic careful preparations had been made to guard against U-boats attacks, which were regarded as inevitable sooner or later. Of course the main task must be to safeguard the egress of the convoys. If the Germans had been able to interrupt these by operations of their U-boats in the Western Atlantic, it would have saved the whole situation for Germany. But it should be stated at once that the German attempts with their submarines off the American coasts never brought about the slightest delay in the rush of troops to France. Much less was there even the threat of an interruption.

Precautions for the safety of the convoys were unremitting. There was never any relaxation of vigilance throughout the many months in which there were no signs of the presence of U-boats. The channels of sailing were as carefully swept, and the convoys as vigilantly guarded by anti-submarine forces, as if there had been frequent U-boat attacks. The decision had been wisely made not to allow this escort duty on our side of the Atlantic to prevent any great number of destroyers from going overseas, and very few destroyers were retained for this service in the Western Atlantic. But the watch over the convoys was all the more painstaking from the very fact that it had to be carried on without them. It was here that the new submarine chasers were of value, and a large force of these craft was especially trained for this purpose. The energetic and adaptable young men who made up the personnel of this naval force performed a most arduous duty, as their activities extended from Halifax to Key West, and few realize what an experience of wind and weather this involved.

Upon our declaration of war, the Coast Guard had become a part of the Naval Establishment for war duty, in accordance with an act of Congress of 1915. Its cruising cutters had been given more powerful guns, and a number of them were sent overseas. The rest rendered most valuable service in this great undertaking of patrolling the Western Atlantic. They were well adapted to our waters and were an important part of the system of cruisers and mother ships which supported the anti-submarine small craft.

The first appearance of German U-boats in the Western Atlantic was heralded by sudden attacks on shipping off the Delaware Capes. Two coastwise schooners were sunk on May 25, 1918, and there were sinkings in the first days of June, most of them on June 2 when seven vessels were sunk. These were coastwise craft, mainly schooners, with the steamship *Carolina* of 5000 tons the most important loss. There were renewed attacks in July, especially off Cape Cod, and again in August. On August 10 no less than nine coastwise schooners were sunk from 50 to 60 miles off Nantucket. "The appearance of enemy submarines in these waters necessitated the putting into effect of the convoy system for coastwise shipping and for the protection of individual ships engaged in the coastwise trade." "To forestall enemy submarine operations in the Gulf and Caribbean, a force was established called the American Patrol Force, and its headquarters was in the vicinity of Key West. . . . As was foreseen, the protection of the oil supplies from the Gulf to our own coast and then abroad was quite vital to the success of the general campaign, and these supplies the patrol detachment was prepared to safeguard by adopting at once the convoy system the instant they were threatened."

Consequently, the German U-boat attacks never won success beyond these depredations against coastwise and incoming individual vessels. The U-boats never came near threatening the regular convoys, which were thus protected by sweeping their channels clear of the mines which the Germans spread, and guarded by escorting patrols of anti-submarine craft. These last were constantly hunting the U-boats with listening devices and depth bombs.

"On the whole the operations of the German submarines against our coast can be spoken of as one of the minor incidents of the war. . . ." That these futile U-boat attacks can be thus dismissed, is evident from the fact that transportation of troops instead of being diminished leapt to the great totals, which have been given, in the very months of these attacks. Only one American fighting ship was lost off our coast, the armored cruiser *San Diego* of the Cruiser and Transport Force. She was sunk by a mine off Fire Island on July 19, 1918, with the loss of six lives, three of these from the explosion.

Not only did these German raids with the U-boats against the

American coast fail to produce any impression that would make us retain naval forces on this side of the Atlantic, but the Germans thus failed absolutely in what must be considered their one necessary object in these U-boat attack—to break the chain of communications which was bringing and sustaining the American reinforcement that meant ruin to the confident military plans of the Germans. The American Expeditionary Forces remained successfully "based on the American Continent." The full measure of German failure was the fact that not one American troopship was torpedoed. And this meant German failure, not only in American waters, but also in the other stages of transportation to the final destination at the ports of disbarkation overseas.

It would be well here to describe the losses in this service, in order to show beyond any question their small effect upon the great volume of American troops which at this stage of the World War poured into France without hindrance from the enemy. In addition to the *San Diego*, the only fighting ship of any size lost by the United States Navy, our Navy lost the destroyer *Jacob Jones*, the armed converted yacht *Alcedo*, the collier *Cyclops*, and the Coast Guard cutter *Tampa* taken over by the Navy.

The *Jacob Jones* was torpedoed December 6, 1917, when on her way alone from off Brest to Queenstown. The *Alcedo* was one of the American armed yachts in French waters, and she was sunk by a U-boat while acting as convoy escort off the coast of France, November 5, 1917. The loss of the collier *Cyclops* was another of the many mysteries of the seas. She had reported at Barbadoes March 4, 1918, for coal, and left for Baltimore. She was never heard from again. The *Tampa* was one of the six Coast Guard cutters overseas, which performed valuable services in the force of the United States Navy based at Gibraltar for escort and protection of convoys. She was acting as escort for a convoy from Gibraltar when she was destroyed in the Bristol Channel on the night of September 26, 1918. "Vessels following heard an explosion, but when they reached the vicinity there were only bits of floating wreckage to show where the ship had gone down. Not one of the 111 officers and men of her crew was rescued. . . ."

Of the transports carrying American troops overseas, the most notable loss from enemy attack was the *Tuscania* (14,348 tons), a chartered Cunard liner under the British convoy system. She was torpedoed off the Irish coast on February 5, 1918, with the loss of 166 missing. The British chartered transport *Moldavia* was also sunk, with the loss of 56 lives. The unbroken record of immunity of the American troopships on their voyages to Europe was not maintained on their homeward voyages. Three of these American transports, *Antilles,* *President Lincoln, Covington,* were sunk on their way back to American ports, with loss of life in each case. The *Mount Vernon* (late German liner *Kronprinzessen Cecile*) and the *Finland* were torpedoed on homeward voyages, but each reached port and was repaired for service. The British chartered steamship *Dvinsk* was torpedoed and sunk on a homeward voyage.

These losses, compared with the great numbers of troopships, which were plying between the United States and Europe to deliver the American reinforcement on the battlefield in France, show most strikingly that the Germans were not accomplishing any appreciable results, so far as concerned preventing this reinforcement from being thrown against their armies on the Western Front. In fact, the battle in France was actually being won on the seas.

Thomas G. Frothingham, *The Naval History of the World War* (Cambridge, Harvard University Press, 1926), III, 223–228 *passim.*

PART XI

AFTERMATH OF THE WAR

CHAPTER XXXIV — THE ARMISTICE AND PEACE

191. The Armistice (1918)

FROM THE NEW YORK TIMES CURRENT HISTORY

Germany's allies had weakened: Bulgaria and Turkey had given up the struggle; Austria-Hungary was on the verge of breaking up. When overtures were made for an armistice, however, President Wilson declined to enter on its negotiation until he had assurance that "a government of the people" had been established in Germany. This meant that the Kaiser and the military party must be out of the picture.—For general bibliography of America in the war, see No. 171 above.

THE war came to an end on Monday, Nov. 11, 1918, at 11 o'clock A. M., French time; 6 o'clock, Washington time. The armistice, which was imposed upon Germany by the Allies and the United States, was signed by the German plenipotentiaries at 5 o'clock A. M., Paris time; midnight, Washington time.

The conclusion of the armistice followed within three weeks after the dispatch of a note from the German Government to President Wilson, in which it was affirmed that a fundamental change had been made in the German Government in "complete accord with the principle of the representation of the people based on equal, universal, secret, direct franchise," with the further announcement that orders had been issued to submarine commanders precluding the torpedoing of passenger ships, and asking that steps be taken to arrange an armistice which would contain no "demand which would be irrecon-

cilable with the honor of the German people and with the opening
of the way to a peace of justice." This note was dispatched on Oct.
21, 1918.

On Oct. 23 President Wilson replied by agreeing to take up with
the Allies the question of an armistice, but said the only armistice
which he would submit for consideration would be one that would
leave the Allies in a position to enforce any arrangement entered
into and make a renewal of hostilities by Germany impossible, with
the significant addition that if the Government of the United States
"must deal with the military masters and the monarchical autocrats
of Germany now, or if it is likely to have to deal with them later in
regard to the international obligations of the German Empire, it must
demand, not peace negotiations, but surrender."

On Oct. 25 the German War Cabinet considered the reply of the
President, and the note was discussed in sectional meetings of the
Reichstag members. It was at this juncture that the first mutterings
of serious discontent with the Government reached the outside world.
On Oct. 25 a dispatch was allowed to go from Berlin stating that an
enormous crowd had assembled before the Reichstag building calling
for the abdication of the Kaiser and the formation of a republic. That
the then existing Government did not contemplate the surrender of
Alsace-Lorraine was indicated by a statement made by the Foreign
Secretary, Dr. Solf, to the Reichstag that "the Cabinet would continue the reforms already undertaken in the government of Alsace-
Lorraine, but would not anticipate the solution of that problem."
The Foreign Secretary contended that "Polish annexation de-
mands were not in accordance with the peace program of President
Wilson."

A vote of confidence was given the Chancellor by the Reichstag
on this day, the vote standing 193 to 52.

On Oct. 27 another note was sent President Wilson by the German
Foreign Secretary declaring that far-reaching changes had occurred
in Germany's constitutional structure and that peace negotiations
were being carried forward by the people's Government, "in whose
hands rests, both actually and constitutionally, the power to make the
deciding conclusions," and closing with the statement that "the
German Government now awaits the proposals for an armistice."

On Oct. 28 matters were advanced by receipt of a note from the

Austrian Government declaring that all the conditions laid down by the President for the entry into negotiations for an armistice were accepted. This note was followed on the 29th by another from the Austrian Government urging that the negotiations for an armistice be hurried, thus indicating that Austria's complete surrender had been decided upon.

Meanwhile in Berlin the Crown Council was practically in continuous session under the Presidency of Emperor William and profound agitation was observed among Reichstag members and extreme nervousness in German military circles. . . .

On Oct. 31 the representatives of the allied Governments held a formal meeting at Versailles to consider the armistice terms for Austria, which would foreshadow the terms to be submitted to Germany. . . .

The Supreme War Council resumed its sessions at Versailles on Nov. 1 to consider the armistice terms which would be submitted to Austria and Germany. . . .

The conference continued its sessions daily, and during this period the political unrest in Germany continued to develop fresh intensity, with extreme agitation in all the larger cities and more pronounced and insistent demands by popular assemblies for the abdication of the Kaiser. During all this time the allied armies on the western front from the North Sea to Switzerland continued to deliver hammer blows on the shattered German lines and the latter were steadily retreating from Belgium and France with enormous losses.

On Nov. 3 the armistice with Austria was signed in the field, imposing drastic terms, and on the same day the German Kaiser issued a decree addressed to the German Imperial Chancellor in which he accepted the transfer of "fundamental rights of the Kaiser's person to the people," and acknowledged the adoption of the changes in the German Government which had been demanded by the Allies. The reports, however, indicated that he was firmly resisting the pressure coming from all sides that he abdicate.

On Nov. 4 the drastic terms of the Austrian armistice were made public and at the same time it was officially announced that the allied Governments and the United States had come to a complete agreement on the terms Germany must accept.

On Nov. 5 a note was handed to the Swiss Minister, who represented

Germany at Washington, by Secretary of State Lansing, in which he stated that Marshal Foch had been authorized to receive German delegates and to communicate to them the terms of an armistice.

The German Government took instant action. On Nov. 6, it was announced from Berlin that a German delegation to conclude an armistice and take up peace negotiations had left for the western front. . . .

The German plenipotentiaries sent to receive the armistice terms from Marshal Foch arrived at allied General Headquarters, Nov. 8, at 6 A. M. The terms were delivered to them, with a formal demand that they be accepted or refused within seventy-two hours.

A message from the German envoys to the Imperial Chancellor and the German high command, sent by the French wireless, was picked up at London Nov. 8. It asked that a courier be sent back as soon as possible with instructions. . . .

The delegates crossed the allied line near La Capelle late on the night of Nov. 7. The white-flag bearers reached the left wing of General Debeney's army at 10 P. M. They arrived at the place indicated by the allied supreme commander within the French lines about 2 o'clock A. M., Nov. 8, and passed the remainder of the night there. They were taken to a house at Rethondes, six miles east of Compiègne and thirty miles from Marshal Foch's headquarters, where preparations had been made to receive them.

The automobiles conveying the delegates carried white flags and were preceded by a trumpeter. Some French soldiers under an officer approached them on the road just outside the lines.

The delegates established their identity and showed their credentials. The members of the German party were then blindfolded and the delegates proceeded to the place where they spent the night.

Generals Winterfeld and von Grünnel wore uniforms of the rank of General. Von Salow was in the uniform of an Admiral of the fleet. Mathias Erzberger and Count von Oberndorff were in plain civilian dress.

They stayed over night at the house to which they were conducted, and were then taken to a place in the Department of the Aisne, which was the meeting place fixed by Marshal Foch. This trip required about four hours.

The delegates were received by Marshal Foch at Rethondes at 9 o'clock on the morning of Nov. 8, in a railroad car, in which the Commander in Chief of the allied force had his headquarters.

When the Germans' credentials had been opened and verified, Mathias Erzberger, leader of the enemy delegation, speaking in French, announced that the German Government had been advised by President Wilson that Marshal Foch was qualified to communicate to them the Allies' conditions and had appointed them plenipotentiaries to take cognizance of the terms and eventually sign an armistice.

Marshal Foch then read the terms in a loud voice, dwelling upon each word. The Germans were prepared by semi-official communications for the stipulations as a whole, but hearing set forth in detail the concrete demands seemed to bring to them for the first time full realization of the extent of the German defeat.

They made a few observations, merely pointing out material difficulties standing in the way of carrying out some quite secondary clauses. Then Erzberger asked for a suspension of hostilities in the interests of humanity. This request Marshal Foch flatly refused.

The delegates, having obtained permission to send a courier to Spa and communicate with that place by wireless, withdrew. Marshal Foch immediately wrote an account of the proceedings and sent it by an aid to Premier Clemenceau, who received it at noon.

With the Commander in Chief at the time of the interview were Major Gen. Maxime Weygand, his assistant; Vice Admiral Sir Rosslyn Wemyss, First Lord of the British Admiralty, and the American Vice Admiral, William S. Sims. Admiral Sims took no part in the negotiations and soon afterward returned to London.

When the French command received the German headquarters' wireless dispatch announcing the start of the armistice delegation, the delegates were directed to present themselves between 8 and 10 o'clock P. M., Nov. 7, at a certain point on La Capelle road. The crossroad was clearly marked by the beams of several searchlights. At the same time the order was given in the French lines that hostilities should be suspended over a distance of several miles in the region of the meeting place.

The three automobiles bearing the German delegates arrived at 9:15 P. M. at the crossroad, preceded by a group of German pioneers charged with making the shell-damaged road passable. The German delegates were received by officers whom Marshal Foch had sent to guide them. These officers got in the automobiles, and, with the window curtains drawn, proceeded to the Château Francfort in Compiègne Forest, belonging to the Marquis de l'Aigle.

Owing to the lateness of the hour, the delegates were conducted to the apartments assigned them, where they took refreshments. The next morning they again entered the automobiles and were taken to the station at Rethondes, where they found Marshal Foch in his special train.

The abdication of the Kaiser and the revolution in Germany occurred the day following the receipt of the armistice terms, Nov. 9, but no decision was announced respecting the acceptance of the armistice.

The German courier bearing the text of the armistice conditions arrived at German headquarters at 10 o'clock A. M., Nov. 10. The courier, Captain Helldorf, was long delayed while the German batteries persisted in bombarding the route he had to follow.

The German delegates had suggested on Nov. 9, that the courier's mission might be attempted by airplane. The French high command saw no objection to this and offered to furnish a machine on condition that the German high command pledge itself that the airplane would not be fired at. A rapid message was sent to German headquarters, which was replied to without delay as follows:

"We grant free passage to the French airplane bringing our courier. We are issuing orders that it shall not be attacked by any of our machines. For the purpose of recognition it should carry two white flags very clearly marked."

The orders from the German headquarters staff, however, were inoperative as regarded the land batteries, for on La Capelle road the enemy's fire, despite reiterated requests to desist, went on without intermission.

A French airplane, piloted by an officer of the French Air Service, was soon available, and the pilot was ordered to hold himself ready to start on his journey. About that time a message came from General Headquarters, announcing that orders for the cessation of fire had been given to the batteries directed against La Capelle road, and that Captain Helldorf was at liberty to start by automobile. Almost immediately the German fire ceased, and the courier set out on the road for Spa at 3:20 o'clock in the afternoon.

German headquarters was notified of his departure, and informed that he might be expected to arrive in the evening. But the road was long and hard, and many delays occurred.

Nineteen hours after the German courier reached the German headquarters—at 5 o'clock A. M. Paris time, Nov. 11—the armistice was signed and the official announcement was made at Washington at 2:40 A. M., Nov. 11, by the Secretary of State. President Wilson was notified immediately by telephone.

Staff article in *New York Times Current History*, December, 1918 (New York), 355–360 *passim*.

---

192. Peace Conference at Versailles (1919)

BY PROFESSOR JOHN SPENCER BASSETT (1926)

Bassett (1867–1928) was Professor of History at Smith College, and author of a number of volumes of historical significance. His account of the election of 1924 is given in No. 197 below. President Wilson s tremendous personal power made him the outstanding individual at the Versailles Conference; but it proved impossible to maintain unselfish principles of statesmanship against the competition of European leaders who insisted on the spoils of war. On the problem of reparations payments, the outgrowth of Allied demands, etc., see No. 208 below.—Bibliography: biographies of Wilson listed in No. 129 above; Haskins and Lord, *Some Problems of the Peace Conference;* House and Seymour, *What Really Happened at Paris;* Robert Lansing, *The Big Four at Paris;* H. V. Temperly, *History of the Peace Conference;* C. T. Temperly, *The Peace Conference Day by Day.*

PRESIDENT WILSON did not originate the idea of a League of Nations. He merely uttered the thought of many others who but desired one in authority to take it up. Wilson's part was that he made it his chief policy of state and carried it through the Peace Conference against the opposition of the old diplomatic school.

In order to do this he decided to go to Paris himself as head of our Peace Commission. The suggestion shocked many people, and his political opponents attributed it to a desire to play a conspicuous part in the negotiations. Yet it seems certain that if he had not gone to Paris there would have been no League. The other members of the Commission were Robert Lansing, Secretary of State, Henry White, formerly an ambassador to France, and described by Roosevelt as "the most useful diplomat in the American service," Colonel

Edward M. House, up to this time a personal adviser of the President, and General Tasker H. Bliss, representing the army. The Commission sailed from New York, December 4, 1918, and arrived at Paris on the 14th.

At that time the position of the United States was high in the world's esteem. Our country had once been considered a clever commercial nation, rich in goods and too new to fight. In a year and a half it had thrown 2,000,000 splendid fighting men into the European struggle, spent wealth and blood as freely as the exigencies of war demanded, and furnished the final energy that turned the scales in the conflict. The Americans were hailed at Paris as the saviors of the world. At their head was President Wilson, whose eloquent speeches had been read with intense sympathy since the nation entered the war; and who arrived in Europe with a message that was to make wars impossible. He was madly acclaimed wherever he went in Europe. Few men stopped to think how difficult a task he had given himself. To establish a régime of peace meant that he would oppose some of the dearest national designs of other peoples; and in doing so he could not help arousing bitter opposition.

Thirty-nine powers, including the British Dominions, came to the Conference to help write the terms of humiliation for Germany and her allies, and to make the world safe against their future aggression. Most of them had in mind definite demands and considered them entirely just and reasonable. These nations were prepared, if necessary, to make combinations among themselves in the old world-congress manner, in order to get what they wished. The only great nation at the Conference that was not seeking advantages for itself was the United States. That was because we were too rich to need Europe's money and too much isolated to be concerned with European territorial rivalries. Wilson's only demand for new arrangements was the League of Nations, and he asked that because he thought it was for the good of all.

The five powers in attendance which had done most of the fighting—Great Britain, France, Italy, Japan, and the United States—must of necessity assume most of the responsibility for making Germany fulfil the treaty which she must sign. It was natural that they should take the lead in the discussions, and also in the results of the Conference.

Hence most of the questions were first decided by the representatives of these five powers; and the decisions were then referred to plenary sessions of the whole Conference, where they were approved. Two persons represented each of the five powers, and this small body became known as the Council of Ten. Experience showed that ten were too many, and the Council was finally composed of only one representative from each power; and since Japan did not attend unless Asiatic or Pacific-Ocean matters were up, most of the business was done by the other members, who came to be known as the "Big Four." These powerful personages were Clemenceau, for France, Lloyd George, for Great Britain, Orlando, for Italy, and Wilson, for the United States.

The position of Wilson among these men was peculiar. Each of the others was Prime Minister in his own country, each had the support of his Parliament, and each believed that what he did was going to be approved by his government. Wilson was the man charged by the Federal Constitution to act for his nation, either by appointees or in person, in making the treaty; and yet he did not represent the Senate, the body that would have to approve the treaty. Frequently a President had negotiated a treaty which the Senate had rejected, but they were always times when the other party was a single state. Now, however, we were called upon to sit in with a Conference of many states. The treaty would have to be such as all would sign: it would necessarily be a compromise made on the spot after conference with the other powers. The ratifying power in the United States could take no part in such a compromise. Wilson was therefore put to the necessity of doing the best he could under the circumstances, trusting to the future to get ratification. As compared with his colleagues at Paris he was in an awkward situation, dependent upon future events in his own country.

The deliberations of the Conference had not gone far when it became evident that the European Powers thought little of the Fourteen Points. It has been said that they threw them over entirely, which is not strictly true; but they pared some of them down and ignored some entirely. The Germans, who were not allowed to take part in the early deliberations, only waiting to know what would be demanded from them, were greatly offended by this action. They had surrendered on the basis of the Fourteen Points and naturally felt they had been deceived after putting themselves beyond the ability to resist. Here was laid the foundation of a deep hostility to Wilson, who, they said, should have left the Conference when it refused to do what he had assured Germany it would do. ⸱

Wilson soon realized that he could not get the Allies to do all they had promised to do. But he thought that if the League of Nations was established in good faith, it would bring about in time all the omitted advantages of his propostition. Accordingly he gave himself to the preparation and adoption of the Covenant of the League, a draft of which was presented to the Conference in plenary session, February 14, 1919. It was not considered at the time, and Wilson departed the next day for Washington, to be present at the approaching close of the Congress. He hoped also to be able to allay to some extent the rising tide of objection to the League in the United States, a hope which the attitude of a Senate in the hands of his political enemies did not warrant.

There was no time to argue the point before his departure. At Paris things began to go against him as soon as he was out of the city. March 5, the day after Congress adjourned, he sailed again for France, arriving to find that the League had been sidetracked. During his absence a vote was passed to decide upon the other matters in the treaty before deciding upon the League. This, it was believed, would mean the defeat of an efficient League. Moreover, it was contrary to a vote of January 25, taken through Wilson's insistence, that the League should be considered an integral part of the treaty.

The reversal of this vote in his absence was a blow at the President and he took occasion after his return to say that reports that the League was to be deferred until the treaty was completed were incorrect and that the vote of January 25 was final.

It was an evidence of his great power in the conferences of the "Big Four" that his interpretation of the situation was allowed to stand. By fighting to the utmost, by never giving up the demand that the Covenant should be part of the treaty, and by finally threatening to withdraw from the Conference he was able to force Lloyd George, Clemenceau, and Orlando to accept his view; and when the treaty of peace was complete it contained the Covenant of the League of Nations. Whatever one thinks about Wilson and the League, it is necessary to admit that he won a hard battle in forcing it into the treaty. As an additional check on Germany President Wilson agreed to recommend that the United States make a three-power treaty with France and Great Britain for the enforcement of the Treaty of Versailles. This recommendation was made by the President but the Senate did not accept it.

The main features of the Covenant were: (1) The chief power was to rest with a council of nine members, one chosen from each of the five Great Powers, Great Britain, France, Italy, Japan, and the United States, and four others, chosen by the Assembly from time to time. (2) An assembly in which each member state was to have one vote. Since five of Great Britain's colonies were members of the Conference this arrangement provided for six votes that were British in sympathy, a provision that aroused much feeling among all who disliked an extensive British influence. (3) A permanent World Court with the power to decide international cases, the League standing in a position to see that its decisions were executed. (4) In Article X it was provided that each state should guarantee the territorial integrity of every other state in the League. (5) In case a member of the League was about to make war on another member the Council would investigate, and if its decisions were violated the other members were pledged to impose economic restrictions, or even to make war against it, until it was willing to accept the arbitrament of the League. The object was to create a power strong enough to make reason take the place of force in the settlement of disputes that ordinarily lead to war.

In matters strictly European, Wilson did not at first take so strong a part. But when he realized the mass of intrigue for gain that filled the Conference he took a stronger stand. In order to keep the conquered German and Turkish colonies from falling into the hands of Britain, France and Japan, he got them recognized as "mandatories" to be administered by nations to whom the League should assign them. . . .

Wilson also asked that reparation payments should be based upon Germany's ability to pay and that the amount should be fixed in the treaty. This provision he did not obtain. Lloyd George and Clemenceau had made excessive promises to their people about forcing Germany to pay for the war, though they knew it was impossible. They did not dare face their people with a fixed amount representing what Germany could pay. It was accordingly provided that she should pay for all damages inflicted on civilians, in all pensions granted on account of the war; and for all "separation allowances," *i. e.*, allowances to families of Allied soldiers in active service. A Reparation Commission was to assess the actual amounts by May 1, 1921. Much trouble arose when it was attempted to execute this feature of the treaty. . . .

On the demand of Japan in the East, Wilson had not the support of Britain and France, and he was, therefore, in a more awkward position. Early in the war Japan took Shantung from Germany, and Japan remained in a position menacing to China. Wilson tried to get her to hand it over to China, from whom it was taken by Germany in 1898 under contract made through duress. Japan promised to give up Shantung, retaining some economic privileges and the right to establish a settlement there. She would not make the promise in writing, claiming her word was sufficient, although in other matters written promises were given and demanded by her. Japan had made special treaties with Britain and France, who supported her in her contention, and Wilson was obliged to content himself with her verbal assurance. China, however, was not satisfied and refused to sign the treaty.

The Peace Conference closed its tempestuous existence with the signing of the completed treaty June 28, 1919. The affair was brilliantly staged in the Hall of Mirrors, at Versailles, where in 1871 the German Empire had been proclaimed. The treaty was ratified by Great Britain, France, and Italy on January 10, 1920. It was never ratified by the United States. A treaty with Austria-Hungary was signed September 12, 1919, but it was not ratified by the United States.

John Spencer Bassett, *Expansion and Reform: 1889–1926* [*Epochs of American History*, Vol. IV] (New York, Longmans, Green, 1926), 280–288 *passim*.

193. Against the Versailles Treaty (1921)

BY SENATOR WILLIAM E. BORAH

For Borah, see No. 128 above.—Bibliography as in No. 192 above.

MR. PRESIDENT, my aversion to the Versailles treaty, to the principles upon which it is built, the old imperialistic policies which have brought the world into sad ruin, makes it impossible for me to ever vote for any treaty which gives even moral recognition to that instrument. That alone would prevent me from voting for this treaty.

I am not forgetful, I trust, of the times and circumstances under which the Versailles treaty was written. They were extraordinary; they were without precedent. All the suffering and passions of a terrible war, led by the intolerant spirit of triumph, were present and dominant. It was a dictated treaty, dictated by those who yet felt the agony of conflict and whose fearful hours of sacrifice, now changed to hours of victory, thought only in terms of punishment. It was too much to expect anything else. We gain nothing, therefore; indeed, we lose much by going back to criticize or assail the individuals who had to do with its making; it was a treaty born of a fiendlike struggle and also of the limitations of human nature. So let its making pass.

But three years have come and gone since the war, and we have now had time to reflect and to contemplate the future. We have escaped, I trust, to some extent the grip of the war passion and are freer to think of the things which are to come rather than upon the things which are past. We have had time not only to read this treaty and think it over, but we have had an opportunity to see its effect upon peace and civilization. We know what it is now, and if we recognize it and strengthen it or help to maintain it, we shall not be able to plead at the bar of history the extenuating circumstances which its makers may justly plead. We see now not alone the punishment it would visit upon the Central Powers, but we see the cruel and destructive punishment it has visited and is to visit upon millions, many of whom fought by our side in the war. We know it has reduced to subjection and delivered over to exploitation subject and friendly peoples; that it has given in exchange for promises of independence and freedom dependence and spoliation. But that is not the worst. "If it were done when it is done," we could turn our backs upon the past and hope to find exculpation in doing better things in the future. But we know this treaty has in it the seeds of many wars. It hangs like a storm cloud upon the horizon. It is the incarnation of force. It recognizes neither mercy nor repentance, and discriminates not at all between the guilty and the innocent, friend or foe. Its one-time defenders now are frank to admit it. It will bring sorrow to the world again. Its basic principle is cruel, unconscionable, and remorseless imperialism. Its terms will awaken again the reckoning power of retribution—the same power which brought to a full accounting those who cast lots over Poland and who tore Alsace-Lorraine from her coveted allegiance. We know that Europe can not recover so long as this treaty exists; that economic breakdown in Europe, if not the world, awaits its execution; and that millions of men, women, and children, those now living and those yet unborn, are to be shackled, enslaved, and hungered if it remains the law of Europe. All this we know, and knowing it we not only invite the lashings of retribution, but we surrender every tenet of the American faith when we touch the cruel and maledict thing.

When the treaty was written it had incorporated in it the so-called League of Nations. I believe it correct to say the treaty proper was only accepted by Mr. Wilson because the league was attached. I have never believed, I have never supposed, he could have been induced to accept this treaty, so at variance with every principle he had advocated and all things for which he had stood, had he not believed the league in time would ameliorate its terms and humanize its conditions. In that, of course, I think he was greatly in error.

In my opinion the league, had it been effective at all, would have been but the instrument to more effectually execute the sinister mandates of the predominant instrument. Under the treaty the league would have quickly grown into an autocracy based upon force, the organized military force of the great powers of the world. But now, so far as we are concerned, the league has been stricken from the document. The sole badge of respectability, the sole hope of amelioration, so far as American advocates were concerned, now vanish. With the league stricken out, who is there left in America, reared under the principles of a free government, to defend the terms and conditions of this treaty? There it is, harsh, hideous, naked, dismembering friendly peoples, making possible and justifying the exploitation of vast populations, a check to progress and at war with every principle which the founders interwove into the fabric of this Republic and challenging every precept upon which the peace of the world may be built. For such a treaty I loathe to see my country even pay the respect of recognition, much less to take anything under its terms.

Some nation or people must lead in a different course from the course announced by this treaty and its policies, or the human family is to sink back into hopeless barbarism. Reflect upon the situation. We see about us on every hand in the whole world around conditions difficult to describe—a world convulsed by the agonies which the follies and crimes of leaders have laid upon the people. Hate seems almost a law of life and devastation a fixed habit of the race. Science has become the prostitute of war, while the arts of statecraft are busy with schemes for pillaging helpless and subject peoples. Trade is suspended, industry is paralyzed, famine, ravenous and insatiable, gathers millions into its skeleton clutches, while unemployment spreads and discontent deepens. The malign shadows of barbarism are creeping up and over the outskirts of civilization. And this condition is due more to the policies which the political dictators of Europe have imposed than any other one thing. Repression, reprisal, blockades, disregard of solemn pledges, the scheming and grabbing for the natural resources of helpless peoples, the arming of Poland, the fitting out of expeditions into Russia, the fomenting of war between Greece and Turkey, and, finally, the maintenance of an insurmountable obstacle to rehabilitation in the Versailles treaty—how could Europe, how can Europe, ever recover? Is there no nation to call a halt? Is there no country to announce the gospel of tolerance and to denounce the brutal creed of force and to offer to a dying world something besides intrigue and armaments?

In this stupendous and bewildered crisis America must do her part. No true American wants to see her shirk any part of her responsibility. There are no advocates of selfishness, none so fatuous as to urge that we may be happy and prosperous while the rest of the world is plunging on in misery and want. Call it providence, call it fate, but we know that in the nexus of things there must be something of a common sharing, all but universal and inexorable in the burdens which these great catastrophies place upon the human family. It is not only written in the great book but it is written in the economic laws of nature—"Bear ye one another's burdens." We do not differ as to the duty of America, we differ only as to the manner in which she shall discharge that duty. . . .

Mr. President, one of the revolting monstrosities born of this war, the illegitimate offspring of secret diplomacy and violence, is the absurd, iniquitous belief that you can only have peace through martial means—that force, force, is the only power left on earth with which to govern men. I denounce the hideous, diabolical idea, and I insist that this Government ought to be counted against all plans, all treaties, all programs, all policies, based upon this demoniacal belief. Let us have an American policy. Or, if the word "American" be considered by some as provincial or distasteful—a term of incivility—then let us have a humane policy, a Christian policy, a policy based upon justice, resting upon reason, guided by conscience, and made dominant by the mobilized moral forces of the world.

William E. Borah, Speech in the United States Senate, September 26, 1921.

CHAPTER XXXV — POLITICAL AND SOCIAL MATTERS

194. Freedom of Speech in War Time (1919)

BY PROFESSOR ZECHARIAH CHAFEE, JR.

Chafee is distinguished as a legal practitioner, as a professor in the Harvard Law School, and as one of the leaders of liberal thought in the United States. He objected to the adoption of what he considered un-American expedients in American administration during the war, and was outspoken in his exposure of defects in the judicial functioning of that time.—Bibliography as in Nos. 108 and 173 above.

NEVER in the history of our country, since the Alien and Sedition Laws of 1798, has the meaning of free speech been the subject of such sharp controversy as to-day. Over two hundred prosecutions and other judicial proceedings during the war, involving speeches, newspaper articles, pamphlets, and books, have been followed since the armistice by a widespread legislative consideration of bills punishing the advocacy of extreme radicalism. It is becoming increasingly important to determine the true limits of freedom of expression, so that speakers and writers may know how much they can lawfully and wisely express. The United States Supreme Court has recently handed down several decisions upon the Espionage Act, which put us in a much better position than formerly to discuss the war-time aspects of the general problem of liberty of speech, and this article will approach the general problem from that side. . . .

Our main task, therefore, is to ascertain the nature and scope of the policy which finds expression in the First Amendment to the United States Constitution and the similar clauses of all the state constitutions, and then to determine the place of that policy in the conduct of war, and particularly the war with Germany. The free speech controversy of the last two years has chiefly gathered about the Espionage Act. This Act contains a variety of provisions on different subjects, such as the protection of ships in harbors, spy activities, unlawful military expeditions, etc., but the portion which concerns us is the third section of Title I. As originally enacted on June 15, 1917, this section established three new offenses: 1. false statements or reports interfering with military or naval operations or promoting the success of our enemies; 2. causing or attempting to cause insubordination, disloyalty, mutiny or refusal of duty in the military and naval forces; 3. obstruction of enlistments and recruiting. . . . Attorney General Gregory reports that, although this Act proved an effective instrumentality against deliberate or organized disloyal propaganda, it did not reach the individual, casual, or impulsive disloyal utterances. Also some District Courts gave what he considered a narrow construction of the word "obstruct" in clause 3, so that as he puts it, "most of the teeth which we tried to put in were taken out." On May 16, 1918, Congress amended the Espionage Act by what is sometimes called the Sedition Act, adding nine more offenses to the original three, as follows: 4. saying or doing anything with intent to obstruct the sale of United States bonds, except by way of bona fide and not disloyal advice; 5. uttering, printing, writing, or publishing any disloyal, profane, scurrilous, or abusive language, or language intended to cause contempt, scorn, contumely or disrepute as regards the form of government of the United States; 6. or the Constitution; 7. or the flag; 8. or the uniform of the Army or Navy; 9. or any language intended to incite resistance to the United States or promote the cause of its enemies; 10. urging any curtailment of the war with intent to hinder its prosecution; 11. advocating, teaching, defending, or suggesting the doing of any of these acts; and 12. words or acts supporting or favoring the cause of any country at war with us, or opposing the cause of the United States therein. Whoever commits any one of these offenses in this or in any future war is liable to a maximum penalty of $10,000 fine or twenty years' imprisonment, or both.

This statute has been enacted and vigorously enforced under a constitution which provides: "Congress shall make no law . . . abridging the freedom of speech, or of the press."

Clearly, the problem of the limits of freedom of speech in war time is no academic question. On the one side, thoughtful men and journals are asking how scores of citizens can be imprisoned under this constitution only for their disapproval of the war as irreligious, unwise, or unjust. On the other hand, federal and state officials point to the great activities of German agents in our midst and to the unprecedented extension of the business of war over the whole nation, so that in the familiar remark of Ludendorff, wars are no longer won by armies in the field, but by the *morale* of the whole people. . . .

At the outset, we can reject two extreme views in the controversy. First, there is the view that the Bill of Rights is a peace-time document and consequently freedom of speech may be ignored in war. This view has been officially repudiated. At the opposite pole is the belief of many agitators that the First Amendment renders unconstitutional any Act of Congress without exception "abridging the freedon of speech, or of the press," that all speech is free, and only action can be restrained and punished. This view is equally untenable. The provisions of the Bill of Rights cannot be applied with absolute literalness but are subject to exceptions. . . .

The true meaning of freedom of speech seems to be this. One of the most important purposes of society and government is the discovery and spread of truth on subjects of general concern. This is possible only through absolutely unlimited discussion, for, as Bagehot points out, once force is thrown into the argument, it becomes a matter of chance whether it is thrown on the false side or the true, and truth loses all its natural advantage in the contest. Nevertheless, there are other purposes of government, such as order, the training of the young, protection against external aggression. Unlimited discussion sometimes interferes with these purposes, which must then be balanced against freedom of speech, but freedom of speech ought to weigh very heavily in the scale. The First Amendment gives binding force to this principle of political wisdom.

Or to put the matter another way, it is useless to define free speech by talk about rights. The agitator asserts his constitutional right to speak, the government asserts its constitutional right to wage war. The result is a deadlock. . . . In our problem, we must regard the desires and needs of the individual human being who wants to speak and those of the great group of human beings among whom he speaks. That is, in technical language, there are individual interests and social interests, which must be balanced against each other, if they conflict, in order to determine which interest shall be sacrificed under the circumstances and which shall be protected and become the foundation of a legal right. It must never be forgotten that the balancing cannot be properly done unless all the interests involved are adequately ascertained, and the great evil of all this talk about rights is that each side is so busy denying the other's claim to rights that it entirely overlooks the human desires and needs behind that claim. . . .

The First Amendment protects two kinds of interests in free speech. There is an individual interest, the need of many men to express their opinions on matters vital to them if life is to be worth living, and a social interest in the attainment of truth, so that the country may not only adopt the wisest course of action but carry it out in the wisest way. This social interest is especially important in war time. Even after war has been declared there is bound to be a confused mixture of good and bad arguments in its support, and a wide difference of opinion as to its objects. Truth can be sifted out from falsehood only if the government is vigorously and constantly cross-examined, so that the fundamental issues of the struggle may be clearly defined, and the war may not be diverted to improper ends, or conducted with an undue sacrifice of life and liberty, or prolonged after its just purposes are accomplished. Legal proceedings prove that an opponent makes the best cross-examiner. Consequently, it is a disastrous mistake to limit criticism to those who favor the war. Men bitterly hostile to it may point out evils in its management like the secret treaties, which its supporters have been too busy to unearth. The history of the last five years shows how the objects of a war may change completely during its progress, and it is well that those objects should be steadily reformulated under the influence of open discussion not only by those who demand a military victory but by pacifists who take a different view of the national welfare. Further argument for the existence of this social interest becomes unnecessary if we recall the national value of the opposition in former wars.

The great trouble with most judicial construction of the Espionage Act is that this social interest has been ignored and free speech has been regarded as merely an individual interest, which must readily give way like other personal desires the moment it interferes with the social interest in national safety. . . . The failure of the courts in the past to formulate any principle for drawing a boundary line around the right of free speech has not only thrown the judges into the difficult questions of the Espionage Act without any well-considered standard of criminality, but has allowed some of them to impose standards of their own and fix the line at a point which makes all opposition to this or any future war impossible. For example:

> No man should be permitted, by deliberate act, or even unthinkingly, to do that which will in any way detract from the efforts which the United States is putting forth or serve to postpone for a single moment the early coming of the day when the success of our arms shall be a fact. . . .

There is no finer judicial statement of the right of free speech than these words of Judge Hand:

> Political agitation, by the passions it arouses or the conflictions it engenders, may in fact stimulate men to the violation of law. Detestation of existing policies is easily transformed into forcible resistance of the authority which puts them in execution, and it would be folly to disregard the causal relation between the two. Yet to assimilate agitation, legitimate as such, with direct incitements to violent resistance, is to disregard the tolerance of all methods of political agitation which in normal times is a safeguard of free government. The distinction is not a scholastic subterfuge, but a hard-bought acquisition in the fight for freedom.

Look at the Espionage Act of 1917 with a post-armistice mind, and it is clear that Judge Hand was right. There is not a word in it to make criminal the expression of pacifist or pro-German opinions. It punishes false statements and reports—necessarily limited to statements of fact—but beyond that does not contain even a provision against the use of language. Clauses (2) and (3) punish successful interference with military affairs and attempts to interfere, which would probably include incitement. The tests of criminal attempt and incitement are well settled. The first requirement is the intention to bring about the overt criminal act. But the law does not punish bad intention alone, or even everything done with a bad intention. A statute against murder will not be construed to apply to discharging a gun with the intention to kill a man forty miles away. . . . Attempts and incitement to be punishable must come dangerously near success. A speaker is guilty of solicitation or incitement to a crime only if he would have been indictable for the crime itself, had it been committed, either as accessory or principal. . . . Consequently, no one should have been held under clauses (2) and (3) of the Espionage Act of 1917 who did not satisfy these tests of criminal attempt and incitement. As Justice Holmes said in Commonwealth *v.* Peaslee, "It is a question of degree." We can suppose a series of opinions, ranging from "This is an unwise war" up to "You ought to refuse to go, no matter what they do to you," or an audience varying from an old women's home to a group of drafted men just starting for a training-camp. Somewhere in such a range of circumstances is the point where direct causation begins and speech becomes punishable as incitement under the ordinary policy of free speech, which Judge Hand applied. Congress could push the test of criminality back beyond this point, although eventually it would reach the extreme limit fixed by the First Amendment, beyond which words cannot be restricted for their remote tendency to hinder the war. In other words, the ordinary tests punish agitation just before it begins to boil over; Congress could change those tests and punish it when it gets really hot, but it is unconstitutional to interfere when it is merely warm. And there is not a word in the 1917 Espionage Act to show that Congress did change the ordinary tests or make any speech criminal except false statements and incitement to overt acts. Every word used, "cause," "attempt," "obstruct," clearly involves proximate causation. Finally, this is a penal statute and ought to be construed strictly. Attorney General Gregory's charge that judges like Learned Hand "took the teeth" out of the 1917 Act is absurd, for the teeth the government wanted were never there until other judges in an excess of patriotism put in false ones. . . .

The courts have treated opinions as statements of fact and then condemned them as false because they differed from the President's speech or the resolution of Congress declaring war. They have made it impossible for an opponent of the war to write an article or even a letter in a newspaper of general circulation because it will be read in some training camp where it might cause insubordination or interfere with military success. He cannot address a large audience because it is liable to include a few men in uniform; and some judges have held him punishable if it contains men between eighteen and forty-five; while Judge Van Valkenburgh, in United States *v.* Rose Pastor Stokes, would not even require that, because what is said to mothers, sisters, and sweethearts may lessen their enthusiasm for the war, and "our armies in the field and our navies upon the seas can operate and succeed only so far as they are supported and maintained by the folks at home." . . .

Although we have not gone so far as Great Britain in disregarding constitutional guarantees, we have gone much farther than in any other war, even in the Civil War with the enemy at our gates. Undoubtedly some utterances had to be suppressed. We have passed through a period of danger, and have reasonably supposed the danger to be greater than it actually was, but the prosecutions in Great Britain during a similar period of peril in the French Revolution have not since been regarded with pride. Action in proportion to the emergency was justified, but we have censored and punished speech which was very far from direct and dangerous interference with the conduct of the war. The chief responsibility for this must rest, not upon Congress which was content for a long period with the moderate language of the Espionage Act of 1917, but upon the officials of the Department of Justice and the Post-office, who turned that statute into a drag-net for pacifists, and upon the judges who upheld and approved this distortion of law. It may be questioned, too, how much has actually been gained. Men have been imprisoned, but their words have not ceased to spread. The poetry in *The Masses* was excluded from the mails only to be given a far wider circulation in two issues of the *Federal Reporter*. The mere publication of Mrs. Stokes' statement in the Kansas City *Star*, "I am for the people and the Government is for the profiteers," was considered so dangerous to the morale of the training camps that she was sentenced to ten years in prison, and yet it was repeated by every important newspaper in the country during the trial. There is an unconscious irony in all suppression.

Those who gave their lives for freedom would be the last to thank us for throwing aside so lightly the great traditions of our race. Not satisfied to have justice and almost all the people with our cause, we insisted on an artificial unanimity of opinion behind the war. Keen intellectual grasp of the President's aim by the nation at large was very difficult when the opponents of his realism ranged unchecked while the men who urged greater idealism went to prison. In our efforts to silence those who advocated peace without victory we prevented at the very start that vigorous threshing out of fundamentals which might to-day have saved us from a victory without peace.

Zechariah Chafee, Jr., in *Harvard Law Review*, June, 1919 (Cambridge, Harvard Law Review Association), 932–973 *passim*. Published also by Harcourt, Brace & Co., New York. Reprinted by permission.

195. President Harding (1923)

BY JUDSON C. WELLIVER

For Welliver, see No. 157 above. Harding became President in 1921 and died in 1923 (see No. 196 below). He was a genial man of moderate abilities. In the Harding administration occurred the misuse of government oil reserves, on which see No. 197 below. He was responsible for the Washington Conference of 1922, for which see No. 207 below.

M R. HARDING came to the Presidency convinced that the tendency to make a dictator of the President was bad. He did not wish to adopt the rôle, and believed it could be avoided. He was all for understanding and coöperation, and from his seat in the Senate Chamber, after he was elected President but before inauguration, he gave assurance of this attitude. McKinley's methods were his ideal, and he clung to them with a sort of despairing hopefulness even when urged by many to use the "big stick" occasionally. It is one of the ironies that among those who pressed him to "use the club" some of the most earnest were members of his own party in Congress. He never came to the point of frankly breaking away from his convictions in this matter; but I know, from conversations with him in the later months of his life, that he had come to realize that his amiability must not be allowed to be mistaken for weakness. Many times, during the period when he was preparing the addresses which were later delivered on his western trip, he talked of the responsibility which he felt for pressing the program outlined in them, and made plain that if the public's reaction to his proposals were favorable, as he was sure it would be, he intended to use all the power of his office to crystallize it into law.

Perhaps that qualification, "if the public's reaction were favorable," should be explained. President Harding was a good deal irked at the manner in which public men, political critics, journalists and editors, are wont inevitably to attach exaggerated importance to rather casual observations of a President; to assume that a suggestion put out with hope of inspiring helpful discussion, is intended as the presentation of a policy. He positively dreaded the microscopic analysis of every suggestive remark, as if a lot of tremendous implications simply *must* be found in it. That is one of the difficulties every President faces. Roosevelt dealt with it by forming an Ananias Club; Wilson, by secluding himself even from members of his cabinet and attempting to do all his thinking in a vacuum; Harding grieved and was endlessly annoyed over it. Once, when a caller had reported some remark of the President in a way that gave it a significance utterly unintended, he walked into his office fresh from the morning newspaper reports of the incident, and an early visitor greeted him with:

"Good morning, Mr. President; a lovely day."

"It does seem that way," he retorted grimly; "but if I mention it to anybody, he's liable to go out and announce that I ordered the Weather Bureau to put on this long dry spell, and try to arouse the farmers against the administration." On another occasion:

"Good day for a golf game, Mr. President," suggested a friend.

"That's your view, not mine," he replied quizzically. "If I commit myself to that sentiment, I'll be accused of ordering golf weather when we need rain."

These whimsicalities were often indulged in, in connection with the minor annoyances incident to his office. He loved golf, and knew that he was criticized for playing it too much. In truth, he played it too little, and felt keenly the vaudeville gibes about his afternoons at golf or week-ends on the *Mayflower*. "I wish I had a little of the genius for play," he once remarked. "It was one of Roosevelt's great attractions. He could play tennis, shoot bears, or do a hundred miles on horseback, and everybody was delighted; if I play golf it's a snobbish game. If I shot a bear it would be heartless slaughter, and if I rode a hundred miles at a stretch the Society for Prevention of Cruelty would want me impeached." He never in his life hunted, because of an intense distaste for killing any living thing. That prejudice didn't run far enough, however, to keep him from being a keen fisherman. "I never saw a fish with any human emotions," was his explanation of this inconsistency. He loved children, and they would always go to him. A dog he had petted was pretty sure to want to follow him.

He couldn't stand against the hard-luck stories that are always coming to people in authority in Washington, about government employees who are losing their places and being left stranded. Yet, finding the government establishment enormously expanded as a result of war excesses, he was determined that it must be reduced sharply, and steeled himself for the task. He announced at the start that he was "going to be hard-boiled about this business" and that under no circumstances would he issue any civil-service executive orders; that is, orders of the President suspending the civil service regulations in a particular case and allowing an applicant to be given a post in the classified service without taking an examination and getting the required rating. On one occasion I weakly listened to the story of a woman in whose behalf I was asked to intercede with the President: widow; three small children; money counter at the treasury; $1200 a year and absolutely no other resources; notified that she would be dismissed on January 1 because the force must be reduced half; had no civil service standing: no chance to be placed elsewhere because reductions were everywhere in progress, unless an executive order could be secured. . . .

He signed the order, handed it to me, and said: "What chance does a President have, anyhow, when everybody's against him! Don't you ever ask for another order of that sort. Good night."

He walked to the door, opened it, turned, and concluded: "You'll really see that she gets it to-night? It'll make a lot of difference in her Christmas, you know." . . .

He had less pride of preconceived opinion than any big man I have known except Theodore Roosevelt. Either of them could be talked out of a long-sustained conviction—if one had a good case—and when won over, they both adopted the new view generously and without any of the odd intellectual resentment that many men would display. If he wanted the opinions of a number of people on anything, he commonly consulted them separately, and seldom let any one of them know he was discussing the same matter with others. This, in my observation, became more and more his method after he was President. It had the effect of making the administration much less an affair of cabinet conference and determination, than most people assume it to have been. Many of the most momentous decisions of the administration were made without cabinet discussion. . . .

To some extent because of this method, the President committed himself to too many losing causes. He was cautious in approach, but when he had decided in his own mind on a given course, he was apt to go ahead with it almost regardless of politics or expediency.

He grew greatly in self-confidence in the period of his presidency. Also, from being at the outset looked upon as a politician of the politicians, a perfectly frank machinist, he came to have an almost intense distaste for the merely political considerations. A member of the cabinet, having occasion to fill the post of assistant secretary, went to him and said: "This is an important place. I can find for it a man almost ideal from the standpoint of the department's work and public usefulness; but his appointment would bring little of political advantage. Or, I can make a perfectly respectable, unobjectionable appointment, and accomplish incidentally some real political advantage. I want your judgment."

The President did not even ask the names of the two men thus described. "The longer I'm here," he said, "the more I'm convinced that political capital acquired in this way is pretty illusory. This Government ought to be run by the best men we can get, for the best interest of the people, and not for the political benefit of anybody who happens to be on the inside. You go ahead and pick the man that will best serve the department and the public, and I'll appoint him."

That declaration would not have come from the Harding of March, 1921. It was strictly characteristic of the Harding of 1923. He said to the present writer many times in the last year, that he didn't care much about the politics, but was determined to give the best government he could; and he meant it. . . .

It was my privilege to live almost at the elbow of President Harding from a few days after his nomination until after his death. I never knew him to make a demagogic utterance. He had a frank disgust for that sort of thing. When he was nominated one of the objections raised to him by some men who had served with him in the Senate was that he was not inured to hard and continuous work, and that as President he was liable to fail at this point. In fact, he proved one of the hardest working of Presidents, although the public was far from a realization of it. He was particularly conscientious about his obligations as the business head of a nation, and twice every week he devoted at least an hour, frequently several hours, to conferences with the Director of the Budget regarding the Government finances. He was anxious to make a reduction of taxes possible as early as might be, but he often said that there was only one way to discharge a debt, and that was to pay off as much as possible whenever it could be done.

He insisted, therefore, that some part of the debt should be discharged every year. From this he would not consider deviating, even when some advisers urged the political advantage of it. Once when he had been besought to consent to some reductions of taxation which ultimately would have meant passing on a larger share of the burden to posterity, he declared that, "posterity didn't get the world into this scrape. Our generation did, and we must pay as much of it as possible."

The President was in his personal affairs an excellent business man, as is attested by the fact that, starting with nothing, he made a fortune approaching the million mark, and yet found time incidentally for a political career of the first importance. He was loved best by those who knew him best, and in 1920 the vote of Marion City and County was certainly a real tribute to one who had been for thirty-five years engaged in the publishing business. Although he had devoted his life to the newspaper business, he was as President a well-nigh hopeless failure in the art of publicity. His trouble was an innate modesty about himself and his accomplishments. His political friends constantly urged that if the Administration would only advertise its accomplishments it would be recognized everywhere as one of the most remarkable in our history, but President Harding always insisted that the record must stand for itself. Nevertheless, he was very proud of having given the Government what he believed was a good business administration, and the speech at Salt Lake City on June 26 was the frankest bit of boasting of which I believe he was ever guilty.

In order to get accurate statistics concerning the cost of state, county and city governments, for comparison with the cost of national government in recent years, he almost turned the Census Bureau inside out for the better part of two weeks. But he got the figures he wanted, and with them made a presentation of the details of national business management, together with a plea for economy and careful administration, such as I believe very few heads of state in all the world could have put forward. It was the sound counsel of a sound business man dealing with the business side of government.

Thirty-nine years ago a country doctor at Marion, Ohio, gave his boy three hundred dollars, saved from a precarious practice, and sent him out into the world. The other day that same country doctor, still practising in Marion, sat in his modest cottage home, and the world brought back his boy. There could be no truer eulogy of that boy's career than is pronounced in that verse from Micah on which it is said his index finger fell when he laid his hand on the Book in taking the oath at his inauguration:

"He has showed thee, O man, what is good; and what doth the Lord require of thee, but to do justly, and to love mercy, and to walk humbly with thy God?"

Judson C. Welliver, *Harding, Man and President*, in *American Review of Reviews*, September, 1923 (New York), CLXVIII, 260–272 *passim*.

------◆------

196. How Coolidge Got the News (1923)

BY LOUIS J. LANG

Vice President Coolidge took the official oath as President immediately on confirmation of the report of Harding's death, August 2, 1923.   Thus precedent was established when the oath was administered by the new President's father, as a notary public.—For Coolidge, see No. 32 above; also, William Allen White, *Calvin Coolidge;* E. E. Whiting, *President Coolidge.*—Bibliography: Calvin Coolidge, *Address at Philadelphia, Pa.*, Sept. 5, 1924, *Adequate Brevity;* compiled by R. J. Thompson; *America's Need for Education and Other Educational Addresses* (1915); *Price of Freedom* (1924); *Thought the Master of Things* (1921); *Foundations of the Republic;* speeches and addresses (1926); *Have Faith in Massachusetts* (1919); C. B. Slemp, ed., *The Mind of the President: as Revealed by Himself in his own Words* (1926); E. E. Whiting, *Calvin Coolidge, His Ideals of Citizenship as Revealed through his Writings* (1924); R. J. Thompson, *Collation and Co-ordination of the Mental Processes of and Reactions of Calvin Coolidge* (1923).

FIVE newspaper correspondents were the first to apprise Calvin Coolidge that he was President of the United States. I was one of them. We did it at one o'clock in the morning of August 3, 1923, by the flare of an ancient kerosene lamp, in the primitive farmhouse of his father, John C. Coolidge, atop the Green Mountains, in Plymouth, Vermont.

The circumstances, abounding in tragedy, pathos, and sweetness too—the last contributed chiefly by Mrs. Coolidge—were these:

At 12:30 A. M. the telephone bell tinkled behind the desk of a tiny hostelry at Ludlow, Vermont.

A yawning night clerk of eighteen years, clad only in trousers and undershirt, answered the call. Three newspaper correspondents, also yawning, in the lobby, were about to seek their couches. The sleepy clerk shouted from the booth, "Is Mr. Roy Atkinson, of the Boston 'Post,' here?"

Mr. Atkinson replied, "Here he is."

"Boston wants you," returned the tousled-headed lad, who held the wire. Mr. Atkinson hurried to the phone. He was in the booth barely a minute. Then he called to us, "Boys, President Harding is dead!"

"Oh, we heard that report last night, and the night before. Who says he is dead this time?" asked James A. Hagerty, veteran political writer of the New York "Times," and myself in duet.

"Secretary Christian has wired the news from San Francisco. It is official," answered Atkinson.

"Well," we agreed, "it means we must awaken Mr. Coolidge and tell him he is President. You know he has no telephone nor telegraph wire 'way up there on Plymouth Notch," I suggested.

The hamlet was asleep. The only available motor-car driver slept. The sole telephone operator was asleep.

President Coolidge was presumably dreaming in the "shack" just across the street from his birthplace, fifteen miles away, up a dark, stony, serpentine mountain path.

How to get the news to him of President Harding's death and give the people of the United States and the world the first message from the new President was our job.

One of us awakened the motor-man by telephone and directed him to bring his fleetest car around. Another awakened the combination station agent and telegraph operator. A third routed out of bed the girl operator who had exclusive charge of the single telephone wire to the region outside.

She was ordered to commandeer every wire she could appropriate in New England and hold it open indefinitely.

The motor car, of the vintage of a quarter of a century agone, rattled up to the hotel door. Then it occurred to Atkinson that two of our comrades were in bed. We yanked them out in their pajamas. They started to dress.

"Dress in the car—the President is dead! We are going to tell the new President about it!" shouted Atkinson and Hagerty in the same breath.

Our comrades grabbed trousers, coats, and shoes, dashed down the stairs, and joined us in leaping into the car.

"Step on her till she busts!" yelled Atkinson to the chauffeur.

The aged boat wheezed, rocked, jerked, and lunged. We were off up the mountain. That drive seemed all but eternal and interminable in its length and anxiety. The car back-fired and shook, crunched rocks, stalled. It careened about road elbows at forty miles an hour. The dim searchlights scarcely punctured the Egyptian gloom. . . .

Painfully laboring up the last series of precipitous hills, we suddenly shot into an open space. Then we narrowly escaped climbing a tree which we had seen the then Vice-President nursing early the day before.

We caught a glimmer of light.

"That's in the President's combination dining and sitting room. Father Coolidge always keeps an old kerosene lamp burning, because he gets up before daylight to milk the cows," said our ancient pilot.

We drew up at the porch of the Coolidge farmhouse. All jumped out. Except for the dim flame just described, the house was an inky blot. Atkinson and I crept on to the porch, on which we had sat with the President-to-be and Mrs. Coolidge the previous morning. Atkinson fumbled for the bell. It could not be found.

"There ain't no bell. We are all honest here. Oh, they don't lock up at night any more than in the day. Walk right into the house," said our bus pilot in a loud whisper.

Atkinson pushed open the door into the mite of a room where the Plymouth Rock lamp sputtered. The Coolidge collie pup barked. "Who is there?" was the husky inquiry from the adjoining room.

Atkinson, who recognized the voice of Father Coolidge, answered: "The newspaper men. President Harding is dead. We must see your son at once."

There was a swish of clothing inside the father's bedroom. Then appeared the aged father of the President. He wore a nightgown tucked into a pair of overalls. His feet were bare. Rubbing his blinking eyes, Father Coolidge said: "Just had a flash from somewhere about it. I'll call Calvin and Grace."

The Plymouth Nestor climbed the stairs to the bedchamber of his son and daughter-in-law. He had hardly mounted the first step when, with a pant and a roar, a motor car stopped outside the door. A breathless, dust-begrimed man rushed into the dingy living-room. "Where is President Coolidge? Tell him President Harding is dead. I have a message from Secretary Christian. I am from the Vermont Telephone Company. I must see the President at once! " he gasped.

We informed the telephone man that Father Coolidge had gone to awaken his son and daughter, and would return soon.

Lights began to gleam through the narrow staircase, at the top of which the President and the future mistress of the White House were presumably dressing. There was a rustling of a skirt. There was shuffling of shoes. Hours seemed to elapse. We correspondents were wondering if the President ever would come downstairs; whether, if he came, he would violate his reputation for taciturnity; whether, if he did, we could ever reach a telephone or a telegraph station in time to catch even an extra edition of our papers.

One-thirty A. M.!

A girlish, brown-haired figure, attired in a simple dotted Swiss gown, came slowly down the rickety, squeaky stairs. Her face wore a sweet but saddened expression. The woman seemed stunned. It happened that the writer stood nearest to the bottom of the staircase when Mrs. Coolidge—for it was she—walked into the room.

Addressing the writer, Mrs. Coolidge said: "It cannot be true! There must be some awful mistake. Poor Mrs. Harding, I do feel so sorry for her! She has been so hopeful, so brave, so loyal and devoted."

Admonished that the news was only too true, the President's wife added: "We are both shocked. We can hardly believe it. We had been assured that President Harding was on the road to recovery. We are simply astounded by the sudden tragedy."

The telephone despatcher handed Mrs. Coolidge this mutilated message, signed by George B. Christian, secretary to the dead President. It was dated San Francisco, August 2, 7:35 P. M.:

"The President died instantaneously and without warning, and while conversing with members of his family, at 7:30 P. M. (11:30 P. M. New York daylight saving time). Death apparently was due to some brain evolvement (this word, through an operator's blunder, read 'environment,') probably an apoplexy.

"During the day he had been free from discomfort and there was every justification for anticipating a prompt recovery."

By the sputtering little lamp Mrs. Coolidge read the message, which had been addressed to the new President. She turned to the writer and said: "That word 'environment' should read 'evolvement.' That means embolism. That means a clot of blood on the brain, the same thing that is reported to have caused the death of former President Roosevelt. Isn't it pitiful?"

"You have no telephone or telegraph service here. We shall gladly wire your message to Mrs. Harding at San Francisco," I suggested.

Mrs. Coolidge expressed her gratitude. She went over to the center table, took up a bit of paper, got a pencil, and wrote:

"Mrs. Warren G. Harding, Palace Hotel, San Francisco, Cal.

"We offer you our deepest sympathy. May God bless and keep you." (signed) "Calvin and Grace Coolidge."

The writer asked the privilege of then taking the message along. Mrs. Coolidge replied: "Please wait until the President has seen it."

Just here there was a step on the stair. There came from the bottom of the flight an apparition in black. A white face was silhouetted in the flutter of flame from the single lamp. It was the face of the new President. It was ashen in hue. This was intensified by a suit of black, a black tie, and black shoes. The habit had been substituted for a much rumpled gray suit the President had worn the morning before, when he sat upon the porch swing and exchanged with the correspondents felicities that President Harding was out of danger.

The new President strode silently, almost majestically, into the room. He greeted each of us with a hand-shake. We each addressed him as "Mr. President."

The new President's keen eyes searched ours as if for information. There was a tense interval. It was broken by Mr. Atkinson, whom the correspondents had selected as their spokesman.

Approaching the President, he said, in solemn dignity: "Mr. Coolidge, you are the President of the United States. We bring you the sad news of the death of Warren G. Harding."

The President's face grew even more pale, were that possible. He waited a full minute. Then he asked, "Is that absolutely authentic?"

"Absolutely," replied Mr. Atkinson.

Mrs. Coolidge then handed the President the message from Secretary Christian. As he leaned over the table and scrutinized the official

report, the President's face grew even sadder. He stoically read and
re-read the message. Then he dropped it upon the table. Speechless, he stood for still another minute. Then he turned to Erwin C.
Geisser, acting secretary. With dignity and precision, he said: "Mr.
Geisser, will you please come with me into the other room?"

The President and Mr. Geisser started for the room on the left.
Father Coolidge had dug up another greasy, flickering lamp. He preceded the President with it. The three disappeared. The door was
closed.

Nearly 2 A. M.! Not a line from the President for the many millions
who awaited it.

Two-fifteen A. M.! The door opened. The President reappeared
with a few sheets of paper. He walked quietly over to Mrs. Coolidge
and handed them to her. "Grace," said he, affectionately, "please
read this and tell me what you think of it."

Mrs. Coolidge carefully examined the manuscript. She handed it
back to the President. She smiled and said, "I think that is fine,
Calvin."

The President was about to turn toward the impatient correspondents when Mrs. Coolidge said: "Wait a minute, dear. I want your
opinion of this message to Mrs. Harding."

The President read it, handed it back, saying, "That is a very sweet
note, Grace."

Mrs. Coolidge gave the message to the writer to wire.

Meantime the President, still silent to the correspondents, handed
them individually this, his first message to the American people:

"Reports have reached me that President Harding is gone. The
world has lost a great and good man. I mourn his loss. He was my
chief and my friend.

"It will be my purpose to carry out the policies which he has begun
for the service of the American people, and for meeting their responsibilities wherever they may arise. For this purpose I shall seek the
coöperation of all those who have been associated with the President
during his term of office.

"Those who have given their efforts to assist him, I wish to remain
in office, that they may assist me. I have faith that God will direct
the destinies of our Nation.

"It is my intention to remain here until I can secure the correct form of oath of office, which will be administered to me by my father, who is a notary public, if that will meet with the necessary requirements. I expect to leave for Washington to-day."

The correspondents glanced hastily through the document. The unprecedented feature was the announcement that the President was to take the oath of office from his father, a mere notary public. I asked the President: "Has it not been invariably the custom that a President should be sworn in by a Justice of the United States Supreme Court?"

The President replied: "Maybe. But it is good law, in my judgment, that a President can be sworn in by anybody who has authority to administer an oath, even if that body happens to be his father."

It is understood that prior to taking the oath the President received an opinion from a very high judicial authority that he was right. This judgment was afterward confirmed by Chief Justice William H. Taft, of the United States Supreme Court.

With the understanding that we should return for the swearing in, if we could, we parted with the new President. . . .

. . . We reached there too late. The oath had been taken. Coolidge was actually President. He had been sworn in at exactly 3:37 A. M. daylight saving time, under additional dramatic circumstances. . . .

Clustered about the President were these witnesses: Representative Porter H. Dale, of Vermont, who had just resigned to become a candidate for United States Senator; President L. L. Lane, of the Railway Mail Association; Joseph H. Fountain, editor of the Springfield (Vermont) "Reporter"; Edwin C. Geisser, the President's assistant secretary; Joseph McInierney, the President's chauffeur; and Mrs. Coolidge. These grouped themselves about the old table, on which still burned the smoky kerosene lamp. The old family Bible was alongside it. Father Coolidge took up his station on one side of the table. The President with Mrs. Coolidge faced him.

Elder Coolidge asked his son to raise his right hand. The President obeyed. Elder Coolidge then read the following oath, the form of which had been phoned from Washington but a few minutes before:

"I, Calvin Coolidge, do solemnly swear that I will faithfully execute the office of President of the United States, and I will to the best of my ability preserve, protect, and defend the Constitution of the United States."

The President with deep emotion repeated each word of the oath after his father. Then came a pause. Suddenly the President, his hand still uplifted, exclaimed:

"So help me, God."

The President paused again. Then he tenderly embraced and kissed his wife. The proud father walked over and seized his son's hand with a crushing grip. The witnesses shook the President's hand. Then neighbors trooped in, and there was quite an affectionate exchange of mingled grief and congratulations.

It was near daylight. The President said to his wife: "We are due at Rutland at 9 A. M. Better hurry with your grip." Mrs. Coolidge disappeared, first to prepare a breakfast of corn-cakes and coffee, and then to get ready for her first journey to Washington as the First Lady in the Land.

Louis J. Lang, in *Outlook*, September 5, 1923 (New York), CXXXV, 22–25 *passim*.

---

197. Issues of the Election of 1924

BY PROFESSOR JOHN SPENCER BASSETT (1926)

For Bassett see No. 192 above.—Bibliography: M. R. Ravage, *Teapot Dome.*

IN the same year, 1924, alarming facts came to light in Washington, seriously reflecting on the correct management of three of the executive departments under President Harding. The occasion was the lease of naval oil reserves in California to E. M. Doheny, and in Wyoming, the Teapot Dome field, to H. F. Sinclair. By law these reserves were under the control of the Secretary of the Navy, but that official, Denby, had with the approval of President Harding transferred the naval reserves to the Department of the Interior, A. B. Fall, Secretary; and the Attorney-General, H. M. Daugherty, had rendered a supporting opinion. Fall lost no time in leasing these lands to Doheny and Sinclair on terms very advantageous to the lessees. Rumor said that these actions were not square, and finally the Senate Committee on Lands began an investigation in 1923. Day after day astonishing revelations came out. Doheny testified that he lent Fall $100,000 in currency two days before the lease was signed, and it was shown that Sinclair had lent him $25,000 about the same time. Fall refused to testify before the committee alleging it might incriminate him and resigned his office. He was indicted for fraud and ordered to trial. Public opinion would not hear of the Attorney-General, who would ordinarily have been the prosecutor, taking charge of the case, and special counsel was appointed. The case, with cases against Doheny and Sinclair, is still in the courts in 1926.

The action of Secretary Denby in transferring the reserves brought suspicion against him and a loud clamor was raised for his dismissal. President Coolidge stood by him stoutly on the ground that nothing was proved against Denby. Then the Senate by resolution demanded his dismissal, but Coolidge replied that the demand was beyond the scope of Senatorial power and that he would not dismiss Denby to satisfy unproved charges. But the pressure of public opinion continued strong and after several weeks of delay the President accepted Denby's resignation.

The next man to fall was Attorney-General Daugherty. The things that were brought to light showed that he was not the man to prosecute violators of laws made to restrain "big business," which is specifically the duty of an Attorney-General. The Senate, with only one dissenting vote, ordered a special committee to investigate his Department. Daugherty refused to allow the books of the Department to be examined by the committee, and on this ground the President demanded his resignation. The testimony before this committee was startling. Although much that was said was unproved it was enough to show that the office had been run in a very lax manner. Daugherty's friends attacked the reputation of the chairman of the investigating committee, Senator Wheeler, and he was indicted for unlawfully accepting a retainer from oil men in Montana. On later prosecution the charges collapsed completely, and when the matter came before the Senate that body supported Wheeler by a vote of 56 to 5. So far as the Harding administration was concerned the net result of the investigations was that three members of the cabinet were discredited and the country was convinced that one part of that cabinet had been constituted on a very unfortunate basis. The confidence of the people in Hughes, Mellon, and Hoover was unshaken.

When the oil scandal came before the public the Democrats were disposed to make capital of it; but Doheny, who proved himself a willing witness, took away that hope by testifying that William G. McAdoo, then a prominent candidate for the coming Democratic presidential nomination, had been retained after leaving the cabinet to look after Doheny's interests in Mexico and had received a large fee. McAdoo replied that his services had nothing to do with oil interests out of Mexico; but in the excited state of the public mind, opinion, stimulated by his enemies, turned strongly against him. It was also shown that Franklin K. Lane, another member of Wilson's cabinet, had been retained by oil men after leaving the cabinet. The result was that the Democrats lost the political advantage they expected to reap.

The election of 1924 proved to be a tame affair. Coolidge was nominated by the Republicans without opposition, with General Charles G. Dawes for Vice-President. In the Democratic convention a strong split occurred. The faction that had supported the Wilson reforms of 1913–1914 and announced a progressive policy for the future now appeared in support of McAdoo, Bryan acting with it. The old Champ Clark following appeared with Governor Al. Smith, of New York, at its head. The prohibition question played an important part, but it was kept as much in the background as possible. More evident was the religious question. Smith, a Catholic, was made to stand out against McAdoo, who was said to have the sympathy of the Ku Klux Klan. Many conservative Democrats from the South stood out for favorite sons, and in many ways showed their determination to defeat the nomination of McAdoo, who was the leading candidate. They were able to prevent his success under the two-thirds rule, with the result that after more than a week of struggle John W. Davis was nominated, with Charles W. Bryan, of Nebraska, for Vice-President. Davis was as conservative as Coolidge, and in the end the voters of the country had to choose between two men whose views were much the same on important questions, with the result that they took the Republican conservative by a majority of 382 against 136, with the 13 votes of Wisconsin for La Follette,

who had run as a Progressive. The popular vote was 15,748,356 for
Coolidge, 8,617,454 for Davis, and 4,686,681 for La Follette.

John Spencer Bassett, *Expansion and Reform: 1889–1926* [*Epochs of American History*, IV] (New York, Longmans, Green, 1926), 303–306.

◆

198. The Ku-Kluxer (1924)

BY GERALD W. JOHNSON

Johnson is a newspaper writer; on the editorial staff of the Baltimore *Sun* since
1926. The Ku Klux Klan was originally organized in post-Civil War days in the
South. Civil power in some states was in the hands of irresponsible negroes and
carpet-baggers. The Klan was an extra-legal secret organization, which used whipping and sometimes death as a means of breaking up state governments founded
on negro suffrage. The modern Klan was a money-making organization, active
in various communities and provided with substantial credit and other means of promotion. In this article the author satirizes a type of well-meaning but rather stupid
and provincial American who made the new Klan profitable to its proprietors.

I THINK that my friend Chill Burton is an Exalted Cyclops, although he may be only a Fury, or a lesser Titan, for my knowledge
of the nomenclature of the Ku Klux Klan is far from exact. At any
rate, he is an important personage among klansmen in our town, but
rather insignificant in the State organization. He may therefore be
classified as a klansman ranking slightly above the average, but not
far enough above to it be in any way identified with the Atlanta
potentates, who are a breed different altogether from the ordinary
members. So if one might determine what made Chill Burton a
member of this curious organization, I believe that the secret of its
rapid growth would be made plain, for an argument that would convince him would unquestionably convince millions of other obscure
and worthy Americanos.

In the first place, the lurid imaginings of many writers on the Klan,
particularly in the North, may be dismissed at once. It was not the
prospect of participating in the celebration of some revolting Witches'
Sabbath that fetched Chill, for he isn't that sort of a man. He is
fifty years old, a pillar of the church, an exemplary husband and the
father of six head of healthy children. He believes in the verbal in-

spiration and literal interpretation of the Scriptures, and accepts the Athanasian Creed and the Democratic Platform with unquestioning faith. You might entrust your purse or your daughter to Chill with quite as much confidence as you might entrust either to the right reverend ordinary of the diocese, or to the pastor of the First Baptist Church. He will *not* take a drink, and he *will* pay his debts. In brief, if Pope was right, Chill is one of the noblest works of God.

Chill goes through life surrounded by the machinations of occult and Machiavellian intelligences. He walks briskly, planting his square-toed shoes with decision. He is sturdy, the least bit stooped, decently garbed in clothing of inconspicuous cut and neutral tint, and his iron-gray hair is growing thin on the top of his head. Occasionally his eyes light up with a pale blue flame, and his mouth tightens into a grim slit; but otherwise he gives no outward indication of the fact that his soul is tormented by tremendous and ghastly visions and his mind appalled by the perils that threaten the very existence of true religion and unpolluted Anglo-Saxon blood.

These visions and perils, and nothing base, were the considerations that made of Chill what is colloquially known in North Carolina as a "klucker." He certainly does not thirst for the heart's blood of Mary Amanda Emmeline Seymour Pleasure Belle Caroline Kearns, who presides in his kitchen. He is on perfectly friendly, if not intimate, terms with J. Leroy Goldstein, the pawnbroker, and Chris Skalchunes, who keeps the fruit stand, and he treats the Rev. Father Paul O'Keefe with faultless, frosty courtesy. Chill would sincerely deplore the lynching of any of these individuals; most emphatically would he refuse to have anything to do with their molestation, even in as mild a form as a cow-hiding, or a coat of tar and feathers. Yet from the bottom of his soul he believes that the dominance of the Anglo-Saxon is hourly imperilled by the Negro; that if the Nordic strain is polluted by infusion of any other blood, American civilization will collapse and disappear; that if the Protocols of Zion were fraudulent, then something worse exists still unrevealed; and that secret agents of the Pope, infiltrating the Bureau of Engraving and Printing, strove treacherously to convert America to Catholicism by introducing crosses, snakes and pictures of His Holiness among the decorations on the dollar bill of 1917. Therefore, when less scrupulous brother knights of the Invisible Empire commit outrages under cover of darkness,

Chill's attitude is that while lawlessness is always to be regretted, it is better that a few individuals should suffer injustice than that our civilization, our religion and our very race should be exposed to the secret assaults of foes without scruples and of superhuman cunning.

Nor is his belief a proof of insanity any more than it is a proof of insanity for his small son to believe that Cæsar overcame the Nervii. The boy has no legal evidence that either Cæsar or the Nervii ever existed in fact; the schoolmaster has simply taught him that the battle occurred, and that settles it for him. Equally oracular authorities, the pastor and the politician, had filled Chill with fear and distrust of Negroes, foreigners, Jews and Catholics long before William Joseph Simmons, of Atlanta, began to dream of a throne. The explanation is absurdly simple. Devil-drubbing is always easier and safer if the particular devil selected for chastisement is feeble, or far away. In the South, where the Ku Klux Klan originated, foreigners, Jews and Catholics are relatively few and far between, and Negroes are politically and socially impotent. Therefore every Southern demagogue, sacred or profane, has for generations covered his significant silence on industrial slavery, on race hatred, on baronial estates supported by legalized peonage, and on election frauds by thundering denunciations of the carpet-bagger, St. Peter, Judas Iscariot and Lenine, none of whom was then and there present or likely to demand embarrassing explanation.

The Cause was furthered in the South by other circumstances. It happens that the South actually was under Negro domination once, and after half a century the memory of that experience still keeps its racial sensibilities abnormally acute. A Northern observer recently pointed out that the Negro is all that it has to worry about, so it has made up for the lack of other major troubles by worrying itself into a pathological condition about the race problem. Thus, in view of the diligent tillage that had been going on for many decades, it is no marvel that the Invisible Empire reaped a rich and instantaneous harvest in the Southern field.

Yet it is commonly reported that the banner Ku Klux State is not Georgia, but Indiana. It is evident, therefore, that the strongest appeal of the Klan is not to prejudice against the Negro—an assumption borne out by the significant fact that only in rare instances in the South have men wearing the regalia of the Klan attacked a Negro.

Nor have the Catholics, Jews, and foreigners furnished the majority of the victims, except at such times as they have offered themselves as candidates and been politically massacred at the polls. The whippings, the tar and feathers, and similar attentions have usually been administered to known or suspected criminals or social outcasts. To this sort of work the klucker of a grade slightly lower than that of my friend Chill goes forth joyously, sublimely confident that he thereby serves the larger cause of white, Gentile, Protestant supremacy, just as the county chairman stuffs the precinct boxes with the county ticket only, thoroughly convinced that he is thereby helping God and the national committee to save the country.

The necromancy by which the guardian of the sacred fires of civilization, race and religion is transformed into a whipper of prostitutes and a lyncher of bootleggers is no mystery. It is no more than the familiar psychological phenomenon of "taking it out on somebody." Chill is profoundly convinced that the Nordic Protestant is in imminent danger; what could be more natural, then, than for him to regard with tolerance, if not with approval, the extra-legal chastisement of any one who violates Nordic Protestant standards in particular? No doubt some Gray Eminence is the man higher up; but he is not within reach, or even identified as yet. . . .

But who impressed Chill with the notion that his duty to obey the law is less than his duty to defend racial, social and religious purity? Who but those who set up the great American fetish of equality, not merely before the law, but in every respect? Chill has been assured from childhood that in the United States of America every man is a king in his own right and so naturally he assumes royal prerogatives. The energy of a monarch in cutting legal red-tape in the cause of justice may very well be a virtue; but it is a virtue that cannot be democratized without disaster. To have a rigid and exacting standard of manners and morals set by an aristocracy may be of great benefit to a nation; but when the proletariat undertakes to confer that benefit—well, we have the result before us in America.

The Ku Klux Klan was swept beyond the racial boundaries of the Negro and flourishes now in the Middle West because it is a perfect expression of the American idea that the voice of the people is the voice of God. The belief that the average klansman is consciously affected by an appeal to his baser self is altogether erroneous. In the voice of the organizer he hears a clarion call to knightly and selfless service. It strikes him as in no wise strange that he should be so summoned; is he not, as an American citizen, of the nobility? Politics has been democratized. Social usage has been democratized. Religion has been most astoundingly democratized. Why, then, not democratize chivalry?

The klansman has already been made, in his own estimation, politically a monarch, socially a peer of the realm, spiritually a high priest. Now the Ku Klux Klan calls him to step up and for the trifling consideration of ten dollars he is made a Roland, a Lancelot, a knight-errant vowed to the succor of the oppressed, the destruction of ogres and magicians, the defense of the faith. Bursting with noble ideals and lofty aspirations, he accepts the nomination. The trouble is that this incantation doesn't work, as none of the others has worked, except in his imagination. King, aristocrat, high priest as he believes himself to be, he is neither royal, noble, nor holy. So, under his white robe and pointed hood he becomes not a Chevalier Bayard but a thug.

The shocked surprise of many prominent publicists and educators in the presence of the phenomenon of the Klan is the crowning absurdity of the farce. These men have spent years and gained great renown making just this thing possible. They have stuffed millions of youths, and filled miles of bookshelves with twaddle about the glory of the masses. By dint of herculean labor they have at length deprived the adjective "common" of its legitimate connotation when it is used to modify the noun "people." To do them justice, they seem to have produced an *un*common people, a people incapable of perceiving any essential difference between St. George and a butcher, a people unwilling to admit that spearing a dragon is a feat requiring mental and spiritual qualities not necessarily possessed by a pig-sticker.

Chill is no more to blame for his delusions than the Knight of the Rueful Countenance was for his. The romances are to blame. Chill, indeed, has an excuse that Quixote could not plead, for Chill's romances were offered and accepted as sober narrations of fact, as histories, as lectures, as sermons. They were offered by and accepted from authorities whom Chill respected too much to question; and whom it is not profitable in any case, and not safe in many cases, for anyone else to question.

Thus they are not merely woven into the fabric of his thinking—
they are the very warp and woof thereof. . . . He has been taught
romance in the name of history to the end that, glorying in the proud
record of American arms, he might present an unfaltering front to
any foe when his every instinct commanded him to go away from
there. But instead of making a patriot of him, it has served merely
to convince him that as an American he is "a mighty tur'ble man,"
one born to command, and disobedience to whom partakes of the
nature of mutiny in the ranks.

To inculcate patriotism, to immunize against foreign radical ideas
and to strengthen the bulwarks of true religion are certainly prominent among the aims of the current program of Americanization,
which is absorbing enormous quantities of money and time and the
energy of innumerable massive brains. I submit that the magical
rise of the Invisible Empire, Knights of the Ku Klux Klan, is one
outstanding proof of the tremendous effect of that program. No
romance that apparently tended to strengthen respect for the flag
and the faith has been rejected by the Americanizers on the ground
that it was blatantly false. But outraged truth has an uncomfortable
habit of avenging itself. Spurious history, spurious ethnology, spurious religion have produced a spurious patriot, none the less existent
because unexpected and undesired. The fact that nobody foresaw
that Chill would blossom into a klansman does not alter the fact that
the klansman is one of the flowers of our democracy.

On the whole, I think that it would have been kinder to him and
safer for the country if America had told him no lies to begin with.

Gerald W. Johnson, in *The American Mercury* (New York, 1924), I, 207–211
passim. Reprinted by permission of the author.

199. The New Generation (1926)

BY MATHER A. ABBOTT

Abbott, a Nova Scotian, was a teacher of boys and a Professor of Latin at Yale, before he became headmaster of the Lawrenceville School. His success as an educator and teacher of boys qualifies him to speak with authority on the supposed radical tendencies of modern youth.—Bibliography: Ben B. Lindsey, *The Revolt of Modern Youth.*

AS I looked over my boys this morning, when we were celebrating Armistice Day in chapel, I said to myself: "The war is an ever-present evil with me. I suffered so much during my three years in the navy—we all suffered so much—that we can never forget it. But not one of these fellows knows anything about it. The oldest boys were only ten years old when the Armistice was signed." Then I saw a picture. I saw a picture of myself at eighteen, and the world as it was then, and a picture of this maelstrom of a world in which our boys are now placed. Think of it, and remember your youth. In the last eight years we have had:

1. Prohibition and all it entails.
2. The ubiquitous automobile.
3. The cheap theater, especially the movies, with its sex problems.
4. The absence of parental control.
5. The ignoring of religion.
6. The emancipation of womanhood, combined with the modern dance.

There are just six things. Now, when we were eighteen, liquor was hardly thought of. We knew there were certain boys that used to drink and we did not often associate with them. As for carrying a pocket flask, it was practically unknown. When we took a girl out for a drive, we had to hire a one-horse rig and we were all properly chaperoned and looked after. We had no cheap theaters and no movies. Our parents were addressed as "sir" and "ma'am," and their word was absolute law. God was an ever-present power, whom we held in deadly awe. Imagine our feelings if a lady, with a cigarette in her mouth and drinking a cocktail, should have shown herself at one of our dinner parties thirty years ago! . . . And the modern dance I saw first in 1902, when I went up the Nile, in certain Ethiopian villages where the tomtom was no louder than the present-day drum! Into this maelstrom the modern youth has come, knowing nothing else, and you and I and all the members of this parental generation are absolutely responsible if youth is going to the devil. But it is not!

I have been in the business of teaching boys for thirty years. I have at present under my charge 540 boys collected from nearly every State, and I have never known a more truthful, clean-living, honorable set of young men. They are different from the boys of my youth as the sun is from the moon—full of nonsense, full of passion, headstrong, mischief-loving, but five times as decent, as truthful, and as manly. Let me describe them to you:

In the first place their leading characteristic is that they must prove everything by trying it. They do not begin where we leave off, as we want them to do; they must go through every experience themselves. They take nothing for granted. They want facts, not camouflage. They can see the false through a ten-inch board. They have an almost devilish intuition—I say "devilish" because I have been caught so often! They will have nothing of what they call "bull" on the part of an older person. I would rather talk to five thousand people of your age than I would to my five hundred boys. I have to be so abominably careful that I can prove every word I say!

Secondly, the absence of religious instruction in their youth. Unfortunately, the mothers are too busy to give the fireside and bedside talks that they used to give the little fellows, and the fathers are too busy in business even to tell them the truth about the sex problem. Now you cannot prove the other world and you cannot prove God, and the modern generation will not accept anything you cannot prove. So, though "the fear of God is the beginning of wisdom," the modern generation is practically without it. Since the great fear which held us is absent, these boys, having the spiritual longings that all boys have, are restless. Unwilling to face the deep questions of life, they try to seek happiness in the material, and most of this desire that we hear so much of for a thrill, for breaking the law, and so on comes from an unanswered longing within, which they think they are going to satisfy with material things, only to find that the material things cannot satisfy. So these lurid tales we hear are usually caused, not by any evil in the boy or girl, but by the untrammeled pursuit of truth which is so evident in all the young of our generation. They want to *realize* everything and, of course, you and I, in our maturity, know that very few things in this world can be realized. In this connection, I wish to use a place near-by as an illustration. This town has suddenly become notorious, but I believe there are 20,000 people in it who are not notorious, who are living lives that are decent and straight and true. But the news of a certain family in the town blackens every paper every morning. So it is with these stories of the youth of today. They are frightful stories, absolutely true, most likely, but I do not believe that 10 per cent of our youth could be thus characterized. If we looked upon the notorious happening in that town as the rule, where would America be going? But it is the great exception. So with these lurid stories; they, too, are the great exceptions.

Now, lastly, the equalization of the sexes: When you and I were boys, woman was on a pedestal; we worshipped her. There was pursuit; there was mystery; there was worship. Did we worship that which was true or that which was false? The worship has gone, disappeared, and I am told that modesty, too, has gone. Perhaps it has, but we are getting at facts; we are getting at companionship; we are getting at the truth. The double standard has vanished. Of course, there are terrific calamities, terrific failures, but out of them there is going to come something remarkable.

To sum up, therefore, what do I find? First, a truth-lover. Second, a word of honor that is never broken. Third, a reasonable being that will not take a rule as final until it is approved. Fourth, and most astonishing, on the whole, a clean-minded individual. And then—what will always happen where God is not regarded as supreme, what has happened throughout history where a nation has given up its God—a restlessness that is always unaccountable, a dissatisfaction of mind which makes the youth probe into things we never thought of going into, which we took on faith. Also, many failures, many disasters, as there always are in a great upheaval, where freedom gets confounded with license. No, gentlemen, the youth of the present generation, as far as I know, and I know five hundred of them very intimately, are on the way to great discoveries, have made a step toward happiness and a step toward self-government far ahead of anything we had in our youth. They need very careful handling. They need all the love and affection that a man can give them, and they are going to bring this old world of ours one step nearer heaven in the end.

Mather A. Abbott, Address before the Rotary Club of Trenton, New Jersey, November 11, 1926.

———————◆———————

200. The Republican Landslide of 1928

FROM THE NEW YORK TIMES

The New York *Times* is a morning paper. This summary is therefore taken from the paper of the second morning after Herbert Hoover, with a long record of scientific achievement, of war-time service as Food Administrator, and eight years as Secretary of Commerce in the Cabinets of Harding and Coolidge, was duly elected President over Alfred E. Smith, four times Governor of New York.

WITH the count of the ballots cast in Massachusetts in Tuesday's election completed last night that State's eighteen electoral votes were added to the meagre score credited to Governor Alfred E. Smith of New York, Democratic candidate for President of the United States, in the nation-wide contest in which he was overwhelmingly defeated by Herbert Hoover of California, his Republican adversary.

Other belated returns from doubtful States were all in Mr. Hoover's favor. North Dakota, North Carolina and Texas increased his triumphant total by thirty-seven. With these put in the Hoover column and Massachusetts included in the Smith tally, the result of the Presidential election expressed in electoral votes was as follows:

Hoover, 444.
Smith, 87.
Total record votes, 531.
Necessary to a Presidential choice, 266.
Hoover's majority over Smith, 357.

How great will be the popular vote is a figure that cannot be determined accurately at this time, but based on returns received with approximately 22,000 missing precincts throughout the United States, it is estimated that as many as 20,000,000 may have voted for Mr. Hoover and perhaps as many as 14,500,000 for Governor Smith. In round numbers this makes a total popular vote that may exceed

35,000,000 with the inclusion of the ballots cast for Presidential candidates of minor political parties.

Definite information that North Carolina and Texas had joined the procession of States whose majority votes went to Mr. Hoover emphasized the widespread character of the defection in the Solid South, consistently Democratic since reconstruction days. Florida and Virginia had gone over to the Republican Presidential candidate on the basis of returns received late Tuesday night and in the small hours of Wednesday morning, leaving to Governor Smith's tally from that section only Alabama, Arkansas, Georgia, Louisiana, Mississippi and South Carolina.

Only two other States were carried by Governor Smith. Their adhesion to him presented a striking contrast to his Solid South showing in that both are New England States, Rhode Island and Massachusetts. He carried the two New England States in the face of the fact that his own State of New York gave its electoral vote to the Republican candidate.

Governor Smith has carried Massachusetts by a majority as yet undetermined, but which has passed the 21,000 mark in the count and will go higher, but not materially so, as few precincts remain to be returned. He ran ahead of Mr. Hoover in most of the large cities and in the towns where plants are located.

The cities of Springfield and Worcester gave pluralities to Mr. Hoover. An ironic incident in Governor Smith's Massachusetts victory is that he carried Northampton, President Coolidge's home city.

But whatever comfort the Massachusetts adherents of Governor Smith's candidacy may be able to obtain by his triumph in that State was overshadowed among the Democracy generally by the emphatic character of the defeat he received at the hands of the Republican nominee for President.

The entire West, dissatisfied farm States and all, gave their suffrages to Mr. Hoover in the face of predictions that he would lose them on account of his opposition to the scheme of agricultural relief embodied in the McNary-Haugen bill.

With the exception of the two New England States which Governor Smith carried, the States of the whole Atlantic seaboard from Maine to South Carolina gave their electoral votes to Mr. Hoover. The Rocky Mountain and Pacific Coast States rallied to his cause. So, too, did the border States of Missouri, Oklahoma, Tennessee and Kentucky, while Wisconsin, credited with being very wet in sentiment and dominated politically by the Progressive element of the Republican Party, most of whose leaders had endorsed Governor Smith's candidacy, also found its way into the Hoover camp.

With Hoover's notable victory went along assurance of that party's control of both Houses of Congress. With some Senatorial and Congressional contests still in doubt, the Republicans have a clear lead in the Senate and the House which should afford promise of the enactment of legislation sponsored by Mr. Hoover as President.

New York Times, November 8, 1928.

CHAPTER XXXVI — THE LEAGUE OF NATIONS AND THE WORLD COURT

201. Wilson on the League of Nations (1919)

BY PRESIDENT WOODROW WILSON

For Wilson, see Nos. 129–132 above. To the President the League of Nations seemed the only possible form of assurance that future wars might be averted. He could not feel that it was enough for peace agreements to restore the status quo. However, although his proposed League of Nations was carried out, a strong domestic opposition blocked his hopes of ratification by the United States. See also Nos. 53, 202 and 204.—Bibliography: Henry Cabot Lodge, *The Senate and the League of Nations;* J. H. Dickinson, *The United States and the League;* Eustace Perry, *Responsibilities of the League;* J. K. Turner, *Shall It Be Again;* and publications of the World Peace Foundation and the League of Nations.

MR. CHAIRMAN:

I consider it a distinguished privilege to be permitted to open the discussion in this conference on the League of Nations. We have assembled for two purposes, to make the present settlements which have been rendered necessary by this war, and also to secure the peace of the world, not only by the present settlements but by the arrangements we shall make at this conference for its maintenance. The League of Nations seems to me to be necessary for both of these purposes. There are many complicated questions connected with the present settlements which perhaps can not be successfully worked out to an ultimate issue by the decisions we shall arrive at here. I can easily conceive that many of these settlements will need subsequent reconsideration, that many of the decisions we make shall need subsequent alteration in some degree; for, if I may judge by my own study of some of these questions, they are not susceptible of confident judgments at present.

It is, therefore, necessary that we should set up some machinery by which the work of this conference should be rendered complete. We have assembled here for the purpose of doing very much more than making the present settlements. We are assembled under very peculiar conditions of world opinion. I may say without straining the point that we are not representatives of Governments, but representatives of peoples. It will not suffice to satisfy governmental circles anywhere. It is necessary that we should satisfy the opinion of mankind. The burdens of this war have fallen in an unusual degree upon the whole population of the countries involved. I do not need to draw for you the picture of how the burden has been thrown back from the front upon the older men, upon the women, upon the children, upon the homes of the civilized world, and how the real strain of the war has come where the eye of government could not reach, but where the heart of humanity beats. We are bidden by these people to make a peace which will make them secure. We are bidden by these people to see to it that this strain does not come upon them again, and I venture to say that it has been possible for them to bear this strain because they hoped that those who represented them could get together after this war and make such another sacrifice unnecessary.

It is a solemn obligation on our part, therefore, to make permanent arrangements that justice shall be rendered and peace maintained. This is the central object of our meeting. Settlements may be temporary, but the action of the nations in the interests of peace and justice must be permanent. We can set up permanent decisions. Therefore, it seems to me that we must take, so far as we can, a picture of the world into our minds. Is it not a startling circumstance, for one thing, that the great discoveries of science, that the quiet studies of men in laboratories, that the thoughtful developments which have taken place in quiet lecture rooms, have now been turned to the destruction of civilization? The powers of destruction have not so much multiplied as gained facility. The enemy whom we have just overcome had at his seats of learning some of the principal centers of scientific study and discovery, and he used them in order to make destruction sudden and complete; and only the watchful, continuous coöperation of men can see to it that science as well as armed men is kept within the harness of civilization.

In a sense the United States is less interested in this subject than the other nations here assembled. With her great territory and her extensive sea borders, it is less likely that the United States should suffer from the attack of enemies than that many of the other nations here should suffer; and the ardor of the United States—for it is a very deep and genuine ardor—for the society of nations is not an ardor springing out of fear or apprehension, but an ardor springing out of the ideals which have come to consciousness in this war. In coming into this war the United States never for a moment thought that she was intervening in the politics of Europe or the politics of Asia or the politics of any part of the world. Her thought was that all the world had now become conscious that there was a single cause which turned upon the issues of this war. That was the cause of justice and of liberty for men of every kind and place. Therefore, the United States should feel that its part in this war had been played in vain if there ensued upon it merely a body of European settlements. It would feel that it could not take part in guaranteeing those European settlements unless that guaranty involved the continuous superintendence of the peace of the world by the associated nations of the world.

Therefore, it seems to me that we must concert our best judgment in order to make this League of Nations a vital thing—not merely a formal thing, not an occasional thing, not a thing sometimes called into life to meet an exigency, but always functioning in watchful attendance upon the interests of the nations—and that its continuity should be a vital continuity; that it should have functions that are continuing functions and that do not permit an intermission of its watchfulness and of its labour; that it should be the eye of the nations to keep watch upon the common interest, an eye that does not slumber, an eye that is everywhere watchful and attentive.

And if we do not make it vital, what shall we do? We shall disappoint the expectations of the peoples. This is what their thought centers upon. I have had the very delightful experience of visiting several nations since I came to this side of the water, and every time the voice of the body of the people reached me through any representative, at the front of its plea stood the hope for the League of Nations. Gentlemen, the select classes of mankind are no longer the governors of mankind. The fortunes of mankind are now in the hands of the plain people of the whole world. Satisfy them, and you have justified their confidence not only but established peace. Fail to satisfy them, and no arrangement that you can make will either set up or steady the peace of the world.

You can imagine, gentlemen, I dare say, the sentiments and the purpose with which representatives of the United States support this great project for a league of nations. We regard it as the keystone of the whole program which expressed our purposes and ideals in this war and which the associated nations have accepted as the basis of the settlement. If we returned to the United States without having made every effort in our power to realize this program, we should return to meet the merited scorn of our fellow citizens. For they are a body that constitutes a great democracy. They expect their leaders to speak their thoughts and no private purpose of their own. They expect their representatives to be their servants. We have no choice but to obey their mandate. But it is with the greatest enthusiasm and pleasure that we accept that mandate; and because this is the keystone of the whole fabric, we have pledged our every purpose to it, as we have to every item of the fabric. We would not dare abate a single part of the program which constitutes our instruction. We would not dare compromise upon any matter as the champion of this thing—this peace of the world, this attitude of justice, this principle that we are the masters of no people but are here to see that every people in the world shall choose its own masters and govern its own destinies, not as we wish but as it wishes. We are here to see, in short, that the very foundations of this war are swept away. Those foundations were the private choice of small coteries of civil rulers and military staffs. Those foundations were the aggression of great powers upon the small. Those foundations were the holding together of empires of unwilling subjects by the duress of arms. Those foundations were the power of small bodies of men to work their will upon mankind and use them as pawns in a game. And nothing less than the emancipation of the world from these things will accomplish peace. You can see that the representatives of the United States are, therefore, never put to the embarrassment of choosing a way of expediency, because they have laid down for them the unalterable lines of principle. And, thank God, those lines have been accepted as the lines of settlement by all the high-minded men who have had to do with the beginnings of this great business.

I hope, Mr. Chairman, that when it is known, as I feel confident it will be known, that we have adopted the principle of the League of Nations and means to work out that principle in effective action, we shall by that single thing have lifted a great part of the load of anxiety from the hearts of men everywhere. We stand in a peculiar case. As I go about the streets here I see everywhere the American uniform. Those men came into the war after we had uttered our purposes. They came as crusaders, not merely to win a war, but to win a cause; and I am responsible to them, for it fell to me to formulate the purposes for which I asked them to fight, and I, like them, must be a crusader for these things, whatever it costs and whatever it may be necessary to do, in honor, to accomplish the object for which they fought. I have been glad to find from day to day that there is no question of our standing alone in this matter, for there are champions of this cause upon every hand. I am merely avowing this in order that you may understand why, perhaps, it fell to us, who are disengaged from the politics of this great Continent and of the Orient, to suggest that this was the keystone of the arch and why it occurred to the generous mind of our president to call upon me to open this debate. It is not because we alone represent this idea, but because it is our privilege to associate ourselves with you in representing it.

I have only tried in what I have said to give you the fountains of the enthusiasm which is within us for this thing, for those fountains spring, it seems to me, from all the ancient wrongs and sympathies of mankind, and the very pulse of the world seems to beat to the surface in this enterprise.

Woodrow Wilson, Address at the Peace Conference, January 25, 1919.

———◆———

202. Henry Cabot Lodge and the League of Nations (1919)

BY BISHOP WILLIAM LAWRENCE (1925)

The author was Episcopal Bishop of Massachusetts from 1893 to 1926, and was an intimate friend of Henry Cabot Lodge. See also Nos. 201 and 204.

CABOT LODGE believed with all his heart in the American ideal, which was that of Washington and which has obtained throughout our history.

As an historian and statesman he distrusted any national or inter-

national action, however well intended, which leaped so far beyond
the traditions and development of each nation as to endanger its
permanence and create a disastrous reaction. He believed that
national and international action must be built up from the people,
their traditions and their intelligent assent, and not imposed from
above. The world is full of the wrecks of noble ideals, pressed into
action by leaders who had not the patience and faith to educate the
world toward them. Hence in his consideration of the Covenant
he met many critical problems; such as these:

No nation, not one of those whose representatives had assembled
in Paris to make and sign the Treaty of Peace, had been commissioned by vote or by the intelligence or knowledge of the people as
to what the League of Nations really meant. It was to be a plan, let
down from above: plans let down from above are not safe or successful in days of democracy.

The Covenant was to be written into the Treaty of Peace in such
a way as to become part of the warp and woof of the whole: and this
at the close of the greatest war of history, when passions and jealousies
were keen, when emotions were on the surface, when sharp reactions
of feelings were sure to come. To be sure, national lines were then
plastic, and the newly formed nationalities could be tied to a new
system for the preservation and enforcement of peace; but the risk
of a sudden casting into mould of those two great issues, both of them
new to history, was very great. Again, the history of sudden alliances
was ominous. Moreover, the prestige of the United States, its
wealth and power, were great temptations to some nations to enter
a plan which could not under that sentiment be impartially considered.

The Covenant as presented, by drawing us into practical alliance
with European and other nations, reversed 'the American policy'
established by Washington, and appeared to negative or wipe out the
Monroe Doctrine—a policy so revolutionary as to demand before
acceptance the intelligent consideration and approval of the American
people.

Senator Lodge had had a part in the framing of scores of treaties,
and knew the value of patient thought, the passage of time for consideration, and exact language. To clarify the terms of a treaty so
that both nations may be practically certain of a common under-

standing of its language is worth months of study; for thereby friction and sometimes war are averted.

The Covenant was practically a treaty or a constitution between forty or more of the nations of the world; and its bearing was not simply upon trade or boundary lines, but upon the issues of international peace and war, the upholding or the punishment of a recalcitrant nation; hence the need of the utmost exactness of language. This Covenant had been struck off in a few weeks, while the critical issues of the Treaty of Peace were also under consideration; and within a week of its publication, statesmen, lawyers, and citizens of every interest were disputing as to the meaning of the most vital sections.

What would happen if under stress of hostile feeling nations hot for war were to depend upon the language of this Covenant? It would be 'a scrap of paper' on the moment. As Mr. Taft, once President and later Chief Justice, an earnest supporter of the ideal of the League, said, 'Undoubtedly the Covenant needs revision. It is not symmetrically arranged: its meaning has to be dug out, and the language is ponderous and in diplomatic patois.' Its terms upon immigration and the tariff were vague. . . .

American policy and practice has always recognized the equality of States. This Nation has always recognized the equality of nations. Upon this principle the Pan-American Union stands. The League of Nations, on the contrary, was and is the glorification of the Great Powers. They made the League. The large States were to be permanently represented in the League: the little States had no representation as of right, only by election. The League is an organization in which it is possible for the Great Powers to control the action of the small Powers: it is not an organization in which the small Powers can control the Great Powers.

The ideal of the nations of the world pledging themselves under certain conditions to insure the peace of the world has appealed to all of us. In national and international relations, however, ideals must meet practical tests. The rôle of an idealist is a noble one, provided he stands true to his ideal. The President, to gain the object of his ambition, became involved in unrighteous compromises, such as the surrender of Shantung to Japan, in order to secure the establishment of the League; and, forsaking his ideal, or seeking to realize it through unjust means, he gained the ill-will and even hatred of peoples which had trusted him, and tended to injure the fair name of the country, won through the sacrifice of her sons.

Important as were these and other considerations in the judgment of Senator Lodge they all held a place secondary to that which, by common popular consent and the understanding of the President and Senate, was the heart of the Covenant, Article 10, which reads:

The members of the League undertake to respect and preserve as against external aggression the territorial integrity and existing political independence of all members of the League. In case of any such aggression, or in case of any threat or danger of such aggression, the Council shall advise upon the means by which this obligation shall be fulfilled.

When I opened the newspaper upon the first publication of the Covenant, I sat down and read it carefully. Coming to Article 10, I read it again and again. Whatever its last clause might mean about advising the members as to how they should fulfill their obligations, the first clause was clear and final—'the members of the League [the United States if she enters] undertake to respect and preserve as against external aggression the territorial integrity and existing political independence of all members of the League.' I read it again; and then I went to my desk and wrote:

My dear Cabot:
I do not see how any true American can stand for Article 10 of the League of Nations.

And I added that the country should know what the Covenant would lead us into.

In answer he wrote:

My dear William,
Your kind note has given me the greatest pleasure. It is a comfort to me to know that you feel just as you do about the League; that the first thing is to consider it thoroughly; that we ought to know, in a matter of such vital importance, just where we are going, and that the American people ought to understand it. . . . The attempt of President Wilson to force it through without consultation with the Senate, equally responsible with him in the making of treaties, is nothing more or less than an attempt to destroy the Constitution.
Always affectionately yours,
H. C. Lodge.

We have not yet, however, struck the fundamental issue of the debate, which was whether the United States would hold to or abandon its historic American Policy or enter into close and organic relations with the nations of Europe and throughout the world.

By our independence we have made unique contributions to the good-will and peace of the world. We have for instance contributed a straightforward, open type of diplomat and diplomacy. The names of Benjamin Franklin, John Jay, Commodore Perry, who was a messenger of peace to Japan, Charles Francis Adams, John Hay, Elihu Root, and others come to mind. . . .

When the President finally presented the Covenant to the Senate for their advice and consent, Senator Lodge, if he had considered only his own judgment, would have voted against it without question or compromise. He always had, however, a keen sense of responsibility for his broader duties. This Covenant was presented to him as a Senator by the President of the United States, and he always felt it his duty to accede to such a call at every point consistent with his principles. He was also leader of the Republican side of the House, and Chairman of the Committee on Foreign Relations: a unique position, and on him to a good degree the peace and unity of the country depended.

Hence, with a solemn sense of responsibility, and with all the force of body, mind, and character, he gave himself to so meeting the objections and opinions of Senator after Senator, adjusting words and sentences, as to obtain a two-thirds vote for the reservation.

The pressure upon Senator Lodge from all parts of the country to alter this or that phrase was tremendous. He was charged with inconsistency, with breaking his word, and evading issues. . . .

In the Senate he had a body of strong and determined men to deal with. Nevertheless, he had the names of the necessary two thirds, Democrats and Republicans, who were ready to vote for the Covenant with the reservations. There were weeks when the Treaty and Covenant were before the Senate when enough Democrats were ready to vote for the Covenant with reservations to have made up a two-thirds vote; but the President had told them that he regarded the reservations as a 'nullification of the Treaty.' Whether this determination was due to promises which he had unhesitatingly made in Paris, or to his temperament or principles, no one may say.

Had the President simply kept silence and allowed those Democratic Senators, strong, conscientious, loyal Americans, to vote according to their judgment, he would have had their consent and approval, and the United States might have been sitting to-day in the League of Nations. Failure to enter the League was not due to the Senate, nor to its leader, Senator Lodge.

William Lawrence, *Henry Cabot Lodge* (Boston, Houghton Mifflin, 1925), 173–186 *passim*. Reprinted by special permission of the publishers.

---

203. World Courting (1923)

BY PROFESSOR MANLEY O. HUDSON

Hudson, Professor of International Law in the Harvard Law School, has been one of the ablest advocates of American participation in the World Court. Service on the Legal Secretariat of the League of Nations has given him first-hand experience of the functioning of both instrumentalities.

WHAT I want to present to you is this: Here is a court which in the first two years of its existence has handed down nine opinions. All nine of those opinions have been promptly accepted and promptly acted upon by the parties in interest.

But there are still some of my friends who talk as if there were before the world a question of *establishing* an International Court. There is no such question today. Forty-seven nations have agreed to the protocol of signature setting up *this* Court. Fifty-four nations are today supporting it, out of their treasuries. It is a Court open to any nation of the world, member of the League of Nations or not member of the League of Nations, on terms of perfect equality. It seems to me to satisfy the general requirements of a world tribunal.

Not only that, but it seems to me to represent a very logical development and fulfillment of what we have been working for in America for the last generation. Our representatives at The Hague Conference of 1899 and at The Hague Conference of 1907 were working for the establishment of a tribunal exactly on this order. In fact, the tribunal has recently been called by a distinguished English lawyer, "A replica of the Supreme Court of the United States."

Now, the Court being in existence, it being a World Court, forty-seven nations having got over the great controversy that prevented us from establishing it before the war, does it not seem a very proper thing for the President of the United States to suggest, as he did, on February 24th last, that the United States should give its support to the maintenance of this institution?

I had the pleasure of speaking here on the very day that the President's proposal was published, the 24th day of last February. I think I mentioned, without knowing the nature of his proposal, conditions very similar to those which Mr. Hughes himself had suggested to President Harding. When the President's proposal was first made there was general acclaim, so far as my contacts went; general acclaim that this represented the fulfillment of an American idea, an American ambition, an American aspiration. But somehow or other, as so frequently happens in these cases, the atmosphere seems to have thinned out very greatly since the twenty-fourth day of February. Opposition which would then have been resented by many people has now come to have a place in our newspapers which must surprise many of us who recall the original enthusiasm for President Harding's proposal.

I would like to take a few minutes to discuss with you the development of that opposition during this period. We are now living over again the comedy which we lived through in 1919 and 1920 with reference to the League of Nations.

We now hear senators say: "We are in favor of *a* court, but not in favor of *the* Court. Of course, we want an international tribunal; the United States has stood for it for a generation; we ourselves have been talking about it for a generation. But this is not the tribunal that we want. So we are going to ask the forty-seven peoples who are parties to the protocol under which this Court is maintained, to abandon their effort altogether and set up something that will be very much better and that will somehow satisfy the susceptibilities of the American people."

Now does anybody propose, does Senator Pepper propose, or does Senator Lenroot propose, that their suggestions make this Court able to perform its functions as an independent judicial tribunal more efficiently? Not at all. And there is nothing in any of the suggestions that are current today, that I can see, that would add in the slightest to the ability of this Court to serve as an independent judicial international tribunal.

There was a suggestion going around last spring—one does not hear it now—that because the Court had a jurisdiction to give advisory opinions to the Council and Assembly of the League of Nations, it was therefore, a tool, a sort of a private adviser of the League of Nations. None of us lawyers who are familiar with the jurisdiction of many American Supreme Courts to give advisory opinions have ever entertained such a view. The Supreme Court of Massachusetts, for instance, has had a jurisdiction of that sort since 1780. And yet it was seriously contended by many people a few months ago that because this Court could give advisory opinions it was not a judicial tribunal.

What I lay before you is this: The record of the Court to date, the attitude of the judges in the discharge of their functions in nine different cases, the attitude of the foreign offices of the world in bringing in this Court in negotiation stages of their efforts to reach the settlement of difficult questions. I think these should leave no doubt in our minds that the Court is the independent tribunal for which the United States has been working for a generation.

My second proposition is that none of the proposals that have been made, with the single exception of the proposal for the compulsory jurisdiction, would in any way increase the possibility of this Court's serviceability in the future.

It seems to me that a great smoke-screen has been erected in front of this Court during the past few months. The American people are now being asked to line up on different sets of reservations with reference to the Court, precisely as they were asked to line up on different sets of reservations with reference to the League of Nations. With reference to the League of Nations, it was contended that we would undertake certain obligations. With reference to the Court what would we undertake if we carried out Mr. Hughes' and President Harding's proposal? We would simply say: "The United States wants to have a part in maintaining this institution. The United States wants the world to know that our moral influence is behind this Court, in the effort of the nations of the world to reach some peaceful settlement of their international disputes."

I think that the generation of which we are a part has a very special opportunity, and I submit to you that that opportunity is about to be thrown away by Senators who are professing to favor *an* international court without ever taking a practical step that would enable us to support *this* Court.

Manley O. Hudson, Address before the Chicago Council on Foreign Relations, December 29, 1923.

---

204. Turning Our Backs (1923)

BY EX-PRESIDENT WOODROW WILSON

For Wilson see Nos. 129–132 above.   For his address to the Peace Conference on the League of Nations, see No. 201 above.

THE anniversary of Armistice Day should stir us to great exaltation of spirit because of the proud recollection that it was our day, a day above those early days of that never-to-be-forgotten November which lifted the world to the high levels of vision and achievement upon which the great war for democracy and right was fought and won; although the stimulating memories of that happy time of triumph are forever marred and embittered for us by the shameful fact that when the victory was won—won, be it remembered, chiefly by the indomitable spirit and ungrudging sacrifices of our own incomparable soldiers—we turned our backs upon our associates and refused to bear any responsible part in the administration of peace, or the firm and permanent establishment of the results of the war—won at so terrible a cost of life and treasure—and withdrew into a sullen and selfish isolation which is deeply ignoble because manifestly cowardly and dishonorable.

This must always be a source of deep mortification to us and we shall inevitably be forced by the moral obligations of freedom and honor to retrieve that fatal error and assume once more the rôle of courage, self-respect and helpfulness which every true American must wish to regard as our natural part in the affairs of the world.

That we should have thus done a great wrong to civilization at one of the most critical turning points in the history of the world is the more to be deplored because every anxious year that has followed has made the exceeding need for such services as we might have rendered more and more evident and more and more pressing, as demoralizing circumstances which we might have controlled have gone from bad to worse.

And now, as if to furnish a sort of sinister climax, France and Italy between them have made waste paper of the Treaty of Versailles and the whole field of international relationship is in perilous confusion.

The affairs of the world can be set straight only by the firmest and most determined exhibition of the will to lead and make the right prevail.

Happily, the present situation in the world of affairs affords us the opportunity to retrieve the past and to render mankind the inestimable service of proving that there is at least one great and powerful nation which can turn away from programs of self-interest and devote itself to practising and establishing the highest ideals of disinterested service and the consistent maintenance of exalted standards of conscience and of right.

The only way in which we can worthily give proof of our appreciation of the high significance of Armistice Day is by resolving to put self-interest away and once more formulate and act upon the highest ideals and purposes of international policy.

Thus, and only thus, can we return to the true traditions of America.

Woodrow Wilson, Radio Address, November 10, 1923.

CHAPTER XXXVII — THE PLACE OF THE UNITED STATES IN THE WORLD

205. The Diplomatic Service (1920)

BY WILLIAM PHILLIPS

Phillips began as private secretary to Joseph H. Choate, Ambassador to Great Britain, a career which has carried him far in the diplomatic service. Between 1914 and 1924 he was Assistant Secretary and Under Secretary of State. Later he was appointed Ambassador to Belgium, and in 1927 became Minister to Canada. See also No. 49 above, and, on the consular service, No. 46 above.—Bibliography: F. Van Dyne, *Our Foreign Service.*

THE foreign service is centered in the Department of State. It is one great machine operating for one purpose—that of facilitating the intercourse of the United States with the rest of the world. This machine is divided into two parts—the Diplomatic Service and the Consular Service. Each part contributes its share to the success of the whole. Neither service stands alone. Each is dependent upon the other and must work in co-operation with the other. The Diplomatic Service is accredited to foreign governments and peoples and has as its principal function the cultivation of good will. The Consular Service is accredited to cities and districts and has as its principal functions the extension of American trade and the protection of Americans residing abroad. Trade and good will go hand in hand, for foreign trade rests upon good will between nations, and without good will it cannot prosper.

The money that we lend abroad, the railroads we construct, the bridges we build, the goods that we sell, raise questions with which both branches of the foreign service must deal. Before equality of treatment in commerce is secured to us, a treaty must be negotiated and its provisions maintained. Our share of the world's foreign trade is subject to all the winds of international politics that blow. Preferential agreements or the opening of a new trade route may close a market to us. Labor conditions or crop failures across the seas may be disastrous to our business year or reveal new and un-expected trade possibilities. Eternal vigilance on the part of the foreign service is the price of our safety in foreign trade. . . .

The diplomatic representative is the embodiment of the Government and people of the United States. He must command the confidence of the Government and people to whom he is accredited, which is not easy unless he has an intimate knowledge of his own country and at the same time a real sympathy with the point-of-view of other nations. Although he has numberless duties to perform, the high purpose of his mission is to strengthen the foundation that will insure for all times intellectual and commercial intercourse of foreign countries with his own country.

The work of consuls is more tangible than that of diplomats. To be successful, a consul must secure immediate results, and result-getting is a factor that brings popularity to the successful performer. The consular officer is in touch with the business men of the community in which he resides and can, therefore, advise American business men of commercial opportunities which open to them. When he returns from his work abroad, he comes personally in touch with American business and is recognized by the business community here as an important asset in the extension and development of foreign commerce. Chambers of Commerce throughout the country have naturally rallied to his support, and because of their interest in his welfare the President and Congress have responded to the needs of the Consular Service and have raised it from a feeble organization, wholly dependent upon the spoils system, to a national institution of dignity and prominence. Young men from all over the country are seeking to become consuls because they feel that the country is behind the Consular Service and they are proud to offer themselves for such an honorable career.

One branch of the Foreign Service—the consular—has come into its own because of its immediate result-getting capacity. The other branch—the diplomatic—without which consular activities cannot function, has not come into its own probably because its results are less tangible and therefore it has failed to arouse interest and support.

Let us see how young America regards the Diplomatic Service. Recently there were about thirty vacancies among the secretaries of embassies and legations and to fill these vacancies an examination was held as required by the regulations governing admission to the service. The State Department made every effort to incite interest in the forthcoming examinations, but, although numbers of inquiries were received, only ten men appeared in Washington for the examination. Fortunately, simultaneously an examination was held in Paris for Americans then in the Army which was a little more successful. But the lesson is plain. Very few will consider for a moment entering upon a career which has so doubtful a future and which has little support or backing from Congress or from the country. It is even more to their credit that, in spite of all drawbacks, there are in the service, now, men who have loyally served the Government for years without proper remuneration or much encouragement. But the highest standard for the service can only be reached if for every vacancy there is competition from among the best elements of young men in the country; and there can be no competition until the service is made more worth while to enter.

The salaries of the diplomatic officers are a farce. A young man is expected to give up the brilliant opportunities offered him at home for services in foreign capitals at a salary of $1500 per annum. If he makes a success of his career and remains in the service for ten or twelve years, he may expect, as the highest reward, a salary of $3000 per annum. It is true that during the war Congress appropriated for the secretaries of embassy or legation a so-called post allowance in order to make up to them the increased cost of living, but this appropriation, when spread over the whole service, does not nearly meet the increased cost of living in foreign countries, is of a temporary nature and may terminate at any time.

And then there is not much assurance given that merit will be recognized by promotion from the rank of secretary to minister. I am seeing constantly the look of discouragement upon the faces of men who deserve the highest consideration from their country for their efficient and loyal service. The discouragement of men of experience pervades the lower ranks of the service and affects the whole system. Granted that Congress increases the salaries of all the secretaries, granted that the Government purchases its own embassies and legations, granted a hundred other needed reforms, there can be nothing permanent, nothing really substantial, nothing which will bring the Diplomatic Service up to the highest standards, until the secretary is assured that, if he makes really good, if he becomes of genuine and far-reaching usefulness to the Government, his field of usefulness will be increased by his promotion to the rank of minister and eventually even to that of ambassador. In other words, merit must be recognized in the Diplomatic Service just as it is now recognized in the Consular Service, and until this is assured, all other reforms may perhaps be waste of time. Do not understand me as recommending that all ambassadors and ministers shall be appointed from the ranks of the secretaries. That would be a grave mistake and would crush that spirit of efficiency which, through competition from within and without the service, we hope to obtain.

Much has been said and written in behalf of the Government owning its embassies and legations instead of permitting each ambassador or minister to rent his own dwelling. A rich man now rents a "palace"; a poor man struggles to find an humble "lodging" within the Government salary, and it is always puzzling to peoples of foreign lands just why all-powerful America should be represented among them first by a "palace," and a year or two later by a "lodging." Of course, the answer is that the Government should require its representatives to adopt a standard of living of suitable dignity and this can be accomplished only by requiring its representatives to occupy a governmental residence and by making it possible for a poor man, through an increased allowance, to live there as well as a rich man. The absurdity of the present lack of system is shown by the allowances which the French, the British and our other competitors in the markets of the world furnish their own diplomatic representatives. In London the French Republic owns a splendid mansion and the French Ambassador receives a salary of $45,000 per annum. The United States has no residence and pays only a nominal salary of $17,500.

I remember shortly after Joseph Choate arrived in London, as American Ambassador, he was obliged to spend weeks of his precious time in hunting for a house. This became a topic of comment and amusement in the English press, and a famous caricature appeared depicting Choate clinging to a lamp-post on a dark and dreary night. A policeman approached and told him to move on home, to which he replied: "Home! home! I have no home; I am the American Ambassador."

In Berlin, both France and England own splendid government

buildings and in addition pay their diplomatic representatives $33,938 and $48,932, respectively, while the United States, of course, owns nothing and pays its usual nominal salary of $17,500. In Siam, the Siamese Government took pity upon the United States and presented it with a piece of land in the hopes that we would build thereon; but no, we accepted the gift but trembled at the thought of spending anything upon it, with the result that a large slice of the land has slipped into the river. We have made a beginning, however, in the right direction by owning diplomatic residences in two or three capitals—but only the merest beginning. Year after year recommendations have been made to Congress looking to improvements—to raising salaries, to purchasing buildings, etc.—and some important reforms have been accomplished, notably the Act of February 5, 1915, grading secretaries and consuls just as officers in the Army and Navy are graded, but it is admitted that without a public opinion in favor of general improvements throughout the service, without the help of American business, no administration can hope to accomplish any great result.

William Phillips, *Cleaning Our Diplomatic House*, in *Forum*, February, 1920 (New York), LXIII, 166–172 *passim*.

---

206. American International Problems (1922)

BY PRESIDENT EMERITUS CHARLES W. ELIOT

This is a scholar's view of the things that were vital to us in international affairs in 1923. For Eliot, see No. 106 above; he is also the author of No. 141 above.

WHEN the armistice was unexpectedly signed on November 11, 1918, the state of mind of the American soldiers in France underwent a sudden change. They all wanted to get home at once, and to resume their civil occupations; and many of them, but by no means all, avowed that they never meant to do any more fighting except in defense of their own country and people. Never again would they encounter the sufferings and hardships of the soldier's life, or run the risk of being killed or disabled, for the sake of any other people or nation, or in any way contribute to the enforcement of any treaties, or alliances which might hereafter be made for the benefit of the Allies, of the nations which had been neutral during the war, or of the new states which had been created or were to be created as results of the war. No more sacrifice of American lives or American savings should be made for the benefit of foreigners.

Shortly after the signing of the armistice, some political leaders at Washington, made aware of this state of mind among the returning soldiers, began to talk about the secure isolation of the United States and the self-sufficiency of their resources, and to preach the dubious doctrines expressed in the phrases "safety first" and "America first." These slogans are both capable of good uses; but these politicians used them in their selfish and ignoble significations. When the probable terms of the Treaty of Versailles became known, a formidable proportion of the members of the Senate gave notice that they should vote against the ratification of any treaty under which the American people might assume an obligation to enforce the decisions of the Assembly and Council of the League of Nations. Partisan politics had something to do with this demonstration in the Senate against the treaty and the League of Nations which was incorporated with it; but there were members of the Senate who really believed that the conduct of the American people towards their late comrades in arms and towards the promotion of human welfare in general, political, economic, or social, might properly be thereafter determined solely by the commercial and financial interests of the American people, and not by any philanthropic or humanitarian emotions or sympathies. The platform of the Republican Party endorsed this demoralizing doctrine. This was an extraordinary departure from the moral principles which the whole experience of the American democracy had inculcated, and the birth of the Republican Party had nobly illustrated.

In November, 1920, the Republican Party returned to power, after an interval of eight years, with an overwhelming majority in both the Senate and the House and complete possession of the administrative organization. The new Administration believed that it had received from the people an emphatic mandate to prevent the United States from incurring any obligation to assist Europe, on either the political or the economic side, to recover from the desolation and chaos which resulted from the war, and particularly to keep the United States out of the League of Nations, because one article in that covenant contemplated the possible use of some international force to prevent outbreaks of war.

Accordingly, the United States have taken no direct official part in any of the international efforts to rescue Europe from its present deplorable condition, although they have sent unofficial observers, or lookers-on, to some of the conferences or meetings on means of rescue. The attitude of the American Government toward all these efforts has been cold and unsympathetic, and as a matter of fact the efforts of the other nations have been crippled by the abstention of the United States. The League of Nations has been well organized, and its membership having been much increased, it has done some effective work toward the re-establishment of order in Europe and the prevention of sporadic fighting; but it cannot accomplish the objects for which it was created until the United States take active part in its work. Why does the American Government maintain this weak and ungenerous attitude? Because it believes that the American people have turned their backs on their history, including that of the five years from 1914 to 1919, and have decided that they will fight no more and suffer no more for other peoples or in the general cause of liberty, justice, and peace for mankind.

There is serious doubt whether any large part of the American people has suffered this moral collapse. . . .

In the two years which have elapsed since the last Presidential election divisions have appeared within the Republican Party itself on such important matters as the Bonus Bill, the Emergency Tariff Bill, and the proper dealing by the government with the strikes which now threaten the comfort and security of the public and the business prosperity of the whole country. Clearly the American public is beginning to desire that their government assume a vigorous and generous attitude both at home and abroad, an attitude determined not by cowardly selfishness or timid circumspection but by brave disinterestedness. It is highly significant that hundreds of college students and young graduates are at this moment attending at their own charges camps for military instruction and training in which the teachers are men who saw service in the late war. These youths propose to be ready to serve effectively when next their country summons them to fight; they do not like the present attitude of the American Government towards suffering humanity, and hope and expect that the American people will shortly return at whatever risk to their traditional policies in favor of arbitration in international disputes, the development of International Law, the maintenance of an International Court with the usual sanctions for its decisions, and the abolition of war for expansion or conquest. These young men constitute an important element in the new voters. The ex-soldiers who rashly say that they will fight no more have no influence with them.

In the hope of making some contribution to the settlement of Europe and the prevention of war, while still keeping America out of European alliances and treaties, the American Government called and led the Washington Conference. In both the original and the revised Agenda prepared by the Department of State reduction of land forces appeared as one of the prime subjects for consideration at the Conference; but when France declared that she could not reduce her army effectively unless she were promised aid by Great Britain and the United States in case she were attacked, the reduction of land forces was dropped incontinently by common consent. The United States would give no such promise. . . .

At the Washington Conference the American Secretary of State carried by great audacity and firmness a serious reduction in the cost of the navies of the leading naval powers; but the reduced navies are to be kept in prime fighting order with all the latest improvements in submarine and aërial activity. This is a gain for the budgets of the few naval powers which is well worth while, but has little effect on the bankrupt condition of the majority of the European powers, and slight if any effect toward the abolition of war. The pacts made at Washington with regard to Pacific Ocean affairs and Far Eastern powers contained no provision for the enforcement of the agreements. If any nation violates or disregards them, the remedy is only more conference. At the Washington Conference the United States did not undertake to use its army or navy, or any part thereof, to enforce on land or sea the agreements into which they entered. The American people seem still to hold the position that they will make no more sacrifices for the promotion in the world of justice, liberty, and peace. How can any lover of his country believe that the American spirit has really sunk so far? How can anyone fail to see that no progress can be made toward the abolition of war until America becomes a full partner in the holy enterprise, and takes all its risks? . . .

One excuse can be offered for the present reluctance of the American people to take their full share in international action. They have always objected to national action in general, not excepting national action in favor of education and the public health. . . . Some recent events have opened the mind of the people to the indispensableness of national action against evils which take effect, or are liable to take effect, all over the country. . . . It was not until prohibition was ordered by a national enactment that a reduction of the monstrous evil of alcoholism became possible and its ultimate extermination probable. The separate states could not deal intelligently with the engineering problem of irrigation from streams that flowed through several states, or along their borders. The immigration problem could not be dealt with in any satisfactory way until the national government took control of it. The Weather Bureau must be supported by the national government. The late war taught emphatically that the state militias must be converted into National Guards, and in wartime brought under the control and direction of the national military authorities. These vivid lessons have taught many Americans that the historical objection to national action requires modification to meet the new conditions of the Federal Union. . . .

What then should American patriots advocate and hope for in respect to American participation in international action to restore stable government to the countries of Europe, old or new, repair the losses in population, public health, means of transportation, and agricultural and manufacturing productiveness, and to efface as fast as possible the distrusts and hatreds which the war engendered? Our government should enter heartily into the existing League of Nations, take a sympathetic share in every discussion broached in the League, and be ready to take more than its share in all the responsibilities which unanimous action of the nations constituting the League might impose. America should cease to keep out of the Paris Covenant, "the greatest step in recorded history in the betterment of international relations," as ex-President Taft said of it in March, 1919, and give over completely every fear of being called upon to fight, no matter where, in support of the decisions of the League. That fear is now and always has been absolutely unworthy of the American people, false to its history, and even falser to its hopes.

The next American contribution to civilization should be full participation in the safe conduct of those world affairs through which the enlightened common interests of mankind are served, first, by joining heartily the League of Nations for the immediate salvation of Europe and the Near East, and then by advocating steadily for all the world Federalism, elastic and progressive Law, coöperative management and discipline in machinery industries, the emancipation of children from fear, harsh domination, and premature labor, the furtherance of preventive medicine and public health, and the opening for everybody of the delightful and sustaining vision of freedom, aspiration, and hope.

Charles W. Eliot, in *Foreign Affairs* (New York, 1923), I, 59–65 *passim*. Reprinted by permission.

---

207. The Washington Conference (1922)

BY MARK SULLIVAN

Sullivan is a widely known journalist, and author of *Our Times*, a history of the United States since 1900. The Washington Conference marked rather larger sacrifices by the United States than by any of the other nations participating, and was really ineffectual in curtailing naval expenditures because there were so many types of ships which it did not affect.   For Harding see No. 195 above.—Bibliography: Mark Sullivan, *The Great Adventure at Washington*.

I SUSPECT that in Harding's mind, as in my own, and in the minds of nearly all the delegates and others in Washington at that time, the two events coming on two succeeding days were merged and seen as one—the burial of the unknown soldier, who symbolized our grief over the sacrifices of the war just passed; and the opening of the Conference, which symbolized our hope of making other such sacrifices unnecessary.   Certain it is that the most earnest and moving part of this speech of Harding's at the Conference opening was the passage in which he spoke the emotions that had come to him the day before:

Here in the United States we are but freshly turned from the burial of an unknown American soldier, when a nation sorrowed while paying him tribute. Whether it was spoken or not, a hundred millions of our people were summarizing the inexcusable causes, the incalculable cost, the unspeakable sacrifices, and the unutterable sorrows, and there was the ever-impelling question: How can humanity justify or God forgive? Human hate demands no such toll; ambition and greed must be denied it. If misunderstanding must take the blame, then let us banish it.

But if this was the most moving part of the speech, the most expressive of that brooding melancholy which still hung over us from the day before, it was a different passage that brought out the most sharply prompt applause, the most deeply ringing approval. That came when Harding spoke in the spirit of stern demand, when he compressed into a single, compact sentence his own and America's determination to bring about the end for which the Conference had been called. Harding's manner, as he raised his eyes from his manuscript and leaned out toward the delegates, took on the same stern quality as his words. There was a completely restrained but nevertheless easily recognizable hint of challenge to any who might oppose—the expression of one with whom it is a rule of life to be placable and gentle, but who, on this occasion, has the unyielding determination of a deeply moved man, a glint of stubborn strength, in a purpose patiently arrived at.

"I can speak officially," he said, "only for the United States. Our hundred millions frankly want less of armament and none of war."

The approval of the audience for this sentiment, which was no less a sentiment than a challenge, was immediate and prolonged. (Incidentally, it was interesting to observe that it was William Jennings Bryan who most quickly caught the import of Harding's words and manner. For the moment, Harding was a fighting man trumpeting out a cause; and it was as one fighting man to another that Bryan dropped his pencil and paper, leaped to his feet, and leaning far out toward the speaker, led the applause with all the fire and fervor of one of his most evangelically inspired moments.) When the applause died down, Harding concluded his address with a less stern note, an appealing call for coöperation in "a service to mankind, . . . a better order which will tranquillize the world."

As Harding ended his address, he again took on his habitual manner of self-effacing modesty. He tried to satisfy the clamoring audience with a smile of appreciation and gratitude as he began to move away toward the door. But Hughes grasped his hand and shook it glow-ingly. That caused the applause to rise again. Harding, still smil-ing and bowing bashfully, kept trying to edge toward the door. But Balfour also grasped his hand, and then Briand and Viviani and all the others who could reach him as he made his way toward the door with as much speed as he could manage without seeming to lack cour-tesy to the applauding audience and to the various delegates who were trying to reach his hand. Finally, he succeeded in edging his way beneath the gallery, and with a last diffident wave of his arm to the audience, stepped rapidly through the door. . . .

The French delegates were highly self-conscious about the proud place their nation had held for six centuries of history, a little un-comfortably aware that that place has become somewhat less elevated, relative to new nations like America and Japan, and acutely sensitive to anything that might seem to diminish France's dignity and ancient prerogatives. One of these prerogatives is the fact that French has long been the official language of diplomacy. In the present confer-ence it would be absurd to so regard it. The Conference was on the soil of an English-speaking country, and the English-speaking peoples participating in it were almost a hundred and seventy millions to France's forty. Nevertheless, France, in this respect as in all others, was at every moment watchfully punctilious about her dignity. . . .

It was in this friendly, warming atmosphere that Hughes began his speech. In the setting he gave to his performance as a whole, Hughes, as all the world now knows, showed a superb sense of the dramatic quality of the relation to the world that he and his country and his purpose had that day. . . .

Then for a moment there came into Hughes' voice the same stern note of imperious demand that had marked a part of Harding's speech. "The world looks to this conference," he said, "to relieve humanity of the crushing burden created by competition in armament, and it is the view of the American Government that we should meet that expectation without any unnecessary delay." At that the audience applauded. That was the kind of talk the crowd wanted. It was American talk, and it sounded like action. . . .

That again was action-talk. Better yet, by this time, Hughes was through with lawyer generalities, and had become thoroughly a fighting man giving voice to a call for instant action. Sentence followed sentence charged with the note of insistent demand. "We can no longer content ourselves with investigations, with statistics, with reports, and with the circumlocution of inquiry. The time has come and this conference has been called not for general resolutions or mutual advice, but for action." . . .

I am happy to say that I am at liberty to go beyond these general propositions and, on behalf of the American delegation, acting under the instructions of the President of the United States, to submit to you a concrete proposition for an agreement for the limitation of naval armament.

Now Hughes went on with the details of what he called America's "concrete proposition"—the very phrase carried crisp and homely implications of something direct and business-like. He read first the four big principles:

(1) That all capital-ship building programmes, either actual or projected, should be abandoned;

(2) That further reduction should be made through the scrapping of certain of the older ships;

(3) That, in general, regard should be had to the existing naval strength of the Powers concerned;

(4) That the capital-ship tonnage should be used as the measurement of strength for navies and a proportionate allowance of auxiliary combatant craft prescribed.

From this, without a pause, Hughes went straight to figures of tonnage and names of ships. He introduced it with the shortest possible sentence, "The United States proposes, if this plan is accepted," and then enumerated:

(1) To scrap all capital ships now under construction. This includes six battle cruisers and seven battleships now on the ways and in course of building, and two battleships launched.

The total number of new capital ships thus to be scrapped is fifteen. The total tonnage of the new capital ships when completed would be 618,000 tons.

(2) To scrap all the older battleships up to, but not including, the Delaware and North Dakota. The total number of these old battleships to be scrapped is fifteen. Their total tonnage is 227,740 tons.

Thus the number of capital ships to be scrapped by the United States, if this plan is accepted, is thirty with an aggregate tonnage (including that of ships in construction, if completed) of 845,740 tons.

Mark Sullivan, *The Conference, First and Last*, in *World's Work*, March, 1922 (Garden City), 550–557 *passim*.

208. Post-War Reparations (1923)

BY PROFESSOR ALLYN A. YOUNG

Young (1876–1929) was Professor of Economics at Harvard.—Bibliography: Bernard M. Baruch, *Reparations and Economic Sections of the Treaty*.

DURING the past three years the Allied Governments and Germany together have managed to make a pretty complete fiasco of reparations. Germany has been derelict in that she has done little or nothing to put her own domestic finances in order—something that must be accomplished before she can make large foreign payments with any regularity. This is a matter of much larger consequence than her "voluntary defaults" under the terms of the treaty. The Allied Governments have been at fault in that they have done much to embarrass and nothing to help the efforts of the German Government to strengthen its domestic political and financial position. The worst single feature in the policy of Germany's creditor has been the French insistence upon the absurd and vicious system of "productive guarantees"—arrangements that produce little and guarantee nothing. It does not appear that until lately the Allied Governments had given any serious consideration to what is, after all, their most important problem, namely, the methods by which maximum payments can be secured from Germany with minimum friction and with a minimum of disturbing effects upon trade and finance.

Before the reparations clauses of the Treaty of Versailles were drafted various estimates were made of the amount Germany would be able to pay. Estimates that were based on her wealth, her total national income, or her taxable capacity may be put to one side, as having no practical importance—for a country cannot export its land, its income, or its taxes. The only estimates that can be given any weight were based on the premise that the limits were set by the means of payment that would be available. Assuming that the payments would be continued for a period, at the most, of not much more than thirty years, the estimates of the present worth or capital value of the maximum payments that Germany could be expected to make ran from 60,000,000,000 gold marks (I know of no careful estimate that gave a larger sum) down to a little more than half that figure.

The differences between the maximum and minimum estimates did not turn upon matters of economic fact. They reflected, in the main, different degrees of optimism respecting the extent to which Germany would be assisted, or permitted, to make the largest payments possible. The policy of the Allied Governments during the past three years has been such as to give comfort to the pessimists. What in 1919 was a possible maximum is now impossible. It must be written down by a third or even a half. Unless there is a definite change in the administration of reparations, and unless the expenses of maintaining the armies of occupation are greatly reduced, the minimum estimates made in 1919 will prove to have been too large.

In most of the estimates a distinction was made between the immediate payments that might be made within the first few years and the later payments that depended upon Germany's ability to send or sell to other countries more than she bought from them. The estimates put the immediate payments at between 12,000,000,000 and 20,000,000,000 gold marks. Such things as the transfer of the German merchant marine, or railway rolling stock, of the Saar mines, or public property in ceded territories, and immediate deliveries in kind were included in the estimates. So far as such items were concerned most of the estimates have proved to be somewhat too large, partly because the credit finally allowed on account of merchant ships and other items was smaller than was indicated by prices prevailing where the estimates were made, and partly because the Allies refused to credit the reparations account with certain items—notably the German state railways in Alsace-Lorraine—which had been allowed for in some of the estimates.

At once the largest and the most uncertain item in the estimate of Germany's cash assets was the amount that might be realized from the sale of the foreign holdings of German citizens. The total value of such holdings before the war was possibly as much as 30,000,-000,000 gold marks—although any estimate is hardly better than a guess. Some of these holdings were sold during the war, some were sequestered in enemy countries and assigned by the treaty to the settlement of other claims, some were small individual properties, and some were in Russia. Foreign holdings at the end of the war in the form of negotiable securities amounted probably to not more than 12,000,000,000 gold marks, and not more than half, or at the most three-fifths, of these were such as could be sold in the international market within a reasonable period of time without heavy loss. Shrunken though these assets were, the failure of the Allied Governments to try to harvest what they could of them seems inexplicable, although in this particular—as in others—the major portion of the blame must be put upon the weakness of Germany's financial policy. The amazing success of the operations attending France's payment of the indemnity of 5,000,000,000 francs in and after 1871 rested very largely upon her ability to induce her citizens to give up their holdings of foreign securities and to accept *rentes* instead. But, it will be remembered, French financial policy at that time was in the able hands of Thiers and Leon Say. In the present juncture, it is clear, France has neither sought nor given weight to the opinions of her competent economists. In Germany, such opinions may have been sought, but it does not appear that they have been followed.

The prospects for such payments as would arise out of a favorable balance of trade are in even worse state. Germany's financial policy has been such as to delay any wholesome and genuine recovery of export trade, while the creditor nations have done much to hinder such a recovery. To pay reparations Germany must export more than she did before the war, or import less, or both. During the past three years the volume of her foreign trade has been no more than two-fifths of what it was before the war. The increasing price of foreign exchange has from time to time given a temporary fillip to Germany's export industries, although it is far from certain that the total *value* of her exports would not have been *greater* if the depreciation of the mark had been less. But imports have consistently exceeded exports. German industries, even the export industries, are largely dependent on imported raw materials. Foods have continued to be imported. In some measure the depreciation of the mark has itself stimulated imports, by prompting importers to seek profits from the probable further rise of foreign exchange and of the prices of imported goods.

Despite the loss of the profits on her former carrying trade, the "invisible" balance of payments, reparations aside, has undoubtedly been in Germany's favor. The disparity between the amount of foreign currency that would buy a mark and what a mark would buy within Germany has led to large investments in German property on the part of capitalists in Holland and other West-European countries. (The gold the United States has been receiving from those countries has probably come, in considerable part, as an indirect result of such operations.) Germans, too, have been exporting capital, but in smaller amounts.

It is out of this favorable balance of imports of capital, no doubt, that the German Government has been able to rake together the small amount of gold exchange it has been able to turn over to its creditors. But Germany and her creditors have allowed larger possible payments of the same sort to slip through their fingers. There has been no attempt at an *efficient* control of *foreign-exchange* market in Germany. Generally the best thing governments can do in such a situation is to get out of the way of the recovery of private business and financial enterprise. But Germany's problem cannot be solved by laissez-faire methods alone. For her a favorable balance of international payments is an *artificial* thing and must be *created* by artificial means. Restricting commodity imports alone, as by higher customs duties, will *not* accomplish the purpose. *In*visible as well as visible imports must be dealt with. The German Government, as a large buyer of foreign exchange, must protect itself in some way against the competition of those of its citizens who want to *export* capital as well as against those who want to *import* goods.

The simplest and probably the most efficient method is to put the foreign-exchange market under *strict* supervision. I do not mean that the government should attempt to fix the rate at which foreign bills should be bought and sold, but that in some way, as by establishing a central market or by an efficient system of licensing, German buyers of foreign bills should be compelled to disclose their purposes and permit them to be passed upon. The export of German capital could in this manner be greatly decreased. . . .

As matters have gone, foreign funds out of which reparation payments might have been made have eluded Germany and her creditors, and the German Government has had to pay a ruinously high price for the funds she has been able to secure. The full price paid is not revealed by the quotations of foreign-exchange rates. The rest of it one will find in the wrecking of the finances and the monetary system of the country. The foreign-exchange operations of the government have been an important cause—not the only cause—of the downfall of the mark. From time to time the German Government, supplied with new marks of its own making, has come into the market as a buyer of foreign bills. To get any considerable part of the small and inelastic supply away from private buyers the price had to be *bid up* to an absurd figure—quite out of line with the general domestic price level. . . . It is impossible for Germany to stabilize her currency until she can create a favorable balance of foreign payments in some other way than by bidding up the price of foreign bills.

Furthermore, as everybody knows, the depreciation of the mark has multiplied the difficulties of Germany's budget. A depreciating currency makes most sorts of taxes unproductive. And as taxes become unproductive larger issues of paper money are needed to make up the *deficit* in the budget. At best German taxation has been inadequate. . . . It is certain that taxes have been very much lighter in Germany than in either Great Britain or the United States. But in Germany there has been in addition a heavy burden of disguised taxation, unequal and unjust in its incidence, in the form of the general downward trend of the purchasing power of money incomes.

Germany, in short, has not done all that she could, or even what might reasonably have been expected of her. Through weakness or the lack of either courage or good-will, she has handicapped herself by her loose management of her finances and of her foreign-exchange operations. It may be, as is claimed in France, that German policy has changed for the worse since the days of Wirth and Rathenau. But the policies of the Allied Governments, and particularly of France, have been equally at fault. Preoccupied with non-productive sanctions, sacrificing ultimate for immediate results, proceeding according to no definite economic program, the Allies have permitted and in a measure compelled Germany to do far less than what, under a wiser régime, she might have done. It is true that they have adjured her to balance her budget. But they have not relaxed the persistent pressure that makes the stabilization of her currency—a necessary preliminary—impossible.

Allyn A. Young, in *Foreign Affairs* (New York, 1923), I, 38–43 *passim*. Reprinted by permission.

INDEX

[The names of the authors of extracts are in **Boldface**. The titles of pieces are in SMALL CAPITALS. The titles of books and articles cited are in *Italics*.]